CYBERSECURITY

ESSENTIALS

Charles J. Brooks

Christopher Grow

Philip Craig

Donald Short

Development Editor: David Clark
Technical Editors: Raymond Blockmon, Chris Culling, Jeff Parker
Production Editor: Athiyappan Lalith Kumar
Copy Editor: Kathy Carlyle
Editorial Manager: Mary Beth Wakefield
Production Manager: Kathleen Wisor
Executive Editor: Jim Minatel
Proofreader: Nancy Bell
Indexer: Johnna VanHoose Dinse
Project Coordinator, Cover: Brent Savage
Cover Designer: Wiley
Cover Image: © ktsdesign/Shutterstock

Published simultaneously in Canada
ISBN: 978-1-119-36239-5
ISBN: 978-1-119-36243-2 (ebk)
ISBN: 978-1-119-36245-6 (ebk)
Manufactured in the United States of America

Library of Congress Control Number: 2018943782

SKY10082327_081924

To my wife Robbie, for all of her understanding, support, and help with these projects, as well as Robert, Jamaica, Michael, and Joshua.

Charles Brooks

To my close friends and family here and gone who have stood by me and encouraged me along my way. Your support through the years, mental, emotional, and financial, has brought me to this point. I dedicate this work to all of you, without which this would not have been possible for me.

Christopher Grow

To my wife Caralee, who has endured many times over the years my travels, my long stays in our nation's capital, and mostly her understanding of the importance of my commitment to cybersecurity. As we celebrate her birthday on September 11 every year, we are reminded of what it means to our daily lives.

Philip Craig

To my family whose grace and support have amazed me for decades. My loving wife of 33 years, Norma, and my children Kenny and Breanne continue to support my efforts and endure the challenges of my entrepreneurial life.

Donald Short

ACKNOWLEDGMENTS

As always, I want to thank the staff at ETG/Marcraft for making it easy to turn out a good product. In particular, thanks to Cathy Boulay and Luke Johns from the Product Development department for their excellent work in getting the text and graphics ready to go and looking good.

Many thanks as well to Jeff Riley, whom I've known and worked with in the book production business for many years. Thanks for putting together another great project.

—Charles Brooks

I would like to start by thanking some of the many people who have made what has become my repository of knowledge and skill available to help make this book possible. First there is my father David P. Grow. His knowledge, mentoring, patience, and understanding started my journey down the career path of computer support and computer networking.

I would also like to thank all of my mentors along the way who have increased my skills and knowledge. Whether they were employers or colleagues, each mentor has made contributions to my knowledge and skill that helped make this all possible. Especially the support staff and leadership here with my current employer at ETG/Marcraft: Charles Brooks, Kevin Smith, Cathy Boulay, Grant Ter-Oganov and any personnel working behind the scenes that I did not meet.

Lastly I would like to thank my close friends and family for all their help and support as I worked through the process of creating my contribution to this book.

—Christopher Grow

To the folks who commit their lives and careers developing new approaches to cybersecurity that protects the immense landscape of computing infrastructures from acts of malicious and sometimes deadly outcomes of cyber attacks, I dedicate these works to you. The next generation of cyber-protectors will gain significant value from this book and hopefully will find its content sparking new dedication to the cyber challenges we will face in the years ahead.

To the leadership at ETG/Marcraft whose vision recognizes the value of the teaching through hands-on experiences and not just the texts, thank you for recognizing and implementing your approach to our trade.

—Philip Craig

I would like to thank my customers and associates from the past 25 plus years who have helped me grow and learn at a rate I would not have thought possible.

—Donald Short

About the Authors

Charles J. Brooks is currently co-owner and vice president of Educational Technologies Group Inc., as well as co-owner of eITPrep LLP, an online training company. He is in charge of research and product development at both organizations.

A former electronics instructor and technical writer with the National Education Corporation, Charles taught and wrote on post-secondary ETG curriculum, including introductory electronics, transistor theory, linear integrated circuits, basic digital theory, industrial electronics, microprocessors, and computer peripherals.

Charles has authored several books, including seven editions of *A+ Certification Training Guide, The Complete Introductory Computer Course*, and *IBM PC Peripheral Troubleshooting and Repair.* He also writes about green technologies, networking, residential technology integration, and IT convergence.

Christopher M. Grow is currently the Technical Services Manager for Educational Technologies Group. He is responsible for product support, solution development, onsite implementation/installation, and instructor support and training for a wealth of cybersecurity and information technology products. He also is involved in program management and contributes in R&D of new products and revisions of current offerings.

Christopher has been a consultant and contractor in the IT industry for over 20 years. As an Information Security and Surveillance manager for a casino in Washington State, Christopher helped design and implement security policies, frameworks, and training to protect and segregate public and private information for the casino and their customers. He also helped to design procedures and train personnel on the physical security aspects of the casino industry.

Philip Craig is the founder of BlackByte Cyber Security, LLC, a consultancy supporting the Pacific Northwest National Laboratory (PNNL) research and national security agendas as well as the National Rural Electric Cooperative Association and National Rural Telecommunications Cooperative.

For many years, Phil served as a Senior Cyber Security Research Scientist at PNNL, where he provided engineering and program management support in the fields of cybersecurity, supervisory control and data acquisition (SCADA) technologies, computing, and communications infrastructure.

This included development of complex system and policy solutions in a variety of critical infrastructures including the nuclear power, electric power, and water sectors. He developed and deployed both strategic and tactical cybersecurity defensive solutions for the electric power and nuclear sectors.

Donald Short is the President of One World Telecommunications, Inc., an Internet Service Provider in Kennewick, Washington, where he both manages the business and programs web and database applications.

Don has been both a pharmacist and computer scientist for over 35 years, working in many programming languages on a variety of network architectures, and has developed large and complex online content and learning management systems.

Contents

Chapter 23 Tools and Utilities 565

Chapter 24 Identifying and Defending Against Vulnerabilities 591

Introduction

Welcome to Cybersecurity Essentials. This book is designed to provide a solid theory and practical platform for cybersecurity personnel. Key information provided in this edition includes:

- Critical infrastructure security systems and devices
- Security for local intelligent computing, and controlling devices and systems
- Security for local area network components and systems
- Cybersecurity for users and networks attached to the Internet

Each chapter begins with a list of learning objectives that establishes a foundation and systematic preview of the chapter.

A wealth of graphic diagrams and screen shots are included in each chapter to provide constant visual reinforcement of the concepts being discussed.

Key thoughts, cautions, and warnings in the chapter are presented in special boxes to call extra attention to them. Key terms are presented in italic type throughout the text. These terms are also defined in a comprehensive glossary at the end of the book that provides quick, easy access to the key terms that appear in each chapter.

Each part concludes with an extensive key-points review of its material.

One of the driving forces in the ongoing development of cybersecurity initiatives in the United States is the National Institute of Standards and Technology's (NIST) Cybersecurity Frameworks. These frameworks have been developed to assist governmental and business organizations in the design and development of systems and techniques to provide security for their critical infrastructure.

Security Challenges

Another outstanding pedagogical feature of this book is the presentation of the scenario-based NIST Security Challenges placed at the beginning of each Part. At the beginning of each Part there are one or more scenario-based Security Challenges that present descriptions of a particular security setting related to the information that will be presented in the chapter. You will be asked to read the scenario, put on your security professional persona, and consider how you might go about exploiting the key assets of the scenario, then contemplate how you could go about establishing systems and strategies to protect those assets.

These challenges are designed to provide you with real, open-ended context that sets the expectation level for the material to be studied. Ideally, you will be considering how the theory and hands-on materials you encounter as you move through the chapter apply to those scenarios.

At the completion of each Part, you will be asked to return to these Security Challenges and create new observations based on your increased knowledge. You will also be asked to compare their observations to those of professional security specialists who have provided their feedback for these scenarios.

Who Should Read This Book

This book is intended for:

- Students preparing for a career in IT, networking, or cybersecurity
- Network professionals who want to improve their network security skills
- Management personnel who need to understand the cybersecurity threats they face and basic options for confronting those threats

If you're interested in certification for the CompTIA Security+ or Microsoft MTA – 98-367 Security Fundamentals Certification exams, this book can be a great resource to help you prepare. See `https://certification.comptia.org/certifications/security` and `www.microsoft.com/en-us/learning/exam-98-367.aspx` for more certification information and resources.

What You Will Learn

You will learn to apply a systematic approach to securing IT networks and infrastructure. This approach begins with addressing physical security concerns from the outer edge of the physical environment to the interior region where the most valuable assets are located. The first half of any security objective is to limit physical access to the assets. If you can't get to it, you can't steal, damage, or destroy it. You will learn to view physical security in terms of three perimeters and to implement the proper tools at each.

After securing the physical environment, you will explore tools and techniques used to secure local endpoint computing devices. Following the three-perimeter strategy developed for physical security, you will address the security of these devices from their outer edge to their most desirable asset: your data.

After the local endpoint devices have been secured, you will turn your attentions to securing the servers, connectivity devices, and transmission media that make up the balance of your local area network. You will learn to secure these devices to protect your IT assets within the connected environment that you control.

Finally, you will explore tools and techniques used to protect your data when it leaves the protection of the network you control and passes through unprotected territory: the Internet. This will include building network structures to protect your network from the bad people hiding in the Internet, as well as how to guard your data when it is traveling through their territory.

What Is Covered in This Book

This book is a basic training system designed to provide a solid theoretical understanding of cybersecurity challenges, tools, and techniques, as well as to develop the foundations of a professional cybersecurity skill set. This is accomplished in a progressive four-section process, as follows:

Part I—Infrastructure Security—This part introduces the concepts and techniques associated with physical infrastructure security devices, systems, and techniques used to combat theft, prevent physical damage, maintain system integrity and services, and limit unauthorized disclosure of information.

Chapter 1 presents two Infrastructure Security Scenarios for the reader to consider and research selected NIST Cybersecurity Framework Functions and Categories and then apply them to the given scenarios.

Chapter 2 deals with common Access Control systems for protecting physical infrastructure assets. This section contains information about different types of physical barriers and their associated monitoring and control systems. The Authentication Systems section that follows is a logical extension of the physical access control materials. Devices and systems covered in this portion of the chapter are used for controlling access and denial of access to key physical assets.

Next the material moves on to examine the components and operation of a typical physical security monitoring and notification system. In this section, security controllers, sensors, and enunciators are covered along with logical implementation strategies.

The material in Chapter 3 flows quite naturally to the addition of visual Surveillance Systems to the security monitoring system. Information contained in this section includes: surveillance cameras, video recorders, modulators, and switchers.

Chapter 4 completes the Infrastructure Security material with a section covering Intrusion detection and reporting systems.

Chapter 5 provides a Summary and Review for the Scenarios and chapters of Part I. This chapter includes a complete list of relevant Summary Points and a Review Quiz. It also returns the reader to the Scenarios that began the Infrastructure Security part so they can update their response to the scenario challenges and then compare them to the response generated by an active Cyber Security Professional.

Part II—Local Host Security—One of the most useful tools ever introduced to business, industry, government, and medicine is the personal computer. This chapter primarily deals with personal computers and focuses on security efforts at the local computer level.

Chapter 6 presents two Local Host Security Scenarios for the reader to consider and research selected NIST Cybersecurity Framework Functions and Categories and then apply them to the given scenarios.

Chapter 7 begins the Part II discussion with sections covering physically securing personal computing devices. Information covered here includes biometric authentication devices such as fingerprint scanners, smart cards, and RFID cards. The material then moves on to physical port access risks and solutions. Options for accessing the PC covered here include the USB and Firewire ports.

Chapter 8 provides an overview of operating system structures, security features, and tools across the spectrum of operating system suppliers. In addition, the chapter covers logical (software-based) authentication methods for access control at the user's level. Topics covered here include passwords and computer locking features. Finally, the chapter provides an overview of operating system auditing and logging utilities and wraps up with a discussion of OS-based encryption tools.

Chapter 9 completes the Local Host Security part by examining security associated with remote access options. Included in this line of discussion are local software-based firewalls, intrusion detection systems, and Internet Browser Security options. The chapter concludes with a detailed discussion dealing with malicious software protection options, such as antivirus and antispyware programs, as well as software updating and patching efforts.

Chapter 10 provides a Summary and Review for the Scenarios and chapters of Part II. This chapter includes a complete list of relevant Summary Points and a Review Quiz. It also returns the reader to the Scenarios that began the

Local Host Security part so they can update their response to the scenario challenges and then compare them to the response generated by an active Cyber Security Professional.

Part III—Local Network Security in the Real World—While networks provide computer users with extended power to communicate and control devices remotely, they also provide a very large window to information stored on different devices attached to the network, as well as control devices operated remotely through the network.

Chapter 11 presents two Local Network Security Scenarios for the reader to consider and research selected NIST Cybersecurity Framework Functions and Categories and then apply them to the given scenarios.

Because modern networking involves so much information, Chapter 12 is designed to provide a basic introduction to networking. This chapter also examines typical network topologies (connection schemes). This is followed by an in-depth discussion of the OSI model that describes the different layers that all modern networks are designed on.

Chapter 13 provides information about network control strategies. These include networking protocols (rules) such as TCP/IP and IP addressing schemes. It concludes with a discussion covering the Ethernet standard.

Servers are the backbone of local area networks. Chapter 14 is dedicated to network servers and security tools and practices associated with them. Items discussed in this chapter include the roles of administrators, physical and logical access controls applied to servers, and steps for hardening server operating systems.

As with previous chapters, the material moves into logical access control for network environments. Topics covered here include user and group access controls instituted through the server's network operating system. Next the chapter covers techniques and tools involved in maintaining server security. These include network-level logging and auditing considerations, conducting backing up operations, and securing network backup media. The chapter concludes with coverage of distributed IDS systems, vulnerability scanning, and remote server monitoring.

Chapter 15 moves on to cover the other major hardware components in the local area network: the different types of connectivity devices used to tie the network together. Topics covered in this chapter include: managed network switches, enterprise routers, gateways, bridges, and wireless access points. The second half of the chapter is dedicated to vulnerabilities and attack types associated with each type of device. The chapter concludes with a discussion of techniques used to harden local area networks.

Chapter 16 concludes the discussion of LAN security by concentrating on the different transmission media types that connect the servers from Chapter 14 and the devices from Chapter 15 together. The first half of the chapter deals with the strengths and weaknesses of the various media types while the second half discusses vulnerabilities associated with each media type.

Chapter 17 provides a Summary and Review for the Scenarios and chapters of Part III. This chapter includes a complete list of relevant Summary Points and a Review Quiz. It also returns the reader to the Scenarios that began the Local Network Security part so they can update their response to the scenario challenges and then compare them to the response generated by an active Cyber Security Professional.

Part IV—Perimeter Security in the Real World—This part of the book builds on the information from the Local Area chapters in Part III to deal with security issues posed by Wide Area Networks (WANs) such as the Internet.

Chapter 18 presents two Perimeter Security Scenarios for the reader to consider and research selected NIST Cybersecurity Framework Functions and Categories and then apply them to the given scenarios.

The first chapter in this part of the book is designed to provide an understanding of the security environment at the edge of the local area network and beyond. It establishes the Basics of Internet Security. Topics covered in this chapter include: TCP/IP, unicasts/broadcasts/multicasts, common TCP/UDP ports, and routing. The chapter concludes with coverage of Internet Services, standards and RFCs, and security organization and standards associated with Internet security.

Chapter 20 is all about hiding the local (private) network from the external, public Internet. It begins with an introduction to the concepts of private networks and then moves on to techniques used to hide them from the outside. Topics covered here include: Network and Port Address Translation schemes, port forwarding and mapping, and network segmentation/segregation techniques. The chapter concludes with an exploration of virtualization techniques (VLANs) to hide network segments from each other.

Chapter 21 is about Protecting the Perimeter. The information presented focuses on protection of the organization from external threats. The most widely used device at the network perimeter is the firewall. This chapter begins with an extensive discussion of different firewall types and functions. It then moves on to discuss other types of devices and structures employed at the network perimeter to provide protection services. These devices and structures include network appliances, proxies, DMZs, honey pots, and Extranets.

Chapter 22 is dedicated to securing data in motion as it moves through the Internet. The key elements of this chapter cover authentication protocols, data cryptography, and data encryption techniques. The chapter continues with coverage of Virtual Private Networks (VPNs) and firewalls.

In Chapter 23 you are introduced to tools and utilities commonly used to monitor, diagnose, and control network environments. Tools covered here include common command line utilities used to test connectivity, packet/protocol analyzers used to inspect network traffic, network mapping tools, and penetration testing tools and utilities.

Chapter 24 deals with identifying and defending against common cyber vulnerabilities. Topics discussed in this chapter include: Zero Day vulnerabilities, software exploits, social engineering exploits, network threats, and other common exploit types.

Chapter 25 provides a Summary and Review for the Scenarios and chapters of Part IV. This chapter includes a complete list of relevant Summary Points and a Review Quiz. It also returns the reader to the Scenarios that began the Perimeter Security part so they can update their response to the scenario challenges and then compare them to the response generated by an active Cyber Security Professional.

Finally, Appendix A is a glossary of terms, Appendix B is a list of acronyms, and Appendix C includes the NIST Preliminary Cybersecurity Framework

The *Essentials* Series

The Essentials series from Sybex provides outstanding instruction for readers who are just beginning to develop their professional skills. Every Essentials book includes these features:

- Multimode instruction, providing specific or hands-on procedures wherever appropriate
- Review questions and/or bonus labs at the end of each chapter, where you can practice and extend your skills

Instructors can access extra supporting materials (suggested short- and long-course syllabi, PowerPoints, and more) by clicking the For Instructors tab at `http://www.wiley.com/go/cybersecurityessentials`.

How to Contact the Author

We're always interested in comments and feedback from our readers as well as information about books you'd like to see from us in the future. You can reach us by writing to `info@marcraft.com`. For more information about our work, please visit my website at `marcraft.com`.

Sybex strives to keep you supplied with the latest tools and information you need for your work. Please check their website at `http://www.wiley.com/go/cybersecurityessentials`, where we'll post additional content and updates that supplement this book if the need arises.

PART I

Securing the Infrastructure

CHAPTER 1

Infrastructure Security in the Real World

The following challenges will provide contextual reference points for the concepts you will learn in Part I. Because you have not yet read the chapters in Part I, the challenges in this chapter are designed to introduce you to the infrastructure security scenarios you'll face in the real world. In this chapter, you'll learn to:

- **Understand the relevance of infrastructure security**
- **Describe the functions, categories, subcategories, and reference structure of the NIST Cybersecurity Framework**
- **Apply the NIST Framework references to specific cybersecurity scenarios**

Security Challenges

The NIST Cybersecurity Framework was developed by the U.S. National Institute of Standards and Technology (NIST) to provide a set of independent guidelines that organizations can use to implement or upgrade their cybersecurity programs. Because the framework is a product-independent tool, it provides guidelines that any organization can tailor to meet its own cybersecurity needs.

The frameworks are divided into five functions (Identify, Protect, Detect, Respond, and Recover) that provide a top-level description of the cybersecurity development process. Each function is then divided into applicable categories that underpin the stated function. Each category is further divided into subcategories and implementation methodology. Finally, the subcategories are supported by lists of reference documents that contain the nuts and bolt of building the cybersecurity program.

This chapter will kickstart your thought processes for what you are about to learn in Part I. It contains two specific cybersecurity scenarios to which you will be asked to apply the NIST Framework in order to produce a cybersecurity solution that meets the desired objectives. In each case, you will be provided with specific subcategories to research, along with some guidance to help you produce your solutions.

In this first pass through the scenarios, you are expected to generate and record *general observations* about securing the infrastructure described, as you have not yet been introduced to the supporting material. As mentioned earlier, this is activity is designed to get your cybersecurity thought processes started.

In Chapter 5, you will return to these scenarios and use what you have learned in Chapters 2, 3, and 4 to revise your initial assessments. You will also compare your observations to those of professional security specialists who have provided their observations and solutions for these scenarios.

Infrastructure Security Scenario 1

You are in charge of planning and implementing a security system for a new electrical substation that will be built next to a new housing development. The substation is equipped with high-voltage electrical switching gear for the surrounding community. It is not manned on a full-time basis but does have a control building that houses instrumentation and communication equipment, as shown in Figure 1.1.

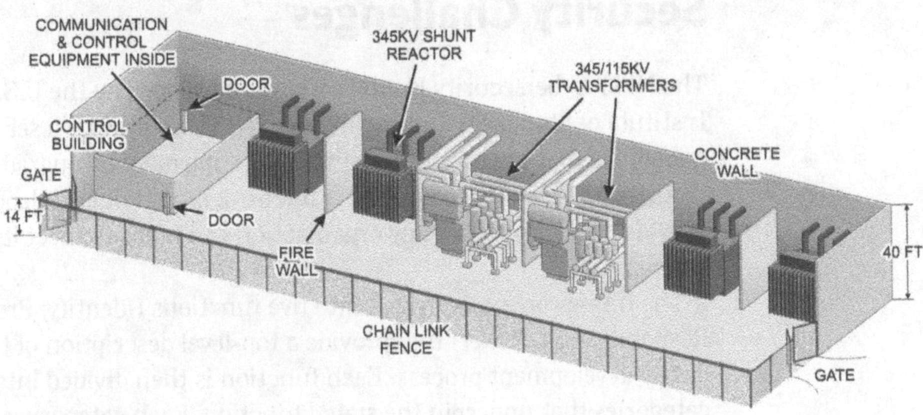

FIGURE 1.1 The Electrical Substation

The high-voltage switch gear accepts electrical power from different sources, which it then conditions and routes to the community users as needed.

The energy arrives on a set of different high-voltage supply lines and leaves the facility via different sets of distribution lines.

The monitoring devices and control systems in the substation communicate with different parts of the utility's transmission and distribution system to route electrical power where and when it is needed. These communication channels include wireless radio signals, signals transmitted across the power lines, and traditional network communications media.

Risk Assessment 1

From the information provided in this first scenario, consider the National Institute of Standards and Technology (NIST) functions detailed in this section and then record your observations as they relate to each category.

See Appendix C for the NIST Cyber Security Framework

A copy of the NIST Cyber Security Framework is available in Appendix C. These frameworks were developed by the U.S. National Institute of Standards and Technology to provide cybersecurity guidelines for Improving Critical Infrastructure Cybersecurity under executive order 13636. The ultimate goal of this initiative is to provide guidelines for the nation's critical infrastructure in business, industry, and utility organizations to reduce their cybersecurity risks.

Identify

Create an inventory of physical assets (devices and systems) within the substation (NIST ID.AM-1).

Understanding NIST References

NIST references include the function, the category, and the subcategory. In the example of ID.AM-1 mentioned earlier, the *function* is Identify (ID); the *category* is Asset Management (AM); and the *subcategory* is 1 (which is "physical devices and systems within the organization are inventoried"). To implement this portion of the Framework for the scenario presented, you may want to refer to an online copy of the designated *Reference* documents listed under this subcategory. The same is true of the following subcategories as well.

Protect

Describe in general how you might go about protecting the physical assets identified in the previous point (NIST PR.AC-2).

Detect

How would you know if someone or something was attempting to access, disable, degrade, or destroy one or more of the devices and/or systems in the substation? How could you detect anomalies and events that might impact the operation of the substation (NIST DE.CM-2, 8)?

Respond

How would you need to respond to the anomalies and events you've identified through the devices, systems, and steps you would implement in the previous point (NIST RS.AN-1, 2, 3)?

Recover

Which steps could be put in place to recover from actions intended to access, disable, degrade, or destroy the assets you previously identified (NIST RC.RP-1)?

Infrastructure Security Scenario 2

Your company is building a new corporate facility, as shown in Figure 1.2, to house its 5,000 headquarters employees. The facility will feature multiple floors. Some management personnel will use traditional offices with doors and windows, but the majority of the employees will work in open cubicles.

Each office and cubicle will be equipped with a telephone and network connection. In addition, many of the employees travel as part of their job roles and require portable computers. Other employees work with desktop personal computers.

The facility will house a cluster of computer servers and network devices that provide workflow and communications between all of the managers and employees. This architecture electronically manipulates, stores, and transmits all of the company's important business information and data. This includes product descriptions, accounting information, legal records, customer records, employee records, and the company's intellectual property.

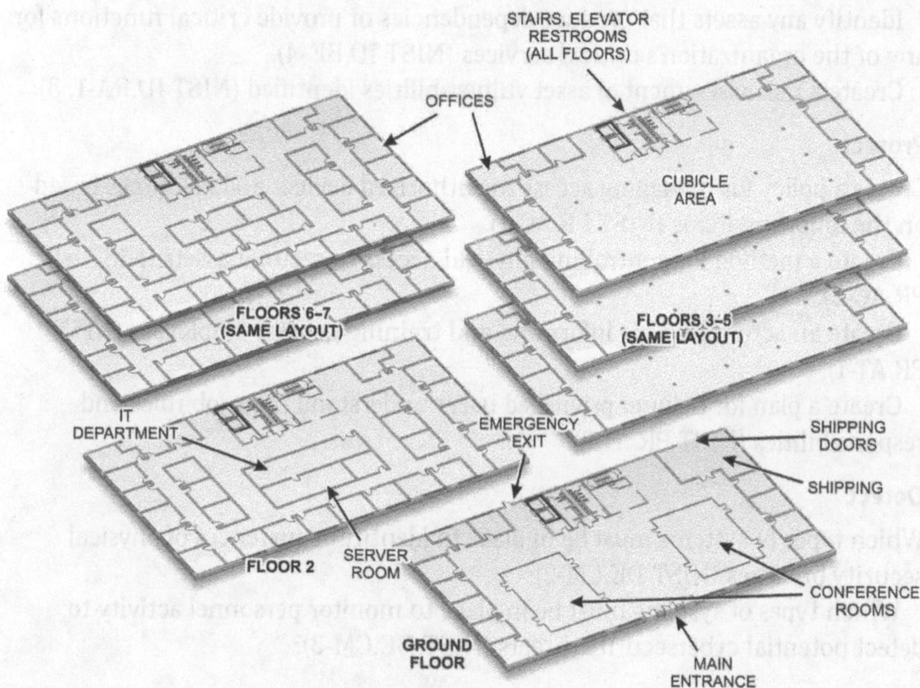

FIGURE 1.2 Headquarters Facility Plans

Risk Assessment 2

From the information provided in the second scenario, consider the NIST functions detailed in this section and then write your observations as they relate to each category.

Identify

Create an inventory of physical assets (devices and systems) within the organization (NIST ID.AM-1).

Create an inventory of cyber assets (software platforms and applications) within the organization (NIST ID.AM-2).

Prioritize the organization's assets based on their criticality or value to the business functions of the organization (NIST ID.BE-3).

Identify any assets that produce dependencies or provide critical functions for any of the organization's critical services (NIST ID.BE-4).

Create a risk assessment of asset vulnerabilities identified (NIST ID.RA-1, 3).

Protect

Create a policy for managing access to authorized devices and resources based on the following items (NIST PR.AC-1).

Create a method for controlling physical access to secured assets (NIST PR.AC-2).

Create an action plan for informing and training general employees (NIST PR.AT-1).

Create a plan for helping privileged users understand their job roles and responsibilities (NIST PR.AT-2).

Detect

Which types of systems must be in place to identify occurrences of physical security breaches (NIST DE.CM-2)?

Which types of systems must be in place to monitor personnel activity to detect potential cybersecurity threats (NIST DE.CM-3)?

Respond

Which type of response plan might be necessary when general physical security is breached at the facility (NIST RS.AN-1, 2, 3)?

Considering the information kept on the company's servers, which type of response plan might be necessary when physical security is breached in the server room (NIST RS.CO-4, 5)?

Recover

Which type of recovery plan might be needed for general physical security breaches that occur at one of the cubicles in the facility (NIST RC.RP-1)?

Which items might a recovery plan include if server security is breached at the facility (NIST RC.CO-1, 2)?

Summary

Record your observations for the risk assessments presented in this chapter. In Chapter 5, you will compare these original thoughts and observations with those you will generate after reading Chapters 2, 3, and 4. You'll also be able to compare your answers to those of professional security specialists.

CHAPTER 2

Understanding Access-Control and Monitoring Systems

If you skipped reading the "Introduction," you might wonder why there's an entire Part I devoted to infrastructure security. However, as the "Introduction" pointed out, without physical security there is no security. Infrastructure security operation and management is based on three basic types of subsystems: access-control and monitoring systems (covered in this chapter), video surveillance systems (covered in Chapter 3), and intrusion-detection and reporting systems (covered Chapter 4). In this chapter, you'll learn to:

- **Understand the application of the following concepts of physical security: access control, physical barriers, and biometrics**
- **Differentiate between authentication and authorization**
- **Identify commonly used physical access-control systems/devices including keypads, card readers, biometric readers, proximity readers, electronic deadbolts, and magnetic locks**

A Quick Primer on Infrastructure Security

The overall aim of any security effort is to establish a peace-of-mind condition (a carefree state free from worries) for an individual, a group, or an organization. This condition is ideally achieved by securing exclusive rights to assets (objects and information), access to those assets, and use of those assets. This condition creates value and provides peace of mind to asset owners.

No Time for Relaxing in the Cybersecurity World

In the cybersecurity realm, a carefree state is never actually achieved. New types of cyber attacks are constantly being devised, causing cybersecurity specialists and administrators to be constantly on guard against potentially damaging occurrences.

A more modern definition for security is the science, technique, and art of establishing a system of exclusion and inclusion of individuals, systems, media, content, and objects. It also provides increased safety and utilization with physical assets such as machinery or processing equipment.

Physical security is the science, technique, and art of establishing a system of exclusion and inclusion for tangible assets. In practice, this involves policies, practices, and steps aimed at combating theft, preventing physical damage, maintaining system integrity and services, and limiting unauthorized disclosure of information.

Similarly, the term *cybersecurity* involves securing physical access to property, systems, and equipment ports while securing intangible assets including electronic, optical, and informational access to the system's data and controls.

In any modern system, security is a function of the synergies of both the physical and cybersecurity domains. Both entities are necessary to support a strong overall security posture and program.

When physical security initiatives are applied to providing security for the basic physical and organizational structures needed for the operation of an enterprise, an organization, or society, this is known as *infrastructure security*.

Although we may think of infrastructure security in simple physical terms such as a lockable door, a patrolling security guard, or as some other method used to protect our assets; there are several additional components that go into constructing an effective infrastructure security system. Such systems generally involve a combination of several critical security procedures that have been well planned and tested to meet or exceed operational and organizational security needs.

As shown in Figure 2.1, there are three general layers to designing and implementing a plan to physically secure an infrastructure asset (a property, building, physical space, system, or device):

The Outer Perimeter Securing this space involves controlling who can move (walk, drive, fly) across the legal or physical line that marks this perimeter.

Examples of typical physical outer perimeters include property lines or the exterior walls of a building or complex.

The Inner Perimeter This perimeter typically involves physical barriers such as walls, doors, and windows—either exterior or interior, depending on the context of the outer perimeter.

The Interior This is the innermost level of security and consists of the interior of the building, office, cubicle, etc. that is surrounded by the inner and outer perimeters.

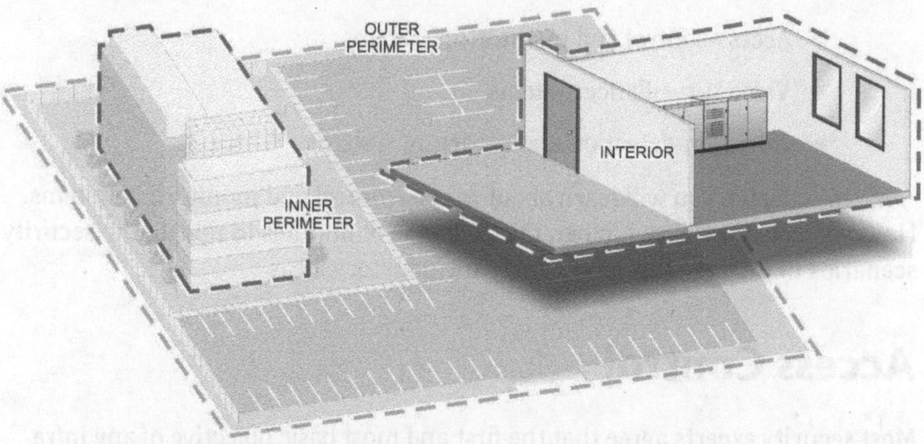

FIGURE 2.1 The Three Perimeters

In a comprehensive security plan, control of all three layers is addressed. Security at each layer typically consists of a formulation of specifically selected devices working together to provide an effective physical security system.

Securing Logical Perimeters

Cybersecurity also deals with securing logical perimeters. They are covered in later chapters having to do with computing and control systems, networks, and the Internet. The same security concepts developed here will be applied to those topics as they are encountered.

At each layer there are two concepts at work:

Natural Access-Control Methods Natural access control involves using natural design elements, such as structures and landscaping, to guide people as they enter and exit spaces.

Territorial Reinforcement Territorial reinforcement employs structures, systems, and devices to prevent unauthorized entry and create a clear difference between what is public and private.

Infrastructure security operation and management is based on three basic types of subsystems:

- Access-control and monitoring systems
- Video surveillance systems
- Intrusion-detection and reporting systems

In this chapter, you will learn about access-control and monitoring systems. However, before reading further, take a couple of minutes to update the security scenarios in Chapter 1 to reflect these introductory ideas.

Access Control

Most security experts agree that the first and most basic objective of any infrastructure security system is to deter potential intruders, as shown in Figure 2.2. This is the goal of access control. You can't damage, destroy, or steal what you can't physically access.

FIGURE 2.2 Access Control

The basis of designing efficient access-control systems involves three terms: ingress, egress, and regress. By definition, *ingress* is the right of an individual to enter a property, while *egress* is the legal right to leave a property. Similarly, *regress* is the term used to describe the legal right to reenter a property.

On a physical security basis, ingress can be defined as the physical path of an individual to properly enter a property, while egress is the physical path to properly leave a property.

In security terms, a *right* is a legal privilege or permission granted to someone, or some group, by some recognized source of authority. This source can be a government, a legally recognized governmental agent, or a legally recognized owner of an asset. By extension, a person who has the right to access an asset is said to be *authorized* (by the recognized authority), while anyone who has not been given this right is labeled as *unauthorized*. When unauthorized people attempt to gain access to an asset they do not have rights to access they become *intruders*.

Therefore, access control involves being able to control the ingress, egress, and regress to an asset based on authorization, as depicted in Figure 2.3. In particular, limiting the access of unauthorized personnel to important assets is the most fundamental security step that you can take.

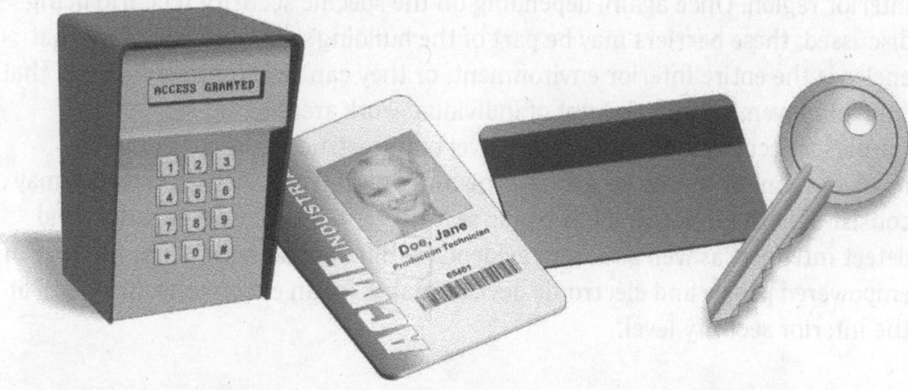

FIGURE 2.3 Authorization

From the list in the previous section, you can see that access control begins at the outer perimeter. Depending on the specific example being studied, this may be the property line of the organization's physical property or the front door of their facilities.

Recall that the goal at the outer perimeter is to control who can walk or drive across the perimeter. Control at this point can be as simple as planting hedges at the edge of the property or including appropriate visual signs to warn unauthorized people to stay out, or as complex as a barbed-wire fence with gates and armed guards.

Access-control efforts typically extend into the area between the outer and inner perimeters. These efforts can include natural access-control techniques such as strategic placement of employee and guest parking, as well as the use of landscaping features to channel people to selected entrances and exits and inhibit access to other possible entry/exit points. This also extends to clearly marking ingress and egress approaches to facilities and properties.

Crime Prevention Through Environmental Design (CPTED)

CPTED is a set of building and property design principles based on anticipating the thought processes of potential intruders to discourage them from follow through.

Inner perimeter control of a physical infrastructure involves the use of physical structures such as walls, windows, and doors that can act as barriers that impede the ability of an intruder to advance from the outer perimeter to the interior region. Once again, depending on the specific security scenario being discussed, these barriers may be part of the building's external structure that encloses the entire interior environment, or they can be interior structures that control movement into and out of individual work areas.

Interior security is the innermost level of infrastructure security, and it involves monitoring the area inside the inner perimeter. Such monitoring may consist of both human and electronic security systems to observe, track, and detect intruders as well as record evidence of different activities. The mixture of empowered people and electronic devices makes for an effective security tool at the interior security level.

Security Policies

A key component that brings all three levels of security together is a well-designed security policy that states how security is implemented at each level. Businesses and organizations develop comprehensive security policies that define who is authorized to access different assets and what they are allowed to do with those assets when they do access them.

For example, allowing employees and visitors to have free access to all the departments inside the organization provides a variety of security risks. You will want to maintain access control to create an environment that reduces the human nature of temptation. If everyone can move freely within the interior of the organization, it is much more difficult to implement safeguards to prevent them from accessing or taking physical or cyber assets. You also need to maintain access control to prevent accidents.

For example, you do not want a sales representative accidentally spilling their coffee on one of the production servers in your engineering department.

Instead, develop a cohesive access-control policy at each level that provides authorized people with appropriate levels of access to selected assets, while inhibiting access to assets by people who are not authorized. Then enforce those policies with the correct types and numbers of access-control devices (sensors, barriers, logs, ID badges, or security guards) as deemed appropriate.

A Word About Security Guards

Although access-control devices may be cheaper than human guards, guards are able to make valuable judgmental decisions based on the actions of a potential intruder. They offer a symbol of security, can initiate human judgment, and they can provide timely intervention during an incident.

Frequently, badges or smartcards are used to control access. Employees may also be identified by a Radio Frequency Identification (RFID) transponder as they move within proximal range of an RFID sensor. Transponders store access codes and use radio receivers and transmitters.

These access-control techniques, systems, and devices are discussed in detail throughout the remainder of this chapter.

Physical Security Controls

Enforcing access-control measures may initially include placing locks on doors that access offices and separating departments or networking sections with similar physical barriers. Many companies have a front door or an entranceway that includes a receptionist to control access. During business hours, the receptionist acts as a physical barrier, inquiring about the nature of clients' visits, as illustrated in Figure 2.4.

FIGURE 2.4 Physical Barriers

In some institutions, the visitor may be required to be accompanied by an escort to physically limit their movement through the company. For additional access control, a human guard could be employed to control access to specific, restricted interior locations, such as a laboratory, or to an elevator that services a restricted area, such as a basement.

At night, the physical barrier may simply be a locked door. However, the door may also be equipped with a sensor and an alarm. The alarm could be a local annunciator such as a siren, or it could be linked directly to an external monitoring system or to the police department.

Locks and Keys

The primary physical barrier in most security perimeters is the lockable door. The door provides the physical barrier but in itself will only keep honest people out. The lock, on the other hand, provides the authentication function of the barrier through its key. Having the key signifies that the person either possesses or knows the information required to gain access through the door.

Many different types of locks are used with security barriers. Likewise, many different types of keys are used to disengage the locking mechanism. Depending on the type of lock being used, the key can be either physical or logical.

In most organizations, only select personnel who work in a particular office may possess a key to access their working environment. Maintaining tight key control and using numbered keys that are clearly coded for nonreproduction helps to maintain the locked door as an effective physical barrier.

ENFORCE A STRICT KEY CONTROL POLICY

A strict key control policy is required to successfully protect equipment and ideas behind locked doors.

Standard Key-Locking Deadbolts

Standard key-locking deadbolts have a locking mechanism similar to that of the electronic solenoid-operated deadbolt but are engaged or withdrawn with a key. They provide an added level of security for doors that can be operated manually. A key-locking deadbolt is available with a single or double cylinder, as shown in Figure 2.5.

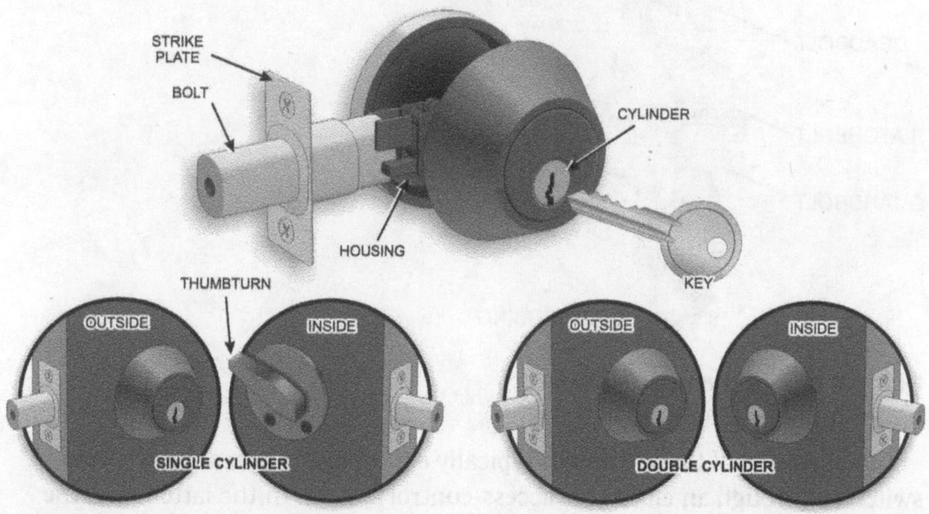

FIGURE 2.5 Key-Locking Deadbolt

Solenoid-Operated Deadbolt Locks

Electronically operated deadbolt locks offer an increased level of security for the perimeter. Adaptable to any security system, electric deadbolts perform well as auxiliary locks on doors where access control is desired.

The main actuation component of solenoid-operated deadbolt locks, like the one displayed in Figure 2.6, are electrically activated solenoids. When electric current is applied to the solenoid's coil, an electromagnetic field is developed around it. The electromagnetic field applies magnetic pressure on the core in the center of the coil, causing it to move. This movement either engages (activates) the physical locking mechanism or it disengages (deactivates) the locking mechanism.

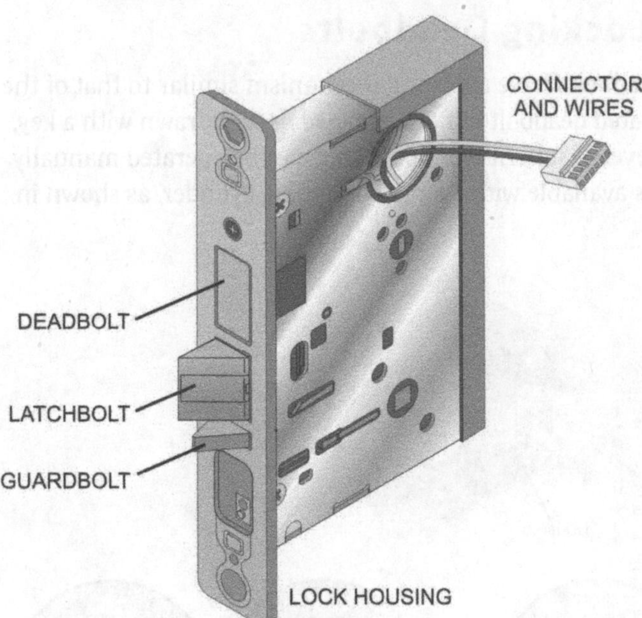

FIGURE 2.6 Electronic Deadbolt

The operation of the solenoid is typically controlled by a remotely located switch or through an electronic access-control system. In the latter case, the system is typically actuated by input from intelligent identification card-access devices.

Solenoid-operated deadbolts can be set to either lock or unlock when energized and are listed by Underwriters Laboratories (UL) as burglary-protection devices. In security applications, the solenoid lock is typically configured so that it automatically moves to the locked position when the door is closed. This helps prevent tailgating, where an unauthorized person slips past the locking door closely behind someone who is authorized to pass through it.

However, some doors that use automatic locks need to be configured to operate in a fail-safe manner (unlocks when power is removed). This type of configuration must be used to enable employees to exit through the door in case of emergency.

A dead-bolted door configured to operate in a fail-secure manner (locks when the power is removed) would not be suitable for use as an emergency exit, because it could not be used to exit the perimeter in an emergency. With a fail-secure lock, the door would default to the locked condition and would not open because of the lack of electricity to operate it.

Electronic deadbolts can be used with swinging, sliding, power-operated, and vertical-lift doors, as well as on fence gates.

Cipher Locks

Cipher locks requiring personal access codes known by the user are often used in access-control and management systems. These locks operate by unlocking magnetic door locks when the correct programmed code is entered by the user on the cipher-lock keypad. They provide an added level of security for perimeter entry areas. An example of a cipher lock is shown in Figure 2.7.

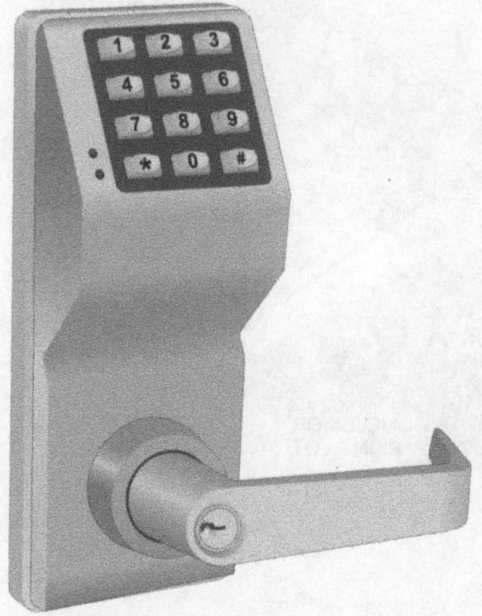

FIGURE 2.7 Cipher Lock

While electronic door pads may offer a more secure physical barrier, their entry codes need to be periodically changed for such pads to be effective over time.

Access-Control Gates

Like a door, a gate is a type of physical barrier that can be swung, drawn, or lowered to control ingress and egress through a wall or fence. Access-control gates can be classified into two main types:

- Sliding gates
- Swinging gates

Both types can be opened or closed through the use of a motorized operator. The size of the gate operator is determined by the width of the pathway and the weight of the selected gate.

Sliding Gates

Sliding gates, such as the one shown in Figure 2.8, are used where high levels of operational safety and security are needed.

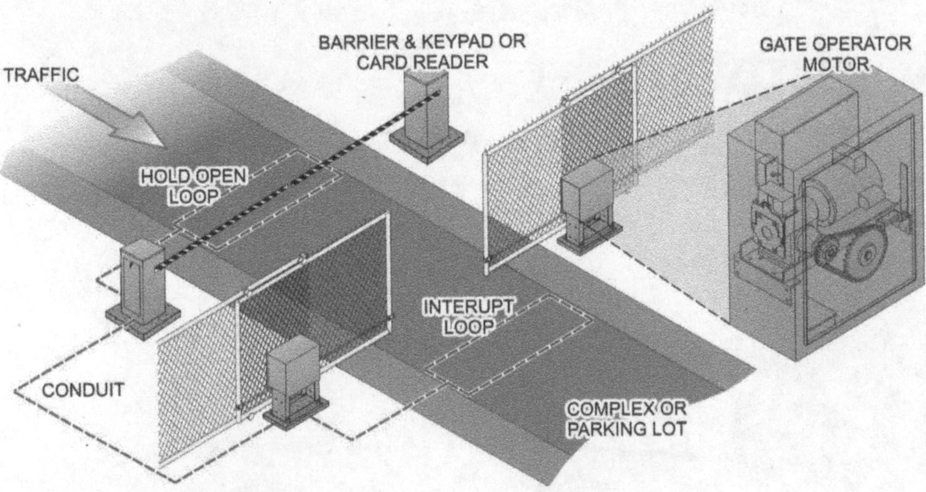

FIGURE 2.8 Sliding Gate

Swinging Gates

Swinging gates, like the one depicted in Figure 2.9, are equipped with fully adjustable hinges that allow the gate to swing through 180 degrees. An articulated arm, which runs from the operator to the gate, pulls or pushes the gate open and closed. Manufacturers sometimes use a piston/cylinder configuration as the actuator for the arm.

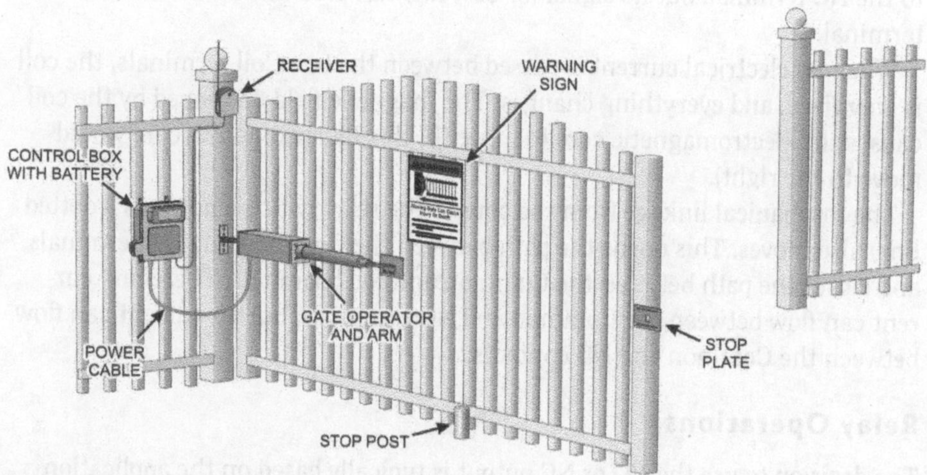

FIGURE 2.9 Swinging Gate

Control Relays

Relays are electromechanical devices that employ safer, low-voltage/low-current control signals to be used to control higher-voltage/higher-current devices. In access-control settings, relays are commonly used to control the operation of electric gates and door locks, garage door openers, and other remote devices.

Figure 2.10 shows a schematic diagram of a simple single-pole, single-throw (SPST) relay. As the diagram illustrates, the relay consists of a coil with two external connections, a Common connection, and two output connections.

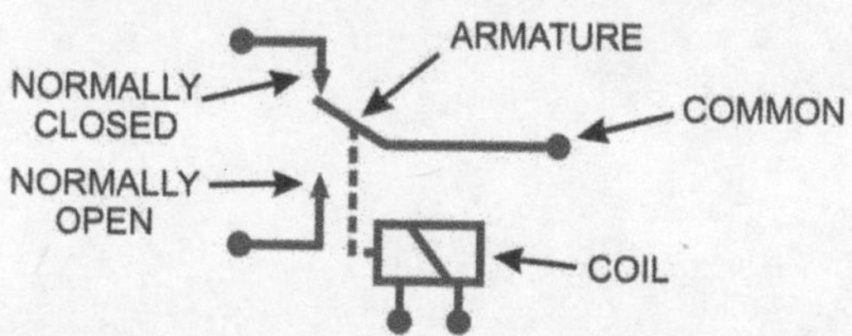

FIGURE 2.10 SPST Relay Schematic

The output connections are specified by their relationship to the Common connection when no energy is applied to the coil. One output is called the Normally Open (NO) contact and the other is the Normally Closed (NC) contact.

When no signal is applied to the coil, the relay is at rest, and there is a physical connection from the Common terminal to the NC terminal. Conversely, there is no physical connection between the Common and NO terminals. In this state, any signal (current) applied to the Common terminal will pass through to the NC terminal, but no signal (or current) can pass through to the NO terminal.

When an electrical current is passed between the two Coil terminals, the coil is energized, and everything changes. The magnetic field developed by the coil causes the electromagnetic core to move (in this illustration the core would move to the right).

The mechanical linkage from the core to the relay switch (shown as a dotted line) also moves. This opens the path between the Common and NC terminals and closes the path between the Common and NO terminals. Therefore, current can flow between the Common and NO terminals, but no current can flow between the Common and NC contacts.

Relay Operations

The decision to use the NO or NC output is typically based on the application the relay is being used to control. In many cases, control circuits are designed so that they provide either fail-safe or fail-secure performance. A fail-safe circuit is designed so that in the event of a power or component failure, the system being controlled will remain in its safe condition (either on or off).

The fail-secure circuit is one that fails in a most secure condition. For instance, if the power fails to an automated security gate, the system should fail in a manner that keeps the operation of the gate secure (it should remain closed unless it is opened manually from a secure location).

Activating relays are frequently built into the keypads, key fobs, door locks, or gate actuators. The relay kit shown in Figure 2.11 is designed for use as a gate controller and provides a view of the relay and associated components. The accompanying key fob is typically used to operate the controller.

FIGURE 2.11 Gate Controller Relay and Associated Components

Authentication Systems

Authentication is the process of determining that someone is who they say they are. Recall that effective access control involves being able to control the ingress, egress, and regress to an asset based on authorization. In particular, limiting the access of unauthorized personnel to important assets is the most fundamental security step that you can take. Therefore, authorization is based on authentication.

Multiple factors are involved in authentication:

- *Knowledge:* Something you know or something that only the designated person should know
- *Possession:* Something you have or something that only the designated person should have
- *Inheritance*: Something you are or something that only the designated person is
- *Location:* Somewhere you are or somewhere that only the designated person is

Many physical authentication systems are based on single authentication factors that depend on possession, such as possessing a key device that opens a lock. The key can be a physical or virtual key as needed to open physical or virtual locking mechanisms.

More intelligent and effective authentication methods involve two-factor authentication (a process that requires two of the factors to grant authorization) based on *knowledge* (something you know) and *possession* (something you have).

Advanced authorization and authentication methods include multifactor authorize and authenticate systems. In these systems, information must be presented to an authentication device that, in turn, passes it to the security controller's authentication system. A number of different authentication devices are used routinely in access-control systems. The major device types are covered in the following sections of the chapter.

Magnetic Stripe Readers

A *magnetic stripe card* is a physical credit-card-like device that contains authentication information in the form of magnetically coded spots on a magnetic stripe, as illustrated in Figure 2.12. The cardholder uses the information on the card to access physical spaces or assets by passing the stripe on the card through a magnetic card reader.

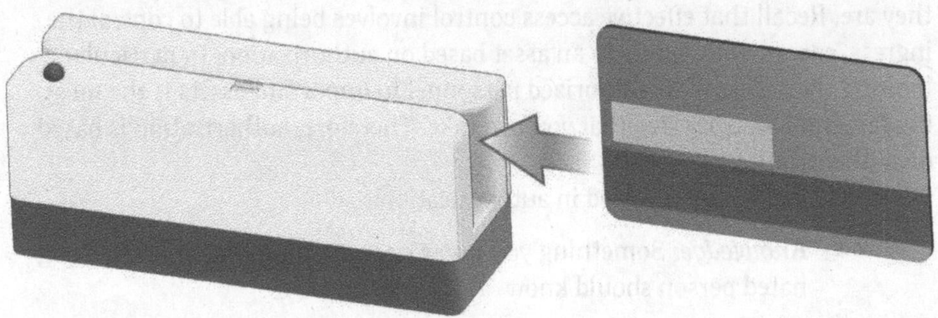

FIGURE 2.12 Magnetic Stripe Card System

The card reader reads the magnetically encoded information as it passes through the reader's magnetic sensor and translates it into digital data that it passes to a host system. The programming of the host system determines whether the information on the card is relevant to provide authorization and access for the cardholder.

Smart Cards

Smart cards are also credit-card-like devices that often resemble magnetic stripe cards, as shown in Figure 2.13. However, they offer improved data security due to the presence of intelligent circuitry that can be used to hide the user's data until an authentication process has been performed. They typically contain information about their owners, such as their passwords, personal identification numbers (PINs), network keys, digital certificates, and other Personally Identifiable Information (PII) that can be used in the authentication process.

A Word About PII

PII is considered any information that has the ability to identify an individual. Examples of PII include: first and last name, home address, Social Security number, date of birth, fingerprints, and other information that may distinguish one individual from another.

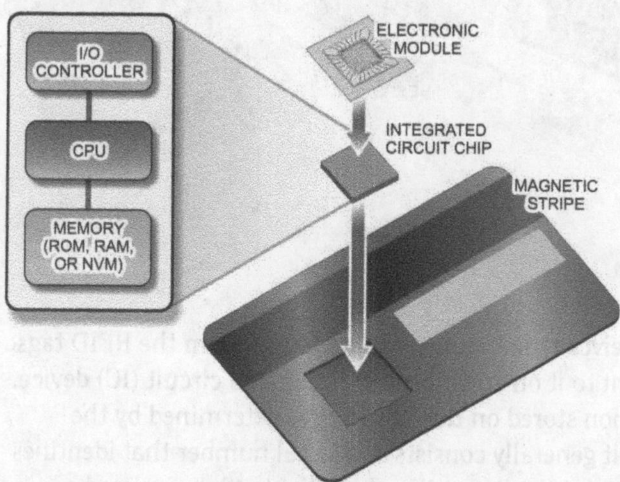

FIGURE 2.13 Smart Cards

Physically, smart cards are intelligent, credit-card-like devices, ID badges, and plug-in devices that communicate with a smart card reader.

Internally, all smart card designs contain a microprocessor and a memory device that are embedded in the card's structure. The smart-card memory section holds user-specific identification information, as well as all the programming the card needs to communicate with the host security system.

Some organizations that use smart cards issue their employees single cards that they can use to get into their buildings, log on to their computers, and access appropriate applications.

Smart cards are designed to be resistant to tampering. Tampering with a smart card generally disables it. In addition, some care must be taken with smart cards as even bending one may render it unusable.

RFID Badges

Radio Frequency Identification (RFID) badges provide hands-free access-control tools that improve on the bar code, magnetic stripe, and proximity reader technologies. The RFID system employs radio signals to identify unique items using an RFID reader device and RFID tags, as illustrated in Figure 2.14.

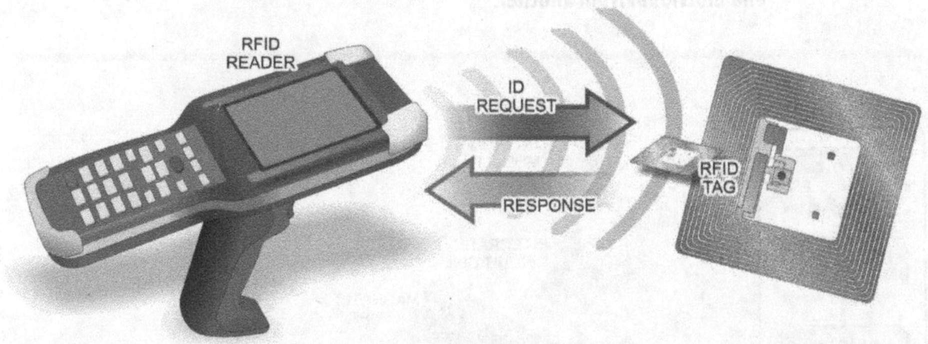

FIGURE 2.14 RFID System

The reader sends and receives radio frequency data to and from the RFID tags. Each tag stores the data sent to it on an embedded integrated circuit (IC) device. While the specific information stored on the RFID tag is determined by the RFID system programmer, it generally consists of a serial number that identifies it, along with information about the item with which the tag is associated.

When the system wants to know something associated with the tag, such as what (or who) it is associated with or where it is at, it simply sends out a request which causes the addressed RFID tag to radiate its information from its built-in antenna. The reader receives the data from the tag and relays it to its host computer for processing. The most interesting part of this technology is that the passive RFID tags are able to perform their task without the presence of an external power source.

Biometric Scanners

Biometrics is the term used to describe access-control mechanisms that use human physical characteristics to verify individual identities. Biometric authentication involves using uniquely personal physiological characteristics to verify people are who they say they are.

Every human possesses unique physical characteristics that differentiate them from other humans. Even identical twins have separate and distinctive voice patterns, fingerprints, eye features, and other characteristics. The qualities most often involved in biometric authentication include voice patterns, fingerprints, palm prints, signatures, facial features, and retinal and iris scans, as shown in Figure 2.15.

In each case, a biometric scanning device is required to convert the physiological quantity into a digital representation. The results are stored in a database where they can be used in an authentication process. The underlying application will use the truly unique qualities of the data as a basis to compare with future access requests. If the data from a future authentication request matches the key points of the stored version, then access will be granted.

However, not all biometric scanning devices are equally accurate at authenticating users. In Table 2.1, U.S. government data shows how different biometric scanning devices rate in terms of their abilities to accurately authenticate people.

TABLE 2.1 Biometric Device Comparisons

	False Positive Rate	False Negative Rate
Palm Print	1.43%	4%
Facial Structure	0.1%	0.8 – 1.6%
Voice Patterns	2 – 5%	5 – 10%
Eye (Retina or Iris)	0.1%	1.1 – 1.4%
Signature	0.49%	7.05%
Fingerprint	2.2%	2.2%

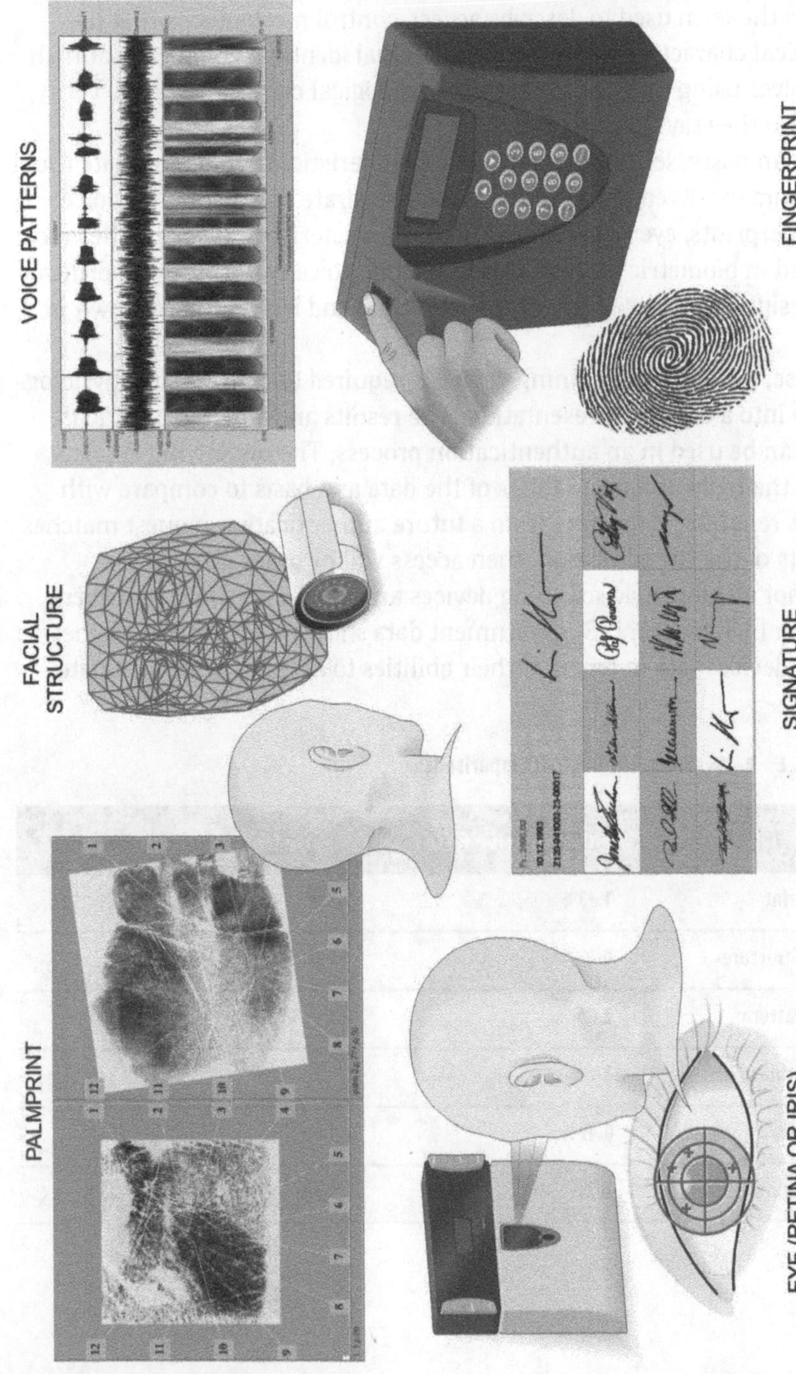

FIGURE 2.15 Typical Biometric Authentication Methods

In general, the characteristics of the human eye—iris and retinal scans—tend to make it the most reliable source of authentication. Of the remaining biometric variables in the list, fingerprint readings tend to be more accurate than voice scans. However, fingerprints can be stored on a clear surface and used later. On the other hand, illnesses and user stress levels can affect voiceprints.

As shown in Table 2.1, there are two basic types of authentication failure:

Type 1 – False Rejection or False Negative Failures This is a report that produces an incorrect rejection of the individual, thereby locking them out of a facility or security area that they should have been able to access.

Type 2 – False Acceptance or False Positive Failures This is a report that incorrectly authenticates the individual, which could lead to providing access to equipment or data that this person should not be able to access. Of the two types of authentication failures, this is the most significant in that it could grant access to malicious people.

Because of the potential for false reporting and inaccuracies, a second method of access control may need to be used in conjunction with biometric devices. In areas requiring higher security, a passport, additional fingerprints, or some other type of verification could be used to ensure that the individual was not mistakenly authenticated.

Remote-Access Monitoring

Remote monitoring refers to monitoring or measuring devices from a remote location or control room. In the security realm, this involves having external access to the security system through a communication system.

Remote-access monitoring systems are used to notify supervisory security personnel when an unauthorized access is attempted. In these systems, the controller monitors the open/close conditions of the infrastructure's sensors. When a sensor such as a magnetic switch or a motion detector is activated, the system automatically identifies it as an intrusion and notifies specified security personnel of the occurrence.

The notification can come in the form of a visual notification on a security control panel, a call via telephone, an instant messenger notice, or a text message to a smart phone. The notification can also involve activating strobe lights and high intensity sirens to call attention to the intrusion attempt. Figure 2.16 shows different options for remotely accessing a typical security system.

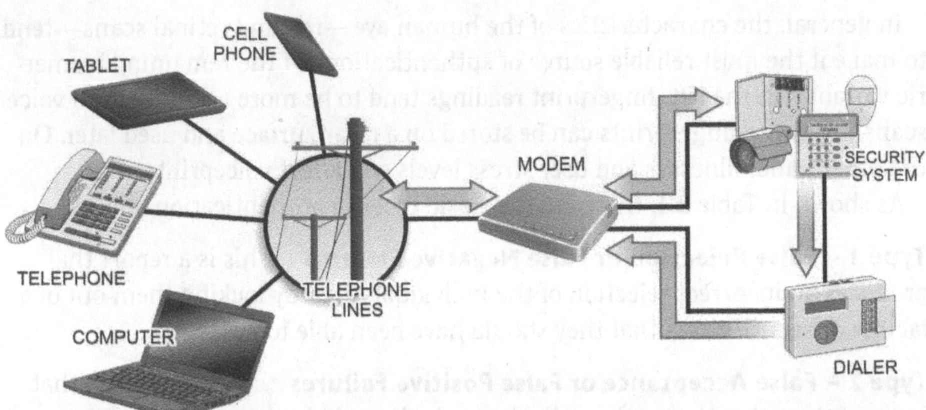

FIGURE 2.16 Remote-Access Communication Options

Opened- and Closed-Condition Monitoring

Various sensors can be used to detect the opened, closed, locked, or unlocked condition of an automated door or gate. They can also be configured to initiate an opened, closed, locked, or unlocked condition at a specified door or gate.

A Word About Sensors

Because open and closed conditions are not the same as locked and unlocked conditions, a single sensor cannot differentiate between these two sets of conditions. A second or different type of sensor needs to be installed and monitored to perform this differentiation.

A simple magnetic sensor and a matching set of contacts for a movable barrier (door, gate, or window) are shown in Figure 2.17. The sensor's transmitter sends a signal either to a control panel or to an emergency dialer when the magnetic switch contacts are broken as the door is opened.

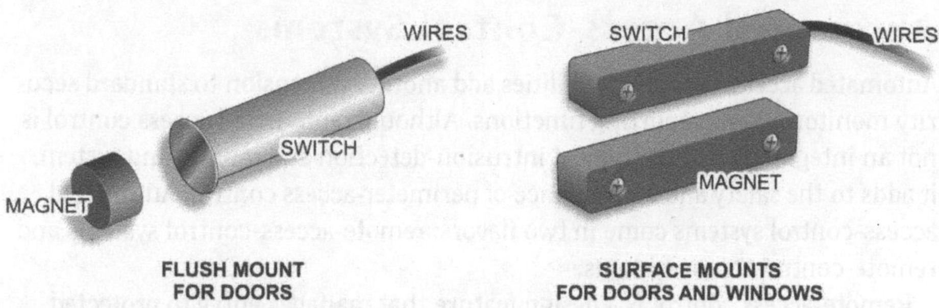

FIGURE 2.17 Window Sensor with Magnetic Switch Contacts

Signaling and reporting between the sensor and the controller is continuous during the elapsed time between the opening and closing of the barrier. If the barrier is left open for a specified time, that information is also noted and recorded by the system. The condition-monitoring system includes an event log, detailing the times and dates of various events. For example:

Locked-Condition Monitoring Locked monitoring is a feature that allows the security supervisor to confirm that a door is locked. In addition to monitoring the locked status of a door or gate, the condition-monitoring system can also provide details as to how long and during what time periods the door or gate has remained locked.

Unlocked-Condition Monitoring The condition-monitoring system can record and signal each time a specific gate or door is unlocked (granting access) and what type of access was granted. Unlocked monitoring can also identify who was granted access.

Time-of-Day Settings Most automated access-control systems base decisions about valid or invalid entry requests, also called *transactions,* on preconfigured time-of-day settings. This is normal because any entry request that does not fit the predefined time profile or time schedule of an identified user is subject to suspicion.

Such a situation might occur for a daily delivery that arrives later than normally expected. The user, in this case a recognized delivery agent, has been identified but is seeking entry at an unauthorized time. An authorized human supervisor will need to intervene to accept the delivery.

Automated Access-Control Systems

Automated access-control capabilities add another dimension to standard security monitoring and reporting functions. Although automated access control is not an integral part of the typical intrusion-detection and monitoring system, it adds to the safety and convenience of perimeter-access control. Automated access-control systems come in two flavors: remote-access-control systems and remote-control access systems.

Remote-access control is a design feature that manages entry to protected areas by authenticating the identity of persons entering a secured area (security zone or computer system) using an authentication system located in a different location than the access point.

This can be accomplished by a number of methods including password readers, magnetic key cards, and secret-cipher lock codes.

Although the differences are minor, the design considerations for remote-control access systems are different from those for remote-access systems. Remote-control access is a design feature that works with remote monitoring systems to monitor, control, and supervise doors, gates, and conveyances from a distance. Figure 2.18 shows the typical components involved in a remote-access-control system.

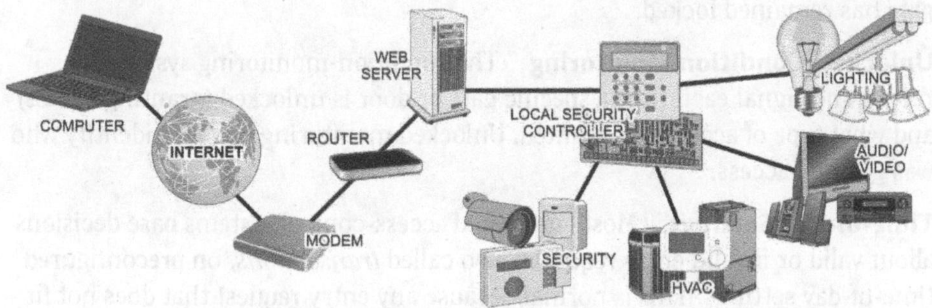

FIGURE 2.18 Remote-Control Operations

The Remote Control function enables the security specialist to initiate communications with a remote site, enter an access code, obtain current conditions, and set system parameters. A closed-circuit television (CCTV) system may be added to the security system to provide visual recognition functions to the remote-control options. Some remote-monitoring and control systems, such as the one depicted in Figure 2.19, can also be used or obtain status messages concerning any sensor that has detected a value outside of programmed values such as heat, cold, water leakage, loud noises, alarm history, or other custom features.

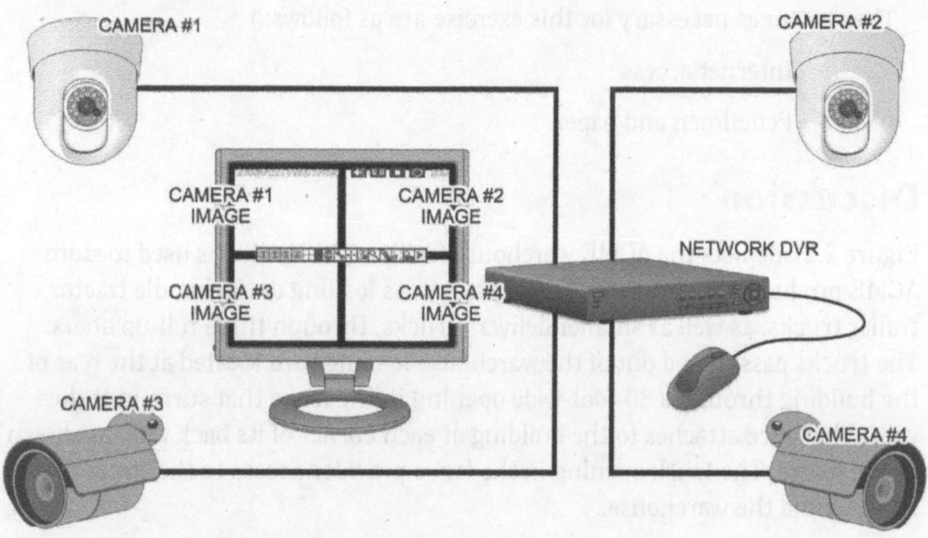

FIGURE 2.19 Remote-Monitoring Systems

Wireless communications devices are often used to connect the components of an automated access-control system. This type of connectivity is an economical solution that eliminates the need for new wiring between control devices, intercoms, and electrically operated security gates and doors.

Hands-On Exercises

In this exercise, you will learn how to secure the outer perimeter. The objectives include:

- For a given facility, define its outer perimeter, inner perimeter, and interior areas, and determine key vulnerabilities associated with each layer.
- For the specified facility and its vulnerabilities, perform research to determine what components (devices and systems) are available to secure these points and what the cost options are for the components you find.
- Design an access-monitoring and control system for the outer perimeter of the facility that will enable the customer to implement the security system required to monitor and control access to their facility.

The resources necessary for this exercise are as follows:

- Internet access
- Pencil/pen and paper

Discussion

Figure 2.20 depicts the ACME warehouse facility. This facility is used to store ACME products that are ready for shipment. Its loading docks handle tractor trailer trucks, as well as smaller delivery trucks, through three roll-up doors. The trucks pass in and out of the warehouse loading yard located at the rear of the building through a 30-foot-wide opening in the fence that surrounds the yard. The fence attaches to the building at each corner of its back wall, as shown in the figure. The truck opening in the fence provides access to the street that runs behind the warehouse.

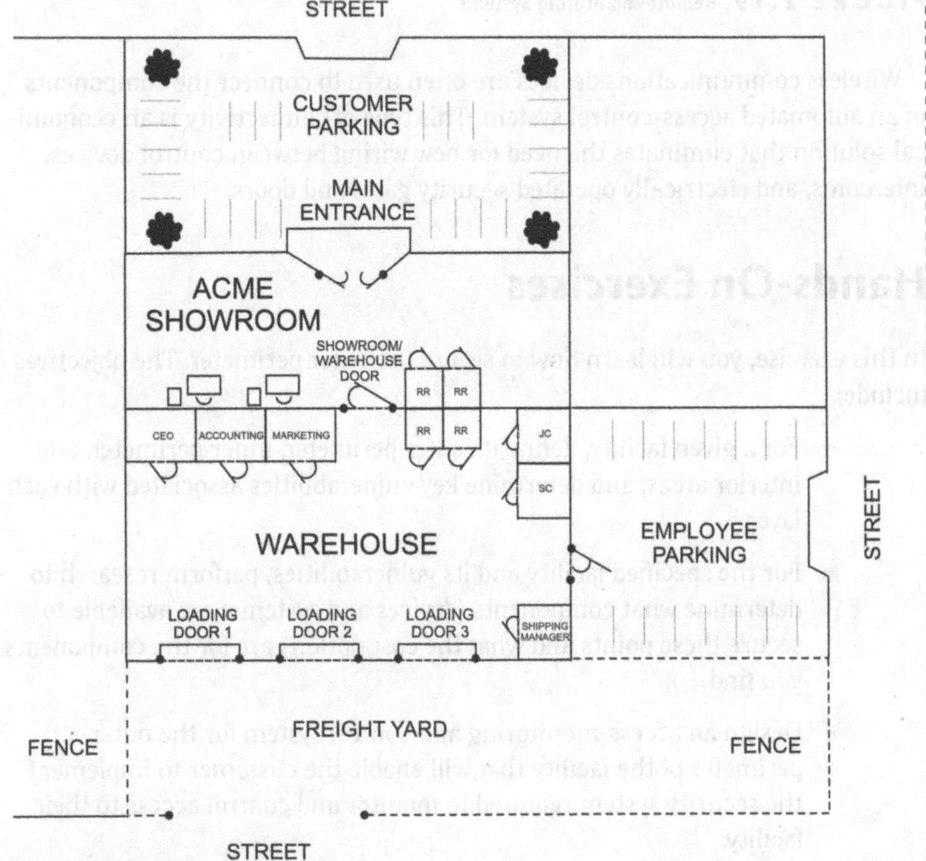

FIGURE 2.20 The Facility

Customers enter the building from the front where there is an open parking area and an attractive customer entrance featuring double glass doors. This parking area is open to the street and has no fencing around it. The customer showroom and sale staff desk areas occupy the front of the building, while the warehouse and management offices are in the rear of the building. Employees can transition between the warehouse and the showroom through an interior pedestrian door between the two portions of the building.

ACME personnel park in an employee parking area along the side of the building. They enter the facility through an employee pedestrian door that faces their parking area. The employee parking area is open and also has no fencing around it. Each ACME employee (warehouse, showroom, and management) will be issued a company ID device. The access-monitoring and control system should be capable of determining which employees have authorization to enter the warehouse portion of the facility.

The warehouse also houses the management offices and a pair of supply closets. Each office has a single window that faces the showroom and a door that opens into the warehouse area. The supply closets are equipped with a solid door and no windows.

The facility is nearing completion, and the ACME Company has asked you to research and recommend security and surveillance systems that will enable them to monitor and control the flow of people into and out of their warehouse.

Procedure

In this procedure, you will use whatever resources you have available to research physical security devices and systems that can be used to secure the outer perimeter of the ACME facility in preparation for developing a comprehensive physical-security proposal.

1. Examine Figure 2.21 and create/label a three-perimeter, multilayer security topology for the ACME facility.
2. After establishing the three perimeters of the security topology, return to the figure to identify and mark the physical access points associated with the facility's outer perimeter.
3. Use the Internet or other available research tools to research access-monitoring and control devices and systems that can be used to secure the access points you've identified in Step 2. Use Table 2.2 through Table 2.10 to organize the specified details about the access-monitoring and control products you find there. For each item, try to locate at least two vendors.

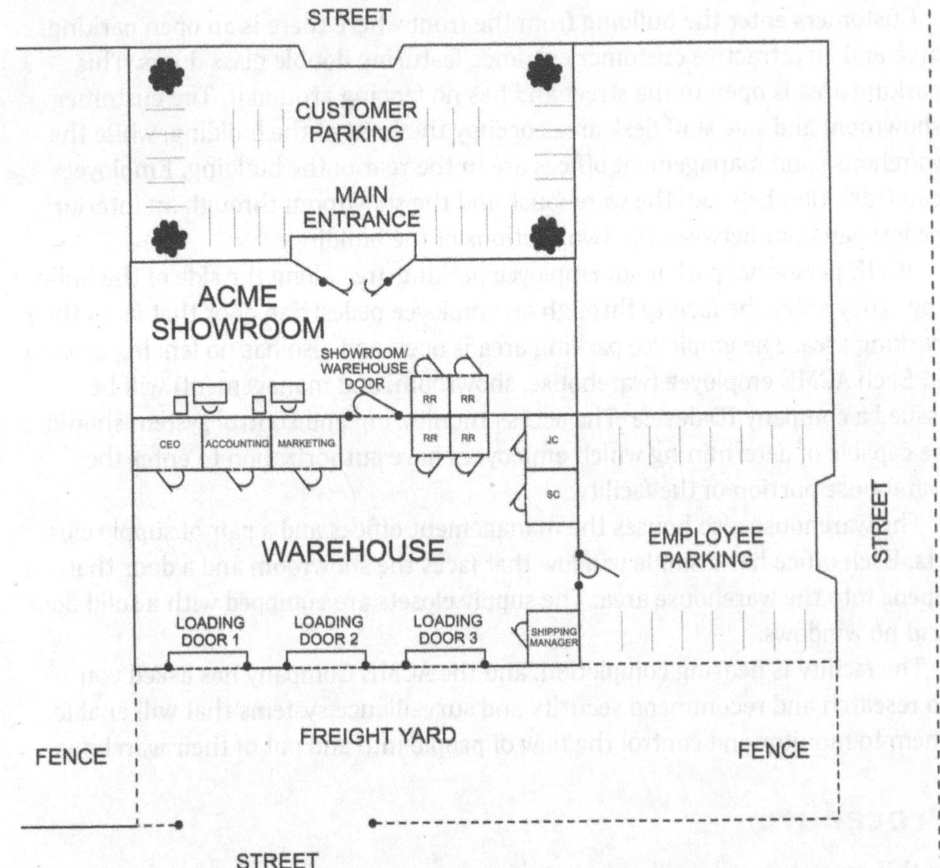

FIGURE 2.21 Security Perimeters

TABLE 2.2: Access-Control Gates

	Product Description	Vendor	Number Required	Cost Per Unit	Total Price
A	Slide Gate Op.	DoorKing	1	$889.00	$889.00
B	Slide Gate Op.	Viking	1	$1,048.00	$1,048.00
C	Slide Gate Op.	LiftMaster	1	$1,499.00	$1,499.00

4. List your selection for the access-control gate/gates you think should be recommended to ACME to secure the entrance to the truck-loading yard.

____

Answer: Viking meets the desired specifications for length and anticipated weight requirements to open a 30-foot sliding gate for the best price point. Vendors can be given access through RFID card or programmable access code.

TABLE 2.3: Access-Control Doors

	Product Description	Vendor	Number Required	Cost Per Unit	Total Price
A	Electronic Keyless Door Lock	Gino Development	1	$89.99	$89.99
B	Mag Door Lock Kit	Entry Vision	1	$274.99	$274.99
C	Cobra Controls Lock Kit	Maglocks.com	1	$1,699.99	$1,699.99

5. List your selection for the access-control doors that you think should be recommended to ACME for controlling their outer perimeter.

For the Warehouse Pedestrian Door: ____________________

Answer: The Entry Vision unit can use programmable keycards to allow all employees access to enter the building at the beginning of their work day. Manual deadbolt locks can secure the door at night.

For the Showroom Entry Doors: ____________________

Answer: Manual deadbolt with actuation to inside of showroom only.

TABLE 2.4: Door/Gate Actuators

	Product Description	Vendor	Number Required	Cost Per Unit	Total Price
A	Chain Drive	Genie	3	$185.88	$557.64
B	Jackshaft	LiftMaster	3	$273.39	$820.17
C	Screw Drive	Genie	3	$229.00	$687.00

6. List your selections for the any access door/gate actuators you think should be recommended to ACME.

____

Answer: The LiftMaster model can be configured to meet the needs of business, can be tied into security system to trigger if activated after an alarm is set or bypassed, and can be remotely operated by management or CEO if tied into network for after hours or weekend deliveries.

TABLE 2.5: Security Controllers

	Product Description	Vendor	Number Required	Cost Per Unit	Total Price
A	HAI OmniPro II	Leviton	1	$1,094.90	$1,094.90
B	Honeywell Intrusion	Ademco	1	$345.53	$345.53
C	Mercury Security EP4502	Mercury Security	1	$1,495.90	$1,495.90

7. List your selection for a security controller you think should be recommended to ACME to monitor and control the access points in their outer perimeter.

____

Answer: Leviton HAI OmniPro II. It offers the best price point for the features. The OmniPro II is Leviton's flagship security and automation control system. Boasting the largest feature set, it can control the maximum number of devices and is designed to provide security and automation for large residences and small commercial installations such as restaurants, offices, and franchise locations. This allows all security considerations to be tied into one controller with multiple zone configurations for varying perimeter requirements. It can cover up to 176 zones so you can segregate or integrate as needed.

TABLE 2.6: Security Keypads

	Product Description	Vendor	Number Required	Cost Per Unit	Total Price
A	Omni 33A00-4	Leviton	1	$192.00	$192.00
B	Honeywell Lynx 7000	Alarm Liquidators	1	$204.95	$204.95
C	Interlogix CaddX Keypad	Home Security Store	1	$94.65	$94.65

8. List your selection for the security keypad you think should be recommended to ACME to enable and disable functions of the security system controller.

____

Answer: Omni 33A00-4 is the best selection because it can be expanded for increased control over loading-bay doors and a slide gate in the freight yard, and it is guaranteed to be compatible with the selected controller.

TABLE 2.7: Door Contacts/Sensors

	Product Description	Vendor	Number Required	Cost Per Unit	Total Price
A	Door Sensor Wired	SensaPhone	8	$9.00	$72.00
B	Gate & Com. Door Sensor	Gogogate	8	$35.00	$280.00
C	SDC MC-4	Grainger Industrial	8	$53.95	$431.60

9. List your selection for the door sensor types you think should be recommended to ACME for their outer perimeter access points.

____

Answer: The Gogogate sensors with an integrated indoor and outdoor sensor system utilizing magnetic contact sensors should be used for eight units. There is a wide enough gap for commercial and residential applications, so they should work well with delivery bay and pedestrian doors as well as the freight gate to monitor access.

TABLE 2.8: Driveway Sensors

	Product Description	Vendor	Number Required	Cost Per Unit	Total Price
A	Driveway Sensor	Mighty Mule	1	$180.78	$180.78
B	Direct Burial Sensor	CarSense	1	$208.46	$208.46
C	WPA 3000 Magnetic Probe	Absolute Automation	1	$249.00	$249.00

10. List your selection (if any) for driveway sensors that you think should be recommended to ACME for the truck gate.

____

Answer: The CarSense unit can be used to automate the opening of the gate for delivery trucks leaving, and it can be tied into/bypassed from the security system to trigger an alarm if activated by a vehicle leaving after hours.

TABLE 2.9: Authentication Devices/Systems

	Product Description	Vendor	Number Required	Cost Per Unit	Total Price
A	Mag Door Lock Kit	Entry Vision	1	$274.99	$274.99
B	Electronic Keyless Door Lock	Gino Development	1	$89.99	$89.99
C	Cobra Controls Lock Kit	Maglocks.com	1	$1,699.99	$1,699.99

11. List your selection for any authentication devices/systems you think should be recommended to ACME for controlling personnel access through their outer perimeter.

    ____

    Answer: RFID passcards should be used to enter through the pedestrian door to the warehouse from outside. The Mag Door Lock Kit already has this feature integrated as part of its design.

    Also specify where you would employ the authentication devices/systems.

    ____

    Answer: They should be used to enter through the pedestrian door to warehouse from employee parking outside.

TABLE 2.10: Door Locks

	Product Description	Vendor	Number Required	Cost Per Unit	Total Price
A	Mag Door Lock Kit	Entry Vision	1	$274.99	$274.99
B	Electronic Keyless Door Lock	Gino Development	1	$89.99	$89.99
C	Schlage B581	Doorware.com	2	$52.00	$104.00

12. List your selection for the access-control door locks you think should be recommended to ACME. Also specify where you would employ the door locks you are recommending.

    ____

    Answer: The Mag Door Lock Kit should be applied to the outside warehouse pedestrian door for entry authentication and control. The Electronic Keyless Door Lock should be applied to the pedestrian door between the warehouse and showroom. It can be actuated without any authentication steps from inside the warehouse, but it requires a key or passcode to operate the door from inside the showroom. Schlage B581 should be used outside the showroom and outside the warehouse pedestrian door to secure the perimeter during closed hours.

13. On Figure 2.22, record the types of devices and deployment locations you would recommend to ACME's management to secure the outer perimeter of their new warehouse facility. Explain the reasoning for your recommendations on the lines provided.

____

____

____

____

Answer: Apply the Mag Door Lock Kit to the outside warehouse pedestrian door for entry authentication and control. Apply the Schlage B581 to the outside showroom and outside warehouse pedestrian door to secure the perimeter during closed hours. The CarSense unit can be used to automate the opening of the gate for delivery trucks leaving, and it can be tied into/bypassed from the security system to trigger an alarm if activated by a vehicle leaving after hours. Use seven Gogogate sensors as an integrated indoor and outdoor sensor system utilizing magnetic contact sensors. The gap is wide enough for commercial and residential applications, so they should work well with the delivery bay and pedestrian doors, as well as the freight gate to monitor access. The Leviton HAI OmniPro II has the best price point for its features. The OmniPro II is Leviton's flagship security and automation control system. Boasting the largest feature set, it can control the maximum number of devices and is designed to provide security and automation for large residences and small commercial installations such as restaurants, offices, and franchise locations. This allows all security considerations to be tied into one controller with multiple zone configurations for varying perimeter requirements. It can cover up to 176 zones, so you can segregate or integrate as needed. The Liftmaster model can be configured to meet the needs of the business. It can be tied into a security system to trigger if activated after an alarm is set or bypassed. It can be remotely operated by management for after hours or weekend deliveries if tied into the network. Viking meets the desired specifications for length and anticipated weight requirements for opening a 30-foot sliding gate for the best price point. Vendors can be given access through an RFID card or a programmable access code.

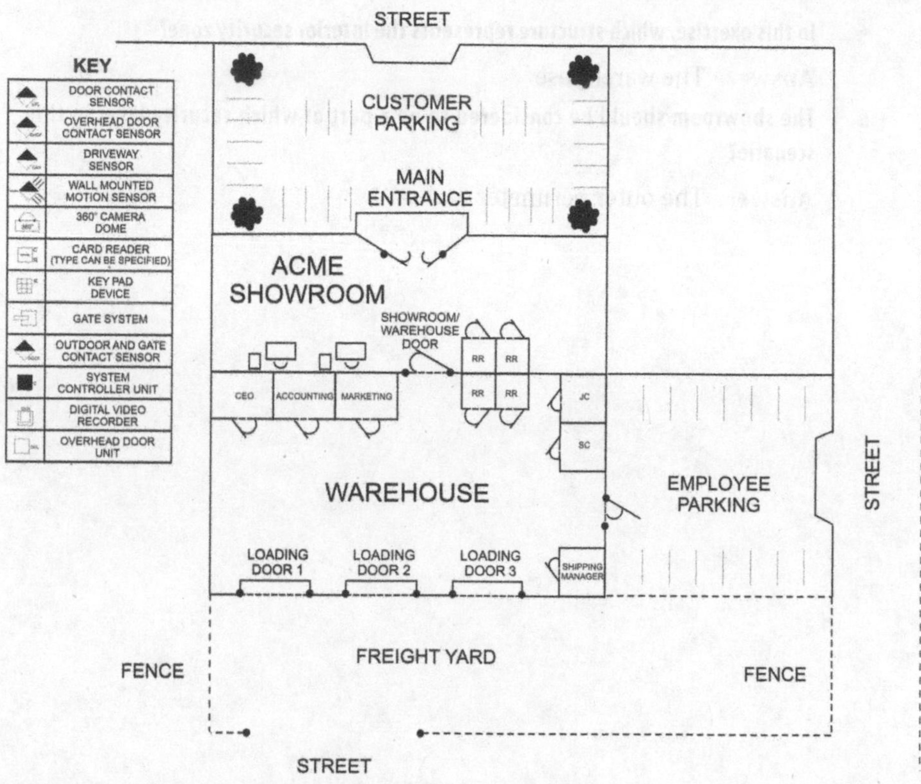

FIGURE 2.22 Device Locations

Review Questions

1. **Which access points are associated with the outer perimeter of the facility?**

   Answer: The street access opening in the fence for trucks to come and go, the warehouse employees' entrance door, and the main entrance door to the showroom

2. **The access door between the showroom and the warehouse are considered to be part of which security perimeter?**

   Answer: The inner perimeter

3. **Which access points are associated with the inner perimeter?**

   Answer: The access door between the warehouse and the showroom, the loading dock doors, and the pedestrian door into the warehouse from employee parking

4. **In this exercise, which structure represents the interior security zone?**

   Answer: The warehouse

5. **The showroom should be considered to be a part of which security layer in this scenario?**

   Answer: The outer perimeter

CHAPTER 3

Understanding Video Surveillance Systems

Video surveillance systems—the second of the three basic types of subsystems introduced in Chapter 2—are important elements of most commercial security systems. Many organizations include visible cameras in their infrastructure security systems to inhibit unlawful activity and to record events that occur at the perimeter or key interior levels. In this chapter, you'll learn to:

- **Identify strengths and weaknesses of different types of security and surveillance systems and devices**
- **Select appropriate camera types when given specific scenarios**

Video Surveillance Systems

Video surveillance systems are based on closed-circuit television (CCTV) systems. The name is derived from the type of the system that transmits signals over a "closed circuit" or private transmission circuit rather than over a standard television broadcast system. Figure 3.1 shows the major components of a basic video surveillance system. Common components include:

- One or more video cameras
- A time-lapse video recorder
- A switcher (optional)
- A video display monitor

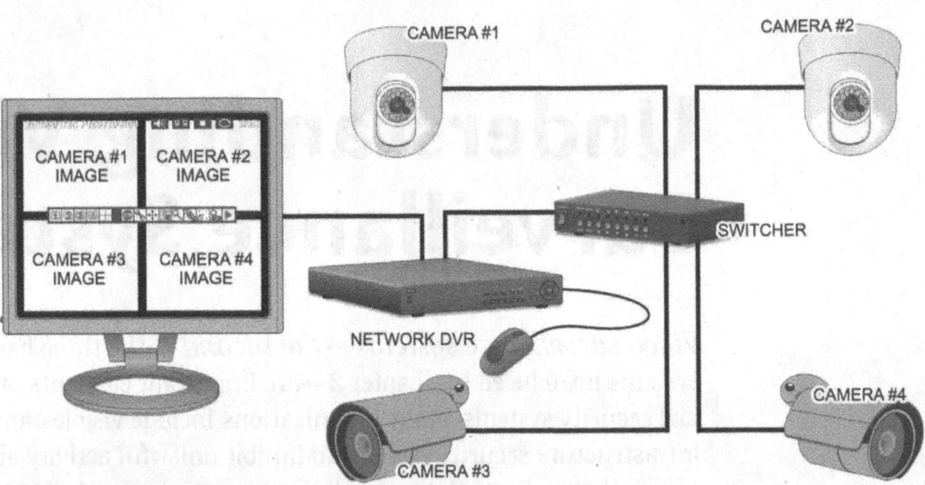

FIGURE 3.1 A Basic Video Surveillance System

In this basic system, the cameras monitor their fields of vision and pass the information to the video-processing equipment. In most cases, this equipment consists of a digital video recorder of some type.

In some cases, the flow of video information from the cameras is controlled by passive infrared (PIR) detectors. If there is no PIR signature (created by body heat) in the PIR detector's field of view, the video information is not transmitted. However, during event periods of motion detection, the video information flows from the camera to the video recorder. In such events, the cameras can be instructed to speed up the number of frames recorded per second to provide finer detail.

Some systems are based on coaxial cable for component connectivity, while others are IP-based and rely on wireless Wi-Fi communications or traditional network cabling.

The digital video-processing equipment can provide video output directly to a video display, or the video output can be channeled to a video switcher. In some cases, the video-processing component may offer its own integrated switcher.

These components are covered in greater detail in the following sections.

Cameras

Surveillance systems use video cameras that convert a viewed image into standard video-transmission formats (composite video, component video, S-Video, or

HDMI signals) for display on a video output device, such as a monitor, television display, or personal computing device.

The best surveillance cameras employ Charged Coupled Device (CCD) technology. They have high-resolution, low-operating light requirements, less temperature dependence, and high reliability. A typical CCD camera used in video surveillance systems is illustrated in Figure 3.2.

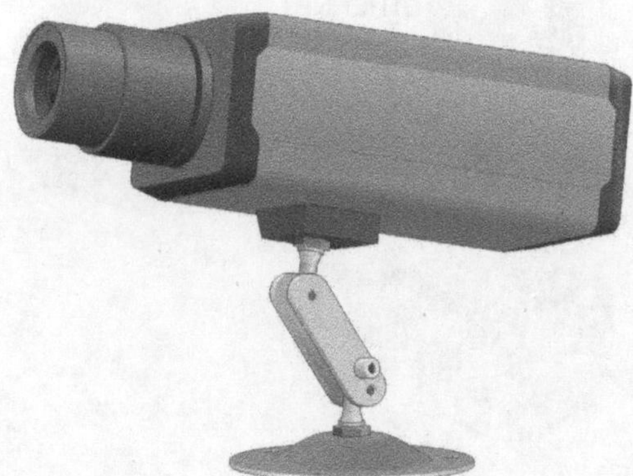

FIGURE 3.2 Video Surveillance Camera

Surveillance cameras are available that use digital or analog interface technologies. Digital cameras convert the images they detect directly into digital signals that can easily be transmitted to and manipulated by digital computing devices. Analog cameras are based on older analog television signal and resolution standards. Cameras of this type require a separate coaxial cable to connect to a monitor or recording device.

Digital cameras generally offer superior performance over analog cameras. Analog cameras are more susceptible to quality degradation of the information being transmitted.

IP Cameras

IP cameras are actually digital IP (Internet Protocol) devices that have IP addresses that can be connected directly to a network, or to the Internet, rather than directly to a host controller or computer. The advantage of using an IP camera, like the one depicted in Figure 3.3, is that it can be viewed from anywhere in the world where Internet access is available.

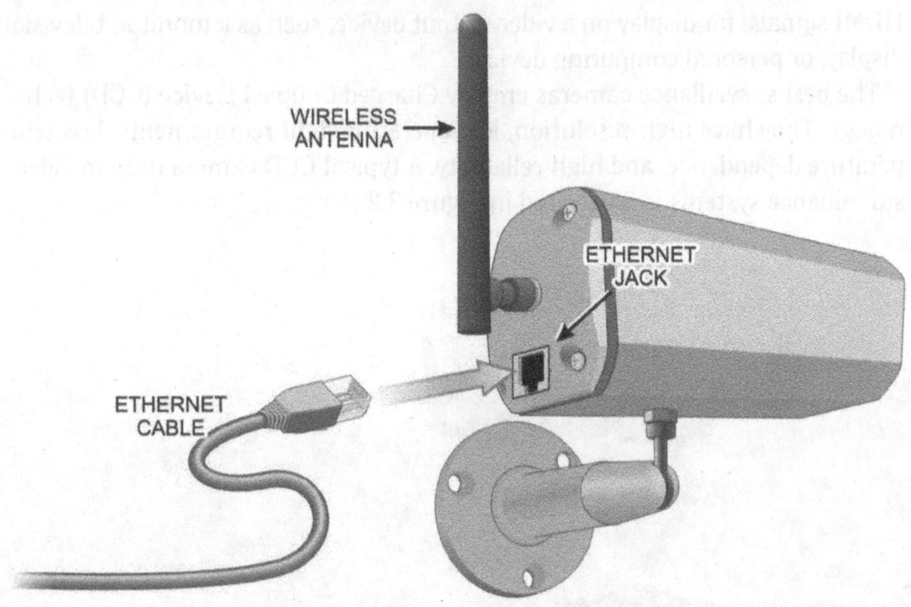

FIGURE 3.3 IP Camera

What sets IP systems apart from other video technologies are the abilities to email notification of motion sensing, process simultaneous user logins, and conduct FTP upload operations. An additional benefit of these cameras is that they can be powered by Power over Ethernet (PoE), whereby power is provided through the network cable rather than from a dedicated power supply for each camera.

Pan-Tilt-Zoom Cameras

A network IP camera with Pan-Tilt-Zoom (PTZ) capabilities, like the one depicted in Figure 3.4, is a standalone device that permits users to view live full-motion video from anywhere. This type of camera is designed for use either on a proprietary computer network or over the Internet using only a standard web browser as its display unit.

Not only is manual Pan-Tilt-Zoom control provided, the ability to remotely direct dozens of positions for each PTZ-capable camera is also possible.

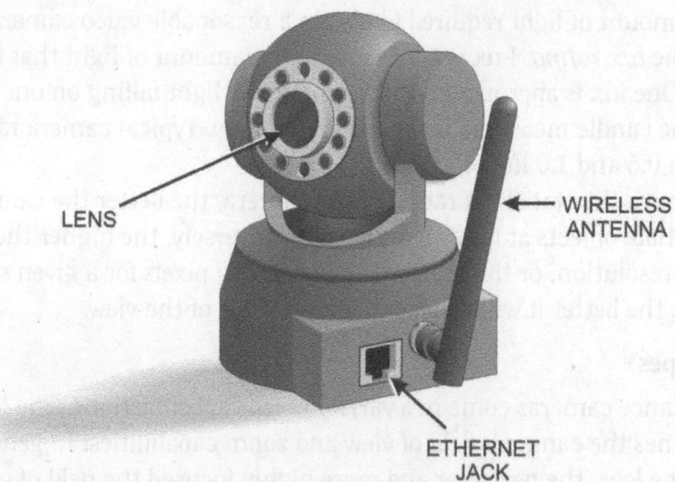

FIGURE 3.4 Pan-Tilt-Zoom Camera

Camera Specifications

The two important specifications that influence the cost of cameras are light-sensitivity rating and resolution. The camera's resolution-specification method depends on whether it is an analog camera or a digital camera.

Resolution for an analog camera is specified as the number of horizontal lines it is capable of generating from top to bottom of the display. With digital cameras, the resolution is expressed in terms of the X-by-Y (horizontal-to-vertical) dot (picture elements or pixels) matrix format it produces. Figure 3.5 illustrates the meanings of the different camera-resolution specifications.

DIGITAL

ANALOG

FIGURE 3.5 Analog and Digital Camera Resolution

The amount of light required to obtain a reasonable video camera image is called the *lux rating.* Lux is a measure of the amount of light that falls on an object. One lux is approximately the amount of light falling on one square meter from one candle measured from one meter away. Typical camera ratings range between 0.5 and 1.0 lux.

The lower the stated lux rating of the camera, the better the camera is able to differentiate objects at lower light levels. Conversely, the higher the number of lines of resolution, or the greater the number of pixels for a given surveillance camera, the better it will display the fine details of the view.

Lens Types

Surveillance cameras come in a variety of lens specifications. The lens size determines the camera's field of view and zoom capabilities. In general, the larger the lens, the narrower and more highly focused the field of view will be.

For example, a fixed lens rated at a 3.6 mm focal length is designed to provide a field of view of approximately 72 degrees, while a 6 mm focal length lens should provide a 44-degree field of view. As a general rule, the shorter the focal length of the lens, the wider the field of view.

On the other hand, a lens with a shorter focal length will also produce a view that provides less image detail. At a distance of 16 feet (5 meters), a 3.6 mm fixed lens may only provide a general description of the objects in a parking facility, while the same camera with a 12 mm lens would provide sharper details of objects in the field of view (such as faces and license plate numbers) but might only cover a fraction of the facility.

You must also determine the objectives of having surveillance cameras. Are they to provide a visible deterrence? Are they to be used for gathering legal evidence? It is always important to select surveillance cameras with lens specifications that will capture the desired viewing area. Common security-camera-lens types include:

Varifocal Lens These are optical assemblies containing several movable elements that permit the effective focal length (EFL) to be changed. Unlike a zoom lens, a varifocal lens needs to be refocused with each change. If a surveillance camera has a fixed lens, it can see only one fixed position. If it has a varifocal lens, it can focus at multiple mm settings based on the user's preference.

Fixed Focal Length Lens Lens that can't be refocused regardless of the distance to the subject.

Wide-Angle Lens Lens that provides the ability to see a wider image in confined areas than standard lens types.

Telephoto Lens The best type of lens for seeing details at long ranges.

Fish Eye Lens A type of lens that allows you to see an entire room, but with some distortion of the image.

Pinhole Lens Lens used for applications where the camera/lens must be hidden. The front of the lens has a small opening to allow the lens to view an entire room through a small hole in a wall.

Black and White versus Color

There is a common misconception that color CCTV cameras offer better pictures than black-and-white (B&W) CCTV cameras. The reality is that although color cameras are more enjoyable to view, both types of cameras are fully capable of providing quality pictures. The real question is what type of camera is better suited for a particular situation.

The most important practical difference between color and black-and-white cameras is that only color cameras can offer a full and accurate clothing and vehicle description. Law enforcement relies heavily on the reported colors of clothing and suspect vehicle when responding to calls for service. Being able to look for specified colors greatly increases the likelihood of catching a suspect.

IR Illumination

Cameras with infrared illumination of the image area permit viewing in low-light conditions. This also provides the ability to maintain a degree of secrecy by using illumination that is outside of the visible light spectrum.

An infrared security camera has infrared LED lighting (light from a region of the electromagnetic spectrum than humans cannot see) installed around the outside of the camera lens. This lighting allows the camera to capture a good image in no-light settings. With a small amount of light (a low-light setting), the infrared camera can capture a picture that looks just like daytime. A typical IR camera is shown in Figure 3.6.

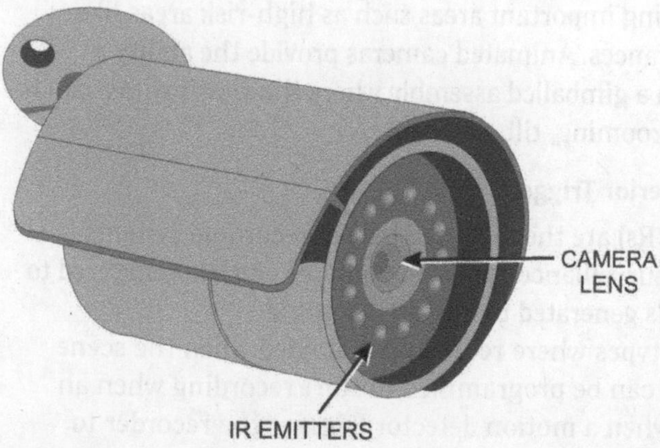

FIGURE 3.6 IR Camera

Camera Applications

Surveillance cameras can be mounted outside the facility to provide the ability to recognize someone wishing to enter the security perimeter area such as a front door or driveway gate. The cameras should be located where no blind spots exist or where it is not practical to use other types of sensors. Cameras can be mounted on any surface area of the facility where coverage is required, as long as the area is illuminated sufficiently at all times after dark.

There are certain legal implications involved in using video surveillance cameras. In particular, there are privacy concerns that must be taken into account when deploying surveillance cameras. They should not be used where there is a reasonable expectation of privacy by individuals, such as in a restroom. This obviously does not apply to a person breaking into a facility.

Other applications for cameras are discussed in the following sections.

Indoor/Outdoor

Indoor cameras are usually less expensive than outdoor types because outdoor cameras must be housed in weatherproof enclosures. The cabling for outdoor cameras must also be suitable for temperature extremes and seasonal weather conditions.

Day/Night

Cameras are available that can switch from color imaging in the daytime and black-and-white for night operation when the illumination is too low for color. This provides the best tradeoff between good color resolution during daytime monitoring and black-and-white during night hours when the light levels are not sufficient for color imaging.

Fixed versus Animated

Cameras that are mounted in a fixed configuration always show the same areas. They are useful for monitoring important areas such as high-risk areas like parking areas and door entrances. Animated cameras provide the ability to move. They are mounted on a gimballed assembly where the viewing area can be changed, and they support zooming, tilt, and pan.

Recording and External/Interior Triggers

Digital Video Recorders (DVRs) are the preferred type of recording systems rather than older VCRs for surveillance cameras. Cameras can be configured to record only when a trigger is generated to initiate recording.

Triggers can be internal types where recording is started when the scene changes. External triggers can be programmed to start recording when an alarm condition exists or when a motion detector triggers the recorder to begin recording.

Sequencing versus Multiplexing

Sequencing allows several cameras to be used with a single monitor. A switcher can be programmed to cycle through all of the cameras in a surveillance system or to dwell on each camera for a specified length of time, usually in the range of 1 to 60 seconds.

Multiplexers route the images from the surveillance system to a specific display device and are capable of recording all of the camera images at the same time by tiling them on the monitor.

Camera Deployment Strategies

The purpose for investing in security cameras is to be able to view activity in critical areas or where critical assets are located. In addition to determining what specifications security cameras must possess for a given role, it is equally important to map out a camera deployment strategy to maximize the surveillance investment.

To accomplish this, cameras should be positioned to capture important events in all critical security areas. In particular, they should be installed in passageways and in locations where their field of vision covers important assets (physical equipment and/or personnel).

Passageways include chokepoints in the physical facility where people or other traffic must pass through a portal, such as a gate, doorway, hallway, or access street/road. Cameras in passageways are typically placed there to document entry, exit, and movement through a facility, as illustrated in Figure 3.7.

FIGURE 3.7 Monitoring Passageways

Security cameras are routinely installed in positions that cover important assets and activities within the facility. This enables management to monitor activities around and associated with those important assets.

Bank lobbies are great examples of both placement strategies. Cameras are positioned to record activities around the bank's parking area and exterior, as well as in hallways that lead to the vault and offices, as illustrated in Figure 3.8. In addition, most banks have cameras arranged so they can focus on each teller station to monitor the handling of money and transactions.

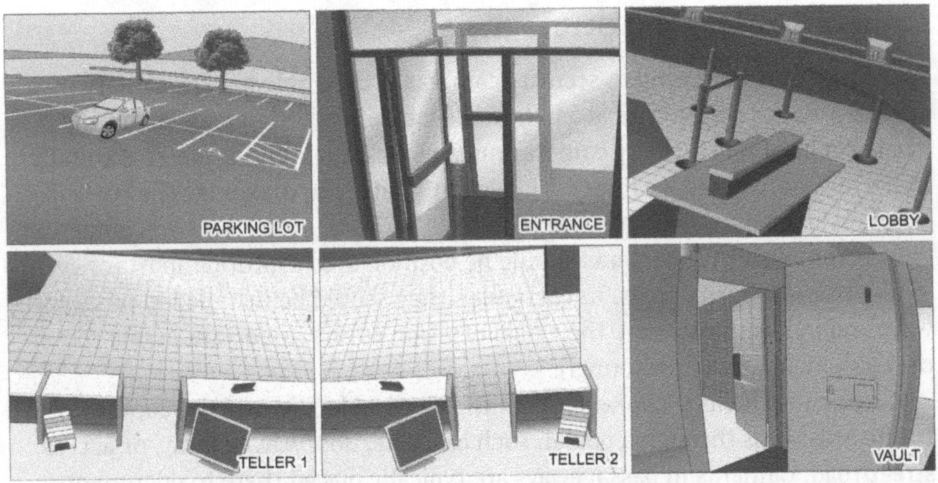

FIGURE 3.8 **Asset Monitoring**

Determining actual camera placement is a matter of first deciding whether the camera is required to provide an overview or detailed view. An overview generally covers a wide field of view, such as over a parking lot or warehouse floor. Conversely, a detailed view is required for targeting relatively narrow fields of view featuring specific areas of interest, such as the bank teller stations mentioned earlier.

The number of cameras involved in the installation depends on the number of passageways and assets that have been identified for viewing/monitoring. In some cases, this depends on the size of the organization; in others, it depends on the value of the assets and physical geography involved.

For example, a small operation may only need to install a single camera to provide surveillance of their key assets. For medium-sized operations, it is far more common for installations to involve dozens of cameras. In large organizations, hundreds of cameras may be deployed to meet their security and surveillance needs. The goal is to effectively cover the areas and assets identified through risk-analysis procedures.

After the installation points have been determined, the next step in the deployment strategy is to determine the specifications for the cameras to be used at each installation point. In general, the following four questions should be answered:

- Is a fixed or movable field of view required?
- Which type of image display is required?
- Which level of display definition is required?
- Which type of signal processing and transmission is best suited for the installation?

Fixed or Movable Field

Fixed cameras are typically employed for overview functions. They provide a fixed field of view, so they must be set up to effectively cover the desired passageway or asset. Therefore, they must have the desired focal length and angle to cover these items.

A remotely controlled PTZ camera is generally used where a detailed view is required. However, in some cases, it may be more economical to install several fixed cameras in different locations than to mount a single PTZ camera that requires an attendant to operate it effectively.

Image Display

From the previous discussion in Chapter 2, you should recall that common image display options include:

Color Color cameras are the default, general-purpose cameras in video surveillance applications today. The one application where color cameras lag behind other camera technologies is in low-light situations. In such cases, infrared or thermal cameras are generally advised.

Infrared Infrared cameras provide clear black-and-white images in very low-light settings. However, they tend to be significantly more expensive than color cameras.

Thermal Thermal cameras tend to be very expensive and produce only silhouettes. However, they also require no light to work.

Display Definition Levels

Is a standard video display acceptable for the view being addressed or is something with a higher definition required? One of the biggest complaints associated with standard definition systems is their inability to deliver a signal that enables law enforcement and the courts to positively identify criminal suspects after a crime.

Signal Processing and Transmission

As described earlier in the chapter, the choices here include analog, digital, and IP cameras. IP cameras continue to gain acceptance over other types of cameras due to their ability to capture and transmit data electronically.

IP cameras also provide more robust connectivity options than traditional analog and digital cameras. They can work directly with a host computer without additional hardware. They are also more compatible with wireless networking options than other camera technologies.

Video Recorders

CCTV has traditionally been recorded using Videocassette Recorders (VCRs); however, such systems tend to be highly labor-intensive. The wear and tear on tapes is a constant problem, along with the need to perform periodic system maintenance.

The introduction of Digital Video Recorders (DVRs) has greatly reduced the dependence on storage media quality and operator intervention. The migration of video recording to digital media has permitted the storage of images to disk and has provided additional advantages such as:

- Ease of use
- Advanced search capabilities
- Simultaneous record/playback functions
- No image degradation
- Improved compression storage techniques
- Integration with other digital systems
- Remote system-management capabilities

Some video-processing systems feature built-in web server functions that provide remote access to either live images or recently recorded ones.

These web interfaces are capable of permitting viewing from one or multiple remote locations.

An example of a video-processing unit with built-in web access capabilities is shown in Figure 3.9. Units like this are capable of conducting Internet monitoring activities from remote locations.

FIGURE 3.9 A Video Recorder

Saved recordings can be searched according to date and time or according to activity/alarm mode options using real-time Video Motion Detection (VMD) technology. Active alerting can also be provided through email transmissions from the observing location.

Two of the most important considerations when recording video for security purposes are how much video needs to be stored and for how long. The answers to these questions enable the organization to determine its storage capacity needs.

Security video by its nature requires a substantial amount of storage space. As such, there is always a tradeoff between storage costs and the risk the organization faces. A single video surveillance camera can consume multiple gigabytes of storage capacity in a single day. With this in mind, the requirement for how long the organization needs to store surveillance video becomes a major decision point. Depending on the nature of the organization and the types of risks they face, the storage requirements may require that several weeks or months of video be stored for each camera they install.

As mentioned earlier, most organizations do not employ a single camera for their surveillance needs—they may employ dozens or hundreds of cameras. To store video data coming from so many cameras can easily require hundreds of terabytes of data storage.

Three common video-storage types can be employed to meet such needs:

Internal Storage Video information can be stored on the internal disk drive (or drives) in the DVR. This solution is practical only for small organizations that use few cameras and store the video information only for a short time.

Peripheral Storage or Direct-Attached Storage (DAS) This technique employs additional disk-drive storage devices that are attached directly to the DVR via USB or eSATA connections, as depicted in Figure 3.10. Direct-Attached Storage does not involve using an IP address to offload the video to the external device.

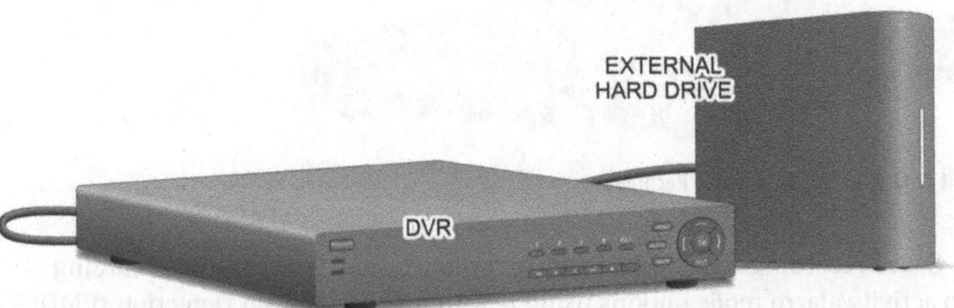

FIGURE 3.10 DAS Video Storage

Networked Storage This storage method uses networking techniques to store IP-based video on remote computers or video servers. The most common techniques for doing this include Network Attached Storage (NAS) and Storage Area Network (SAN) technologies, as shown in Figure 3.11.

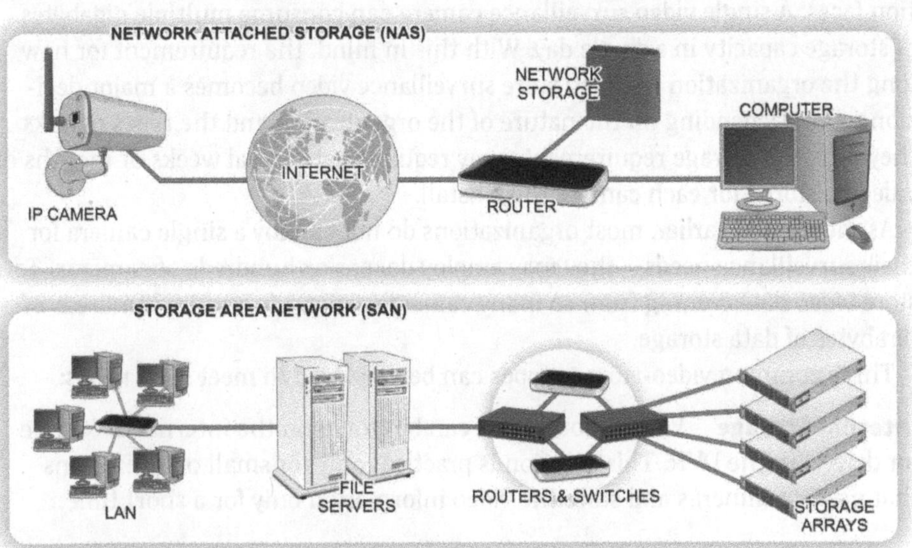

FIGURE 3.11 NAS and SAN Storage Systems

Switchers

Switchers are devices used with multiple-camera surveillance systems. They allow several cameras to be used with a single monitor. A switcher can be programmed to cycle through all of the cameras in a surveillance system or to dwell on each camera for a specified length of time, usually in the range of 1 to 60 seconds. Exterior sensors can detect movement and cause cameras to start recording on a video recorder.

A Word About Switchers

Four images can be displayed by a "quad" switcher. More advanced systems often provide simultaneous video recording, viewing, and playback activities using 4-, 9-, 16-, or 25-camera capacities.

A *quad* is a switcher that allows the viewer to simultaneously record and monitor four cameras at a time. It does this by splitting the monitor screen into four sections. The normal configuration for connecting a quad switcher with a sensor and a video recorder is shown in Figure 3.12, which illustrates the connections between a quad switcher, a monitor, and four surveillance cameras. The monitor can view all four images at the same time. The sensor detects movement that triggers the video recorder to capture a recording of the event.

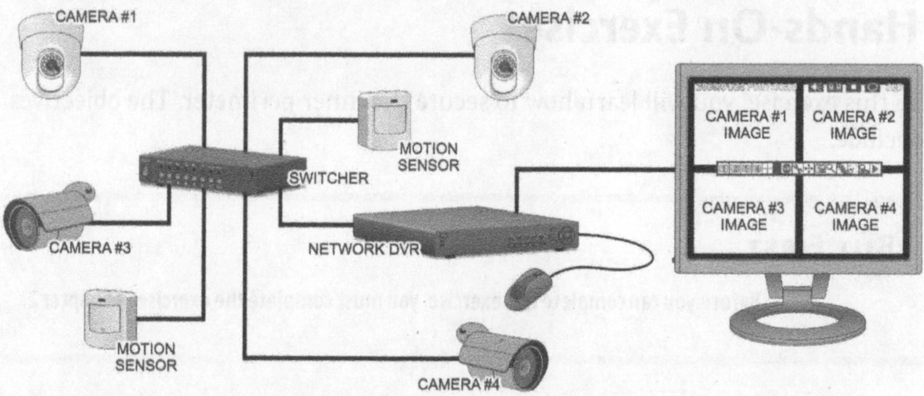

FIGURE 3.12 Quad Camera Switcher with a Sensor and Video Recorder

Typically, live images can be observed from one camera at a time or from multiple cameras simultaneously. Security personnel can use the interface to browse through and play back recordings from a specified camera, using fully adjustable built-in VMD.

Security Monitors

Monitors are video display systems similar to computer displays or televisions. They display video information that is obtained from the cameras and processed by video processing devices, such as the DVR. They may also be connected to programmable switchers that receive inputs from several cameras so as to show multiple images on a single screen.

The quality of the image produced on the screen is a function of two factors: the *refresh rate* (the speed at which the image is retraced on the screen) and the number of pixels (picture elements) on the screen. The more pixels on a given screen size, the higher the image quality.

As with cameras, this quantity is referred to as the display's *resolution,* and is often expressed in an X-by-Y format. Using this format, the quality of the image is still determined by how big the viewing area is (for example, an 800 × 600 resolution on a 14-inch-wide display will produce much better quality than the same number of pixels spread across a 27-inch display).

CCTV monitors are available for black-and-white or color display, depending on the resolution and camera selection. Black-and-white monitors have resolutions in the range of 700 to 1,000 lines. Color monitors are available with 350 to 400 lines. They are designed for extended 24-hour operation.

Hands-On Exercises

In this exercise, you will learn how to secure the inner perimeter. The objectives include:

BUT FIRST

Before you can complete this exercise, you must complete the exercise in Chapter 2.

- For the ACME facility, define its inner perimeter and determine the vulnerabilities associated with that perimeter.
- For the specified perimeter and its vulnerabilities, perform research to determine what components or systems are available to secure the inner perimeter and what the cost options are for the components you find.
- Design a video surveillance and notification system that ACME can implement to secure this portion of their facility in the most cost-effective manner.
- Design an access-monitoring and control system for the inner perimeter of the facility.

The resources necessary for this exercise are as follows:

- Internet access
- Pencil/pen and paper
- Completion of the exercise in Chapter 2

Discussion

After the outer perimeter has been established and designed, the next step in a multilayer physical-security topology is to define the inner perimeter. Often, this involves monitoring the spaces between the outer and inner perimeters using video surveillance equipment. When properly designed and implemented, the surveillance system provides detection and notification capabilities that will cover specific passageways and key assets, as well as any areas requiring wide areas of view.

The other major component of securing the inner perimeter is to monitor and control its access points that lead to the interior. This process is similar to the one you performed in the previous procedure for the outer perimeter.

Procedure

1. Review Figure 3.13 and identify/label the inner perimeter of the warehouse facility. Hint: Do not include the showroom as part of the inner perimeter.

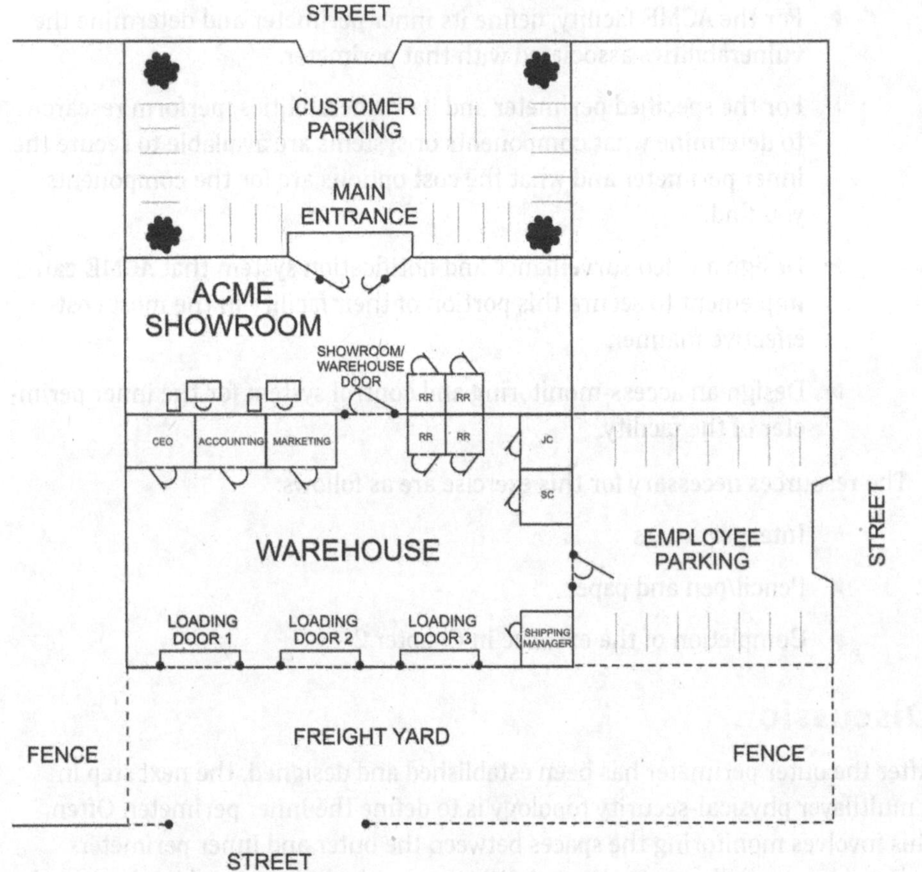

FIGURE 3.13 The Inner Perimeter

2. After examining the layout, identify at least two security areas between the outer and inner perimeters that would be suitable candidates for video surveillance. Highlight these areas on the drawing and record your reasons for selecting these areas on the following lines:

____

____

____

____

Answer: There are at least three areas: the loading bay doors into the warehouse, the pedestrian door into the warehouse from outside, the pedestrian door between the showroom and warehouse, and any possible windows. These are all conventional means of entry and likely sources of intrusion.

3. Identify and mark the physical access points associated with the interior perimeter of the facility on the figure.

4. On the diagram, identify and mark the locations where surveillance cameras might be mounted for maximum effectiveness in monitoring these areas between perimeters.

Video Monitoring

1. Use the Internet to research video surveillance/monitoring devices and systems that can be used to effectively secure the *areas* and *access points* you identified in the previous section. Use Table 3.1 through Table 3.3 to organize the specified details about the video surveillance products listed there. For each item, try to locate at least two vendors.

TABLE 3.1 Video Cameras

	Product Description	Vendor	Number Required	Cost Per Unit	Total Price
A	360-Degree Panoramic Camera 20MP	Arecont Vision	3	$1,468.00	$4,004.00
B	Home Network Surveillance Dome 360 Degree	Digital Watchdog	3	$425.00	$1,275.00
C					

Use caution when you're selecting cameras. Make certain to differentiate between camera types and the specifications that best fit the different locations you've noted.

2. List your selections for any video surveillance cameras you think should be recommended to ACME for controlling access to their inner perimeter.

Answer: Arecont Vision for the truck- loading- yard cameras.

Answer: Arecont Vision for the showroom cameras, also covers warehouse/showroom pedestrian door.

Answer: Arecont Vision for the inside warehouse space covering both the warehouse/outside pedestrian door and the loading bay doors.

3. Specify where you would deploy the cameras.

Answer: Centered inside warehouse to cover warehouse/outside man door, warehouse/showroom pedestrian door, and all three loading bay doors.

Answer: Central ceiling inside showroom to cover warehouse/showroom pedestrian door and for the showroom areas including the front, public entryway, and showroom floor.

Answer: Outside corner of building in truck yard to cover outside of loading bay doors and truck yard.

4. Specify the power and connectivity requirements for the different camera types you select.

Answer: Utilizing 360-degree indoor/outdoor cameras all with POE capability (Power over Ethernet), a powered switch will be required on the network hosting the DVR and cameras.

Answer: (Optional answer if student is using dissimilar cameras in their design.)

TABLE 3.2 Digital Video Recorders

	Product Description	Vendor	Number Required	Cost Per Unit	Total Price
A	4 CH DVR	TW Vision	1	$51.99	$51.99
B	4 CH DVR	Lorex	1	$89.99	$89.99
C	4 CH HD DVR	Samsung	1	$475.00	$475.00

A Word About Compatibility

Make certain the video recorder you select is compatible with the camera types you've already specified.

5. List the DVR that you would recommend to ACME for recording and storing the video surveillance data related to their inner perimeter.

Answer: The Samsung unit. It is compatible with IP cameras and its remote-access capabilities meet the desired specifications. This unit has a reasonably large hard-drive capacity for data storage, and it has the ability to use a USB device to burn video for evidentiary purposes.

TABLE 3.3 Additional Video Monitoring Software

	Product Description	Vendor	Number Required	Cost Per Unit	Total Price
A	Android APP	Samsung	Dependent on number of authorized users	$0.00	$0.00
B	Apple APP	Samsung	Dependent on number of authorized users	$0.00	$0.00
C	Windows/Mac Browser	Native to operating system of workstation	Dependent on number of authorized users	$0.00	$0.00

Be Aware of ACME Specifications

Make certain the video monitoring software associated with the camera types and video recorder you've already specified meets the requirements laid out by the ACME specification. In particular, make certain that it will enable all of the ACME managers to access the current camera views as well as review past activities captured by the system.

6. List your recommendations for any video monitoring software you think should be recommended to ACME in addition to the native software offered by the DVR manufacturer.

Answer: For remote access via website or smartphone app, no additional software should be needed.

7. As part of your video surveillance research, investigate the local and remote notification capabilities associated with each surveillance system you list. Use the following lines to describe the capabilities of the system you would recommend to ACME.

____

____

____

Answer: Remote access via website or smartphone app. Record and playback. Camera-view auto sequencing. Capability to manage and set permissions for multiple users/groups. Camera privacy settings. PTZ control. Tamper detection.

Inner Perimeter Access Controls

In addition to the surveillance system, you must also determine what types of access controls (if any) are required between the area inside the outer perimeter and the interior zone of the facility (the warehouse). The major access point between these two zones in the ACME warehouse is the showroom/warehouse door.

The movement of personnel between the showroom and the warehouse needs to be monitored and controlled. Only warehouse management personnel should be able to move freely between the two areas. Sales and customer service personnel should not be allowed in the warehouse area.

1. Use the Internet to research access control devices and systems that can be used to secure the access points you've associated with the inner perimeter. Use Table 3.4 through Table 3.6 to organize the specified details about the intrusion-detection products listed there. For each item, try to locate at least two vendors.

TABLE 3.4 Authentication/Access-Control Devices and Systems

	Product Description	Vendor	Number Required	Cost Per Unit	Total Price
A	**Electronic Keyless Door Lock**	**Gino Development**	**1**	**$89.99**	**$89.99**
B	**Mag Door Lock Kit**	**Entry Vision**	**1**	**$274.99**	**$274.99**
C	**Cobra Controls Lock Kit**	**Maglocks.com**	**1**	**$1,699.99**	**$1,699.99**

2. What authentication devices/systems would you recommend to ACME to control access through their inner perimeter?

Answer: An RFID pass card to enter through the pedestrian door to the warehouse from outside. The Mag Door Lock Kit has this feature integrated as part of its design. The Electronic Keyless Door Lock to be applied to the pedestrian door between the warehouse and the showroom can be actuated without any authentication steps from inside the warehouse, but it requires a key or passcode to operate the door from inside the showroom.

3. Specify where you would employ the authentication devices/systems.

Answer: Authentication devices should be at both inner-perimeter pedestrian doors; they should require different levels of authentication for the different departmental levels of employees.

TABLE 3.5 Door Contacts/Sensors

	Product Description	Vendor	Number Required	Cost Per Unit	Total Price
A	Door Sensor Wired	SensaPhone	7	$9.00	$54.00
B	Gate & Com. Door Sensor	Gogogate	7	$35.00	$210.00
C	SDC MC-4	Grainger Industrial	7	$53.95	$377.65

4. List your selections for the door sensor you would recommend to ACME for their inner-perimeter access points.

Answer: Gogogate Magnetic contact sensors for the pedestrian doors and roll-up loading-bay doors.

Answer: (An optional secondary sensor package if using dissimilar sensors for roll-up doors or pedestrian doors.)

TABLE 3.6 Door Locks

	Product Description	Vendor	Number Required	Cost Per Unit	Total Price
A	Jackshaft	LiftMaster	3	$273.39	$820.17
B	Electronic Keyless Door Lock	Gino Development	1	$89.99	$89.99
C	Mag Door Lock Kit	Entry Vision	1	$274.99	$274.99

5. List the door locks you would recommend to ACME for their inner-perimeter access points.

   ____

   Answer: The Electronic Keyless Door Lock to be applied to the pedestrian door between the warehouse and showroom. It can be actuated without any authentication steps from inside the warehouse, but a key or passcode is needed to operate the door from inside of showroom.

   ____

   Answer: The Jackshaft LiftMaster for the three roll-up doors. The devices will keep the doors secure in a fail-safe design unless manually disengaged from inside the warehouse.

   ____

   Answer: An RFID pass card to enter through the pedestrian door to the warehouse from outside. The Mag Door Lock Kit already has this feature integrated as part of its design.

Review Questions

1. **Which two areas of the ACME facility are good candidates for video monitoring?**

   Answer: The loading yard and the showroom. The loading yard provides direct access to the warehouse through the three roll-up doors, while the showroom provides direct inside access to the showroom/warehouse pedestrian door.

2. **Which access points are associated with the inner perimeter of the facility?**

   Answer: The three loading dock doors and the showroom/warehouse door.

3. **Which type of camera is best suited for monitoring the area inside the fence of the truck loading yard and the gate at the driveway entrance?**

   Answer: Any outdoor-rated camera with an adequate zoom/focus/frame rate that is compatible with the surveillance system desired by the client.

4. **Which type of camera is best suited for monitoring the showroom and the pedestrian door that leads to the warehouse?**

   Answer: Any indoor-rated camera with an adequate zoom/focus/frame rate that is compatible with the surveillance system desired by the client.

5. **ACME wants to include a hardware device that will enable all the members of their management staff to simultaneously display the output from the video cameras on the PCs located at their desks. Which type of hardware should you install to provide this level of functionality?**

   Answer: A DVR that offers network access and a web interface for remote access.

Understanding Intrusion-Detection and Reporting Systems

While preventing unauthorized access is the first line of defense in physical security, layers of additional security measures are crucial to preventing intrusions from escalating into serious events. A closely related second tier of defense is intrusion detection, which enables potential intruders to be detected and removed before they can cause problems. This level of security involves detection devices that are monitored or that can create an alarm. In this chapter, you'll learn to:

- **Describe components of a typical, physical intrusion-detection and reporting system**
- **Explain the purpose for creating physical security zones and common techniques for defining them**
- **Identify common sensor types employed in a physical intrusion-detection system.**

Intrusion-Detection and Reporting Systems

The components of a basic commercial security system, as depicted in Figure 4.1, come together to provide a functional intrusion-detection and reporting system. This system includes an intelligent control panel connected by wires (or radio signals) to sensors at various locations throughout the facility.

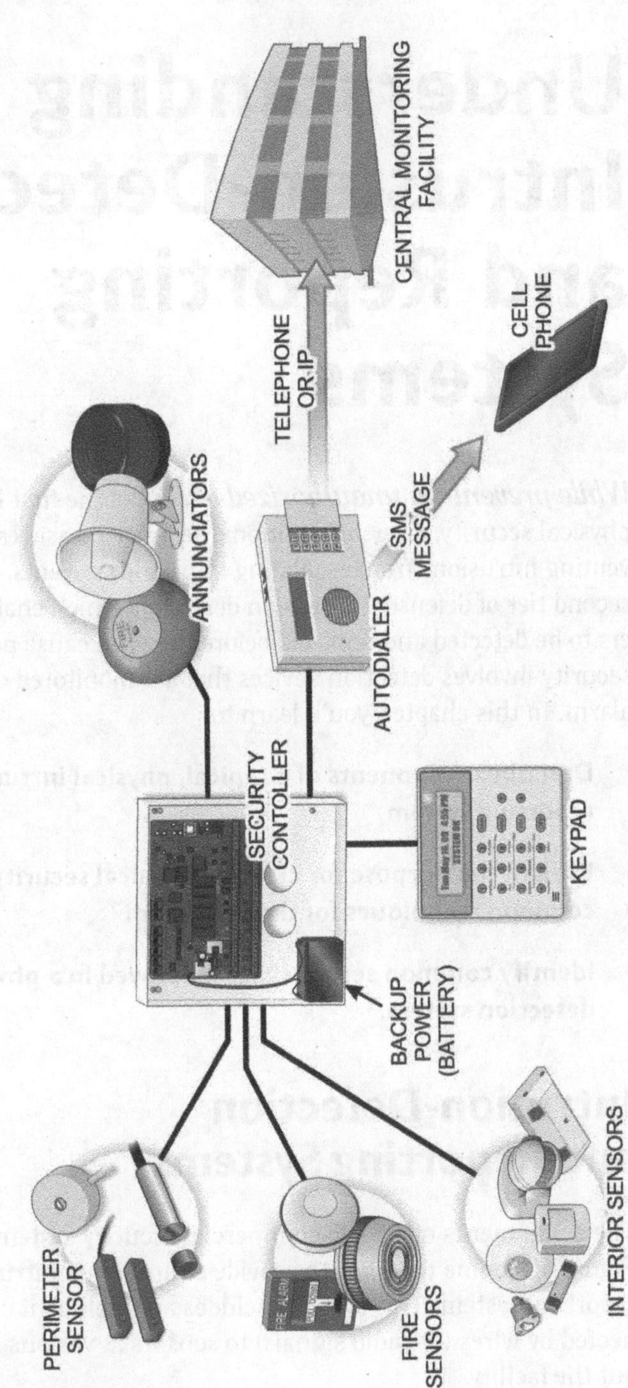

FIGURE 4.1 Basic Intrusion-Detection and Reporting System

The control panel includes the electronic components and central processor, which monitors and controls the entire system. The processor accepts input information from the various sensors attached to it. In a basic security system, these inputs can be divided into three distinct types: perimeter, interior, and fire.

Perimeter area inputs to the control panel typically include sensors at every perimeter opening including doors, windows, garage doors and windows, and doors to crawl spaces. Additional perimeter protection may include using sound, vibration, and motion-detector sensors to guard against entry through broken windows.

Some interior areas may also be protected with various types of sensors, such as motion detectors and interior door sensors. Most security systems also include inputs capable of handling adequate smoke and fire sensors.

When the controller receives an active input signal from one of its input sensors, it evaluates the conditions presented according to its programming (and the type of emergency response required), and if necessary, sends the appropriate output signals to annunciators (sirens or bells). It may also communicate with designated security contacts (security supervisors, monitoring services, or law enforcement/fire agencies) as directed by its programming.

Commercial security systems may use any of several notification methods to notify designated security personnel when an alarm condition is triggered. Some alarm systems use a telephone dialer to alert the remote security contacts that an alarm condition exists. These systems are designed to react when no one is present by placing the call over a standard telephone line or cell phone. Special digital codes are used to inform the security contacts as to what type of condition caused the alarm.

It is also possible to have a prepared text-messaging system, such as SMS, relayed by a cell phone to the designated security contacts. Another option is IP-based notification, which is used to notify the monitoring station via an IP network, such as the Internet, concerning an alarm condition.

Most security systems typically employ some type of keypad to provide the control interface for supervisors to arm and disarm the system using a programmed access code. The keypad may be designed to provide some level of visual and audible output signals to help monitor the status of the system.

Finally, most security systems include some type of emergency backup power (a backup battery or uninterruptable power supply) to provide emergency power to the security system when commercial power outages occur.

The choices for access-control and management system components and subsystems are extensive. The following sections of this chapter will explain the various subsystems typically found in the intrusion-detection and reporting portion of a typical infrastructure security system.

Security Controllers

The center of any intelligent security system is the *controller*. The security controller, shown in Figure 4.2, is typically installed in an enclosure that contains the security controller board, all of the electronic components, wire termination points, backup battery packs, and telephone termination wiring.

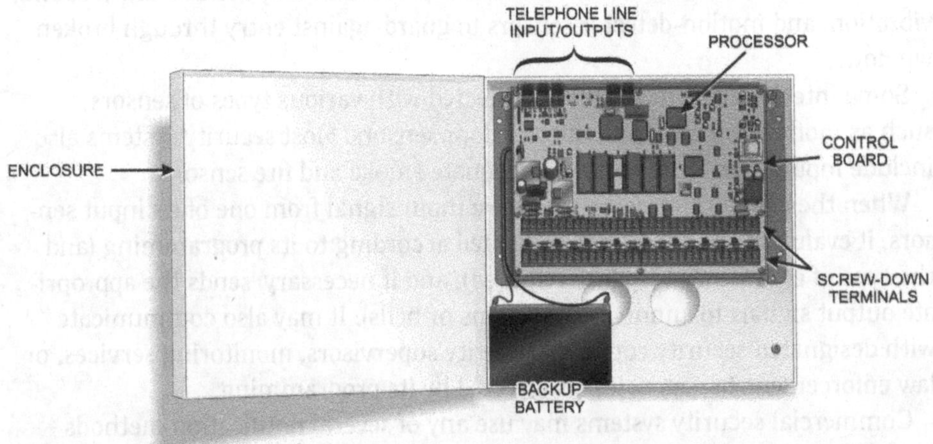

FIGURE 4.2 Control Box with Panel and Battery

A given security controller model will be designed to handle a specific number of programmable zones. A *zone* can be a single point of protection such as a motion detector, or multiple points can be combined into a single zone. For example, two hallway motion detectors could be connected to form a zone, or a stairway motion detector could be combined with the hallway sensors to form a single zone.

The security controller is the command center and distribution point of the intrusion-detection and reporting portion of the security system to which all input and output devices are connected. Each sensor receives power and is managed from the security controller.

The controller must have enough capacity and functionality to connect to and manage all the security devices that will be part of the security system, in addition to providing remote access capability for remote monitoring and control.

The controller's enclosure should be mounted out of plain view and near a 120-volt AC outlet, where a plug-in transformer can supply low-voltage power to the total system.

Security Zones

As mentioned earlier, security controllers possess a fixed number of detection circuits that can be used to create physical security zones. For instance, a typical, commercial security controller may possess as few as eight zones and up to 250 zones or more. Typically, one of these inputs is dedicated to the fire detection system. Figure 4.3 shows a typical eight-zone security controller connection scheme.

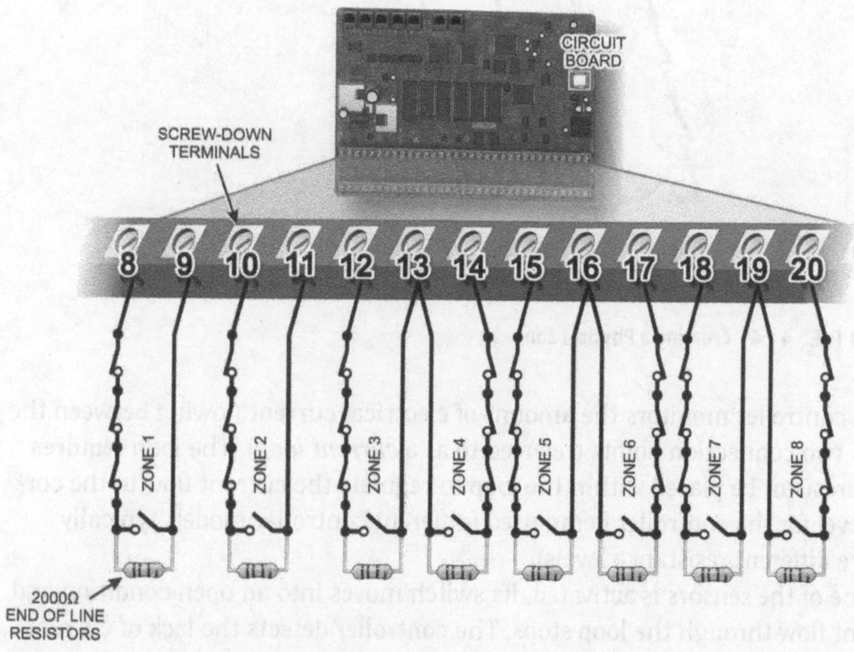

FIGURE 4.3 Security Panel Zone Inputs

Suppose that the facility in which you are installing the security system has fourteen windows, two personnel entrance doors, and a roll-up receiving door for the warehouse. In addition, it has two major hallways to monitor and an integrated fire-detection system.

How should you physically install and configure the controller so that it provides full protection for the facility? The answer is to logically group related sensors together to create a security zone. This is accomplished by connecting all of the related sensor switches (all sensors appear as switches to the security controller) together in a serial format as illustrated in Figure 4.4.

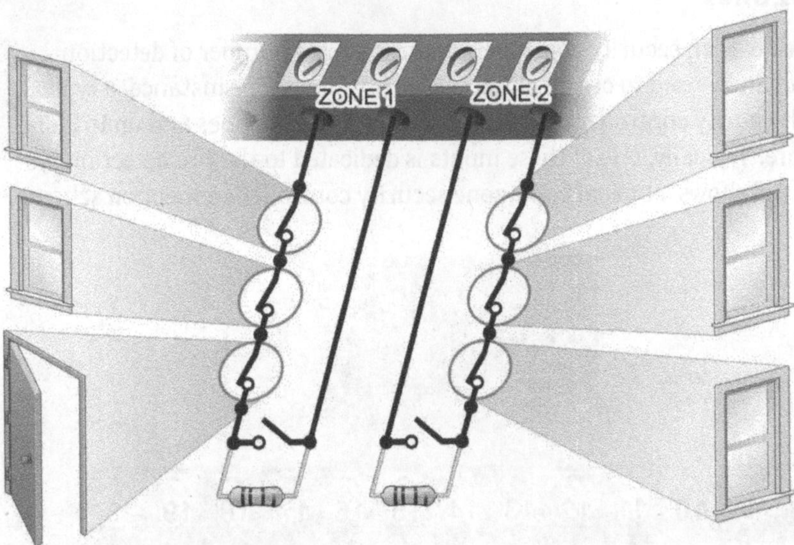

FIGURE 4.4 **Creating a Physical Zone**

The controller monitors the amount of electrical current flowing between the zone's two connection points (referred to as a *current loop*). The loop requires that a resistor be placed within the loop to regulate the current flow to the correct level for the controller being used (different controller models typically require different resistance levels).

If one of the sensors is activated, its switch moves into an open condition and current flow through the loop stops. The controller detects the lack of current flow and processes the input according to its configuration programming.

The fact that a certain level of current must be flowing helps to make tampering with the loop more difficult. If the system used normally opens switches that close when activated, the system could be circumvented by simply cutting a wire in the loop; no signal would ever be presented to the controller.

For the sample installation presented earlier, it might be logical to wire all of the west-side window sensors into one input that could be reported as the West Side Windows. Likewise, the two personnel entry doors can be configured together because they will require special settings to allow exit and entry times for setting and disarming the system when leaving or entering the structure. Conversely, the other door may be connected into a different door zone or incorporated into one of the window zones since it has no timing requirement.

Zoning also enables the system to instantly sound an alarm for intrusion detection in a specific area, while other sensor alerts in a specific zone (such as the main front door) may require a short delay before sounding the alarm. This enables security personnel to arm the system by entering a secret code on a keypad when exiting the facility (exit delay).

It also allows them to enter a protected area when arriving at the facility and disarm the system through the entry area keypad within a specified entry-delay interval (usually 30 to 45 seconds). This feature allows keypads to be installed inside the facility near the exit door to avoid vandalism and tampering with keypads from the outside area.

Interior motion sensors that guard the hallways may be integrated into a window or a door zone. However, they are more likely to be configured separate from the exterior sensors so that they can be disabled at night when people may need to move around during the night but want the perimeter to be protected from outside intruders. Figure 4.5 describes a possible zoning solution for this example.

The use of zoning also enables security personnel to arm only portions of the system, such as the perimeter doors and windows, while bypassing interior motion detectors in a specific zone. A bypass mode setting is normally accomplished by entering a predetermined numerical code through the keypad. When personnel leave the facility, all zones including the interior detectors can be armed as required.

A zoned security-system layout can also be used by an external monitoring service to know which sensor in a designated zone is causing an alarm. If a sensor is reported as just Sensor 3, Zone 5, this could mean that the event occurred just about anywhere. If the sensor was reported as Sensor 3, Zone 5 perimeter, this would inform the operator that the violated area is on the outside of the premises.

Zones also provide ease of troubleshooting. For example, if a sensor in the Zone 3 perimeter is reporting a problem, there is no need to troubleshoot sensors that are located in the interior of the system.

Sensors

Sensors are a class of input devices that convert physical activity into a signal that can be presented to the security controller. They are available in a variety of configurations including magnetic switches for doors and windows, acoustic detectors, vibration detectors, motion detectors, and glass-break detectors. Sensors protect the perimeter, selected outside areas, and the open spaces inside the facility.

As mentioned earlier, perimeter devices primarily protect doors and windows. The most common perimeter sensors are magnetic door switches, window vibration, and window acoustical detectors to detect breaking-glass sounds.

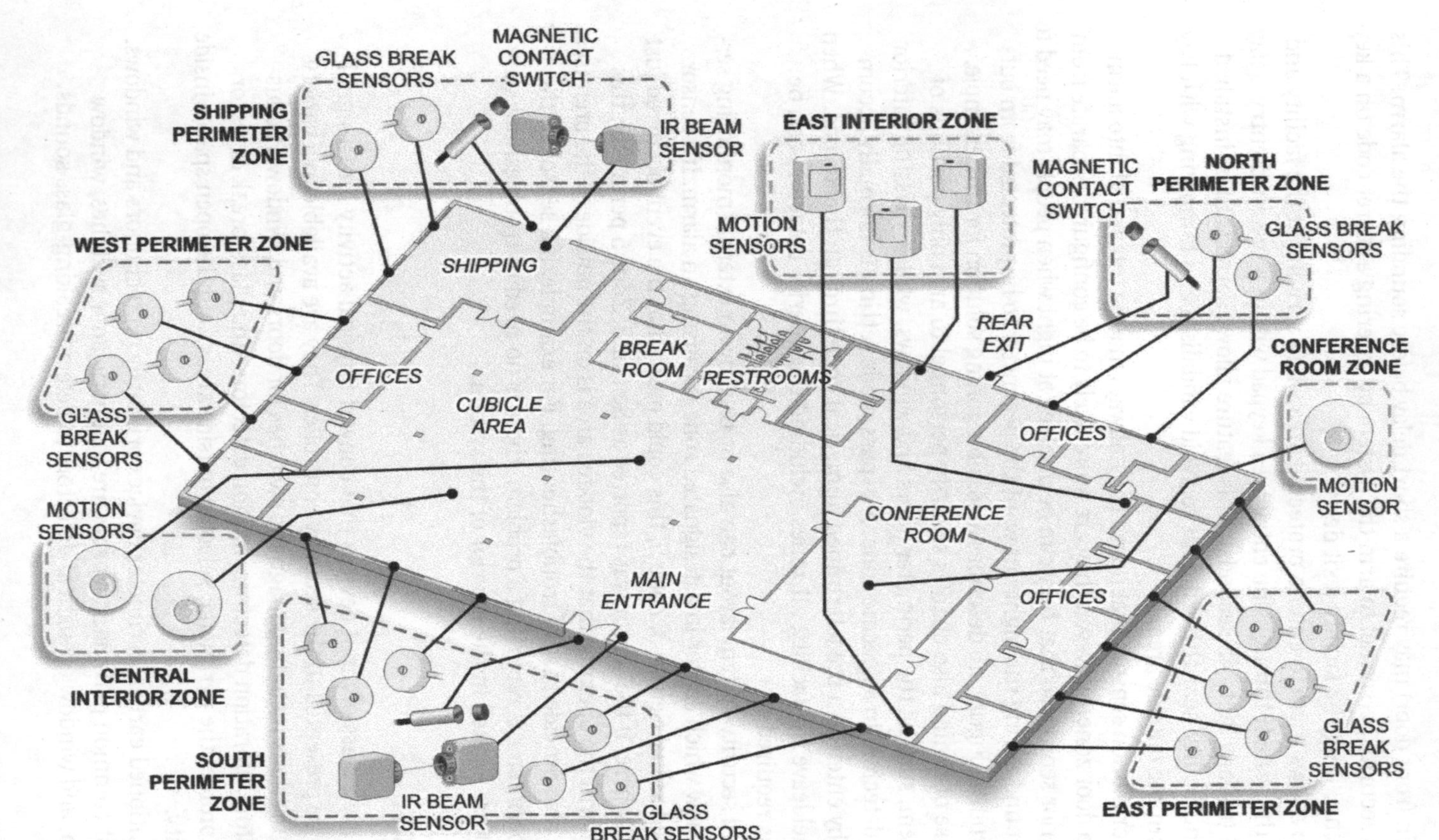

FIGURE 4.5 Zoning Concepts

Open-space-protection sensors called *motion detectors* cover interior rooms and hallways. Outside motion detectors activate security lights when movement is detected. Indoor motion detectors can detect an intruder who has been able to defeat a perimeter device. Exterior motion detectors and motion-activated security lights are also used. The following paragraphs describe the sensors included in basic security and surveillance systems.

Magnetic Contact Switches

Magnetic contact switches basically consist of a two-part magnetic switch. One piece of the sensor is a magnet, while the other side is a switching mechanism, called a *reed switch,* that is sensitive to a magnetic field. The switch portion is mounted on the fixed structure (frame) of the barrier, as shown in Figure 4.6. Wires from the switch are routed to the security system's control panel.

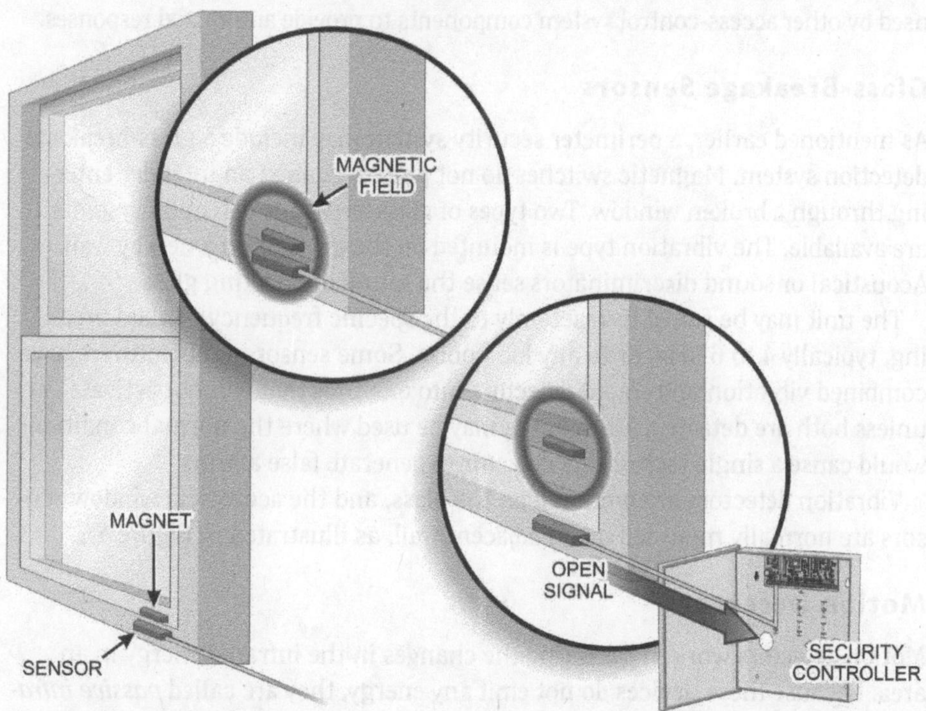

FIGURE 4.6 Sensor Mounting

The magnet portion of the sensor is mounted on the movable barrier so that it is in close proximity to the switch when the barrier is closed. This also keeps the switch closed. Opening the barrier moves the magnet away from the switch and opens the switch, which is sensed by the central control panel, and activates an alarm.

This simple magnetic-switch sensor can be used to protect doors and windows or any other moving barrier. It alerts security managers when someone attempts to gain entry through a passageway through illegal or unauthorized means. Its magnet and reed-switch mechanism detects any intrusion and signals an alarm.

This type of sensor can be used to indicate the open/closed condition of a movable barrier, but it cannot determine whether the barrier's locking mechanism is locked or unlocked. As mentioned earlier, some types of electrically operated door locks are equipped with sensors for determining whether the locking mechanism is locked or unlocked.

Even though up to 70 varieties of barrier sensors are available, a sensor alone cannot offer true control other than detection and warning. Its signal, however, can be used by other access-control system components to provide automated responses.

Glass-Breakage Sensors

As mentioned earlier, a perimeter security system may include a glass-breakage detection system. Magnetic switches do not protect against an intruder entering through a broken window. Two types of glass-breakage detection systems are available. The vibration type is mounted on the glass or on a nearby wall. Acoustical or sound discriminators sense the sound of breaking glass.

The unit may be tuned to react only to the specific frequency of glass breaking, typically 4 to 6 kHz, or to any loud noise. Some sensor manufacturers have combined vibration and sound detectors into one unit that will not activate unless both are detected. These units may be used where the normal conditions would cause a single technology detector to generate false alarms.

Vibration detectors are mounted on the glass, and the acoustical window sensors are normally mounted on an adjacent wall, as illustrated in Figure 4.7.

Motion Detectors

Motion detectors work by detecting the changes in the infrared energy in an area. Because these devices do not emit any energy, they are called *passive infrared (PIR) detectors*.

PIR detectors use a lens mechanism in the sensor housing to detect any change in infrared energy across the horizontal sectors covered by the sensor. This type of detector is insensitive to stationary objects but reacts to rapid changes that occur laterally across the field of view. PIR detectors are the most common and economical type of motion detectors.

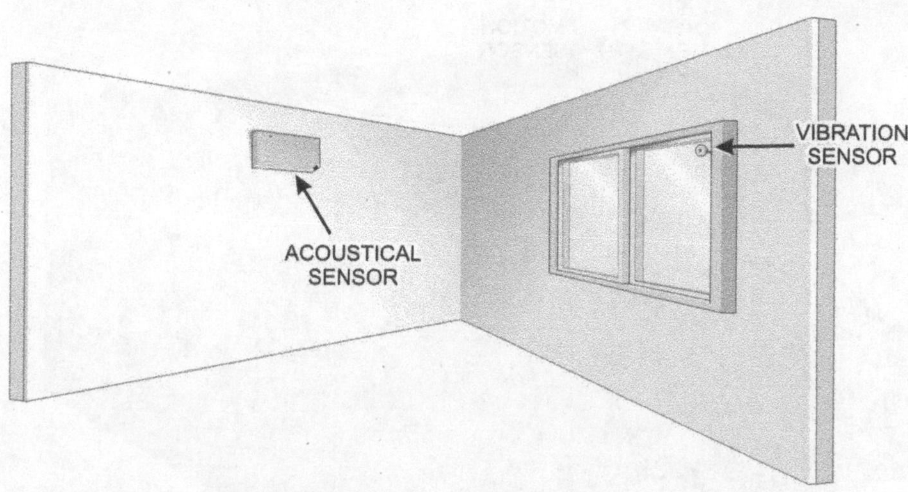

FIGURE 4.7 Glass-Breakage Sensors

Motion detectors should be installed in open areas that cannot be protected by window or door sensors. An example of a PIR motion detector for interior use is shown in Figure 4.8.

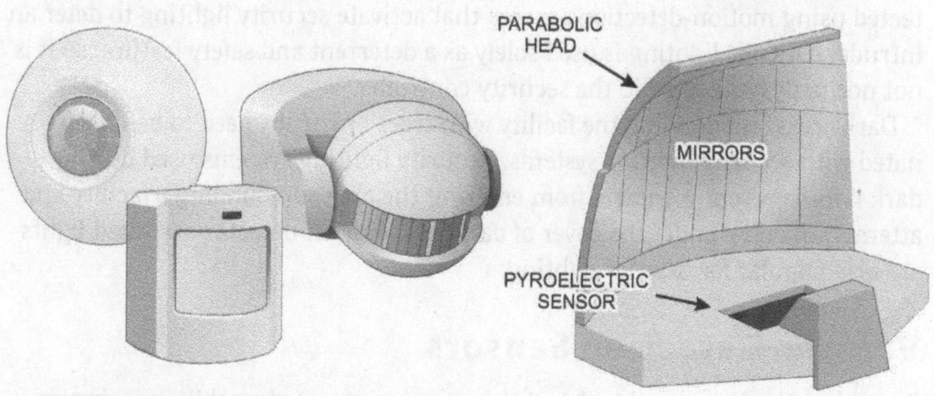

FIGURE 4.8 A PIR Motion Detector

Motion Detector Locations

Motion detectors are normally mounted in the corner of a room. This allows the detector to cover a 90-degree field, as illustrated in Figure 4.9. Motion detectors are sensitive to movement across the sensor's field of view.

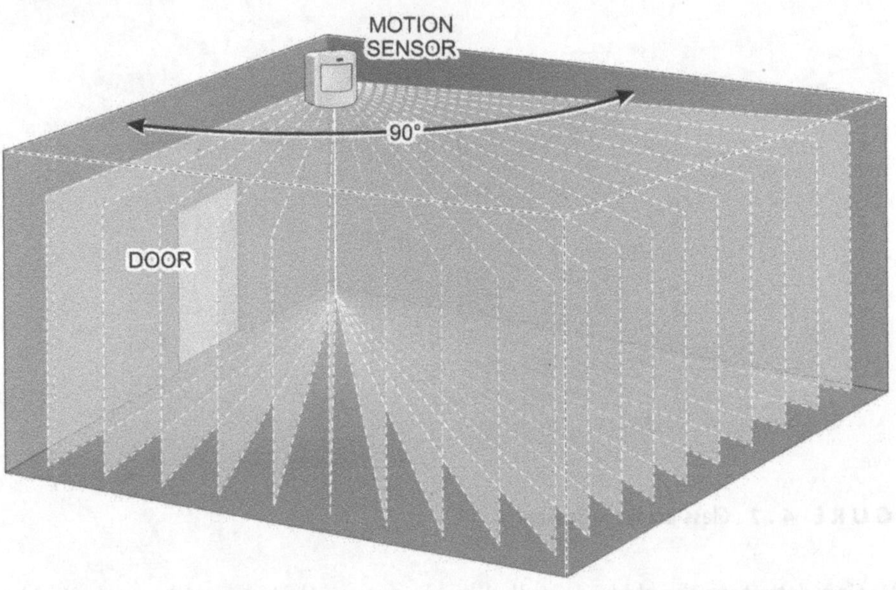

FIGURE 4.9 PIR Field of View

Exterior lighting is often used to illuminate dark areas or areas to be protected using motion-detection sensors that activate security lighting to deter an intruder. Outside lighting is used solely as a deterrent and safety feature, so it is not normally connected to the security controller.

Dark areas surrounding the facility with trees or shrubs need to be illuminated with security lighting systems. Security lighting systems used during dark hours prevent intruders from entering the area surrounding a facility and attempting entry under the cover of darkness. Motion-detector-activated lights are also popular for exterior lighting.

Vehicle-Detection Sensors

Several methods are used to detect the presence of an automobile entering an area near a facility. The most common type of sensor used for this purpose is a motion detector placed above the entrance to the garage. Pressure sensors can also be employed to detect a vehicle on a driveway or garage area.

Photoelectric Beam Devices A photoelectric sensor is an optical control that detects a visible or invisible beam of light and responds to a change in the received light intensity. Photoelectric beam devices use this feature by having a narrow beam of light aimed through an area of interest such as a parking lot gate, as shown in Figure 4.10. When the light beam is interrupted, the photoelectric device is used to sound an alarm, or in the case of garage door safety system, to stop or reverse an automatic garage door's lifter motor.

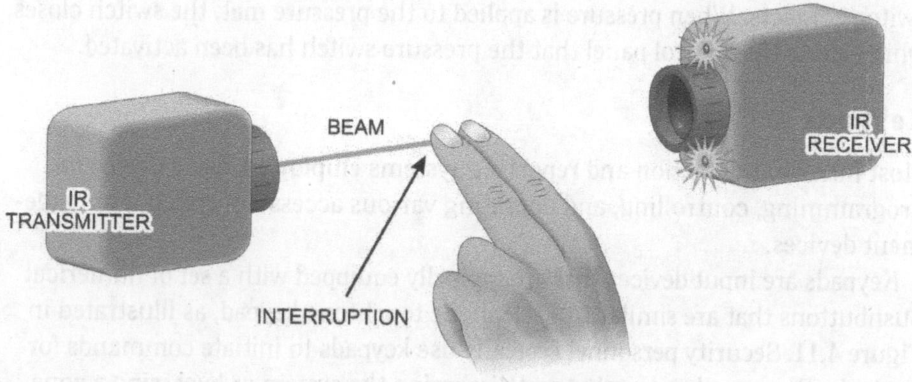

FIGURE 4.10 Photoelectric Beam System

Microwave Beam Devices This device emits microwaves from a transmitter and detects microwaves at a receiver, either through reflection or reduction in beam intensity. The transmitter and receiver are usually combined inside a single housing for indoor applications and separate housings for outdoor applications. By generating energy in the microwave region of the electromagnetic spectrum, the detector operates as an active device that responds to:

- A Doppler shift frequency change. These devices are based on the Doppler Effect phenomenon, which observes frequency changes in energy waves (in this case, microwaves) in motion relative to a listener or receiver. These detectors emit microwaves of a specific frequency into a given environment and then analyze the frequencies of any waves reflected to it. Changes from its normal frequency reception cause the sensor to signal an alarm condition.
- A frequency phase shift. These devices also rely on changes in reflected energy waves caused by motion. Like the Doppler sensors, these sensors emit specific microwave frequencies into an area and measure phase shift of reflected waves, which are directly proportional to the velocity of the moving object.
- A motion causing reduction in received energy. These devices respond to changes in the level of energy between a transmitter and a receiver caused by some or all of the transmitted energy wave being blocked by an obstacle moving into its path.

Pressure Sensors Pressure mats are a type of sensor that can be placed under rugs in hallways or on stair treads. They react and alarm due to pressure from footsteps activating the alarm. Pressure sensors typically use normally open switch contacts. When pressure is applied to the pressure mat, the switch closes, which alerts the control panel that the pressure switch has been activated.

Keypads

Most intrusion-detection and reporting systems employ a keypad device for programming, controlling, and operating various access-control and management devices.

Keypads are input devices that are typically equipped with a set of numerical pushbuttons that are similar to a telephone touchtone keypad, as illustrated in Figure 4.11. Security personnel typically use keypads to initiate commands for control options such as arming and disarming the system or bypassing a zone.

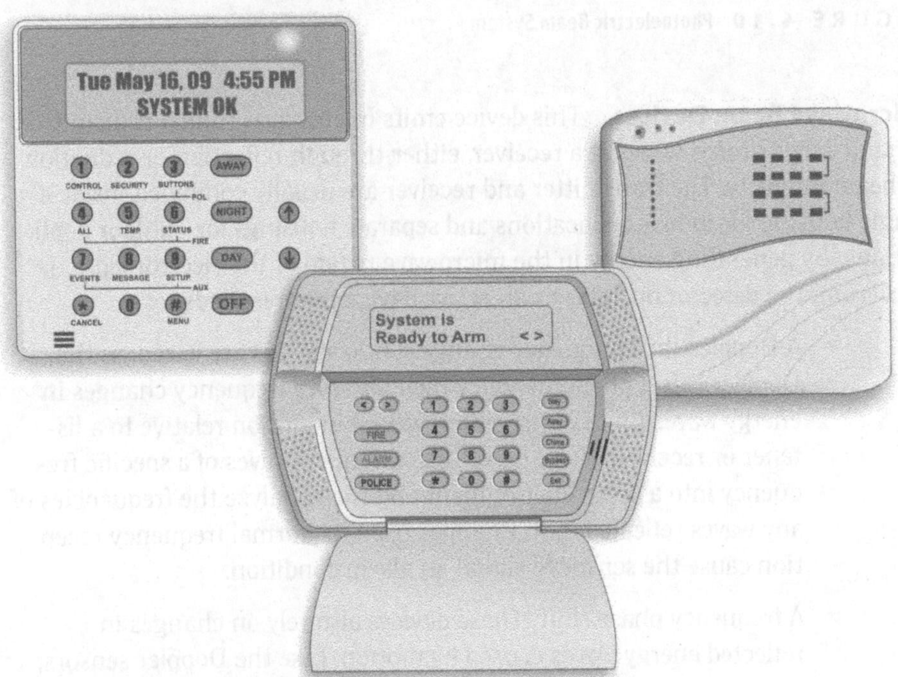

FIGURE 4.11 Controller Keypad

Keypads can be located in any area of a facility that is convenient for security personnel to operate external gates and doors. However, many new security systems typically include software that runs on a tablet computer or a smart phone app to perform these functions from anywhere.

Key Fobs and Panic Buttons

A key fob is a wireless keychain device similar to the type used to lock, unlock, and alarm a vehicle. Convenient and easy-to-use remote-entry key fobs enable security personnel to arm and disarm a security system with a push of a button when outside the facility. The key fob often features a panic button function that allows the user to contact help in case of emergency. An example of a key fob is shown in Figure 4.12.

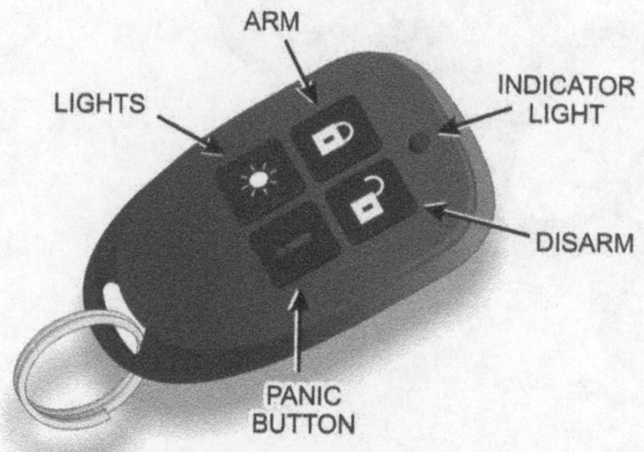

FIGURE 4.12 Security Key Fob

Panic buttons are devices that allow immediate triggering of an alarm system when facing an emergency situation such as the discovery of an intruder. As indicated in the previous paragraph, panic buttons are often integrated with a key fob but may also be mounted permanently at key locations inside the facility.

Fire-Detection Sensors

Many intrusion-detection and reporting systems include a fire-detection and alarm function as an integral part of the system. However, for larger or more complex security systems, standalone fire-detection and reporting systems may be used.

Two common types of fire-detection sensors are available: heat sensors and smoke detectors. They operate by detecting heat rise or the presence of smoke particles in the facility.

Heat sensors operate using a different technology than smoke detectors. The basic design features of each type are summarized in the following paragraphs. *Heat sensors* detect a rapid rise in temperature. They also set off an alarm when a fixed temperature is reached. On the other hand, smoke detectors, such as the one shown in Figure 4.13, do not react to heat but use one of two common sensor designs to detect smoke.

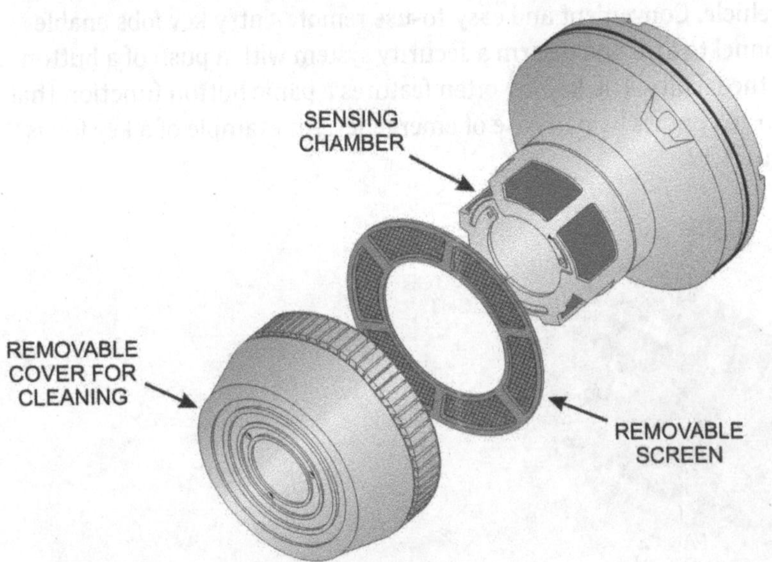

FIGURE 4.13 **A Typical Smoke Detector**

Ionization detectors form an electrical path inside a small chamber with a very small amount of radioactive material. When smoke enters the chamber, the particles attach themselves to the ions and change the electrical current.

Photoelectric detectors work by using a photoelectric cell and a light source. Normally, the light does not reach the photoelectric cell; but when smoke is present, the light is dispersed, and the detector triggers an alarm signal.

The main difference between the two detector types is that photoelectric types are more sensitive to large particles and ionization types are more sensitive to small particles.

Carbon Dioxide and Carbon Monoxide Detectors

Carbon dioxide (CO_2), a natural byproduct of normal respiration, is different from the toxic carbon monoxide (CO) gas—and much less dangerous. Outdoor air usually contains about 400 ppm (parts per million) of carbon dioxide, while carbon monoxide levels should normally be less than 0.2 ppm.

Although CO is a colorless and odorless compound produced by incomplete combustion, it is lethal at high levels. When dangerous levels of CO are detected, the detector sounds an alarm, giving people in the area an opportunity to safely leave the residence—or to apply immediate ventilation.

Carbon monoxide is generated through the incomplete burning of natural gas, kerosene, fuel oil, coal, or gasoline, and not by appliances that use only electricity. If the furnace, water heater, space heater, stove, or oven does not burn gas or fuel, it will not generate carbon monoxide. Accurate carbon monoxide data require that suspect appliances be operating before any readings are taken.

When a CO alarm activates, personnel need to call emergency services, the fire department, or 911. They must immediately move to a source of fresh air, either outdoors or by an open door or window. A head check should be taken to ensure that all personnel are accounted for. No one should return into the facility or move away from the fresh air source until the emergency services arrive and give the all clear.

Output Devices

Physical intrusion-detection systems typically include three basic types of output devices: visual notification, audible annunciators, and remote messaging. The visual and audible annunciators provide a local and general call for attention to a predefined alarm condition, while the remote messaging element is employed to notify specific personnel or organizations that an alarm condition exists. The following sections describe the various output signals and devices employed in a basic security system.

Sirens

The control panel provides the voltage for driving the external electronic siren or strobe light. The controller activates these devices when an alarm condition exists. Various types of audible annunciators (sirens, horns, buzzers, klaxons, and bells) are used to attract attention when an alarm condition is activated.

These different devices produce different levels of volume for use in various locations. Audible alarm sounders are used not only to attract the attention of others outside the facility or away from the area of the intrusion, but also to create a sufficiently high level of sound to discourage an intruder. Commercial security systems typically employ solid-state electronic sirens like the one shown in Figure 4.14. These sirens provide a higher level of sound output as well as a variety of tones and pitches.

Interior sounders installed in concealed areas within the facility are designed to operate at maximum sound levels to frighten an intruder into making a fast exit. This is because the sound masks any outside approaching police siren. Interior sirens are available from several vendors that operate at sound levels in the 110 to 120 dB range, which is near the threshold of pain.

FIGURE 4.14 Electronic Siren

Strobe Lights

Many security system installations include at least one strobe light to provide a visual indicator. These lights are typically mounted on the outside of the facility to attract attention of people in the vicinity of the intrusion and to discourage would-be intruders. Security strobe lights operate from various DC voltage levels provided by the security controller panel.

Security strobe lights, like the one depicted in Figure 4.15, produce light output levels specified in either foot-candles, or *candelas,* of light. A foot-candle is a measure of *luminance* (or light intensity) used by the lighting industry. Likewise, one candela is equal to foot-candles multiplied by distance squared:

$$C = fc \times d^2$$

FIGURE 4.15 Strobe Light

Security strobe lights are available in a number of different colors including red, blue, amber, and clear.

Remote Notification Systems

While strobe lights and sirens call general attention to alarm conditions in a localized environment, it is often necessary to notify specific people (such as a security specialist) or organizations (such as third-party security companies, fire departments, or police services) to respond to different types of alarm conditions.

The most common remote notification systems involve the use of a telephone line by the security-system control panel to automatically call a remote monitoring facility or key personnel when an alarm condition exists. When the security controller receives an active input signal from one of its zones, it activates the telephone dialer unit and causes a digital data message to be transmitted to a predetermined recipient. The message recipient can also use remote access to check on the status of the security system when away from the facility.

Some intrusion-detection and reporting systems employ a separate telephone dialer like the one depicted in Figure 4.16, or a built-in dialer. However, a growing number of systems utilize built-in cellular communications systems. Such systems provide additional dependability in that they can function even if the physical telephone lines are damaged.

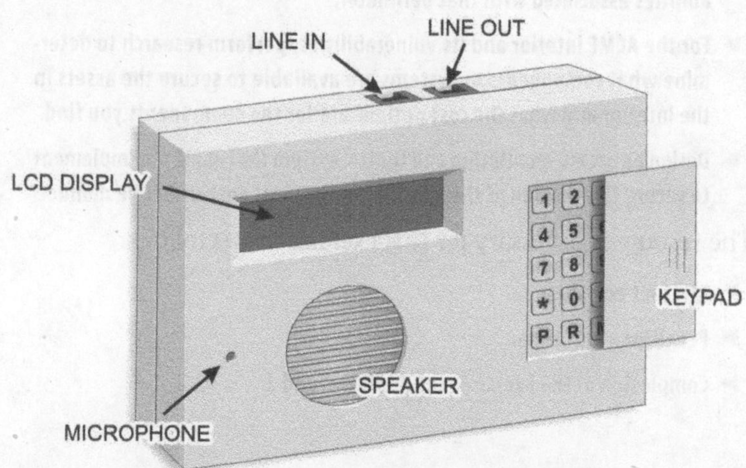

FIGURE 4.16 Automatic Voice/Pager Dialer Console

Third-Party Alarm-Monitoring Services

Depending on the nature of the organization, the intrusion-detection and reporting system may be totally based on employees of the organization.

However, in many organizations, the security systems are supported by professional third-party alarm-monitoring companies.

These companies provide 24-hour/7-days-per-week monitoring services for a monthly fee. When they receive an alarm notification, they perform a response action based on their contractual agreement with the subscriber (client) company.

The sequencing of the response typically corresponds to the nature of the alarm notice they receive and when they receive it. They may initially try to contact designated personnel or contact law enforcement or fire department agencies when an unanswered alarm condition occurs. They may also dispatch armed or unarmed security personnel from the monitoring company to investigate the alarm.

Hands-On Exercises

In this exercise, you will learn how to secure the interior. The objectives are as follows:

Before You Begin

Before you can complete this exercise, you must complete the exercises in Chapters 2 and 3.

- **For the ACME facility, define its security interior and determine the vulnerabilities associated with that perimeter.**
- **For the ACME interior and its vulnerabilities, perform research to determine what components or systems are available to secure the assets in the interior and what the cost options are for the components you find.**
- **Design an access-monitoring and control system that ACME can implement to secure this portion of their facility in the most cost-effective manner.**

The resources necessary for this exercise are as follows:

- **Internet access**
- **Pencil/pen and paper**
- **Completion of the exercises in Chapters 2 and 3**

Discussion

Returning again to the ACME Warehouse project presented in the previous lab procedures, the last preparation step before creating your recommendations to be delivered to the ACME management staff is to research and design the intrusion-detection plan for the interior security zone of the facility.

In the previous procedures, you researched the options for monitoring and controlling access through the outer and inner perimeters, as well as monitoring the areas between those perimeters using video surveillance components.

In this procedure, you will be tasked to research components and strategies that can be used to monitor and control activity within the interior security zone. You will also be expected to make recommendations for implementing the most cost-effective solution that will provide the necessary levels of security.

Figure 4.17 depicts the ACME warehouse area. This portion of the facility is used to store ACME products for shipping to buyers and distributors. As the figure indicates, this area also contains the company's local offices, including:

- The CEO's office
- The shipping manager's office
- The accounting office
- The marketing office
- A supply closet for office supplies
- A janitorial closet for cleaning supplies

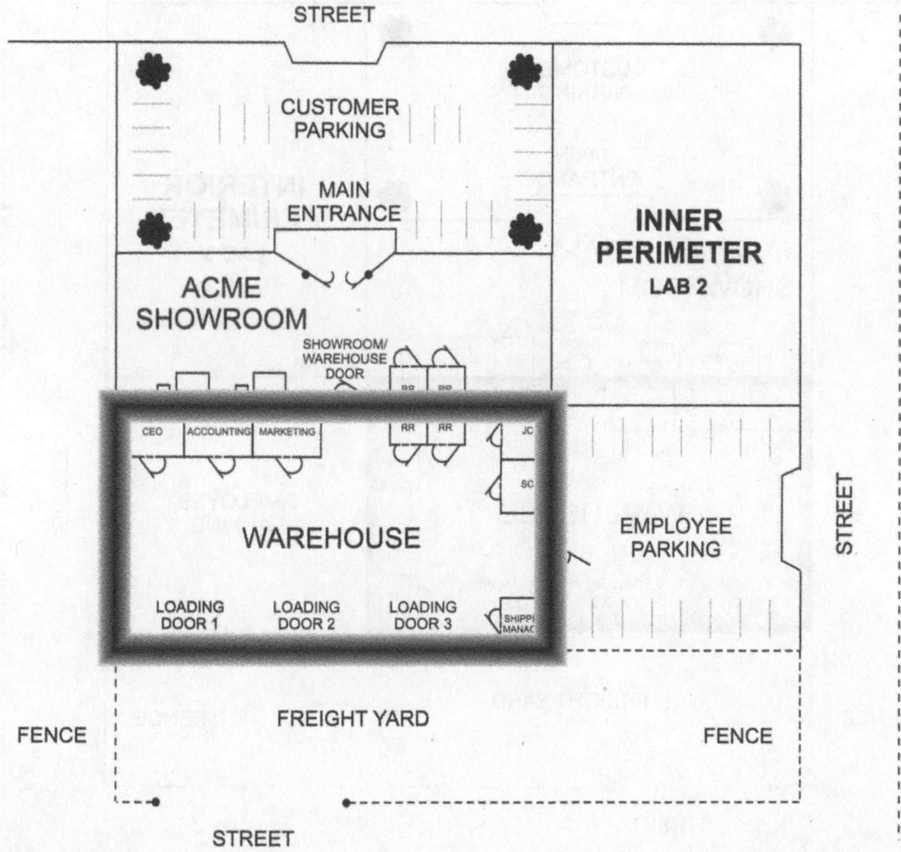

FIGURE 4.17 The Warehouse Area and Offices

The remainder of the warehouse area is open floor space filled with rows of shelving racks that hold ACME products.

It should be apparent that there are two security matters to be considered for the warehouse interior area:

- What are the interior security needs when the warehouse is in operation?
- What are the interior security needs when the warehouse operation is shut down for evenings and weekends?

Procedure

1. Review Figure 4.18 and identify/label the assets of the warehouse facility that should be monitored.

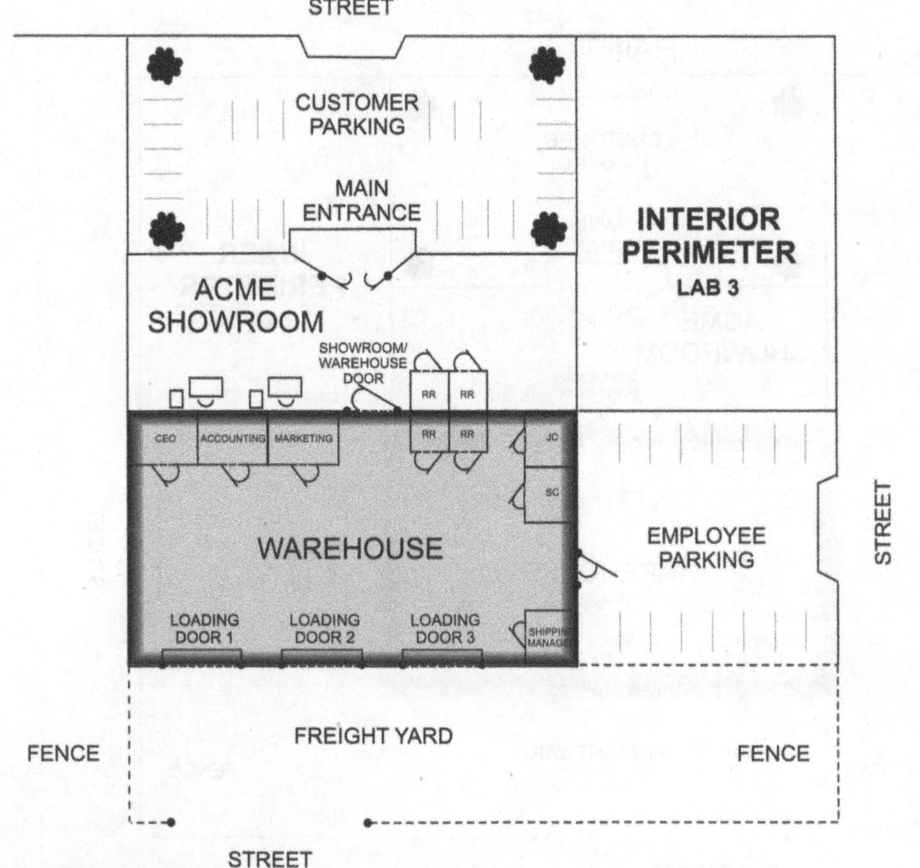

FIGURE 4.18 The Interior Security Zone

2. Use the Internet or other available research tools to research access-monitoring and control devices and systems that can be used to secure the access points you identified in the previous step.

3. Use Table 4.1 through Table 4.3 to organize the specified details about the access-monitoring and control products you find there. For each item, try to locate at least two vendors.

TABLE 4.1 Door Locks

	Product Description	Vendor	Number Required	Cost Per Unit	Total Price
A	Mag Door Lock Kit	Entry Vision	1	$274.99	$274.99
B	Electronic Keyless Door Lock	Gino Development	4	$89.99	$359.96
C	Schlage B581	Doorware.com	1	$52.00	$52.00

TABLE 4.2 Door Contacts/Sensors

	Product Description	Vendor	Number Required	Cost Per Unit	Total Price
A	Surface Mount	Seco-Larm	4	$1.90	$7.60
B	Wireless Surface	Insteon	4	$25.00	$100.00
C	Recessed Mount	Interlogix	4	$6.86	$27.44

TABLE 4.3 Motion Detectors

	Product Description	Vendor	Number Required	Cost Per Unit	Total Price
A	PIR Motion Sensor	Vedard Alarm	2	$8.50	$17.00
B	Pir 360 Motion Audio Sensor	Lithonia	2	$117.00	$234.00
C	PIR 360 Motion Sensor	Optex	2	$54.00	$108.00

4. List your recommendation for the access-control door locks you think should be utilized by ACME.

Answer: Mag Door Lock Kit, Electronic Keyless Door Locks, Schlage B581 deadbolt.

5. Where you would utilize the door locks you are recommending?

Answer: The Mag Door Lock Kit should be applied to outside warehouse pedestrian door for entry authentication and control. Electronic Keyless Door Locks should be installed for the CEO's office, the shipping manager's office, the accounting office, and the marketing office. The locks can be actuated without authentication steps from inside the offices, but require keys or passcodes to operate doors from inside of warehouse. Schlage B581 should be used for the outside showroom and the outside warehouse pedestrian door to secure the perimeter during closed hours.

6. List your selection for the door sensor types you would recommend to ACME for their interior assets.

Answer: The Interlogix Recessed Mount should be utilized to provide additional tracking of people's movement into sensitive offices such as the CEO's, both during operating hours and after hours of operation.

7. List your recommendation for the motion detectors ACME should use for their interior security zone.

Answer: The Lithonia 360 PIR Motion and Audio Sensors will allow full coverage/cross coverage of the warehouse floor after hours to trigger the security system if any other sensor fails before an intruder actually enters the security zone.

Review Questions

1. **Which type of access-control devices might be good recommendations for securing the CEO's office door?**

   Answer: A biometric ID device, a cipher lock, or a keyed lock. The information available in most executive offices typically requires some level of protection. The level of security depends on the organization's tolerance for risk and should be based on a risk assessment. This typically holds true for other management offices (for example, accounting and sales/marketing offices).

2. **Which type of access-control devices might be good recommendations for securing the doors of the supply and janitor's closets?**

   Answer: Either a simple keyed lock or no lock at all. These closets do not contain valuable assets and are often shared by various levels of employees requiring access so they may not require any security beyond a door.

3. **Where would infrared motion detectors be an appropriate choice for the ACME facility?**

   Answer: In the open floor area of the warehouse. There are no access points to monitor, so motion detectors can provide good wide-area monitoring for interior zones. Of course, these devices would only be effective during the evening and weekend time periods when the warehouse operation was closed down and unattended.

CHAPTER 5

Infrastructure Security: Review Questions and Hands-On Exercises

Review the following summary points before proceeding to the "Review Questions" and "Exam Questions" sections at the end of this chapter to make sure you are comfortable with each concept. After completing the review, answer the review questions to verify your knowledge of the material covered in Part I.

Summary Points

- *Security* is the science, technique, and art of establishing a system of exclusion and inclusion of individuals, systems, media, content, and objects.
- *Physical security* is the science, technique, and art of establishing a system of exclusion and inclusion for tangible assets. In practice, this involves policies, practices, and steps aimed at combating theft, preventing physical damage, maintaining system integrity and services, and limiting unauthorized disclosure of information.
- *Cybersecurity* involves securing physical access to property, systems, and equipment ports while securing intangible assets including electronic, optical, and informational access to the system's data and controls.
- *Infrastructure security* refers to physical security initiatives that are applied to providing security for the basic physical and

organizational structures needed for the operation of an enterprise, organization, or society.

- Securing the outer perimeter involves controlling who can move (walk, drive, fly) across the physical or logical line that marks that perimeter. Examples of typical physical outer perimeters include property lines or the exterior walls of a building or complex.
- The inner perimeter typically involves physical barriers such as walls, doors, and windows—either exterior or interior depending on the context of the outer perimeter.
- The *interior* is the innermost level of security and consists of the interior of the building, office, cubicle, etc. that is surrounded by the inner and outer perimeters.
- Natural access control involves using natural design elements, such as structures and landscaping, to guide people as they enter and exit spaces.
- Territorial reinforcement employs structures, systems, and devices to prevent unauthorized entry and create a clear difference between what is public and private.
- Infrastructure security operation and management is based on three basic types of subsystems: access-control and monitoring systems; intrusion-detection and reporting systems; and video surveillance systems.
- Access control is the first major component of a physical security system. The first and most basic objective of any infrastructure security system is to deter potential intruders. This is the goal of access control. Intruders can't damage, destroy, or steal what they can't get to.
- A *right* is a legal privilege or permission granted to someone, or some group, by some recognized source of authority. This source can be a government, a legally recognized governmental agent, or a legally recognized owner of an asset.
- A person who has the right to access an asset is said to be *authorized* (by the recognized authority).
- Anyone who has not been given this right is labeled as *unauthorized*. When unauthorized people attempt to gain access to an asset they do not have rights to access, they become *intruders*.

- A key component that brings all three levels of security together is a well-designed security policy that states how security is implemented at each level.
- A cohesive access control policy at each security level provides authorized people with appropriate levels of access to selected assets, while inhibiting access to assets by people who are not authorized.
- *Authentication* is the process of determining that someone is who they say they are.
- Effective access control involves being able to control the ingress, egress, and regress to an asset based on authorization. In particular, limiting the access of unauthorized personnel to important assets is the most fundamental security objective.
- Multiple factors are involved in authentication:
  - Knowledge—Something that only the designated person should know (something you know)
  - Possession—Something that only the designated person should have (something you have)
  - Inherence—Something that only the designated person is (something you are)
  - Location—Somewhere you are
- Many physical authentication systems are based on single authentication factors that depend on possession.
- Intelligent authentication methods involve *two-factor authentication* (a process that requires two of the factors to grant authorization) based on knowledge and possession.
- *False rejection* or false negative failures are reports that produce an incorrect rejection of the individual, thereby locking them out of a facility or security area to which they should have access.
- *False acceptance* or false positive failures are reports that incorrectly authenticate the individual, which could provide access to equipment or data that this person should not be able to access. Of the two types of authentication failure, this is the most significant in that it could grant access to malicious people.

- *Remote monitoring* refers to monitoring or measurement of devices from a remote location or control room. In the security realm, this involves having external access to the security system through a communication system.
- Remote-access monitoring systems are used to notify supervisory security personnel when an unauthorized access is attempted.
- Because open and closed conditions are not the same as locked and unlocked conditions, a single sensor cannot differentiate between these two sets of conditions. A second or different type of sensor needs to be installed and monitored to perform this differentiation.
- Remote-access control is a design feature that manages entry to protected areas by authenticating the identity of persons entering those secured areas (security zone or computer system) using an authentication system located in a location other than the access point.
- Remote-control access is a design feature that works with remote-monitoring systems to monitor, control, and supervise doors, gates, and conveyances from a distance.
- A functional intrusion-detection and reporting system typically includes an intelligent control panel connected by wires or radio signals to sensors at various locations throughout a facility or organization.
- Each security controller model is designed to handle a specific number of programmable zones. A zone can be a single point of protection such as a motion detector, or multiple points can be combined into a single zone.
- *Sensors* are a class of input devices that convert physical activity into a signal that can be presented to the security controller. They are available in a variety of configurations including magnetic switches for doors and windows, acoustic detectors, vibration detectors, motion detectors, and glass-break detectors. Sensors protect the perimeter, selected outside areas, and the open spaces inside the facility.
- Physical-intrusion-detection systems typically include three basic types of output devices: visual notification, audible annunciators, and remote messaging.
- Two types of fire-detection sensors are available: heat detectors and smoke detectors. They operate by detecting heat rise or smoke in the home.

- Digital video recorders (DVRs) are the preferred technology for recording surveillance video.
- Motion detectors work by detecting the changes in the infrared energy in an area.
- The use of multiple physical security zones has several purposes. It allows the user to arm only portions of the system, such as the perimeter doors and windows, while bypassing the interior motion detectors in a specific zone.
- An IP camera can be viewed from anywhere in the world where Internet access is available.
- The two important specifications that influence the cost of cameras are light sensitivity rating (lux rating) and resolution.
- Surveillance cameras should not be used where there is a reasonable expectation of privacy by individuals.
- In addition to determining what specifications security cameras must possesses for a given role, it is equally important to map out a camera deployment strategy to maximize the surveillance investment.

Security Challenge Scenarios

In Chapter 1, you were asked to record your observations for the risk-assessment challenges presented there. At that point, you may have had little or no knowledge of the security tools and techniques required to secure the environments presented in those scenarios.

Now that you have read the first four chapters, complete the information requested in the following section and compare that information to the original assessments you generated in Chapter 1 to measure how much you've learned.

Infrastructure Security Scenario 1

Identify: ____________________

Protect: ____________________

Detect: ____________________

Respond: ____________________

Recover: ____________________

Infrastructure Security Scenario 2

Identify: ____________________

Protect: ____________________

Detect: ____________________

Respond: ____________________

Recover: ____________________

Professional Feedback

In this section, you will compare your observations to those of a working security specialist—in this case, Philip Craig, the founder of BlackByte Cyber Security—to improve your understanding of cybersecurity.

About Philip Craig

Philip Craig is the founder of BlackByte Cyber Security, LLC, a consultancy supporting the Pacific Northwest National Laboratory (PNNL) research and national security agendas, as well as the National Rural Electric Cooperative Association and National Rural Telecommunications Cooperative.

For many years, Phil served as a Senior Cyber Security Research Scientist at PNNL, where he provided engineering and program management support in the fields of cybersecurity, supervisory control, and data acquisition (SCADA) technologies, computing, and communications infrastructure.
This included the development of complex system and policy solutions in a variety of critical infrastructures including the nuclear power, electric power, and water sectors. He developed and deployed both strategic and tactical cybersecurity defensive solutions for the electric power and nuclear sectors.

The Insights of a Practicing Professional

Practicing security professionals have a significant advantage when determining the most effective security solutions for many deployments very quickly. After repeatedly practicing the trade in the field, you too will be able to create certain models that will remain effective in the future.

Here is a time-proven approach that opens with three very basic questions that will position you to enter the initial assessment phase. Always ask your client:

1. What are we trying to protect?
2. Who are we trying to protect it from?
3. Why do we need to provide protection?

The first answer is always a physical thing (e.g., some material, component, product, etc.) that you can physically see, taste, touch, and smell. It may be a sensitive device or instrument in development or it may have a high monetary value. It also may be some material that has environmental sensitivity or that may be dangerous to the general public if protection methods are not utilized correctly.

The second answer is focused on a person (potentially an adversary).

The last answer could originate from a business need supporting the economic strength of the corporation or the requirement to follow a particular regulation. Needless to say, you can throw as many of your newly learned techniques as you can at the solution, but without the information you discern from asking these questions, you are wasting a significant amount of your time—and more importantly, your client's money.

Let's review your scenario. Consider the following construct:

- A building (containing multiple floors and spaces)
- An office environment (containing spaces for offices and cubicles)
- A cubicle (containing computing resources)

As you learned earlier, there are many physical and cybersecurity considerations. They exist in external, internal, and interior contexts with many attributes that influence the access to each. We will need to consider these influences and begin to provide physical and logical separations that are often called perimeters or demarcations.

Figure 5.1 represents a reliable model that provides a consistent approach for handling these considerations. For security purposes, we're always concerned primarily with threats, so this threat-informed model will always apply.

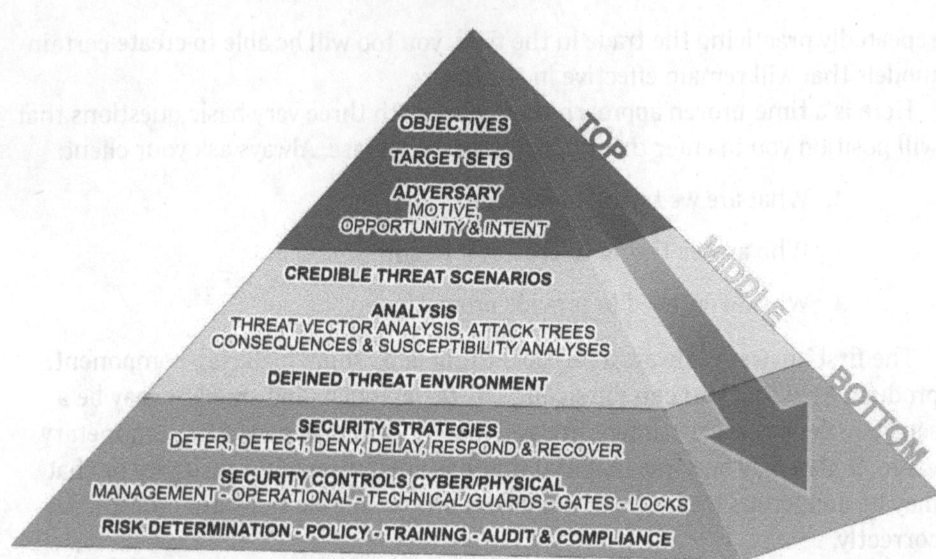

FIGURE 5.1 Threat-Informed Pyramid

Securing the Top Region

The items to deal with in the upper region of the threat-informed model include:

- *Objectives:* The adversary's overall objective is to disrupt, destroy, or steal a target
- *Target Sets:* The assets that represent the best opportunity to upset, compromise, damage, or otherwise discontinue functions and/or operations of a system.
- *Adversary:* An agent who is determined to carry out a particular objective driven by MOI (motive, opportunity and intent). Each adversary attribute will govern the adversary's overall decision-making process to determine what is necessary to reach an objective and complete a mission.

Securing the Middle Region

The activities called out in the middle region of the threat-informed model include:

- *Credible Threat Scenarios:* A set of activities, when scripted or arranged in a particular sequence, would have the highest success of achieving an attack objective. Therefore, you must concentrate your efforts on identifying all these scenarios.

- *Analysis:* Those activities (threat vector analysis, attack trees, consequences, and susceptibility analysis) that must be performed to evaluate the best, most likely, most effective, or most probable means of a potential attacker's success in reaching an objective along with a description of the impacts of such success.
- *Defined Threat Environment:* The Defined Threat Environment represents the culmination of all the attributes associated with the topics above it in the "upper" and "middle" regions of the pyramid.

Securing the Bottom Region

The activities called out in the bottom region of the threat-informed model include:

- *Security Strategies (Detect, Deter, Deny, Delay, Respond, Recover):* Based on the defined threat environment, those strategies are formulated to ensure security functions to deter, detect, deny, delay, respond, and recover from an attack.
- *Security Controls Cyber/Physical (Management, Operational, Technical/Guards, Gates, Locks):* Mechanisms that are employed to ensure that the security strategies are effective.
- *Risk Determination – Policy – Training – Audit and Compliance:* The supporting programmatic elements necessary to document measures to determine the effectiveness of an overall security program.

All too often organizations are too quick to apply a comprehensive security policy and then build a program to ensure the policy is met. From a practicing security professional's standpoint, that is completely backward from how it should be approached. However, at your first job, or on any new job, you're going to likely step into an operational security program. It is important that you still take this approach or you'll struggle with the reasons that decisions have already been made.

So now you've been given a means to understand what, who, and why, as well as a model to enable a good process to assess and evaluate the security environment, what is next? How can you tackle the task?

Tackling the Task at Hand

First, you need to establish your perspective. We'll call it the "you are here" dot on a map of your environment. Two different perspectives are used: an outside-in and an inside-out. Picture a castle. In the days when castles were prevalent, they were actually giant fortified structures created to keep people out. This perspective is an "outside-in" perspective. The architects busily constructed methods that from an outside perspective protected their castles from being penetrated. Although many physical security methods still employ this perspective (and should), a more comprehensive approach is to use the "inside-out" perspective. This approach will ensure that the most interior areas are considered and you will be able to build a security posture using graded methods as you reach the most outer areas. This is called a *graded approach*. It allows security professionals to prescribe security controls as necessary so they don't overprescribe them and amass excessive costs or expend unnecessary resources or effort.

What Am I Protecting?

Document the object, material, and property. It can be a box of diamonds or intellectual property like the Colonel Sanders Kentucky Fried Chicken recipe.

Who Am I Protecting My Asset From?

You play the adversary! From an inside-out perspective, start at the most interior area (cubicles) and look for any artifacts that could challenge your security controls.

Make sure you are familiar with and understand the physical pathways: from the cubicles to the office areas to the building itself. Look for both physical and cyber ingress and egress. Always think like an adversary (the top of our triangle).

Why Am I Providing Protection?

Is it the asset's value? Is it a production process that could result in millions of dollars of lost revenue if disrupted? Is it some material that could cause challenge the safety of your employees or the public? Are there regulatory or other legal or contractually binding requirements?

Executing Your Plan

Prioritize and select the appropriate (necessary) security controls that will detect, deter, deny, delay, respond, and recover your security posture. Properly documented installation processes and procedures should be in place to help ensure that your security controls are properly installed.

Implement your plan as constructed. Make sure all physical and cyber methods are installed as required.

Check your implementation by procedure. When you are operational, there needs to be a method to constantly check to ensure that your security controls are effective. These controls usually range from simple internal email-phishing exercises, rattling doors and windows, to actually executing a combined cyber/physical challenge exercise constructed to test your response and mitigation capability.

Improve your posture as you execute periodic assessments and exercises that may expose any weaknesses and opportunities to provide corrective or augmented capabilities. Without this cycle, you'll never be able to defend your operational budgets or get support from management.

There are hundreds if not thousands of ways to provide secure and trusted environments depending on the what, who, and why of any company or organization. The methods that are successful are those that you can defend with proper arguments that are well documented. Your future employer won't just keep you around because you're good, they'll keep you around because you're thorough.

Review Questions

The following questions assess your knowledge of the material presented in Part I.

1. **_______________ is the science, technique, and art of establishing a system of exclusion and inclusion for tangible assets.**

   Answer: Physical security. In practice, this involves *policies, practices,* and *steps* aimed at combating theft, preventing physical damage, maintaining system integrity and services, and limiting unauthorized disclosure of information.

2. **_______________ is a report that incorrectly authenticates the individual, which could provide access to equipment or data that this person should not have.**

   Answer: False acceptance or false positive failures

3. **Define *lux rating* as it applies to surveillance cameras and describe the typical range of lux ratings for these devices.**

   Answer: The amount of light required to obtain a reasonable video camera image is called the *lux rating*. Lux is a measure of the amount of light that falls on an object. One lux is approximately the amount of light falling on one square meter from one candle measured from one meter away. Typical camera ratings range between 0.5 and 1.0 lux.

4. **Using natural design elements such as structures and landscaping to guide people as they enter and exit spaces is referred to as_______________.**

   Answer: Natural access control

5. **Which type of security device is used for programming, controlling, and operating access control and management devices?**

   Answer: Most intrusion-detection and reporting systems employ a *keypad* device for programming, controlling, and operating various access-control and management devices.

6. **Which type of cameras provides the best resolution in low-light conditions?**

   Answer: An IR camera. An infrared security camera has infrared LED lighting (light from a different region of the electromagnetic spectrum than we are normally used to seeing) installed around the outside of the camera lens. This lighting allows the camera to capture a good image in no light at all. With a little bit of light (called low light), the infrared camera can capture a picture that looks just like daytime.

7. **Which type of image sensor is used in cameras designed to produce the highest quality images?**

   Answer: CCD. The best surveillance cameras employ *Charged Coupled Device (CCD)* technology. They have high resolution, low-operating light requirements, less temperature dependence, and high reliability.

8. **Describe the primary uses for keypads in security systems.**

   Answer: Most intrusion-detection and reporting systems employ a *keypad* device for programming, controlling, and operating various access-control and management devices.

9. **Describe the technologies used to report alarm conditions to key personnel or remote monitoring organizations.**

   Answer: The most common *remote notification systems* involve the use of a telephone line by the intrusion-detection and reporting system's control panel to automatically call a remote monitoring facility or key personnel when an alarm condition exists. Some systems employ a separate *telephone dialer* or a built-in dialer. However, a growing number of systems possess built-in *cellular communications* systems. Such systems provide additional dependability in that they can function even if the physical telephone lines are damaged.

10. **______________________ employs structures, systems, and devices to prevent unauthorized entry and create a clear difference between what is public and private.**

    Answer: Territorial reinforcement

11. **With______________________, the condition monitoring system can record and signal each time a specific gate or door is unlocked (granting access) and what type of access was granted. Unlocked monitoring can also identify who was granted access.**

    Answer: Unlocked condition monitoring

12. **List the locations in which perimeter-area input sensors are typically placed in an intrusion-detection and reporting system.**

Answer: Perimeter-area inputs to the control panel typically include sensors at every perimeter opening including doors, windows, garage doors and windows, and doors to crawl spaces. Additional perimeter protection may include using sound, vibration, and motion-detector sensors to guard against entry through broken windows.

13. **Which physical technique is used to create a physical security zone on a security controller?**

    Answer: Logically group related sensors together to create a security zone. This is accomplished by connecting all of the related sensor switches (all sensors appear as switches to the security controller) together in a serial format that connects to a specific set of contacts on the controller's panel.

14. **List the four factors that are commonly employed in authentication systems.**

    Answer: There are multiple factors that can be used to establish authentication: Knowledge—something you know, possession—something you have, inherence—something you are, and location—where you are.

15. **Name the two major concerns associated with storing video surveillance information, particularly in larger enterprises.**

    Answer: How much video needs to be stored? For how long does it need to be stored? The answers to these questions enable the organization to determine its storage capacity needs.

Exam Questions

1. **Securing which of the following involves controlling who can move (walk, drive, fly) across the physical or logical line that marks this perimeter, such as property lines or the exterior walls of a building or complex?**

    A. **The interior space**

    B. **The inner perimeter**

    C. **The outer perimeter**

    D. **The primary zone**

    Answer: C

2. **Which of the following is *not* a subsystem involved in infrastructure security management?**
   - **A. Access-control and monitoring systems**
   - **B. Intrusion-detection and reporting systems**
   - **C. Video surveillance systems**
   - **D. Corporate cyber security policies**

   Answer: D

3. **Which of the following options represent physical barriers? (Select all that apply.)**
   - **A. A locked door**
   - **B. A receptionist**
   - **C. An RFID badge reader**
   - **D. A surveillance camera**

   Answer: A and B

4. **Which type of surveillance camera can be viewed from virtually anywhere in the world?**
   - **A. A digital camera**
   - **B. A digital IP camera**
   - **C. An analog camera**
   - **D. A hybrid camera**

   Answer: B

5. **From the following report types, which options would produce an incorrect rejection of the individual, thereby locking him out of a facility or security area to which he should have access? (Select all that apply.)**
   - **A. False rejection**
   - **B. False acceptance**
   - **C. False negative failures**
   - **D. False positive failures**

   Answer: A and C

6. **Which sensor detects a beam of light (visible or invisible) and responds to a change in the received light intensity?**
   - **A. Microwave sensor**
   - **B. Pressure sensor**
   - **C. Motion sensor**
   - **D. Photoelectric sensor**

   Answer: D

7. **Which lens enables you to view an entire room but with some distortion of the image?**
   A. **Fish-eye lens**
   B. **Telephoto lens**
   C. **Fixed-focal-length lens**
   D. **Varifocal lens**

   Answer: A

8. **Which of the following best describes the meaning of *lux rating* as it applies to surveillance cameras?**
   A. **Rating for the size of the camera lens**
   B. **Amount of light required for an acceptable image**
   C. **Resolution of the camera lens**
   D. **Specifies the color resolution of a camera**

   Answer: B

9. **Which of the following cameras provides the ability to maintain a degree of secrecy by using illumination that is outside of the visible light spectrum?**
   A. **CCD camera**
   B. **Infrared security camera**
   C. **Black-and-white camera**
   D. **Color camera**

   Answer: B

10. **Which of the following cameras features the best set of specifications for monitoring a 24/7 cash machine that must operate in both daytime and low-level night-time lighting conditions, while providing a high-resolution, detailed view to monitor the different banking functions the machine is used for?**
    A. **Camera 1 – 800 × 600 pixel resolution, 1.0 lux rating**
    B. **Camera 1 – 2240 × 1680 pixel resolution, 0.5 lux rating**
    C. **Camera 1 – 1024 × 768 pixel resolution, 0.75 lux rating**
    D. **Camera 1 – 1536 × 1180 pixel resolution, 0.9 lux rating**

    Answer: D

PART II

Securing Local Hosts

CHAPTER 6

Local Host Security in the Real World

The following challenges provide contextual reference points for the concepts you will learn in Part II. Because you have not yet read the chapters in Part II, the challenges in this chapter are designed to introduce you to the local host scenarios you'll face in the real world.

In this chapter, you'll learn to:

1. Apply applicable categories and sub-categories of the NIST Cyber Security Framework's "Identify" function to a specific scenario to document the network's assets and their possible vulnerabilities.
2. Use applicable categories and sub-categories of the "Protect" function to generate specific policies and actions that can be used to secure the network's assets for the specified scenario.
3. Apply applicable categories and sub-categories of the "Detect" function to identify technologies, policies, practices, and strategies that can be used to monitor the network in the scenario to determine whether security events are occurring.
4. Apply applicable categories and sub-categories of the "Respond" function to create an incident response plan to cover specific security events associated with the scenario presented.
5. Apply applicable categories and sub-categories of the NIST Cyber Security Framework "Recover" function to the scenario to implement solutions for recovering from specific cyber events.

Security Challenges

This chapter will kickstart your thought processes for what you are about to learn in Part II. Instead of simply trying to absorb all of the information you're about to learn in these chapters, you'll begin here by gaining a better understanding of the real-world relevance of that information.

In Chapter 10, you will return to these scenarios and apply what you learned in Chapters 7, 8, and 9. You will also compare your observations to those of the professional security specialists who have provided their observations and solutions for these scenarios.

Computing Device Security Scenario 1

You have been assigned to develop a local security policy and the configuration specifications for the desktop computers used by in-house employees at your firm. These PCs are mounted in special openings under the desk in each cubicle.

The computers are physically identical, and they all run the same operating system. However, they may have different types of job-specific company software installed, as shown in Figure 6.1. These computers are equipped with the following:

- Detachable keyboards and mice
- Six built-in USB connection ports
- Separate video display monitors
- UTP local area network connection ports
- Microsoft Windows 7 Professional operating systems
- Microsoft Office 2013 software
- Dual built-in DVD disc drives

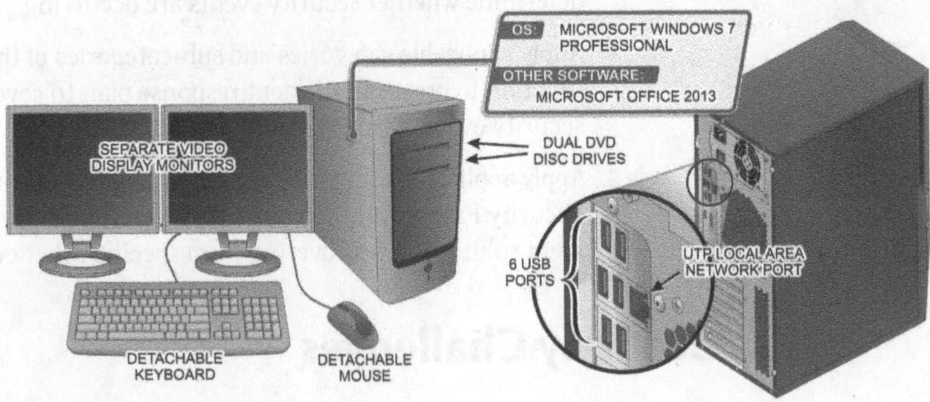

FIGURE 6.1 Corporate Desktop PC

Risk Assessment 1

From the information provided in this first scenario, consider the National Institute of Standards and Technology (NIST) functions detailed in this section and then write your observations as they relate to each category.

Identify

Create an inventory of physical and software assets associated with the user computers described here. Identify potential pathways that could provide unauthorized personnel with access to the physical and software assets associated with these computers (NIST ID.AM-1, 2; ID.RA-1).

Protect

Describe how to go about managing the identities and credentials of authorized users at the local level (NIST PR.AC-1, 2, 4; PR.PT-1, 3).

Detect

Using the computers and environment identified at the outset of this section, how might you determine whether someone was attempting to gain access to the computers described or the software and intellectual property stored on them (NIST DE.CM-1,4; DE.AE-1,2,3,4)?

Which types of systems must be in place to identify occurrences of physical security breaches (NIST DE.CM-2, 3)?

Respond

Describe how to respond to a suspected security breach of one or more local host units (NIST RS.RP-1; RS.CO-2, 3, 4, 5; RS.AN-1, 2, 3; RS.MI-1, 2, 3; RS.IM-2).

Recover

List the policies and steps that should be put into place to recover from actions that might be taken to access, damage, or destroy the assets described in this scenario (NIST RC.RP-1).

Which items might a recovery plan include if local host security is breached (NIST RC.CO-1, 2, 3)?

Computing Device Security Scenario 2

Because you did such an outstanding job of creating the security policies and configurations for the company's desktop computers, you have been asked to produce the same type of materials for the notebook computers used by the organization's sales people.

These computers typically contain product information the sales people need to do their jobs when they are meeting with customers. As such, confidential company and customer information (such as proprietary price lists for different customers, customer contact and purchase history information, confidential communications between the sales person and the customers, as well as with company supervisory personnel, and information about products under development but not yet announced) is stored on these devices.

Obviously, these computers are portable PCs that work in the office and at different locations on the road. As depicted in Figure 6.2, these computers are equipped with the following:

- ► Built-in keyboards and displays
- ► Two built-in USB connection ports
- ► UTP local area network connection ports
- ► Microsoft Windows 7 Professional operating systems
- ► Microsoft Office 2013 software
- ► Dual SD card reader slots
- ► Built-in wireless networking capabilities
- ► External VGA display connection ports
- ► Built-in DVD disc drives

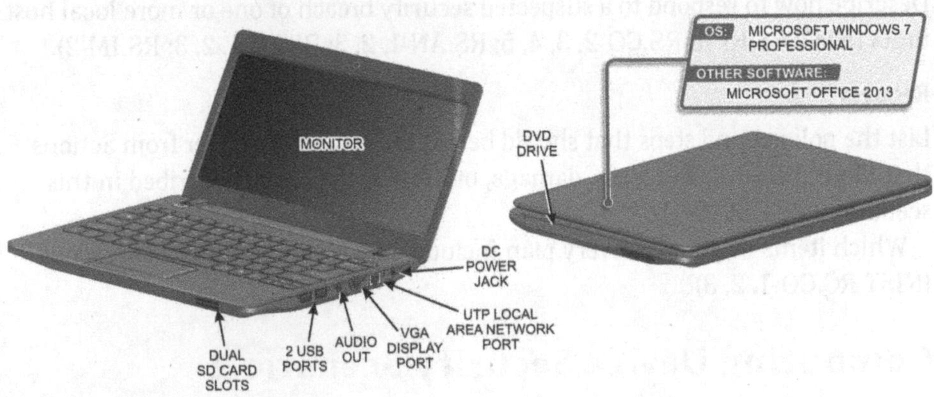

FIGURE 6.2 Notebook PC

Risk Assessment 2

From the information provided in the second scenario, consider the NIST functions detailed in this section and then write your observations as they relate to each category.

Identify

Create an inventory of physical devices and systems associated with the user computers described here (NIST ID.AM-1).

Create an inventory of software used on the company notebook computers (NIST ID.AM-2).

Map the organization's communications and data flow with these portable computers (NIST ID.AM-3).

Describe the risks associated with the environment and the computing devices described in this scenario. Create a risk assessment of identified asset vulnerabilities (NIST ID.RA-1, 2, 3, 4, 5).

Protect

For the equipment package described, determine which assets must be in place to mitigate the risks identified previously (NIST PR.AC, AT, DS, IP, and PT).

Describe how to manage the identities and credentials for the authorized users of these computers (NIST PR.AC-1).

Create a plan to determine how remote access will be provided and protected when the mobile devices are used away from the corporate facilities (NIST PR.AC-3).

Describe how data on the mobile computers will be secured as well as how it will be protected when communicated to and from the devices (NIST PR.DS-1, 2).

Detect

Establish a security plan to monitor these information systems to identify cybersecurity events and verify the effectiveness of protective measures (NIST DE.CM-1-8; DE.AE-1-5).

Which types of systems must be in place to monitor remote communications from these devices to detect potential cybersecurity events (NIST DE.CM-1)?

Which types of systems must be in place to monitor personnel activity to detect potential cybersecurity threats (NIST DE.CM-3)?

Respond

Create a plan to ensure that response processes and procedures are in place to provide timely responses to detected cybersecurity events (NIST RS.RP-1; RS.AN-1).

Considering the information kept on these mobile host devices, which type of response plan might be necessary if security is breached on one of the systems (NIST RS.CO-4, 5)?

Recover

Which steps should be put into place to recover from actions intended to access, damage, or destroy the assets you've identified (NIST RC.RP-1)?

Summary

Record your observations for risk assessments presented in this chapter. In Chapter 10, you will compare these original thoughts and observations with those you will generate after reading Chapters 7, 8, and 9. You'll also be able to compare your answers to those of professional security specialists.

## CHAPTER 7

Securing Devices

Based on the scenarios in Chapter 6, you can see that protecting standalone Information Technology (IT) assets offers many challenges. Local host (Computing and Intelligent Control Device) security is implemented on multiple levels that include physical denial of use, limited access to system resources, and active protection against individuals and software intent on corrupting or stealing data. In this chapter, you'll learn to:

- **Identify three security perimeters associated with an end point computing device**
- **Provide physical security for end point computing devices**
- **Evaluate BIOS/CMOS Security Options**

The Three Layers of Security

If you think of standalone IT or ICS devices in terms of the three layers of security described in Chapter 2, you can think of the *outer perimeter* as the space around the outside of the physical device and its housing. The *inner perimeter* should be viewed as the device's operating system and application programs. Finally, the interior of the device consists of the intangible data assets of the information created, obtained, and stored electronically in the device. Figure 7.1 graphically illustrates these layers.

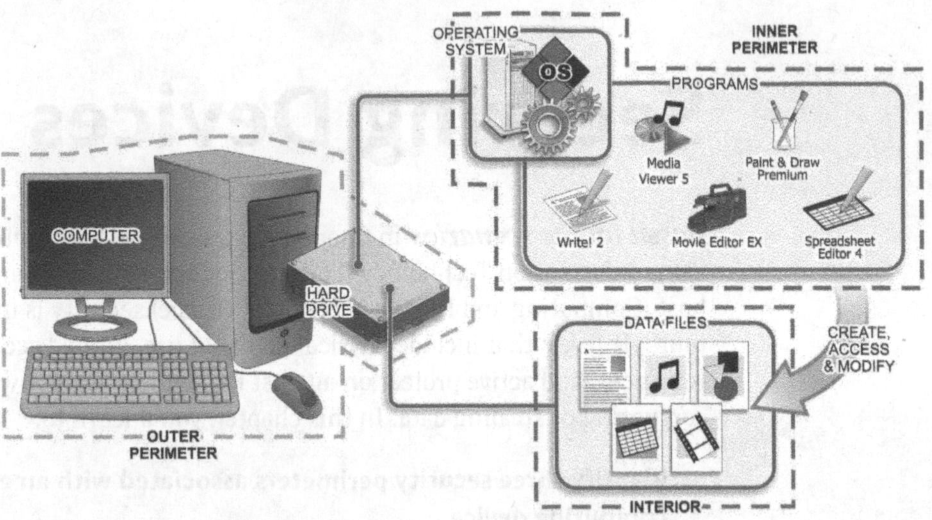

FIGURE 7.1 The Three Layers

The first level of securing your intelligent devices is to control access to them. Once again, an intruder can't damage, destroy, or steal what they can't get to. This applies to intelligent computing and control devices as well. So, the first step is to control physical access to the devices as much as is practical.

Autonomous or semiautonomous ICS devices, such as Programmable Logic Controllers (PLCs) or standalone microcontrollers, can normally be placed in secure, lockable enclosures where access is limited to only those people possessing the key. These devices tend to be prevalent in industrial control and utility environments.

In this chapter, the primary asset we will be dealing with is the personal computer (PC). For the most part, it is not practical to lock up desktop and portable PC systems that may be used by different people. In many cases, a given computer may routinely be used by different personnel—for example, a day shift employee and a night shift employee. In such applications, administrative security measures must be in place to guarantee proper authentication and access control.

Securing Host Devices

Protecting local computing and control devices begins with a locked door or an enclosure when possible. However, in business and industrial settings, many such assets are used in relatively open environments. In these environments, locking security cables, like the one depicted in Figure 7.2, may be used to physically attach the computing equipment to desks or other nonportable structures to make them more difficult to remove.

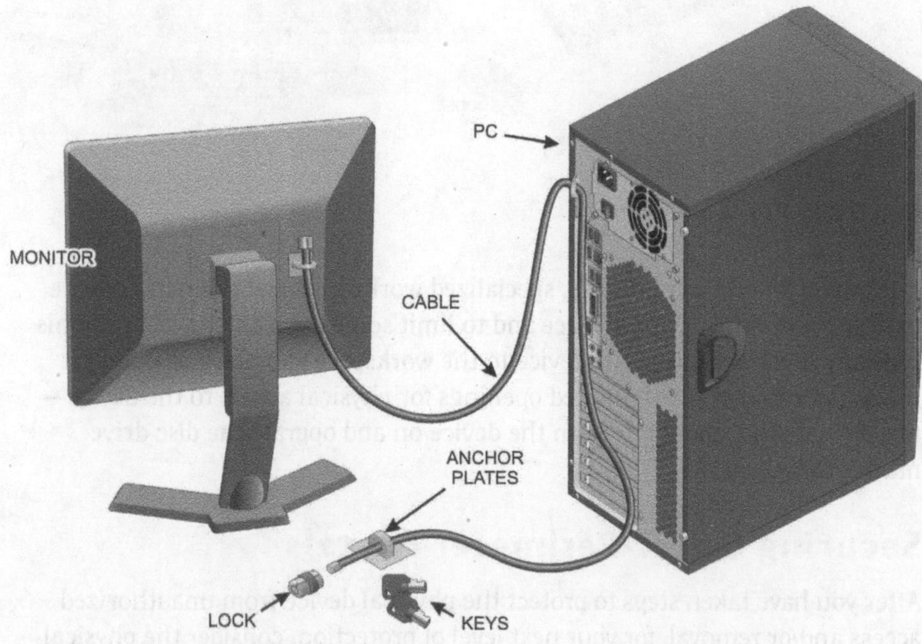

FIGURE 7.2 PC Security Cable

Docking stations like the one illustrated in Figure 7.3 are accessories designed for use with portable computing devices. The primary function of the docking station is to enable portable users to travel with their portable devices, yet still employ full-size peripheral and connectivity devices when they are in the office environment.

The second function of many docking stations is to provide a lockable attachment to the desktop to prevent unauthorized users from picking up the portable unit while it is not in use and simply carrying it away.

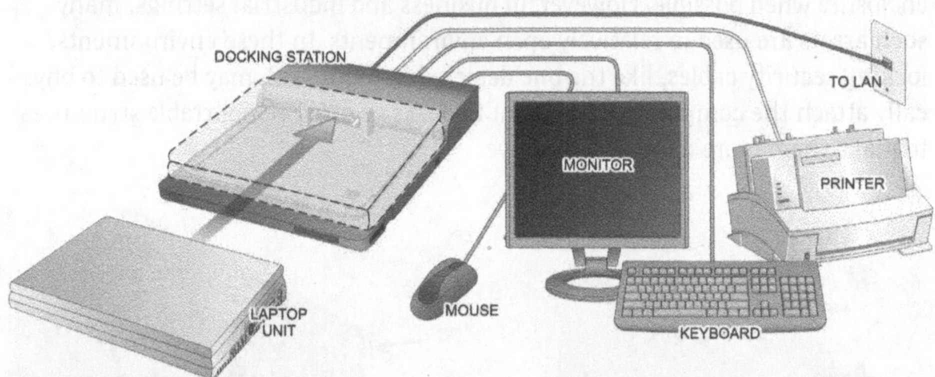

FIGURE 7.3 A Docking Station

In many office environments, specialized work desks and cabinetry can be used to secure the device in place and to limit some access to the device. This typically involves bolting the device to the workspace cabinetry or hiding it inside the cabinetry with limited openings for physical access to the device—maybe just large enough to turn the device on and operate the disc drive mechanisms.

Securing Outer-Perimeter Portals

After you have taken steps to protect the physical device from unauthorized access and/or removal, for your next level of protection, consider the physical case of the local computer or intelligent control device as its outer perimeter.

Also, remember what malicious people really want from such devices—they want the programs and data located inside the machine. So, where can such people access these items in order to damage, destroy, or steal them? In both computing and intelligent control devices, there are three general locations where they can gain access to these items:

- While it's in memory
- While it's in storage on devices such as hard drives and flash drives
- When it is being transferred from one place to another

In the case of the personal computers, depicted in Figure 7.4, how would you penetrate their cases to get to the intangible valuables inside?

FIGURE 7.4 Typical PCs

The most obvious point of access through the outer perimeter of a PC would be its basic input devices: its keyboard and mouse or touch-sensitive display. If someone can simply sit down in front of the system and freely use its input devices (keyboard, mouse, touchpad, or touchscreen), they have an avenue for accessing the information inside. All they have to do is push the On/Off button and wait for the device to boot up.

DISPLAYS AND THEIR INPUT CAPABILITIES

Unless a display has an input capability, such as a USB port, it is not considered to be an access device that can be exploited. The same holds true for nonwireless printers or other output-only devices.

BIOS Security Subsystems

There is one basic security tool built into the hardware of most personal computers that offers some basic protection before the operating system bootup completes. The Basic Input/Output System (BIOS) offers basic hardware security options that can be set through its BIOS Setup utility, also called the CMOS Setup utility. Figure 7.5 displays a typical Security Configuration screen.

Normally, these options include setting user passwords to control access to the system and supervisory passwords to control access to the CMOS Setup utility.

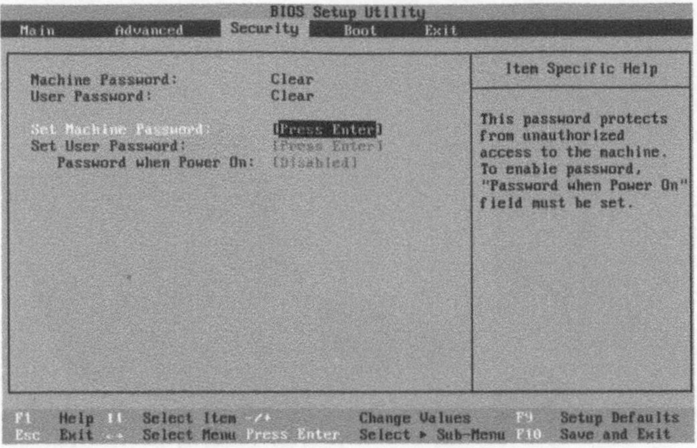

FIGURE 7.5 CMOS Security Configuration

The Set User Password option enables administrators to establish passwords that users must enter during the startup process to complete the boot process and gain access to the operating system. Without this password, the system will never reach an operational level that an intruder could use to access its internal perimeter and interior information.

However, this password does not provide access to the CMOS Setup utility where the user and supervisory password options are configured. A supervisory password option must be used to establish a password that can be employed to access the CMOS Setup utility.

The Security Configuration screen may also include options for setting virus check and backup reminders that pop up periodically when the system is booted. In addition to enabling these settings, administrators can also specify the time interval between notices.

One of the main sets of security options in the CMOS Setup utility consists of those that can be used to control access to the system's inner perimeter and interior assets. For the most part, these options cover such things as limiting access permitted through the asset's physical ports and removable media systems, as well as access to the boot sector of the system's disk drive.

Because the CMOS password controls access to all parts of the system, even before the bootup process occurs, there is some inconvenience in the event that the user forgets a password. When this occurs, it will be impossible to gain access to the system without completely resetting the content of the CMOS RAM. On some motherboards, this can be accomplished by shorting a special pair of jumpers on the board.

With other systems, you must remove or short across the backup battery to reset the CMOS information. You will also have to unplug the power from the commercial outlet to reduce the voltage to the CMOS registers. When the content of the CMOS is reset, you must manually restore any nondefault CMOS settings being used by the system.

Local System Hardening

In computer and networking environments, the term *hardening* is used to refer to the process of making a system more secure. Computer hardening efforts begin with hardware, but also extend to the local host's operating system, its file system, and its applications.

At the hardware level, the primary area of hardening is the system BIOS and any other firmware add-ons that may have been introduced to the system. Because *firmware* by definition is a software product enclosed in a hardware device, it comes preinstalled in the system or on one of its devices.

To make firmware more secure than it already is requires updating. Depending on the physical structure of the firmware, these updates may involve physical or logical updates. Hardware manufacturers provide firmware updates to improve their existing, installed products—including upgrading their security tools. Their intent is to improve the reliability, security, or attractiveness of their product.

In most cases, firmware updates are designed to provide solutions to hardware incompatibilities or to provide the Data Link layer drivers necessary for the firmware to work with a particular operating system. However, some product improvements may simply extend the product's capabilities but may not necessarily make it more secure.

Additional Inner-Perimeter Access Options

In addition to the basic input devices used with personal computers, there are several other pathways built into most computer systems that provide access to the inner perimeter. Even non-networked, standalone computers may be susceptible to exploitation from outside sources through removable media systems and physical access ports (connection points).

Physical Port Access

Physical hardware ports enable the basic PC system to interact with optional, removable devices, as shown in Figure 7.6. They also provide a potential security threat because individuals with malicious intent can gain access directly into the computer internal communication and processing system through these ports.

FIGURE 7.6 Physical PC Ports

Hardware ports provide access to the computer's internal communications buses that link all of its internal components, including its data bus, memory, and internal storage devices (the three areas listed for gaining access to programs and data). Figure 7.7 depicts the layout of a typical PC's internal bus structure. The only component standing between someone with physical access to the port connection and the system's internal structure is the bus controller interface that is part of the computer's internal chipset. The operation of this circuitry is controlled by the system's BIOS and operating system.

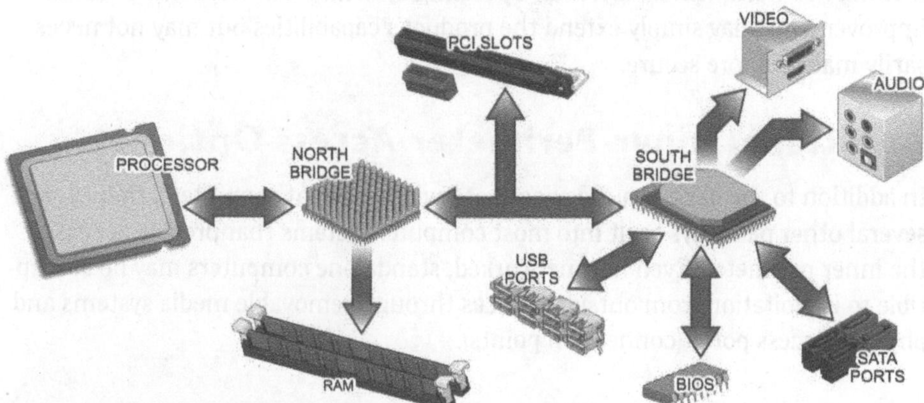

FIGURE 7.7 Pathways to the Vital Components

A Clarification of the Word Port

Be aware that the term *port* is also used to refer to logical TCP/UTP software ports used in computer network communications. You will encounter this version of the term shortly when you are introduced to firewalls.

Data can be downloaded into removable media devices through these ports and quickly carried away. Likewise, malicious programs, such as viruses and worms that you will be introduced to later in this chapter, can be uploaded into the machine from the removable media source. Once these programs have been introduced to the host system, they infect it and can damage or destroy data and programs stored on it.

Securing Connection Points

A PC may possess several different hardware connection points. Not all of these connections pose a security threat. Only those connection ports that provide access directly to the system's internal bus structure need to be considered. For example, a standard VGA video port is an output-only connection that does not provide access to the system's internal operation.

The most widely used hardware connection ports in newer PCs are USB ports. However, you may still encounter older legacy ports such as IEEE 1394, RS-232, and RS-485 serial communication ports, as well as parallel printer ports and eSATA ports if the system supports them.

Securing Network and Wireless Connections

It is also possible and common for intruders to penetrate the PC's outer perimeter and access its internal buses, memory, and storage devices through network and wireless connections. These access routes and how to secure them are discussed in detail in Chapter 12.

Universal Serial Bus Ports

The most popular hardware port found in modern personal computers is the Universal Serial Bus (USB) port, depicted in Figure 7.8. This high-speed serial interface has been developed to provide a fast, flexible method of attaching up to 127 peripheral devices to the computer.

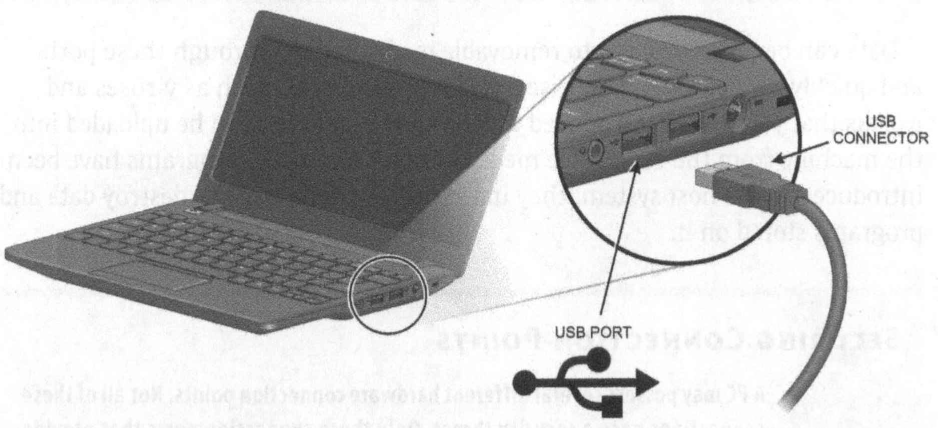

FIGURE 7.8 A USB Port

USB peripherals can be daisy-chained or networked together using connection hubs that enable the bus to branch out through additional port connections. A possible USB desktop connection scheme is presented in Figure 7.9.

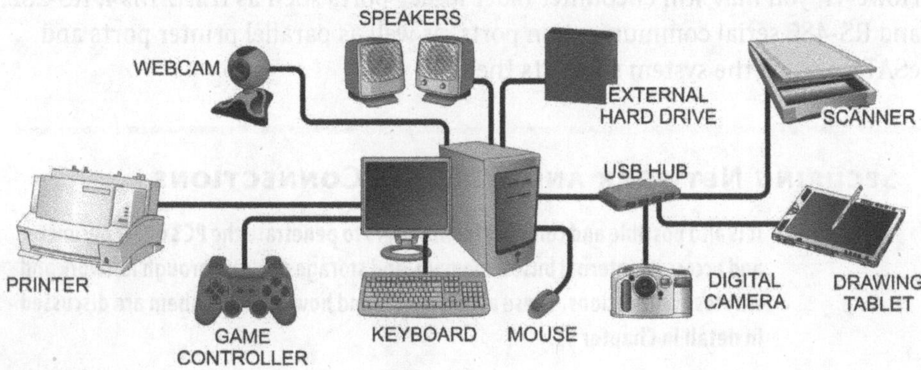

FIGURE 7.9 USB Desktop Connections

USB devices can be added to or removed from the system while it is powered up and fully operational. This is referred to as *hot-swapping* or hot-plugging the device. The Plug and Play capabilities of the system will detect the presence (or absence) of the device and configure it for operation.

The USB specification defines two types of plugs: series-A and series-B. Series-A connectors are used for devices where the USB cable connection is oftentimes permanently attached to devices at one end. Examples of these devices are keyboards, mice, and hubs.

Conversely, the series-B plugs and jacks are designed for devices that require detachable cabling (printers, scanners, and modems, for example). Both are four-contact plugs and sockets embedded in plastic connectors, as shown in Figure 7.10.

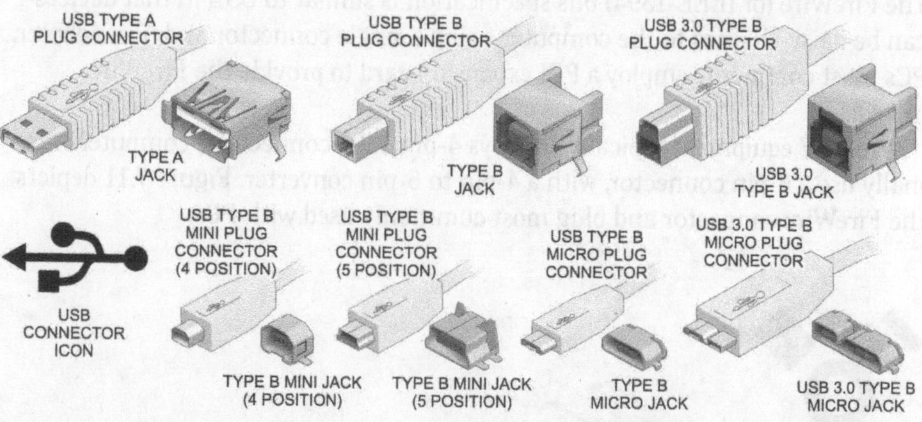

FIGURE 7.10 USB Connectors

Smaller 5-pin USB plugs and jacks (referred to as Mini-A and Mini-B) have been developed for the USB 2.0 and 3.0 specifications, and an even smaller Micro-USB connector version has been developed for the 3.0 version. USB 3.0 plugs are commonly blue in color. These connectors are intended for use with smaller devices such as digital cameras and cell phones. These structures are designed to provide rugged connections that are not prone to damage from repeated or incorrect usage.

The connectors for both series are keyed so that they cannot be plugged in backward. The connectors are designed so that the A- and B-series connections cannot be interchanged.

USB devices can be quite small and are easy to conceal and transport. Therefore, they provide an excellent vehicle for injecting malicious software into local host computers and intelligent control devices that might be very well protected from network access. For this reason, it is very important to control access to USB ports on the computer, as well as to control the reasons for which individual users can use the ports.

In the case of USB ports built into the computer's motherboard, the operation of the port connections is controlled by settings in the motherboard's CMOS Setup utility. For the security reasons cited previously, it may be necessary to access the CMOS Setup utility to disable its USB function.

IEEE-1394 FireWire Bus Ports

The FireWire (or IEEE-1394) bus specification is similar to USB in that devices can be daisy-chained to the computer using a single connector and host adapter. PCs most commonly employ a PCI expansion card to provide the FireWire interface.

While AV equipment typically employs 4-pin 1394 connectors, computers normally use a 6-pin connector, with a 4-pin to 6-pin converter. Figure 7.11 depicts the FireWire connector and plug most commonly used with PCs.

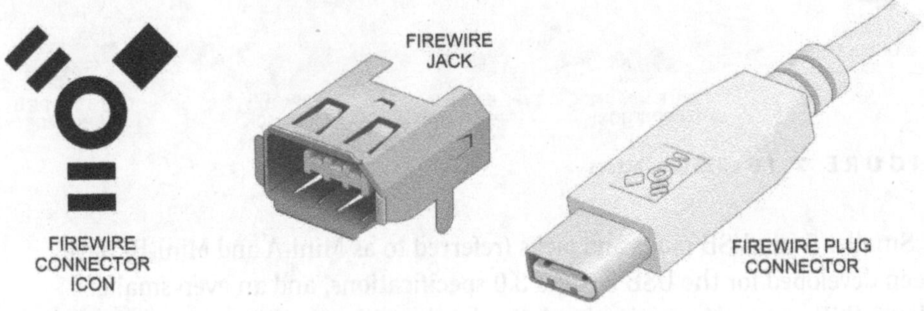

FIGURE 7.11 FireWire Plug and Connector

eSATA Ports

External SATA (Serial AT Attachment), or eSATA ports, are physical interfaces that link eSATA-compatible device with the system's internal SATA bus. This bus is the standard bus for connecting disk drive units to PC systems.

Figure 7.12 illustrates the implementation of a typical eSATA interface port. A shielded eSATA cable connects an external drive unit to the eSATA hardware port mounted on an expansion slot cover. Internally, a standard SATA cable connects the port to a SATA connector on the motherboard.

FIGURE 7.12 eSATA Interface Connections

Because these ports provide direct access to the buses that connect the disk drives to the system, they pose a security concern.

Legacy Ports

There are some older legacy hardware ports you might not encounter too often. Table 7.1 summarizes the physical port types used with PCs. They are most often located on the back of the PC, but some models may feature some of these ports on the front panel for convenience. The physical appearance of these ports is described in Figure 7.13.

TABLE 7.1 Typical and Legacy I/O Ports

Port	Connector
Keyboard	PS/2 6-pin mini-DIN
Mouse	PS/2 6-pin mini-DIN
COM1	DB-9M
COM2	DB-9M
LPT	DB-25F
VGA	DE-15F (3 row)
Game	DE-15F (2 row)

(Continues)

TABLE 7.1 *(Continued)*

Port	Connector
Modem	RJ-11
LAN	BNC/RJ-45
Sound	RCA 1/8" minijacks or 3/32" sub minijacks
SCSI	Centronics 50-pin
USB	4-pin USB Socket

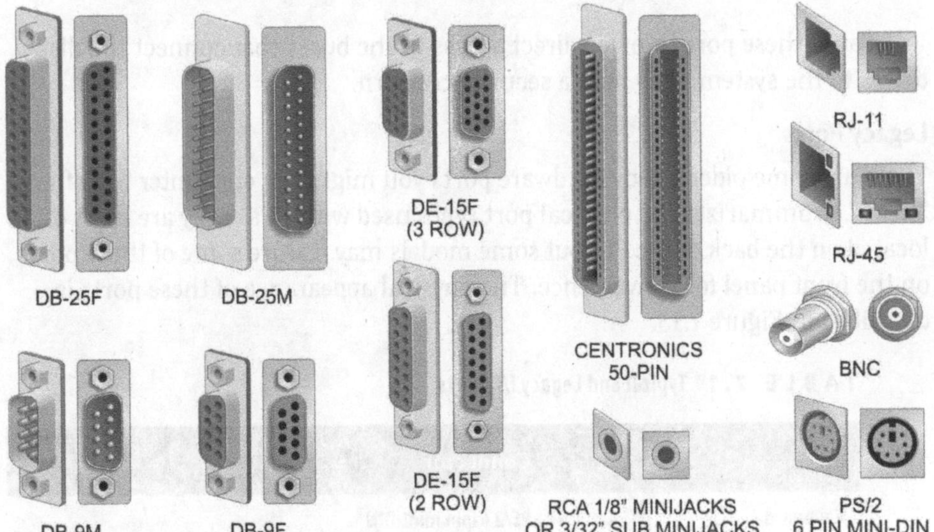

FIGURE 7.13 Typical IO Port Connectors

If you encounter these ports, the ones that pose a security risk include the RS-232/422/485 serial COM ports, Small Computer System Interface (SCSI), and the LPT parallel printer ports. These ports are all capable of handling two-way communications with the system's internal devices.

BIOS Port-Enabling Functions

It is common for a system's BIOS to offer device control options that provide control over the computer's external hardware connection ports. By disabling these ports, users and administrators can help to ensure that unauthorized users cannot use the ports to gain unauthorized access to the system, transfer information out of the system, or download malware programs into the system.

In addition to controlling access through the USB and IEEE-1394 ports, the BIOS may also offer control over serial ports, parallel ports, flash media readers, smart card slots, card bus slots, and eSATA ports, if the system possesses them, as shown in Figure 7.14.

```
BIOS Setup Utility
Main   Advanced   Security   Boot   Exit

I/O Port Access                          Item Specific Help

Parallel Port           [Enter]          Select whether to
-Current Setting        [Enabled]        enable or disable
                                         individual I/O
USB Port                [Enter]          devices.
-Current Setting        [Enabled]
                                         [Enabled]
CarBus Slot             [Enter]          Enable use of Device
-Current Setting        [Enabled]
                                         [Disable]
PCI Express Slot        [Enter]          Disables use of device
-Current Setting        [Enabled]        and keeps it disabled
                                         in the OS environment.
Memory Card Slot        [Enter]
-Current Setting        [Enabled]

CD-ROM Drive            [Enter]
-Current Setting        [Enabled]

F1   Help  ↑↓ Select Item  -/+         Change Values         F9   Setup Defaults
Esc  Exit  ↔  Select Menu  Press Enter Select ▸ Sub-Menu     F10  Save and Exit
```

FIGURE 7.14 Port-Enabling Options

Removable Media Access

Removable computer media presents multiple security risks. These risks include potential loss of data through theft due to the portable nature of the media, as well as the potential to introduce destructive malware into the host system.

Figure 7.15 shows different types of removable media associated with PC systems. These typically include:

- Magnetic storage media such as external hard drives and backup tapes
- Optical storage media such as CD and DVD drives and discs
- Electronic storage devices such as USB flash or thumb drives, MMC memory sticks, and SD cards

All three of these media device types provide access to the computer's internal system through its drives and hardware connection ports.

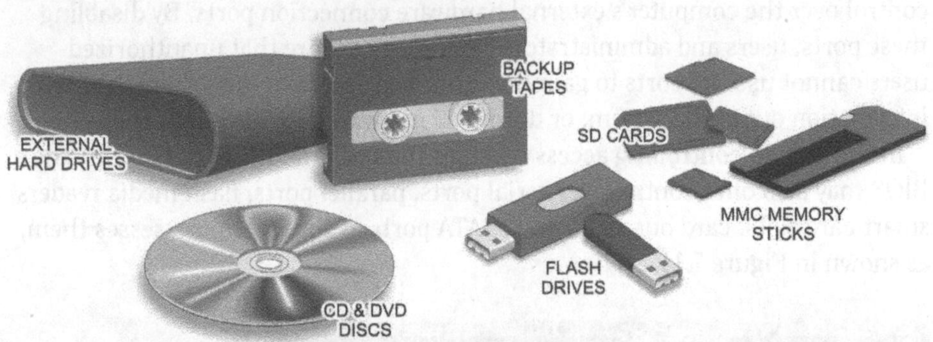

FIGURE 7.15 Removable Media

BIOS Boot Device/Sequence Controls

Most BIOS provide boot device enabling, disabling, and sequencing functions that should be used to control the circumstances of how the computer can be booted up for operation. Typically, the BIOS offers users and administrators the option to enable or disable the following types of devices:

- Optical disc drive(s)
- Hard disk drive(s)
- USB devices
- SD cards
- eSATA devices

Unless it is necessary to routinely boot the system from other devices, all boot options except the primary hard disk drive option should be disabled to provide the best security option.

Microsoft Autorun Feature

Similarly, some versions of Microsoft's operating systems include a featured called Autorun that automatically runs executable programs found on removable media devices as soon as it detects the presence of the media in the drive or reader. This feature provides a very serious security threat as malware programs located on the media will run automatically and infect the host device.

This feature is blamed for up to 50 percent of all malware infections in older Windows systems. The threat can be removed simply by disabling the Autorun feature in Windows by downloading an app to turn off Autorun. The other alternative is to modify the Windows Registry to turn off Autorun.

Hands-On Exercises

In this lab, you will examine the settings available in BIOS. First, you will find and examine the USB port control. Then you will examine the Administrator and User-access BIOS settings. Finally, you will examine various options in the boot menu, including boot order and Secure Boot.

Objectives

- Enter the BIOS.
- Navigate the BIOS.
- Find the settings to improve system security.

Procedure

1. Turn off the PC workstation.

   Pay attention to the workstation monitor when you turn it on in the next step. When you see the motherboard or computer manufacturer, there should be an option at the bottom of the screen. It will instruct you on how to enter the BIOS. Frequently used buttons include F2, F10, and Delete. The actual button you need to use will depend on the motherboard manufacturer; therefore, it is important to pay attention to the instructions on the screen.

Record the button you need to use on the following line:

____

2. Turn on the PC workstation. Attempt to enter the BIOS by pressing the correct button. If you are unsuccessful, turn off the workstation and try again.

NOTE **You may be prompted to repeat the required keystroke multiple times.**

BIOS menu interfaces differ greatly among system manufacturers and motherboard vendors. Figure 7.16 is merely an example.

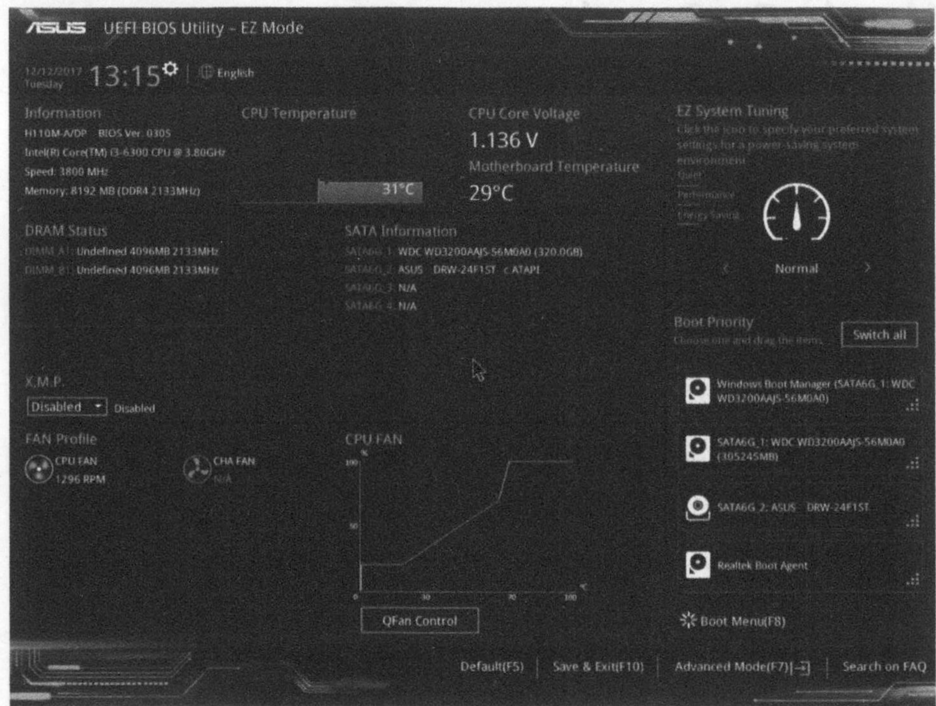

FIGURE 7.16 Sample BIOS Initial Settings Screen

The lab may end right now if your BIOS settings have already been password-protected by a system administrator. If this happens, the lab is over and you have one of three options to proceed:

a. Skip to the end of the chapter and answer the questions as best you can.

b. Try to get the administrator password to unlock and clear this setting.

c. If capable, you may have a jumper to reset the CMOS to factory defaults and clear the password. (Option C should be executed only by a competent technician.)

3. If your lab didn't end, use the arrow keys to navigate the menus. Press Enter to select a highlighted option. You can also use the Tab key if you are unable to highlight a desired option. Navigate to Advanced Mode or your equivalent. See Figure 7.17 and Figure 7.18.

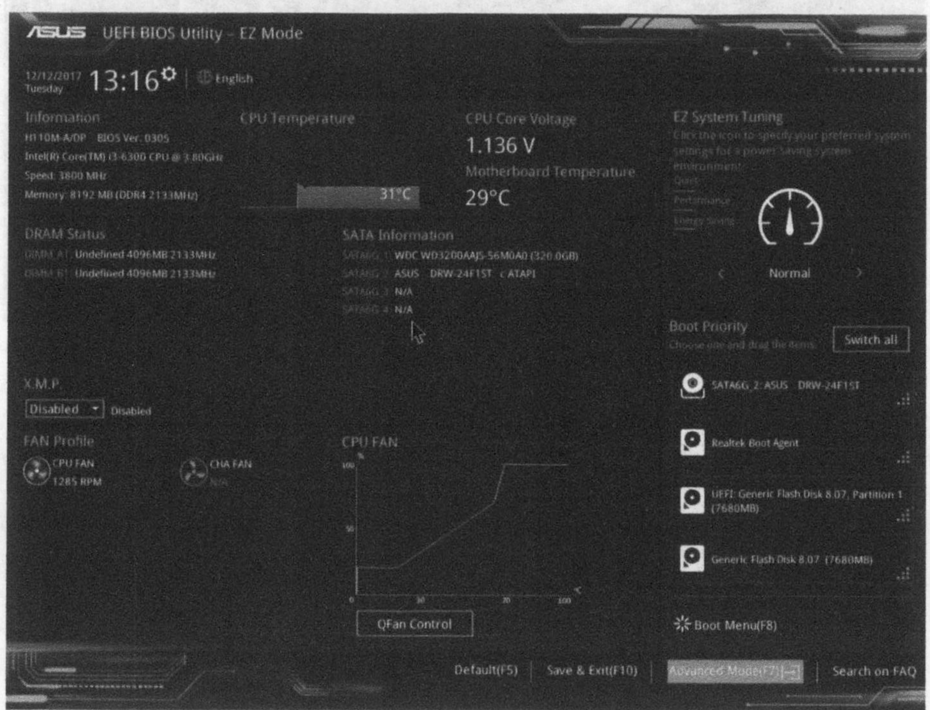

FIGURE 7.17 Advanced Mode Highlighted

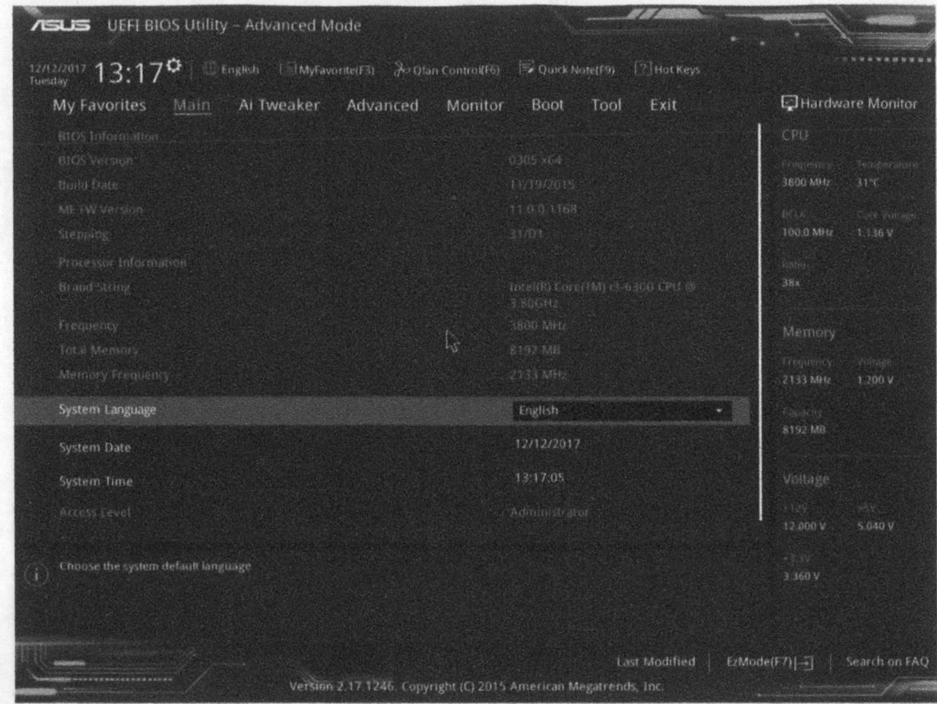

FIGURE 7.18 Advanced Mode Initial Menu

4. Figure 7.19 shows USB Configuration highlighted. Look for a menu or setting option like this.

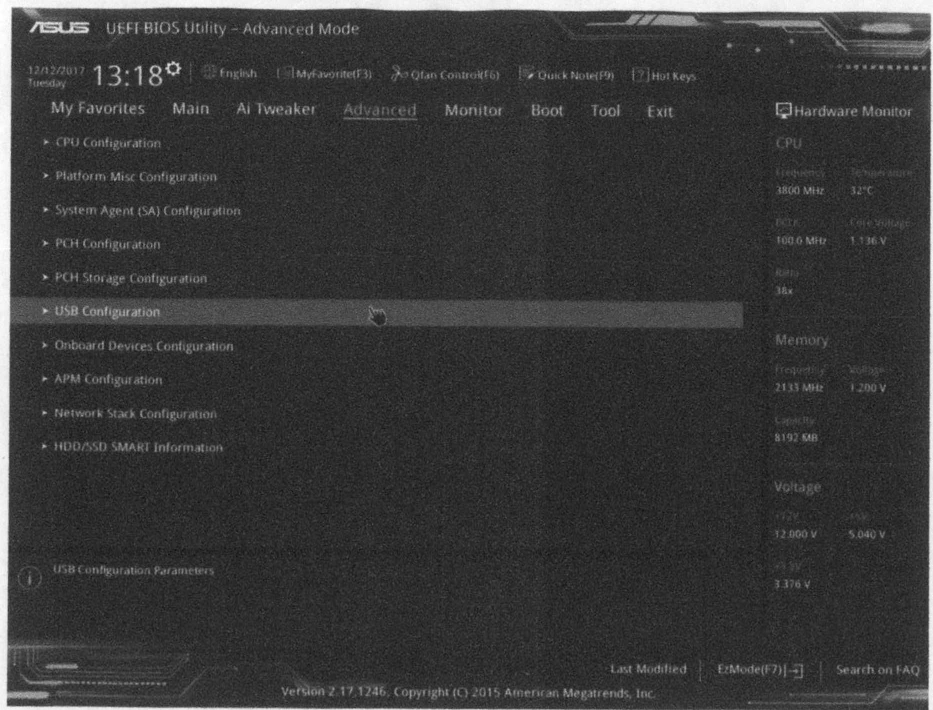

FIGURE 7.19 USB Configuration

5. From here, there should be some options. Look for an option that most closely matches USB Single Port Control (see Figure 7.20). This option could have a different name for your BIOS settings. Figure 7.21 shows where to enable or disable the USB ports.

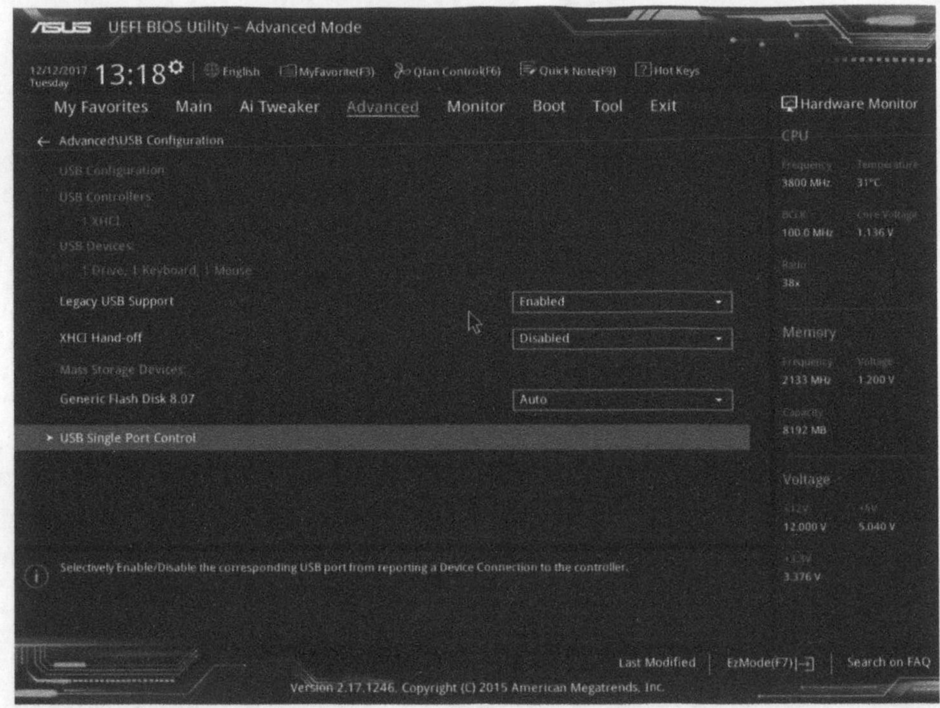

FIGURE 7.20 USB Single Port Control

6. Find a setting that lets you set up Administrator or User passwords for the BIOS. Do not change these settings. Leave the passwords empty. In this case (see Figure 7.22), the setting is simply labeled Security under the Main settings. Figure 7.23 shows the BIOS Administrator Password and the User Password settings.

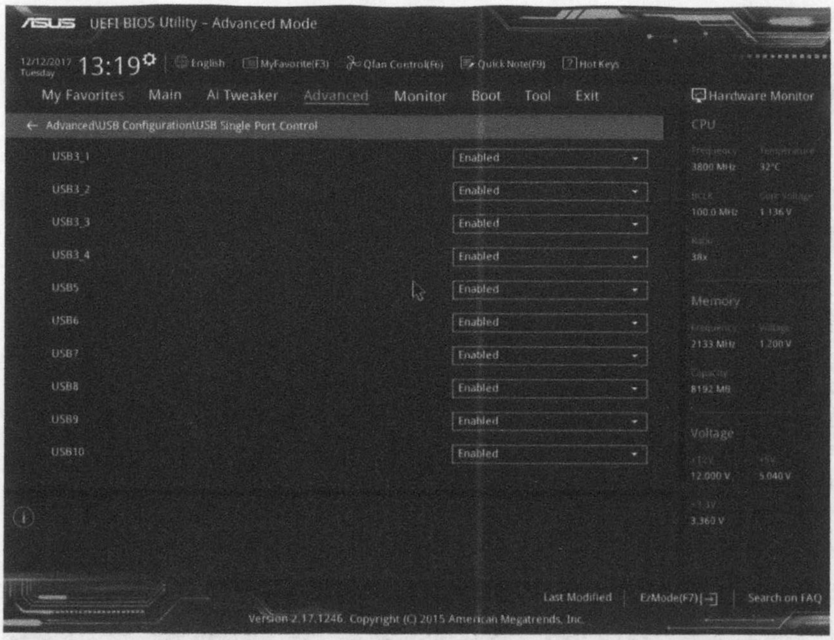

FIGURE 7.21 Enable or Disable USB Ports

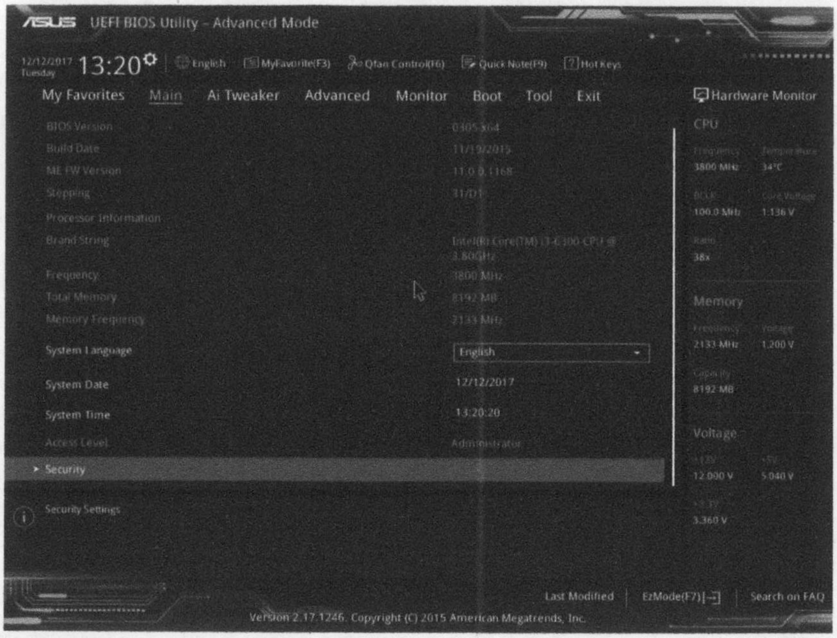

FIGURE 7.22 Security Settings

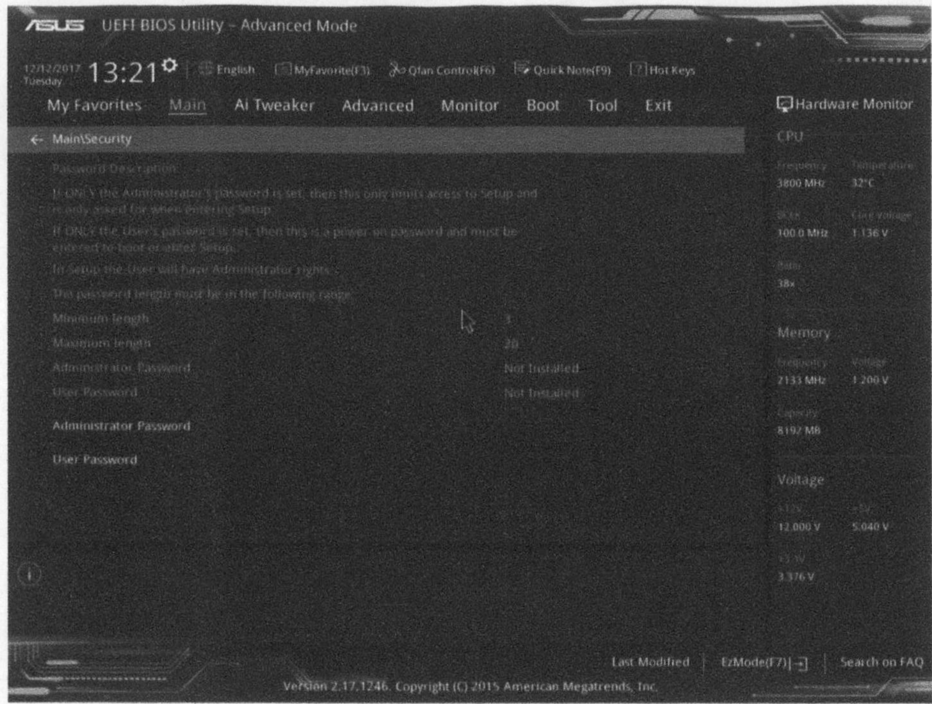

FIGURE 7.23 BIOS Administrator and User Password Settings

7. Navigate to the boot menu (see Figure 7.24). The boot menu lets you configure various settings related to system boot up.
8. Find the setting that controls the boot order (see Figure 7.25). For these BIOS settings, the boot order settings were about halfway down the boot menu. Each number corresponds to the order in which the motherboard will attempt to boot.

ASUS UEFI BIOS Utility – Advanced Mode
13:23
My Favorites Main Ai Tweaker Advanced Monitor Boot Tool Exit
Hardware Monitor
Fast Boot Enabled
Next Boot after AC Power Loss Normal Boot
Boot Logo Display Auto
POST Delay Time 3 sec
Boot up NumLock State Enabled
Wait For 'F1' If Error Enabled
Option ROM Messages Force BIOS
Interrupt 19 Capture Disabled
Setup Mode EZ Mode
CSM (Compatibility Support Module)
Enables or disables boot with initialization of a minimal set of devices required to launch active boot option. Has no effect for BBS boot options.
Last Modified EzMode(F7) Search on FAQ
Version 2.17.1246. Copyright (C) 2015 American Megatrends, Inc.

FIGURE 7.24 Boot Menu

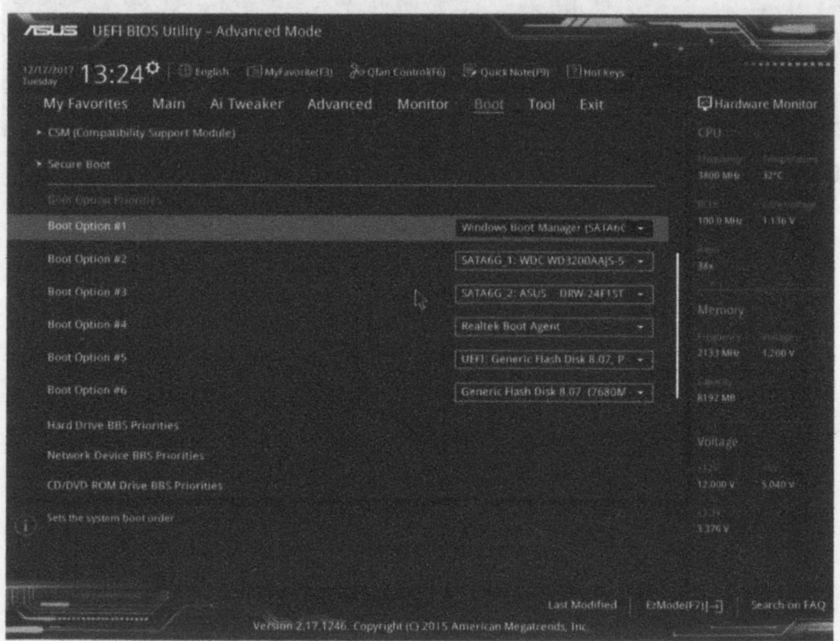

FIGURE 7.25 Boot Option #1 Attempted to Boot First

9. Find the Secure Boot option (see Figure 7.26). *Secure boot* is a relatively universal term, so you can look for these words, and you will most likely find the same option.

10. Choose the option that lets you interact with your keys.

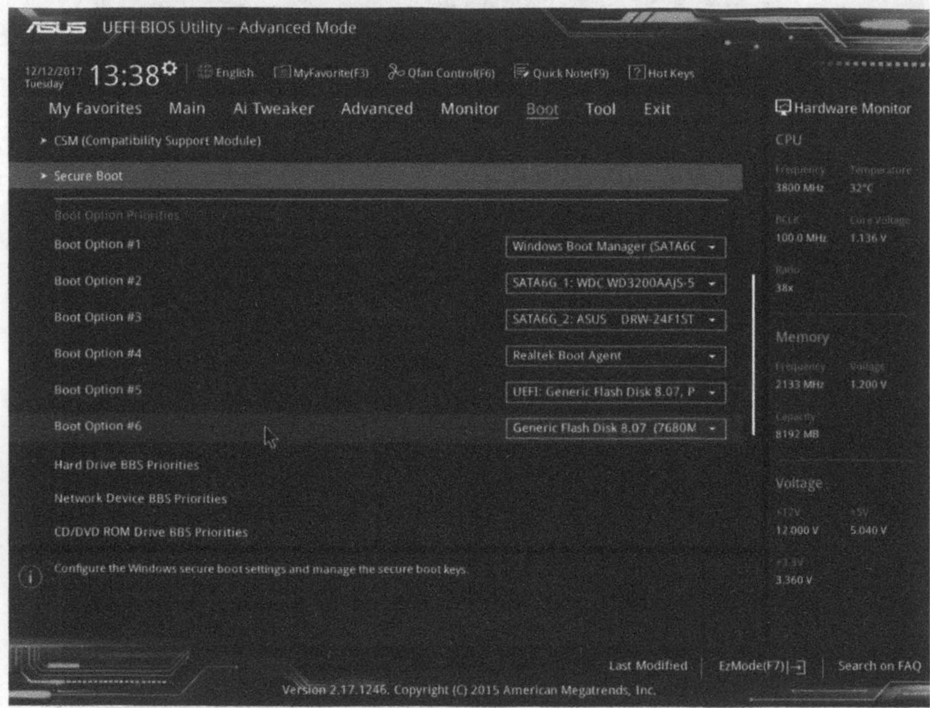

FIGURE 7.26 Secure Boot

11. If possible, read any available documentation about secure boot keys. See Figure 7.27 and Figure 7.28.

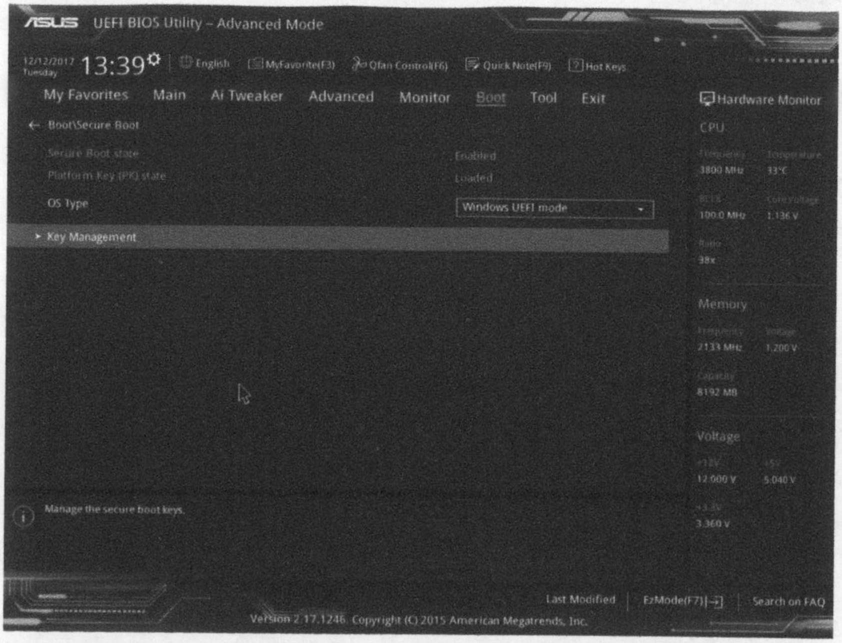

FIGURE 7.27 Key Management

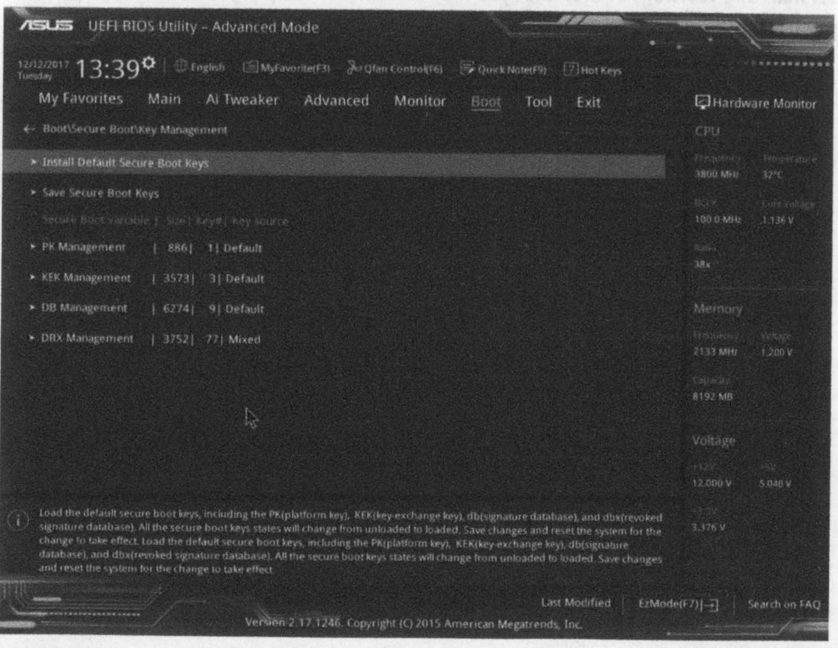

FIGURE 7.28 Key Management Settings

Review Questions

If your lab ended early, answer these questions.

1. Have you tried to visit the BIOS before this lab?
2. What was your reason for visiting the BIOS?
3. Why would you set an administrative password on your BIOS?

If you completed the lab, answer these questions.

1. Which options are available for accessing the various areas of your BIOS under your BIOS advanced settings or equivalent?
2. Where did you find the USB port settings?
3. Where did you find the BIOS Administrator and User Password settings?
4. What is the order of your boot devices?
5. What did you read about Keys in the BIOS?

NOTE **All of the answers will be specific to your particular BIOS. There are many versions and revisions of BIOS that you may be using, so simply go back through your particular BIOS and list your answers.**

## CHAPTER 8

Protecting the Inner Perimeter

In general, after you get past the outer perimeter defenses, you can think of the inner perimeter as part of the three-level structure illustrated in Figure 8.1. Consider this perimeter as consisting of the operating system and its application programs that form the gateway to the data stored in the interior zone (folders and files).

- **Describe Local Login and User Configuration Options for Host Devices.**
- **Compare and Contrast the Security Features of Common Operating Systems.**
- **Identify Common Logging and Auditing Options for Windows and Linux Based Systems**
- **Explain Options for Encrypting Data at Rest in Different OS Environments**

The Inner Perimeter

The valuable information we're trying to protect is generally the digital data stored in the computer hardware in the form of different types of files. These files are created and interpreted by application programs. Without the application to interpret the data, it is very difficult to determine what the data actually means. See Figure 8.1.

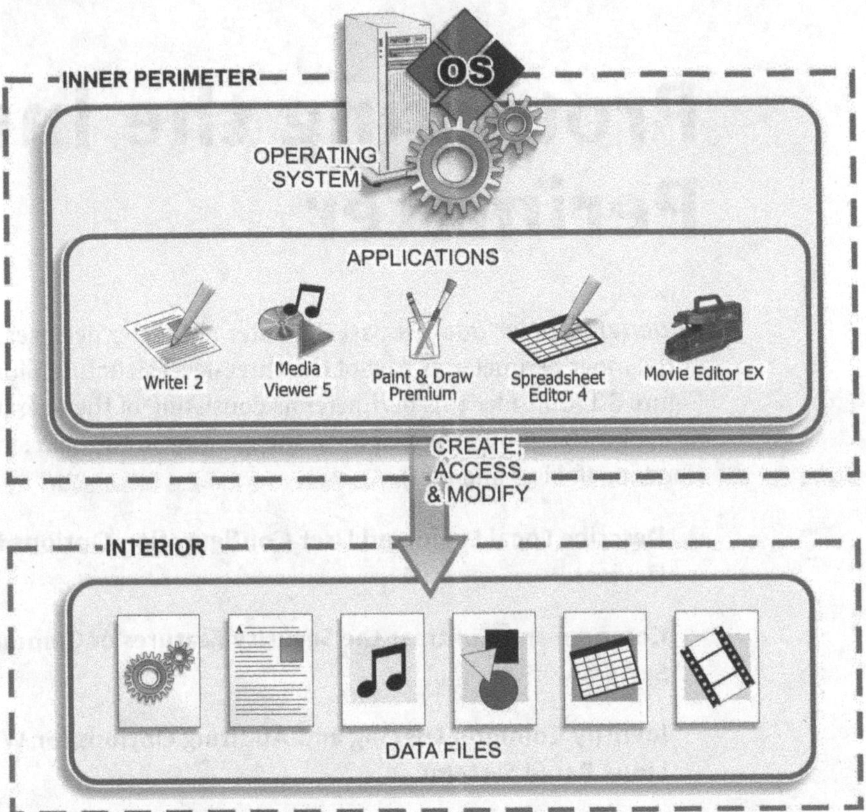

FIGURE 8.1 The Inner Perimeter

The operation of the application program and access to the files are controlled by the operating system (OS). The operating system coordinates the operation of the hardware system and devices with the software applications. Applications are designed to run on specific operating systems, so they are dependent on those operating systems. They will not run on another operating system without some sort of translator being involved.

The operating system is also responsible for keeping track of where data is stored in the system and how it can be located and accessed. Without the operating system's file management system (FMS), there is no way to know how to find the data to steal, damage, or destroy it. Each major OS supplier uses a different FMS.

Therefore, to access data on a computer, you must gain access to the running system, which is controlled by its operating system. Then you need to be able to locate the file, which requires the ability to navigate the OS file system. Finally, you will need to open the file, which requires the application software or software designed to examine data at the digital-code level.

There is not much actual value in the operating system or common application programs for thieves to steal. These types of software are commonly available, relatively inexpensive, and hard to transfer and use between systems. These programs are basically just tools for creating and manipulating information. However, they are interesting to would-be hackers because they can be accessed and repurposed for malicious and illegal operations.

On the other hand, the data files stored on the computer can be very interesting to thieves. As you are no doubt aware, quite a bit of digital information exists about most people and it is all stored on computers somewhere. If someone can locate and gain access to those data files, they can find a way to extract the information from them.

Once they have access to the file (or a copy of it), they can either open it on their system using the same application originally used to create the file, or they can extract the information from the digital code. The latter tends to be somewhat more involved and difficult to accomplish and typically requires someone with hacker skills and tools to operate at that level.

However, not every malicious operator wants to steal information. Some people, organizations, and governments just want to damage or destroy data for one reason or another. This type of activity could arise from many different motives, as described in the Introduction to this book

So how do you keep unwanted persons from gaining access to these programs? Let's first look at typical operating systems from different suppliers and see what security options they offer. As you will see in the following sections, operating systems tend to have many security tools and options built into them.

Operating Systems

Operating systems are programs designed to control and coordinate the operation of the computer system. As a group, they are easily some of the most complex programs ever devised.

In all microprocessor-based environments, the operating system accepts commands from a program or an input source (such as a computer user) and carries them out to perform some desired operation. Likewise, the operating system acts as an intermediary between nearly as complex software applications and the computer hardware they run on.

Some Clarity on Operating Systems

Unless the display has input capability, it is not considered to be an access device that can be exploited. The same holds true for printers or other output-only devices.

The most widely used operating systems in the world have nothing to do with personal computers. These operating systems are found in automobiles and consumer electronics products. They receive input from sensing devices such as airflow sensors (instead of keyboards and mice), process a control program according to a set of instructions and input data, and provide output to electro/mechanical devices such as fuel injector pumps (not video displays and printers). They also don't have much to do with disk drives.

A disk operating system (DOS) is a collection of programs used to control overall computer operation in a disk-based system. These programs work in the background to allow the user of the computer to input characters from the keyboard, to define a file structure for storing records, or to output data to a monitor or printer. The disk operating system is responsible for finding and organizing your data and applications on the disk.

As illustrated in Figure 8.2, the disk operating system can be organized according to four distinct sections:

- *Boot files* take over control of the system hardware from the ROM BIOS during start-up. They bring the OS kernel files into RAM memory so they can be used to control the operation of the system.
- *Kernel files* are the fundamental logic files of the operating system responsible for interpreting commands obtained from software programs for the central processing unit. These files are created to work with specific hardware architectures (microprocessors and chipsets).
- *File management files* enable the system to manage information within itself. These files are responsible for storing, tracking, and retrieving data into RAM memory where the microprocessor can access it.
- *Utility files* are programs that permit the user to manage system resources, troubleshoot the system, and configure the system.

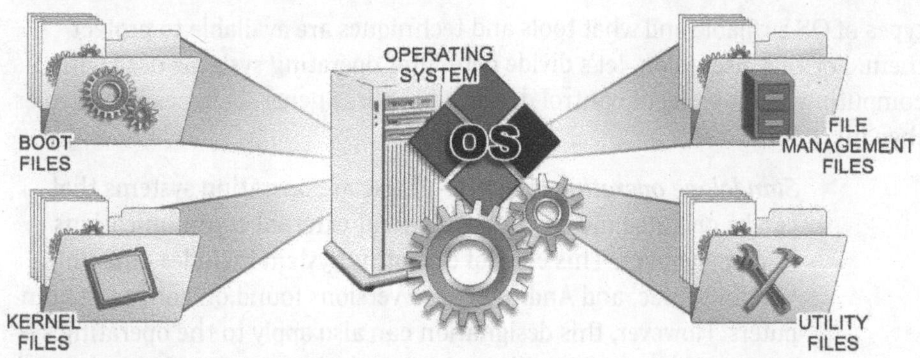

FIGURE 8.2 Basic OS File Structure

The operating system acts as a bridge between application programs and the computer hardware, as described in Figure 8.3.

These application programs enable the user to create files of data pertaining to certain applications such as word processing, multimedia delivery, remote data communications, business processing, and user programming languages.

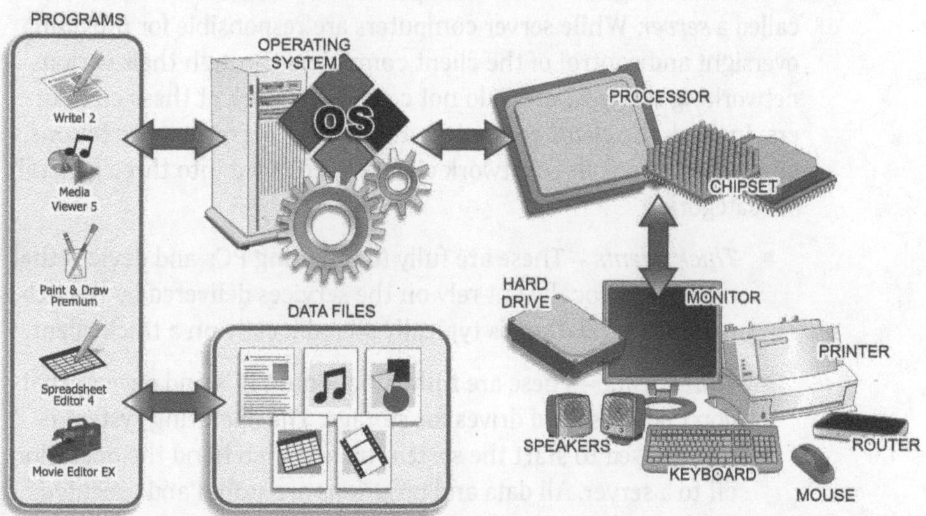

FIGURE 8.3 The Position of the OS in the Computer System

Because the operating system is a major part of the electronic gateway to the computer's applications and data, you must be aware of the different general types of OS available and what tools and techniques are available to protect them. For this discussion, let's divide computer operating systems used with computing and intelligent control devices into three general classes by the roles they fill:

- *Standalone operating systems* – These are operating systems that can be operated independently without external communications or management. This class of operating system includes different Windows, Mac, and Android-based versions found on consumer computers. However, this designation can also apply to the operating systems used in many intelligent control devices employed in industrial and manufacturing applications.

While these OS versions may be operated in a standalone manner, most modern versions possess some networking abilities that allow them to communicate with other intelligent devices or the Internet.

- *Client operating systems* – Client operating systems are designed to work in a network environment. In particular, they are designed to take advantage of the services provided by a master computer called a *server.* While server computers are responsible for providing oversight and control of the client computers through their various networking services, users do not commonly work at these computers. Instead, the client computers and devices serve as workstations, or autonomous nodes. Network clients are divided into three general subcategories:
    - *Thick clients* – These are fully functioning PCs and devices that could work locally but rely on the services delivered by the network server(s). Data is typically stored locally on a thick client.
    - *Thin clients* – These are fully functioning PCs and devices that don't possess hard drives for storage. The operating system is simply used to start the system up and then hand the operation off to a server. All data and programs are stored and executed on the server.
    - *Terminal clients* – These are server-dependent PCs and devices where the operating system does not exist on the client. Instead, the client actually boots up to a remote server and all programs and data are located and executed on the server.

- *Server operating systems* – These operating systems are designed to run on specialized server computers that function as the center of a client/server network environment. Server operating system versions are typically responsible for:
  - Data and resource security for the network and its devices
  - Centralized network administration
  - Cost benefits to the business or enterprise
  - Server operating systems provide security for the network and its clients by controlling access to:
    - Resources (disk drives, printers, directories, and files)
    - Services (email, Internet connectivity, messenger services, databases, and so on)
    - Administrative tools (user accounts, local and network utilities, computer management tools)

Network Operating Systems

Network Operating Systems (NOS) are designed to extend the control of disk operating systems to provide for communications and data exchanges between computers connected by a communication media. Notable network operating systems include Windows Server OS versions, Linux Server distributions, and Unix.

Server operating systems are some of the primary tools responsible for security in a network environment. These operating systems and their security tools are explored in depth in Chapter 14. The remaining sections of this chapter deal with security tools that are available and can be implemented at the local standalone or client computer level.

Notable standalone, or client disk operating systems, include: Microsoft Windows versions, Apple Computer's MAC OS X, a variety of Linux operating system distributions, and the Android operating system from Google.

Operating systems and the programs and data they control are attacked from two common areas:

- By manipulating the operation of the OS kernel
- By attacking its file management system

The following sections address these two common areas of attack.

OS Kernel Security

Figure 8.4 illustrates the position of the OS kernel between the system's hardware and applications. Due to this positioning, it should be apparent that if you can get to the programming code in the OS kernel and disable it, you have disabled the operation of the entire computer system. However, if you can access the kernel and manipulate the code, you have taken over operation of the computer.

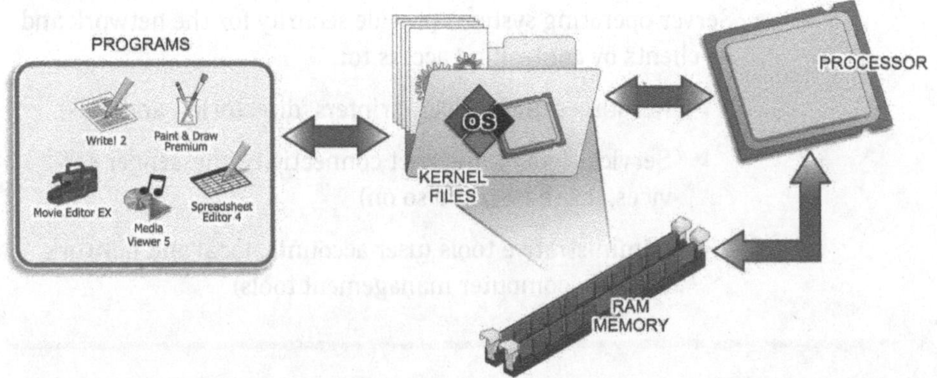

FIGURE 8.4 The Position of the Kernel

Attackers who possess enough knowledge of a given operating system's memory-handling strategy can exploit the OS kernel in a number of different ways:

- They can change the value of a variable in the kernel programming to change its behavior.
- They can change the return address of some standard OS function so that when the OS tries to return to its basic pipeline of instructions, it is rerouted into code supplied by the attacker.
- They can change a pointer in the program that directs the execution of the instruction code to an exception handler supplied by the attacker.
- They can insert malicious code into an application's code that has been loaded into RAM memory for execution. The inserted code is designed to overwrite kernel components that interact with the application.

All of these attacks rely on gaining access to specific areas of the computer's memory where the OS kernel operates.

Most operating systems utilize a feature built into microprocessing hardware to protect certain areas of memory that contain specific blocks of instruction code. This feature is referred to as the *No eXecution (NX) bit,* or the eXecute Disable (XD) bit. NX bit technology is used to flag certain areas of memory as storage-only.

Any section of memory marked with the NX attribute means it's only for storing data. Therefore, processor instructions cannot be stored there. This is a popular technique for preventing malicious software from taking over computers by inserting their code into another program's data storage area and then running that code from within this section, as they would with a buffer overflow attack.

Some operating systems ship with built-in executable-space-protection features, referred to as Data Execution Prevention (DEP) modes, to defeat these types of attacks. The operating system accomplishes this by creating unique, isolated memory regions for each application running on the machine. Each isolated memory region becomes a virtual environment managed by the microprocessor's virtual memory management module.

In Unix, Unix-like, and Linux operating systems, this function is provided as an advanced implementation of its standard `chroot` operations (its system for creating and managing multiple virtualized copies of the operating system).

File System Security

The *file management system* is extremely important in protecting the existence and integrity of data stored on a hard drive or removable storage device. If the file system is destroyed or becomes corrupted, the data becomes inaccessible and is lost. In addition, if unauthorized users are given access to the file system and its stored data, they have been given the opportunity to damage, destroy, or steal it.

One of the main tools for protecting the file system and its data is the use of access control lists (ACLs) to provide Resources Access Control. The file management system uses ACLs to grant or deny specific users access to its different files, as well as to control what types of activities the individual can perform once access has been granted. For example, you may be given the capability to run a file, read it, write it, or perform other actions on it under the control of the file management system.

The operating system's ACLs are also used to control access to other objects such as TCP/UDP ports as well as I/O devices. Their ACL tables maintain records that identify which access rights each user has to a particular system object.

Depending on the operating system, resource access control can be implemented in the form of Mandatory Access Control (MAC) or Role-Based Access

Control (RBAC). Unix and Linux systems typically offer MAC approaches, while Microsoft's Windows platforms provide RBAC control.

POSIX (Portable Operating System Interface)

POSIX (Portable Operating System Interface) is a set of interoperability standards developed to standardize variations of Unix and Unix-like operating systems. POSIX-compliant systems (Unix, Linux, and Apple OS X systems) support some type of ACL for managing traditional Unix file-access permissions.

In MAC versions, the operating system takes action based on the administrator's policy configuration settings to determine who can do what and to what extent they can do it. Under RBAC, the system restricts or permits access to objects based on the user's role within the organization. The RBAC structure is typically the access control method employed in large enterprises.

In Microsoft Windows environments, these capabilities are assigned to folders and files in the form of permissions. *Permissions* can also be defined as privileges to perform an action. In Unix and Linux-based systems, users are assigned *access rights* to files.

Another tool for protecting data is to encrypt it so that becomes unusable without a key to decrypt it. The encryption/decryption process can be performed on data when it's stored and retrieved from a device (PR.DS-1, data at rest) or when it is being moved from one location to another (PR.DS-2, data in motion).

The Primary Cybersecurity Guidelines

The NIST Framework for Improving Critical Infrastructure Cybersecurity specifies protection strategies for protecting "Data at Rest" (PR.DS-1) and protecting "Data in Transit" (PR.DS-2).

Most of the major disk operating systems available offer some type of data encryption capabilities through their file management systems. Depending on the design of the operating system, encryption may be applied at the device level, the disk (or volume) level, or the file and folder level. Third-party encryption applications are available for use with many of these operating systems as well.

The data encryption services available with different operating systems are discussed in the following sections. Data encryption techniques are covered in detail later in this chapter.

The following section compares and summarizes the key structural and security features of the most widely used operating systems. This comparison involves the operating system's versions, kernel architecture, file management systems, and native data-encryption capabilities.

File System Attacks

Typical attacks mounted on OS files systems include:

- Using race condition attacks
- Using data streams to hide files
- Performing directory traversals

Using Race Condition Attacks

A *race condition* exists when an attacker exploits the timing of consecutive events in a multiuser/multitasking environment to insert malicious code into the system between the events.

For example, a time of check-time of use (TOCTOU) condition exists when an operating system creates a temporary file. During the time between when the OS checks to see if a file by that filename exists and when it actually writes the file, the attacker executes a program to save a malicious code package using the filename of the temp file.

The malicious code could contain higher access permissions so the attacker can read or manipulate the file, or it could contain a link to a script file that grants access to the password file where the administrative password is stored.

Using Alternative Data Streams to Hide Files

Advanced hackers use this NTFS OS compatibility feature to hide root kits or other hacker tools to establish an anonymous base to launch attacks on the system.

The ADS feature was originally built into NTFS to provide support for Apple's Hierarchical File System (HFS) file system, which sometimes "forks" data into different files. However, this technique has been adopted for storing file metadata and to provide temporary storage.

As mentioned earlier, hackers use the ADS feature to hide their tools from the system as it is virtually impossible to detect with native user interfaces.

After the hidden ADS files have been embedded in some standard OS file, they can be executed without being detected as an illegitimate operation. The only sign of an ADS operation is an illegitimate timestamp on the file where the hidden tools have been injected.

Performing Directory Traversals

These attacks exploit poorly secured software applications to access files that should not be accessible in order to "traverse" to a higher level folder or directory, as shown in Figure 8.5. Such attacks are also referred to as *backtracking, directory climbing attacks,* or *canonicalization attacks.*

Hackers use this form of HTTP exploitation to access a web server's directory tree. After the hacker has gained access, they can navigate the tree to view restricted files or execute commands on the server. Such attacks are launched using common web browsers against poorly configured web servers.

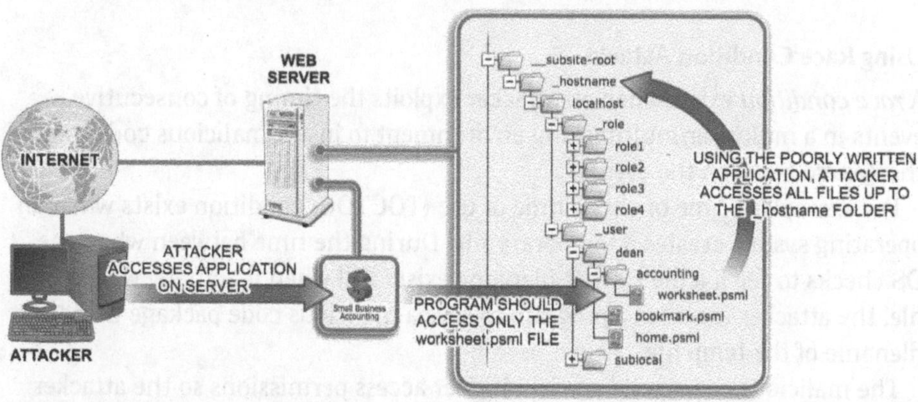

FIGURE 8.5 Directory Traversal

These attacks can be minimized through careful web server configuration, filtering web browser input, and using vulnerability scanner software.

The following section compares and summarizes the key structural and security features of the most widely used operating systems. This comparison involves the operating system's versions, kernel architecture, file management systems, and native data-encryption capabilities.

Microsoft Windows

The Windows line of operating systems from Microsoft offers the most widely used disk operating systems with personal computers. Windows is a graphical user interface (GUI)-based operating system that enables users to navigate through the system using a series of pop-up windows and menus.

- Windows Client versions – Windows XP, Windows Vista, Windows 7, Windows 8, and Windows 10
- Windows Server versions – Windows Business and Small Business Server (SBS) versions 2003, 2008, 2012, and 2016

All Windows operating systems are designed to work with x86 32-bit and x86 64-bit processor types from Intel, AMD, and VIA. Windows operating systems after Windows XP SP2 and Windows Server 2003 support XD-bit operations on some 32-bit x86 processors, as well as on 64-bit x86 processors that offer NX-bit support.

Windows operating systems support the following basic file system formats:

- FAT/FAT16/FAT32 – The File Allocation Table series of FMS are cluster-based versions of an older file management system that was developed to manage data storage on floppy disks. Because of its widespread use in Microsoft DOS and early Windows versions, it has evolved and remained in use until the present.

  The number in the FAT title represents the number of bits in the table entry that tracks the location of the data cluster on the disk. The original FAT standard employed a 12-bit table entry and could track the locations of 4096 (1 × 212) table entries. The FAT file system is still commonly found on USB storage devices, SD cards, and other flash memory devices, as well as many other portable and embedded devices. FAT file system versions offer relatively little in the way of security tools for the data stored in their structures.
- NTFS – The New Technology File System is Microsoft's proprietary and default file management system for its operating systems. NTFS brought with it enhanced security features including access control lists (ACLs) and the encrypting file system (EFS).
- ISO 9660 (CDFS) – The Compact Disc File System is the standard file management system for optical disc storage.
- UDF – Universal Disk Format is the successor of the CDFS file management system. In particular, it is widely used in DVD and advanced optical storage devices.

The Windows operating systems include file- and folder-level encryption through its encrypting file system (EFS) feature. Full disk-level encryption is provided on some high-end Windows OS versions through a native utility called BitLocker. These utilities are discussed in detail later in this chapter.

Microsoft Windows operating systems provide an integrated Windows Firewall feature that enables the local administrator (or owner) to establish and configure a local firewall to control the flow of information into and out of the local host computer from an external network connection through a process called *packet filtering*.

Local and Network-Based Firewalls

The operation of local firewalls is covered in Chapter 9. Network-based firewalls, which are designed to control the flow of data into and out of a network, will be discussed in Chapter 12.

Unix

The Unix line of operating systems provides modular, multitasking, multiuser OS environments originally developed to run on mainframe and minicomputers. Proprietary versions of the Unix OS include several BSD (Berkley Software Distribution) variations, along with Apple's OSX and iOS operating systems. Several notable Unix-like operating systems have been derived from the basic Unix operating system, including multiple Linux distributions.

Different Unix OS versions have been designed to work with a number of different microprocessors. Likewise, different Unix OS versions provide support for number of different file systems formats:

- UFS – The UNIX File System was the first structure designed for the original UNIX operating system and continues in use with UNIX and its derivatives. The structure of this file system standard presents a unified tree structure beginning at a main directory known as root (/).
- NFS – The Network File System was developed by Sun Microsystems to enable client computers to access files across a network. Because NFS was developed as an open protocol standard any company can (and have) incorporate it into their own suite of supported protocols. It is used primarily in UNIX OS versions, but is also supported in Microsoft Windows and Apple's MAC OSs.

Some Unix operating systems include built-in encrypted file system capabilities. The original encryption tool included as a standard part of the Unix operating system is *crypt*. However, this tool is considered to be a very low-powered encryption tool that is relatively easy to crack. For that reason, it is not widely used. The Data Encryption Standard (DES) is a stronger encryption tool used with many Unix distributions. Pretty Good Privacy (PGP) is another widely used Unix encryption tool. This tool does both private and public key encryption/decryption and offers a very strong method to secure data.

Unix distributions based on the Free BSD kernel offer encryption services through PEFS, GELI, and GBDE utilities. Private Encrypted File System (PEFS) is a file-based encryption system. GELI and GEOM Based Disk Encryption (GBDE) are disk-level encryption utilities. Another notable encryption tool for other Unix or Unix-like operating systems is EncFS.

FreeBSD and OpenBSD distributions also offer multiple built-in firewall utilities to control the flow of data into the local computer. These options include ipfirewall (ipfw), IPFilter, and Packet Filter (PF). As with the integrated Windows Firewall mentioned earlier, these applications enable the local computer to control the flow of incoming and outgoing data through a process called *packet filtering*. Local firewalls and packet filtering are covered in detail later in the chapter.

A Word About Encryption Tools

Many countries have created laws outlawing the use of strong encryption. Therefore, different operating systems may be available with and without different encryption tools based on where they are being sold.

Linux OS Distributions

Many personal computer users run versions of a freely distributed, open-source operating system called Linux. Linux is a very powerful, command-line operating system that can be used on a wide variety of hardware platforms including Windows PC and Apple Mac systems.

A community of programmers works with the Linux oversight committee to continually upgrade and enhance the basic Linux structure to keep it current and competitive. In addition, several companies have developed proprietary additions to the basic Linux structure to produce their own distributions (Linux-speak for versions) of the operating system:

- Major Linux client distributions – Ubuntu, Red Hat, SUSE, Slackware, Mandrake, Fedora, FreeBSD, Debian, and others
- Linux Server distributions – Red Hat Linux Server, Ubuntu Server, SUSE Server, and others

Different Linux OS distributions have been designed to work with x86 and x86 64-bit microprocessor types from Intel, AMD, and VIA, as well as Motorola/IBM-PowerPC processors and Sun Microsystem's SPARC processors. The Linux kernel supports the NX-bit on some x86 processors, as well as on x86-64, PowerPC microprocessors, and other 64-bit processors that offer NX-bit support.

Linux Distributions and Capabilities

The Linux name is actually used to describe a number of different distributions with differing capabilities.

Linux OS distributions commonly provide support for several different file system types:

- ext/ext2/ext3/ext4 – The ext series of Extended File Systems are the primary file management systems designed for the Linux kernel. Ext2/3 is widely used in SD cards and other flash-based storage devices.
- ReiserFS – The Linux kernel provides support for the Reiser file system which is the default system on some Linux distributions. It is a journaling file system (one that keeps track of changes in a circular log file, referred to as a journal, before committing them to the file system). ReiserFS includes UNIX permissions, ACLs, and attribute security features, but does not include any data encryption services.
- Linux OS – Linux OS distributions also commonly provide support for the ISO9660, FAT, and UDF file system formats described for Windows files systems.

The major Linux operating systems provide built-in file-system-level encryption services through a package called eCryptfs. This level of encryption enables the encryption service to be applied at the individual file or directory without significant disk management overhead.

Linux distributions offer built-in local firewall functions through a kernel utility called Netfilter. In addition to providing packet filtering for local firewall implementation, this utility offers additional protection through processes called network address translation (NAT) and port address translation (PAT) for directing packets through a network in addition to masking the private IP address from hosts outsider the network.

Apple OS Versions

Apple Inc. produces personal computers that are not intrinsically compatible with PCs. They have distinctly different hardware designs and do not directly run software packages developed for the Win/PC environment.

All newer Apple Mac computers run on a proprietary version of Unix called Apple OS X. While the structure of OS X is Unix-based, the user interaction portions of the system employ Apple's trademark GUI-based desktop. This gives the Mac a very powerful and stable engine with very user-friendly interfaces with which to work:

- Apple client versions: macOS, OS X, and Mac OS X
- Apple Server versions: macOS Server, Mac OS X Server, and OS X Server

MacOS was designed to work with x86 and x86 64-bit microprocessor types from Intel, Cyrix, VIA, and AMD, as well as PowerPC processors from IBM and Motorola. These microprocessors all support NX-bit functions to protect certain areas of memory from virus manipulation.

MacOS supports the ISO9660, FAT, NFS, UFS, and UDF file system formats described earlier. In addition, support for the following FMS standards is provided in different macOS versions:

- HFS/HFS+ – The Hierarchical File Systems are proprietary Apple file systems developed as the primary file system for their Mac line of computers using macOS. It is also used in Apple's line of iPod music devices. Support for the updated HFS+ version has been included in non-Apple operating systems including the Linux kernel and Windows (including support in Microsoft's Xbox360 gaming console).
- SMBFS/CIFS – The Server Message Block File System, also known as the Common Internet File System, was developed to provide shared

access to files and devices, along with network communications. This FMS is mostly used with computers running Windows prior to the advent of Active Directory. However, support for newer SMB releases has continued through all current Microsoft OS versions in addition to making its way into several non-Microsoft operating systems.

Apple macOS operating systems include disk-level-based data encryption through a service called FileVault; FileVault2 macOS users can also use the built-in disk utility to encrypt their disk and store subsets of their home directory.

iOS

iOS is a proprietary Apple mobile operating system designed to support Apple's line of iPhones and iPads. While iOS shares many structures with macOS, it is not compatible with macOS applications.

iOS is designed to work with reduced instruction set computing (RISC) processor types from the Acorn RISC Machines (ARM) Ltd company. These devices use significantly less energy and produce much less heat than their x86 complex instruction set computing (CISC) rivals. This makes RISC processors a natural for use in small, battery-powered devices such as phones, tablets, and pads. From the ARMv6 version forward, this architecture has supported an Execute Never (XN) page protection feature.

The iOS system includes integrated device-level file encryption to protect the data if the device running is lost or stolen. It also offers protection from unauthorized users using or modifying the data. In addition to its hardware encrypting feature, iOS offers a class-based tool called Data Protection. With this protection tool, file-based encryption keys are created each time data is written to the device's flash memory structure.

Android OS

The Android operating system was developed for use with tablet and smart phone devices that primarily use touchscreen gestures for operation and control. It is currently the most popular mobile operating system in use due to the number of smart phone and tablet devices it is used in, as shown by the graph in Figure 8.6.

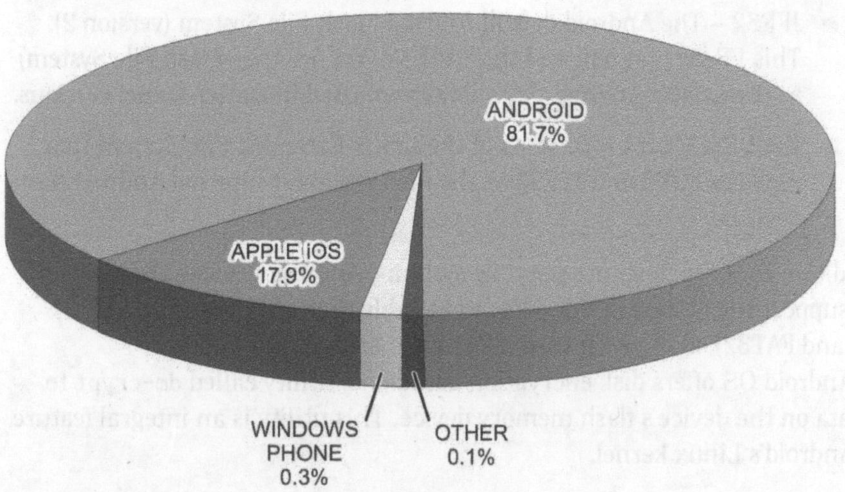

FIGURE 8.6 2014 Smartphone OS Graph

Android is based on the Linux OS kernel but typically includes a wrapper of proprietary user interfaces, utilities, and applications. Because of its open-source availability, Android has been embraced by a development community and made its way into a number of devices in consumer, military, business, and educational applications.

The Android OS is designed to run on 32- and 64-bit ARMv7/8 processors. This includes proprietary I.MX5/i.MX6 ARM processors from Freescale Semiconductors (a former division of Motorola). These microprocessors support the XN page-protection feature. There is also a version of the Android OS kernel designed to support x86 architectures. Of course, these processors support the XD-bit or NX-bit feature.

The kernel configuration of different Android devices supports different file systems that are specific to that device. However, there are some flash memory file systems that are common to Android systems:

- exFAT – Microsoft's extended File Allocation Table file system for flash memory devices.
- F2FS – Samsung's Flash-Friendly File System (version 2) is an open-source Linux file system for flash storage devices.

- JFFS2 – The Android default Journal Flash File System (version 2). This FS version replaced the YAFFS2 (Yet Another Flash File System) as the default Android flash file system used in earlier kernel versions.
- Ext2/Ext3/Ext4 – Versions of the Linux Extended File System that replaces F2FS and JFFS2 as the file system for internal Android flash devices.

In addition to these flash-memory file systems, Android devices also commonly support the Microsoft File Allocation Table (FAT) file systems (FAT12, FAT16, and FAT32), along with their VFAT extension.

The Android OS offers disk encryption based on a utility called `dm-crypt` to store data on the device's flash memory device. This utility is an integral feature of the Android's Linux kernel.

Operating System Security Choices

Because of its popularity, Microsoft Windows presents the biggest target for both mischievous and malicious malware and *grayware* (annoying unwanted software) writers. Therefore, Windows receives an unrivaled percentage of all the attacks associated with viruses and spyware.

This fact has led some Windows customers to adopt other operating system platforms such as Linux or macOS, which are much less of a malware target. Table 8.1 summarizes some common security features associated with various operating systems.

TABLE 8.1 Operating System Security Comparisons

Name	Resource Access Control	Subsystem Isolation Mechanisms	Integrated Firewall	Encrypted File Systems	No Execute (NX)
Linux	POSIX, ACLs, MAC	`chroot`, capability-based security, seccomp, SELinux, AppArmor	Netfilter, varied by distribution	Yes	Hardware/Emulation
macOS	POSIX, ACLs	`chroot`, BSD file flags set using chflags	PF	Yes	Hardware/Emulation

Name	Resource Access Control	Subsystem Isolation Mechanisms	Integrated Firewall	Encrypted File Systems	No Execute (NX)
Windows Server	ACLs, privileges, RBAC	Win32 WindowStation, desktop, job objects	Windows Firewall	Yes	Hardware/ Emulation
Windows	ACLs, privileges, RBAC	Win32 WindowStation, desktop, job objects	Windows Firewall	Yes	Hardware/ Emulation

Common Operating System Security Tools

After the system has booted up, steps can be taken to prevent unauthorized personnel from accessing the operating system and its applications. These steps include:

- Implementing local login requirements
  - Establishing user and group accounts
  - Setting up password policies
  - Establishing lockout policies
- Implementing additional authentication options
  - Using biometric authentication devices
  - Using physical authentication devices
- Using Local Administrative Tools
  - Enabling system auditing and event logging
  - Implementing data encryption tools
  - Overseeing application software security
- Providing remote access protection
  - Establishing firewall settings
  - Configuring browser security options

- Establishing and implementing malicious software protection
- Applying security updates and patches

Figure 8.7 shows the Local Security Policy/Security Settings options available in a Microsoft Windows control panel. The first set of options includes password and account lockout policy choices to locally control access to the system. You can also implement local admin policies for system auditing, users rights, and security policies.

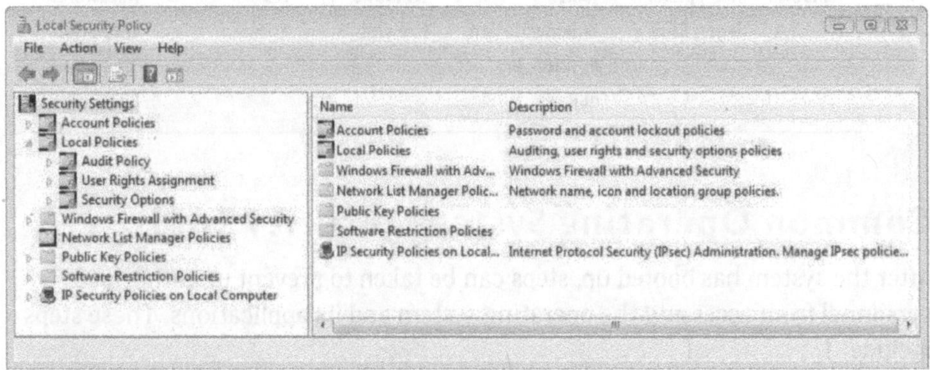

FIGURE 8.7 Local Security Policy/Security Settings

The Windows Firewall and Advanced Security tools enable the local administrator (or owner) to establish and configure a local firewall as described earlier.

The remaining tools shown in Figure 8.7 are security tools that enable local policies to be established to control the local computer's interactions with an external network. In the following sections, you will learn how to implement them for best local-host security practices.

A Word About Security Tools

It should be apparent from a quick look at the tools in Figure 8.7 that the policies are designed to control the interaction of the local computer with an external network. While the tools are local, they are also used in networked environments. There are cases where both local and network administrative policies cover the same security elements. In these cases, the network policy will override the local policy if they are configured in conflict with each other.

Implementing Local Login Requirements

The main user authentication tool used with personal computing devices is the username and password login. In general, there are three types of user-related logons with which to contend:

- A logon to the local machine
- A logon to a specific software application
- A network logon

At the local computer level, the local logon is typically required. This level of logon validates the user for using the local computer's resources (files and devices). However, in a shared computer environment where multiple users may be enabled to use the same computer, local user and group credentials are created and configured through a user accounts database that is stored on the local computer.

A Word About Local Logons

In a network environment, the network login typically supersedes and replaces the local login option. This logon level confirms the user's credentials for accessing remote resources.

These credentials are used to gain initial access to the computer, control access to its local resources, and control access to network resources. In a Windows environment, these accounts are created and managed through the Local Users and Groups utility under Computer Management, as depicted in Figure 8.8.

The first time a standalone system is started an administrator's account is automatically created in the operating system's local accounts database. The administrator has rights and permissions to all of the system's hardware and software resources. The administrator, in turn, creates other users and then grants rights to them and permissions to system resources as necessary.

The administrator can deal with users on an individual basis or may gather users into groups that can be administered uniformly. In doing so, the administrator can assign permissions or restrictions on an individual or an entire group. The value of using groups lies in the time saved by being able to apply common rights to several users instead of applying them one by one.

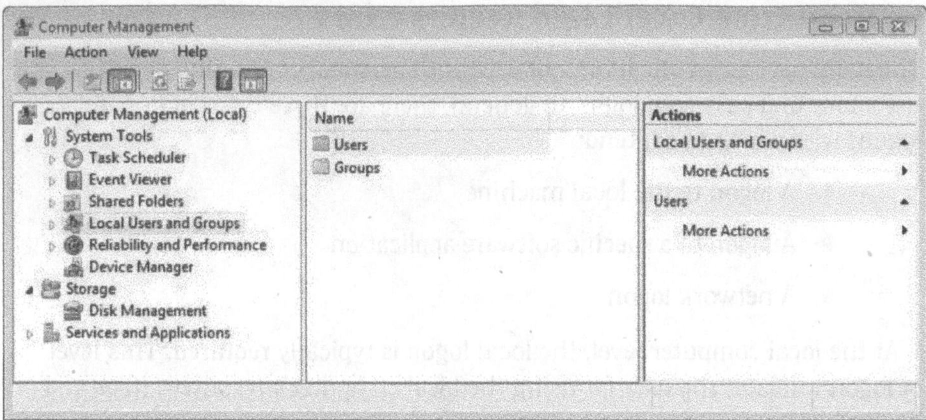

FIGURE 8.8 Microsoft Local User and Group Accounts

The other default group created when the operating system first starts is a type of account known as a Guests group. This default group typically has minimized access to the system, and all of its members share the same user profile. The Guest user account is automatically a member of this group.

Each user and group in the local environment has a profile that describes the resources and desktop configurations created for them. Settings in the profile can be used to limit the actions users can perform, such as installing, removing, configuring, adjusting, or copying resources.

When users log into the system, it checks their profiles and adjusts the system according to their information. These credentials are used to gain initial access to the computer and control what access each user has to its local resources. In addition, access to certain software applications and other resources may be controlled by additional application-level passwords.

Passwords

For a password to be effective it must possess a certain amount of complexity. Its length, width, and depth must be such as to thwart the efforts of the previously mentioned password-cracking techniques.

The length of a password directly affects the ease with which it can be cracked. The longer the password is, the more difficult it will be to crack. It is generally recommended that passwords should consist of at least eight characters. If permitted by the OS, longer passwords can be used, provided the employees or clients can remember them.

The width of a password relates to the number of different types of characters that can be incorporated, including those not belonging to the alphabet. Combinations of numbers, special characters, and uppercase and lowercase letters make passwords stronger, especially when an operating system considers uppercase and lowercase letters as completely different characters.

Passwords can contain control characters, alternative characters, and even spaces in some operating systems. Ideally, all the following character sets should be drawn from when users are required to create strong passwords.

- Uppercase letters such as A, B, C
- Lowercase letters such as a, b, c
- Numerals such as 1, 2, 3
- Special characters such as $, ?, &
- Alternative characters such as @, %

The depth of a password involves how difficult it is to guess its meaning. Although a good password should be easy to remember, it should nevertheless be difficult to guess. For a number of years, the top two passwords overall have been "123456" and "password." Attackers know common terms and techniques used in creating passwords as well, such as appending and replacing.

Appending is the act of adding a set of characters to the end of another set of characters (example123). *Replacing* is using a set of characters to replace another set of predictable characters (ex@mple). The meaning of a password should not be something that could be easily guessed or deduced through simple reasoning. One approach that seems to work well is to think in terms of phrases rather than simply words.

Mnemonic phrases are often incorporated, allowing the creation of passwords that cannot be easily guessed, but yet do not need to be written down to be remembered. Mnemonic phrases can be spelled phonetically, using, for example, "UraTygr!" instead of "You're a tiger!" Alternatively, the first letters in each word of a memorable phrase can be incorporated, such as "Ihnybtf," which is abbreviated from "I have not yet begun to fight!"

Another effective method is to choose a meaningful phrase that can be easily recalled. Then, the initials of some words in the phrase can be converted into alternative characters. For example, the number "4" could be substituted wherever the letter "f" is used.

Additional Password Security

The need for additional password security has become more recognized with the increased ease with which scam artists continue to steal them. Passwords have ultimately been gathered as easily as simply asking for them. Personnel should simply never talk about passwords with anyone, no matter how harmless or legitimate such conversations might seem.

Although standard password-protection practices may be adequate to keep some would-be intruders at bay, certain situations require a more sophisticated approach. In these cases, extra protection can be afforded through the use of encryption techniques and one-time passwords (OTP).

Password encryption is the process of taking a standard password and applying an algorithm to it in such a way as to make it meaningless to sniffers, crackers, or other eavesdroppers. Two-factor authentication, such as one-time passwords, are good only for one transaction but add another valuable layer of security.

Best password practices include the following:

- Use a consistent naming convention across the organization so that users can understand theirs and not resort to recording them so they can be found by others.
- Always supply a password to an account and make the user change it upon first login.
- Protect passwords (don't write them down in open spaces).
- Do not use default passwords.
- Educate users to create strong passwords.
- Enforce password policies at all levels of an organization.

SAFEGUARDING PASSWORDS

True password security involves users safeguarding their passwords from others.

Account Lockout Policies

Operating systems provide password lockout policy settings that enable administrators to enact password policies that prevent attackers from repeatedly trying to access the system. This prevents the attackers from using brute force attacks to guess the account password so they can break into the system.

Brute force attacks involve the repeated use of login attempts to try to guess the password. As shown in Figure 8.9, typical lockout policy settings include:

- Account Lockout Duration – How long (in minutes) the account will be locked out before it automatically unlocks. Setting this value to 0 will prevent the account from unlocking until the administrator manually resets it.
- Account Lockout Threshold/Max Failures – How many times account access can be attempted before the account is locked out. The default value for this setting is 0, which disables the account lockout function.
- Reset Account Lockout Counter After/Lockout Duration – The amount of time that can pass before the account lockout value is returned to 0.

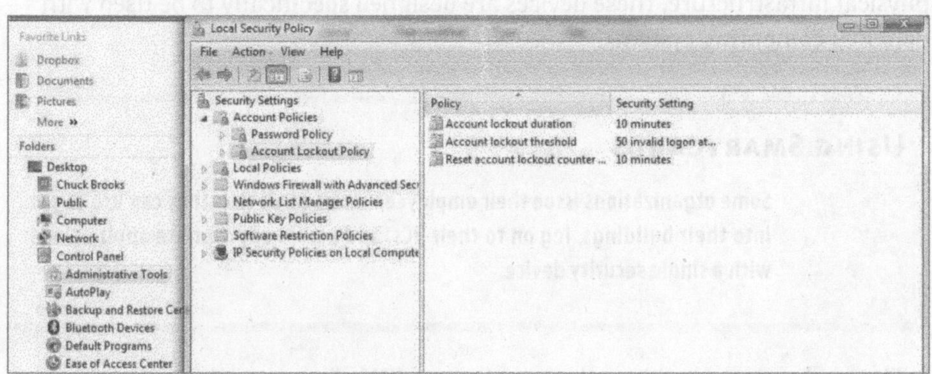

FIGURE 8.9 Windows Lockout Options

Computer Locking

Users should never leave their computer unattended after they have logged on. Doing so opens the door for others to access and manipulate their computer, data, and network. All users should be trained to either log off or lock their computers when they are away from them, even if only for a few minutes.

Locking the computer protects it from intruders and preserves the current system state. When the computer is unlocked, the applications and data that were active in the system are still open, making it much easier for the user to pick up where they left off.

Users should also be instructed to make sure they log off at the end of the day. This closes all applications and ensures that data files are saved.

Implementing Additional Authentication Options

Recall from Chapter 2 that authentication is defined as the process of determining that someone is who they say they are. At the local computing or control device level, authentication can be implemented in terms of physical or biometric authentication systems to replace or augment password authentication methods.

Physical Authentication Devices

There are hardware devices that can be used to make personal computer systems unusable by people other than authorized users. These devices include items such as smart cards and biometric devices similar to the ones described in the preceding chapter. However, unlike the devices designed to protect access to physical infrastructure, these devices are designed specifically to be used with personal computing systems.

Using Smartcards

Some organizations issue their employees smart cards that they can use to get into their buildings, log on to their PCs, and access appropriate applications with a single security device.

The card system combines the users' secret PINs (i.e., something the users alone know) with tokens generated by the network's Certificate Authority authentication system to generate a unique pass code. The pass code validates the user and their access to different resources.

Biometric Scanners for Personal Computing Devices

As discussed in Chapter 2, biometric scanners are becoming significantly more sophisticated, including facial scanning devices, searchable databases, and supporting application programs.

In addition to serving as authentication devices for facility access, many biometric scanning devices have evolved for use with personal computers. However, the biometric authentication device most widely used with personal computers is the fingerprint scanner. Figure 8.10 shows different fingerprint scanner devices designed for use with PCs.

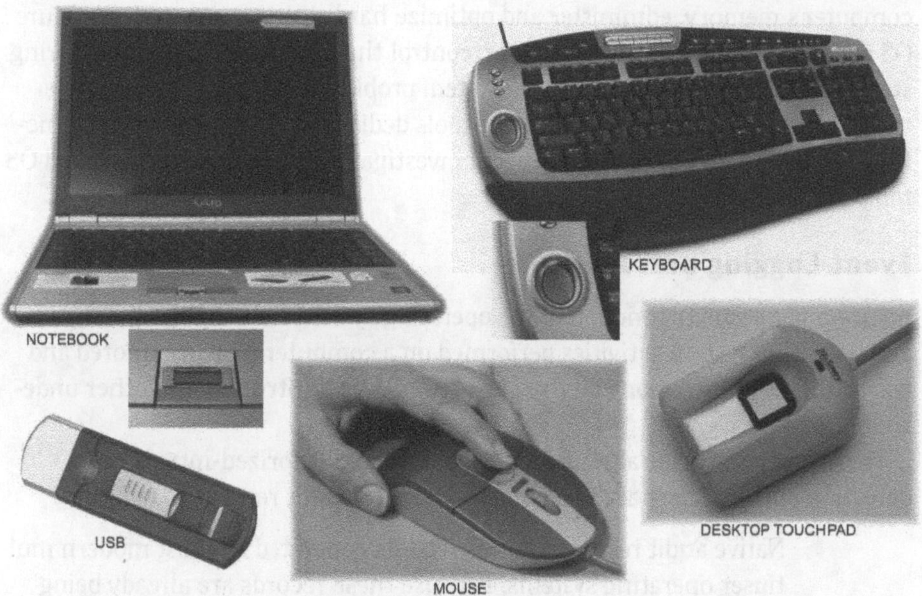

FIGURE 8.10 Fingerprint Scanners

Some fingerprint scanner manufacturers offer miniature touchpad versions that sit on the desk and connect to the system through a cable and USB connector. Other fingerprint scanners are built into key fobs that simply plug directly into the USB port. Some manufacturers even build these devices into the top of the mouse.

Some models actually store the scanned images and account access information on the device. This allows the identification file to travel with the user if they work with different computers at different locations.

After the fingerprint scanner software has been installed and configured, the password manager will prompt you to scan in your fingerprint rather than type a password on future log-in attempts.

Using Local Administrative Tools

All of the different operating systems discussed previously offer management tools to control who, when, and how the local computer is used. Collectively, these tools are referred to as *administrative tools* (in Microsoft Windows OS versions, the Control Panel applet where these tools are configured and launched is titled "Administrative Tools").

These tools typically include programs designed to control the usage of the computer's memory, administer and optimize hard-disk-drive usage, configure OS services running on the computer, control the hardware/OS handoff during startup, and troubleshoot operating system problems. However, in each case there is a subset of these management tools dedicated to security-related functions. In the following sections, we will investigate common security-related OS tools and their implementations.

Event Logging and Auditing

Auditing is a security function of the operating system that enables the user and operating system activities performed on a computer to be monitored and tracked. This information can then be used to detect intruders and other undesirable activities.

These entries provide a fundamental tool for unauthorized-intrusion-detection efforts. There are two common types of audit records to consider:

- Native audit records – Event records generated by most modern multiuser operating systems. Because these records are already being generated by the operating system, they are always available, but they may not contain the desired events or be in a readily usable form.
- Detection-specific audit records – Records generated to provide specific information about desired actions or events. These actions or events can be based on operating system activities, application events, or security events.

The auditing systems available with most operating systems consists of two major components:

- Audit policy (or audit rules), which defines the types of events that will be monitored and added to the system's security logs
- Audit entries (or audit records), which consist of the individual entries added to the security log when an audited event occurs

Windows Auditing Tools

In a Microsoft Windows environment, audit entries are maintained in the security log file. Figure 8.11 shows a typical security log displayed in the Windows

Event Viewer utility. For auditing to be an effective security tool, the security log should be reviewed and archived regularly.

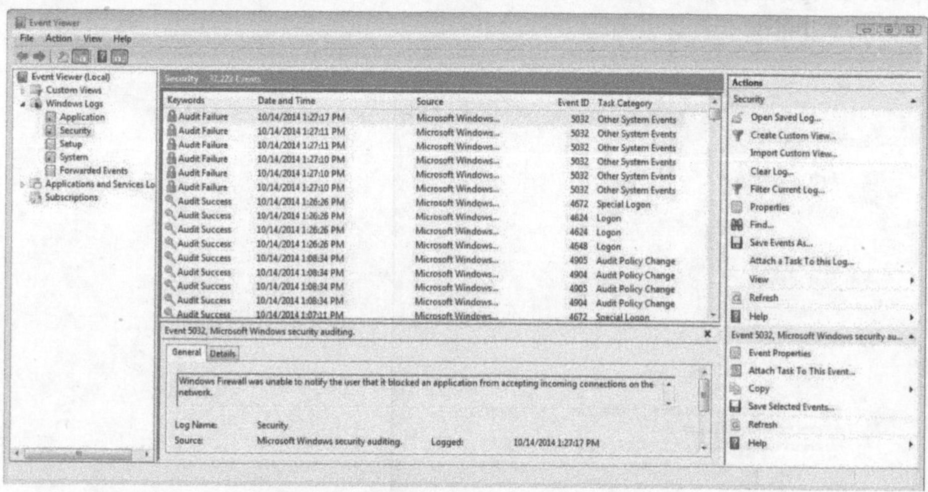

FIGURE 8.11 Viewing Security Audit Logs

In Windows, auditing is configured through the Local Security Policy option located under the Administrative Tools menu, as shown in Figure 8.12.

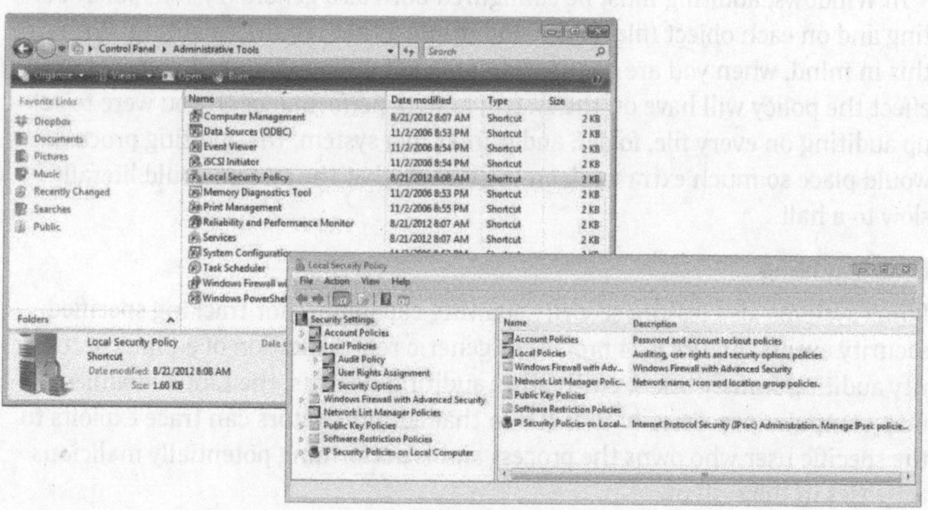

FIGURE 8.12 Configuring Auditing in Windows

Selecting a policy to be configured in the right pane will produce the Local Security Setting window, depicted in Figure 8.13. Place check marks beside the option or options that should be tracked and audited. You can check Success, Failure, or both.

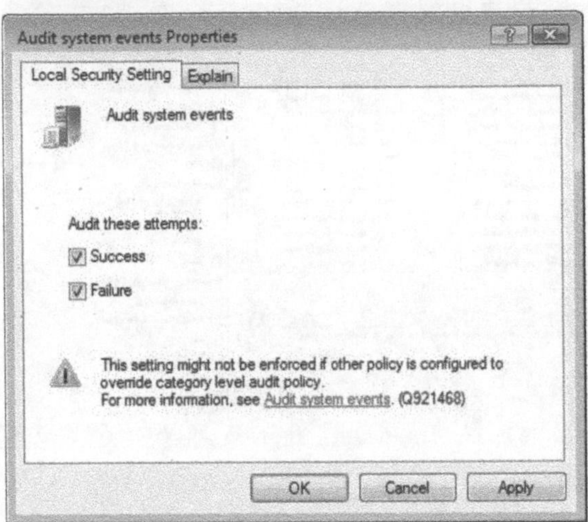

FIGURE 8.13 Establishing a Local Security Policy Setting

In Windows, auditing must be configured both as a general system policy setting and on each object (file, folder, and printer) that requires auditing. With this in mind, when you are configuring an audit policy, you must consider what effect the policy will have on the system and its performance. If you were to set up auditing on every file, folder, and printer in a system, the auditing process would place so much extra work on the system that the system could literally slow to a halt.

Linux Auditing

Linux systems also feature security auditing capabilities for tracking specified security events. Figure 8.14 provides a generic representation of a Linux security auditing framework. As with other auditing systems, the Linux modules map computer processes to user IDs so that administrators can trace exploits to the specific user who owns the process and is performing potentially malicious activities in the system.

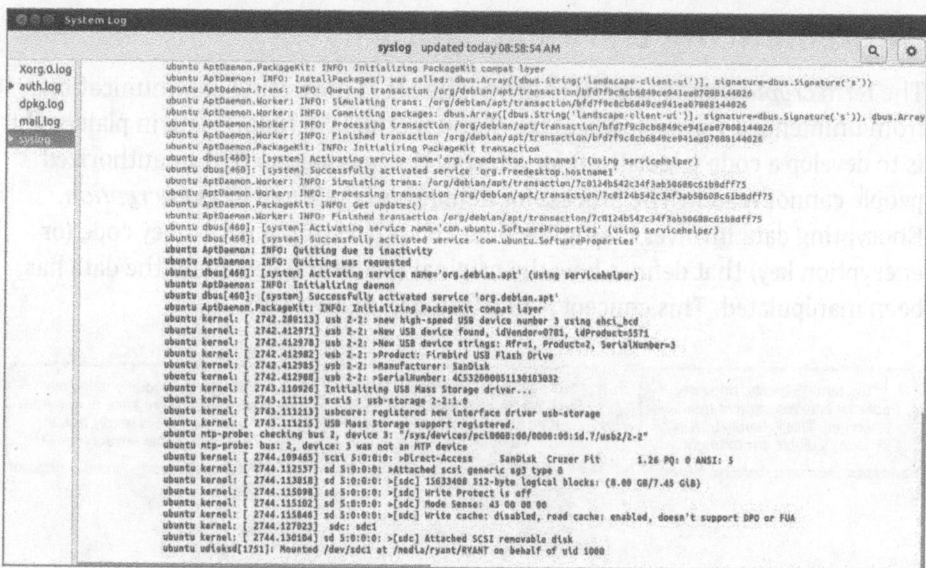

FIGURE 8.14 Linux Auditing

At the heart of the system is the audit daemon that works with the Linux kernel's audit module to record relevant events and write them to a log file on the disk. Audit rules are configured in a file that is executed when the system boots up. The audit controller utility employs the parameters in these rules to determine which system events are tracked and how they are written to the audit log file.

When an application encounters a situation that triggers a preconfigured audit event, a message is presented to the kernel's audit interface and passed to the audit controller. Under the direction of the audit controller, the audit daemon writes the event away to the audit event log.

Linux auditing systems also include a report generation tool that the administrator can use to generate custom security reports. It may also include a search utility to provide quick/specific examination of log entries for specific events.

As with Windows Group Policy configurations, you must consider the level of auditing you want the Linux audit system to perform on the computer and its operational consequences.

Implementing Data Encryption

The term *cryptography* is used to define the art of protecting communications from unintended viewers. One of the oldest methods of hiding data in plain sight is to develop a code (algorithm) for altering the message so that unauthorized people cannot read it. The process for doing this is referred to as *encryption*. Encrypting data involves taking the data and processing it with a key code (or encryption key) that defines how the original (plaintext) version of the data has been manipulated. This concept is illustrated in Figure 8.15.

FIGURE 8.15 Data Encryption

Anyone who is given the encryption key can use it to decode the message through a decryption process. *Symmetric encryption* uses the same key to encrypt and decrypt data. *Asymmetric encryption,* described in the following paragraph, uses two different keys to encrypt and decrypt information.

A particularly effective asymmetric key system is Public Key Encryption (PKE). This technique employs two keys to ensure the security of the encrypted data: a public key and a private key. The *public key* (known to everyone) is used to encrypt the data, and the *private* or *secret key* (known only to the specified recipient) is used to decrypt it. The public and private keys are related in such a way that the private key cannot be decoded simply by possessing the public key.

Data encryption in a digital device or network can occur at many levels:

- As file-system level (file and folder level) encryption
- As disk-level encryption
- As transport-level encryptions

Disk-level encryption involves using technology to encrypt the entire disk structure. This technique offers value in that it protects everything on the disk from unauthorized access including the operating system files and structure.

Disk encryption in a personal computer system may be performed at the software or hardware level. At the software level, disk encryption technology is available through most major disk operating system versions as well as through third-party suppliers.

The disk encryption software runs at a level between the operating system's device drivers and the higher-level applications. For the most part, computer programs and designated users are not aware that the encryption/decryption process is occurring. Figure 8.16, illustrates a simplified version of the encryption/decryption process.

During the initial disk encryption process an encryption key is generated and stored on the system. This key is stored in an encrypted format that requires a password or passphrase to decrypt. When a user supplies the password or passphrase, the system applies the decryption key to the data, unlocking it for the computer's applications to use. When new data is generated, it is encrypted before it is stored on the disk drive.

Hardware-Level Disk Encryption

Many computer motherboard designs include a built-in microchip called a Trusted Platform Module (TPM) that is used to store cryptographic information, such as encryption keys. Information stored on the TPM is more secure from external software attacks and physical theft.

This technology protects the operating system and user data to ensure that a computer is not tampered with, even if it is left unattended, lost, or stolen. The encryption managers in these operating systems prevent access to a hard drive by encrypting the entire drive.

If the computer motherboard is equipped with a compatible TPM chip, disk operating systems use the TPM to lock the encryption key that protects the data stored on the hard drive. The key cannot be accessed until the TPM has verified the state of the computer during startup.

During the computer startup process, the TPM compares a hash code derived from important operating system configuration values with a snapshot of the system taken earlier. If the codes match, the operating system will release the decryption key that unlocks the encrypted disk drive. In doing so, this process verifies the integrity of the operating system's startup process, as shown in Figure 8.17. The key will not be released if the TPM detects that the operating system installation has been altered.

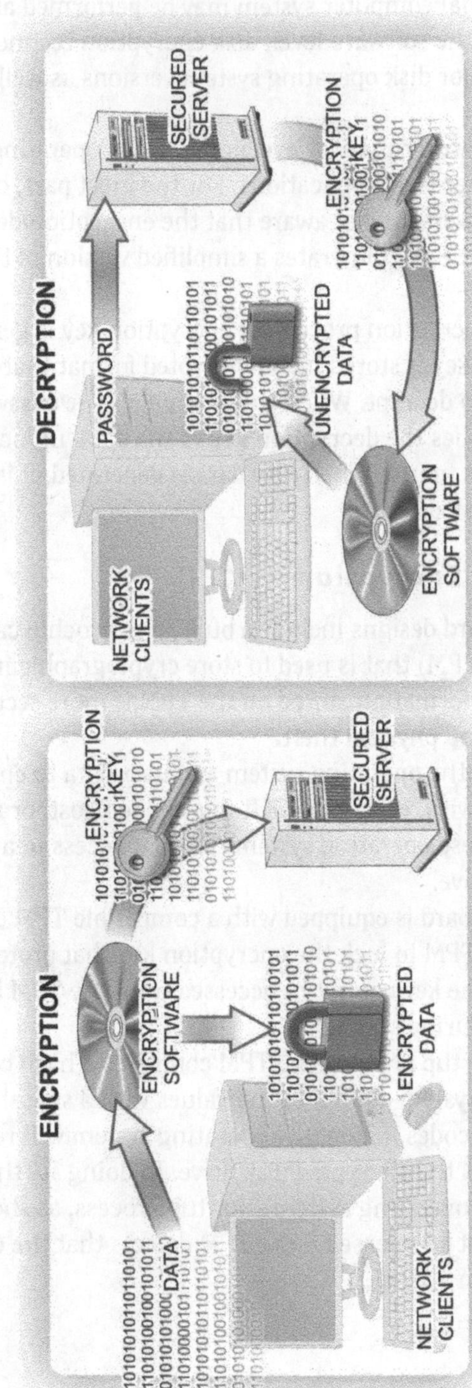

FIGURE 8.16 The Encryption/Decryption Process

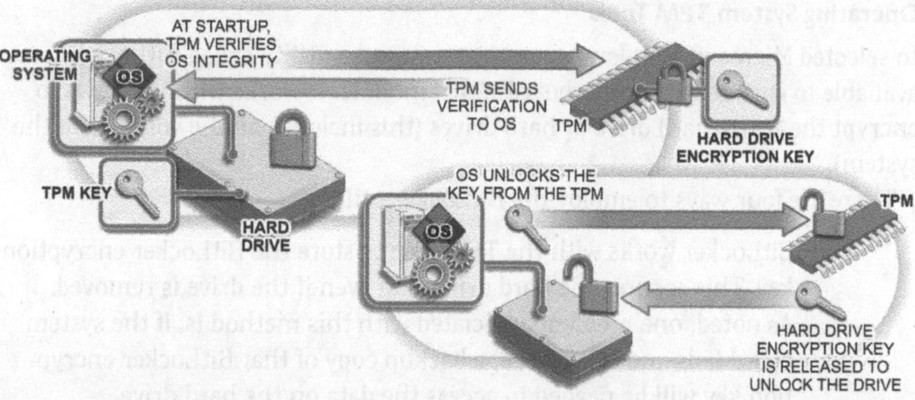

FIGURE 8.17 Using the TPM

The theory is that the data on a hard drive would be safe if the computer were stolen because the operating system would not allow the hard drive to be accessed. One problem associated with this method is, if the motherboard fails and is replaced, a backup copy of that startup key will be needed to access the data on the hard drive.

Moving TPM Chips

A TPM chip cannot be moved from one motherboard to another.

This drive must be present to unlock the data stored on a volume. In such cases, it is recommended that you make backups of the startup key. The most secure option is to require that a PIN or password be used any time the computer is started along with the automated TPM process.

Backing Up Startup Keys

Be aware that if the TPM fails or all the copies of the startup key become lost or corrupted, the recovery of the data will prove to be very difficult. Individual computer users must determine whether their security needs warrant going this "extra mile" to protect their personal computers. However, in a business environment, this requirement is typically dictated by the system administrator.

Operating System TPM Tools

In selected Microsoft Windows operating systems, a utility called BitLocker is available to engage the motherboard's TPM module. It works with Windows to encrypt the entire hard drive or hard drives (this includes all the volumes in the system).

There are four ways to employ the BitLocker utility:

- BitLocker works with the TPM chip to store the BitLocker encryption key. This secures the hard drive data even if the drive is removed. As noted, one problem associated with this method is, if the system board fails and is replaced, a backup copy of that BitLocker encryption key will be needed to access the data on the hard drive.
- If the computer is not equipped with a TPM chip, the startup key on a USB flash drive must be inserted in the system prior to bootup.
- Startup keys can also be used on computers that do possess TPM chips. One problem associated with this method is the tendency of users to leave the flash drive installed in the computer.
- The most secure option is to require that a PIN be used along with the automated TPM process any time the computer is started.

Linux operating systems also possess tools to engage the TPM encryption capabilities of compatible motherboards. In these systems, it is necessary to confirm that the Linux kernel involved supports the TPM version on the motherboard. The three kernel modules involved in TPM configuration are `tpm_bios`, `tpm`, and `tpm_tis`. The generic `tpm_bios` and `tpm` modules are loaded first and then the `tpm_tis` module is loaded with specific parameters.

Several Linux software tools are available to manage TPM on Linux-based machines. Trousers is an open-source daemon that controls all of the communications with the TPM through a single module. Likewise, the TrustedGrub module is capable of detecting and supporting TPM functionality in Linux systems. It is a downloadable extension of the Grub bootloader that has been modified for this purpose.

When you initialize the TPM, the module will request an owner password and a Storage Root Key (SRK) password that it can use to generate the cryptographic key. The owner password is required to perform administrative tasks on the system, while the SRK is required to load a key into the TPM. These keys must be maintained and can never be lost because continued access to the system would be nearly impossible without them.

File- and-Folder-Level Encryption

As the title implies, file-and-folder-level encryption is applied to individual files and folders. File- and-folder-level encryption tools enable users to encrypt files stored on their drives using keys that only the designated user (or an authorized recovery agent) can decode. This prevents data theft by those who do not have the password or a decoding tool. It greatly enhances the security of files on portable computers by enabling users to designate files and folders so that they can only be accessed using the proper encryption key.

This type of encryption is typically implemented as an attribute setting that can be established for specified files or folders and is linked to the authorized users in the system. These users can open these files and folders just as they would any ordinary files or folders. However, if someone gains unauthorized access to the computer, they will not be able to open the encrypted files or folders.

Microsoft File Encryption Tools

Windows provides effective local hard-drive security through its encrypting file system (EFS) feature, as shown in Figure 8.18.

The EFS feature enables the user to encrypt files stored on the drive using keys that only the designated user (or an authorized recovery agent) can decode. This prevents data theft by those who do not have the password or a decoding tool.

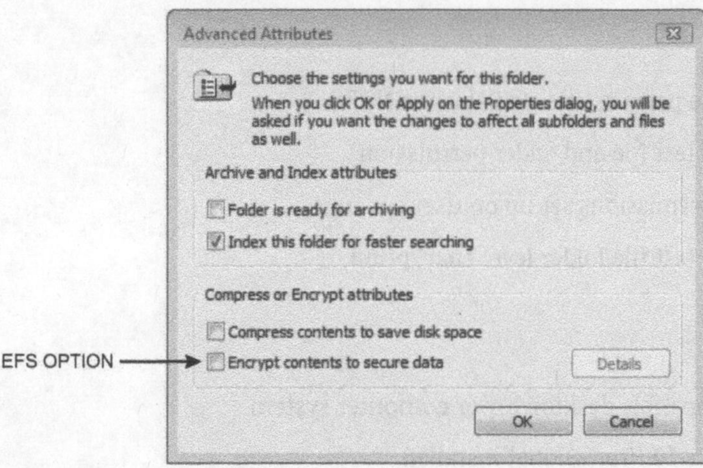

FIGURE 8.18 Windows Drive Encryption Options

Windows users can implement the EFS option to encrypt their files and folders on NTFS drives. To do so, they simply click the Encrypt Contents To Secure Data check box in the file or folder's Advanced Attributes windows. Users can open these files and folders just as they would any ordinary files or folders. However, if someone gains unauthorized access to the computer, they will not be able to open the encrypted files or folders. EFS is simple to use because it is actually an attribute that can be established for files or folders.

The EFS feature further enhances the security of files on portable computers by enabling users to designate files and folders so that they can only be accessed using the proper encryption key.

A Word About EFS

EFS prevents files from being accessed by unauthorized users, including those trying to bypass the operating system and gain access using third-party utilities. It uses both symmetric and asymmetric encryption when securing the information.

Hands-On Exercises

Objectives

- Describe permissions available for NTFS.
- Set and test file and folder permissions.
- Verify permissions set up on user accounts.
- Set and test file/folder level encryption.

Resources

- PC-compatible desktop/tower computer system
- Windows 10 Professional installed
- TestUser accounts setup on your PC/workstation
  - User: TestUser1 with Password: testuser1

- ▶ User: TestUser2 with Password: testuser2
- ▶ Both accounts should be set as standard users.
- ▶ AxCrypt installed (`https://www.axcrypt.net/download/`)

Discussion

The New Technology File System is Microsoft's proprietary and default file management system for its operating systems. NTFS brought with it enhanced security features including access control lists (ACLs) and the encrypting file system (EFS).

NTFS permissions can be configured as Allow or Deny options within the associated access control list. This is an example of a discretionary access control list, in which the user who is considered the owner of a file or folder chooses the permissions of said information. Figure 8.19 illustrates an ACL.

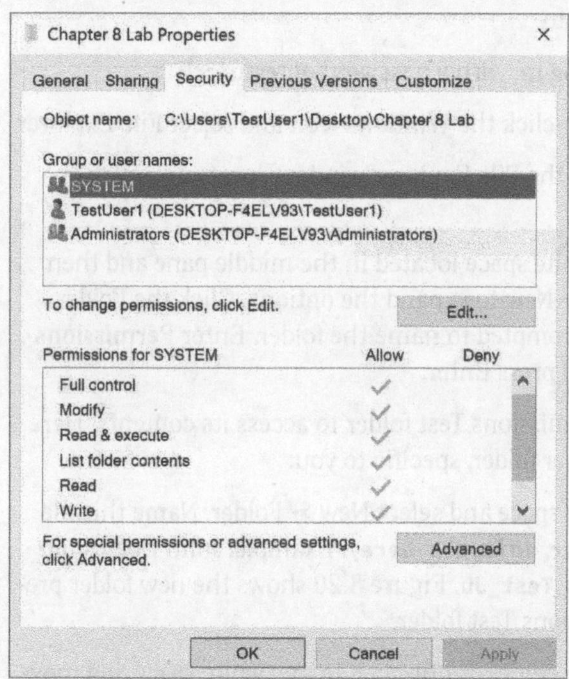

FIGURE 8.19 Access Control List

In this lab, you will manage and test permissions, and you will explore encryption at a file level with AxCrypt. Keep in mind that these procedures provide an introduction to permissions. This lab will explore permissions management on a local host computer. This lab will not feature share permissions, server permissions, inheritance, or Linux file permission management. You will manage file and folder permissions for a select set of users. Finally, you will test various permission settings to gather a better understanding of the importance and power of ACLs.

Procedures

Setting Up and Creating Files and Folders

To be able to test the NTFS permissions you will put into place, you must first become the owner of files and folders. The owner of a file has the discretion to allow or deny access to other users.

1. Power on the computer, and if necessary choose Windows 10 Professional to log into.
2. Select TestUser1 to log in, with a password of **testuser1**.
3. Once logged in, right-click the Windows icon and select File Explorer.
4. Along the left side of the File Explorer window, locate and click on the C: drive.
5. Right-click in any white space located in the middle pane and then hover the cursor over New to expand the options. Click the Folder option. You will be prompted to name the folder. Enter **Permissions** Test as the name and press Enter.
6. Double-click the Permissions Test folder to access its contents. Here you will create another folder, specific to you.
7. Right-click the white space and select New ➢ Folder. Name this file **`Perm_Test_`*`(add your initials here)`***. Example: John Doe would name his folder **`Perm_Test_JD`**. Figure 8.20 shows the new folder prepared in the Permissions Test folder.
8. This folder should be empty. Right-click in any white space and move the cursor to hover over New. Here you will select Text Document. Name the file **`test1`** and press Enter.

9. Repeat Step 8 three times to create files **test2**, **test3**, and **test4**.
10. There is no information in these files, so open each .txt document by double-clicking and typing This is a test. This is only a test. into each file. Save and close each text file.

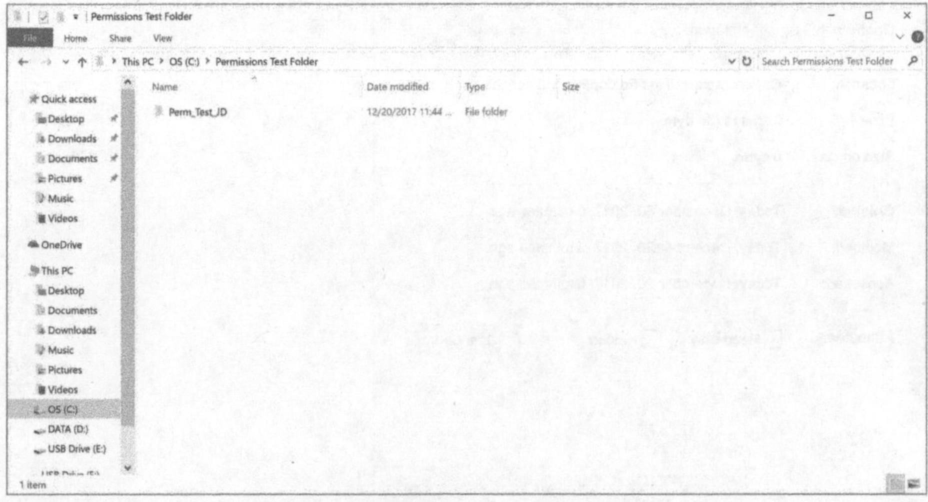

FIGURE 8.20 Perm_Test **Folder Created**

Creating File Permissions

In this section, you will explore the options available to restrict certain users' access to the files and folder you just created. You can prevent specific users or groups from executing, reading, writing, and modifying files that you have deemed important. This is accomplished through the ACL as part of each individual file.

1. Verify that you are within the Perm_Test folder you created in the previous steps. Right-click test1 and click Properties. This will launch the test1 Properties window, as shown in Figure 8.21.

The Properties window may not have all of the tabs listed in the example. At this point, the only necessary tab you will be working with is the Security tab.

2. Click the Security tab. Note the types of permissions available and record them in Table 8.2. This window is the file's associated access control list.

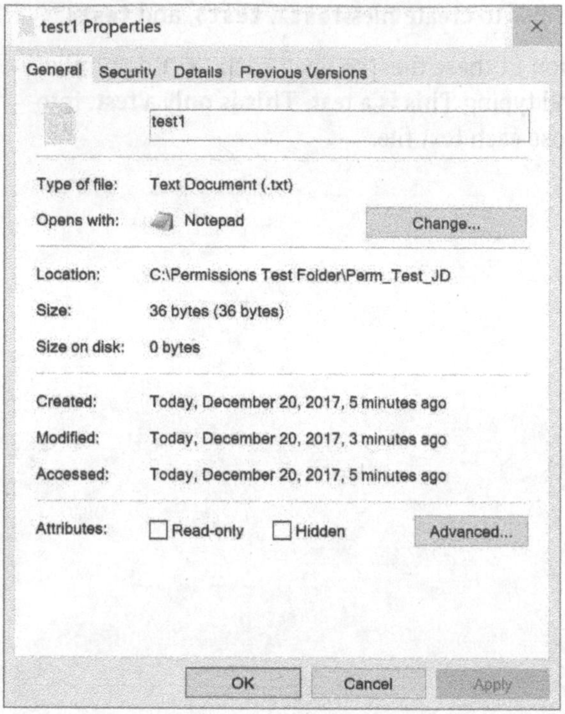

FIGURE 8.21 File `test1` Properties window

Currently, the only permissions granted or denied on this object are those associated with the group the user became a member of at its creation. To limit specific users' access to this file, you must add them to the ACL and select the permission level you want them to have.

TABLE 8.2 Permissions Available in `test1` ACL

3. Click Edit to open the `test1` Permissions window.
4. Click Add to navigate to the Select Users Or Groups window.
5. Under Enter The Object Names To Select (Example):, enter TestUser2. Click Check Names to confirm the user account. Click OK to continue.

This is the same window in which you can add groups to grant or deny access to anyone associated with a known group. Groups are better utilized within a networked environment; therefore, you will not set or test group permissions in this lab.

Notice that the user TestUser2 is now included in the ACL. Here you can fine-tune the permissions for this user on the file you created. The default permissions given are to allow Read and Read & Execute.

6. Under the Deny column head, click the Write check box. Figure 8.22 shows the Permissions allocated to TestUser2.

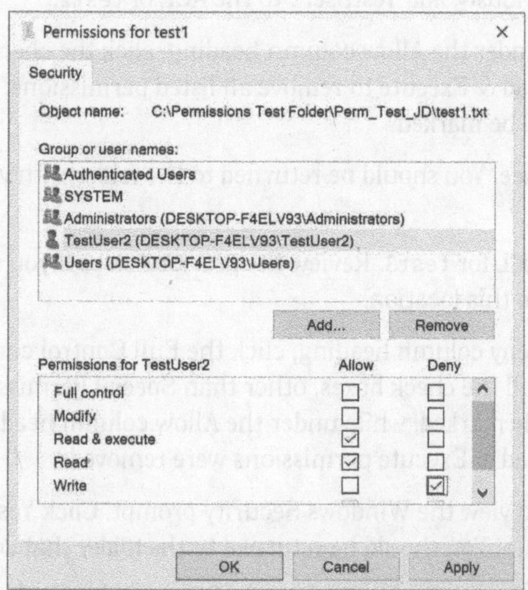

FIGURE 8.22 **Permissions for `Test1` Given to TestUser2**

7. Click the Apply button. Read the Windows Security prompt, and then click Yes. You are directed back to the `test1` Properties window. Click OK to exit this window.

In regard to permissions, there are a number of rules that apply:

- *Deny permissions* take precedence over *allow permissions* in most scenarios. When a deny permission is applied to an object, in this case a `.txt` document, it is called an *explicit deny*.

- *Explicit permissions* are those applied directly to an object, and they take precedence over permissions that have been inherited. This will be discussed in later labs.
- Permissions are cumulative among users and groups. Permissions will be combined to achieve what is called the *effective permissions* for that object.

8. Right-click `test2` and click Properties.
9. Click the Security tab and click Edit.
10. As done previously, add TestUser2 to the ACL of `test2`.
11. For `test2`, under the Allow column heading, click the check boxes for Read and Read & Execute to remove all listed permissions. No check boxes should be marked.
12. Click OK twice. You should be returned to the folder with your test files.
13. Access the ACL for `test3`. Review the previous steps if you need help navigating to this location.
14. Under the Deny column heading, click the Full Control check box. Notice that all the check boxes, other than Special Permissions, were automatically marked, while under the Allow column heading, the Read and Read & Execute permissions were removed.
15. Click OK and view the Windows Security prompt. Click Yes, and then click OK again. You should be returned to the folder that contains your test files.

Applying File-Level Encryption

In this procedure, you will be using freeware by the name of AxCrypt. AxCrypt is an open-source file-encryption program that can be integrated with Windows Explorer. This feature makes it easy to use and convenient. It also password-protects the encrypted files, giving another layer of security.

1. Right-click on the file `test4`. Locate and hover the mouse cursor over AxCrypt. There are a few options, but for now you will just click the bold Encrypt.
2. To encrypt the file, you must passphrase-protect it as well. Enter the passphrase marcraft and verify the passphrase by entering it again.

3. Click on both check boxes to mark Remember This For Decryption and Use As Default For Encryption. The window should look the same as Figure 8.23.

FIGURE 8.23 Using AxCrypt to Encrypt the `test4` File

4. Click OK. You will notice the icon next to `test4` has changed, as well as the name and extension of the file. If you double-click it though, the file will open as normal in Notepad, with the same data inside.

Setting Folder Permissions

Folder permissions provide the same basic permission choices as file permissions. This can be deceiving, as the meaning of each Allow or Deny is slightly different. For instance, the Allow – Read option on a file permits the opening and viewing of its contents. On the other hand, the Allow – Read option on a folder will only let the specified user list the contents of the folder. The latter can be used when a user needs to be able to access a folder, but not all of the files within the folder.

1. Click the Back button, or Permissions Test in the address bar, to see the folder you created named `Perm_Test_`*`(your initials here)`*.
2. Right-click the folder and click Properties.

   Notice the options for permissions. They are the same as file permissions, with the inclusion of one more option: List Folder Contents.
3. Click Edit.
4. Click Add and add TestUser2 to the folder's ACL. This process is the same as you performed before with individual files. Return to the

"Creating File Permissions" section if you need to review how this is done.

5. The default permissions for the folder are Allow – Read & Execute, List Folder Contents, and Read. Under the Deny column heading, click the Read & Execute check box. You will notice that all of the Allow permissions have been removed, and the subsequent Deny permissions replace all three.
6. Click the check box to select Allow – Write.
7. Click OK, acknowledge the Windows Security prompt, and click Yes. Click OK to close the Properties window.

Testing Folder Permissions

Now it is time to test all of the options you have put into place. You will need to close all open windows and log onto TestUser2. Choose to Switch User, rather than the Log Off option.

1. Close all open windows and select Switch Users. (Logging off completely would serve the same function; however, it would take much longer.)
2. After selecting the Switch User option, type in the username TestUser2. Enter the password testuser2.
3. Navigate to the location of the folder you created at the beginning of this lab: Permissions Test. Your personal testing folder will be there.
4. Double-click your folder. Were you able to access the contents? Input your findings into Table 8.3.

TABLE 8.3 TestUser2 Access Levels

File/Folder	Permissions for Testuser2	Access?
Perm_Test_folder access		
test1		
test2		
test3		
test4		

5. Right-click the folder and click Properties to try to access the ACL. Click the Security tab. What are the results?

The Deny – Read & Execute, List Folder Contents, and Read permissions override any group permissions that may have previously allowed this. This is an easy way to keep certain users out of important information that they should not access.

6. Leave the Permissions Test window open and switch users. You will need to access TestUser1 again.
7. After entering the username and password, you should be back to the desktop. Once again, navigate to the Permissions Test folder.
8. Right-click the `Perm_Test_`*`(your initials here)`* folder and click Properties. In order to grant access to TestUser2, you will need to remove the Deny options.
9. Click the Security tab. Click TestUser2 under Group Or User Names.

When you click on the username, you will notice the check marks for permissions are black. If you click on another user or group, you will notice the check marks for permissions are gray. This means you are unable to change them. Only those check marks that are black can be modified.

In this lab, you are dealing with the DACL (Discretionary Access Control List). This means when a user creates a file, they are considered the owner and have the right to grant or deny permissions as they so choose. However, users with administrative privileges have the right to change the ownership and permissions of a file or folder.

10. Click Edit. The Permissions window loads. Click TestUser2 in the top panel. Change the permissions by clicking the Allow – Read & Execute permissions. This will remove all Deny permissions previously in place and fill in the three Allow permissions as they were originally.
11. Click the OK button to save the permissions.
12. Close all windows and switch users. Log into TestUser2 by supplying the username and password.
13. The desktop will load with the window of the Permissions Test folder still open. Attempt to read the contents by double-clicking the `Perm_Test_`*`(your initials here)`* folder. Were you able to access it this time?

Testing File Permissions

1. Within this folder, you should see the four text documents that you created as TestUser1. Double-click `test1` to attempt opening it. Were you allowed?

If you recall from earlier, `test1` was given a Deny – Write permission.

2. Adjust the text in the file by deleting it all and typing This is no longer a test. Click File and then click Save. You are asked to confirm the name; click Save. You are asked to Confirm the Save As to replace the file; click Yes.
3. A prompt appears. Was this the expected outcome? List your findings in Table 8.3. Click OK to accept the Access Is Denied prompt.
4. Click the X in the upper-right corner of the file window to close the window. You are asked if you want to save changes, but you already know that you do not have the proper permissions to accomplish this. Click Don't Save. You are now back to the contents of the folder.
5. Double-click `test2` to attempt to open it. Were you allowed?
6. Adjust the text in the file by deleting it all and typing This is no longer a test. Click File, and then click Save. Were you prompted for any reason? Record your results in Table 8.3.

You previously removed all permissions for TestUser2 on `test2`. No permissions were granted or denied; however, you are still able to read, modify, and write to this file. Why is that?

TestUser2 is also part of the group Users, which is granted Read & Execute, Read, and Write permissions by default. As mentioned earlier, permissions are cumulative, and the result is the Effective Permissions. Only in the case of a Deny, will an Allow be overridden.

7. Close the `test2` file by clicking the X in the upper-right corner.
8. Double-click `test3` to attempt to open it. Were you allowed? Note the results in Table 8.3.

Deny – Full Control was issued for this particular file. Therefore, TestUser2 is not allowed to access it in any way.

Testing File Encryption

You no doubt have noticed that `test4` has a green shield next to it. The filename and extension are still in their changed format. All indications are that this file is encrypted. You will now try to access the information.

1. Double-click `test4` to attempt to open. Were you allowed?

As a different user, you must supply a password to decrypt the file for access. Assuming the password is not known to another user, this is a good preventative measure.

2. Click Cancel.
3. You will now attempt to view the encrypted text. Right-click `test4`. Hover the cursor over Open With.
4. Click Choose Default Program. The window suggests you open the file with AxCrypt; however, you are unable to access it in this way. Under Other Programs, find and select Notepad.
5. Before clicking OK, look to be sure Always Use The Selected Program To Open This Kind Of File is unchecked. Now click OK.
6. The test document opens. Can you read it? It should look something like Figure 8.24.
7. Adjust the text by deleting and adding random characters to it. Click File, and then click Save. Were you able to save? Record your results in Table 8.3.
8. If you haven't received an error yet, try to access `test4` by double-clicking the file. An error has occurred.

Although encrypting safeguards the information from TestUser2, the permissions were unchanged. This allowed TestUser2 to open the file, change its contents, and finally save it. The result is a corrupted file, which can no longer be read. So even though encryption can hide the contents, permissions still need to be set in order to truly protect the data.

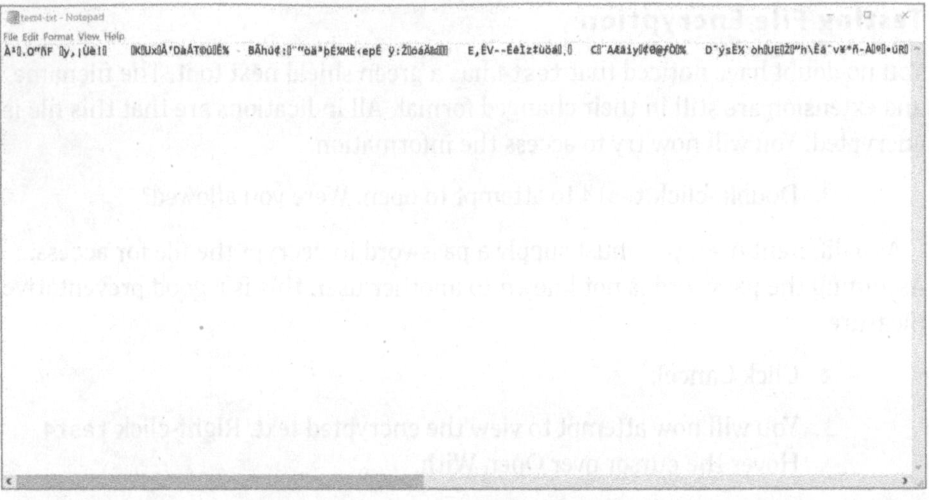

FIGURE 8.24 Encrypted Data in `.txt` Document

9. Close all the windows and log off as user TestUser2.
10. Log onto TestUser1.
11. Navigate to the Permissions Test folder and access your `Perm_Test_(your initials here)` folder. Attempt to open the `test4` AxCrypt file. Were you able to open it?

Unfortunately, this information is lost.

12. Close all the windows and shut down the computer.

Tables

TABLE 8.2 Permissions Available in `test1` ACL

Full Control	Modify	Read & Execute
Read	Write	Special Permissions

TABLE 8.3 TestUser2 Access Levels

File/Folder	Permissions for TestUser2	Access?
Perm_Test_ folder access	Allow – Write Deny – Read & Execute, List Folder Contents, Read	No access to contents of folder or the ACL
test1	Allow – Read & Execute, Read Deny – Write	Can access file but cannot change/ save file
test2	No explicit permissions given	Can access, change, and save file
test3	Deny – Full Control	Denied any access
test4	Allow – Read & Execute, Read, Write.	Can access, change, and save file

Lab Questions

1. **Which permission do folders have that files do not?**

   Answer: Folder permissions include List folder contents. File permissions only have Read and Read & Execute.

2. **What are effective permissions?**

   Answer: Effective permissions are the cumulative permissions granted by all sources. Individual and group sources are combined to give an overall permission within an ACL.

3. **Does encryption alone make your data safe?**

   Answer: No. As shown in the lab, the information may be protected, but it is not untouchable. Without setting proper permissions, a malicious person might choose to corrupt your information. Even worse, another person might not know exactly what they are doing and accidentally affect the data in an irreversible way.

4. **If a User tries to access a file that has an Allow – Read & Execute permission, and a Deny – Read & Execute permission assigned to them from different sources, will they be able to access the file?**

   Answer: No. In most cases, a Deny permission overrides the Allow permission. The Allow permission granted is voided, and the User will not have access.

5. **If you remove all permissions, Allow and Deny, from a specific user will they be able to access the file or folder?**

   Answer: Depending on the group or groups they are associated with, yes. Users are generally added to the Users groups, and as such they are given the default Allow – Read & Execute, Read, and Write on most files.

6. **As a basic user, can you change the permissions on any file or object?**

   Answer: No. A user without administrative properties cannot change any file or folders permissions. A user is allowed to change only the permissions of files to which they are considered the owner.

## CHAPTER 9

Protecting Remote Access

As you learned earlier in Part II, computers do not have to be connected to other computers to be at risk. Although many computers might not be part of a corporate network, almost all modern personal computers at least occasionally get attached to the largest data network in the world: the Internet. As such, these standalone computing and control devices are exposed to corruption and exploitation from remote sources.

- **Analyze and Differentiate Between Anti-Virus/Anti-Malware Products.**
- **Secure the Web Browser of a Standalone Computing Device.**
- **Configure and Test a Local Firewall Installation.**
- **Explain the Importance of Application Security.**
- **Audit Local Operating System Services and Events.**
- **Establish a Local Security Policy on a Standalone Host Device.**
- **Describe the Importance of Conducting Local Updates and Patch Maintenance Activities.**

Protecting Local Computing Devices

There are nine basic steps for protecting local computing devices from Internet-based threats:

1. Use a secure connection.
2. Establish and configure a firewall to control the flow of information between the computing device and the Internet.

3. Install and use anti-malware on the local computer.
4. Remove unnecessary software from the computer.
5. Disable any nonessential services running on the computer.
6. Disable unnecessary OS default features.
7. Secure the web browser.
8. Apply operating system and application software updates and patches.
9. Require strong passwords.

Using a Secure Connection

One of first steps in securing an Internet connection is to implement security options on the local router. If a particular connection does not include a router, you may want to consider installing one, as well-configured routers offer one of the best initial lines of defense. Routers and other network connectivity devices are covered in detail in Part III.

Some basic items to consider when configuring a router's security features include:

- Change the login username and default password. (The defaults are published in the user's setup instructions and, therefore, are known to everyone.)
- For wireless network connections, change the default SSID setting.
- Configure the wireless network with the highest level of encryption available—preferably WPA2-AES for maximum data confidentiality.
- Identify trusted wireless connections by conducting MAC address filtering.

Establishing and Using a Firewall

You should always establish and configure a firewall to control the flow of information between the computing device and the Internet. For standalone or local computers, this can be addressed through the local software firewall available with the operating system and/or through the protective router. Local firewall configurations are discussed later in this chapter.

Installing and Using Anti-Malware Software

Anti-malware software can be installed using an inclusive malware-prevention product or by combining different types of specific prevention programs, such as antivirus and antispyware products from different vendors. Different malware types and prevention methods are discussed in detail at the end of this chapter.

Removing Unnecessary Software

Keeping unused software products on a computer provides additional avenues of possible attack and exploitation. If you don't know what a suspected software program does, research it and get rid of it if it is not important to the operation of that system.

Disabling Nonessential Services

Some viruses are designed to exploit nonessential services in order to migrate from device to device. In particular, disengage any file-sharing or device-sharing services that are running, unless they are somehow required for proper operation of the system (this is almost never the case in nonconsumer usage).

Photo-sharing and music-sharing services should always be disabled, while file and printer should be disabled unless required to pass information from one device to another to perform work tasks. (This would pertain to a networked computer, which is discussed in detail in Part IV.)

Disabling Unnecessary OS Default Features

As mentioned earlier, Autorun is a highly exploitable feature of the Microsoft line of operating systems. When this feature is enabled, the OS will detect the presence of the removable media and execute its contents. If the SD card or CD/DVD contains a virus, it will automatically be executed and infect the host computer.

Securing the Web Browser

The web-browsing class of application software has attracted an increasing number of attacks. Initial browser configurations may not offer much in the way of security. As such, it is usually necessary to configure a new browser's security options to safeguard the system from attack through this portal. Steps for securing different web browsers are discussed later in this chapter.

Applying Updates and Patches

People and groups that produce malware are always busy designing the next exploit. For this reason, operating systems and applications must constantly be updated to counteract these efforts. This requires a planned methodology for obtaining and applying the latest upgrades and security patches for each software product on the system.

Requiring Strong Passwords

The main user authentication tool used with personal computing devices is the *username and password login*. In general, there are three types of user-related logons with which to contend:

- Logons to the local machine
- Logons to a specific software application
- Network logons

For a password to be effective, it must possess a certain amount of *complexity*. Its length, width, and depth must be designed to thwart the efforts of the previously mentioned password-cracking techniques. Refer back to Chapter 8 for an in-depth discussion of passwords.

Implementing Local Protection Tools

Five common tools are used at the local level to protect computing devices from exploitation through the Internet world:

- Local firewalls
- Host-based intrusion-detection systems
- Browser security options
- Antivirus/anti-malware tools
- Software updates and patches

Each topic is discussed in greater detail later in this book. The materials presented in this chapter are specific to local host security. However, each topic expands in scope as the local hosts are attached to larger networks and Internet systems.

Software-Based Local Firewalls

Computers connected directly to the Internet are vulnerable to attacks from outsiders. One way to protect standalone computers from outside attacks is to install a local firewall. A *firewall* is a device or a program that is placed between a local device and an outside network such as the Internet.

Local software-based firewalls can be installed on an individual computer to protect it from malicious activities introduced through the Internet connection. In some cases, the operating system provides a built-in firewall option that can be used to protect the local computer.

A Word About Firewalls

Local software firewalls are designed to provide protection from outside attacks by preventing unwanted connections from Internet devices. Software-based firewall services are designed to protect individual computers that are directly connected to the Internet through dial-up, LAN, or high-speed Internet connections.

The firewall inspects all traffic going to and coming from the outside connection and can be configured to control traffic flow between the Internet and the local device based on desirable properties, as illustrated in Figure 9.1. Firewalls are configured so they will only pass data to and from designated IP addresses and TCP/UDP ports.

Normally, firewall filters are configured around services recognized by the TCP and UDP networking protocols. These protocols use port numbers to identify specific processes such as HTTP or FTP and are used to refer incoming packets to a software application that will process them. Many of the port numbers are standardized and are referred to as *well-known ports.* Similarly, their associated applications are called *well-known services.*

Table 9.1 lists several well-known port numbers and their associated services. The Internet Assigned Numbers Authority (IANA) has assigned standard port numbers ranging from 0 to 1023 to specific services. Port numbers from 1024 through 49151 are called *registered ports* and are used in vendor applications. Ports 49152 through 65535 are *dynamic,* or ephemeral, ports and are used by computer applications to communicate with other applications.

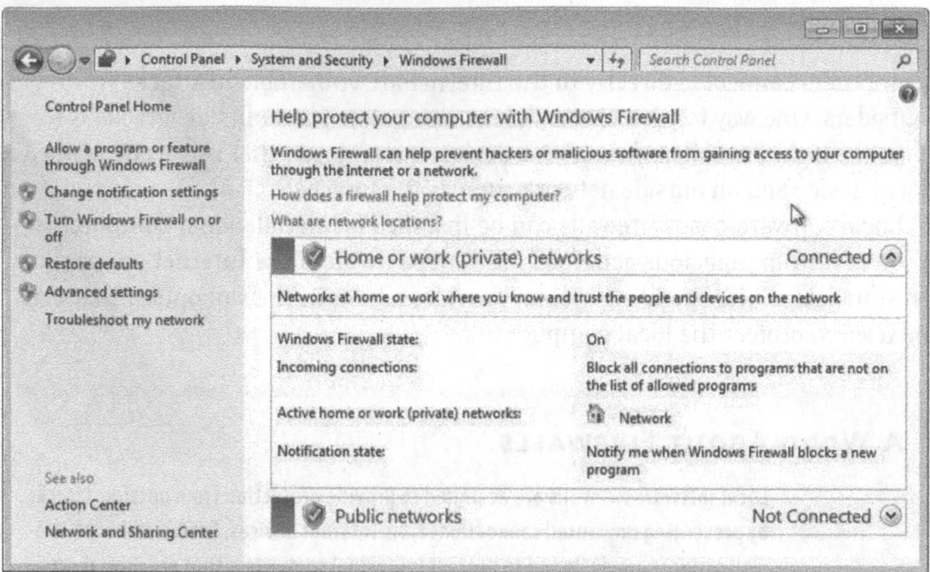

FIGURE 9.1 Firewall Operation

TABLE 9.1 Typical I/O Ports

Service	Well-Known Port Number
FTP	20, 21
Telnet	23
SMTP Mail	25
HTTP (WWW)	80
POP3 (Mail)	110
News	144
HTTPS	443
PPTP	1723
IRC	6667

When the firewall examines the incoming packet, it can read the source and destination IP addresses of the packet and any TCP/UDP port numbers, as shown in Figure 9.2. It will use the IP address and port information in the packet headers to determine if an incoming packet should be routed into the internal network.

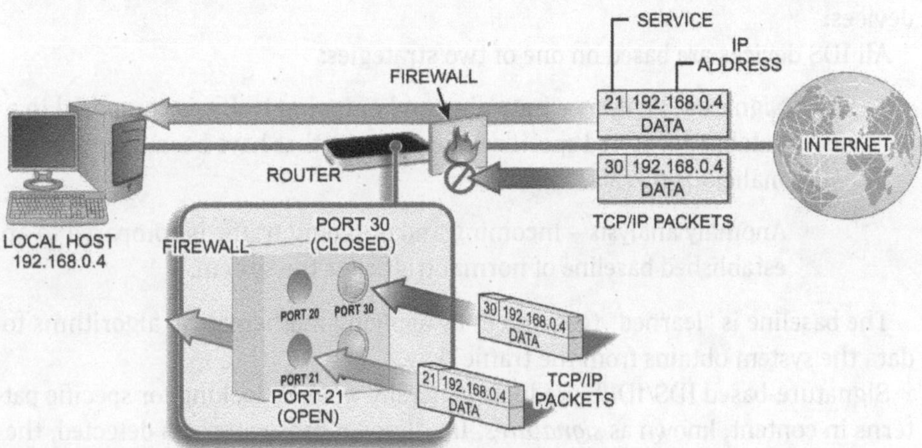

FIGURE 9.2 Firewall Functionality

If you have configured the firewall with the IP address of an internal computer that provides FTP services and opened ports 20 and 21, the firewall will recognize the IP address and port numbers in the incoming header as valid and route the packet to that computer. However, all other incoming requests will still be blocked.

Using Local Intrusion-Detection Tools

As with physical security efforts, preventing unauthorized access is the first line of security at the local computing and control-device level. However, it is just as important at this level to be able to detect the occurrence of an intrusion and notify the proper authorities of its nature.

Computer-based Intrusion Detection Systems (IDS) can be implemented in two ways: as network-based IDS (NIDS) or as host-based IDS (HIDS). In both cases, the system is designed primarily to monitor the system (local computer or network environment), log key events and policy violations, and report them as directed.

Intrusion Prevention Systems (IPS), also referred to as Intrusion Detection and Prevention Systems (IDPS), provide an additional level of protection aimed at preventing the detected threat from succeeding.

As their definitions imply, HIDS and NIDS operate in different areas of the computer/network environment. For now, we will hold off on the discussion of NIDS. Instead, we will focus on HIDS tools that run on individual hosts or devices.

All IDS devices are based on one of two strategies:

- Signature analysis – Incoming and outgoing traffic is compared to a database of stored specific code patterns that have been identified as malicious threats.
- Anomaly analysis – Incoming and outgoing traffic is compared to an established baseline of normal traffic for the system.

The baseline is "learned" (generated) by applying mathematical algorithms to data the system obtains from the traffic flow.

Signature-based IDS/IDPS products generally work by looking for specific patterns in content, known as *signatures*. If a "known bad" pattern is detected, the appropriate actions can be taken to protect the host. However, because of the dynamic nature of programming languages, scripting in web pages can be used to evade such protective systems.

The signature-based IDS database is typically generated and distributed by its manufacturer in response to observed malicious signatures. Therefore, the malicious code is already in existence before a signature can be identified and added to the database to be acted on. The time delay between the release of the malicious code and the issuing of its signature presents its own security issue.

Anomaly-based IDS/IDPS systems apply statistical analysis techniques to the data stream to determine whether it is "normal" or "anomalous" at any given time. There are two common methods of implementing statistical anomaly detection:

- Profile-based anomaly-detection systems
- Threshold-based anomaly-detection systems

Profile-Based Anomaly-Detection Systems

These systems use mathematical algorithms to monitor normal data traffic and develop a "profile" of rules that describe what normal traffic for that system looks like. The profile developed reflects evaluations of users' past behaviors and is configured to signal when deviations from these behaviors reach a certain level (or *threshold*).

- Rule-based anomaly detection – This detection method analyzes audit records to generate rules based on past usage patterns to generate the "rules" set. The system then monitors the traffic looking for patterns that don't match the rules.
- Penetration detection – These systems generate rules based on known penetration occurrences, system weaknesses, or behavior patterns. For this reason, they are normally specific to a given host system. They also typically include rules generated by security experts that are current with security activities.

Threshold-Based Anomaly-Detection Systems

These IDS systems are designed to track the number of occurrences of specific events over time and generate an intrusion warning if the number of events exceeds a predetermined number.

Most commonly available IDS systems are designed for use on local host systems. However, there is an increasing effort in producing network-based IDS systems to provide a more effective intrusion-detection-and-prevention arsenal. Network-Based Distributed Intrusion Systems are described in Part IV.

IDS Notifications

In all IDS types, the administrator is notified when a potential attack is detected.

Configuring Browser Security Options

Web browsers are designed to be highly flexible to offer users as many usage options as possible. They are also designed to appeal to users who by and large are nontechnical. Coupled together with the abundance of people connected to the Internet who use their access to the web for less-than-honorable purposes and you have a huge security window into your local system.

For example, Figure 9.3 shows a sample of the Internet options available with the Windows Internet Explorer (IE) web browser. As you can see, some of these options are personal preferences, such as colors, fonts, and toolbars. However, there are a variety of security-related activities that involve the browser and searching the Internet.

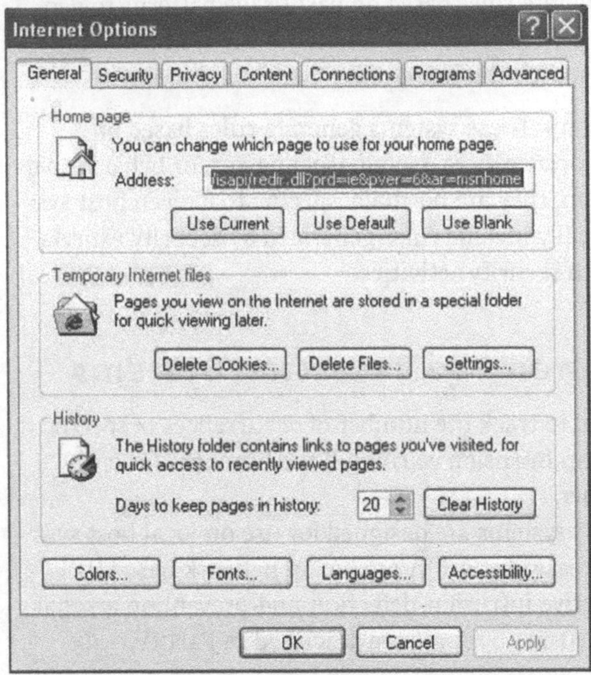

FIGURE 9.3 Internet Options

As the figure illustrates, web browsers routinely offer a variety of user-selectable security options that can be established to compensate for the added vulnerability Internet browsing and searching brings to the system. These options include:

- Configuring security levels
- Configuring scripting
- Configuring proxies
- Controlling cookies

Although each browser is designed differently, they all tend to provide similar web security options. The user may have to search for specific tools to configure their browser for secure operation, but the same basic configuration techniques apply to all browsers.

Configuring Security Levels

Because the browser is the portal to the wider outside world, its security settings are very important. In addition, other Internet tools on the machine may rely on components of the browser to perform their functions. These applications may bring with them enhancements that create additional vulnerabilities. These features should be evaluated and turned off if they do not contribute to the operation of the system.

As with other applications, browsers come with a preconfigured set of security levels. In Microsoft IE, these functions are located on the Security tab depicted in Figure 9.4.

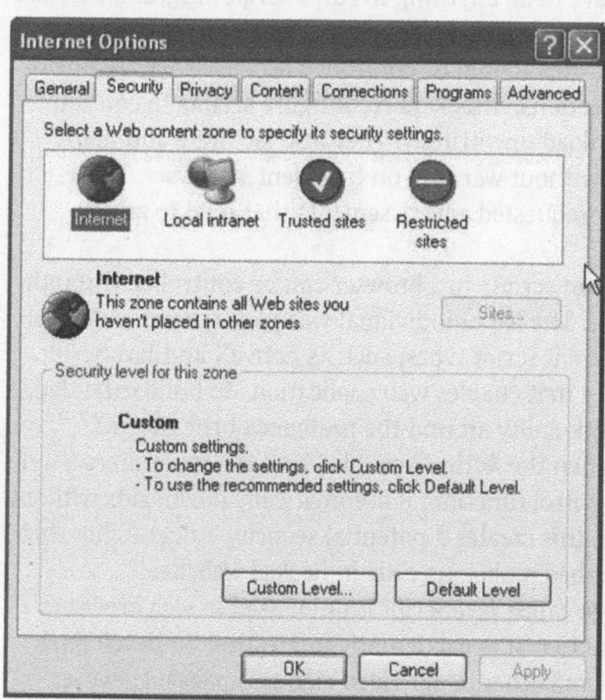

FIGURE 9.4 IE Security Tab

In this browser example, Internet sites may be categorized under different Internet security *zones* that enable sites listed in each zone to be governed by security restrictions that apply to that group (Internet, Local Intranet, Trusted Sites, and Restricted Sites).

This allows different websites to be accessed with different security restrictions. Trusted Sites could be established to work with less security overhead, while Restricted Sites can be assigned heightened security settings. The Internet zone option is the default zone for all sites not assigned to one of the other zone options.

The best option for configuring security levels is to set them as high as possible without restricting the browser to the point where sites do not load or function correctly.

Configuring Script Support

Scripts are executable applications that provide interactive content on websites. They are also capable of retrieving information in response to user selections. However, the user may not have to do anything to run a script program; they are simply embedded in the website being accessed.

Scripts encountered on websites should be controlled because they are one of the main sources of virus infections. Attackers reconfigure scripts to contain viruses that clients may download unwittingly. They also facilitate automatic pop-up windows that appear without warning on the client's browser. These windows normally contain unrequested advertisements that tend to annoy users.

The capability to load and run scripts in a browser can be controlled through the browser's Security feature. The list of individual web page components that you can control includes different script types, such as ActiveX and JavaScript.

ActiveX is a Microsoft utility that enables web applications to build extended, interactive features, and functionality around the presence of the ActiveX framework in the browser. When the ActiveX-enabled browser encounters a web page calling for an ActiveX control function, it automatically downloads without involving the user. Of course, this creates a potential security vulnerability that can be used by crackers to embed malicious code in hacked websites.

A similar scripting language called JavaScript is often used in web browsers to make websites more interactive. It is particularly interesting for developing interactive content in games and other audio/video-rich web pages. However, it is also widely used to transmit information about remote activities, such as browsing and reading habits for use in advertisement tracking and analysis. It does this without reloading the page where the information was gathered and without notifying the reader. This again creates a potential portal for malicious (or at least unwanted) activities.

A Word About VBScript

VBScript is another scripting language that is unique to Microsoft Windows Internet Explorer. VBScript is similar to JavaScript, but it is not as widely used in websites because of limited compatibility with other browsers.

Another area of concern in the interaction between websites and browsers is the use of plug-ins to add new features to existing software applications, such as search engines and antivirus functions. These script controls are similar to ActiveX controls but cannot be executed outside of a web browser. Adobe Flash and QuickTime Player are the most recognized examples of web browser plug-ins.

Most browsers support various plug-ins by default and rely on them for some portion of their operation. Along with the automatic nature of these components comes an increasing vulnerability both in terms of design deficiencies and as potential hacking targets. Historically, ActiveX controls, Adobe's PDF Reader and Flash products, as well as Apple's QuickTime product have represented the highest number of documented vulnerabilities among script products.

As with the other security objects, the browser can typically be configured to Enable, Disable, or present a user prompt whenever it encounters these scripted items on a page. As a rule of thumb, all add-ons (including Java, JavaScript, Flash, and ActiveX) should be disabled on websites unless you know that they can be trusted.

Controlling Cookies

Cookies are small files that web servers send to web browsers when their pages are accessed. The legitimate use of these files is to enable the server to automatically recognize the client browser any time it connects to the server. The basic HTTP page transfer process is described in Figure 9.5.

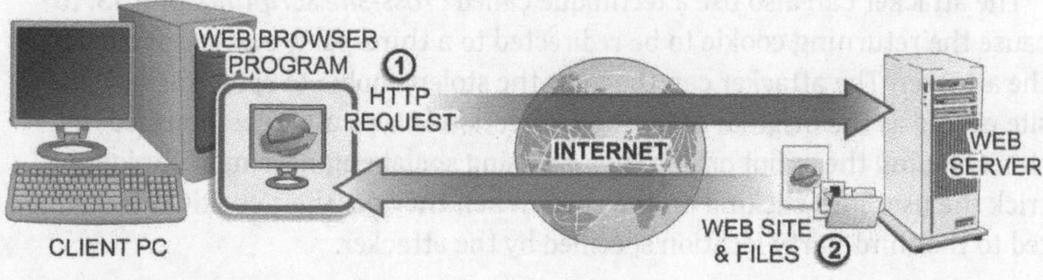

FIGURE 9.5 HTTP Transfer Operations

Web page transfers are initiated on the client side through the local web browser. The browser sends an HTTP request to the designated web server, which in turn sends back the requested page along with an HTTP response message. One piece of information in the message may be a request for the browser to set (accept and store) cookies, so that a more efficient, automated page transfer process can be carried out.

The cookie may also contain several pieces of configuration information known as *cookie attributes*. One key security-related attribute is the setting for when the cookie expires. There are basically two varieties of cookies to be concerned with: session cookies and persistent cookies. *Session cookies* are cleared when the browser is closed, and *persistent cookies* will remain on the computer until the specified expiration date is reached. Persistent cookies pose a higher risk than session cookies because they remain on the client computer for a longer period of time.

Cookies were originally developed to keep users logged into online shopping environments while they moved from page to page and placed items in online shopping baskets. However, the use of cookies has expanded to include a lot more than just shopping baskets. They may be designed to gather and track any information that a website is designed to place in it—for example, they may track information about the sites the user visited or credentials used to access the site. Cookies designed to perform these types of functions are called *tracking cookies*.

This is the type of information that makes cookies attractive to crackers. If a website uses cookies for authentication, then an attacker may be able to acquire unauthorized access to that site by obtaining the cookie. This is referred to as *cookie theft*.

The attacker only needs to employ a packet sniffer utility to monitor the network traffic and capture the cookie in order to gain access to their credentials (username, passwords, network address, and so on). With this information in hand, the attacker has the ability to pretend to be the original user when they access other sites.

The attacker can also use a technique called *cross-site scripting*, or XSS, to cause the returning cookie to be redirected to a third-party server operated by the attacker. The attacker can then use the stolen cookie to spoof the original site posing as the original user. The redirection is typically accomplished by simply hiding the script on the site and using social engineering techniques to trick the user into clicking on the code. When they do, their cookie is transmitted to the third-party location specified by the attacker.

In addition, the attacker may simply alter the contents of a stolen cookie to perform an attack on the original web server. For example, if the cookie was the product of an ecommerce sales site, it might include pricing information about products in a shopping cart. The attacker could alter that information and send it back to the original server, causing it to charge the customer a lower price for the item. This type of attack, as depicted in Figure 9.6, is a form of a man-in-the-middle (MITM) attack referred to as *cookie poisoning*.

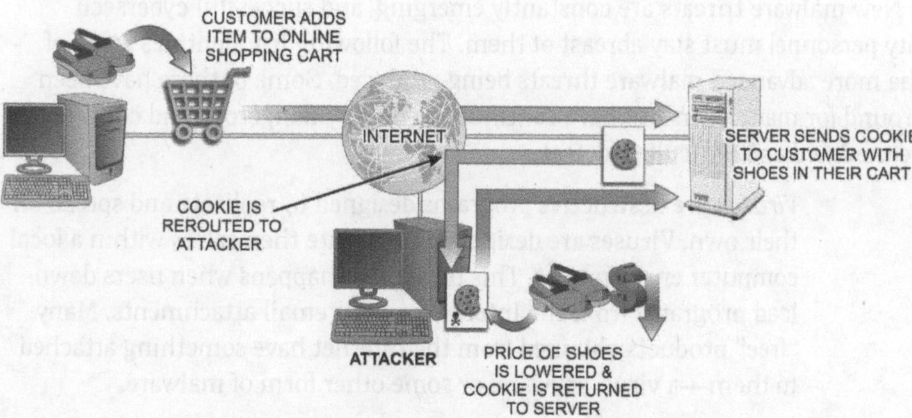

FIGURE 9.6 Cookie Poisoning

Virtually all browsers support cookies by default. Some offer the user the option to completely enable or completely disable cookies, while others provide a more robust cookie manager that enables the user to view and select individual cookies to remove from the system.

For security purposes, the best recommendation for handling cookies is to disable the option to Always Set Cookies. In addition, use transmission encryption to prevent third parties from being able to read the cookies if they are intercepted along the way. This is particularly important when using Wi-Fi communications. If the wireless link is not encrypted, attackers can easily intercept and then read the data including the cookies sent.

The use of secure socket layer (SSL) links provides data encryption security for the transmitted data (including the cookies) and prevents unauthorized access to the data as it moves across the communication link. SSL links are always identified as `HTTPS://` sites instead of simply `HTTP://`.

Defending Against Malicious Software

Increased connectivity through networks and the Internet have made personal computers vulnerable to an array of different types of malware and grayware. *Malware* is the term used to describe programs designed to be malicious in nature. The term *grayware* describes programs that have behavior that is undisclosed or that is undesirable.

New malware threats are constantly emerging, and successful cybersecurity personnel must stay abreast of them. The following list identifies some of the more advanced malware threats being produced. Some of these have been around for many years but have continued to be very dangerous and continue to be modified and difficult to detect:

- *Viruses* are destructive programs designed to replicate and spread on their own. Viruses are designed to replicate themselves within a local computer environment. This most often happens when users download programs from the Internet or open email attachments. Many "free" products obtained from the Internet have something attached to them—a virus, spyware, or some other form of malware.

- *Worms* (sometimes referred to as network viruses) are circulated through a network connection. Unlike a virus, worms do not need a host program in order to infect your computer. Worms search for vulnerabilities to exploit in an application. Once the worm has taken advantage of the vulnerability, it seeks to replicate to another computer on the network. While initially intended to slow down network environments, worms often leave payloads on systems to cause further malicious activity.

- *Trojans* appear to be a legitimate program that might be found on any system. They are made to appear to be actual applications so that users will be tricked into using them. Although they function and work properly, they have malicious code that initiates when the application is launched.

- *Rootkits* are a type of software designed to gain administrative control of a computer system while remaining undetected. Normally, the purpose is to enable malicious operations to occur on a target computer without the knowledge of its users or system administrators. Rootkits can occur in hardware or software by going after the BIOS, boot loader, OS kernel, and sometimes applications or libraries.

Rootkits are designed to operate at the root level of the operating system and appear as a benign entity at that level. After the rootkit has been installed in a system, it will take measures to hide itself from detection. They modify the behavior of the operating system's core components by altering drivers or kernel modules. These programs have the ability to steal PINs, account passwords, credit cards, and other sensitive information. They can infect nearly any operating system type.

- *Ransomware* is software designed to keep the user from their data and hold it hostage for payment. Spam email is the most common delivery vehicle for spreading the malware. It is then activated by the user clicking an attachment or a link in the email message. It then disables essential system services or even locks the computer so that the user cannot gain access to it.

  Hackers can encrypt personal files on the computer keeping the user from gaining access to their data. The hacker will normally prompt the user to enter a code that can be attained only after wiring payment through cryptic means such as Bitcoin cryptocurrency. They will also typically try to get the user to purchase a legal decryption or removal tool. The author (hacker) is the only person(s) who knows the required private decryption key.

- *Spyware* programs are generally introduced to the system through Internet downloads that appear to be useful programs. Unlike viruses and Trojans, spyware typically does not self-replicate. Once spyware is installed on a system, it monitors the system's operation and collects information such as usernames, passwords, credit card numbers, and other PII.
- *Adware* programs introduce unwanted, unsolicited advertising displays to web browsers. They can also be designed to gather user selection information from the browser, constructing a more personalized advertising scheme. Adware is typically introduced to the system through downloads such as free software (freeware).
- *Logic bombs* are a type of malware typically used to delete data. A logic bomb is computer code that, much like other malware, is attached to a legitimate program. The code sits idle until a specific logical event is concluded. This includes a number of days passing, a number of programs being opened, or executing a program in a

specific manner. Logic bombs are hard to detect because they are often included in large programs with thousands of lines of code.

- *Zombies* are infected computers that can be placed under the remote control of a malicious user. Zombies can be used to create Denial of Service (DoS) attacks that flood targeted networks to slow down and sometimes stop servers completely. Computers are often infected and become zombies by way of viruses, worms, and Trojans.
- *Botnets* are a large collection of zombies, or bots, controlled by a bot herder. This type of network can consist of literally millions of unsuspecting computers. Botnets can be used to send out spam (usually through email lists) originating from unsuspecting users' computers. It is estimated that 50 to 80 percent of spam worldwide is created by zombie computers.

It is common to install a number of different defensive products to protect PCs and their data from unauthorized access and malicious interference. Most products these days include protections against multiple fronts. The products most widely used for these purposes include:

- Antivirus programs
- Antispyware programs
- Spam blockers
- Pop-up blockers

Using Antivirus Programs

Every computer should have some means of protecting itself against computer viruses. The most common means of virus protection involve installing a virus-scanning (antivirus) program that checks disks and files before using them in the computer. Several companies offer third-party virus-protection software that can be configured to operate in various ways.

If the computer is a standalone unit, it might be nonproductive to have the antivirus software run each time the system is booted up. It would be much more practical to have the program check any removable media attached to the system, only because this is the only possible non-network entryway into the computer.

All computers with connections to the Internet should be protected by an antivirus solution before they are ever attached to the Internet. In these cases, setting the software to run at each bootup is more desirable. In addition, most antivirus software includes utilities to check email and files downloaded to the computer through network or Internet connections.

As indicated earlier, when an antivirus application is installed on the system, it can be configured to provide different levels of virus protection. You will need to configure when and under what circumstances you want the virus software to run.

Using Antispyware

As shown in Figure 9.7, there are basically two types of antispyware products available: those that find and remove spyware after it has been installed and those that block spyware when it is trying to install itself. Both of these methods stand a better chance of keeping computers free from spyware when they are combined with user information about how to avoid spyware.

FIGURE 9.7 Antispyware Product Types

The detect-and-remove method is by far the simpler type of antispyware product to write. Therefore, there are several commercially available products that use this method. Like antivirus software packages, this type of antispyware product relies on databases of existing definitions to recognize spyware threats. These databases must be updated frequently to recognize new spyware versions that have been identified.

The real-time-prevention type of antispyware product does not rely on historical data to identify spyware. Instead, it monitors certain configuration parameters and notifies the user when suspicious installation activity occurs. The user then has the option to allow or block the installation effort. Some antispyware products incorporate both methods of dealing with spyware.

In addition to installing antispyware applications, users can fight spyware in a number of other ways:

- Install a web browser other than Internet Explorer (for example, Chrome or Firefox).
- Download the newest browser version that offers better security features.
- Work with an ISP that uses their firewalls and proxies to block sites that are known to distribute spyware.
- Download only software from reputable sites to prevent spyware that comes attached to other programs.

Hardening Operating Systems

As noted earlier, the second level of hardening local computer systems against attacks is to secure their operating systems. This involves updating vulnerable code segments of the OS as they become known. OS hardening occurs through the application of new programming in the form of:

- Service packs
- Patches
- Updates

Service Packs

After an operating system has been in the field for some time, vendors may combine several product improvements and distribute a numbered *service pack* for the specific operating system being upgraded. Critical files should always be backed up in the event that the service pack or OS fails to work after installing the service pack.

Patches

Patches are general improvements to a given operating system that have been released for distribution. Many patches and updates are purely cosmetic and convenient add-on features, while others are critical security upgrades designed to respond to a particular virus, discovered threat, or weakness found in the operating system.

Updates

An *update* is a service pack or patch that improves the reliability, security, or attractiveness of an operating system. The most reliable source of operating system updates is the OS manufacturer. These organizations are always seeking ways to improve their products. Some updates may make the OS more convenient but may not necessarily make it more secure. Therefore, they should be tested before implementing. Consider backing up critical files in the event that the patch or OS fails to work after installation.

Overseeing Application Software Security

Software application packages operate as extensions of the operating system. Depending on the type of operating system being used, an application program may directly control some system resources, such as printers and network interfaces, while the operating system lends fundamental support in the background. In more advanced systems, the operating system supplies common input, output, and disk management functions for all applications in the system.

Some applications include built-in security tools that control access to the application beyond the levels presented by the operating system. However, many applications are written with very little concern for security issues. The focus of such programs is functionality and sharing, leaving security issues to the operating system and security utilities.

Software Exploitation

The term *software exploitation* is used to describe cyber attacks designed to take advantage of vulnerabilities or weaknesses in software products—operating systems and applications. These vulnerabilities may be the result of software that is created with little or no thought for security issues, or they may be the product of software that has been inadequately tested before being released for use.

There are two very conflicting objectives in the computer software industry:

- Make the product as open and easy to use as possible so that otherwise nontechnical users will be able to work with it.
- Make the application bullet proof so that nothing bad can happen to it—ever.

Software programmers are asked to meet both of these objectives in the same product.

In some cases, the programmers may be trying to create a truly open product without concerns about how it might be exploited by malicious people. In other cases, they may not be experienced enough to envision how their product might be exploited. With the worldwide pool of programmers continuously growing, there are many individuals with a significant knowledge base of how to test, manipulate, and modify programming. This includes black hat hackers.

A Word About Black Hat Hackers

A *black hat hacker* is an individual who possesses extensive programming skills and uses them to breach or bypass network security structures for malicious or criminal purposes. People in this category of hacker are also known as *crackers* or *dark-side hackers*.

There are also *white hat* and *gray hat hackers* who also seek to exploit Internet security vulnerabilities and weaknesses, but not for malicious reasons (for example, to perform security system analysis checks).

Modern operating system and application programming is very complex. When programmers initially develop a product, they may make coding mistakes or create portions of a product that do not work well with elements created by other programmers in the development team. Attackers will often use software vulnerabilities to insert and hide malicious code that can be used to disrupt services or operations.

In particular, the attacker may alter the existing code to create a condition in the computer's memory known as a *buffer overflow,* which results in erratic behavior, memory access errors, and/or system crashes. The system is effectively disabled to the point where the user cannot use it. This kind of attack is a type of Denial of Service (DOS) attack.

Applying Software Updates and Patches

From the previous section, you can see that due to the nature of product development and the pressures on software producers to bring new products to the market, new software releases never seem to be complete or perfect. As security issues are revealed with software products, their producers are forced to issue security patches for their product that correct the weakness.

Security patches are updates issued for the specific purpose of correcting an observed weakness to prevent exploitation of the vulnerability. Microsoft issues security patches for its products once a month. Other software developers use dedicated security teams to develop and issue security patches as soon as possible after a vulnerability has been discovered.

For security and stability reasons, you should always patch operating systems on computing devices that are connected to the Internet. However, this is not the case with all PCs. Stable PC systems that are not connected to the Internet should not be patched unless doing so resolves some sort of existing problem.

Hands-On Exercises

Objectives

- Manage the local firewall configuration.
- Explore Windows Firewall with Advanced Security.
- Recognize the need for outbound filtering.
- Create a port filtering rule.
- Create an ICMP filtering rule.

Resources

- PC-compatible desktop/tower computer system
- Windows 10 Professional installed
- User account with Administrative access
- Internet access from a network connection

Discussion

Computers connected directly to the Internet are vulnerable to attacks from outsiders. One way to protect standalone computers from outside attacks is to install a local firewall.

Local software-based firewalls can be installed on an individual computer to protect it from malicious activities introduced through their Internet connection.

In some cases, the operating system provides a built-in firewall option that can be used to protect the local computer.

In this lab, you will explore the options associated with Windows Firewall to apply the local (software) firewall. You will also recognize the need for inbound and outbound filtering and testing various security options. In some scenarios, you may want to download a software-based firewall, but Microsoft includes Windows Firewall, as well as Windows Firewall with Advanced Security, with their operating system.

Procedures

Accessing Windows Firewall Basic Settings

To access the basic Windows Firewall settings, follow these steps:

1. Power on the computer, and choose Windows 10 Professional if given a choice.
2. Log on to your administrative account.
3. Click on the embedded search bar on your taskbar, type **Control Panel**, and then click on Control Panel in the menu presented.
4. If necessary, switch to viewing the Control Panel with the View by: Small Icons, locate and click Windows Firewall. Figure 9.8 shows the basic Windows Firewall settings.

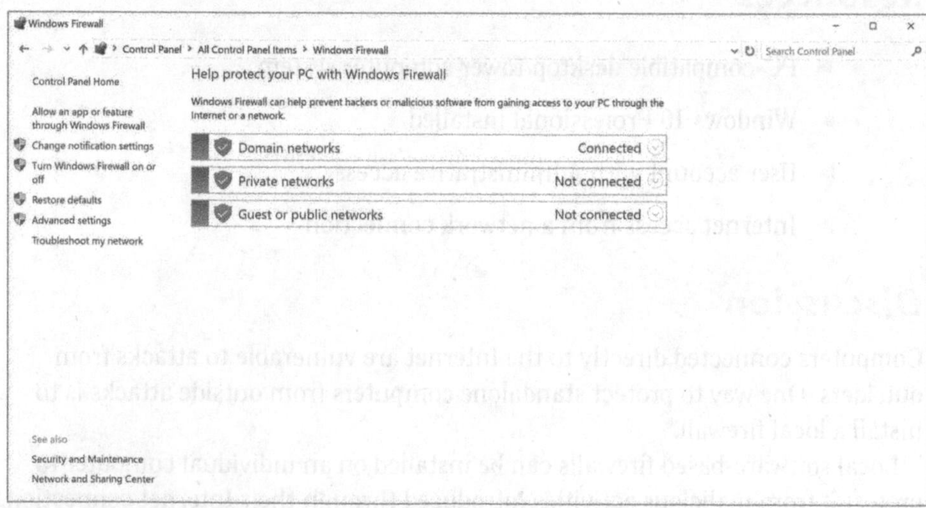

FIGURE 9.8 Basic Windows Firewall Settings

In this window, you can see the current firewall states for each type of network.

5. Expand each network type by clicking the down arrows located in the top-right of each network. Examine the current states and the rules associated with each. List the three types of networks in Table 9.2.
6. In the left pane, click Turn Windows Firewall On Or Off, located next to a Windows Defender Shield indicating Administrative access is required.

In the left pane, Turn Windows Firewall On Or Off and Change Notifications lead to the same window. Figure 9.9 depicts the Customize Settings window.

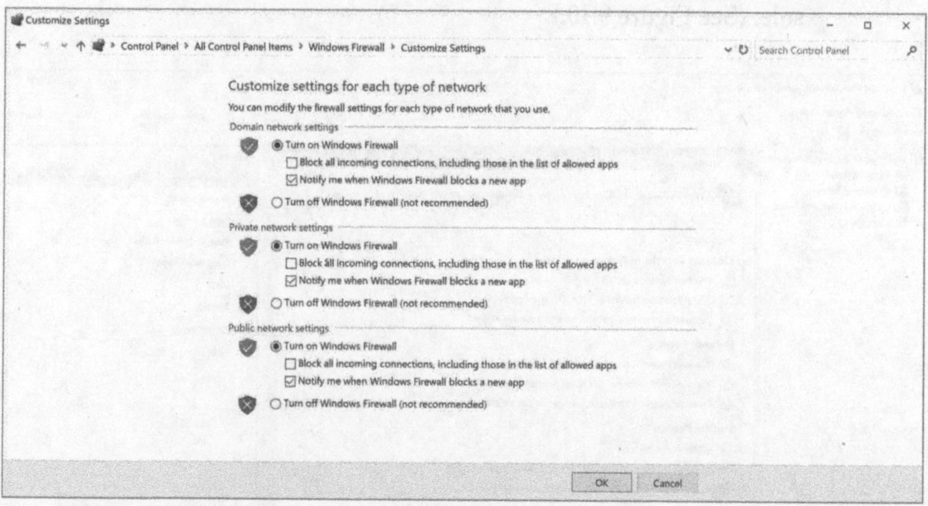

FIGURE 9.9 Customize Settings Window for Windows Firewall

This window shows the basic options associated with each type of network. You turn on or off the firewall. If the firewall is turned on (recommended), you can decide if you want to block all incoming traffic and if you want to be notified if and when a program is blocked.

The firewall inspects all traffic going to and coming from the outside connection and can be configured to control traffic flow between the Internet and the local device based on desirable properties. Firewalls are configured so they will only pass data to and from designated IP addresses and TCP/UDP ports.

There are very few reasons to turn off Windows Firewall (not recommended).

7. If any network type has Turn Off Windows Firewall selected, click Turn On Windows Firewall. Click OK to exit the Windows Firewall Customize Settings.

Examining Windows Firewall with Advanced Security

To examine Windows Firewall with Advanced Security, follow these steps:

1. In the left pane, click Advanced Settings, next to a Windows Defender Shield, to launch the Windows Firewall with Advanced Security console. (See Figure 9.10.)

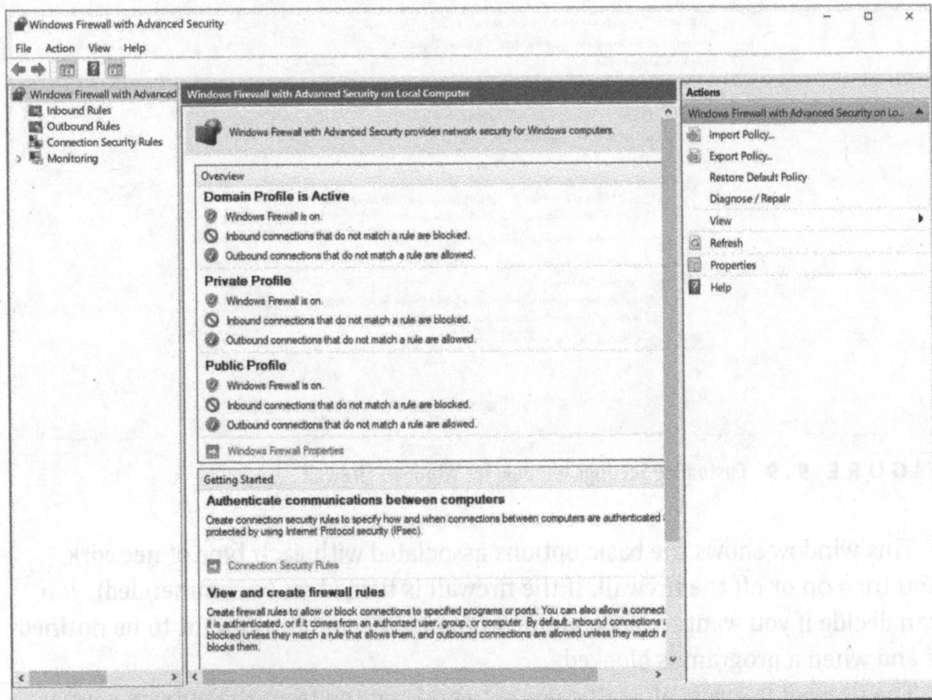

FIGURE 9.10 Windows Firewall with Advanced Security Console

This opening view in the console shows an overview of the current state of the firewall, along with a basic Getting Started tutorial that includes:

- ▶ Authenticate communications between computers
- ▶ View and create firewall rules
- ▶ View current firewall and IPsec policy and activity

2. At the bottom of the Overview section, select Windows Firewall Properties to launch the Windows Firewall with Advanced Security on Local Computer Properties window, as shown in Figure 9.11.

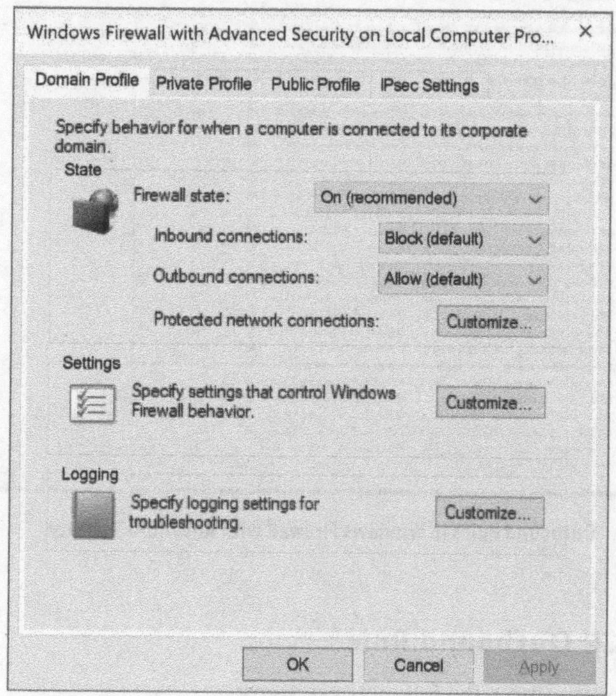

FIGURE 9.11 Windows Firewall with Advanced Security on Local Computer Properties

This window gives you another option to control settings for each of the three types of networks. You can also customize the various settings and set rules for logging.

3. Explore the tabs without changing the configurations and then click Cancel to close out this window.

4. In the left pane, select Outbound Rules. The central and right panes will be similar to Figure 9.12.

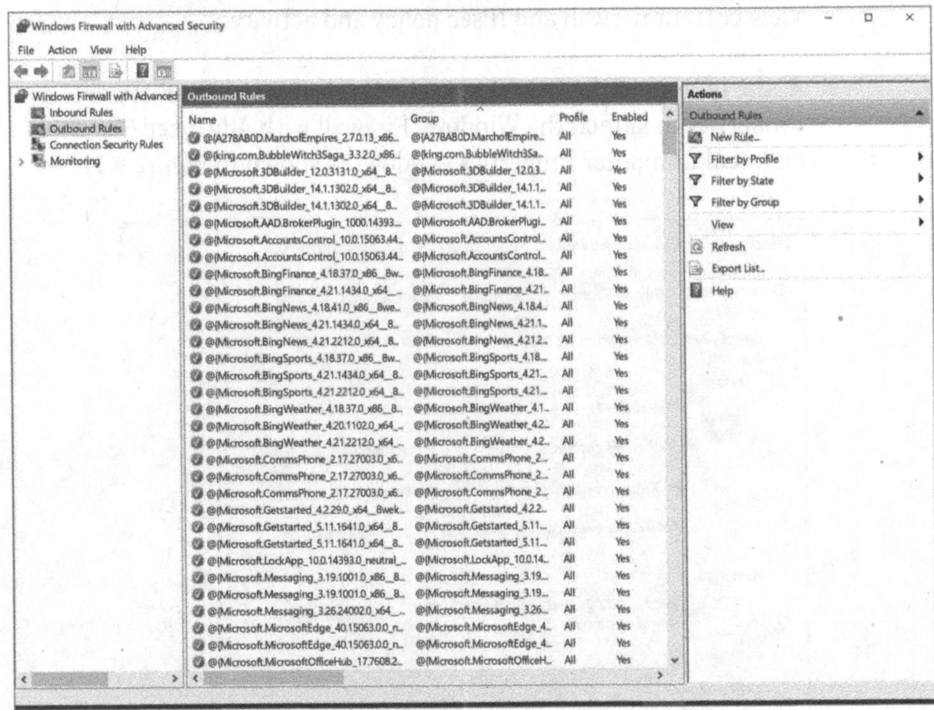

FIGURE 9.12 Outbound Rules in Windows Firewall with Advanced Security

Creating a TCP Outbound Rule

To create a TCP outbound rule, follow these steps:

1. In the right pane, click New Rule. The New Outbound Rule Wizard will appear, as shown in Figure 9.13.

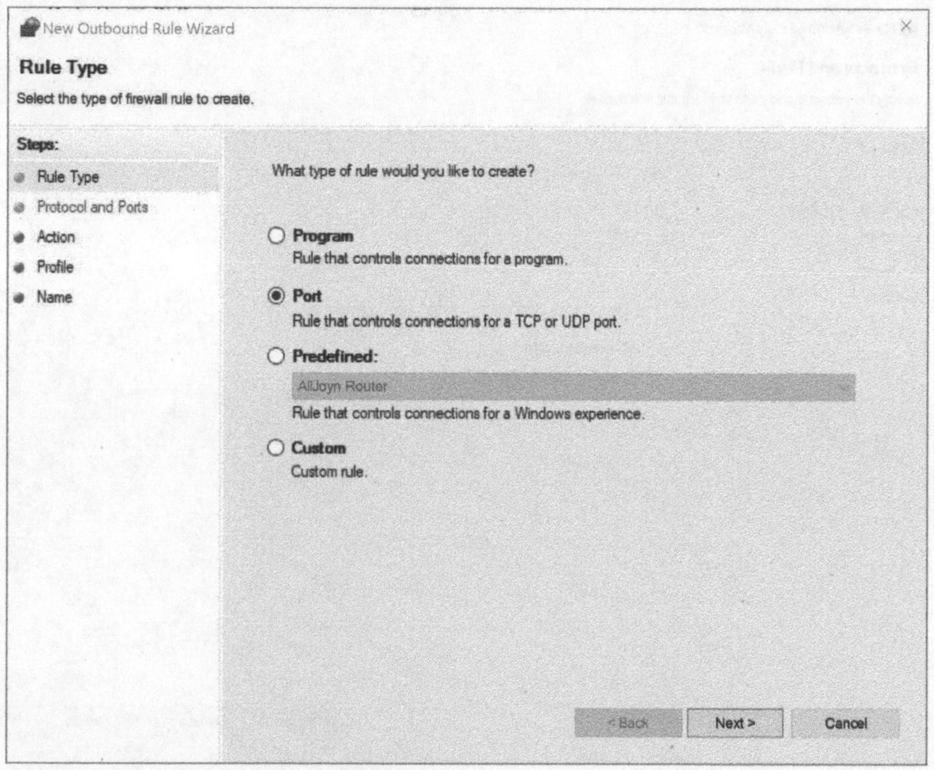

FIGURE 9.13 New Outbound Rule Wizard

On any page within the New Outbound Rule Wizard, you can learn more about the options by selecting the Learn More About (Subject) link located near the bottom of each page.

2. Select the Port radio button, and then click on the Next button to continue the steps in the left pane, as shown in Figure 9.14.
3. In the Protocol and Ports window that appears, make sure the TCP radio button is selected along with the Specific Remote Ports radio button. Input 135 into the text field.

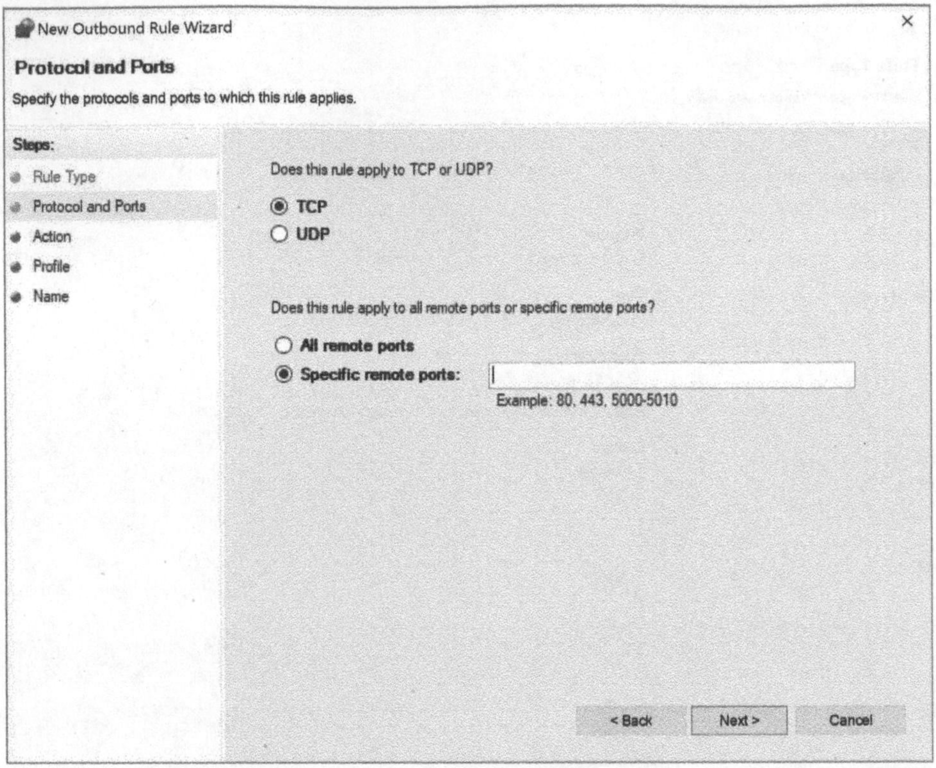

FIGURE 9.14 New Outbound Rule Wizard Steps: Protocol and Ports

TCP port 135 is one of many ports through which malware often attempts to initiate network requests via `NetBIOS/SMB/RPC`. Creating an outbound block rule will prevent your system from connecting to malicious external hosts.

4. Click the Next button to proceed to the Steps: Action page.
5. Examine the options, but leave the Block The Connection radio button selected. Click the Next button to continue onto the Steps: Profile page.

6. Here you will decide the type of network to which your rule should apply. Leave all three check boxes marked to apply the rule to all networks. Click Next to continue to the Steps: Name page.

7. On the Name page, enter **My First TCP Rule** into the Name text box. Type **This is my first TCP outbound rule** into the Description (Optional): field box. Figure 9.15 shows the Steps: Name page with the information entered.

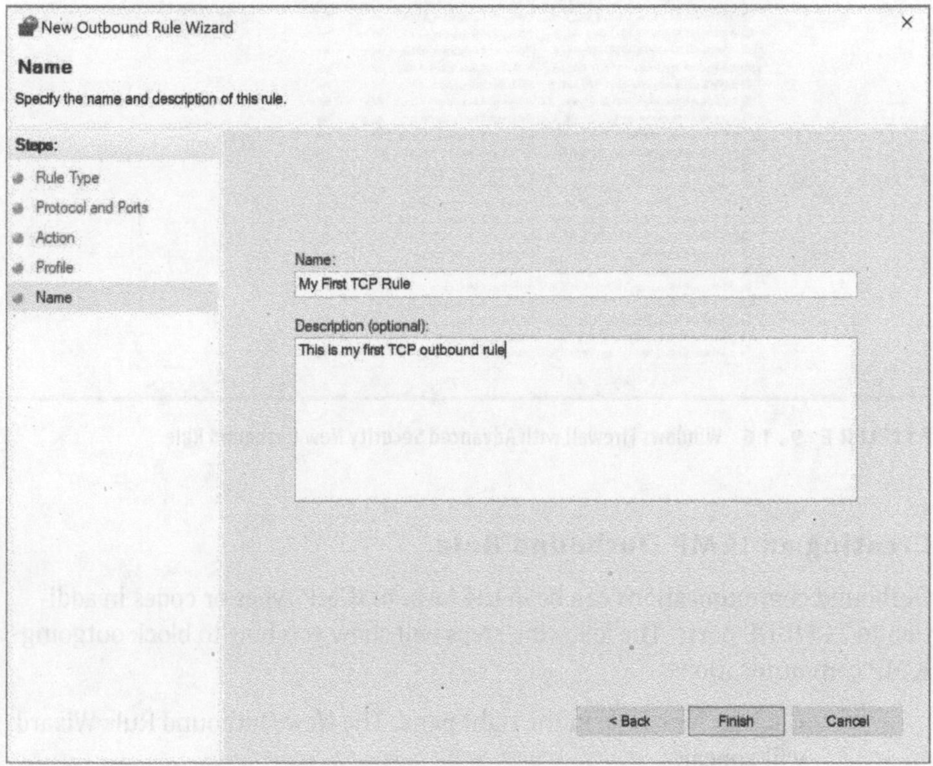

FIGURE 9.15 New Outbound Rule Wizard Steps: Name Page

8. Click Finish. You should see your rule in the Rules list in the center pane, as shown in Figure 9.16.

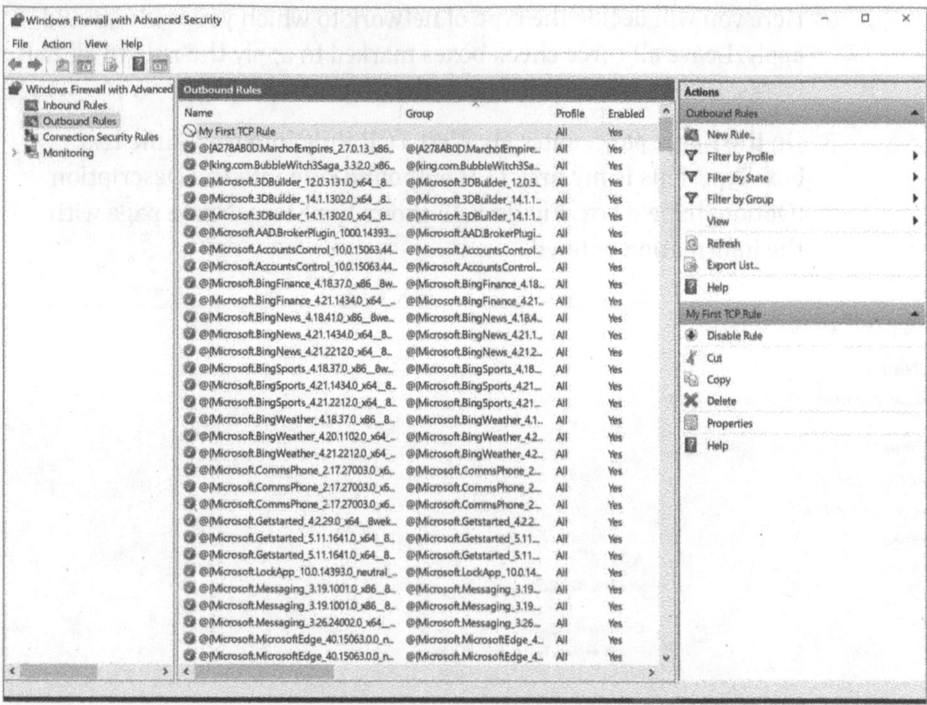

FIGURE 9.16 Windows Firewall with Advanced Security New Outbound Rule

Creating an ICMP Outbound Rule

Outbound communications can be in the form of ICMP types or codes in addition to TCP/UDP ports. The following steps will show you how to block outgoing ICMP communications.

1. Click on New Rule in the right pane. The New Outbound Rule Wizard will appear.

2. Select the Custom radio button. Notice that the Steps located in the left pane have grown in numbers. Click Next to continue.

3. Leave the All Programs radio button selected, as shown in Figure 9.17.

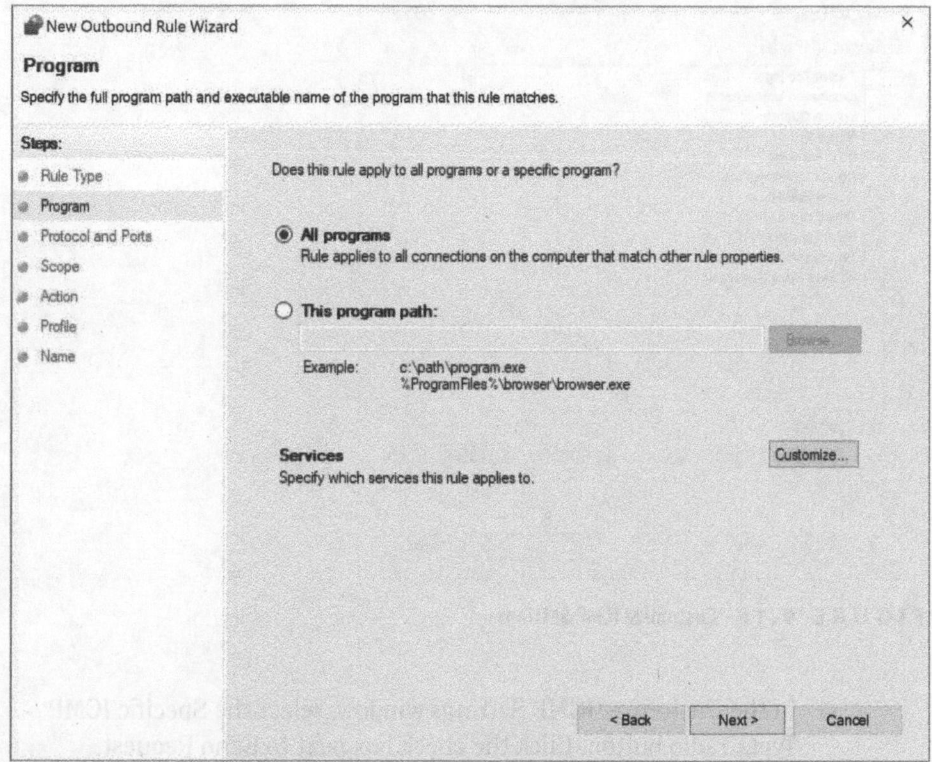

FIGURE 9.17 New Outbound Rule Wizard Steps: Program Page

4. Click Next to continue to the Steps: Protocol and Ports page.

5. Select ICMPv4 from the Protocol Type drop-down menu. Click on the Customize button to access the Customize ICMP Settings, as shown in Figure 9.18.

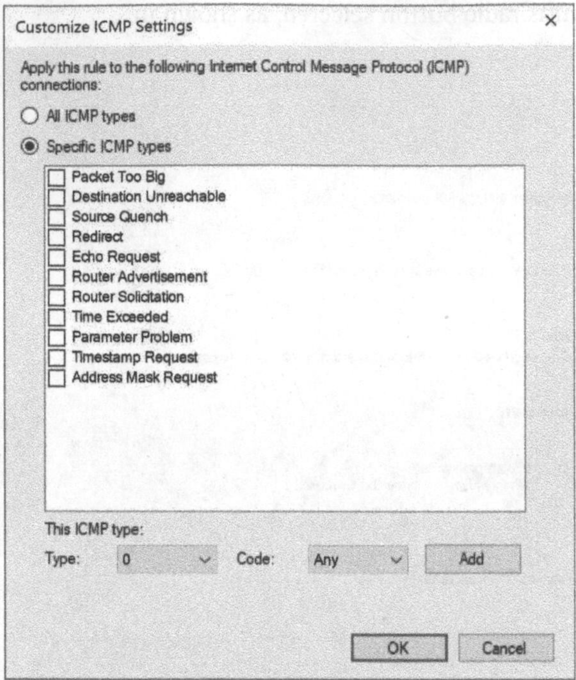

FIGURE 9.18 Customize ICMP Settings

6. In the Customize ICMP Settings window, select the Specific ICMP Types radio button. Click the check box next to Echo Request.

   You can block outbound ICMP echo requests, also known as `pings`, when your machine has been affected by malware and is now part of a botnet. In this instance, the botnet may be sending ICMP requests to create a `ping` flood (DoS attack).

7. Select OK to return to the Steps: Protocol and Ports page.
8. Click Next to continue to the Steps: Scope page, as shown in Figure 9.19.
9. Leave the Any IP Address radio buttons selected and then click Next to continue to the Steps: Action page.

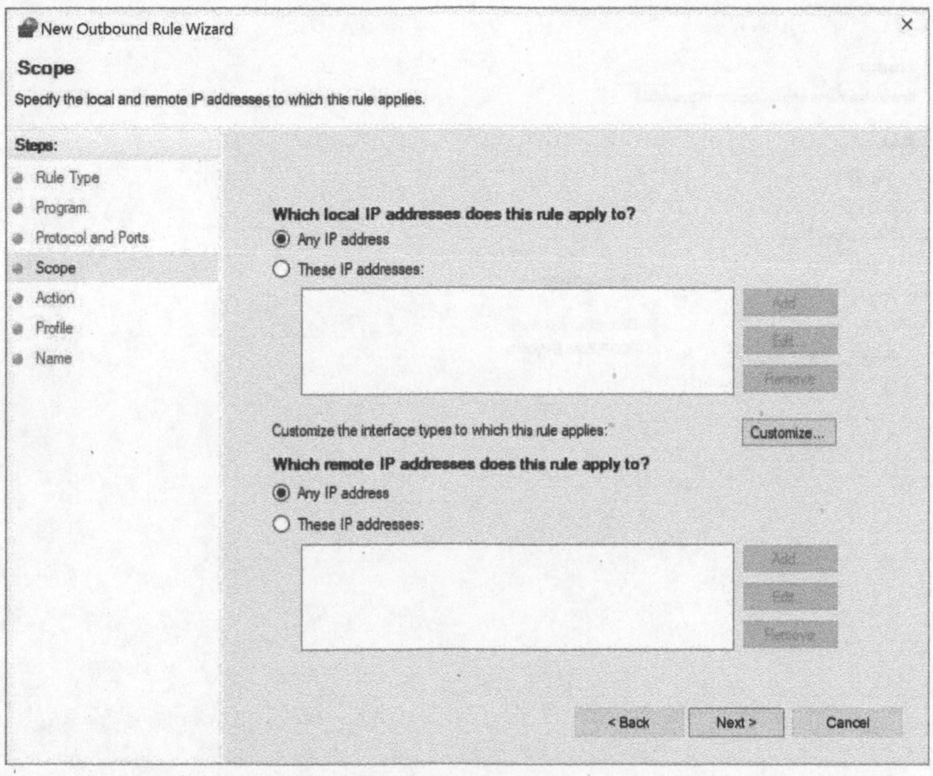

FIGURE 9.19 New Outbound Rule Steps: Scope Page

10. Leave the Block The Connection radio button selected, and then click Next to continue to the Steps: Profile page.
11. Leave all the profile check boxes marked, and then click Next to continue to the Steps: Name page.
12. In the Name text box that appears, enter My First ICMP Rule. Enter ICMP Echo Requests into the Description (Optional) text box. Figure 9.20 shows the completed Steps: Name page.
13. Click Finish to complete and exit the New Outbound Rule Wizard.

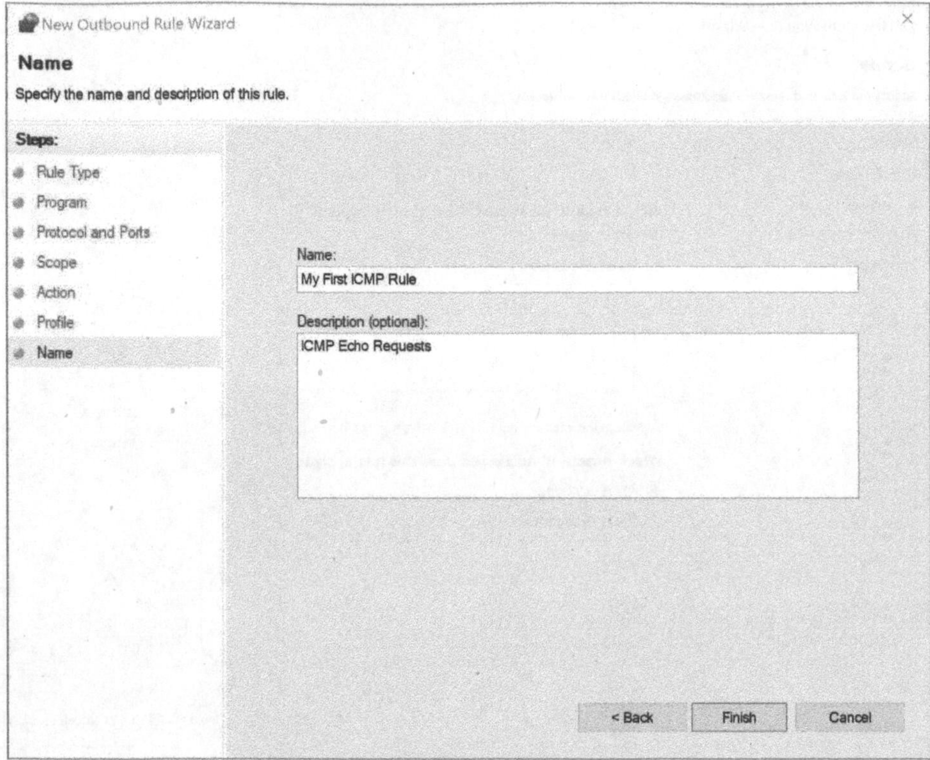

FIGURE 9.20 New Outbound Rule Wizard Steps: Name Page

You should see your rule in the Rules list in the center pane, as shown in Figure 9.21.

Testing ICMP Outbound Rule

Now it is time to test the previously made ICMP Echo Requests rule. This is completed in a command-line operation involving the PING utility.

1. Leave the Windows Firewall with Advanced Security console open.
2. Click the embedded search bar on the taskbar and enter **cmd**. This is the quick method to access the command line. Press Enter to launch the command line.
3. To test the ICMP rule, `ping` a well-known server of Google. Type **`ping 8.8.8.8`** into the command line, and then press Enter.

Notice that there is a general failure. The outbound rule has effectively blocked ICMP echo requests. Figure 9.22 shows the failure to `ping` (100% loss).

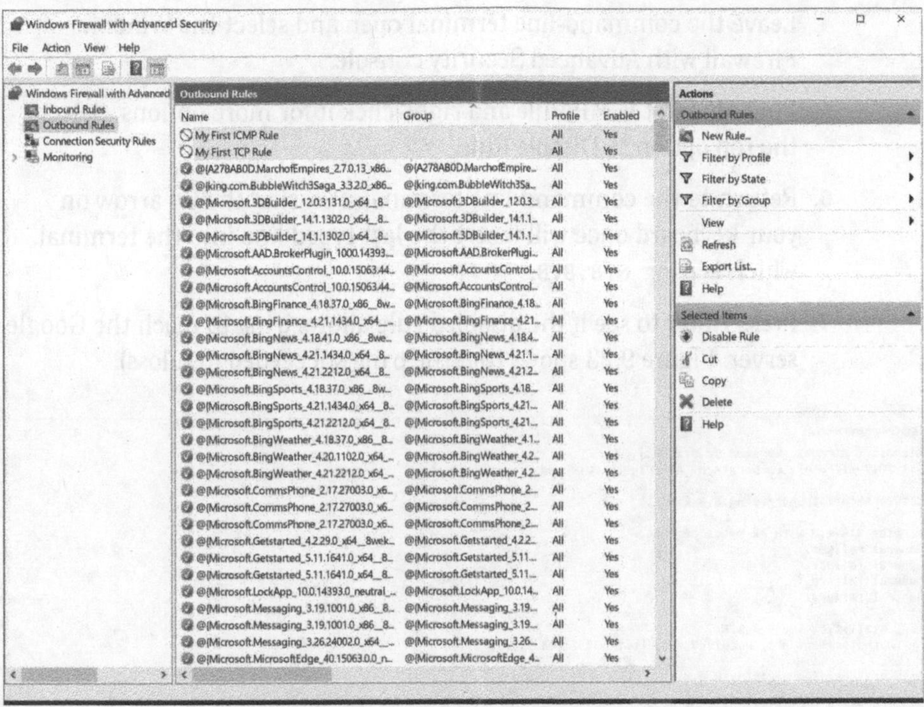

FIGURE 9.21 New Outbound Rule in Windows Firewall with Advanced Security

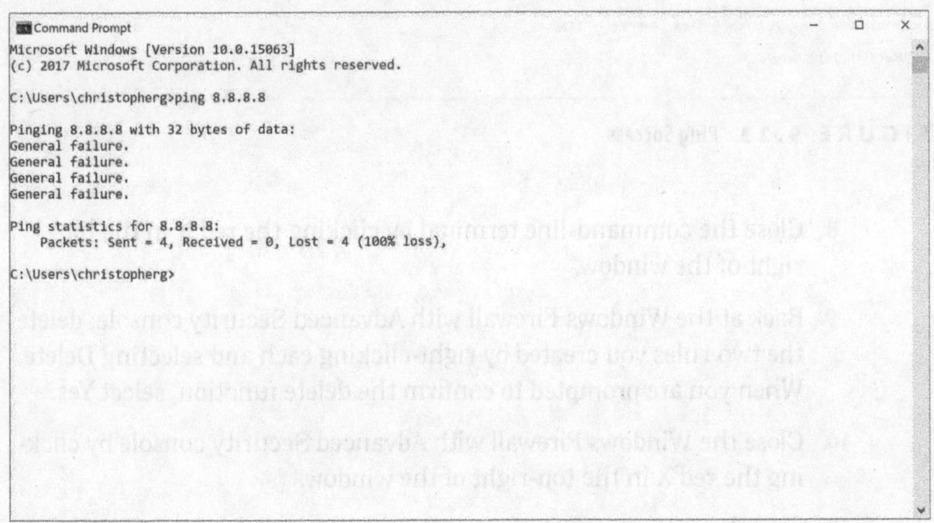

FIGURE 9.22 Ping Failure

4. Leave the command-line terminal open and select the Windows Firewall with Advanced Security console.
5. Find My First ICMP Rule and right-click it for more options. Select the top option to Disable Rule.
6. Return to the command-line terminal. Pressing the Up arrow on your keyboard once will insert the last typed line into the terminal, which is `ping 8.8.8.8`.
7. Press Enter to see if the disabled rule allows `ping` to reach the Google server. Figure 9.23 shows that the `ping` succeeded (0% loss).

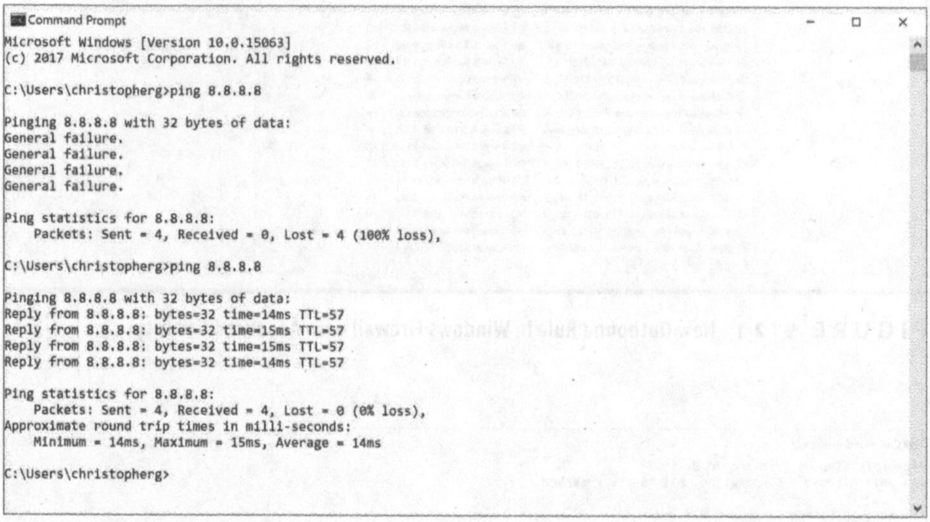

```
Command Prompt
Microsoft Windows [Version 10.0.15063]
(c) 2017 Microsoft Corporation. All rights reserved.

C:\Users\christopherg>ping 8.8.8.8

Pinging 8.8.8.8 with 32 bytes of data:
General failure.
General failure.
General failure.
General failure.

Ping statistics for 8.8.8.8:
    Packets: Sent = 4, Received = 0, Lost = 4 (100% loss),

C:\Users\christopherg>ping 8.8.8.8

Pinging 8.8.8.8 with 32 bytes of data:
Reply from 8.8.8.8: bytes=32 time=14ms TTL=57
Reply from 8.8.8.8: bytes=32 time=15ms TTL=57
Reply from 8.8.8.8: bytes=32 time=15ms TTL=57
Reply from 8.8.8.8: bytes=32 time=14ms TTL=57

Ping statistics for 8.8.8.8:
    Packets: Sent = 4, Received = 4, Lost = 0 (0% loss),
Approximate round trip times in milli-seconds:
    Minimum = 14ms, Maximum = 15ms, Average = 14ms

C:\Users\christopherg>
```

FIGURE 9.23 Ping Success

8. Close the command-line terminal by clicking the red X in the top-right of the window.
9. Back at the Windows Firewall with Advanced Security console, delete the two rules you created by right-clicking each and selecting Delete. When you are prompted to confirm the delete function, select Yes.
10. Close the Windows Firewall with Advanced Security console by clicking the red X in the top-right of the window.
11. Shut down the computer.

See Table 9.3 and Table 9.4 at the end of the Procedures exercise for lists of ports, ICMP types, and codes to close in order to exercise best practices.

Tables

TABLE 9.2 Types of Networks

Domain networks	Home or work (private) networks	Public networks

TABLE 9.3 Recommended Ports to Close

Port Name	TCP or UDP	Port Number(s)	Reason for Closure
MS RPC	Both	135	Windows systems use these ports to send out queries. This can leak information or be construed as an attack by another network.
NetBIOS/IP	Both	137–139	
SMB/IP	TCP	445	
Trivial File Transfer Protocol	UDP	69	Closing this prevents a hacker from moving their toolkit onto your system.
Syslog	UDP	514	Both of these send out information about the network topology, which is something to avoid.
Simple Network Management Protocol	UDP	161–162	
SMTP (all but your mail server)	TCP	25	This prevents your network infrastructure from being turned into a Spam relay, which could get your network on one or more blacklists.
Internet Relay Chat	TCP	6660–6669	These are used by hackers to send and receive communications from the systems that they infect.

TABLE 9.4 Recommended ICMP Types and Codes to Close

ICMP Name	Type	Code	Reason for Closure
Echo – Replies	0	0	These are used for covert communications.
Host Unreachables	3	1	Host Unreachables are used by hackers to map out networks and to identify which hosts are online and offline.
Time Exceeded in Transit	11	0	Closing these prevents some network-mapping tools from functioning.

Lab Questions

1. **What are the three main types of networks that Windows Firewall handles?**

   Answer: The three types of networks include: Domain networks, Home or work (private) networks, and Public networks.

2. **It is important to turn Windows Firewall off. True or False?**

   Answer: False. There are only a few legitimate reasons to turn off Windows Firewall. Overall, it is a necessary security tool within the Windows environment.

3. **What are the four Rule types that you can create with the New Rule Outbound Wizard?**

   Answer: The four types of rules that are listed for you to choose from within the New Outbound Rule Wizard include: Program, Port, Predefined, and Custom.

4. **What is an easy way to test ICMP echo requests?**

   Answer: An easy way to test ICMP echo requests is to use the ping function inside a command-line terminal—for example, `ping 8.8.8.8`.

5. **You have the option to block all incoming traffic. True or False?**

   Answer: True. If the firewall is turned on (recommended), you can decide if you want to block all incoming traffic and if you want to be notified if and when a program is blocked.

CHAPTER 10

Local Host Security: Review Questions and Hands-On Exercises

Review the following summary points before proceeding to the "Review Questions" and "Exam Questions" sections at the end of this chapter to make sure you are comfortable with each concept. After completing the review, answer the review questions to verify your knowledge of the material covered in Part II.

Summary Points

- The first level of securing intelligent computing and control devices is to control access to them.
- The most obvious point of access through the outer perimeter of a PC would be its basic input devices: its keyboard, mouse, and touch-sensitive display. If someone can simply sit down in front of the system and freely use its input devices (keyboard, mouse, touchpad, or touchscreen), they have an avenue for accessing the information inside.
- The User Password option enables administrators to establish passwords that users must enter during the startup process to complete the boot process and gain access to the operating system. Without this password, the system never reaches an operational level that an intruder could use to access its internal perimeter and interior information.
- A Supervisory Password option must be used to establish a password that can be used to access the CMOS Setup utility.

- In computer and networking environments, the term *hardening* refers to the process of making a system more secure. Computer hardening efforts begin with hardware, but also extend to the local host's operating system, its file system, and its applications.
- Physical hardware ports enable the basic PC system to interact with optional, removable devices. They also provide a potential security threat because individuals with malicious intent can gain access directly into the computer internal communication and processing system through these ports.
- It is common for system's BIOS to offer device control options that provide control over the computer's external hardware connection ports. By disabling these ports, users and administrators can help to ensure that unauthorized users cannot use the ports to gain unauthorized access to the system, transfer information out of the system, or download malware programs into the system.
- Removable computer media presents multiple security risks. These risks include potential loss of data through theft due to the portable nature of the media, as well as the potential to introduce destructive malware into the host system.
- The *inner perimeter* can be considered as consisting of the operating system and its application programs.
- One of the main tools for protecting the file system and its data is the use of access control lists (ACLs). The file management system uses ACLs to grant or deny users access to its different files, as well as to control what types of activities the individual can perform once access has been granted.
- In Microsoft Windows environments, these capabilities are assigned to folders and files in the form of *permissions.* In Unix and Linux-based systems, users are assigned *access rights* to files.
- The main user authentication tool used with personal computing devices is the username and password login. In general, there are three types of user-related logons with which to contend: a logon to the local machine, a logon to a specific software application, and a network logon.
- In a shared computer environment where multiple users may be enabled to use the same computer, local user and group credentials

are created and configured through a user accounts database that is stored on the local computer.

- For a password to be effective, it must possess a certain amount of complexity. Its length, width, and depth must be such as to thwart the efforts of the previously mentioned password-cracking techniques.
- *Password encryption* is the process of taking a standard password and applying an algorithm to it in such a way as to make it meaningless to sniffers, crackers, or other eavesdroppers.
- Operating systems provide password-lockout policy settings that enable administrators to enact password policies that prevent attackers from repeatedly trying to access the system. This prevents the attackers from using *brute force attacks* to guess the account password so they can break into the system.
- *Authentication* is defined as the process of determining that someone is who they say they are. At the local computing or control device level, authentication can be implemented in terms of physical or biometric authentication systems to replace or augment password authentication methods.
- There are hardware devices that can be used to make personal computer systems unusable by people other than authorized users. These devices include items such as smart cards and biometric devices.
- *Auditing* is a security function of the operating system that enables the user and operating system activities performed on a computer to be monitored and tracked. This information can then be used to detect intruders and other undesirable activities.
- The auditing systems available with most operating systems consist of two major components: an *audit policy* (or audit rules), which defines the types of events that will be monitored and added to the system's security logs, and *audit entries* (or audit records), which consist of the individual entries added to the security log when an audited event occurs.
- At the heart of the Linux audit system is the audit daemon that works with the Linux kernel's audit module to record relevant events and write them to a log file on the disk. Audit rules are configured in a file that is executed when the system boots up. The audit controller

utility employs the parameters in these rules to determine which system events are tracked and how they are written to the audit event log file.

- The term *cryptography* is used to define the art of protecting communications from unintended viewers.
- One of the oldest methods of hiding data in plain sight is to develop a code (algorithm) for altering the message so that unauthorized people cannot read it. The process for doing this is referred to as *encryption*.
- *Disk-level encryption* involves using technology to encrypt the entire disk structure. This technique offers value in that it protects everything on the disk from unauthorized access, including the operating system files and structure.
- Many computer motherboard designs include a built-in microchip called a Trusted Platform Module (TPM) that is used to store cryptographic information, such as the *encryption key* (also known as start-up key).
- File- and folder-level encryption is applied to individual files and folders. File- and folder-level encryption tools enable users to encrypt files stored on their drives using keys only the designated user (or an authorized recovery agent) can decode. This prevents theft of data by those who do not have the password or a decoding tool.
- Local software-based *firewalls* can be installed on an individual computer to protect it from malicious activities introduced through the Internet connection.
- Firewalls are configured so they will only pass data to and from designated IP addresses and TCP/UDP ports.
- Computer-based Intrusion Detection Systems (IDS) can be implemented in two ways: as network-based IDS (NIDS) or as host-based IDS (HIDS). In both cases, the system is designed primarily to monitor the system (local computer or network environment), log key events and policy violations, and report them as directed.
- Intrusion Prevention Systems (IPS), also referred to as Intrusion Detection and Prevention System (IDPS), provide an additional

level of protection aimed at preventing the detected threat from succeeding.

- Signature-based IDS/IDPS products generally work by looking for specific patterns in content, known as *signatures*.
- Anomaly-based IDS/IDPS systems apply statistical analysis techniques to the data stream to determine whether it is "normal" or "anomalous" at any given time.
- Internet sites may be categorized under different security "zones" that enable sites listed in each zone to be governed by security restrictions that apply to that group (Internet, Local Intranet, Trusted Sites, and Restricted Sites).
- *Scripts* are executable applications that provide interactive content on websites. They are also capable of retrieving information in response to user selections. However, the user may not have to do anything to run a script program—they are simply embedded in the website being accessed.
- *Cookies* are small files that web servers send to web browsers when their pages are accessed. The legitimate use of these files is to enable the server to automatically recognize the client browser any time it connects to the server.
- *Malware* is the term used to describe programs designed to be malicious in nature.
- The term *grayware* describes programs that have behavior that is undisclosed or that is undesirable.
- All computers with connections to the Internet should be protected by an antivirus solution before they are ever attached to the Internet.
- There are basically two types of antispyware products available: those that find and remove spyware after it has been installed and those that block spyware when it is trying to install itself.
- The second level of hardening local computer systems against attacks is to secure their operating systems. This involves updating vulnerable code segments of the OS as they become known. OS hardening occurs through the application of new programming in the form of service packs, patches, and updates.

- The term *software exploitation* is used to describe cyber attacks designed to take advantage of vulnerabilities or weaknesses in software products, operating systems, and applications.

Security Challenge Scenarios

Now that you have completed this review chapter, once again use your portfolio to record your new observations for the Security Challenge Scenarios presented at the beginning of the chapter. Afterward, create a short comparison of your original assessment to the information you acquired through the chapter and its associated lab procedures.

Computing Device Security Scenario 1

Identify: ____________________

Protect: ____________________

Detect: ____________________

Respond: ____________________

Recover: ____________________

Computing Device Security Scenario 2

Identify: ____________________

Protect: ____________________

Detect: ____________________

Respond: ____________________

Recover: ____________________

Professional Feedback

In this section, you will compare your observations to those of a working security specialist—in this case, Philip Craig, the founder of BlackByte Cyber Security—to improve your understanding of cybersecurity.

About Philip Craig

Philip Craig is the founder of BlackByte Cyber Security, LLC, a consultancy supporting the Pacific Northwest National Laboratory (PNNL) research and national security agendas as well as the National Rural Electric Cooperative Association and National Rural Telecommunications Cooperative.

For many years, Phil served as a Senior Cyber Security Research Scientist at PNNL, where he provided engineering and program management support in the fields of cybersecurity, supervisory control, and data acquisition (SCADA) technologies, computing, and communications infrastructure.

This included development of complex system and policy solutions in a variety of critical infrastructures including the nuclear power, electric power, and water sectors. He developed and deployed both strategic and tactical cybersecurity defensive solutions for the electric power and nuclear sectors.

The Insights of a Practicing Professional

The most basic activities you'll face in everyday cybersecurity include the challenges of securing the devices within your networked or distributed environments. Part II is focused on the host, so this will account for any of the security controls that will be implemented on any particular host computer for which you are responsible. Many of these security controls have centralized management features, but in some cases they may not be part of an overall managed environment. An example may be a remote sales force that uses their own devices, or your company may be implementing cost reductions by implementing bring-your-own-device (BYOD) programs. Here you have to assume that you're dealing with completely unsecure devices.

This solution will focus on the constraints listed in the scenarios, which are very common to a personal computer used in any business.

Computing Device Security Scenario 1

You have been assigned to develop a local security policy and configuration specifications for the desktop computers used by in-house employees at your firm. These PCs are mounted in special openings under the desk in each cubicle. The computers are physically identical, and they all run the same operating system. However, they may have different types of job-specific company software installed. These computers are equipped with the following:

- Detachable keyboards and mice
- Six built-in USB connection ports
- Separate monitors
- UTP local area network connection ports
- Microsoft Windows 10 Professional operating systems
- Microsoft Office 2016 software
- Dual built-in DVD disc drives

Although these recommendations aren't specified down to the NIST level, they can be used to provide the basis for selection. Based on risk of loss, selecting Low-Risk=Low implementation, Med-Risk=Medium implementation, and, of course, High-Risk=Hi-Implementation of the selected security control is appropriate. As an example, simple USB locking devices, shown in Figure 10.1, are available. Certainly, they can be defeated, but in order to do so, combined with disabling the port in firmware, you have a pretty nefarious insider threat at this point—or, you may just have an indignant employee. Either way, your company will likely take action upon your discovery of the compromised system.

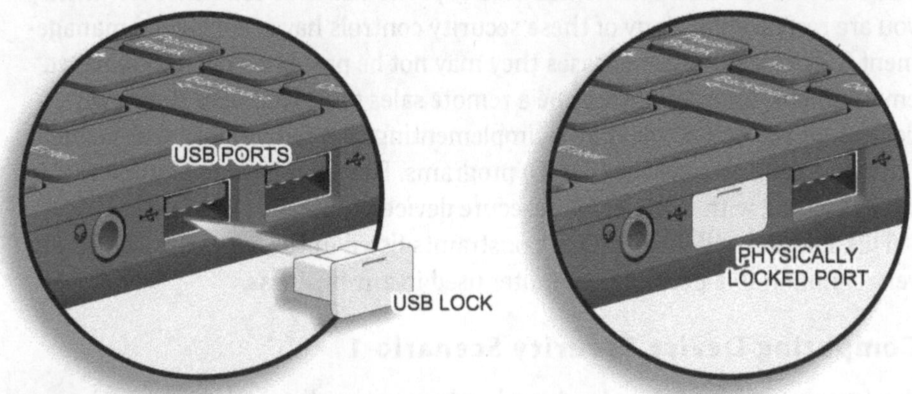

FIGURE 10.1 USB Port Locks

First, you need to quantify the problems you might experience by simply diagramming them, as shown in Figure 10.2.

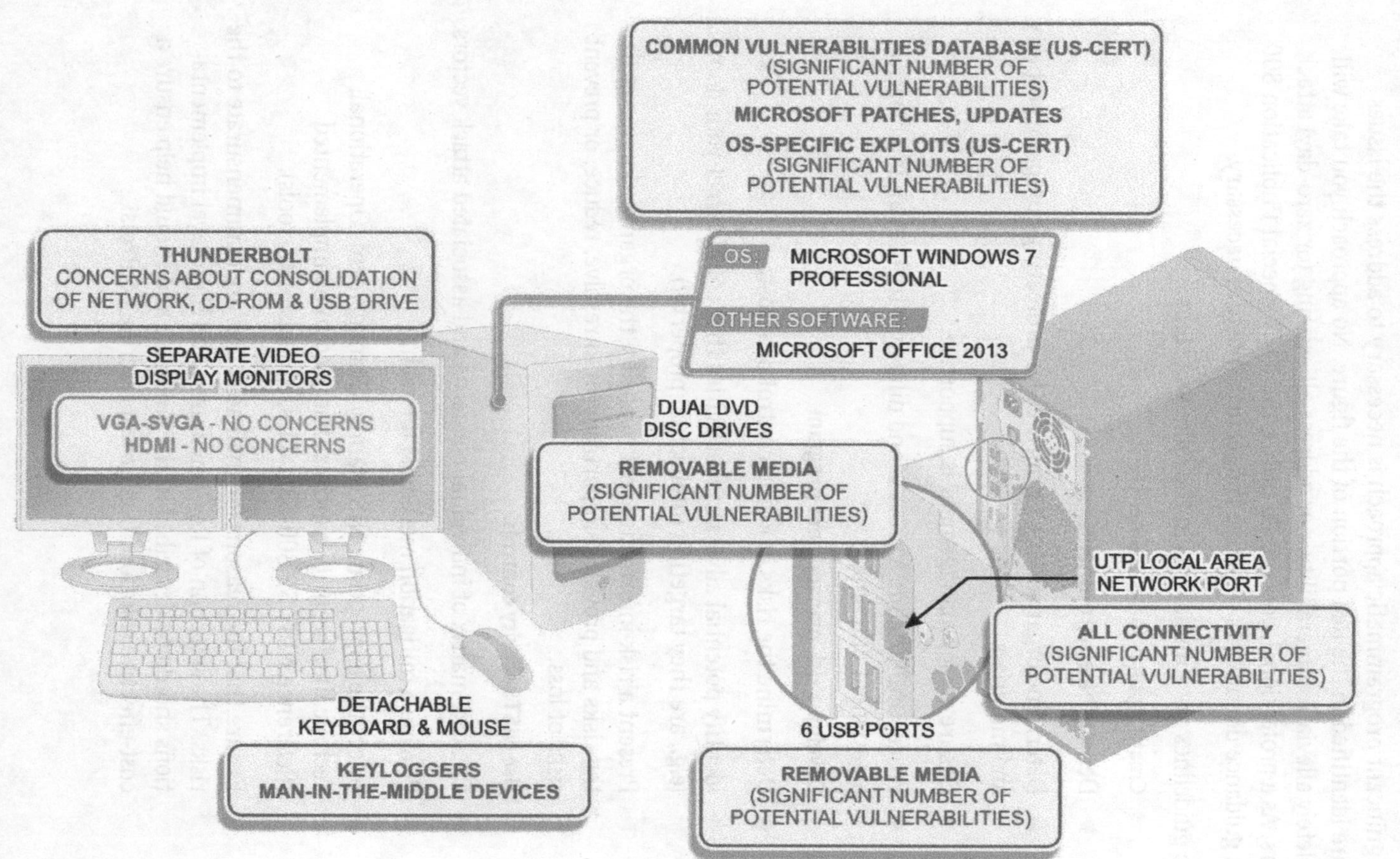

FIGURE 10.2 Known Vulnerabilities

A significant programmatic approach is necessary to address the issues that are identified in the Red portion of the figure. No approach you take will completely alleviate vulnerability, nor address all existing (or zero-day) attack vectors. As a professional, you should utilize the NIST Special Publication 800 series guidance documents to define the security posture necessary.

Those guidelines are summarized in the following steps.

Create a policy for assessments.

- Define the environment.
- Determine organizational priorities for protecting company property and materials.
- Ensure senior management is supportive.
- Procedurally define a process and diligence to form an informative assessment outcome.

Develop a risk-management program.

- Determine the risks of losing control of a host.
- Identify potential adversarial activities that could target your domain (e.g., are they targeting intellectual property?).
- Present a risk-informed report to ensure the organization recognizes the risks and provides support/buy-in to resolve, reduce, or prevent risks of loss.

Use NIST security controls.

- Create a matrix of individual concerns and associated attack vectors.
- Provide a mitigation method(s) for each.
- Select the appropriate NIST family (Management, Operational, Technical) of security controls that need to be implemented (Reference NIST SP 800-53, tables, spreadsheets, tools).
- Ensure that the reasons for their selection are commensurate to the risks. The selection of low-, medium-, and high-level implementations should be described in the guidance and should help ensure a cost-effective solution. Don't overprescribe controls!

Deploy security hardware and software.

- Select, configure, and deploy commercially available solutions, or determine effective open-source security solutions. In many cases, the open-source community has provided very effective tools that should be evaluated for use.

Create an effective audit program.

- Provide effectiveness tests that challenge your security posture. (For example, use open-source or commercial password-hacking tools to challenge your domain or local password repository.) Tests will provide impact and awareness to your users if they are using simple passwords that do not comply to organizational security policy.
- Execute physical walk-downs (physically inspect keyboards and mice for key-loggers). As an example, you could implement the procedures listed in Figure 10.3.

  The physical walk-down can be broken down into the following areas of concern:

Detachable Keyboards and Mice

- Do not allow personally owned keyboards and mice.
- Physically inspect the mice for man-in-the-middle devices.

Six Built-in USB Connection Ports

- Disable USB ports and, if necessary, provide physical locks on them.
- Encourage or require the use of network storage for all company-related business.

Separate Monitors (Thunderbolt Ports)

- Discourage or disable connectivity to external ports.
- Provide detection/audits of externally connected devices. Disable ports.

UTP Local Area Network Connection Ports

- Provide network access controls, such as Layer 2 protective mechanisms (ACL, port authorization, etc.).

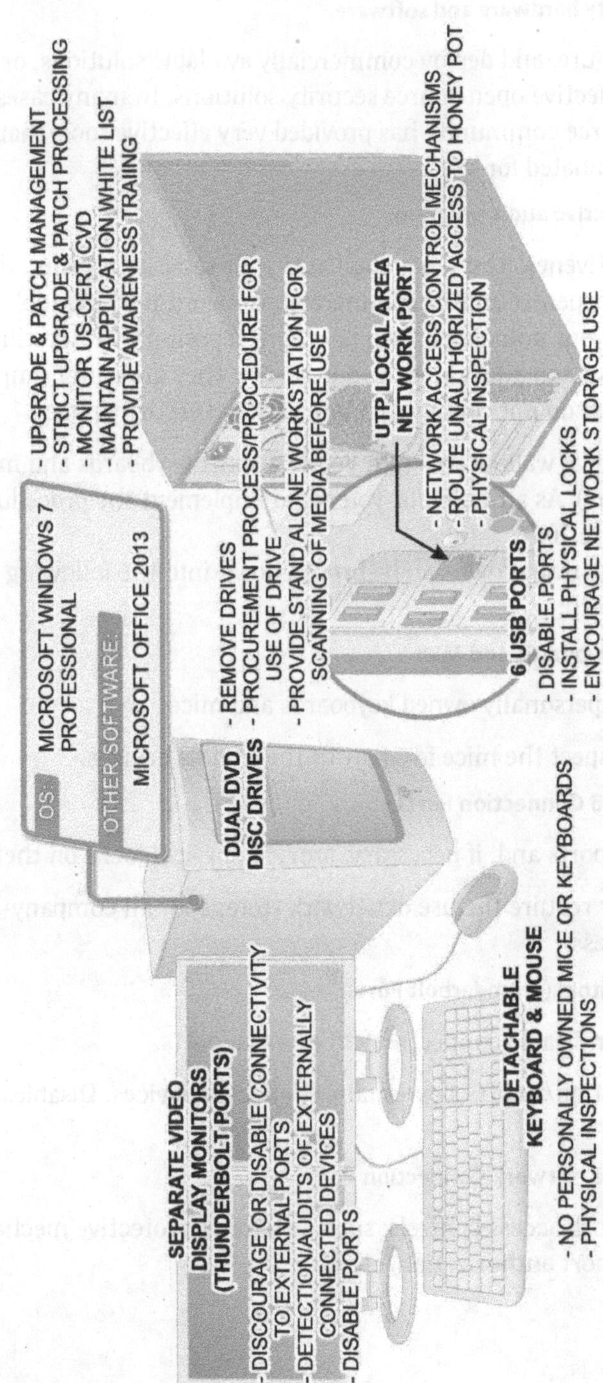

FIGURE 10.3 Implementation

- Route unauthorized connectivity to a local honeypot for capture and analysis.
- Physically inspect for man-in-the-middle devices.

Microsoft Windows 7 Professional Operating Systems and Office 2013 Software

- Upgrade and patch management policy.
- Strict processing is required.
- Monitor US-CERT.
- Maintain a list of approved applications.
- Enforce user policy to disallow installation without system administration approval and IT support.
- Provide strong awareness training and extend security principles into your organization and workforce.

Dual Built-in DVD Disc Drives

- Remove DVD disc drives or other media controllers.
- Provide a procurement process or procedure that requires written justification and approval of these devices.
- Provide standalone workstation to scan media before using on host computers.

Computing Device Security Scenario 2

Because you did such an outstanding job of creating the security policies and configurations for the company's desktop computers, you have been tasked to produce the same type of materials for the notebook computers used by the organization's sales people.

Obviously, these computers are portable PCs that work in the office and at different locations on the road. These computers are equipped with the following:

- Built-in keyboards and displays
- Two built-in USB connection ports
- UTP local area network connection ports
- Microsoft Windows 10 Professional operating systems

- Microsoft Office 2016 software
- Dual SD card-reader slots
- Built-in wireless networking capabilities
- External VGA display connection ports
- Built-in DVD disc drives

Without completely repeating the previous scenario, let's just say that there are many different methods to deal with the same problem. Focusing on a mobile computer (laptop, tablet, iPad, etc.) is more difficult based on what the user is tasked to do with it from a business perspective, and what you can control with electronic policy and written policy. It is very likely that removable devices will be used frequently. Remote connectivity, hotel/kiosk connectivity, and physical control of the device itself may offer unique challenges. In such cases, many companies simply utilize virtualization (or a *business sandbox,* as it is sometimes referred) to isolate the user and their interaction with the business. In the case of the laptop, you will want to at minimum ensure the following:

Use strong antivirus protection.

- Check applications, encrypted files, and removable media.

Use strong authentication methods to ensure appropriate access.

- Multifactor at a minimum utilizing hardware tokens.

Deploy a diligent auditing process as the device is connected to your local business network and from remote networks.

- VPN tunneling to proxy and DMZ environments even while in the local office is recommended.
- Review logs to reveal how many and what types of connectivity, media, or users have accessed or attempted to access the device.

Create an electronic policy for administration of the device

- Enforcement of access control by role, user, and application is sometimes necessary.

A Note About Electronic Devices

Ensure the device is used only for business purposes. Most people carry a number of electronic devices, so it is not that inconvenient to limit the employee to using the company device only for business access and not for movies and browsing the web while on travel.

Review Questions

The following questions test your knowledge of the material presented in Part II.

1. **How is securing a portable PC different than securing a cabinet mounted desktop computer?**

   Answer: For the most part, it is not practical to lock up desktop and portable personal computer (PC) systems that may be used by different users and, in many cases, are portable. In many cases, a given computer station may routinely be used by different personnel—such as a day shift employee and a night shift employee. In such applications, administrative security measures must be in place to guarantee proper authentication and access control. One of the main functions of a docking station is to provide a lockable attachment to the desktop to prevent unauthorized users from picking up the portable unit while it is not in use and simply carrying it away.

2. **List three locations where malicious individuals typically gain access to programs and data to damage, destroy, or steal them.**

   Answer: In both computing and intelligent control devices, there are three general locations where individuals typically gain access to *programs* and *data*: while it's in memory, while it's in storage on devices (such as hard drives and flash drives), and when it is being transferred from one place to another.

3. **The _____ option must be used to establish a password that can be used to access the CMOS Setup utility.**

   Answer: User Password

4. **What microprocessor/operating system feature is designed to protect certain areas of memory to prevent malicious software from taking over the computing device by inserting its code into another program's data area?**

   Answer: The No Execute (NX) bit or the eXecute Disable (XD) bit feature.

5. **Describe one of the main tools that operating systems use to protect their file systems and stored data.**

   Answer: Access control lists (ACLs)

6. **Which tool is considered to be the main user-authentication tool used with computers and networking equipment?**

   Answer: User Names and Passwords

7. **Where are local user and group credentials created and stored in the local host computer?**

   Answer: The users account database stored on the local computer

8. **What administrative tool enables administrators to create password policies that prevent attackers from using brute force attacks to obtain account passwords so they can use them to break into the system?**

   Answer: Password lockout policy settings

9. **In Linux systems, what tool works with the Linux kernel's audit module to record relevant events on disk?**

   Answer: The audit daemon

10. **Describe the steps associated with data encrypting processes.**

    Answer: Encrypting data involves taking data and processing it with a key code (or encryption key) that defines how the original version of the data has been manipulated. Anyone who is given the encryption key can use it to decode the message through a decryption process using a decryption algorithm (or decryption key).

11. **If you configure the local firewall and then find that no email has been received by the local host, what logical TCP port should be checked to see if it is being blocked?**

    Answer: Port 110 – POP3

12. **When using a web browser, how do you know that SSL links are being used to provide encryption services to prevent unauthorized access to the data during transmission across the Internet?**

    Answer: SSL links are always identified as `HTTPS://` sites instead of simply `HTTP://`.

13. **List three steps that can be taken at the local host computer to fight spyware.**

Answer: In addition to installing antispyware applications, users can fight spyware in a number of other ways, including:

- Install a web browser other than Internet Explorer (for example, Chrome or Firefox).
- Download the newest browser version that offers better security features.
- Work with an ISP that uses firewalls and proxies to block sites that are known to distribute spyware.
- Download software only from reputable sites to prevent spyware that comes attached to other programs.

14. **Where are controls for managing scripts located in the local host systems?**

Answer: The capability to load and run scripts in a browser can be controlled through the browser's Security feature.

15. **What type of attack is being conducted when attackers exploit poorly written computer code by inserting their own malicious code to corrupt a computer's memory so that its operation is degraded so badly that the machine becomes virtually unusable?**

Answer: An attacker may alter existing code to create a condition in the computer's memory known as a *buffer overflow,* which results in erratic behavior, memory access errors, and/or system crashes. The system is effectively disabled to the point where the user cannot use it. This type of attack is referred to as a Denial of Service or DOS attack.

Exam Questions

1. **From the following options, select the most obvious pathway for attackers to gain access to computing equipment.**

   A. Through the keyboard

   B. Through a USB port

   C. Through an open network port

   D. Through email attachments

   Answer: A

2. **Without this password, the system will never reach an operational level that an intruder could use to access its internal perimeter and interior information.**
   A. **Administrator**
   B. **Supervisory**
   C. **User**
   D. **SuperUser**
   Answer: C
3. **Which of the following areas of a local host system is the first location for hardening the system?**
   A. **Hardware**
   B. **File systems**
   C. **Operating system**
   D. **Applications**
   Answer: B
4. **Which type of physical access port is most likely to be used to inject malicious software into computing and intelligent control device that might be very well protected from network access?**
   A. **IEEE-1394 FireWire ports**
   B. **HDMI connectors**
   C. **USB ports**
   D. **Parallel ports**
   Answer: C
5. **From the following options, select the type of attack that is not associated with the operating system's file system.**
   A. **Buffer overflow attacks**
   B. **Race condition attacks**
   C. **Alternate data streams**
   D. **Directory traversals**
   Answer: A
6. **What type of login is typically required to validate users and supply access to the local host's resources?**
   A. **Administrative login**
   B. **Network login**

C. Application login

D. Local login

Answer: D

7. Which of the following options does not represent a typical level for encrypting data?

A. At the file/folder level

B. At the microprocessor level

C. At the disk level

D. At the network transmission level

Answer: B

8. Select the type of firewall typically used with a local host computing device.

A. A hardware firewall device

B. A 1394 firewall card

C. A software firewall

D. A static firewall card

Answer: C

9. Which type of intrusion-detection systems are designed to look for specific patterns in software code?

A. Signature-based detection systems

B. Profile-based anomaly detection systems

C. Rule-based anomaly detection

D. Threshold-based anomaly detection systems

Answer: A

10. What type of utility would an attacker employ to monitor data traffic looking for cookies to steal?

A. An intrusion device

B. A scripting utility

C. A packet sniffer utility

D. A man-in-the-middle (MITM) utility

Answer: C

PART III

Securing Local Networks

CHAPTER 11

Local Network Security in the Real World

The following challenges provide you with contextual reference points for the concepts you will learn in Part III. Because you have not yet read the chapters in Part III, the challenges in this chapter are designed to introduce you to the local host scenarios you'll face in the real world. In this chapter, you'll learn to:

- Apply applicable Categories and Subcategories of the NIST Cyber Security Framework's Identify function to a specific scenario to document the network's assets and their possible vulnerabilities.
- Use applicable Categories and Subcategories of the Protect function to generate specific policies and actions that can be used to secure the network's assets for the specified scenario.
- Apply applicable Categories and Subcategories of the Detect function to identify technologies, policies, practices, and strategies that can be used to monitor the network in the scenario to determine whether security events are occurring.
- Apply applicable Categories and Subcategories of the Respond function to create an incident response plan to cover specific security events associated with the scenario presented.
- Apply applicable Categories and Subcategories of the NIST Cyber Security Framework Recover function to the scenario to implement solutions for recovering from specific cyber events.

Security Challenges

This chapter will start your thought processes for what you are about to learn in Part III. Instead of simply trying to absorb all of the information that you're about to learn in these chapters, you'll begin here by gaining a better understanding of the real-world relevance of that information.

In Chapter 19, you will return to these scenarios and apply what you have learned in Chapters 12 through 18. You will also compare your observations to those of the professional security specialists who have provided their observations and solutions for these scenarios.

Local Network Security Scenario 1

You have been tasked with making recommendations for equipping a new data network for a small educational content development company (fewer than 20 employees). The new company has outgrown its old network and computing equipment and wants to start out in the new facility with a network that meets their current needs.

Because their business is based on the creation of IP (intellectual property) in a market that is highly competitive, they have asked for equipment and configuration recommendations to establish the most secure physical networking environment they can afford.

In particular, the customer has asked that you provide comprehensive recommendations for implementing their server-related security policies and standards. Figure 11.1 provides an overview of the company's electronic workflow structure.

The company's major functions can be organized as follows:

- Executive Staff – The executive staff conducts the following electronic activities:
  - Conducting electronic banking activities via the Internet
- Administrative Staff – The administrative staff is involved in the following electronic functions:
  - Managing server-based accounting, warehousing, and inventory programs
  - Managing electronic employee payroll and time-keeping records

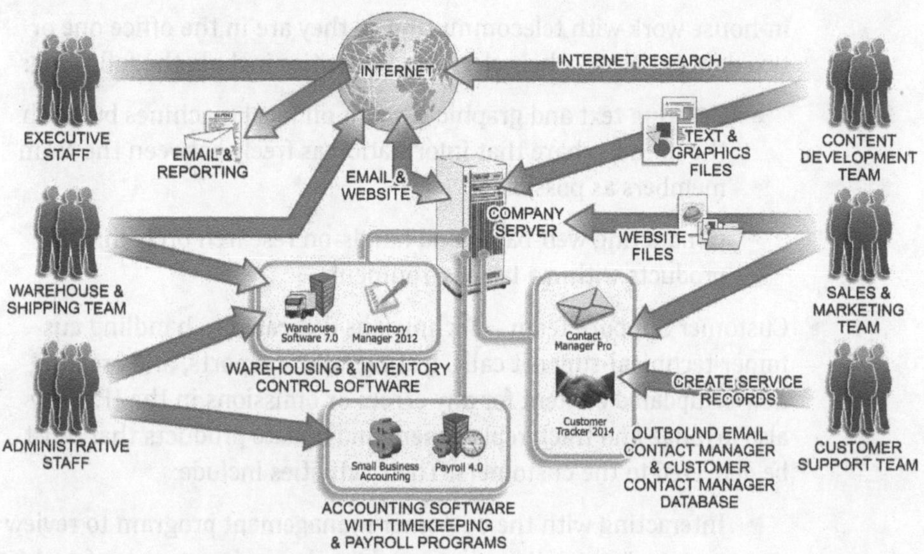

FIGURE 11.1 The Company Layout

- Sales and Marketing Team – Sales and marketing personnel who work in-house and on the road as required to prospect for customers, interact with outside sales representatives, and make customer visits and presentations. They are involved in the following electronic activities:
  - Handling incoming emails and customer sales calls
  - Operating an outbound email contact manager
  - Tracking customer interactions using a server-based customer-management database program
  - Interacting with the home office when traveling to retrieve documents, product updates, emails, and other communications
  - Interacting with their Internet ISP and their internal content development team to manage and update the company's website
- Content Development Team – Writers, editors, and artists. Some of these workers are located in the company facility, some live and work remotely and never physically access the facilities, and some combine

in-house work with telecommuting so they are in the office one or two days per week. Their electronic activities include the following:

- Creating text and graphic content on local machines but with the need to share that information as freely between the team members as possible
- Conducting web-based and hands-on research on technical products within a lab environment

- Customer Support Team – Technicians dedicated to handling customer technical-support calls, testing failure reports, and creating new or updated content for any errors or omissions in the IP. They also arrange and track replacement and update products that must be delivered to the customers. Their activities include:
  - Interacting with the customer management program to review past customer interactions and create service records of problem calls and resolution actions
  - Interacting with the Content Development Team to share content problems reported by customers and offer rough revision materials as required
- Warehouse and Shipping Team – Workers involved in the receiving, storage, inventory tracking, and shipping of products. These employees have the following electronic activities associated with their jobs:
  - Interacting with the warehouse and inventory portion of the company's accounting software to update and track product receiving and shipping, as well as current inventory levels
  - Interacting with Federal Express, United Parcel Service, and over-the-road trucking companies via the Internet to schedule and track shipments

Take note that many of the organization's software packages may not be the most current versions. While the IT world would like us to believe that everyone is running the latest versions of every software package, this is simply not true, even for larger organizations. There are still plenty of servers and computers running Windows 2003 Small Business Server and Windows XP/Vista in organizations like the one in this scenario—even though support for those versions has been discontinued.

With this scenario in mind, provide suggestions as to how you would implement their server functions and which security measures should be set in place to provide security for their corporate resources. Recommendations should include, but are not limited to, physically securing the server and server room, establishing policies to protect the company's intellectual property and personal information, and establishing procedures for maintaining the company's servers.

Risk Assessment 1

From the information provided in this scenario, consider the following NIST functions and generate thoughts about the Categories and Subcategories listed for each function. With these considerations in place, you will then be introduced to specific information about how to implement the functions requested.

Identify

Create an inventory of physical assets associated within the server systems (NIST ID.AM-1). Itemize the software platforms and applications required to carry out the company's network operations (NIST ID.AM-2). Identify possible asset vulnerabilities associated with the servers for the scenario presented (NIST ID.RA-1). Determine the information security roles and responsibilities associated with the company's servers (ID.GV-2).

Protect

Describe in general how you might go about protecting the physical assets identified in the previous point (NIST PR.AC-2). How will identities and credentials be managed for authorized server users (NIST PR.AC-1)? Describe how remote access to the servers will be managed (NIST PR.AC-3). Document how access permissions will be managed for the servers (NIST PR.AC-4). Document the strategy for protecting the confidentiality, integrity, and availability of data stored on the servers (NIST PR.DS-1, NIST PR.IP-4, NIST PR.PT-1).

Detect

How would you know if someone or something was attempting to access, disable, or destroy devices and/or systems associated with the server room? How could you detect anomalies and events that might impact the operation of the servers (NIST DE.CM-2, 8)?

- Which types of systems do you need to have in place to monitor personnel activity to detect potential cybersecurity threats associated with the servers (NIST DE.CM-1, 3)?

Respond

Which type of response plan might be necessary when physical security for the servers or server room is breached (NIST RS.AN-1, 2, 3)?

- Considering the information kept on the company's servers, which type of response plan might be necessary when physical security is breached in the server room (NIST RS.CO-4, 5)?

Recover

Which type of recovery plan might be needed for general physical security breaches that occur at one of the cubicles in the facility (NIST RC.RP-1)?

- Which items might a recovery plan include if server security is breached at the company (NIST RC.CO-1, 2)?

Use your portfolio to record your observations for this challenge. You will be asked to access this information again at the conclusion of the chapter to assess your original knowledge concerning this scenario and compare it to the information you have acquired throughout the chapter and its associated lab procedures. You will also be able to compare your observations with those of a working security specialist to improve your understanding of the subject.

Local Network Security Scenario 2

Your server-consulting task has been extended to include providing suggestions for the organization's communications media and network connectivity devices, as well as techniques to implement the physical network architecture.

With the information previously provided, design a network to securely connect the company's users together, taking care to consider which types of information and services require different levels of security. Figure 11.2 provides an overview of the projected company's network structure.

Risk Assessment 2

From the information provided in this challenge, consider the following NIST functions and generate thoughts about the Categories and Subcategories listed for each function. With these considerations in place you will then be introduced to specific information about how to implement the functions requested.

Identify

Create an inventory of physical assets (devices and systems) involved in the company's network architecture (NIST ID.AM-1, PR.PT-3, 4). Create a map of the organization's communications and data flow (NIST ID.AM-3). Create a map of the organization's external information systems (NIST ID.AM-4). Determine whether the information security roles and responsibilities associated with the company's networks are the same as those recommended for the servers in the previous scenario (ID.GV-2). Identify and document network asset vulnerabilities (NIST ID.RA-1).

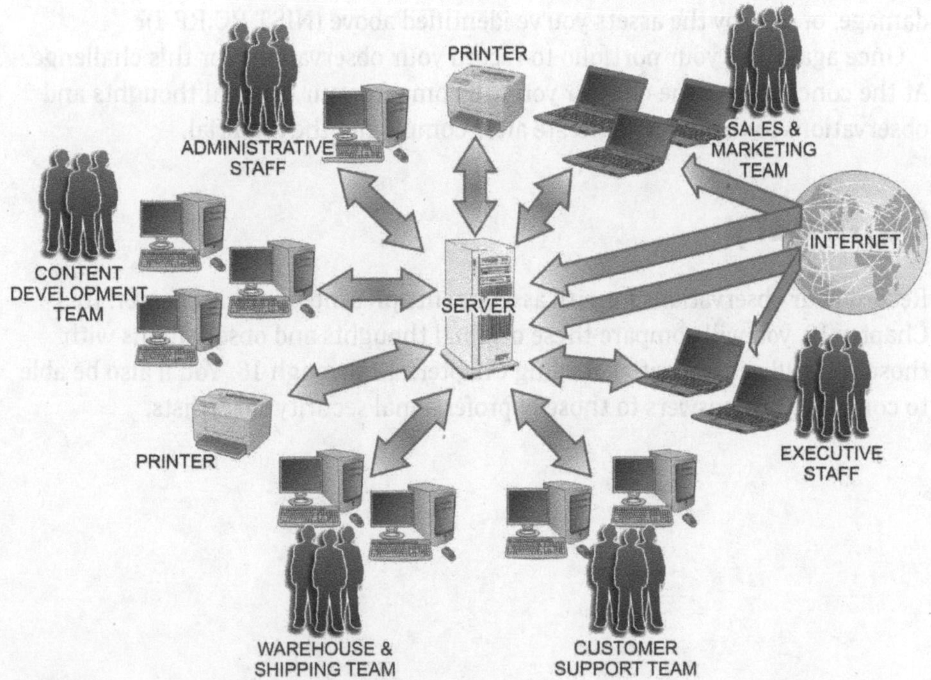

FIGURE 11.2 The Company Network Layout

Protect

Describe in general how you might go about protecting the physical assets identified in the previous point (NIST PR.AC-1, 2, 3, 4). Determine how you will protect data moving through the company's network (NIST PR.DS-2).

Detect

How would you know if someone or something was attempting to access, disable, or destroy one or more of the devices and/or systems in the network? How could you detect anomalies and events that might impact the operation of the network (NIST DE.CM-1, 2, 8)?

Respond

How would you need to respond to the anomalies and events you've identified through the devices, systems, and steps you would implement in the previous point (NIST RS.AN-1, 2, 3)?

Recover

Which steps could you put in place to recover from actions intended to access, damage, or destroy the assets you've identified above (NIST RC.RP-1)?

Once again, use your portfolio to record your observations for this challenge. At the conclusion of the chapter you will compare your original thoughts and observations to those you generate after completing the material.

Summary

Record your observations for risk assessments presented in this chapter. In Chapter 19, you will compare these original thoughts and observations with those you will generate after reading Chapters 12 through 18. You'll also be able to compare your answers to those of professional security specialists.

CHAPTER 12

Networking Basics

When only two intelligent devices are connected, simple direct connections can be made using cables, light signals, or radio waves. The interconnected devices only need to speak the same digital language and use an agreed-upon communication control method to manage the flow of information between them. However, when more than two intelligent digital devices are linked together, a network is formed. When a third device is added to the system, additional control methods must be put into place to not only control the conversations between the devices, but to make sure the correct parties on the network receive the information and that information not intended for other parties is kept private. In this chapter, you'll learn to:

- **Identify the characteristics of common network types**
- **Describe the primary function of the different layers of the OSI networking model**
- **Discuss how the layers of the OSI model correspond to the generation of network data transmission packets**
- **Explain how different OSI model layers apply to cybersecurity issues**
- **Describe standard networking topologies**

Understanding the Basics of Networking

In the Information Technology (IT) world, there are two basic types of networks:

- Networks that exist in a relatively confined geographical area are referred to as local area networks (LANs).
- Networks distributed over wider geographical areas are referred to as wide area networks (WANs).

There are several less-well-defined versions of these basic area network types, as described in this section.

In all of the following network types, two fundamental considerations must be in place to implement communications between the network's devices: its physical or logical connection method (topology) and the rules governing its communication processes (or protocols). You must be able to link the network components together, and they must all use the same signal types and language.

Campus Area Networks or Corporate Area Networks (CANs)

Campus area networks or corporate area networks (CANs) are combinations of interconnected local area networks inside a limited geographical area.

Metropolitan Area Networks (MANs)

Metropolitan area networks (MANs) are widespread combinations of interconnected local area networks inside a medium-sized geographical area. This designation is applied to networks that operate between LANs and WANs and most likely connect different LANs to a WAN.

Wireless Local Area Networks (WLANs)

Wireless local area networks (WLANs) are local area networks of more than two devices that are connected by wireless radio communication methods. These networks may also interconnect through a wireless access point, which also attaches the LAN to a wide area network, such as the Internet.

Storage Area Networks (SANs)

Storage area networks (SANs) are a network of dedicated storage devices configured for the express purpose of providing consolidated data storage. These devices act in a transparent manner so that they appear to be an integral part of the network's server(s).

The OSI Networking Model

Networks are complex, multifaceted structures that require a tremendous amount of interaction between computer designers, network equipment designers, operating system manufacturers, and networking application providers. Several initiatives have been put forward to provide models to serve as blueprints for these groups to follow in designing their products. While you should be aware that different hierarchical networking models exist, the most widely discussed initiative is the open systems interconnection (OSI) model put forward by the International Standards Organization.

The OSI model helps us conceptualize how data is handled between two networked systems. To do so, the OSI model divides the working flow of data into abstract *layers*. Although the layers are not literal in any sense, nor do they provide any actual barrier for product design, the layers do help people respect and understand the flow of how data gets managed.

The layers of the OSI model are shown in Figure 12.1. In the figure, each layer on the left is matched with a group of protocols that operate within it on the right. As you can see, many protocols are at work in network architectures.

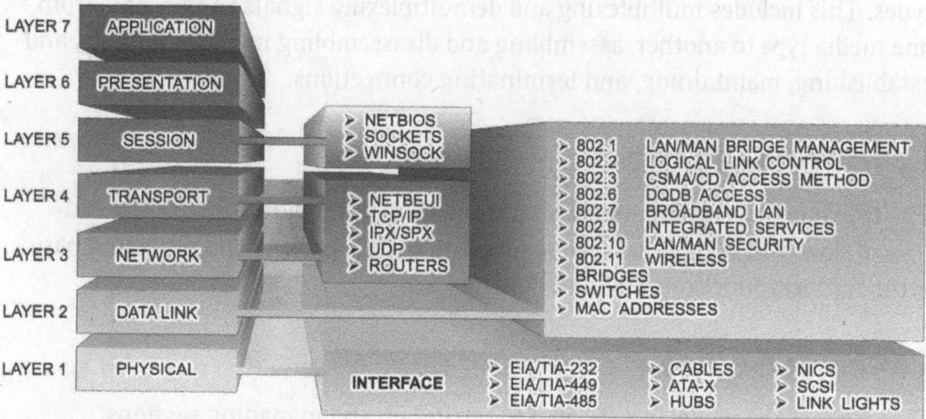

FIGURE 12.1 The OSI Networking Model

The primary functions of the layers are summarized in the following sections.

Layer 1: Physical

This layer is concerned with the transmission media used to move data. Functions associated with this layer include moving the data onto the transmission media, providing electrical or light signals, the mechanical compatibility between the communications port and the media, and activation and deactivation of the physical connection.

Layer 2: Data Link

This layer involves controlling how the data is packaged and moved between communication points. At this layer, the data is formatted into frames suited for transmission. Components at this level also add error detection and correction functions to the frames, as well as media access protocols and specific information about transmission to specific nodes on the same network segment.

Layer 3: Network

Elements of the network layer are responsible for controlling the routing of data packets between different communication nodes, network segments, or media types. This includes multiplexing and demultiplexing signals as they pass from one media type to another, assembling and disassembling message packets, and establishing, maintaining, and terminating connections.

Layer 4: Transport

The transport-level components are responsible for providing an orderly end-to-end flow of data that includes sequencing of data packets and providing basic error-recovery functions and flow control.

Layer 5: Session

This layer of the model is dedicated to setting up and managing sessions between applications as well as providing parameters such as security. Activities conducted by components at this level include stopping and starting data transfers, controlling the flow of data between applications, and providing network failure recovery options. This layer deals with management of transmission security options such as authentication and tunneling protocols.

Layer 6: Presentation

The elements of this level are tasked with controlling how the data looks to the user at the destination end. Functions provided by components at this level include visually formatting and presenting data, dealing with data compression and encryption functions, and starting/stopping control of sessions.

Layer 7: Application

The highest level of abstraction for the OSI model is concerned with the network handling of data for end-user applications. Services such as email and the web browser are application examples where the application layer is functioning. At this level of the model, user IDs and passwords are authenticated and user services are provided.

Data Transmission Packets

When data is moved from one communication node to another, the elements associated with each level of the OSI model add a header to the message that contains the information necessary to carry out the transfer. Technically, at some OSI layers, a small footer is also added to create an envelope. But for the sake of discussion, we'll focus on the headers. The data could be digitized text, numbers, voice, video, or any other type of digitized information. When the command is given to move the data at the sending node (for example, by pressing Send on an email message), the packeting process progresses as described in Figure 12.2.

As the data packet leaves the application, an additional *header* (block of information) is added to the message as it moves through the different OSI layers on its way to the transmission media. On the receiving end, the entire message is brought into the designated receiving node, where each layer's header is examined, the appropriate header removed, and the message acted on by its corresponding layer.

The steps involved in the communication process are typically carried out without any intervention from the user who is sending the message. The different headers and activities are functions of the application, the physical network adapter, and all the "layers" in between.

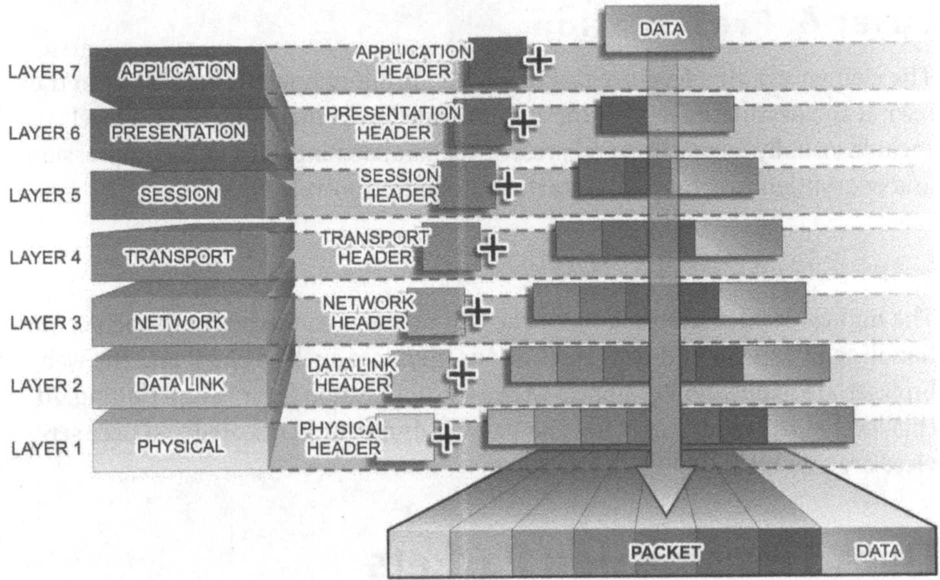

FIGURE 12.2 Building Transmission Packets

OSI Layer Security

Every networking course examines the OSI model in terms of which types of devices, protocols, and functions exist at each level. However, different cybersecurity challenges may be present at each level. Table 12.1 lists the security focus related to each layer.

TABLE 12.1 OSI Layer Security

OSI LAYER	Network Security Model	Exploit Type	Security Focus
1) Physical Layer	7) Physical Level	Physical Tampering/ Break-in	Physical Security
2) Data Link Layer	6) VLAN Level	Network Scanning Local/Internal	Access Security

OSI LAYER	Network Security Model	Exploit Type	Security Focus
3) Network Layer	5) ACL Level	Network Scanning Complete/Internal	Domain Security
4) Transport Layer	4) Software Level	Software Specific Exploits	Port Security
5) Session Layer	3) User Level	Social Engineering – Users	Authentication/ Encryption
6) Presentation Layer	2) Administrative Level	Social Engineering – Administrators	Authentication
7) Application Layer	1) IT Department Level	Social Engineering – IT Staff	ID/Authentication

You can also apply the three-layered rings of security developed in the previous chapters to the layers of the OSI model. As a matter of fact, the three-layer ring actually exists in two places—the transmitting device and the receiving device. Therefore, the outer perimeter is established at the physical termination or connection point of each device. The cable or airwaves between the devices connect their outer perimeters.

The outer perimeter corresponds to the Layer 1 components of the OSI model. Securing the physical layer in a network involves securing the physical media, as well as the networking and communication equipment.

Likewise, the inner perimeter is associated with the Layer 2 components of the model. The components working at this level represent the first layer of logical defense. At this level data can be accepted, discarded, or forwarded based on its identity.

Finally, the interior ring can be viewed as including Layer 3 through Layer 7. Each of these layers provides options for preventing unauthorized movement to a higher level. For example, port-blocking mechanisms associated with firewalls work at Layer 4.

However, the Layer 7 components represent the most desired targets of a cyber attack. Attacks aimed at this level are designed to gain control of physical assets or compromise the operation of software applications.

Throughout Part III, you will learn about the operation of different network components, their positions in the OSI architecture, and their related security vulnerabilities and remedies.

Network Topologies

Network topologies are Layer 1 physical (or logical) connection strategies that fall into four basic configurations, as illustrated in Figure 12.3.

- Bus
- Ring
- Star
- Mesh

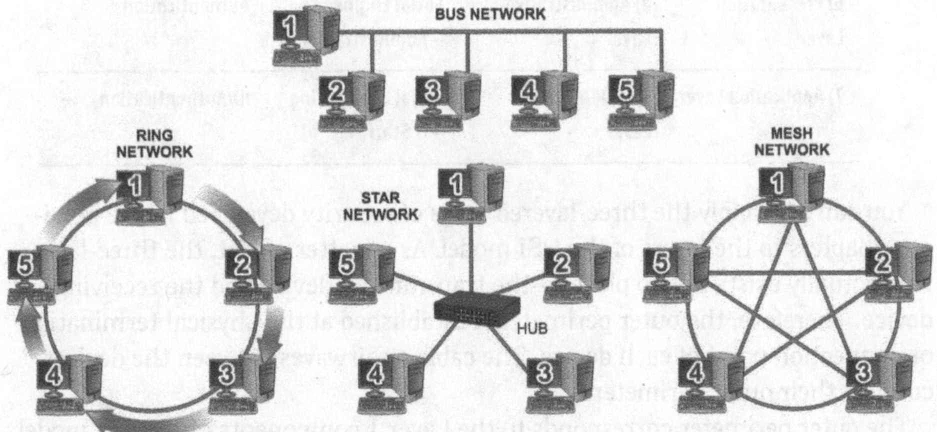

FIGURE 12.3 Bus, Ring, Star, and Mesh Configurations

Bus Topology

In the bus topology, the *nodes,* or stations, of the network connect to a central communication link. Each node has a unique address along the bus that differentiates it from the other users on the network. Information can be placed on the bus by any node. The information must contain the network address of the node, or nodes, for which the information is intended. Other nodes connected to the bus will ignore the information.

Ring Topology

In a ring network configuration, the communication bus is formed into a closed loop. Each node inspects the information on the network as it passes by.

A repeater, built into each the network adapter of each node, will regenerate every message not directed to it and send it to the next appointed node. The originating node eventually receives the message back and removes it from the ring.

Ring topologies tend to offer very high data-transfer rates but require additional management overhead. The additional management is required for dependability. If a node in a ring network fails, the entire network fails. To overcome this, ring designers have developed rings with primary and secondary data paths as depicted in Figure 12.4. If a break occurs in a primary link, the network controller can reroute the data onto the secondary link to avoid the break.

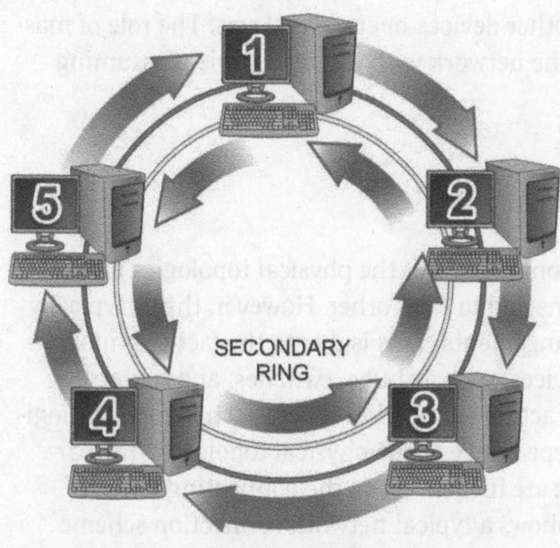

FIGURE 12.4 Primary/Secondary Ring Topologies

Star Topology

In a star topology, the logical layout of the network resembles the branches of a tree. All the nodes are connected in branches that eventually lead back to a central unit. Nodes communicate with each other through the central unit.

The central station coordinates the network's activity by polling the nodes, one by one, to determine whether they have any information to transfer. If so, the central station gives that node a predetermined slice of time to transmit. If the message takes longer to transmit than the time allotted, the message will be chopped into small packets of information that are transmitted over several polling cycles.

Mesh Topology

The mesh network design offers the most basic network connection scheme and the most extensive management scheme. In this topology, each node has a direct physical connection to all the other nodes in the network. Mesh topologies are employed in two very large network environments—the public telephone system and the Internet, as well as in small, wireless piconet communication networks that include Bluetooth and ZigBee networks.

Piconets are small, short-range networks of devices grouped together to communicate on the same channel. One of the devices operates at the master device, or coordinator, while the other devices operate as slaves. The role of master device can circulate through the network with different devices assuming that role as it becomes available.

Logical Topologies

It would be easy to visualize the connections of the physical topologies just described if the nodes simply connected to each other. However, this is typically not the case in most network arrangements. This is due to the fact that most networks employ connectivity devices, such as hubs, switches, and routers, which alter the appearance of the actual connection scheme. Therefore, the logical topology will not match the appearance of the physical topology—the particulars of the connection scheme are hidden inside the connecting device.

As an illustration, Figure 12.5 shows a typical network connection scheme using a connecting device to consolidate connections in a single location. The physical topology appears as a star. However, the internal wiring of the connecting router provides a logical bus topology. It is not uncommon for a logical ring or mesh topology to be implemented in a physical star topology.

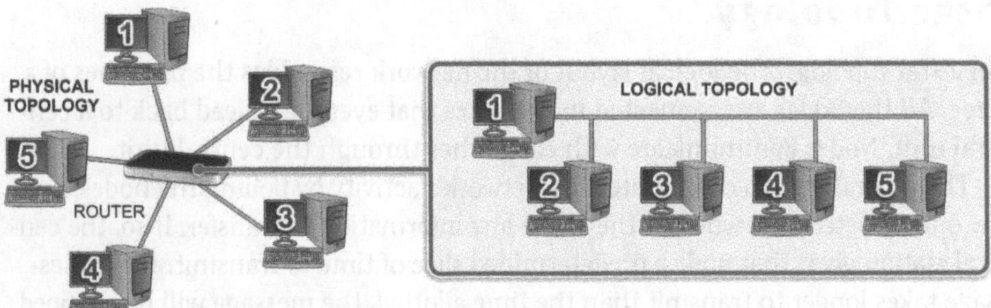

FIGURE 12.5 Logical Topologies

Hands-On Exercises

Objectives

- Describe the purpose of IPsec.
- Create a Connection Security rule.
- Explore the options of creating a Connection Security rule.
- Define "integrity and confidentiality" as they apply to IPsec.

Resources

- Customer-supplied desktop/laptop hardware system
- Windows 10 Professional installed (This procedure will also work successfully on PCs running Windows 10 Home Edition.)
- An account with administrative privileges

Discussion

Internet Protocol Security (IPsec) is an open standard using a suite of protocols for encrypting and authenticating IP communication that is commonly used in VPNs.

Protocols in this suite include:

- Authentication Headers (AH) provide data integrity and origin authentication to protect against *replay attacks* (attacks where a recorded transmission is replayed by an attacker to gain access). Encapsulating Security Payloads (ESP) offers origin authentication as well as encryption. ESP encrypts and encapsulates the entire TCP/UDP datagram within an ESP header that does not include any port information. This means that ESP won't be able to pass through any device using port address translation (PAT).
- Security Associations (SAs) offer a number of algorithms and frameworks for authentication and key exchange.
- Internet Key Exchange (IKE) is the protocol used to set up a security association in IPsec.

Unlike SSL, IPsec operates at Layer 3 in the OSI model and secures everything in a network. IPsec also differs from SSL in that it is implemented on a client system, whereas SSL is built into a browser. All of this combined leads to a safer environment for transferring data, usually at a faster rate. There are two modes of IPsec:

- Transport mode – The IP payload is encapsulated only.
- Tunnel mode – The entire IP packet is encapsulated.

Connection Security includes authenticating two computers prior to communication and then ensuring the confidentiality between them. Windows employs IPsec to achieve Connection Security.

Procedure

In this procedure, you will discover how and where IPsec is configured. You will create a new Connection Security rule, and explore the options associated with IPsec. This procedure is intended to instruct you on how to create an IPsec communication; however, you will not be able to test it in this environment.

Accessing IPsec

IPsec is located within Windows Firewall with Advanced Security. It has been renamed Connection Security; however, it is generally stated that Connection Security is achieved by using IPsec rules.

1. Power on your machine.
2. Log on to Windows using your administrative account.
3. At your desktop, in the search bar embedded in your taskbar, type wf.msc and press Enter.
4. This should launch the Windows Firewall with Advanced Security.
5. Click the Connection Security Rules entry, as illustrated in Figure 12.6. The middle pane should have no current rules established.
6. Expand Monitoring and then Security Associations by selecting the arrow next to each, as illustrated in Figure 12.7.

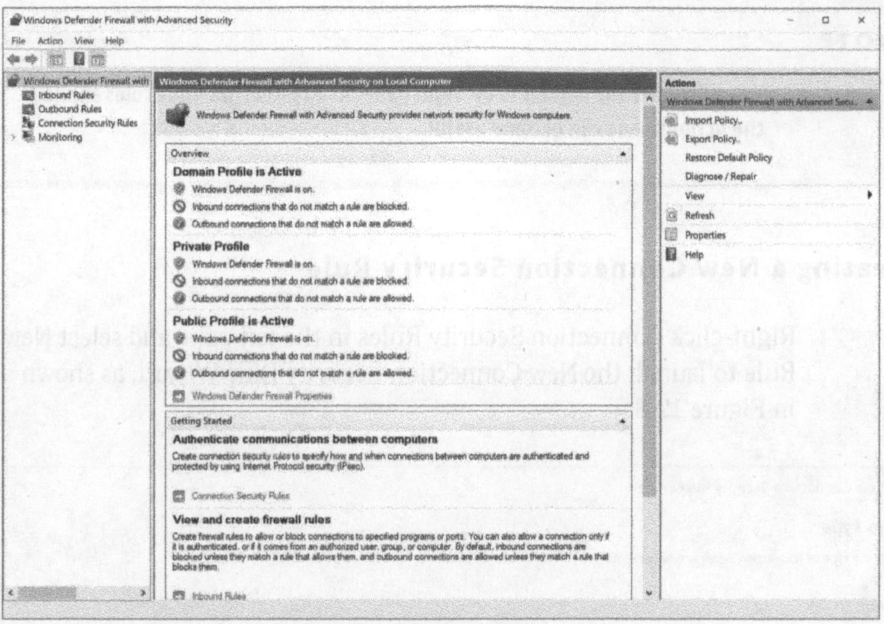

FIGURE 12.6 Windows Firewall with Advanced Security

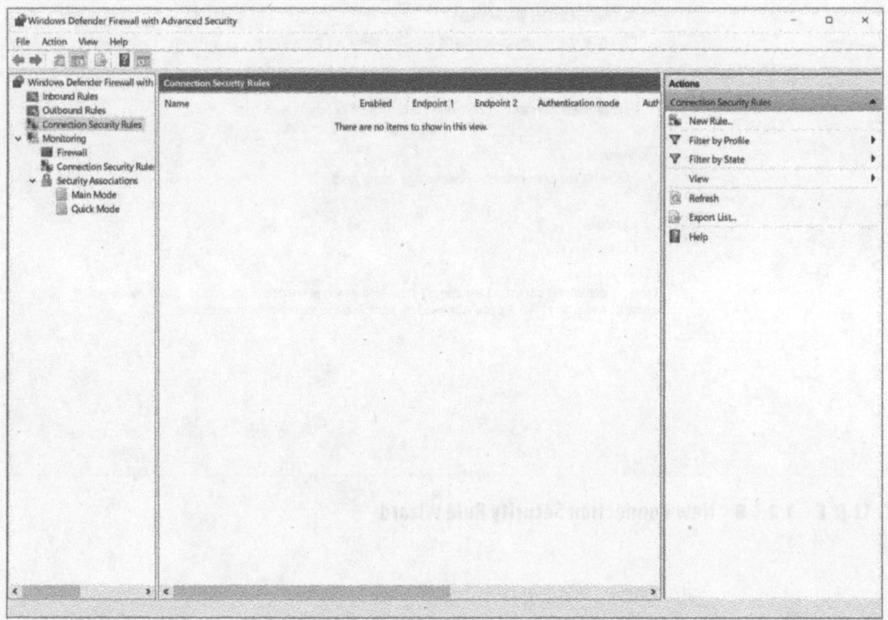

FIGURE 12.7 Expanded Monitoring and Security Associations Items

NOTE

You will notice the Actions in the right pane. As a system has more rules applied, the Actions pane can become useful.

Creating a New Connection Security Rule

1. Right-click Connection Security Rules in the left pane and select New Rule to launch the New Connection Security Rule Wizard, as shown in Figure 12.8.

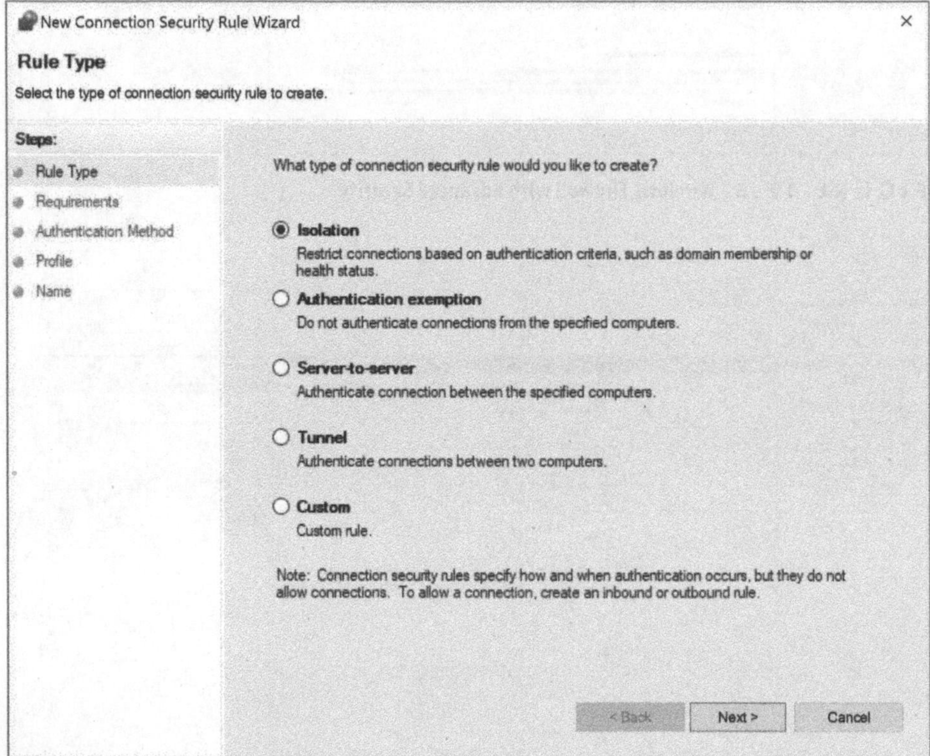

FIGURE 12.8 New Connection Security Rule Wizard

Depending on the Rule Type selected, there are anywhere from four to seven steps. Each step has multiple options from which to choose.

2. Record the Rule Types in Table 12.2. Pay special attention to the definitions of each.

TABLE 12.2: Rule Types

Isolation	
Authentication exemption	
Server-to-server	
Tunnel	
Custom	

NOTE **Connection Security rules specify how and when authentication occurs. However, this is not the same as allowing connections. To allow a connection, you will need to create an inbound or outbound rule.**

3. Select each radio button next to the Rule Types to explore the different steps necessary for each. When finished, select the radio button associated with Isolation.

   The Rule Type specifies some basic settings based on the intended use of the rule. The Isolation rule will restrict access based on the authentication type and the network profile.

4. Click the Next button to proceed to the Requirements window. The choices here include:

   - Request authentication, but do not require.
   - Require authentication for inbound and outbound.
   - Require inbound, request outbound. A hybrid of the previous two options.

5. Read the definition of each and select Request Authentication For Inbound And Outbound Connections, as illustrated in Figure 12.9.

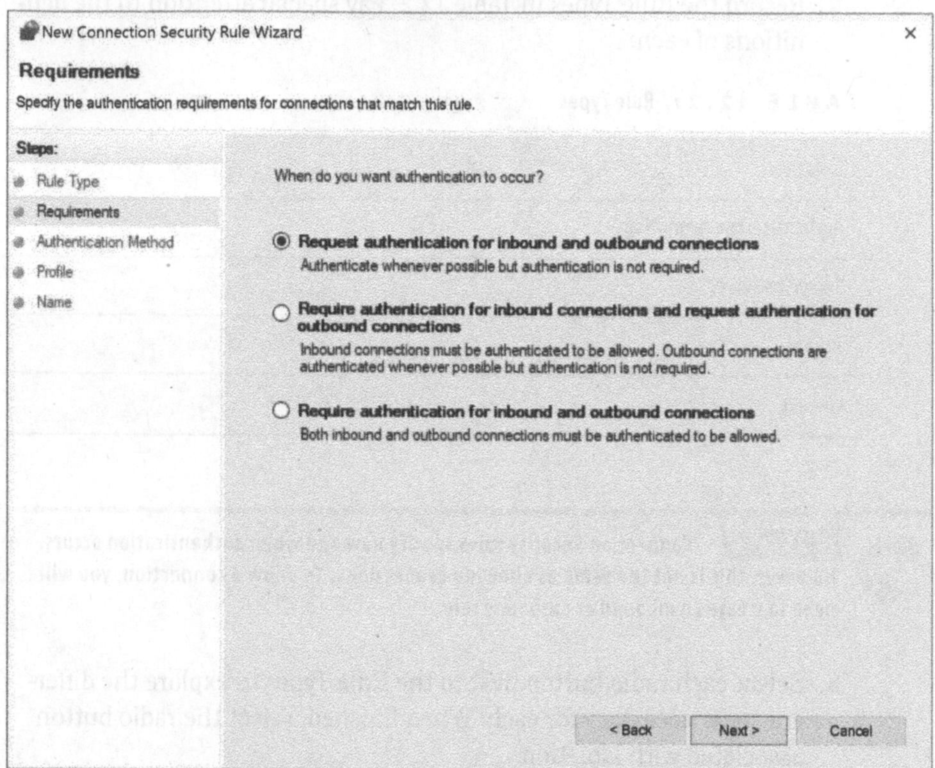

FIGURE 12.9 New Connection Security Rule Wizard – Requirements Window

6. Click Next to view the Authentication Method window.

   Although four options are listed, the two involving Kerberos V5 are restricted to connections made within an Active Directory forest.

7. Select the radio button next to Advanced to make the Customize button available, as shown in Figure 12.10.

8. Click the Customize button to launch a separate Customize Advanced Authentication Methods window, as shown in Figure 12.11.

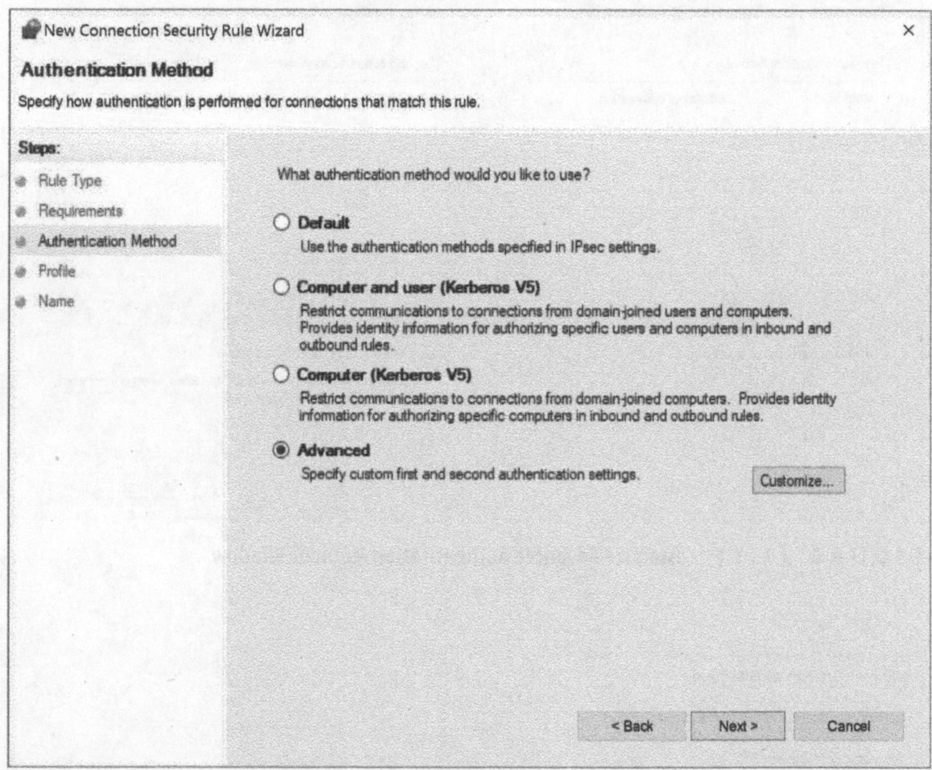

FIGURE 12.10 The Customize button is active.

In this window, you can customize a list of authentication methods to fit your needs. Explore the window carefully.

9. Click the Add button located under First Authentication Methods: The Add First Authentication Method window will appear, as shown in Figure 12.12.

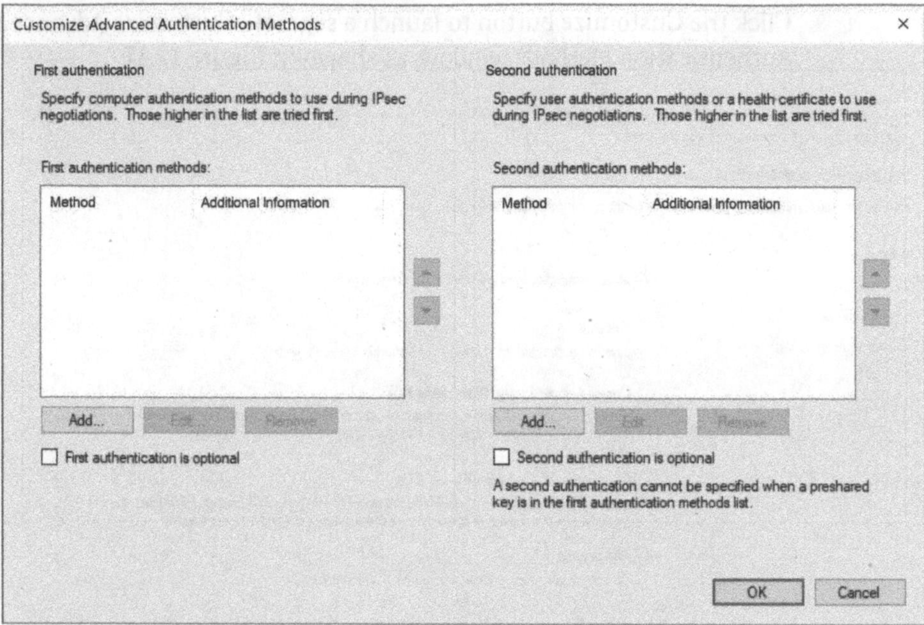

FIGURE 12.11 Customize Advanced Authentication Methods Window

Add First Authentication Method

Select the credential to use for first authentication:

Computer (Kerberos V5)

Computer (NTLMv2)

Computer certificate from this certification authority (CA):

Signing algorithm: RSA (default)

Certificate store type: Root CA (default)

Browse...

Accept only health certificates

Advanced

Enable certificate to account mapping

Preshared key (not recommended):

Preshared key authentication is less secure than other authentication methods. Preshared keys are stored in plaintext. When preshared key authentication is used, Second Authentication cannot be used.

OK

Cancel

FIGURE 12.12 Add First Authentication Method Window

This Add First Authentication Method window offers four possible authentication methods from which to choose:

- ▶ Kerberos V5
- ▶ NTLMv2
- ▶ Certificate
- ▶ Preshared key (not recommended)

10. After exploring the options, click Cancel to exit the window. Click Cancel in the Customize Advanced Authentication Methods window as well.

11. You should be returned to the New Connection Security Rule Wizard – Authentication Method window. Select the radio button next to Default and then click Next. You will be directed to the Profile window.

These selections relate to the network connections in place on the computer. While a standalone computer in a networked office may not need to worry about using a Public network, a traveling laptop will need to ensure integrity and confidentiality over the Internet.

12. Leave all three check boxes selected, as shown in Figure 12.13, and click Next to move to the Name window.

13. Enter **Request IPsec Rule** under Name. Leave the Description (Optional): blank, as shown in Figure 12.14.

14. Click Finish to save the rule. You are brought back to the Windows Firewall With Advanced Security window. The new rule is now located in the middle pane, as illustrated in Figure 12.15.

Notice the right pane. The Actions panel has changed and more options are available.

To create an IPsec connection, another computer would configure a Connection Security rule using the same process. Any time the computers want to transfer information, an IPsec connection needs to be completed.

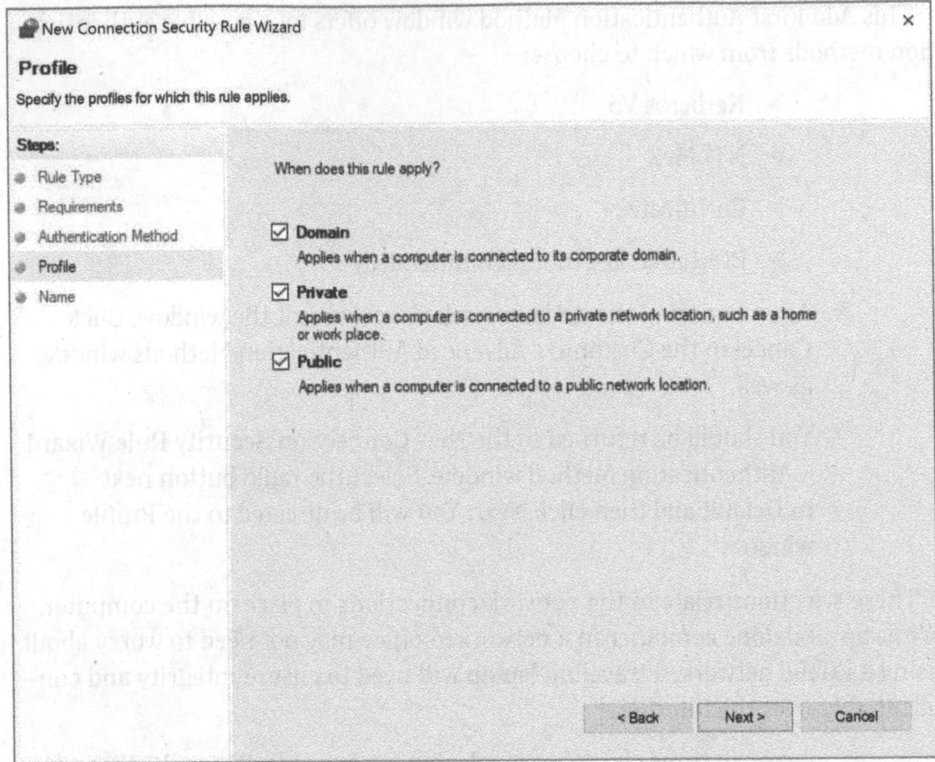

FIGURE 12.13 **New Connection Security Rule Wizard – Profile Window**

Recall that you selected the Request Authentication, Not Required option. Therefore, you can still connect to anyone else without a secure connection.

15. Select the rule in the middle pane to highlight it. In the right pane, click the Properties entry, as shown in Figure 12.16.

Each tab allows you to adjust the settings you selected in the New Connection Security Rule Wizard.

16. Explore each tab, and then click the Cancel button to exit the Properties window.

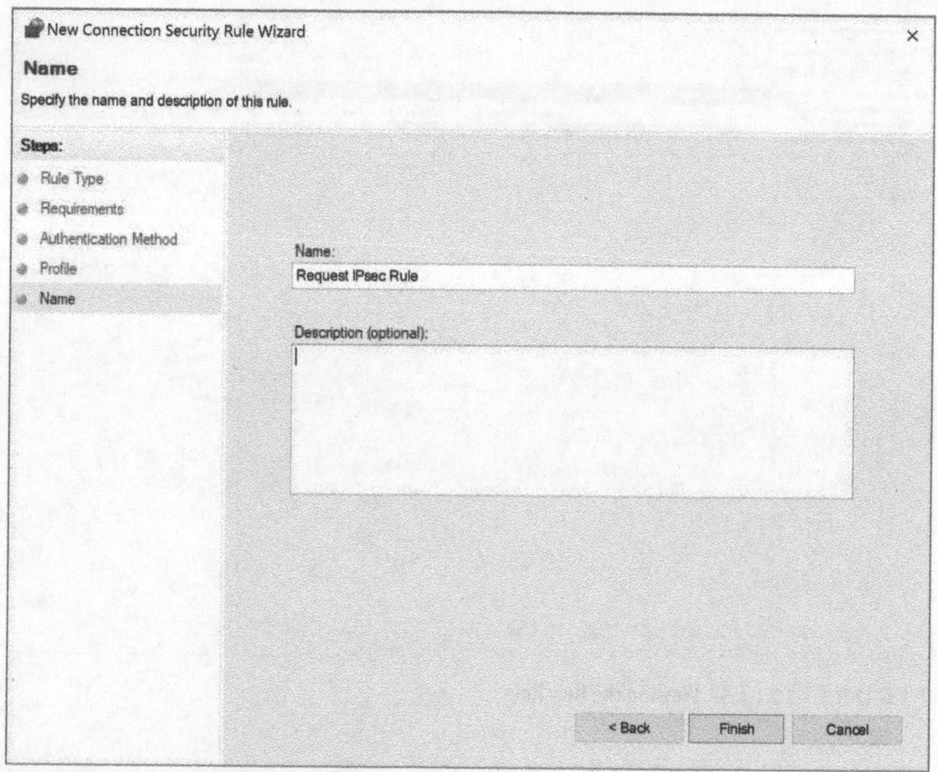

FIGURE 12.14 Naming the Rule

Monitoring IPsec Connections

Under the Monitoring directory, you can view any active rules being used for IPsec. Although you will not see any active rules, it is important to know where to view this information and what it means.

1. If the Monitoring directory and the Security Associations directory in the left pane are not expanded, expand them now by selecting the arrows next to them.
2. Select Main Mode in the left pane. Nothing should be listed in the middle pane.

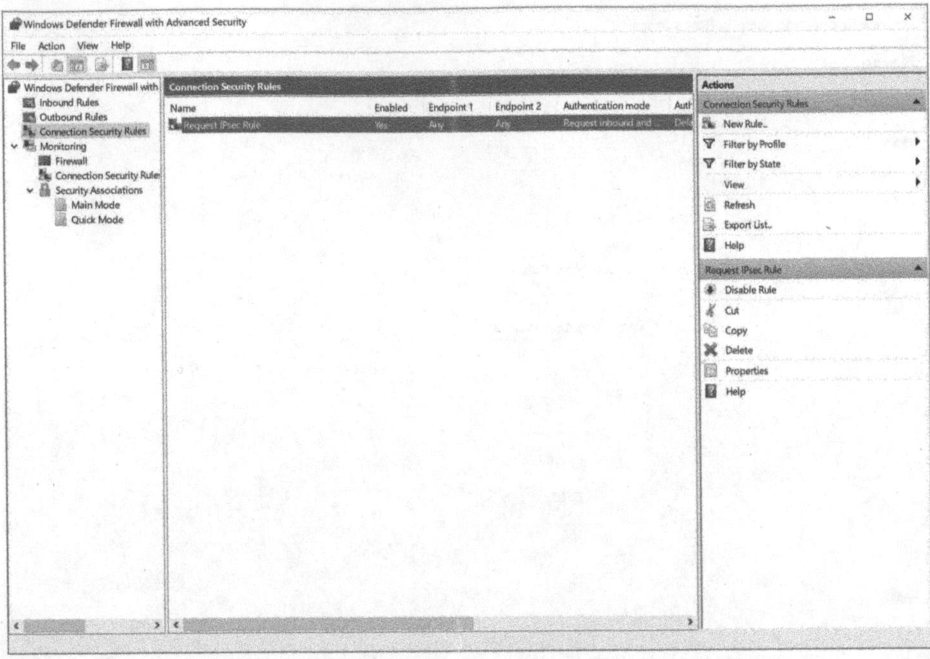

FIGURE 12.15 Viewing the New Rule

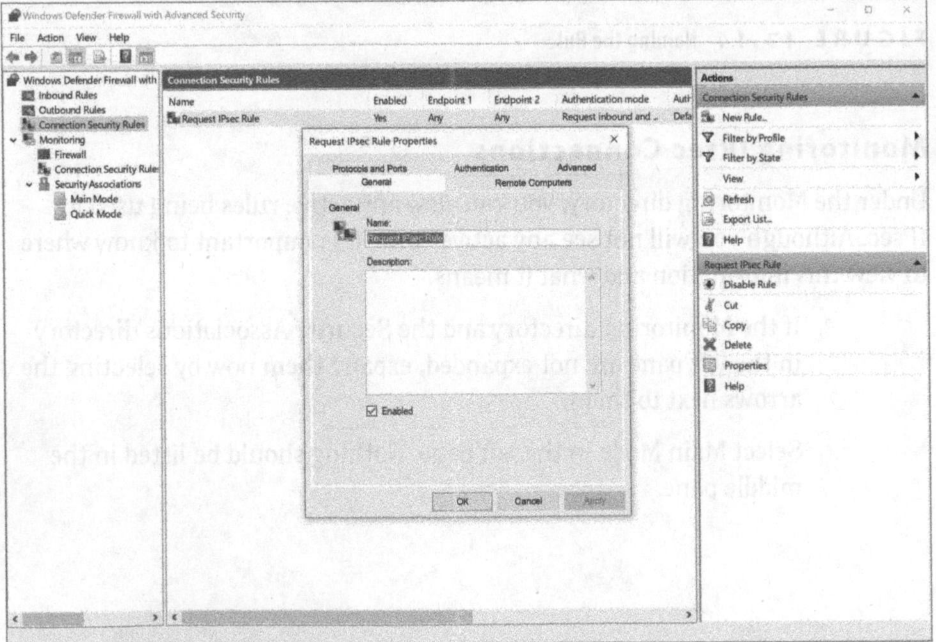

FIGURE 12.16 Request IPsec Rule Properties

Main mode is phase 1 on the IPsec connection. It uses cleartext to establish how it will proceed.

3. Select Quick Mode in the left pane. Again, nothing should be listed in the middle pane.

In Quick mode, which is considered to be Phase 2, communication parameters are negotiated.

If a connection were active, you would be able to see each listed with the applicable AH and ESP protocols in place. AH gives integrity, while ESP provides both integrity and confidentiality.

- Integrity – Confirming that the data packets have not been tampered with. Prevents man-in-the-middle attacks.
- Confidentiality – Confirming that the data packets cannot be viewed by a malicious user. Prevents network sniffers from viewing data.

NOTE **Even though you have created this rule, your firewall may be blocking the connection. Under normal circumstances, you would also create an inbound and outbound rule as necessary.**

Lab Questions

1. What protocols are used in the IPsec standard?
2. At which level of the OSI model does IPsec operate?
3. With regard to authentication, what are the three options for Requirements?
4. Describe the difference between "integrity" and "confidentiality" as it relates to IPsec.
5. Define Connection Security.

Lab Answers

1. The protocols in this suite include:
   - Authentication Headers (AH) provide data integrity and origin authentication to protect against *replay attacks* (attacks where a recorded transmission is replayed by an attacker to gain access).

- Encapsulating Security Payloads (ESP) offers origin authentication as well as encryption. ESP encrypts and encapsulates the entire TCP/UDP datagram within an ESP header that does not include any port information. This means that ESP won't be able to pass through any device using port address translation (PAT).
- Security Associations (SAs) offer a number of algorithms and frameworks for authentication and key exchange.
- Internet Key Exchange (IKE) is the protocol used to set up a security association in IPsec.

2. Unlike SSL, IPsec operates at Layer 3 in the OSI model and secures everything in a network. IPsec also differs from SSL in that it is implemented on a client system, whereas SSL is built into a browser.
3. All of this combined leads to a safer environment for transferring data—usually at a faster rate. The options include:
   - Request authentication, but do not require.
   - Require authentication for inbound and outbound.
   - Require inbound, request outbound. A hybrid of the previous options.
4. The IPsec standard uses a suite of protocols to accomplish its goal of securing data. AH gives integrity while ESP provides both integrity and confidentiality.
   - Integrity – Confirms that the data packets have not been tampered with. Prevents man-in-the-middle attacks.
   - Confidentiality – Confirms that the data packets cannot be viewed by a malicious user.
   - Prevents network sniffers from viewing data.
5. Connection Security authenticates two computers prior to communication and then ensures the confidentiality between them. Windows employs IPsec to achieve connection security.

CHAPTER 13

Understanding Networking Protocols

When more than two computers are involved in the communications pathway, a network is formed and additional controls must be put into place to make certain that information is sent to the correct member of the network. This is in addition to controlling the flow of information on the network connection. These controls are implemented as a set of rules called *protocols*. In this chapter, you'll learn to:

- **Discuss basic network protocols**
- **Identify components associated with different IP addressing standards**
- **Discuss security issues associated with MAC addressing**
- **Identify the components and operation of the TCP/IP protocol suite and identify its vulnerabilities**
- **Provide examples of network subnetting and it uses**
- **Describe the functions and structure of the Ethernet networking standard**
- **Contrast peer-to-peer and client/server network access control methods**

The Basics of Networking Protocols

A *network protocol* is a set of rules that governs how communications are conducted across a network. In order for devices to communicate with each other on the network, they must all use the same network protocol.

In a complex network, such as the Internet, multiple protocol layers are employed to deal with the complex levels created by hosting so many different types of devices and applications. Referring to Figure 12.1 in Chapter 12, you can see that different types of protocols reside in each level of the OSI model up through Layer 5.

For example, at Layers 1 and 2 there are different protocols for different types of communication media (wired networks, wireless networks, fiber-optic networks). Layer 1 components provide physical media standards, while Layer 2 provides for logical transmission standardization. Layers 3 and 4 contain different network routing schemes (to make sure everything winds up where it should go), email handling applications, web applications, and secure transmissions.

MAC Addresses

All network operations depend on a hierarchy of addresses in order to enable the network's devices to exchange information. The most basic address in networking operations is the Media Access Control address (MAC address) that serves as a unique identifier for every device attached to a network. These addresses are typically assigned to the devices by their manufacturers and stored in their firmware.

The standard 48-bit format for generating a MAC address specifies six pairs of hexadecimal digits. For display purposes, the number is written as six number pairs separated by hyphens (-) or colons (:)—for example,

```
13:A2:00:40:6B:8E:66
```

This original 48-bit format is known as the EUI-48 (Extended Unique Identifier) in IEEE terms. This format corresponds to the original Ethernet IPv4 addressing scheme for networking and is used in wireless 802.11 and Bluetooth networking technologies.

The EUI-64 bit version of the MAC address code enlarges the code to eight pairs of hexadecimal digits. For example, a given device could be assigned the MAC address = 00:13:A2:00:40:6B:8E:66. This format corresponds to the IPv6 addressing scheme and is included in Firewire, ZigBee, and 802.15 technologies.

As you recall from Table 12.1 in Chapter 12, MAC addressing is associated with OSI Layer 2 operations. Recall that this layer is responsible for establishing the logical access and connectivity to and from each network port. Different network connectivity devices, such as switches and routers, rely on MAC addresses as the basis for building and using internal content addressable memory (CAM) tables. The devices use these tables to route messages they receive from one network segment to a location on another network segment based on the hardware port to which the intended recipient is connected.

Many connectivity devices build and maintain their CAM tables through a MAC learning and discovery process. As they interact with devices connected to their physical ports, they read message headers to acquire the sending and receiving devices' MAC addresses and record them in the CAM along with their port information.

TCP/IP

While there are many different types of network protocols in use throughout the world, the TCP/IP (Transmission Control Protocol/Internet Protocol) suite of protocols forms the most popular network protocol currently in use. Although this is partially due to the fact that the Internet is based on it, TCP/IP has solidified its place as the protocol of choice for corporate networks because most operating systems support this protocol. It can also be used on any topology (for example, Ethernet, Token Ring, and so on).

This fact becomes very useful when you are trying to network different types of systems to one another (for example, Microsoft Windows computers and devices, Apple computers and devices, and Linux computers and devices). In addition, TCP/IP is a routable protocol, so its packets can be transferred across many different types of networks before they reach their final destination.

The U.S. Department of Defense originally developed the TCP/IP protocol as a hacker-resistant, secure protocol for transmitting data across a network. It is considered to be one of the most secure of the network protocols. In addition, because the U.S. government developed it, no one actually owns the TCP/IP protocol, and so it was adopted as the transmission standard for the Internet.

No matter what type of computer platform or software is being used, information must move across the Internet in the form of TCP/IP packets. This protocol calls for data to be grouped together in bundles called *network packets*. The TCP/IP packet is designed primarily to allow for message fragmentation and reassembly. It exists through two header fields, the IP header and the TCP header, followed by the data field, as illustrated in Figure 13.1.

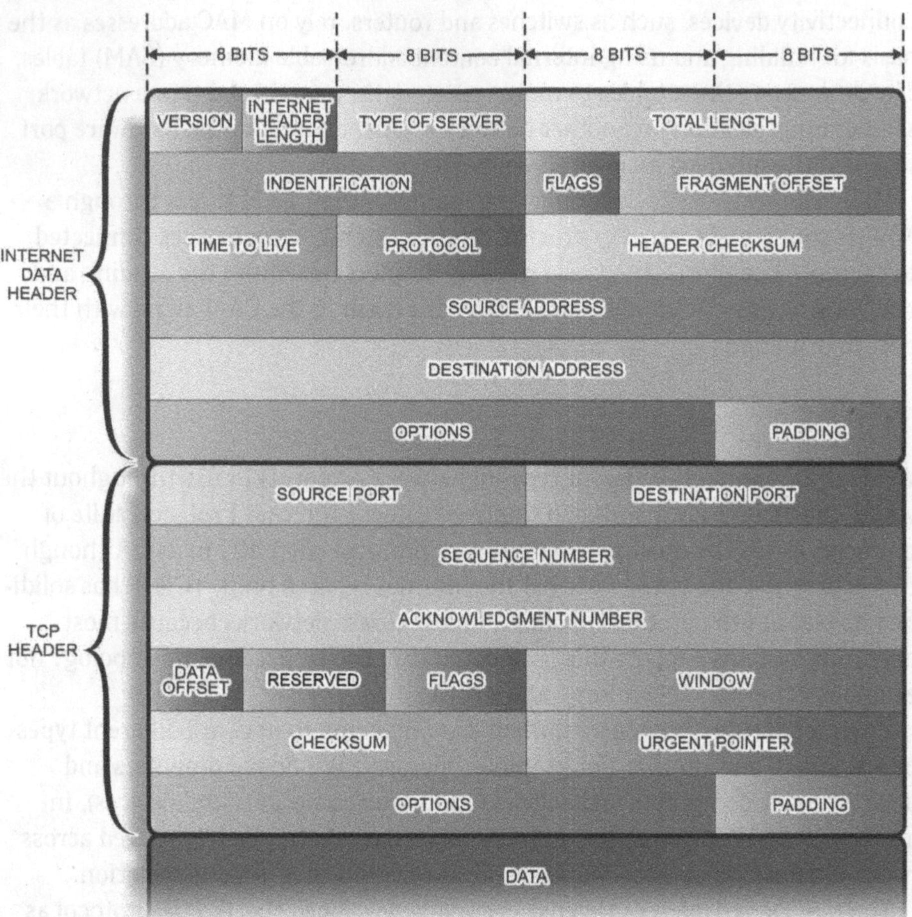

FIGURE 13.1 TCP/IP Packet

The major parts of the TCP/IP protocol rest on the two core protocols that give it its name: TCP and IP. The IP portion of TCP/IP protocol operates at Layer 3 of the OSI model, while the TCP portion of the combined protocols standard operates at Layer 4. As such, the IP portion is responsible for the packets and their actual delivery, while TCP is responsible for tracking the individual segments into which the message gets divided.

The conceptual divide between layers is not to be taken as exact. For example, the protocol Internet Control Message Protocol (ICMP) resides at Layer 3, despite offering no packet routing or addressing information, because it assists the Layer 3 IP in doing its job. On the other hand, as another example, Bridging Control Protocol (BCP) is a routing protocol but is carried by TCP at Layer 4.

One other important element to be aware of is how the TCP/IP protocols initiate connections. This is accomplished in a three-way handshaking arrangement that begins with a Synchronize (SYN) packet being sent from a client to a server. In response, the server sends back a Synchronize/Acknowledge (SYN/ACK) packet to the client. Upon receipt of the SYN/ACK packet, the client returns an Acknowledge (ACK) packet to the server, and the conversation between them can begin. Figure 13.2 illustrates the SYN/ACK sequence.

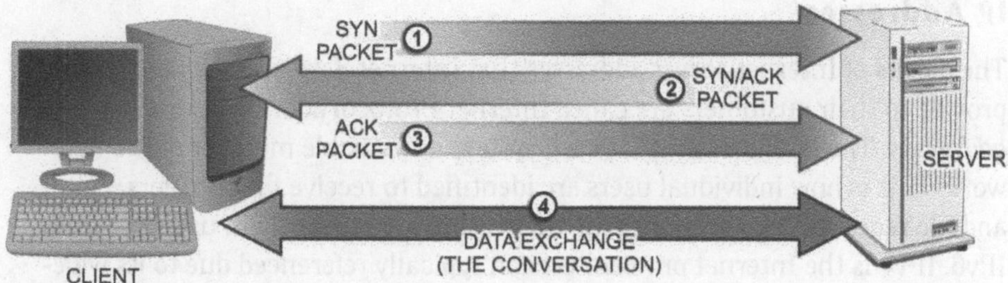

FIGURE 13.2 SYN/ACK Sequence

TCP/IP Vulnerabilities

Because a TCP/IP packet is made up of many different sections and fields, attackers often exploit the makeup of the packets. With the proper tools, it is fairly easy to manipulate the IP headers of TCP/IP packets to falsify addresses to hide an attacker's identity. In the case of manipulating the source and/or destination network address, this manipulation process is known as *IP spoofing* and is the basis for many types of network and internetwork attacks. The idea behind IP spoofing is similar to MAC spoofing, which is discussed in the previous section of this chapter.

Another common attack method directed against TCP/IP packets is a SYN flood that exploits the three-way handshake TCP/IP employs to initiate connections between network nodes. In this type of attack, the attacker sends the SYN request to the server, but manipulates the handshake to either spoof a different IP address in the SYN packet or simply withhold the ACK packet from the server.

In the first instance, the server will send the SYN/ACK packet to the spoofed address, which will not respond because it did not send the original SYN packet. In both cases, the fact that the server does not receive an ACK packet causes it to wait for some period of time. The attacker will typically send a wave of SYN requests to the server so that it fills up with half-opened connections that tie up its resources.

When the full capability of the server's ability to handle these requests is reached, it will stop supplying service due to its lack of resources to handle the volume. This is known as a *Denial of Service (DoS) attack*.

The tools, attacks, and prevention methods associated with TCP/IP manipulation are discussed in detail later in this chapter in conjunction with network servers and connectivity devices that service Layers 2, 3, and 4 of the ISO model.

IP Addresses

The blocks of Internet access addresses that Internet Service Providers (ISPs) provide to their customers are called Internet Protocol addresses, or *IP addresses*. The IP address makes each system a reachable member of the network. This is how individual users are identified to receive file transfers, email, and file requests. Two versions of IP addressing are currently in use: IPv4 and IPv6. IPv4 is the Internet protocol version typically referenced due to its widespread use.

IPv4 Addressing

IPv4 addresses exist in the numeric format of `XXX.YYY.ZZZ.AAA`. Each address consists of four 8-bit fields separated by dots (.). This format of specifying addresses is referred to as dotted decimal notation. The decimal numbers are derived from the binary address that the hardware understands. For example, a binary network address of:

`10000111.10001011.01001001.00110110` (binary)

corresponds to:

`135.139.073.054` (dotted - decimal)

You will also find that IP addresses are referred to in terms of octets. An *octet* is simply a grouping of eight consecutive bits. In the binary example just given, the most significant octet would be `10000111` (or 135). The least significant octet would be `00110110` (or 054). The entire address occurs in four-octet fields like the previous example.

Within the four octets, each IP address consists of two parts: the network address and the host address. The network address identifies the entire network;

the host address identifies an intelligent member within the network. Three classes of standard IP addresses are supported for LANs: Class A, Class B, and Class C:

- Class A addresses are reserved for large networks and use the last 24 bits (the last three octets or fields) of the address for the host address. The first octet always begins with a 0, followed by a 7-bit number. Therefore, valid Class A addresses range between `001.x.x.x` and `126.x.x.x`. This allows a Class A network to support 126 different networks with nearly 17 million hosts (nodes) per network.
- Class B addresses are assigned to medium-sized networks. The first two octets can range between `128.x.x.x` and `191.254.0.0`. The last two octets contain the host addresses. This enables Class B networks to include up to 16,384 different networks with approximately 65,534 hosts per network.
- Class C addresses are normally used with smaller LANs. In a Class C address, only the last octet is used for host addresses. The first three octets can range between `192.x.x.x` and `223.254.254.0`. Therefore, the Class C address can support approximately two million networks with 254 hosts each.

Subnets

Sections of the network can be grouped together into subnets that share a range of IP addresses. A protective gateway is employed to act as an entry and exit point for the segmented subnet. These groups are referred to as *intranets*. An intranet requires that each segment have a protective gateway to act as an entry and exit point for the segment. In most cases, the gateway is a device called a *router* or a *switch*. A router is an intelligent device that receives data and directs it toward a designated IP address. A Layer 2 switch is also an intelligent device, but it directs the data toward a designated MAC address.

Some networks employ a firewall as a gateway to the outside. A firewall is a combination of hardware and software components that provide a protective barrier between networks with different security levels. Administrators configure the firewall so that it will only pass data to and from designated IP addresses and TCP/IP ports.

Subnets are created by *masking off* (hiding) the network address portion of the IP address on the units within the subnet. This, in effect, limits the mobility of the data to those nodes within the subnet because they can reconcile only addresses from within their masked range. This concept is illustrated in Figure 13.3. Three common reasons to create a subnet include the following:

To isolate one segment of the network from all the others. Suppose, for example, that a large organization has 1,000 computers, all of which are connected to the network. Without segmentation, data from all 1,000 units would run through every other network node. The effect of this would be that everyone in the network would have access to all the data on the network, and the operation of the network would be slowed considerably by the uncontrolled traffic.

To efficiently use IP addresses. Because the IP addressing scheme is defined as a 32-bit code, there are only a certain number of possible addresses. Although 126 networks with 17 million customers might seem like a lot, in the scheme of a worldwide network system, that's not a lot of addresses to go around.

To utilize a single IP address across physically divided locations. For example, subnetting a Class C address between remotely located areas of a campus would permit half of the 253 possible addresses to be allocated to one campus location, and the other half to be allocated to hosts at the second location. In this manner, both locations can operate using a single Class C address.

The subnet is established by entering numbers to block any or all of the addresses associated with each octet of the IP address. For example, a subnet mask value of 255 blocks the entire octet, while a value of 254 would block all but one of the addresses in the octet.

The default subnet mask for a Class A IP address is `255.0.0.0`, while a Class B IP address typically uses a subnet mask of `255.255.0.0`. For a Class C address, which is typically used in small organizations and residential networks, a subnet mask of `255.255.255.0` is commonly used. This blocks the first three octets (the network portion of the address) and leaves the addresses from the lower octet open for use with hosts. When you enter an IP address in Windows, the default subnet mask value for that class of IP address is automatically filled in.

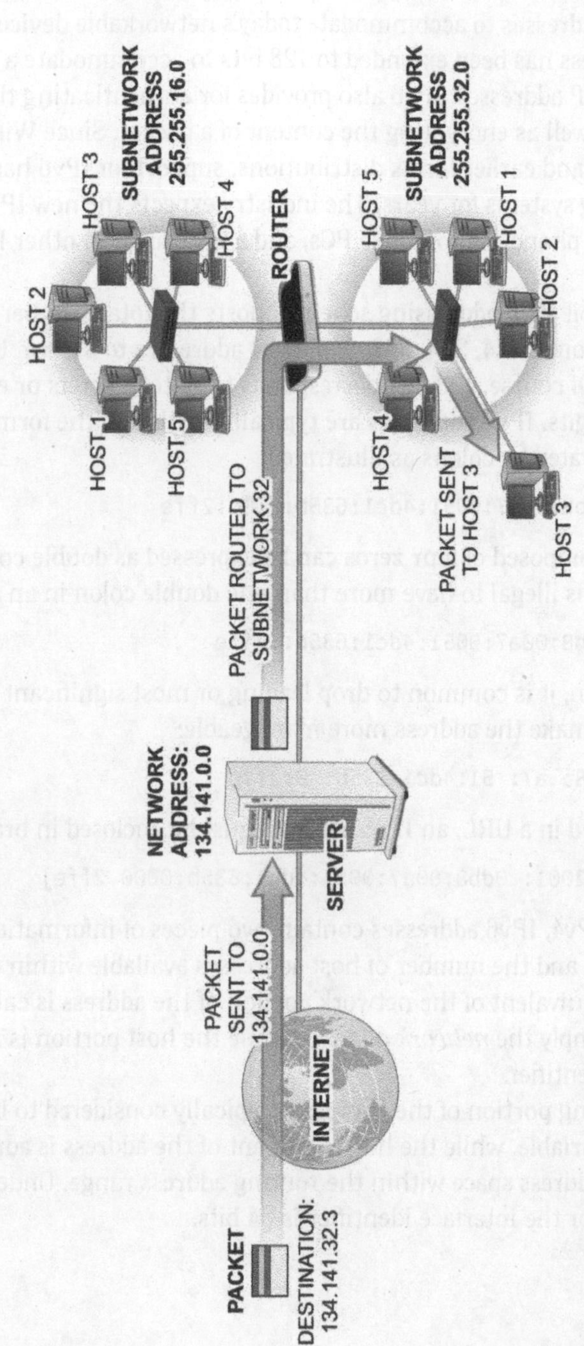

FIGURE 13.3 Subnetting with IPv4

IPv6 Addressing

IPv6 is a newer IP addressing protocol developed to cope with the lack of available IPv4 addresses to accommodate today's networkable devices. Under IPv6, the IP address has been extended to 128 bits to accommodate a tremendous number of IP addresses. IPv6 also provides for authenticating the sender of a packet as well as encrypting the content of a packet. Since Windows Vista, Windows 7, and earlier Linux distributions, support for IPv6 has been included in operating systems for years. The industry expects the new IP version to support mobile phones, automobile PCs, and a wide array of other IP-based personal devices.

The 128-bit IPv6 addressing scheme boosts the total number of usable IP addresses from 2^{32} (4, 294, 967, 296) IPv4 addresses to 21^{28} or 3.4×10^{38} IPv6 addresses. Of course, 128 bits corresponds to sixteen octets or eight hexadecimal (base 16) digits. IPv6 addresses are typically written in the form of hexadecimal digits, separated by colons as illustrated:

```
2001: 0db8:00a7:0051:4dc1:635b:0000:2ffe
```

Groups composed of four zeros can be expressed as double colons (::). However, it is illegal to have more than one double colon in an address.

```
2001: 0db8:00a7:0051:4dc1:635b::2ffe
```

In addition, it is common to drop leading or most significant zeros from the number to make the address more manageable:

```
2001: db8: a7: 51:4dc1:635b: 0:2ffe
```

When used in a URL, an IPv6 address must be enclosed in brackets:

```
http://[2001: 0db8:00a7:0051:4dc1:635b:0000.2ffe]
```

As with IPv4, IPv6 addresses contain two pieces of information: the number of networks and the number of host addresses available within those networks. The IPv6 equivalent of the network portion of the address is called the *routing prefix* or simply the *network address,* while the host portion is referred to as the interface identifier.

The routing portion of the address is typically considered to be an externally managed variable, while the hosts segment of the address is administered locally using the address space within the routing address range. Under IPv6, the minimum size for the interface identifier is 64 bits.

Therefore, when referring to the network portion of an IPv6 address, the first address in the block of contiguous addresses would begin with the network portion of the address followed by a string of all zeros:

```
2001: db8: a7:0000:0000:0000:0000:0000
```

and would end in the network address plus a string of "f16"s (for 1111[2] or 15[10]):

```
2001: db8: a7: ffff:ffff:ffff:ffff:ffff
```

It is also common to see ranges of IPv6 addresses written in CIDR notation. Under IPv6, this system uses the routing prefix portion of the address followed by the slash (/) character and a decimal number that represents the number of bits reserved by the prefix. Applying this to the block of addresses just described produces the following notation:

```
2001:0db8:00a7:/48
```

The /48 value is calculated by taking the number of places held by the routing prefix (12) and multiplying the number of places by the 4 bits required to represent each hexadecimal place.

A Note About Leading Zeros

The leading zeros have been restored in this example for ease of calculations. They would not normally be in place in a real CIDR address.

The IPv6 transmission packet format is not the same as the IPv4 packet. Therefore, they are not interchangeable (IPv4 devices are not directly compatible with IPv6 devices). Newer computing devices and networking equipment possess IPv6-ready detection and connectivity capabilities.

While both IPv4 and IPv6 networks can be divided into subnetworks, there is no equivalent term for subnet masking in IPv6.

Private IP Classes

Because the Internet is basically a huge TCP/IP network in which no two devices connected to it can have the same address, if companies utilized Internet routable addresses for every system, the world would have exhausted the IP addressing scheme many years earlier.

Instead, a private network can use a special IP addressing scheme as long as that network does not need to be routable to the Internet. This is referred to as a private network. When configuring a private network, you must design an IP addressing scheme to use across the network. Although, technically, you could use any IP addressing scheme you want in a private network without consulting an ISP, the risk remains that any accidental connectivity to the Internet would allow private network traffic to continue outward across the Internet.

To fix this, special ranges of network addresses in each IP class have been reserved for use with private networks. This is according to RFC 1918. These reserved addresses are not registered to anyone on the Internet and, more importantly, traffic using these private ranges is not publically routable. This means all routers managing Internet traffic will refuse to forward on network traffic using those private addressing.

If you are configuring a private network, you should use one of these address options rather than create a random addressing scheme. The total number of clients on the network typically dictates which IP addressing class you should use. The following list of private network IP addresses can be used:

- An IP address of `10.0.0.0`, with the subnet mask of `255.0.0.0`
- An IP address of `169.254.0.0`, with the subnet mask of `255.255.255.0` (the Microsoft AIPA default)
- An IP address of `172.(16-32).0.0`, with the subnet mask of `255.240.0.0`
- An IP address of `192.168.0.0`, with the subnet mask of `255.255.0.0`

A Word About Address Ranges

Under IPv4, the `127.x.x.x` address range is a special block of addresses reserved for testing network systems. The U.S. government owns some of these addresses for testing the Internet backbone. The `127.0.0.1` address is reserved for testing the bus on the local system.

In addition, remember that all hosts must have the same network ID and subnet mask and that no two computers on your network can have the same IP address when you are establishing a private IP addressing scheme.

Ethernet

While the TCP/IP protocol has emerged as the dominant data packaging and transfer method, the Ethernet family of standards has become the dominant force in hardware and electrical signaling interfacing as well as for providing media access control. The original Ethernet standard specification was developed by Xerox in 1976 and published by the International Electrical and Electronic Association (IEEE) as the IEEE-802.3 Ethernet protocol.

Local area networks are designed so that the entire network runs synchronously at one frequency. Therefore, only one set of electronic signals may be placed on the network at one time. However, data can move in both directions between network locations. By definition, this makes local area network operations half-duplex in nature (that is, information can travel in both directions, but not at the same time).

In such a network, some method must be used to determine which node has use of the network's communications paths and for how long it can have it. The network's access protocol handles these functions, and it is necessary to prevent more than one user from accessing the bus at any given time. If two sets of data are placed on the network at the same time, a data collision occurs, and data are lost.

The Ethernet methodology for access control is referred to as carrier sense multiple-access with collision detection (CSMA/CD). Using this protocol, a node that wants to transfer data over the network first listens to the LAN to determine whether it is in use. If the LAN is not in use, the node begins transmitting its data. If the network is busy, the node waits for a predetermined length of time for the LAN to clear and then takes control of network media.

If two nodes are waiting to use the LAN, they will periodically attempt to access the LAN at the same time. When this happens, a data collision occurs, and the data from both nodes are rendered useless. The receiver portion of the Ethernet controller monitors the transmission to detect collisions. When it senses the data bits overlapping, it halts the transmission, as does the other node. The transmitting controller generates an abort pattern code that is transmitted to all the nodes on the LAN, telling them that a collision has occurred. This alerts any nodes that might be waiting to access the LAN that there is a problem.

The receiving node (or nodes) dumps any data that it received before the collision occurred. Other nodes waiting to send data generate a random timing number and go into a holding pattern. The timing number is a waiting time that the node sits out before it tries to transmit. Because the number is randomly generated, the odds against two of the nodes trying to transmit again at the same time are very low.

The first node to time out listens to the network to determine whether any activity is still occurring. Because it almost always finds a clear LAN, it begins transmitting. If two of the nodes do time out at the same time, another collision happens, and the abort pattern/number generation/time-out sequence begins again. Eventually, one of the nodes will gain clear access to the network and successfully transmit its data.

While the Ethernet strategy provides for up to 1,024 users to share the LAN, from the description of its collision-recovery technique, it should be apparent that with more users on an Ethernet LAN, more collisions are likely to occur, and the average time to complete an actual data transfer will be longer.

The Ethernet Frame

Under the Ethernet standard, information is collected into a package called a *frame*. Figure 13.4 depicts a typical Ethernet frame. The frame carries the following six sections of information:

- A preamble
- A destination address
- A source address
- A type field
- The data field
- The frame check error-detection and correction information

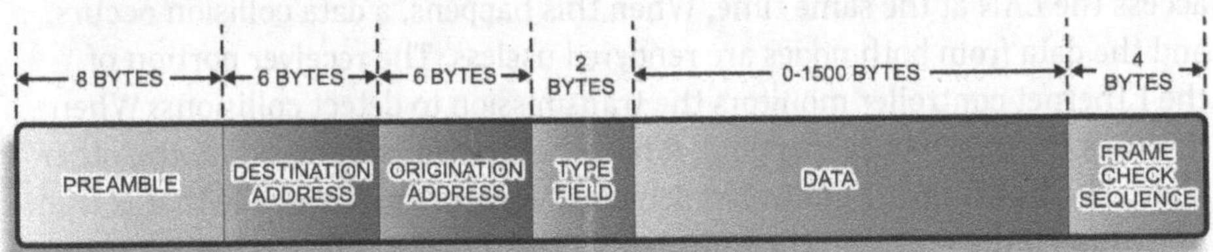

FIGURE 13.4 A Typical Ethernet Frame

As you can see from the figure, an Ethernet frame brings together many pieces of information that can be required to navigate a network. In particular, it brings together source and destination MAC addresses (discussed earlier in the chapter) as well as the IP packet header and data.

In addition, the Ethernet frame adds an error-checking and correcting section, which enables the receiver at the destination to check what it has received for correctness. If not, the communication system will generate a message back to the original address to resend the damaged frame.

Ethernet Topologies

The Ethernet protocol is classified as a bus topology that has been implemented across several different network media, including:

- Coaxial cable (IEEE 802.3 – 10BASE-2 or -5)
- Twisted-pair copper cable (IEEE 802.3 – 10/100/1000BASE-T)
- Fiber-optic cable (IEEE 802.3 – 10/100/1000BASE-Fx, Lx or Sx)
- Wireless RF (IEEE 802.11a-h)

All of these topologies may be present in a given utility's generation and distribution networks. Therefore, the power technician needs to be familiar with wired and wireless IP-networking devices and strategies, as well as fiber optic and radio communications systems.

Network Control Strategies

When you begin to connect computers and devices together so that they can share resources and data, the issue of who will control the network (and how) comes up very quickly. In some applications, such as developing a book like this one, it is good for the author, artists, and pagination people to be able to share access to text and graphics files, as well as access to devices such as printers. However, in a business network, companies must have control over who can access sensitive information and company resources, as well as when and how much access they should have.

Control of a network can be implemented in two ways:

- As a *peer-to-peer* network where each computer is attached to the network in a ring or bus fashion and is equal to the other units on the network.
- As a *client/server* network where dependent workstations, referred to as *clients,* operate in conjunction with a dedicated master computer called a *server.*

Figure 13.5 illustrates a typical peer-to-peer network arrangement. In this arrangement, the users connected to the network can share access to different network resources, such as hard drives and printers. In a peer-to-peer network, control of the local unit is fairly autonomous. The nodes in this type of network configuration usually contain local hard drives and printers over which the local computer has control. These resources can be shared at the discretion of the individual user. A common definition of a peer-to-peer network is one in which all the nodes can act as both clients and servers of the other nodes under different conditions.

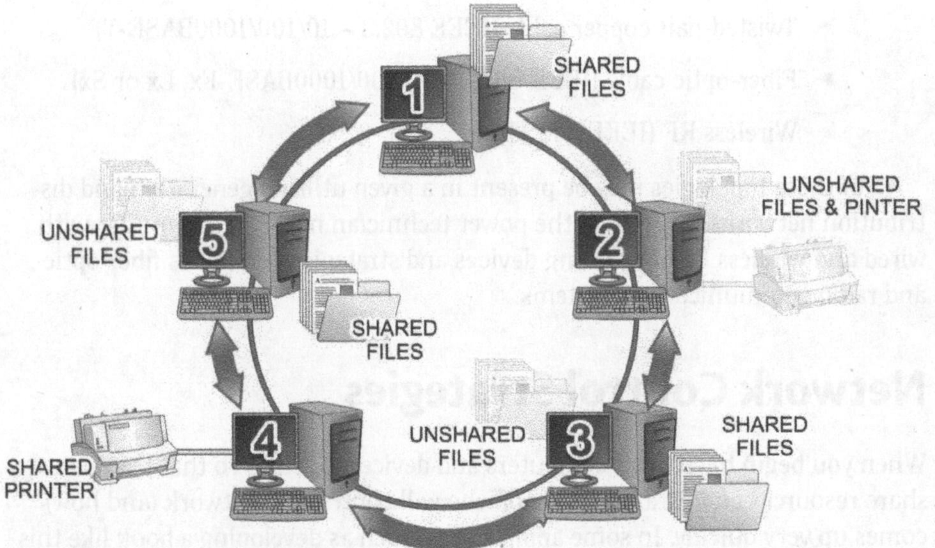

FIGURE 13.5 A Peer-to-Peer Network

Figure 13.6 depicts a typical client/server LAN configuration. In this type of LAN, control tends to be very centralized. The server typically holds the programs and data for its client computers. It also provides security and network policy enforcement.

The major advantages of the client/server networking arrangement include:

- Centralized administration
- Data and resource security
- Network services

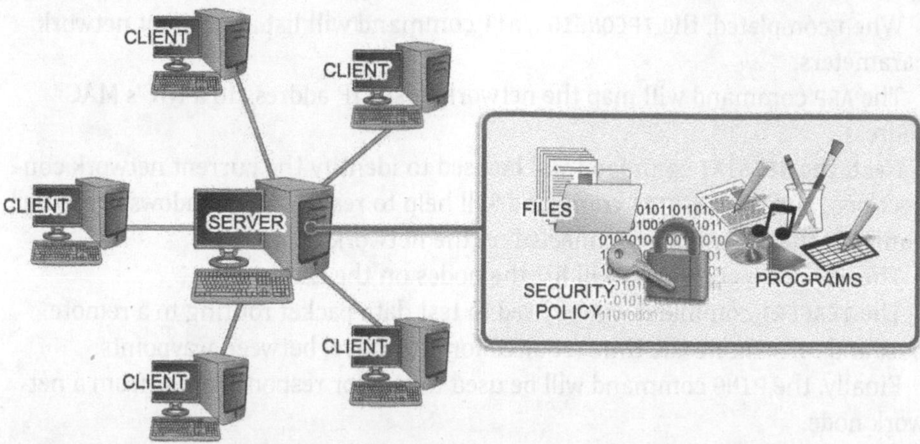

FIGURE 13.6 A Client/Server Network

In some cases, the client units do not include a local hard drive unit. The bootup process is performed by an onboard BIOS, and no data is stored at the client machine. This type of client is referred to as a *diskless workstation*.

While peer-to-peer networks enable users to share resources and have a limited amount of local control over resources, they do not typically provide services for the different computers and devices attached to the network. In a client/server-based network, special computers running server operating systems can be tasked with automatically providing services to the network members.

Hands-On Exercises

Objectives

In this exercise, you will use TPC/IP networking utilities to test network connectivity and properties.

Discussion

In the following procedure, the Command Prompt window will be modified to increase the visibility of the displayed information and add a shortcut to the desktop.

When completed, the `IPCONFIG /all` command will list all current network parameters.

The `ARP` command will map the network host's IP address to a NIC's MAC address.

Next, the `NETSTAT` command will be used to identify the current network connections, and the `NBTSTAT` command will help to resolve the Windows computer names of the other nodes connected on the network.

The `NET VIEW` command will list the nodes on the LAN.

The `TRACERT` command will be used to test data packet routing to a remote host and to examine the time required for it to travel between waypoints.

Finally, the `PING` command will be used to test for responsiveness from a network node.

Keep in mind that the information actually displayed when these utilities run will vary greatly depending on the particular network configuration. The examples provided here will not precisely match the actual results.

Procedures

Modifying the Command Prompt Window

Modify the Command Prompt window to increase visibility.

1. Boot your PC to the Windows 10 desktop.
2. In the Search box located on the taskbar, type the word **command**, as shown in Figure 13.7.
3. Right-click on the Command Prompt option and select Pin To Taskbar to create a shortcut for it directly on the taskbar.
4. Click on the Command Prompt shortcut you just created to open the Command Prompt window.
5. In a blank area at the top of the Command Prompt window, right-click and then select Properties from the menu that appears.

The first option you will change is the font size. In particular, you will change the size of the font to a size that makes viewing comfortable and is within the capabilities of the monitor being used with your PC.

6. Select the Font tab and change the font type to Lucidia Console.
7. Click on the Bold fonts checkbox to create a check mark in the box just below the Font list. Your Fonts tab should look similar to Figure 13.8.

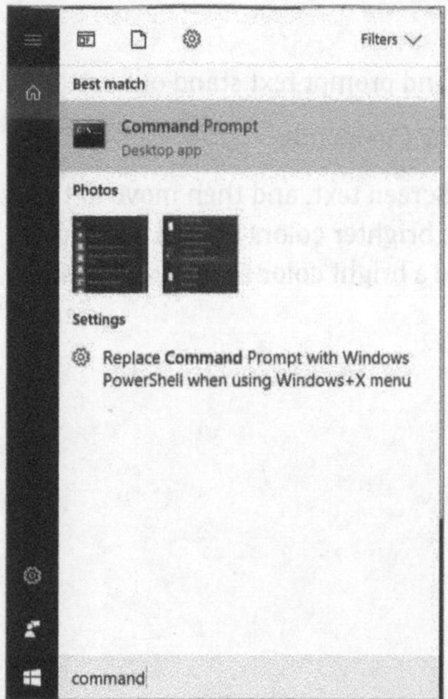

FIGURE 13.7 Accessing the Command Prompt

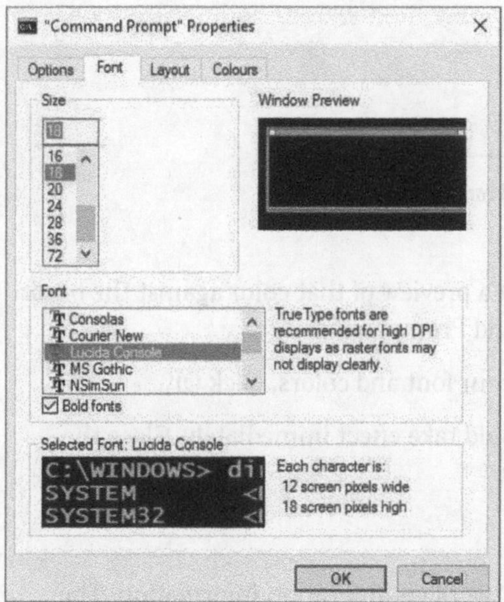

FIGURE 13.8 Changing the Command Prompt Font Type and Size

Changing the Color Options

Change the color options to make the command prompt text stand out better.

1. In the Properties window, select the Colors tab.
2. Click on the radio button next to Screen text, and then move to the color options and select one of the brighter colors toward the end of the color chart. You should choose a bright color that is easy to see, as illustrated in Figure 13.9.

FIGURE 13.9 Changing the Command Prompt Colors

3. Click on the color to obtain a preview of that color against the black background of the Command Prompt window.
4. After you finish adjusting your font and colors, click OK.
5. The changes you make should take effect immediately. Close the Command Prompt window.

Using the IPCONFIG Utility

Use the IPCONFIG utility to obtain network configuration information. The IPCONFIG utility permits the observation of the local computer's current IP address and other useful network configuration information.

The `IPCONFIG /all` command will display the complete network information for the computer being used. As illustrated in Figure 13.10, this utility will identify the current network configuration, including the IP address and the physical MAC address.

When using DHCP to provide an IP address, the `ipconfig /release` and `ipconfig /renew` switches can be used to force the DHCP server to withdraw the current IP address lease and obtain a new one.

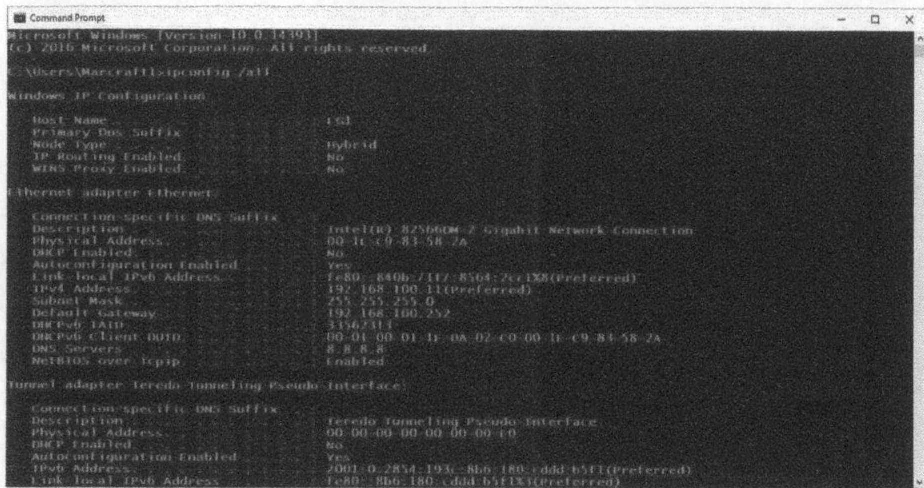

FIGURE 13.10 Listing the Network Configuration

1. Click on the Command Prompt shortcut that you previously pinned to the taskbar to open a Command Prompt window.
2. At the command prompt, type **`ipconfig ?`** and then press Enter to review the IPCONFIG options. You can scroll up to review buffered parts of the text that may have cycled off screen.
3. At the command prompt, type **`ipconfig /all`** and press Enter.
4. Record the requested information from the results for your PC in the designated areas of Table 13.1.

TABLE 13.1 LAN Information

Using the ARP Utility

The Address Resolution Protocol (ARP) utility can be used to identify addressing information by examining the contents of the ARP caches on either the client or the server. It is primarily used to map IP addresses to physical MAC addresses belonging to active network connections.

1. At the command prompt, type **arp** and then press Enter. Review the usage notes for the ARP utility.

2. At the command prompt, type **arp -a** and then press Enter. This will display information similar to Figure 13.11.

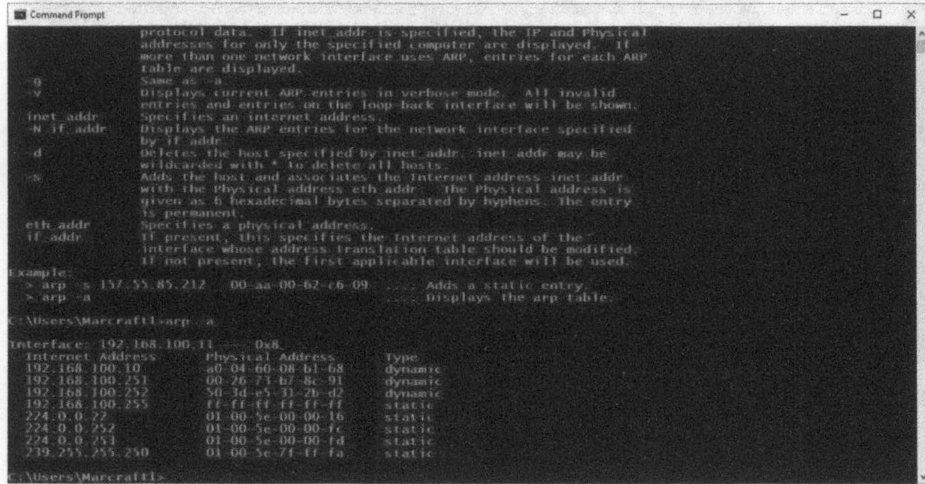

FIGURE 13.11 Mapping IP Addresses to MAC Addresses

3. Record the IP address of the host computer, as shown in the Interface line, on the following line:

____

4. View the IP and physical MAC addresses of the network connections.

Using the NETSTAT Utility

The `netstat -e` command will be used to display the number of data packets transmitted and received, as well as the number of errors generated during the data transfer. The `netstat -r` command will display a list of all current connections as well as indicate which ones are active.

1. At the command prompt, type **netstat ?** and press Enter. Review the usage notes for the NETSTAT utility.

2. Back at the command prompt, type **`netstat -e`** and press Enter to display packet statistics similar to those shown in Figure 13.12.

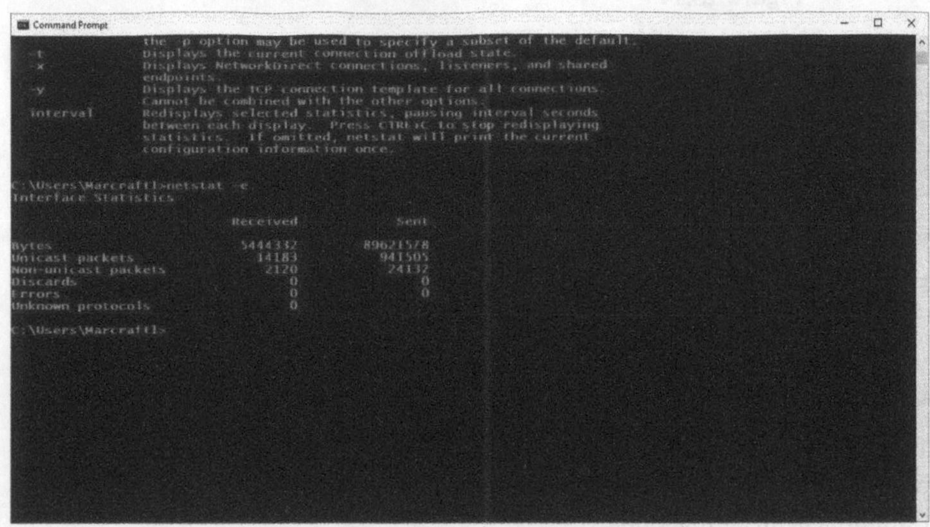

FIGURE 13.12 Observing Data Packet Statistical Information

3. Type **`netstat -r`** at the command prompt and press Enter to display the routing table of connected nodes, as illustrated in Figure 13.13.

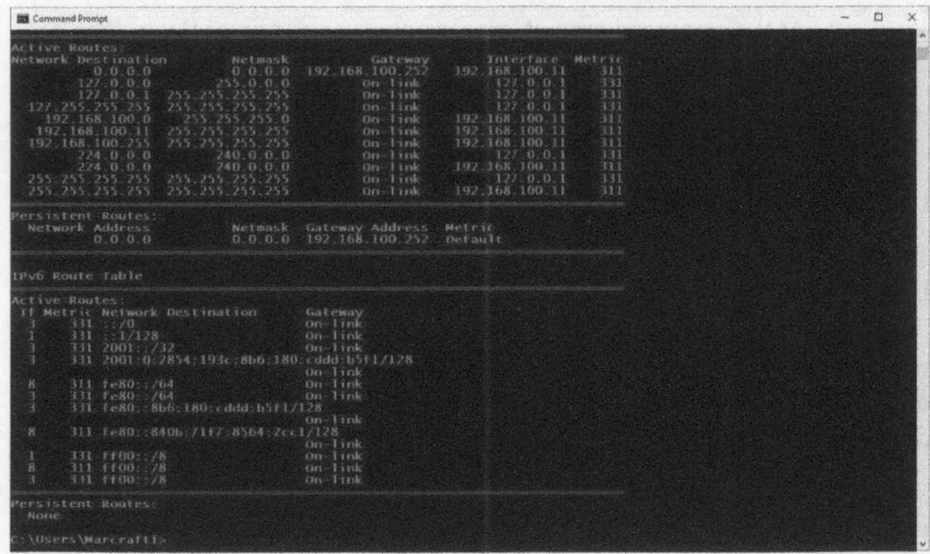

FIGURE 13.13 Displaying the Routing Table

4. At the command prompt, type **`netstat -n`** and press Enter to display addresses and port numbers in numerical form, as shown in Figure 13.14.

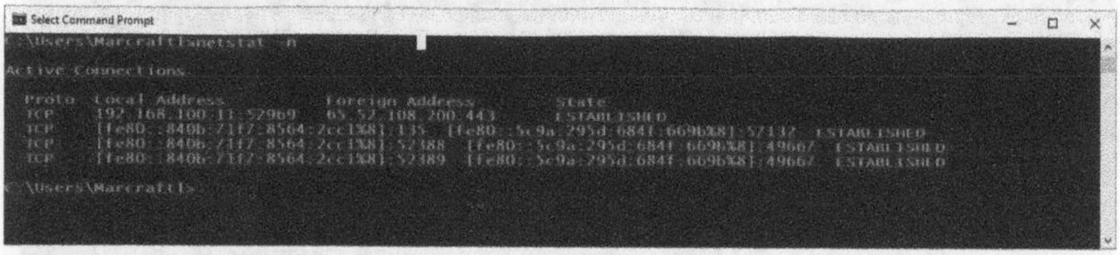

FIGURE 13.14 Numerical Address and Port Connections

Using the NBTSTAT Utility

The NetBIOS over TCP STATistics (NBTSTAT) utility displays the Windows NetBIOS names for connected computers, lists their IP addresses, and reports the status of all connections.

The `nbtstat -c` command will display the NetBIOS names of all connected hosts and the IP addresses to which they map. You can use the NBTSTAT utility to resolve current network connections.

1. At the command prompt, type **`nbtstat`** and press Enter. Review the usage notes for NBTSTAT.

2. At the command prompt, type **`nbtstat -c`** and press Enter. Review the displayed Remote Host Identification information, similar to that shown in Figure 13.15. This information was obtained from the Student PC1x machine.

Using the NET VIEW Utility

The NET VIEW utility lists all of the computers currently connected to the LAN. It can also display all shared devices associated with a particular network host.

The format for displaying shared devices is `net view \\`*`your server name`*, where the server name is the actual NetBIOS name of the workstation, or server, on which the command is executed. For example, `net view \\accounting` will display a list of all shared devices supported by the server named `accounting`.

1. At the command prompt, type **`net view ?`** and press Enter. Review the usage notes for NET VIEW.

2. At the command prompt, type **`net view`** and press Enter to list all of the nodes connected the local LAN. The results should be a list similar to the one depicted in Figure 13.16.

```
C:\Users\Marcraftl>nbtstat

Displays protocol statistics and current TCP/IP connections using NBT
(NetBIOS over TCP/IP).

NBTSTAT [ [-a RemoteName] [-A IP address] [-c] [-n]
        [-r] [-R] [-RR] [-s] [-S] [interval] ]

  -a   (adapter status) Lists the remote machine's name table given its name
  -A   (Adapter status) Lists the remote machine's name table given its
                        IP address.
  -c   (cache)          Lists NBT's cache of remote [machine] names and their IP addresses
  -n   (names)          Lists local NetBIOS names.
  -r   (resolved)       Lists names resolved by broadcast and via WINS
  -R   (Reload)         Purges and reloads the remote cache name table
  -S   (Sessions)       Lists sessions table with the destination IP addresses
  -s   (sessions)       Lists sessions table converting destination IP
                        addresses to computer NETBIOS names.
  -RR  (ReleaseRefresh) Sends Name Release packets to WINS and then, starts Refresh

  RemoteName   Remote host machine name.
  IP address   Dotted decimal representation of the IP address.
  interval     Redisplays selected statistics, pausing interval seconds
               between each display. Press Ctrl+C to stop redisplaying
               statistics.

C:\Users\Marcraftl>nbtstat -c

Ethernet:
Node IpAddress: [192.168.100.11] Scope Id: []

    No names in cache

C:\Users\Marcraftl>
```

FIGURE 13.15 Identifying Remote Host Connections

FIGURE 13.16 Creating a List of Nodes on a LAN

3. Record the host names listed by NET VIEW on the following lines:

____

4. At the command prompt, type **`net view \\host name`** (replacing ***`host name`*** with the NetBIOS name of one of the hosts listed in Step 3).

5. Press Enter and observe any shared devices on the selected host computer, as illustrated in Figure 13.17.

```
Select Command Prompt
Microsoft Windows [Version 10.0.14393]
(c) 2016 Microsoft Corporation. All rights reserved.

C:\Users\Marcraft1>net view
Server Name            Remark

-------------------------------------------------------------------------------
\\LG1                  StudentPC2-A
\\PCB                  PC-A
The command completed successfully.


C:\Users\Marcraft1>net view \\LG1
Shared resources at \\LG1

StudentPC2-A

Share name                  Type   Used as  Comment

-------------------------------------------------------------------------------
Documents                   Disk
FTPLAB                      Disk
Labpair1a pictures folder   Disk
LG1                         Disk
LG1share                    Disk
My Shared Docs              Disk
Student PC1 Lab Group 1     Disk
StudentPC1A Printer         Print           StudentPC1A Printer
StudentPC1A test file       Disk
Users                       Disk
The command completed successfully.


C:\Users\Marcraft1>
```

FIGURE 13.17 Creating a List of Shared Host Devices

Running *TRACERT*

The `TRACERT` *`hostname`* command (where *`hostname`* is the IP address or DNS name of a remote host) will trace the path of a network connection to that named host. The display includes the number of *hops* required and the IP addresses of routers through which a data packet has passed in reaching the remote host. A hop is generated each time a packet moves from one network device to another on the path to its designated destination. Therefore, TRACERT generates a hop count to trace the number of intermediate devices the packet passes through between its source and destination addresses.

The utility will also measure the time (in milliseconds) taken by the data packet to travel from point to point on the route. When a problem occurs while connecting to a specific destination, the question arises as to where the problem lies. Is the problem at the destination or at one of the routers along the way?

`TRACERT` will detect whether a particular router along the communication path is not functioning. When a particular router does not respond, the response time values are marked with an asterisk [*], indicating where the data packet timed out.

`TRACERT` also indicates when a particular router is slow. This can be determined by looking at the time taken for a packet to get through a particular router.

As shown in Figure 13.18, time delays are calculated three times for each router in the chain. The average of the three values should be used to evaluate the amount of time it took for the data packet to navigate through the router.

```
Command Prompt
Microsoft Windows [Version 10.0.14393]
(c) 2016 Microsoft Corporation. All rights reserved.

C:\Users\Marcraftl>tracert -h 10 www.microsoft.com

Tracing route to e1863.dspb.akamaiedge.net [23.199.225.204]
over a maximum of 10 hops:

  1     1 ms    <1 ms    <1 ms  192.168.100.252
  2     2 ms     1 ms     1 ms  192.168.254.254
  3     9 ms     8 ms     8 ms  adr01.knwc.wa.frontiernet.net [74.42.148.105]
  4    10 ms     8 ms     8 ms  172.76.20.121
  5    17 ms    14 ms    14 ms  ae4---0.cor02.sttl.wa.frontiernet.net [74.42.149.105]
  6    14 ms    13 ms    13 ms  ae1---0.cbr01.sttl.wa.frontiernet.net [74.40.5.126]
  7    13 ms    77 ms    50 ms  ix-ae-19-0.tcore1.0DS-Seattle.as6453.net [64.86.123.133]
  8    45 ms    13 ms    14 ms  a23-199-225-204.deploy.static.akamaitechnologies.com [23.199.225.204]

Trace complete.

C:\Users\Marcraftl>
```

FIGURE 13.18 Tracking a Data Packet with TRACERT

1. At the command prompt, type **`tracert`** and press Enter.
2. Review the usage notes for `TRACERT`.
3. At the command prompt, type **`tracert -h 10 www.microsoft.com`** and press Enter to trace the hops in the route to the Microsoft web server.
4. Record the number of hops required to reach the destination on the following line:

   ____

5. Record the IP address associated with `www.microsoft.com` on the following line:

   ____

6. Press the keyboard's up arrow (↑) key to show the last entered command and then press Enter to run `TRACERT` again.
7. Record the IP address now associated with `www.microsoft.com` on the following line:

   ____

8. Is the second address identical to or different from the one recorded in Step 5? Why?

   ____

   ____

Running *PING*

The PING command is one of the key tools for troubleshooting TCP/IP. It causes a data packet to be sent to a specified IP address and then returns it to the initiating machine. If the IP address is not currently active, a message will arrive stating that the transaction has timed out.

When there is a problem connecting to a network, PING can be used to test the functionality of TCP/IP on the machine trying to connect. If a successful PING between the *loopback address* (127.0.0.1) and the initiating device's own network IP address is achieved, it is fairly certain that TCP/IP on the host device is working properly.

The next step is to test the IP address for the network server and/or the default gateway.

As a final test, PING the IP address of a remote host server.

NOTE For the IP address of the initiating computer, or the IP address of the local server, run IPCONFIG or look up the data in Table 13.1.

1. At the command prompt, type **ping** and press Enter. Review the usage notes for PING.
2. At the command prompt, type **ping 127.0.0.1** and press Enter to test TCP/IP on your local host computer.
3. At the command prompt, type **ping *xxx.xxx.xxx.xxx*** (where *xxx.xxx.xxx.xxx* is the host IP address listed in Table 13.1).
4. Press Enter to test the local TCP/IP connection. A screen similar to Figure 13.19 should appear.

```
Command Prompt
C:\Users\Marcraft1>ping 127.0.0.1

Pinging 127.0.0.1 with 32 bytes of data:
Reply from 127.0.0.1: bytes=32 time<1ms TTL=128
Reply from 127.0.0.1: bytes=32 time<1ms TTL=128
Reply from 127.0.0.1: bytes=32 time<1ms TTL=128
Reply from 127.0.0.1: bytes=32 time<1ms TTL=128

Ping statistics for 127.0.0.1:
    Packets: Sent = 4, Received = 4, Lost = 0 (0% loss),
Approximate round trip times in milli-seconds:
    Minimum = 0ms, Maximum = 0ms, Average = 0ms

C:\Users\Marcraft1>ping 192.168.100.11

Pinging 192.168.100.11 with 32 bytes of data:
Reply from 192.168.100.11: bytes=32 time<1ms TTL=128
Reply from 192.168.100.11: bytes=32 time<1ms TTL=128
Reply from 192.168.100.11: bytes=32 time<1ms TTL=128
Reply from 192.168.100.11: bytes=32 time<1ms TTL=128

Ping statistics for 192.168.100.11:
    Packets: Sent = 4, Received = 4, Lost = 0 (0% loss),
Approximate round trip times in milli-seconds:
    Minimum = 0ms, Maximum = 0ms, Average = 0ms

C:\Users\Marcraft1>
```

FIGURE 13.19 Testing the Local Host and TCP/IP

5. At the command prompt, type **`ping 8.8.8.8`** and press Enter to test your connection to `www.google.com`.

6. A screen similar to the one displayed in Figure 13.20 should appear.

```
Command Prompt
Microsoft Windows [Version 10.0.14393]
(c) 2016 Microsoft Corporation. All rights reserved.

C:\Users\Marcraft1>ping 8.8.8.8

Pinging 8.8.8.8 with 32 bytes of data:
Reply from 8.8.8.8: bytes=32 time=14ms TTL=57
Reply from 8.8.8.8: bytes=32 time=16ms TTL=57
Reply from 8.8.8.8: bytes=32 time=24ms TTL=57
Reply from 8.8.8.8: bytes=32 time=13ms TTL=57

Ping statistics for 8.8.8.8:
    Packets: Sent = 4, Received = 4, Lost = 0 (0% loss),
Approximate round trip times in milli-seconds:
    Minimum = 13ms, Maximum = 24ms, Average = 16ms

C:\Users\Marcraft1>ping www.google.com

Pinging www.google.com [216.58.193.68] with 32 bytes of data:
Reply from 216.58.193.68: bytes=32 time=16ms TTL=54
Reply from 216.58.193.68: bytes=32 time=14ms TTL=54
Reply from 216.58.193.68: bytes=32 time=14ms TTL=54
Reply from 216.58.193.68: bytes=32 time=67ms TTL=54

Ping statistics for 216.58.193.68:
    Packets: Sent = 4, Received = 4, Lost = 0 (0% loss),
Approximate round trip times in milli-seconds:
    Minimum = 14ms, Maximum = 67ms, Average = 27ms

C:\Users\Marcraft1>
```

FIGURE 13.20 Pinging the Remote Google Server Cluster

NOTE **This example shows the results of pinging the `8.8.8.8` Google property and then the `www.google.com` domain name so you can see both results.**

7. Close all open windows and shut down both student PCs.

Lab Questions

1. Which command-line utility program is used to find the primary DNS suffix, IPv4 and IPv6 addresses for your computer?

2. The ____________________ command causes a data packet to be sent to a specific IP address and then returns to the initiating machine.

3. Which command detects whether routers along a communication path are functioning?

4. Which utility program is used to examine current network connections?

5. The ____________________ utility is used to map IP addresses to MAC addresses.

6. Which utility command is used to examine a list of all the shared devices on a LAN?

Lab Answers

1. `ipconfig`
2. `ping`
3. `tracert`
4. `netstat`
5. `ARP`
6. `net view`

## CHAPTER 14

Understanding Network Servers

Network servers are specialized computers designed to operate efficiently in a multiuser, multiprocessor, multitasking environment. Often they are based on physical configurations that are very different from those of common, consumer computing devices. Typically, they employ multiple processors, use large disk-drive arrays, and are housed in rack mount or pedestal-type cases. These characteristics are critical to providing the expanded computing power needed to support a business network. In this chapter, you'll learn to:

- **Understand server security**
- **Understand the role of network administrators**
- **Understand the importance of server software security**
- **Understand the two classes of users in a network**
- **Understand network authentication options**
- **Understand how to establish resource controls**
- **Understand how to maintain server security**
- **Understand how to scan for vulnerabilities**

The Basics of Network Servers

Servers are often housed in special rack-mount cabinets like the one shown in Figure 14.1. These racks are primarily designed to allow service personnel easy access to troubleshoot, repair, or replace server components. Pullout rails and easy-access panels are rack-mount features that facilitate maintenance. These features are important for application in business client/server environments to limit or eliminate entirely downtime due to maintenance or component replacement. Remember that in business it's all about money, and the longer a server is down, the more money it costs the organization.

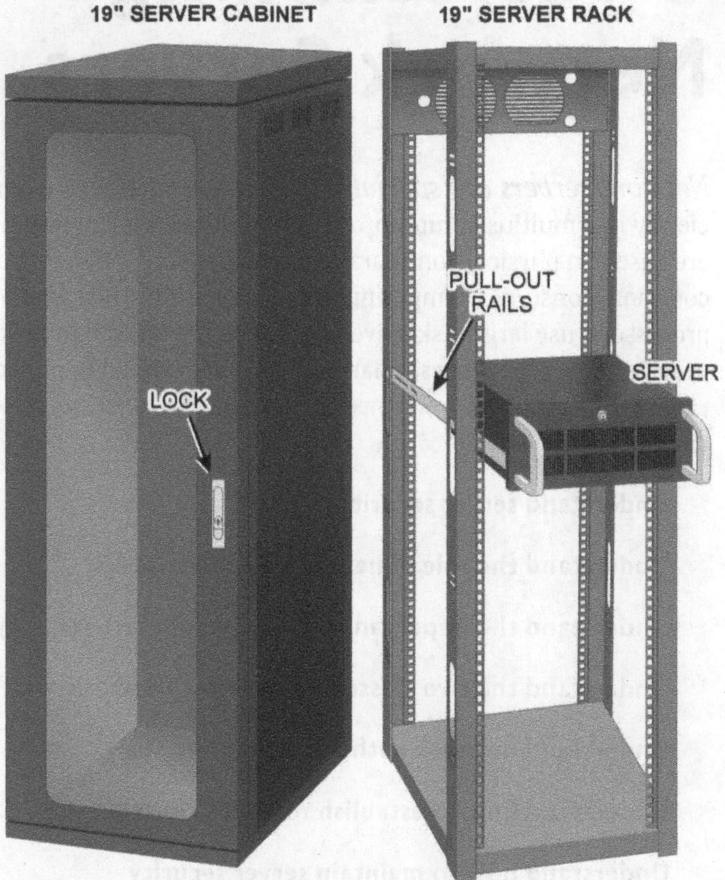

FIGURE 14.1 Typical Rack-Mount Server Cabinet

All servers perform the basic functions we've described so far; however, in practice they may vary significantly in the primary application they perform for the network's clients. The following list describes some of the various implementations found in different types of networking environments:

- General-purpose servers are employed in most small businesses for multiple purposes such as handling departmental email and providing file, print, and web services running on standard network operating systems.

- Appliance servers are specialized servers that provide specifically bundled hardware and software components. This makes for relatively easy installation and administration.
- Application servers run programs accessed by multiple users, and they often interact with informational databases.
- Mail servers are client/server types of application servers used to receive and store electronic mail messages in private mailboxes, even when users are not actually logged directly on to the network.
- Firewall servers control the connections between two networks, such as acting as an Internet gateway, where access control blocks unwanted traffic while allowing acceptable communications.
- Proxy servers act as intermediaries between network computers and the Internet.
- Web servers host web pages for intranet and/or Internet access and can be configured to host more than one site, depending on the server's underlying OS.
- Database servers are used to store and process data in response to client queries, where organizations must manage large quantities of data.
- Terminal servers are special-purpose computers fitted with multiported asynchronous modem connections, as well as ports designed to interface with host machines acting as terminals on one side and with a LAN, on the other side.
- DNS (Domain Name Service) servers contain database listings used to resolve human-readable computer names to IP addresses.
- Gateway servers provide interfacing between different types of networks, protocols, or mechanisms to provide access to another system.
- Router servers manage the shared resources of all other routers in the network, as well as the various transmission speeds and different protocols being used within an organization's network.
- Bridge servers use multiple network interfaces to connect groups of computers. They translate between protocols and help to reduce network traffic.

- FTP (File Transfer Protocol) servers transfer files across the Internet, an extranet, or an intranet through the use of FTP client software.
- NAS (Network Attached Storage) servers move storage out from behind the file server and put it directly on the transport network, permitting any network user with access rights to directly access stored NAS data.
- SAN (Storage Area Network) servers operate in enterprise storage environments with disk array controllers and tape libraries attached. They are capable of providing large-scale data protection and retrieval.
- RAS (Remote Access System) servers allow clients to dial in to a computer from a remote site, even if they are not connected to a LAN.
- Print servers help to decrease the administrative and management workload by streamlining both local and remote printer control.
- DHCP (Dynamic Host Configuration Protocol) servers are used to temporarily assign dynamic IP addresses to both network workstations and Internet clients.

Server Security

Servers require special security consideration and placement within the network. As the previous list illustrates, several different servers may be operating in an organization's network, delivering a variety of services to its users. In most cases, this involves supplying at least one critical service to multiple users. Therefore, the organization's users are dependent on these servers to perform their work.

Some of the network's servers, such as database servers, may be tasked with storing large amounts of data. Some or all of that data may contain critical or secret information such as confidential user information, including medical, financial, or personnel records. Network servers may also be used to process and store proprietary organizational information such as trade secrets, patents, inventions, or production information.

For these reasons, networked servers represent the most interesting targets for attackers. While part of the attackers' work involves getting past all the protective equipment in the network, the goal of their operation is either accessing, or disrupting access to, the data held on the servers. Therefore, servers require special consideration and placement within the network's security structure:

- Access to a server's shared resources should be limited to those users who have both a need and the proper authorization to gain such access. Controls must be in place to make sure that unauthorized employees do not gain access to confidential materials.
- Network access to some types of servers should typically be protected by one or more firewalls that limit traffic to the server.
- Subnets or routers should be used to create secure network segments or zones for different types of servers. For example, a given department, such as the accounting department, may be protected within their own secure subnet and possess their own departmental server resources.
- Because servers are frequently employed for user authentication, the server's password should be hashed (encrypted) as a preventative measure.
- Critical server resources should be audited periodically to identify potential problems before they escalate into real problems.

Network Administrators

The sheriff on any network is the network administrator. In network environments, the administrators are responsible for implementing the organization's security policies. These policies should be designed to reflect the three objectives associated with the classic model of information security—confidentiality, integrity, and availability (CIA).

Network administrators also use another implementation to keep information secure—authentication, authorization, and accounting (AAA). *Authentication* is ensuring that an individual is who they say they are. *Authorization* is applying approval of access to information, after the individual authenticates. Finally, *accounting* supplies a tracking of events, through logs or other means.

In some organizations, the network administrator may also be responsible for generating the company's security policies—including physical and logical access controls. As you've seen in all the previous chapters, all security efforts begin at the physical access level. If an unauthorized person can gain physical access to the network servers, media, or connectivity devices, then there is no security.

In larger organizations, specialized administrative roles are typically created to handle different aspects of the network's operation. This may include having separate server and network administrators. The server admin is responsible for the design, implementation, and maintenance of the server computers, while the network administrator provides the same functions for the network and its media and connectivity devices.

Division of administrative duties may also involve a special security administrator who is responsible for performing information security tasks for the servers, hosts, and connectivity devices in the network. In these settings, the separation of administrative duties should be as distinct, defined, and controlled as possible.

The system's administrators are generally responsible for the following activities associated with servers:

- Installing, configuring, and maintaining the servers and network components in compliance with the organizational security policies
- Establishing and maintaining user and group accounts as needed
- Implementing authentication options
- Performing system maintenance activities in a secure manner
- Conducting timely system backup and software updating operations
- Enabling system auditing and event logging
- Using intrusion detection and auditing tools to monitor network integrity, protection levels, and security-related events
- Establishing firewall settings
- Establishing and implementing malicious-software-protection policies
- Following up on detected security anomalies associated with their information system resources
- Using vulnerability scanning and penetration testing tools to conduct security tests on the network and its components as required

Physical Server Access Control

At a most fundamental level, network administrators must have control over their physical server environment to provide a comprehensive security setting. This is accomplished by strictly limiting physical access to the servers. This is most commonly accomplished by placing them in protected server rooms that have automatic locks on the door and computer racks.

Depending on the management structure of the network, the server (or network) administrator is generally responsible for determining which personnel can access the server room and may log access for anyone working inside the server room. The presence of unauthorized individuals in the server room should be reported to the administrator immediately. Violations of any server-room security measures should be reported to the appropriate administrator for corrective action.

Alternatives to Separate or Centralized Server Rooms

Reasonable alternatives to a separate or centralized server room include using a locked cabinet or even using a secure rack.

To provide hardware security, companies and utilities often place physical-intrusion-detection systems, such as motion sensors, card readers, cameras, and alarms in server rooms and on their servers and racks. They also install locks on the doors of the server rooms as well as on each individual server rack. They may also lock each server chassis or rack of servers. Figure 14.2 illustrates typical server security measures.

Server Room Door Locks

Physical locks should be on server-room access doors. The door to a server room should be a solid door that will prevent anyone from getting into the room. If the door has windows in it for viewing purposes, they should be made of security glass that has wire screens embedded in the glass to prevent individuals from gaining access by breaking the glass.

The ideal server-room door lock requires a key for access, and it should lock automatically when it shuts. The server-room lock should not have a button mechanism on the inside that can be used to keep the door unlocked.

Server Rack Locks

Antitheft devices should be in place for the server hardware, too. This begins with the server rack and the server chassis. It is normally a good practice to use server-rack cabinets that include sensors that will send alerts when the cabinet is opened. The system can also use the input from these sensors to log when and for how long the cabinet was open. In addition, the server's security system can be configured so that these alerts are paged or sent via email to network administrators or technicians.

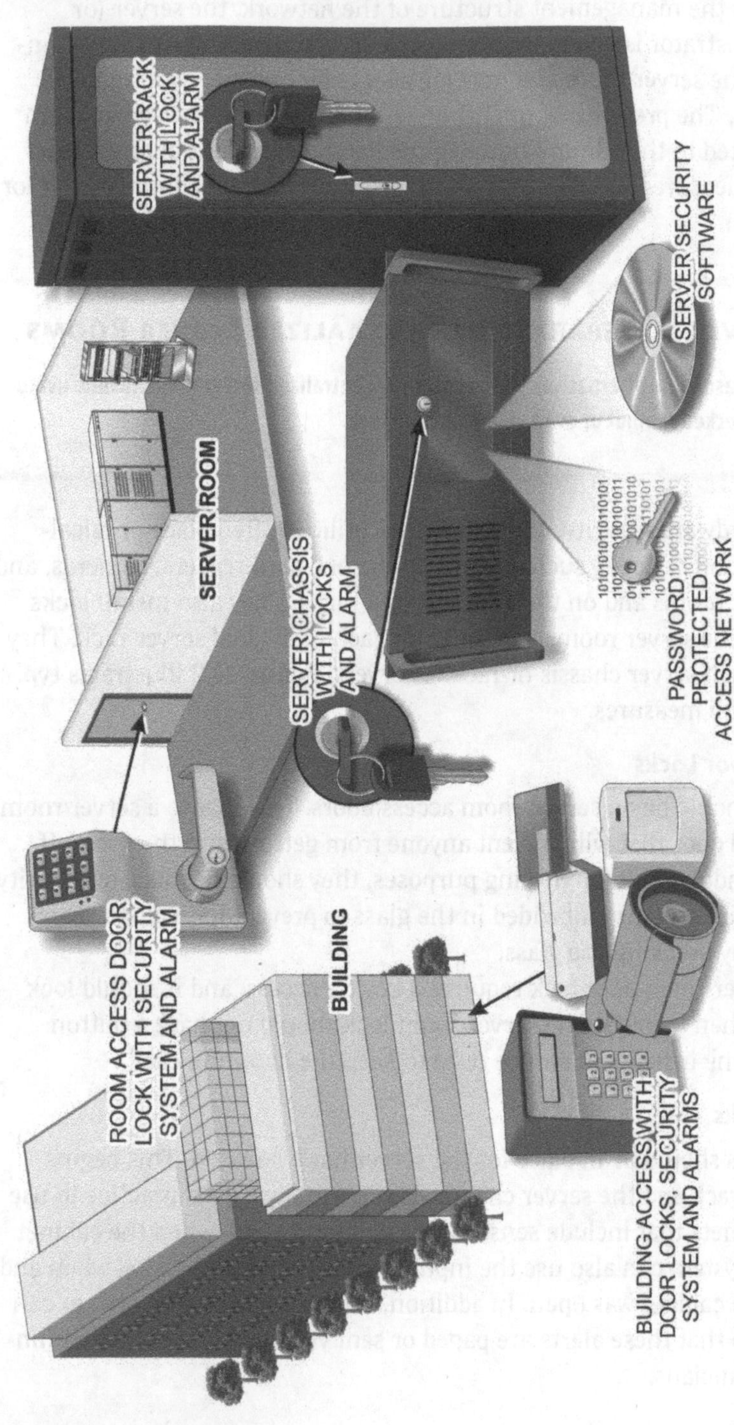

FIGURE 14.2 Server Security Points

Each server chassis in the rack should also have an intrusion sensor on it so that it can send an emergency page to the administrator if the server case or chassis is opened. The case or chassis should include a locking front panel, as illustrated in Figure 14.3. This panel can be used to prevent unauthorized access to the server's drives and front panel controls.

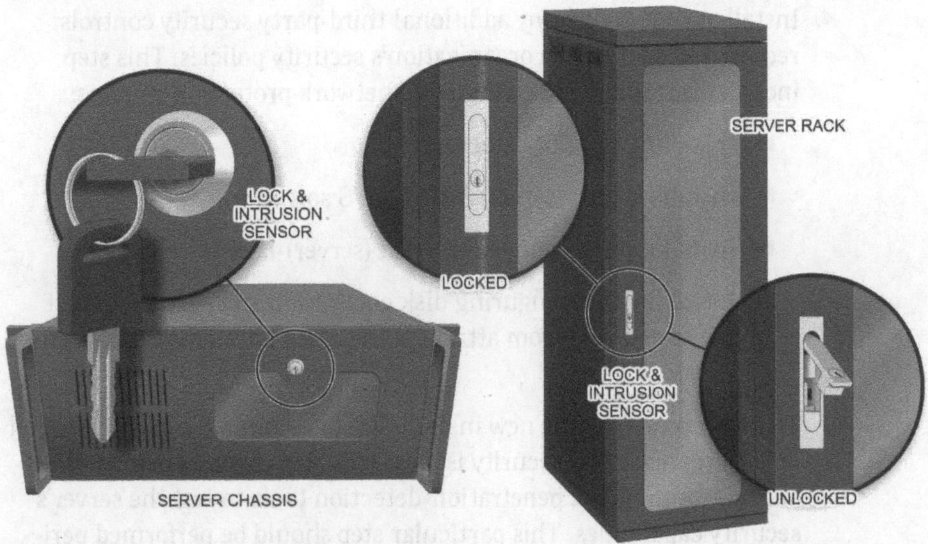

FIGURE 14.3 A Locking Server Chassis

Server Software Security

As with standalone host security, the next level of server security after securing physical access to the system is to secure its operating system and application software. This involves securely installing, configuring, and maintaining the server operating system and software packages selected for use on the server.

The most important server software component is the network operating system. Securing the operating system involves the following five steps:

1. Install the server operating system using the manufacturer's installation guidelines.

2. Patch and update the new installation. The operating system creator cannot know the full security requirements for a given organization's servers. In addition, new security threats are created every day, so there are security gaps that exist between when the software was

created and when it is installed. Applying patches and updates to the new install before it is put into operation should correct any known current vulnerabilities.

3. Configure and harden the new operating system to implement the organization's security policies.
4. Install and configure any additional third-party security controls required to address the organization's security policies. This step includes installing and configuring network protection systems:
   - Installing Rootkit detectors
   - Installing host (server)-based IDPS software
   - Installing and configuring host (server)-based firewalls
   - Installing or configuring disk encryption software to protect the stored data from attackers that gain physical access to the server
5. Test the security of the new installation to ensure that it addresses all of the organization's security issues. This step involves using vulnerability scanning and penetration-detection tools to test the server's security capabilities. This particular step should be performed periodically throughout the life cycle of the server to ensure that its security capabilities remain acceptable.

Configuring/Hardening Server Operating Systems

After the operating system and the desired applications have been installed on the server, the next step in securing the server is to harden the security configuration of the entire server software environment. *Hardening* is the process of taking steps to close as many known vulnerabilities as possible while still offering an acceptable usability level to the network's users/customers:

1. Map the network topology the server will serve and determine what devices are attached to it. Include a detailed record for each local device on its network along with a list of its operating system version, who should have authorized access to it, expected times of operation, and expected network connections.
2. Compare the level of security provided by the operating system with the needs of the organization. Particularly look for open services running on the different servers to determine whether those services

are needed. Turn off services that are not needed or are not being used on the network.

3. Compare the security needs of the organization's users with the capabilities of the operating systems in use.
   - Ensure that the network's operating system is running the most current updates and support available.
     - Antivirus software
     - Anti-malware products
     - Anti-spyware software
   - Disable any guest account on any server installed (unless there is a legitimate reason to have the account enabled on a specific server).
   - Configure Admin and User authentication systems.
     - Rename the default administrator account.
     - Remove or disable any unused default or user accounts, along with their existing authentication settings (usernames and passwords).

A Word of Caution Before Disabling Any Default Services

Before disabling any default services on a server, verify that the service and any dependencies related to it are not required by different network users.

   - Configure resource controls as required.
4. Employ the principle of least privilege to provide services and access permissions to network users. Typical steps involved in this process include:
   - Removing any unnecessary software packages or utilities from the server, including remote access programs, language compilers, and development tools, along with any system and network development tools.

- Removing or stopping unnecessary services, applications and protocols.
    - File and print-sharing services functions
    - Wireless networking services
    - Directory services
    - Email services
- Closing any open TCP/UDP network ports.

Each step requires the administrator to balance security requirements with users' needs. Ideally, the server would be locked down tight and serve a single function. However, as security increases, functionality decreases.

Logical Server Access Control

The network administrator is also responsible for determining who gains access to the operation of the network's servers, network connectivity devices, and data. In most organizations, they implement the organization's policy statements through the network operating system's management tools that control "who" has access to the network and its resources and what they can do with them.

Three standard types of network access control strategies are available to administrators:

Mandatory Access Control (MAC) The system establishes which users or groups may access files, folders, and other resources.

Discretionary Access Control (DAC) The user has the discretion to decide who has access to their objects and to what extent.

Nondiscretionary, Role-Based Access Control (RBAC) Control is determined by the job roles each user has within the organization.

MAC strategies assign sensitivity labels to network objects such as files and folders and granting access to the users based on their permission level, as illustrated in Figure 14.4.

As the figure shows, each user's range of access depends on the clearance level they have been given by their administrators. Personnel with a Top Secret clearance level have access to all objects that have been assigned a Top Secret label. In addition, they are permitted to access all objects labeled with a lesser label—such as Secret and Classified objects.

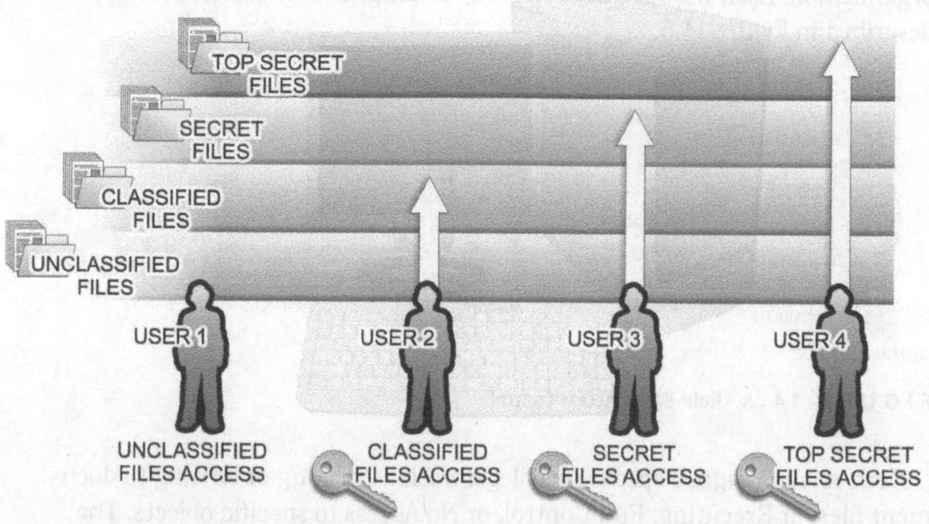

FIGURE 14.4 Mandatory Access Control

DAC involves giving users the discretion to determine what objects should be restricted or shared. Each object has an owner that it responsible for determining who can gain access to the object. This is how permission is assigned in a peer-to-peer networking environment.

Because each object is subject to a permission level, the owner has the option of making some objects more secure than others. In addition, under DAC the access control strategy can be delivered in an identity-based or user-directed manner.

THE FOURTH ACCESS CONTROL METHOD: *RULE*-BASED ACCESS CONTROL

There is a fourth access control method called *Rule*-Based Access Control, also known as *automated provisioning.* In this method, a rule is the basic element of a role. The rule defines what operations the role can perform.

RBAC is a strategy designed for centralized control of all network objects and users. The network administrator is given the authority to specify and implement explicit security policies that carry out the designated policies of the organization. Each network user or group is assigned one or more roles, as described in Figure 14.5.

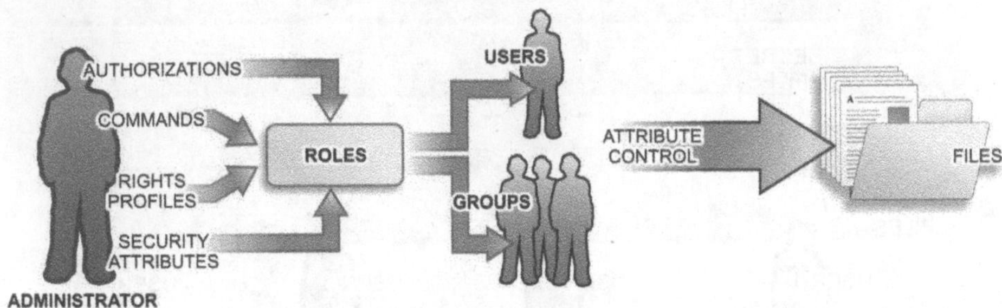

FIGURE 14.5 Role-Based Access Control

Each role is assigned specific privileges such as reading or writing to document files, or Executing, Full Control, or No Access to specific objects. The server is responsible for maintaining an access control list (ACL) database that tracks each user account, including which group accounts they may be assigned to, as well as what rights and permission they have to different objects, as shown in Table 14.1, Table 14.2, and Table 14.3.

TABLE 14.1 RBAC Rights and Permissions

Individual Rights			Group Membership			Other/Nonmember		
Read	Write	Execute	Read	Write	Execute	Read	Write	Execute
0	0	0	0	0	0	0	0	0
0	0	1	0	0	1	0	0	1
0	1	0	0	1	0	0	1	0
0	1	1	0	1	1	0	1	1

In the following sample (File A):

- Individual owner can read, write, and execute the file.
- Group members can read and write the file.
- All others can only read the file.

TABLE 14.2 File A

Individual Rights			Group Membership			Other/Non-Member		
Read	Write	Execute	Read	Write	Execute	Read	Write	Execute
1	1	1	1	1	0	1	0	0

In the following sample (Folder B):

- Individual owner can read and write to the folder.
- Group members can only read the folder contents.
- All others are denied any access to the folder.

TABLE 14.3 Folder B

Individual Rights			Group Membership			Other/Non-Member		
Read	Write	Execute	Read	Write	Execute	Read	Write	Execute
1	1	0	1	0	0	0	0	0

In each strategy type, the principle of least privilege level should be implemented when providing users with access to objects through rights and permissions assignments. Under the least privilege rule, each user is only granted the levels of access required to perform their job rolls. Applying this principle consistently limits the damage that can be inflicted by a security breach to the initial task, process, or user.

User Accounts

Basically, there are two classes of users in a network: administrators and users. These classes may also exist at two different levels:

- In local accounts, databases located on the individual client devices
- In network accounts, databases located on network servers

Recall that network account settings typically take precedence over local settings.

In a Microsoft Windows environment, there are several default user accounts after installation. These accounts include the following:

Administrator This is the main administrative management account that has full access to the system and all its management tools.

Guest Account This is a catchall account used to provide access to users who do not have a user account on the computer. This account should be disabled after user accounts have been established.

HelpAssistant This is a special Windows account used with its Remote Assistance utility to authenticate users connecting through it. This account is enabled whenever a remote assistance invitation is created, and it is automatically disabled when all invitations have expired.

SUPPORT_XXXXX This is a special Microsoft account used to provide remote support through their Help and Support Service utility.

These default user accounts can be renamed but not deleted. The initial Windows administrator accounts password is set up during the installation process.

As with Microsoft-based network environments, Linux systems employ a "users and groups" structure to control access to local and network resources (files, directories, and peripheral devices). Each person who is enabled to access the Linux system must be given a username. With the exception of the root superuser, usernames are created by administrative users as they are required.

Users are added to the Linux system through the `useradd` command-line tool, while existing user account information can be modified through the `usermod` command. The `passwd` command in conjunction with the username created with `useradd` (`passwd username`) will enable you to establish a password requirement for accessing the system as the new user.

A Word About Root Accounts

The root account has unlimited access to the Linux operating system and its configuration parameters, and it is provided for administrative purposes. For security purposes, you may want to lock the root user account after creating users and groups to prevent others from using the default user without a username and password.

A given network may employ a single administrator who has comprehensive control over all aspects of the system including servers, network media, and connectivity devices. However, larger networks typically have multiple administrators who have separate, specific network duties, such as server admin, network admin, and security admin. In these situations, it is considered best practice to have only the number of administrator accounts necessary and have those accounts configured with only the rights necessary to perform their functions.

When it comes to network users who can access the services on the computer, security is always balanced against functionality. Some network environments may have a list of authorized users (employees or agents), but still need to accommodate the general public (unauthorized users or customers). In these cases, authentication methods must be set up to accommodate both types of users. Typically, this involves establishing different group accounts for the diverse classes of users and then very strictly providing the resources needed by each group.

Establishing User and Group Accounts

Administrators in corporate and industrial networks create user and group accounts for network members that include specific access rights and permissions to the network and its resources. Network users are allowed or denied access to read, modify, and examine files and folders based on the access control policy that has been established for them either as individuals or by their position in different network groups.

Authentication may be applied to certain individuals through an inheritance process based on being included in an enabled group. For example, all members of the accounting department may be provided with inherited access to accounting programs and files due to their inclusion in the company's accounting group.

Administrators use group accounts to collectively deal with user accounts that have common needs. Doing so saves time by allowing them to issue user rights and resource access permissions to everyone in the group at once. However, even if a user is granted access to certain resources, the administrator can limit the scope of activities the user can conduct with different files and folders.

Windows Group Accounts

The default group accounts in Windows Server systems include the following:

Administrators Members of this group have full access to the computer and its tools and can perform all management functions. This group automatically includes the Administrator user account as a member.

Guests This default group has minimized access to the system, and all members share the same user profile. The Guest user account is automatically a member of this group.

Power Users Power Users is a special group that has permissions to perform many management tasks on the system but does not have the full administrative privileges of the administrator account. Power Users can create and manage users and groups that they create. Also, they do not have access to files and folders on NTFS volumes unless they are granted permissions to them through other sources. There are no members in this group when it is created.

Backup Operators As the name implies, members of this group can back up and restore all files on the computer. Through the backup utility, members of this group have access to the system's entire file system. There are no members in this group when it is created.

Network Configuration Operators Members of this group can manage different aspects of the system's network configuration. In particular, they can modify TCP/IP properties, enable, disable, and rename connections, and perform IPCONFIG operations. This group is empty when it is created.

Users This is a catchall group with limited default permissions. Except for the guest account, all user accounts created on the system, including the administrator account, are made members of this group by default.

Remote Desktop Users Members of this Windows group have user rights to log on to the system remotely to perform remote desktop activities. The group has no members by default.

Windows Domain Accounts

Windows server systems also support domain user and group accounts when used in a domain environment. In a domain environment, all the members of the network share a common directory database and are organized into various levels. The domain is identified by a unique name and is administered as a single unit having common rules and procedures.

Domain accounts are created on Windows domain controllers through their Active Directory Users and Computers utility and are stored in the Active Directory database. When a Windows client device is placed in a domain environment, some group memberships are automatically changed to reflect this:

- The Domain Admins group is added to the local Administrators group so that domain administrators will have administrative control over all the computers in their domain.
- A Domain Users group is added to the local Users group.
- A Domain Guests group is added to the local Guests group.

These groups are all a function of the Windows domain controllers and exist only in Windows domain environments. The automatic addition of these groups in domain environments makes it easier for domain administrators to configure access to the local computer's resources. The groups are not permanent additions and can be removed at the administrator's discretion.

Linux Group Accounts

As with other multiuser operating systems, individual Linux users are commonly made members of groups for administrative purposes. Because of the relationships that exist within a group, the file generated by the user becomes the property of the members in the group. Figure 14.6 shows how to add users or groups in a Linux distribution.

```
root@ryant-desktop: ~
marcraft@ryant-desktop:~$ sudo -s
[sudo] password for marcraft:
root@ryant-desktop:~# useradd marcraftuser
root@ryant-desktop:~# groupadd marcraftgroup
root@ryant-desktop:~# usermod -g marcraftgroup marcraftuser
root@ryant-desktop:~# id marcraftuser
uid=1004(marcraftuser) gid=1009(marcraftgroup) groups=1009(marcraftgroup)
root@ryant-desktop:~# groups marcraftuser
marcraftuser : marcraftgroup
root@ryant-desktop:~#
```

FIGURE 14.6 Adding Users or Groups in a Linux Distribution

Unlike Windows, the list of default groups that exists after installation varies between different Linux distributions. Some common Linux groups that appear in most distributions include:

Games This group provides access to game software.

Users This is the standard, default Linux users group.

Wheel This is an administrative group that typically provides access to user creation and configuration utilities (su and sudo commands).

Daemon This is a standard, default user/group that has privilege to execute *daemon programs* (background processes) that run without direction from the user. In the Microsoft realm, this type of program is referred to as a terminate-and-stay resident program and most resemble services running in the Windows environment.

Bin This is a standard, default Linux group that historically provided running executable files. The bin reference is based on the binary (executable) file types stored there. The folder contains scripts and commands that can be executed to perform a task. The commands in this directory can be run by every user.

Mail This group has special mail privileges.

Root The Root admin group is a standard, default Linux group that has complete administrative control of the system.

Nobody This is the unprivileged group.

Disk This provides access to "block devices," such as disk drives and optical drives.

This list shows only a few of the common groups that may be installed or added to a given Linux installation. The tool for adding groups in Linux is `groupadd`. Group information is modified through the `groupmod` command, and users are added to the group through the `usermod` command.

Group Account Security

When dealing with group accounts, you should keep a few security-related actions in mind:

- Remove or disable unused default accounts, such as the guest account. Left unattended, these accounts can be used by hackers to exploit them. If default accounts must be retained, change their names as their standard authentication credentials are well known to potential attackers. Also, severely restrict access, along with rights and permissions available, to these accounts.
- Create user groups that encompass the functions associated with different types of users who have common needs and then assign rights and permissions to each group according to the functional needs of the group.
- Create user accounts and assign them to groups according to their job functions in the organization. Using this approach prevents

administrators from having to individually configure each user's account settings. Only create the accounts actually needed as unused accounts can provide security vulnerabilities if discovered.

- Set account passwords to work under the organization's password policy.
- Install and configure any additional authentication systems, such as biometric scanning devices, selected for use with the network.

Network Authentication Options

Even though you are a member of one or more group accounts, you cannot use one of these accounts to log on to the network. You can gain access to a system only by logging on with a legitimate user account.

At the network level, the username and password system is still the first line of authentication options in use. The main difference is that in a client-server network, the authenticated users list is stored on the server, not at the local computer.

Also, at the network level the network logon typically overrides any local system logon. Therefore, administrators control who can log on to any portion of the network through password policy statements.

They also set the network password policy for how often users must change their passwords, as well as setting length and complexity requirements. These options, shown in Figure 14.7, enable administrators to make user accounts and passwords more secure. Password policies apply to all users who log on to the system and cannot be configured for individual users.

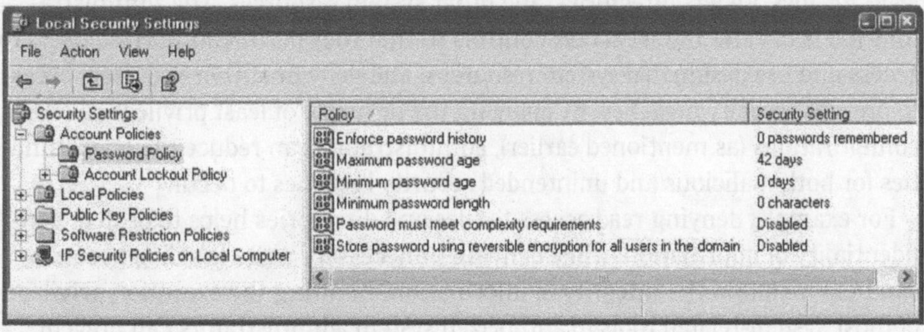

FIGURE 14.7 Password Policies

Typically, network administrators can configure the following password-related settings for network users:

Enforce Password History This option is used to specify the number of passwords that will be tracked for each user. When users attempt to change their password, they will not be permitted to reuse any of the passwords being tracked.

Maximum Password Age/Minimum Password Age These two settings enable administrators to set passwords so that they expire after the specified number of days; they can also prevent users from changing their passwords for some specific number of days. When the password expires, the user is prompted to change it, ensuring that even if a password becomes public, it will be changed within a short period of time to close the security breach.

Minimum Password Length This option is used to specify the minimum number of characters that a password may contain. This allows the administrator to force users to employ passwords that are longer and harder to guess. A password of at least eight characters is recommended for secure systems.

Passwords Must Meet Complexity Requirements Administrators can use this option to force users to use more secure, complex passwords that include some combination of lowercase letters, numbers, symbols, and capitalized characters. The administrator sets the level of complexity by establishing password filters at the domain controller level.

Establishing Resource Controls

Server operating systems provide the capability to specify individual access privileges for files, folders/directories, and other system resources. The administrator's job is to carefully set access controls so that they permit authorized users to access and use designated system resources, and deny unauthorized users access to prevent security breaches. By applying the principle of least privilege to these configurations (as mentioned earlier), administrators can reduce the opportunities for both malicious and unintended security breaches to occur.

For example, denying read access to files and directories helps to protect confidentiality of information, while denying unnecessary write (modify) access can help maintain the integrity of information. Limiting the execution privilege of most system-related tools to authorized system administrators can prevent users from making configuration changes that could reduce security. It also can restrict an attacker's ability to use those tools to attack the server or other hosts on the network.

NTFS Permissions

The NTFS file management system used in Windows environments includes security features that enable permission levels to be assigned to files and/or folders on the disk. NTFS permissions set parameters for operations that users can perform on the designated file or folder. They can be assigned directly by an administrator, or they can be inherited through group settings, such as the default "Everyone" group.

NTFS permissions can be configured as Allow or Deny options. If a user has only Read permissions to a particular folder or file, but is assigned to a group that has wider permissions for that folder or file, the individual would gain those additional rights through the group. On the other hand, if the user is assigned the Deny option for a given permission level, then they would be denied that permission level even if it were granted by another group that they were a part of. In a server environment, the default permission setting for files is No Access.

Standard NTFS folder permissions include the following:

Read This permission enables the user or group to view the file, folder, or subfolder of a parent folder along with its attributes and permissions.

Write This permission enables the user or group to add new files or subfolders, change file and folder attributes, add data to an existing file, and change display attributes within a parent folder.

Read & Execute The Read & Execute permission enables users or groups to make changes to subfolders, display attributes and permissions, and run executable file types.

Modify The Modify permission enables users to delete the folder and makes it possible for users to perform all the activities associated with the Write and Read & Execute permissions.

List Folder Contents This permission enables users or groups to view files and subfolders within the folder.

Full Control The Full Control permission enables the user or group to take ownership of the folder and to change its permissions, as well as perform all of the other activities possible with all the other permissions.

Standard NTFS file permissions include the following:

Read This permission enables the user or group to view the file along with its attributes and permissions.

Write This permission enables the user or group to overwrite the file, change its attributes, and view its ownership and attributes.

Read & Execute The Read & Execute permission enables users or groups to run and execute an application, along with all the options available through the Read permission.

Modify The Modify permission enables users to modify and delete the file and to perform all the activities associated with the Read, Write, and Read & Execute permissions.

Full Control The Full Control permission enables the user or group to take ownership of the file and to change its permissions, as well as perform all of the other activities possible with all the other permissions.

Linux Permissions

Linux operating systems also employ file and directory permissions to protect them from unauthorized accesses. In Linux (and Unix) systems, structures other than documents and executables are defined as files. Other system resources (such as disk drives, optical drives, modems, input and output devices) and network communications are also accessed as files.

Each file in a Linux system also has an owning user and an owning group assigned to them, along with access permissions for each owner type. Permissions are also established for unprivileged users. Three types of access permissions can be configured:

Read (r) When specified, this permission enables the user to read the contents of the file or directory.

Write (w) When specified for a file, this permission enables the user to modify the file by writing to it. When assigned to a directory, the Write permission allows the user to create or delete files in the directory.

Execute (x) This permission enables users to execute files and scripts with this permission assigned. Each permission is established independently for each user category. A typical file permission display (such as that obtained from a list [ls] command) will appear in the following format:

```
drwxrwxrwx user group filesize Jan 01 08:00 filename
```

Each *rwx* segment of the left column displays the active permission setting for owner user, owner group, and others, respectively. The fact that all three permission types are present in this example would indicate that all three groups have all permissions enabled. When a permission is disabled for a particular user, its space contains a simple dash character:

drwxrw-r- user group filesize Jan 01 08:00 filename

In this example, the owning user still has all permissions, but the owning group permissions have been reduced to Read and Write, while other users' permissions have been reduced to simply Read.

When a directory or file is created in a Linux system, it is associated with its creator, who by default becomes its owner. Typically, Linux users will assign permissions of `-rw-r-r-` to their nonexecutable files. This setting will permit others to read their file, but they will not be able to make changes to it. Similarly, directories are often assigned permissions of `-rwxr-xr-x`. This enables others to look through the directory and execute without being able to write new files into it or remove existing files from it.

A Word About Linux Permissions

Linux permission assignments for a file are overshadowed by the permissions assigned to its parent directory. Even though a file may be assigned the permissions `-rwxrwxrwx`, the user will not be able to access the file unless they have read, write, and execute permissions to the directory above the file.

File System Hardening

While the file system is part of the operating system, there are a few file-system-specific techniques that can be used to improve or harden file system security:

- The first step is to employ standardized files systems across the organization if possible.
- Consider separating boot/system files from shared directories and data by placing them in different partitions on each server and user computing device.

For windows systems, place the boot and system files in drive `C:\` and shares in other drives such as `D:\` or `E:\`. For Linux systems, change the mount options in `/etc/fstab` to limit user access. Also, user writable directories such as `/home`, `/var`, and `/temp` should be mounted in other partitions.

- Remove any hidden sharing features from the boot/system partition as well as in any other partition that has information that should not be shared.
- For key folder and file permissions, use individually assigned permissions instead of role-based access control options. Only use RBAC options for information that truly needs to be shared across groups. RBAC and other logical access control strategies were discussed earlier in this Part.
- Employ file and folder encryption options where available.
- Establish periodic auditing and reporting for folders and files that are most critical to the organization's operations.

Maintaining Server Security

After the operating system has been securely installed on the server, its selected applications have been installed, and the server software has been hardened, there are several administrative duties involved in maintaining the server's security. Primary duties associated with ongoing server operations include:

- Logging and auditing server activity
- Conducting regular server-data backup operations
- Performing server-security testing procedures to verify the server's security remains uncompromised. These procedures include:
  - Maintaining the Intrusion Detection Systems
  - Performing routine vulnerability testing
  - Performing penetration testing

Network-Level Auditing and Event Logging

An important part of an administrator's tasks and the overall network security plan is accounting. One form of accounting is auditing. *Auditing* is a preplanned monitoring method to evaluate or determine if problems exist within the area being evaluated or audited. Inherent in nearly all server software are monitoring and auditing tools used to evaluate the performance of that software and the hardware platform that supports it.

However, performing auditing steps that go beyond the normal hardware and system monitoring that is required for performance maintenance is usually called *monitoring*. Instead, network administrators configure auditing software to evaluate specific network objects or events and then track those results in an audit log for evaluation later.

Some firewalls, Intrusion Detection Systems (IDS), and auditing software can be configured to provide immediate alerts or notifications to administrators when unusual patterns or events are recognized.

Auditing all objects and events on a network is impractical and would significantly impact the performance of the network. This would cause the network to come to a screeching halt or at least significantly slow down. Therefore, judicial use of auditing techniques has been the standard approach.

Prior to initiating an audit, considerable thought should be taken to determine which objects and events should be audited and when. Additionally, having too many audit logs could lead to administrative overload and the possibility of not reviewing or identifying the critical events that could have caused a security concern or violation. Of course, auditing requires additional resources, including time and personnel to review audit data.

Although computer performance may be an issue, auditing is an important security feature that must be carefully planned. There are many options as to what should be audited. Success or failure of user logon attempts may provide a clue to cracker activity and should provide information that may lead to modification of the password policy or the need for continued user education.

Auditing results that indicate an attacker has attempted to identify and use passwords, attempts to break through access control lists, or attempts to unscramble encrypted data, may all lead to the conclusion that a cracker is attempting to penetrate the network.

The result of an audit may show that a user account is being used at irregular hours. This audit may indicate that the user's logon account has been compromised. Objects such as restricted folders may be audited for access attempts and improper user access permissions. Usually, individual printers are not audited, although they could be audited for short periods of time.

Audits can be planned to scan for inappropriate activity from within a LAN, an internal audit, or from external activity attempting to penetrate the network. Some companies hire a security team or ask their administrator to turn on auditing tools and attempt to penetrate the network to evaluate the network for potential weaknesses.

Auditing user logon attempts is probably one of the most important ways to identify whether a user's password has been compromised. Network administrators should be aware of the normal work schedule of assigned employees. If an employee works only days or is on a scheduled vacation, their account should not be active at night or when they are gone.

Auditing user privileges is a useful technique for identifying whether a user's computer has picked up a virus that escalates the user's privileges. Privilege escalation refers to users who are able to execute a program with embedded code that gives them administrative privileges after logging onto the server.

Many firewalls are configured to audit which internal users are accessing inappropriate websites. These same firewalls can be configured to identify files, folders, and services that are being accessed by users from the Internet. Results of these audits are placed in audit logs that provide an audit trail. Users that fail to meet company policies can be counseled and in some instances terminated. Audit results may be required if legal action becomes necessary.

Auditing is established at the server level, while event logging can be set up at the local computer level. The auditing functionality enables the user and operating system activities on a computer to be monitored and tracked. This information can then be used to detect intruders and other undesirable activity.

The auditing system consists of two major components: an audit policy, which defines the types of events that will be monitored and added to the system's security logs; and audit entries, which consist of the individual entries added to the security log when an audited event occurs. The system administrator implements the audit policy.

Audit entries are maintained in the security log, which can be viewed by the administrator. Figure 14.8 shows a typical security log. For auditing to be an effective security tool, the security log should be reviewed and archived regularly.

Conducting Backups

One of the network administrator's key security roles is in contingency planning. In this role, the administrator is responsible for implementing a recovery plan that will assure that the network's operation (and that of the organization) can recover in the case of a disaster. One of the first steps of any disaster recovery plan must include the development and implementation of an effective backup policy.

Without backed-up data, there can be no contingency plan for an efficient recovery (or possibly any recovery at all). Backup utilities enable the administrator to create extended copies of files, groups of files, or entire disk drives, for use in the event that a server's disk drive crashes or its contents become corrupt.

Typically, only administrators or specially designated members of the Backup Operators groups are given appropriate permissions to back up and restore all data on the server, regardless of their permissions level. However, any user can back up any local files for which they have at least the Read permission. Likewise, they can restore anything for which they have at least the Write permission. Users generally have these permissions for their own files, so they can perform backups and restores of their data as necessary.

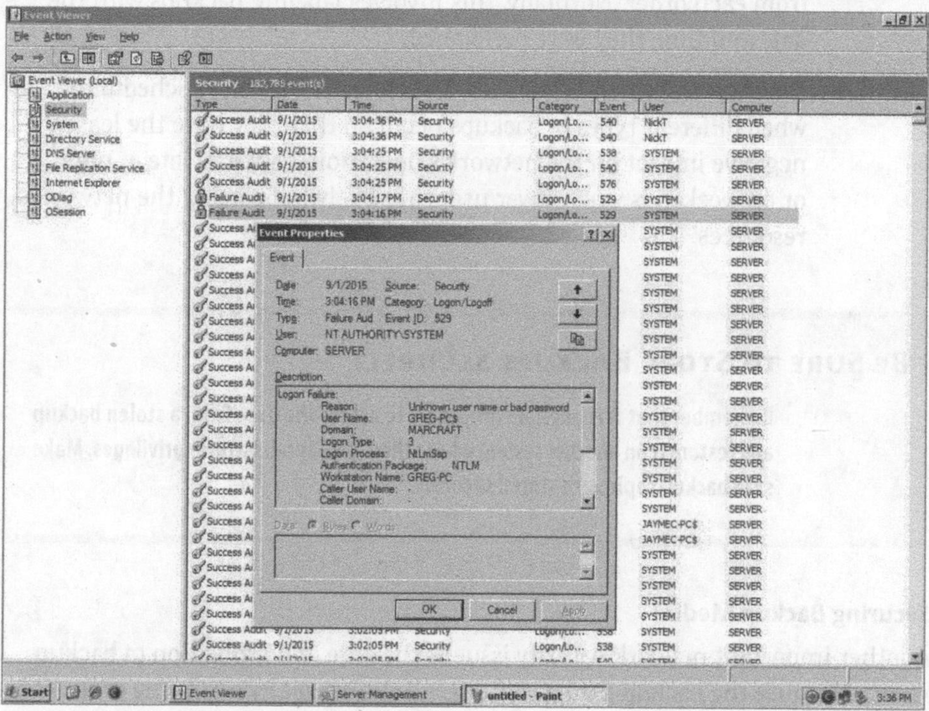

FIGURE 14.8 Viewing Security Audit Logs

Administrative responsibilities associated with implementing a disaster recovery plan include:

- ▶ Establishing types of backups to be performed. This includes configuring the backup utilities to conduct full, differential, incremental, copy, or daily backup options.
- ▶ Defining how to back up. This includes configuring options for verifying the backup and enabling compression (if it's supported by the backup device). Verifying the backup involves comparing the stored data version with the data that was designated to be backed up (to make certain that all information was copied properly during the backup).

- Specifying whether to replace the existing data on the backup media or append the new data to the end of the media.
- Establishing backup labeling so that different backup copies that exist on the backup media can easily be identified and differentiated from each other. Normally, this involves labeling backups with the date and time they were performed.
- Determining when to back up. This selection involves scheduling when different types of backups occur so that they have the least negative impact on the network's operation—such as late at night or on weekends when fewer users are likely to be using the network's resources.

Be Sure to Store Backups Securely

Remember that it is possible for others to access the data from a stolen backup and restore it on another system where they have administrator privileges. Make sure backup copies are stored securely.

Securing Backup Media

Another important network security issue is the care and protection of backup media. Because the backup media contains all the company's valuable proprietary data, if someone gains access to it, they could retrieve the company's privileged information and misuse it. Not only should there be doors that lock with a key on the room where the backup media is stored, there should also be a sign in/out sheet for tracking people entering and exiting the room.

Backup media contain the company's proprietary information, so it should be kept in a secure location, and in a fire-proof safe. Ideally, two sets of backup media should be kept, one on-site and the other off-site. For both the on-site and off-site locations, fireproof safes are the most secure containers for backup media.

For security purposes, only a limited number of people should know where the backups are stored and have access to the safe's key or combination.

Distributed Intrusion Detection Architectures

In Part II, you were introduced to intrusion detection and prevention systems at the local-host level. Historically, local-host intrusion-detection systems have been the dominant implementation choice. However, similar systems are available for network-wide implementation. Ultimately, the most effective IDS/IDPS defense is a combination of the two types of systems working together in what are referred to as distributed IDS systems.

Figure 14.9 shows a sample of a distributed IDS implementation. In this network architecture example, each local host attached to the network has its own IDS module installed. There is also an IDS management module installed in a network server that coordinates the flow of information to and from the individual local IDS modules.

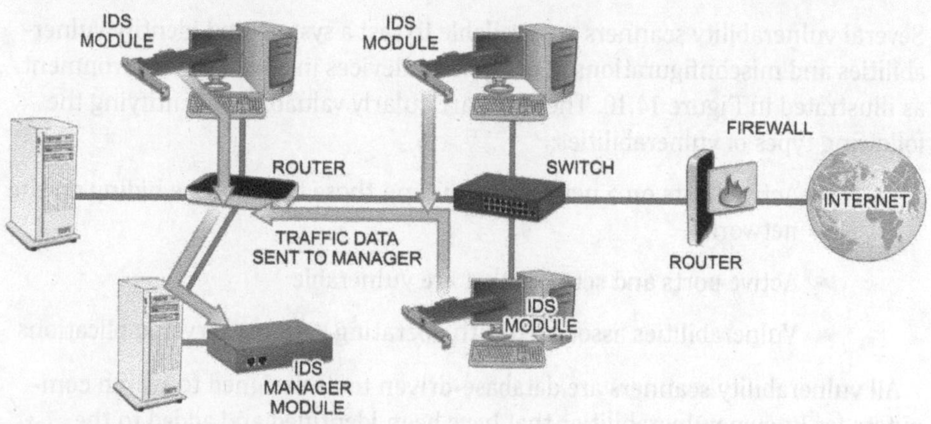

FIGURE 14.9 Distributed IDS

The local IDS modules pass local audit information to the IDS manager, which filters the incoming information to build a signature database. The database can be built on detected anomalies or on known patterns of misuse, or on both types of data. When an action matches one of the signatures stored in the database, the IDS will generate an intrusion alarm under the direction of its configuration manager.

In the case of IDPS systems, the management module forwards the attack signal to a separate countermeasure module that conducts appropriate response activities based on the nature of the detected intrusion signature.

A Word About IDS Performance Factors

When a distributed IDS system is being implemented, there are two major performance factors to consider: security versus efficiency. Likewise, the major *management issues* associated with implementing IDS/IPS systems involve the creation of false positive and false negative alerts—particularly when the system is first installed. However, over time these conditions can be minimized by tuning the IDS/IPS to provide the best level of security with a minimum number of false alarms.

Vulnerability Scanning

Several vulnerability scanners are available to test a system and identify vulnerabilities and misconfigurations of computing devices in a network environment, as illustrated in Figure 14.10. They are particularly valuable in identifying the following types of vulnerabilities:

- Active hosts on a network (including those that may be hiding on the network)
- Active ports and services that are vulnerable
- Vulnerabilities associated with operating systems server applications

All vulnerability scanners are database-driven tools designed to search computers for known vulnerabilities that have been identified and added to the database. As such, they are only as good as their last update. For this reason, it is imperative that all vulnerability scanners be updated just before using them. Results from the scan are displayed for the user to review.

Although using vulnerability scanners is time and resource consuming, doing so is an important part of the ongoing security process. It allows vulnerabilities to be addressed as soon as possible—hopefully, before they are discovered and exploited by others.

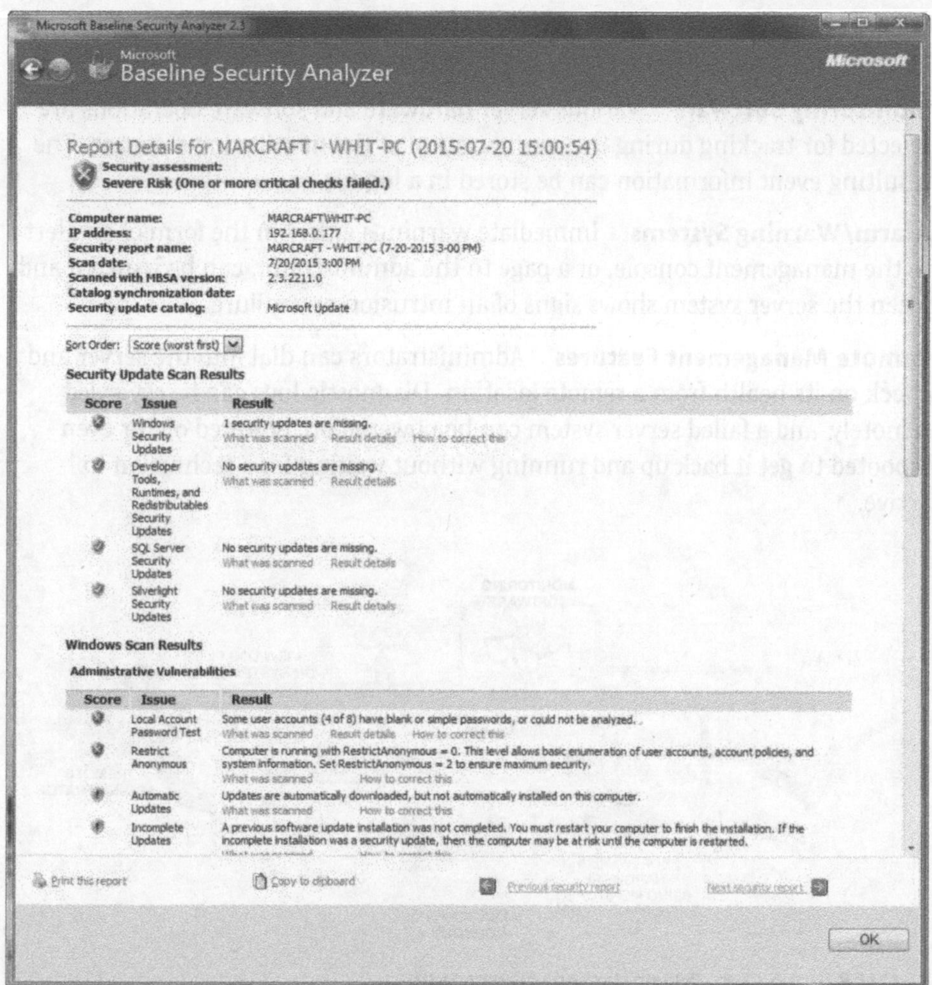

FIGURE 14.10 A Typical Vulnerability Scanner

Remote Monitoring

Server software management components are designed to implement a complete server monitoring solution. As shown in Figure 14.11, the following components are required to provide an effective proactive management and monitoring program:

Monitoring Software Various server hardware and software operations are selected for tracking during the configuration of the monitoring software. The resulting event information can be stored in a log file.

Alarm/Warning Systems Immediate warnings either in the form of an alert to the management console, or a page to the administrator, can be issued if and when the server system shows signs of an intrusion or a failure.

Remote Management Features Administrators can dial into the server and check on its health from a remote location. Diagnostic logs can be reviewed remotely, and a failed server system can be powered on, powered off, or even rebooted to get it back up and running without waiting for a technician to arrive.

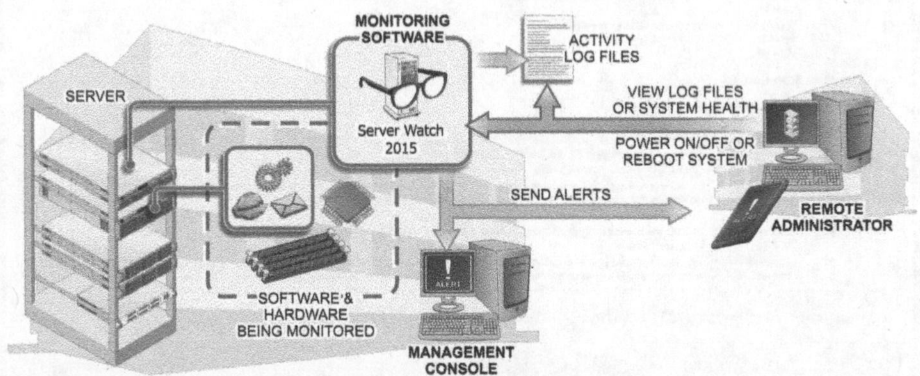

FIGURE 14.11 Remote Monitoring Components

By using these critical software-management components, administrators can proactively monitor and manage servers to optimize their availability. By providing system administrators with advance warnings before failures occur, server management software helps them to recognize and deal with problems before they become catastrophic and cost the company money or business.

Simple Network Management Protocol

Because of the critical nature of a server's function in the network, most servers possess extended management capabilities to keep administrators apprised of their operational status. This is often based on a Simple Network Management

Protocol (SNMP) utility that runs underneath the installed operating system and provides system management and reporting functions across the entire network.

Administrators use SNMP to check server characteristics, and network activity, without actually going through the main network operating system. In this way, the administrator's management activities can be executed without locking up the server's operating system.

It should be obvious why the use of remote monitoring through the use of SNMP is more cost-effective than having a server technician on duty 24/7. Although a daily review of system event logs might reveal the existence of a problem after the fact, using this approach alone provides no advance warning before the problem adversely affects the system.

System monitors should be capable of providing active notifications to administrators when parameters begin slipping. If they do not, the administrator is responsible for upgrading them. In the event of a problem with the server, SNMP sends an alarm message to the administrator about the situation. One drawback with SNMP is that in the event of a processor lockup, the SNMP software also locks up.

Hands-On Exercises

Objectives

- Describe a network intrusion detection system.
- Perform scanning operations with a NIDS.
- Inspect information gathered from a NIDS.
- Explore the results of logged files.

Resources

- Customer-supplied desktop/laptop hardware system
- Windows 10 Professional installed
- An account with administrative access
- Snort installed (`https://www.snort.org/downloads`)
- 7-Zip installed (`http://www.7-zip.org/download.htm`)

Discussion

As with physical security efforts, preventing unauthorized access is the first line of security at the local computing and control-device level. However, it is just as important at this level to be able to detect the occurrence of an intrusion and notify the proper authorities of its nature.

Computer-based Intrusion Detection Systems (IDS) can be implemented in two ways: network-based IDS (NIDS) or as host-based IDS (HIDS). In both cases, the system is designed primarily to monitor the system (local computer or network environment), log key events and policy violations, and report them as directed.

Some systems referred to as Intrusion Detection and Prevention System (IDPS) provide an additional level of activities aimed at actively preventing the detected threat from succeeding. These systems are classified as *reactive* IDS systems, while simple IDS are referred to as *passive* IDS systems.

All IDS devices are based on one of two strategies:

- Signature analysis: Incoming and outgoing traffic is compared with a database of stored, specific code patterns that have been identified as malicious threats.
- Anomaly analysis: Incoming and outgoing traffic is compared to an established baseline of normal traffic for the system. The baseline is "learned" (generated) by applying mathematical algorithms to data the system obtains from the traffic flow.

Procedures

In this procedure, you will use Snort, arguably the most popular open source Network IDS. It uses both signature-based and anomaly-based analysis, and it has a strong community of users who constantly create new rules to employ.

Adjusting the Snort Configuration File

Although Snort is very effective and widely used, it does not contain a GUI to provide for easy administration. This is both a pro and a con. The benefit is that the administrator has complete control, even being able to create his or her own rules. However, one of the drawbacks of Snort is that it has a steep learning curve and requires strong command-line understanding. In this section, you will insert information into the configuration file prior to using the program. This is necessary to run the IDS.

1. Power on your Windows 10 Pro machine.
2. Log on using your administrative account.
3. In the search bar embedded in your taskbar, type **cmd** and then press Enter to launch a command prompt.
4. At the command prompt, type **ipconfig** and press Enter. Figure 14.12 shows the sample results from IPCONFIG. Your results will vary.
5. Record your IPv4 address and subnet mask. In Figure 14.12, the applicable IPv4 address and subnet mask includes:

   IPv4 Address – 192.168.0.182

   Subnet Mask – 255.255.255.0

   IPv4 Address: ____________________

   Subnet Mask: ____________________

```
Command Prompt

Ethernet adapter vEthernet (New Virtual Switch):

   Media State . . . . . . . . . . . : Media disconnected
   Connection-specific DNS Suffix  . :

Wireless LAN adapter Wi-Fi:

   Media State . . . . . . . . . . . : Media disconnected
   Connection-specific DNS Suffix  . :

Wireless LAN adapter Local Area Connection* 2:

   Media State . . . . . . . . . . . : Media disconnected
   Connection-specific DNS Suffix  . :

Ethernet adapter Ethernet:

   Connection-specific DNS Suffix  . : Marcraft.local
   Link-local IPv6 Address . . . . . : fe80::2014:6417:84f1:e918%21
   IPv4 Address. . . . . . . . . . . : 192.168.0.182
   Subnet Mask . . . . . . . . . . . : 255.255.255.0
   Default Gateway . . . . . . . . . : 192.168.0.1

Ethernet adapter Bluetooth Network Connection:

   Media State . . . . . . . . . . . : Media disconnected
   Connection-specific DNS Suffix  . :

C:\Users\christopherg>
```

FIGURE 14.12 IPCONFIG

6. Exit the command prompt by typing **exit** and pressing Enter.
7. Using Windows Explorer, navigate to Computer ➢ C: ➢ Snort. Double-click the Etc folder to view its contents, as illustrated in Figure 14.13.

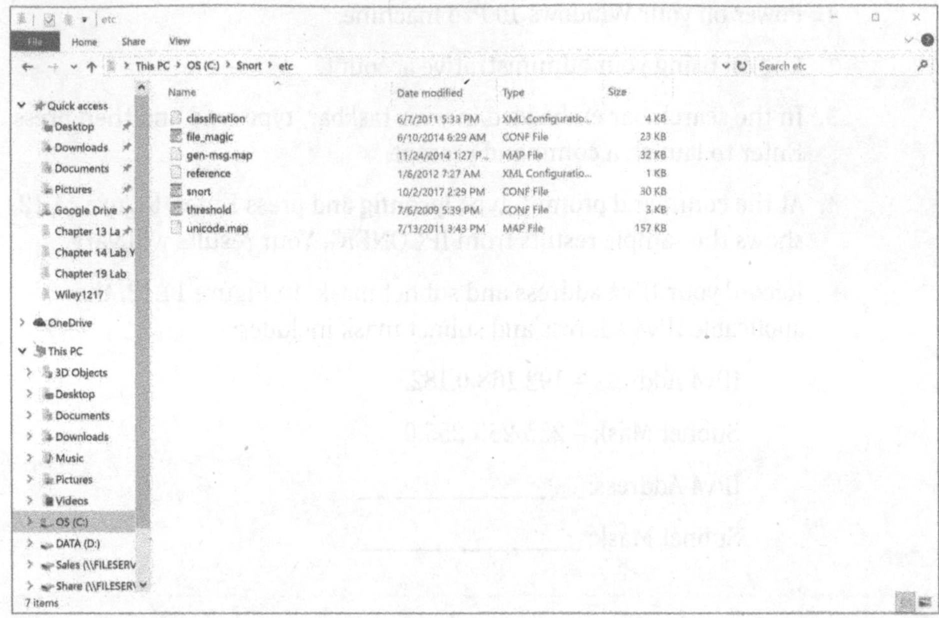

FIGURE 14.13 Contents of the Etc Folder

8. Locate the `snort.conf` file and right-click it, and then select Open. The Windows prompt will ask what you would like to do.

NOTE **If the file extensions do not display, go to Organize Folder And Search Options View, and unclick Hide Extensions For Known File Types.**

9. Click the radio button associated with Select A Program From A List Of Installed Programs and select OK.
10. Select Wordpad or Word and select OK. The `snort.conf` file is now open, as shown in Figure 14.14.

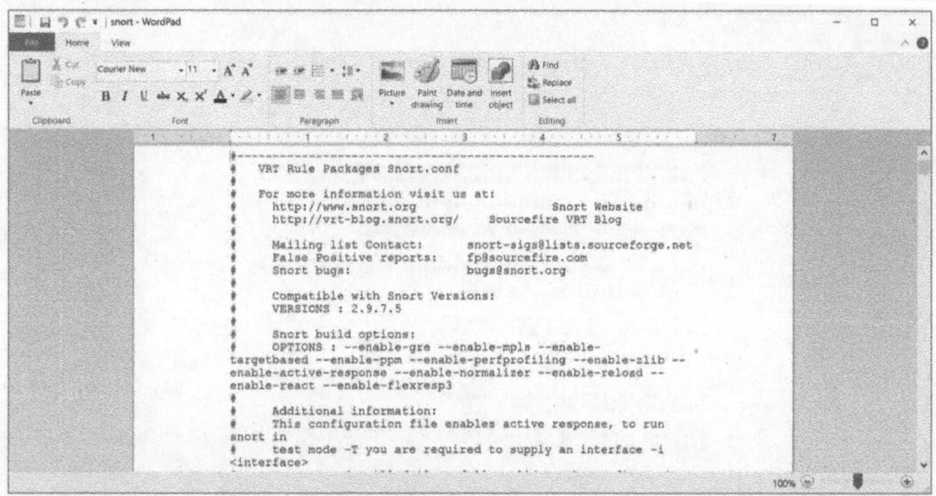

FIGURE 14.14 The Snort Configuration File

NOTE **If the `snort.conf` file has already been changed, the following steps will need to be confirmed and adjusted accordingly.**

11. Under the `snort.conf` Step # 1, locate:

```
# Setup the network addresses you are protecting
ipvar HOME_NET any
```

As shown in Figure 14.15, replace the keyword any with your IPv4 address and subnet mask in CIDR notation. Use the address you recorded in Step 5. For example:

```
ipvar HOME_NET 192.168.0.182/24
```

Supplying your IP address gives Snort the proper reference to check for incoming and outgoing packets.

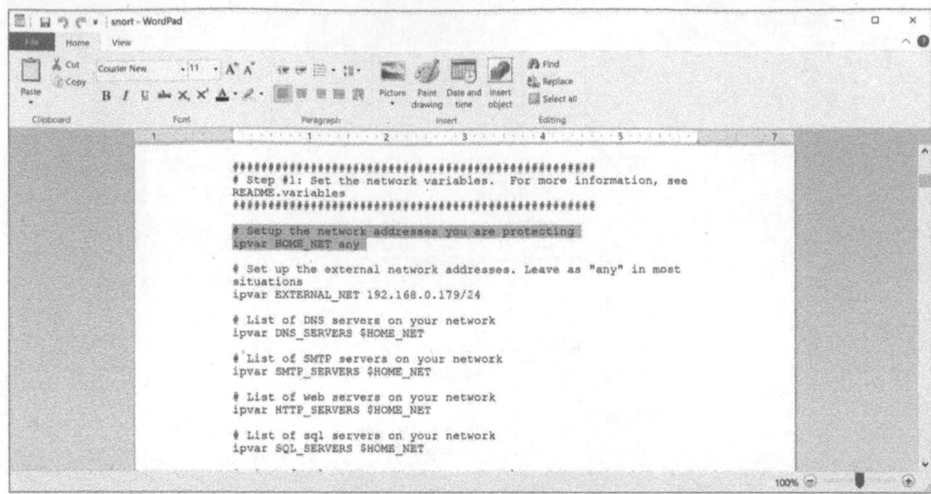

FIGURE 14.15 **Network Address Change**

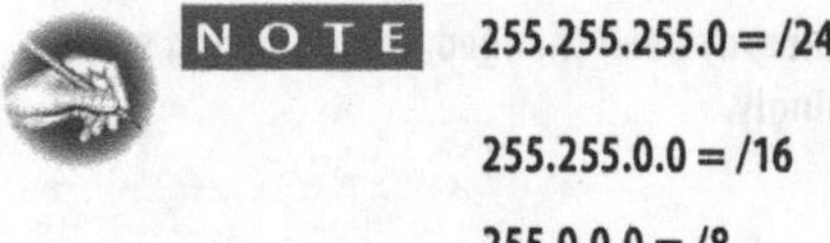

NOTE **255.255.255.0 = /24**

255.255.0.0 = /16

255.0.0.0 = /8

If your subnet mask is different than these, refer to a subnet calculator.

12. While still under the `snort.conf` Step # 1, scroll down and locate:

```
# such as: c:\snort\rules
var RULE_PATH ..\rules
var SO_RULE_PATH ..\so_rules
var PREPROC_RULE_PATH ..\preproc_rules
```

As shown in Figure 14.16, replace each `../` with `c:\snort\`. Also place a pound sign (#) in front of `var SO_RULE_PATH`. This change is needed to define the variables path location for future use inside the configuration file.

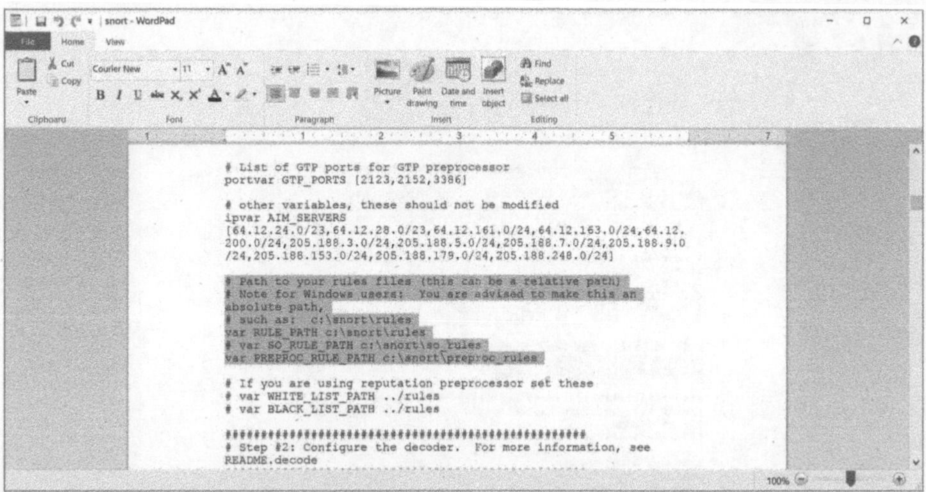

FIGURE 14.16 Rule Paths Changed

13. Finally, under Step # 1, locate:

```
# if you are using reputation preprocessor set these
var WHITE_LIST_PATH ../rules
var BLACK_LIST_PATH ../rules
```

As shown in Figure 14.17, insert a pound sign (#) in front of both variables. You will not be issuing any whitelists or blacklists of sites. By including a pound sign (#), you tell Snort to disregard the entire line; this is often referred to as "commenting the line out."

14. At the very end of Step # 2, locate:

```
# config logdir:
```

Remove the pound sign (#) and insert `c:\snort\log` at the end of the line, as shown in Figure 14.18. Removing the pound sign (#) and adding a path confirms the creation of a log directory, which is needed to audit logging.

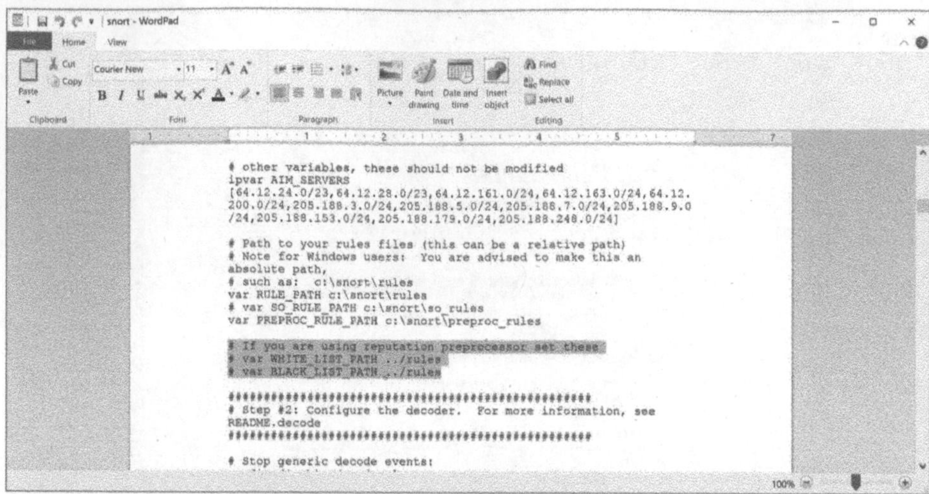

FIGURE 14.17 Whitelist and Blacklist Changed

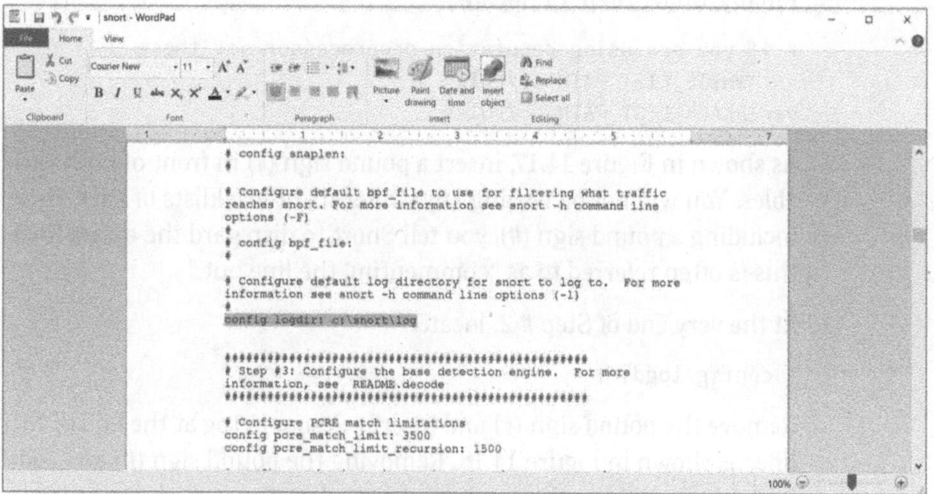

FIGURE 14.18 Configuring Log Directory

15. Skip Step # 3 and proceed to Step # 4. Locate:

```
# path to dynamic preprocessor libraries
dynamicpreprocessor directory
/usr/local/lib/snort_dynamicpreprocessor/
```

Replace the following:

`/usr/local/lib/snort_dynamicpreprocessor/` with the following: `C:\Snort\lib\snort_dynamicpreprocessor`

As shown in Figure 14.19, this defines the path needed to locate the `snort_dynamicpreprocessor`.

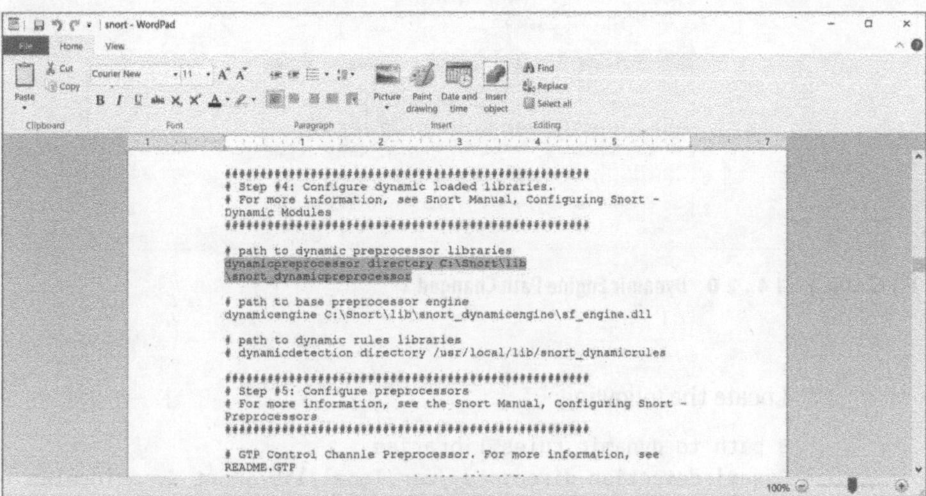

FIGURE 14.19 Dynamic Preprocessor Path

16. Locate the following:

```
# path to base preprocessor engine
dynamicengine /usr/local/lib/snort_dynamicengine/libsf_
engine.so
```

Replace the following:

`/usr/local/lib/snort_dynamicengine/libsf_engine.so`

with the following: `C:\Snort\lib\snort_dynamicengine\sf_engine.dll`

As shown in Figure 14.20, this defines the path to the `snort_dynamicengine` file and changes the name of the file used in Windows (as opposed to Linux).

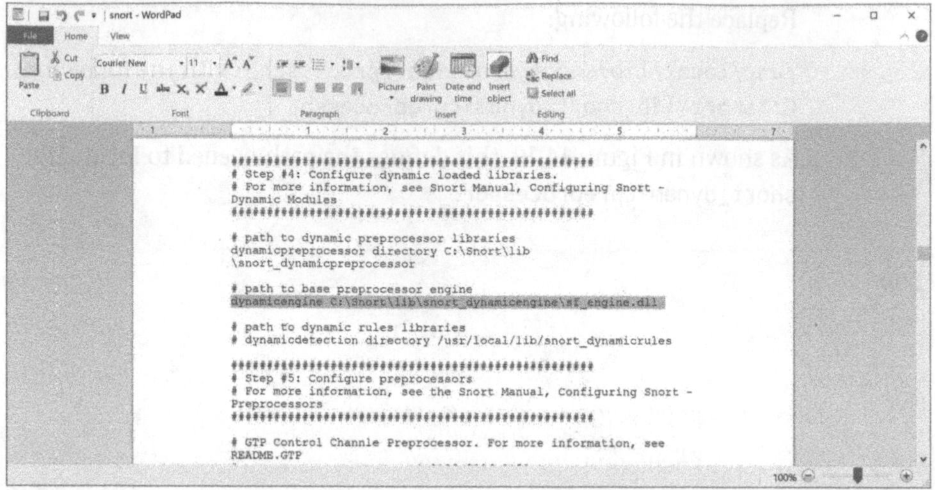

FIGURE 14.20 Dynamic Engine Path Changed

17. Locate the following:

```
# path to dynamic rules libraries
Dynamicdetection directory /usr/local/lib/snort_dynamicrules
```

Insert a pound sign (#) prior to the bottom line, as shown in Figure 14.21. Inserting the pound sign (#) prior to the line removes the usage of the `snort_dynamicrules`.

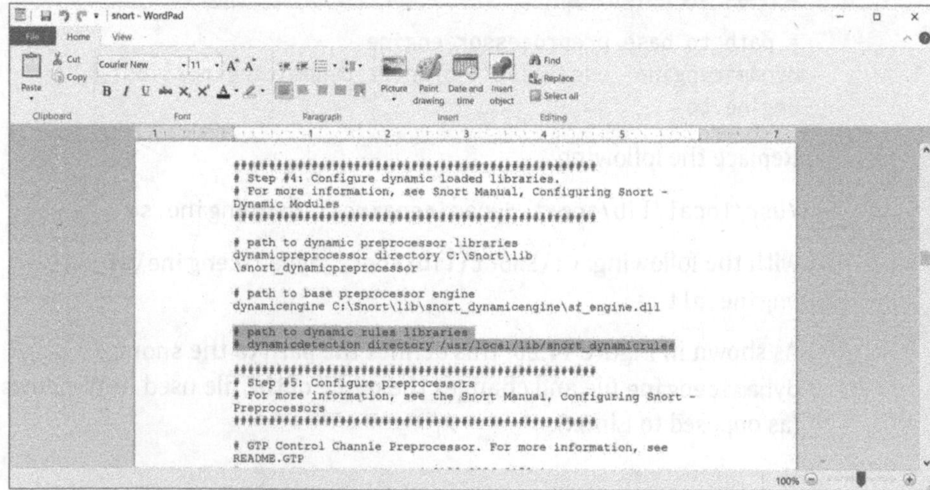

FIGURE 14.21 Dynamic Rules Excluded

18. In Step # 5, locate the following:

```
# Does nothing in IDS mode
preprocessor normalize_ip4
preprocessor normalize_tcp: block, rsv, pad, urp, req_urg,
req_pay, req_urp, ips, ecn, stream
preprocessor normalize_icmp4
preprocessor normalize_ip6
preprocessor normalize_icmp6
```

Insert a pound sign (#) in front of every preprocessor, as shown in Figure 14.22. Windows has issues with the preprocessor functions in this section, so inserting a pound sign (#) prior to each line removes them from the equation.

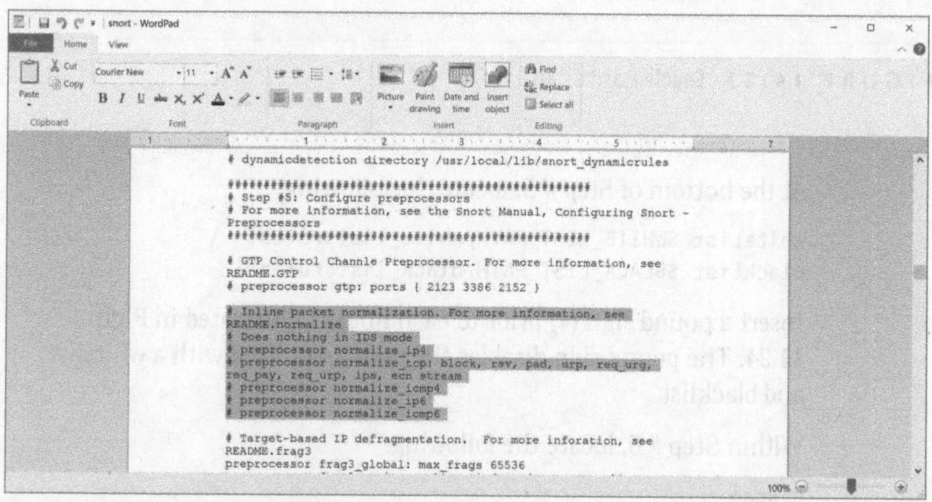

FIGURE 14.22 Inline Packet Normalization Excluded

19. In Step # 5, locate the following:

```
README.sfportscan
# preprocessor sfportscan: proto  { all } memcap  {  10000000
} sense_level  { low }
```

Remove the pound sign (#) to enable port scan detection, as illustrated in Figure 14.23.

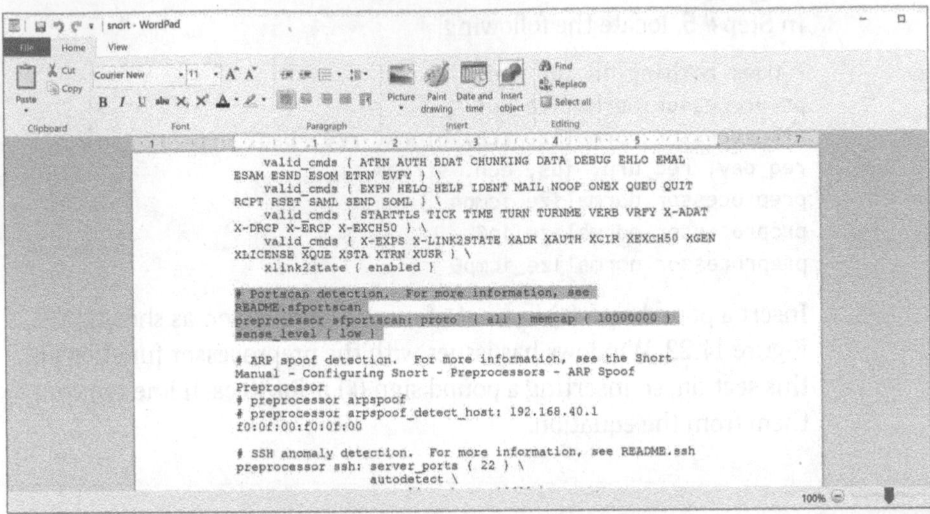

FIGURE 14.23 Enable Portscan

20. At the bottom of Step # 5, locate the following:

```
whitelist $WHITE_LIST_PATH/white_list.rules, \
blacklist $BLACK_LIST_PATH/black_list.rules
```

Insert a pound sign (#) prior to each line, as illustrated in Figure 14.24. The pound sign disables the path associated with a whitelist and blacklist.

21. Within Step # 6, locate the following:

```
# pcap
# output log_tcpdump: tcpdump.log
```

Insert `output alert_fast: alerts.ids` underneath, as illustrated in Figure 14.25. Inserting this line will create a log when alerted during the intrusion-detection mode.

22. You will need to create this file. Without closing the `snort.conf` file, click the Start icon and type **Word** into the search bar. Microsoft Word or Wordpad will appear. Press the Enter key.

23. Select File ➢ Save As. You will need to navigate to C: ➢ Snort ➢ Log. Enter **alert.ids** as the name and select Save. Select Yes if a warning prompt appears.

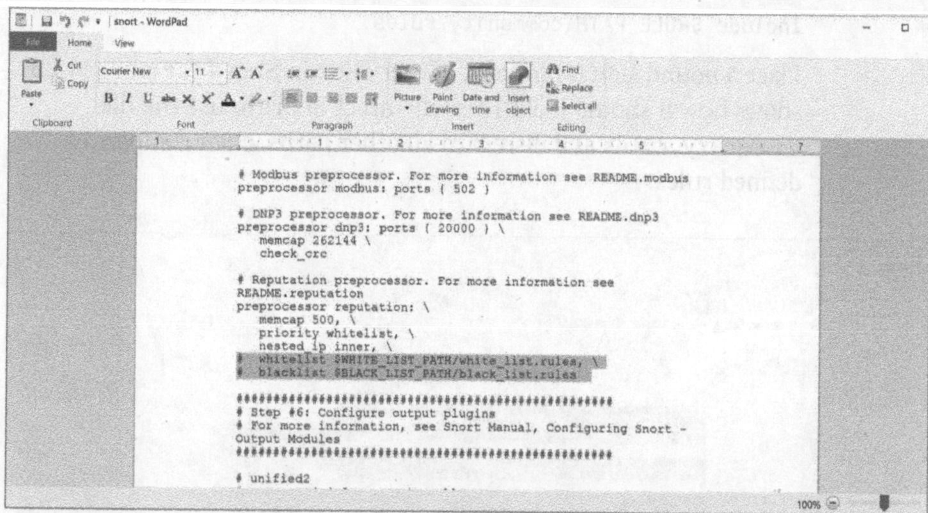

FIGURE 14.24 Whitelist and Blacklist Excluded

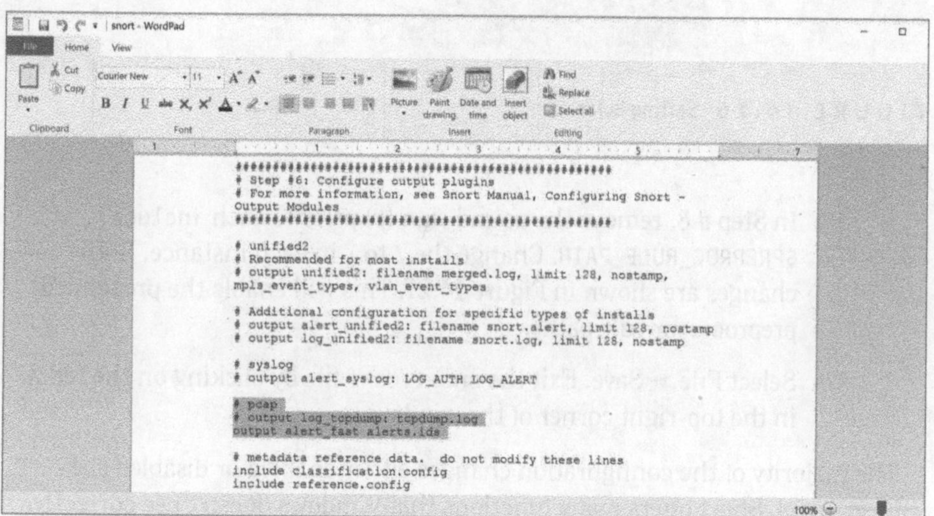

FIGURE 14.25 Output Alert

24. Close the `alert.ids` document. Return to the `snort.conf` file.
25. In Step # 7, under `# site specific rules`, insert the following:

`Include $RULE_PATH\community.rules.`

Place a pound sign (#) in front of every line in Step # 7. Figure 14.26 shows how it should look. This will direct Snort to use the file `community.rules` and disregard all other paths when comparing defined rules.

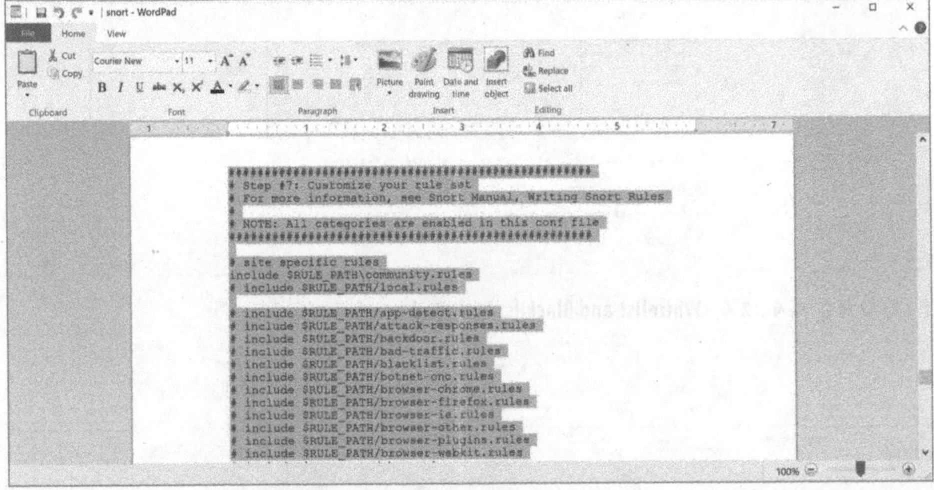

FIGURE 14.26 Setting Rules

26. In Step # 8, remove the pound sign (#) prior to each `include $PREPROC_RULE_PATH`. Change the / to \ in each instance. Both changes are shown in Figure 14.27. This will enable the predefined preprocessor rule paths.
27. Select File ➢ Save. Exit the `snort.conf` file by clicking on the red X in the top-right corner of the window.

The majority of the configuration changes either enabled or disabled specific features. Snort offers many functions that Windows doesn't use correctly. Without going through the configuration file, you would not be able to run Snort.

Adding the Rules

Snort needs rules in order to compare against them. There are three levels of rules: community, registered, and subscriber. For the purposes of this lab, you will be loading the community rules. They may be slightly outdated, but they are useful and necessary.

1. Go to: `https://www.snort.org/downloads` to download the `community-rules.tar.gz`.
2. Go to your downloaded file location and select the `community-rules.tar` file and right-click. Select 7-Zip ➢ Extract Files to launch the Extract window, as shown in Figure 14.28.

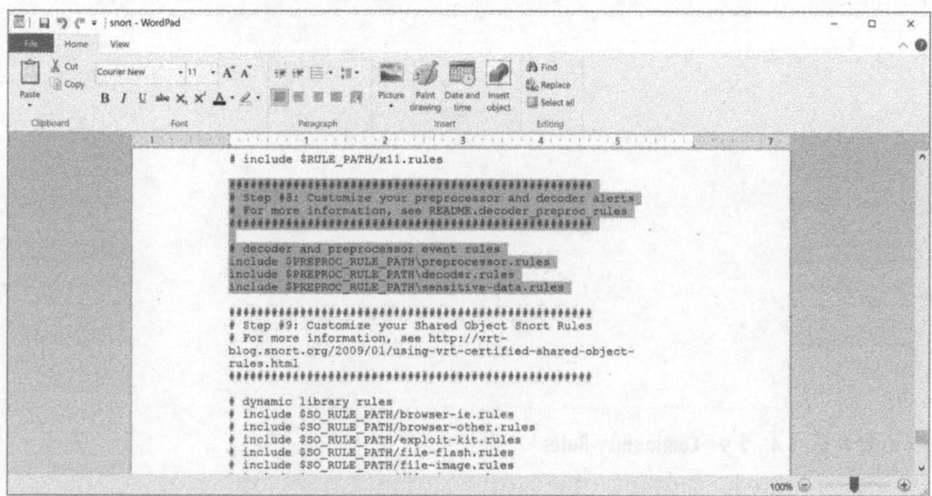

FIGURE 14.27 Step #8 Changes

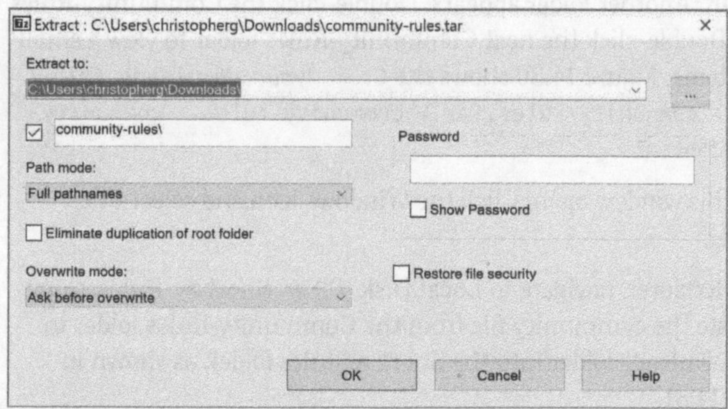

FIGURE 14.28 Extract Window

3. Click OK. A new folder will appear. Double-click the `community-rules.tar` folder to view its contents, as shown in Figure 14.29.

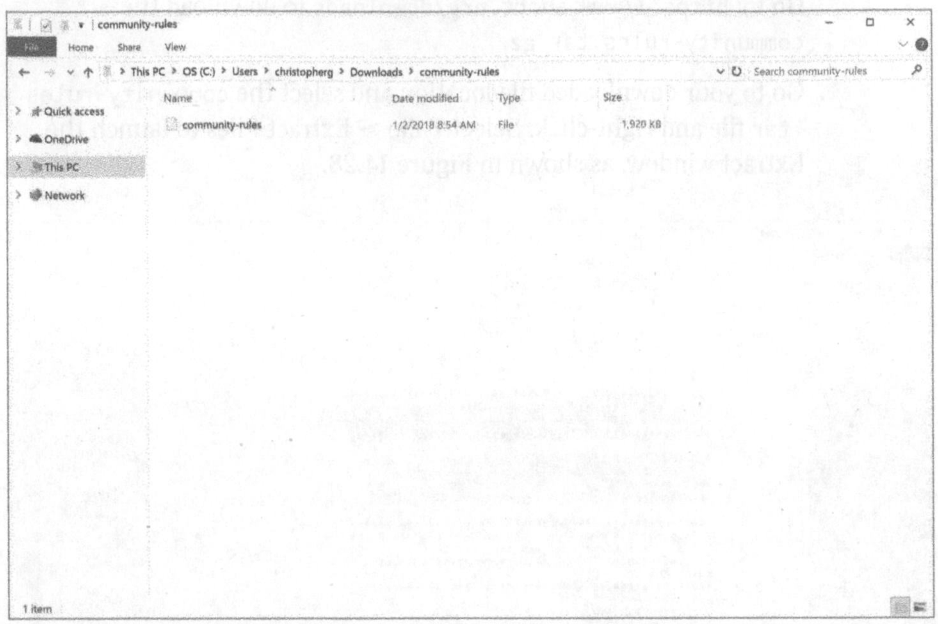

FIGURE 14.29 Community-Rules

4. Right-click the new `community-rules.tar` file, select 7-Zip ➢ Extract Files to launch another Extract window.
5. Click OK. Another folder appears. Double-click the Community-Rules folder. Double-click the next Community-Rules folder to view a small list of items. Figure 14.30 shows the `C: >` *`"your downloads folder path"`* `> community-rules.tar > community-rules > community-rules contents.`
6. Leave this window open. Click the Windows icon and select File Explorer.
7. In File Explorer, navigate to Local Disk (C:) ➢ Snort ➢ Rules. Copy and paste the community file from the Community-Rules folder in your Downloads folder into the Snort ➢ Rules folder, as shown in Figure 14.31.
8. Close all windows by clicking the red X in the top-right corner of the window.

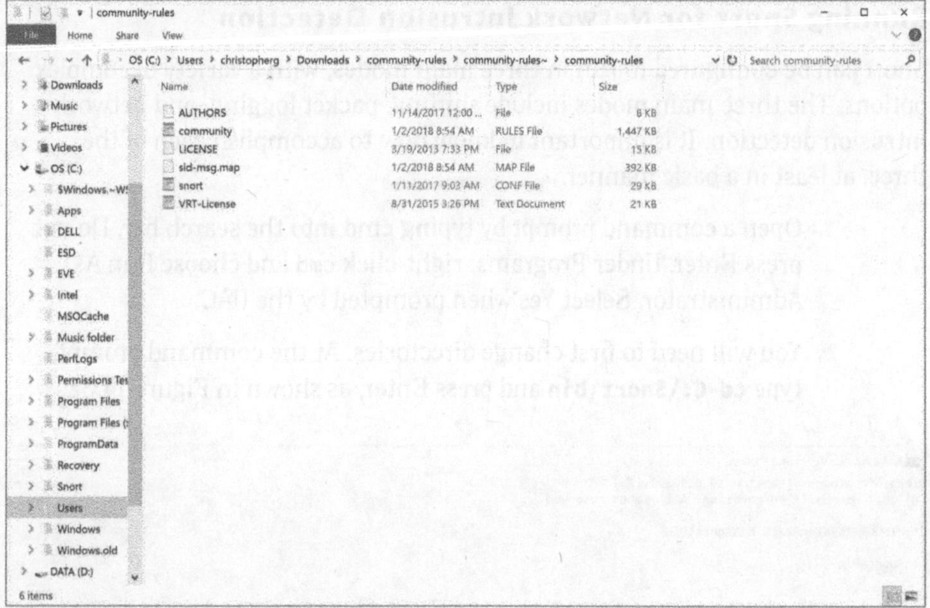

FIGURE 14.30 Community-Rules Folder

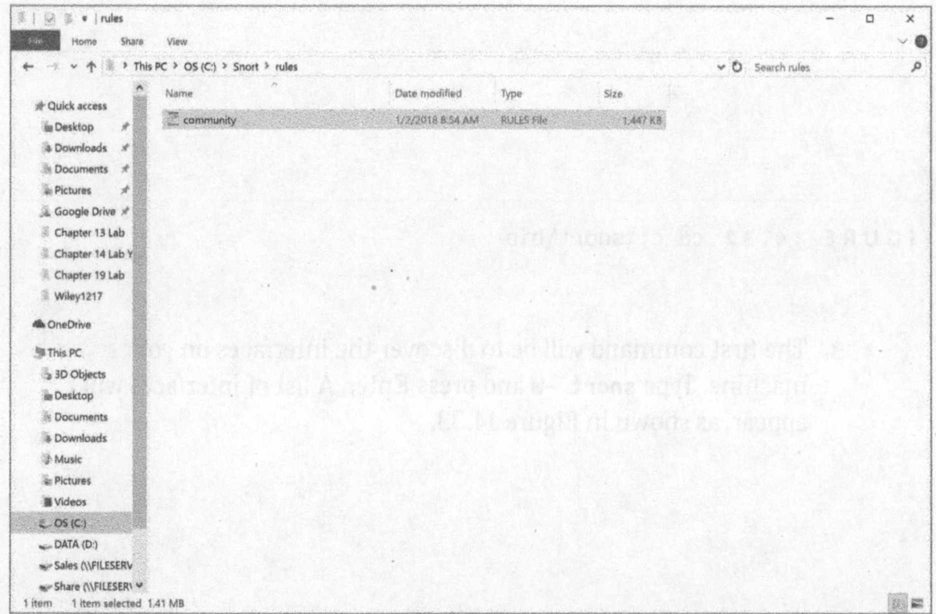

FIGURE 14.31 Community File Moved to Rules Folder

Running Snort for Network Intrusion Detection

Snort can be configured to run in three main modes, with a variety of complex options. The three main modes include sniffing, packet logging, and network intrusion detection. It is important to know how to accomplish each of the three, at least in a basic manner.

1. Open a command prompt by typing **cmd** into the search bar. Do not press Enter. Under Programs, right-click `cmd` and choose Run As Administrator. Select Yes when prompted by the UAC.

2. You will need to first change directories. At the command prompt, type **`cd C:\Snort\bin`** and press Enter, as shown in Figure 14.32.

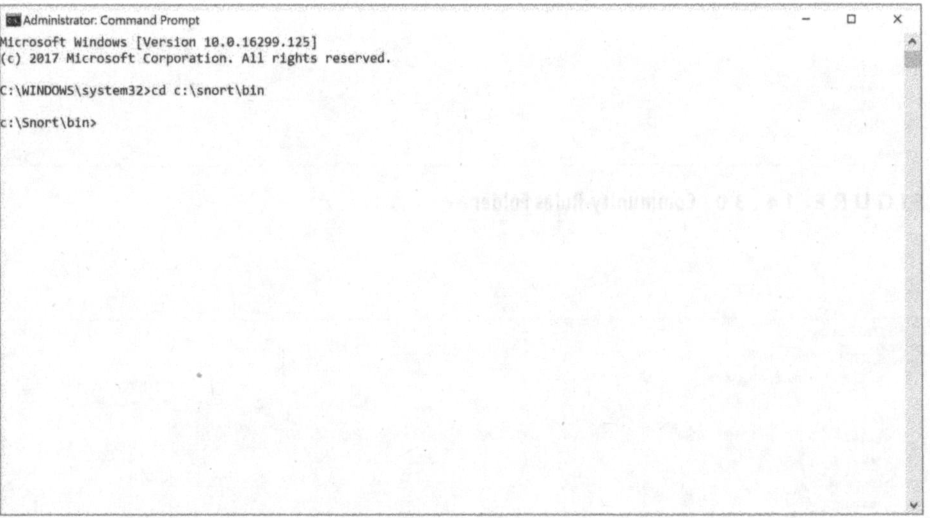

FIGURE 14.32 cd c:\snort\bin

3. The first command will be to discover the interfaces on your machine. Type **`snort -W`** and press Enter. A list of interfaces will appear, as shown in Figure 14.33.

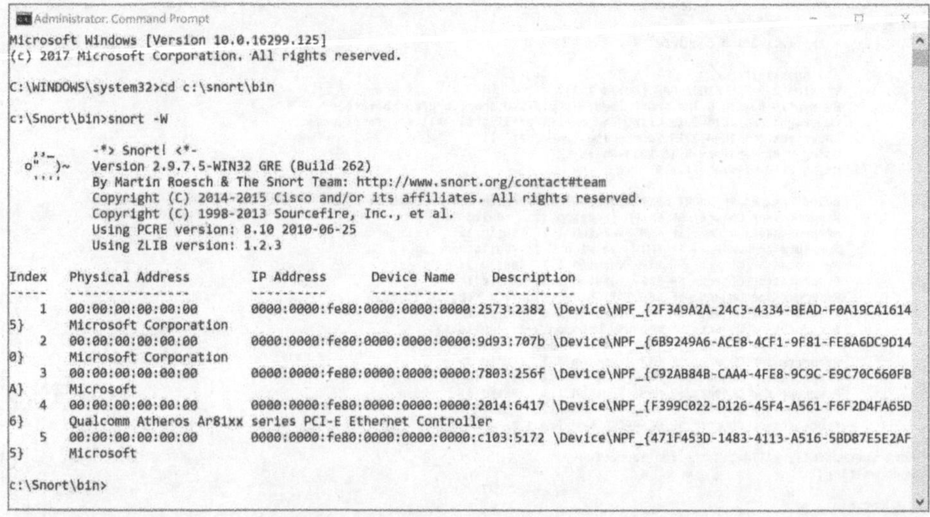

FIGURE 14.33 Snort List of Interfaces

NOTE **You may have more interfaces. It is important to choose the correct one when commanding Snort where to detect.**

4. You will now test the configuration file that was previously edited. Type the following:

   `snort -i 1 -c c:\snort\etc\snort.conf -T`

   This command is telling Snort (`snort`) to use the number 1 interface (`-i 1`) to use the configuration file (`-c`), which is located here (`c:\snort\etc\snort.conf`) and to only test it (`-T`). *Important:* you may need to use another interface number (interface 4 was used for this example).

When completed, as shown in Figure 14.34, a successful validation message will be displayed. You will now run Snort in IDS mode while logging it to a file and simultaneously flashing to the screen.

```
Administrator: Command Prompt
        --== Initialization Complete ==--

   ,,_     -*> Snort! <*-
  o"  )~   Version 2.9.7.5-WIN32 GRE (Build 262)
   ''''    By Martin Roesch & The Snort Team: http://www.snort.org/contact#team
           Copyright (C) 2014-2015 Cisco and/or its affiliates. All rights reserved.
           Copyright (C) 1998-2013 Sourcefire, Inc., et al.
           Using PCRE version: 8.10 2010-06-25
           Using ZLIB version: 1.2.3

           Rules Engine: SF_SNORT_DETECTION_ENGINE  Version 2.4  <Build 1>
           Preprocessor Object: SF_SSLPP  Version 1.1  <Build 4>
           Preprocessor Object: SF_SSH  Version 1.1  <Build 3>
           Preprocessor Object: SF_SMTP  Version 1.1  <Build 9>
           Preprocessor Object: SF_SIP  Version 1.1  <Build 1>
           Preprocessor Object: SF_SDF  Version 1.1  <Build 1>
           Preprocessor Object: SF_REPUTATION  Version 1.1  <Build 1>
           Preprocessor Object: SF_POP  Version 1.0  <Build 1>
           Preprocessor Object: SF_MODBUS  Version 1.1  <Build 1>
           Preprocessor Object: SF_IMAP  Version 1.0  <Build 1>
           Preprocessor Object: SF_GTP  Version 1.1  <Build 1>
           Preprocessor Object: SF_FTPTELNET  Version 1.2  <Build 13>
           Preprocessor Object: SF_DNS  Version 1.1  <Build 4>
           Preprocessor Object: SF_DNP3  Version 1.1  <Build 1>
           Preprocessor Object: SF_DCERPC2  Version 1.0  <Build 3>

Snort successfully validated the configuration!
Snort exiting

c:\Snort\bin>
```

FIGURE 14.34 Snort Successful Validation

5. Type **snort -A console -i 1 -c c:\snort\etc\snort.conf -l c:\snort\log** (the **-l** is a lowercase L) and press Enter (remember that the **-i 1** may be a different number for you).

   At this point, the rules are being compared. If any violations occur, they will be shown on the screen and logged.

6. At any time, press Ctrl+C to exit Snort from the IDS mode.
7. Scroll up to view the information about the session. You can see the protocol breakdown, packet I/O totals, and other information, as shown in Figure 14.35.

NOTE **Your screen may look different.**

In your current networked environment, it is highly unlikely that you will be notified of any intrusion. To show that Snort is providing IDS and can be used for other purposes, you need to *sniff* the network.

8. At the command prompt, type **snort -dev -i 1 -c c:\snort\etc\snort.conf** (recall that **-i 1** may be different in your environment) and press Enter.

After packet processing begins, you will see individual packets with their associated information.

Figure 14.36 shows a few packets in sniffer mode.

```
Administrator: Command Prompt
Packet I/O Totals:
   Received:         3522
   Analyzed:         3514 ( 99.773%)
    Dropped:            0 (  0.000%)
   Filtered:            0 (  0.000%)
Outstanding:            8 (  0.227%)
   Injected:            0
===============================================================================
Breakdown by protocol (includes rebuilt packets):
        Eth:         3518 (100.000%)
       VLAN:            0 (  0.000%)
        IP4:         3450 ( 98.067%)
       Frag:            0 (  0.000%)
       ICMP:            0 (  0.000%)
        UDP:         1541 ( 43.803%)
        TCP:         1902 ( 54.065%)
        IP6:            1 (  0.028%)
    IP6 Ext:            1 (  0.028%)
   IP6 Opts:            0 (  0.000%)
      Frag6:            0 (  0.000%)
      ICMP6:            0 (  0.000%)
       UDP6:            1 (  0.028%)
       TCP6:            0 (  0.000%)
     Teredo:            0 (  0.000%)
    ICMP-IP:            0 (  0.000%)
      EAPOL:            0 (  0.000%)
    IP4/IP4:            0 (  0.000%)
    IP4/IP6:            0 (  0.000%)
    IP6/IP4:            0 (  0.000%)
    IP6/IP6:            0 (  0.000%)
```

FIGURE 14.35 Snort IDS Mode Breakdown

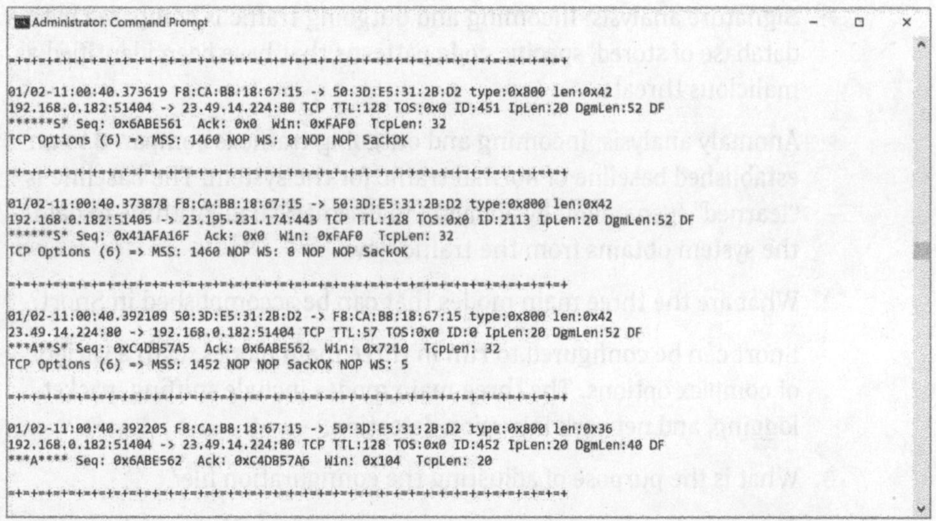

```
Administrator: Command Prompt

=+=+=+=+=+=+=+=+=+=+=+=+=+=+=+=+=+=+=+=+=+=+=+=+=+=+=+=+=+=+=+=+=+=+=+=+=+=+

01/02-11:00:40.373619 F8:CA:B8:18:67:15 -> 50:3D:E5:31:2B:D2 type:0x800 len:0x42
192.168.0.182:51404 -> 23.49.14.224:80 TCP TTL:128 TOS:0x0 ID:451 IpLen:20 DgmLen:52 DF
******S* Seq: 0x6ABE561  Ack: 0x0  Win: 0xFAF0  TcpLen: 32
TCP Options (6) => MSS: 1460 NOP WS: 8 NOP NOP SackOK

=+=+=+=+=+=+=+=+=+=+=+=+=+=+=+=+=+=+=+=+=+=+=+=+=+=+=+=+=+=+=+=+=+=+=+=+=+=+

01/02-11:00:40.373878 F8:CA:B8:18:67:15 -> 50:3D:E5:31:2B:D2 type:0x800 len:0x42
192.168.0.182:51405 -> 23.195.231.174:443 TCP TTL:128 TOS:0x0 ID:2113 IpLen:20 DgmLen:52 DF
******S* Seq: 0x41AFA16F  Ack: 0x0  Win: 0xFAF0  TcpLen: 32
TCP Options (6) => MSS: 1460 NOP WS: 8 NOP NOP SackOK

=+=+=+=+=+=+=+=+=+=+=+=+=+=+=+=+=+=+=+=+=+=+=+=+=+=+=+=+=+=+=+=+=+=+=+=+=+=+

01/02-11:00:40.392109 50:3D:E5:31:2B:D2 -> F8:CA:B8:18:67:15 type:0x800 len:0x42
23.49.14.224:80 -> 192.168.0.182:51404 TCP TTL:57 TOS:0x0 ID:0 IpLen:20 DgmLen:52 DF
***A**S* Seq: 0xC4DB57A5  Ack: 0x6ABE562  Win: 0x7210  TcpLen: 32
TCP Options (6) => MSS: 1452 NOP NOP SackOK NOP WS: 5

=+=+=+=+=+=+=+=+=+=+=+=+=+=+=+=+=+=+=+=+=+=+=+=+=+=+=+=+=+=+=+=+=+=+=+=+=+=+

01/02-11:00:40.392205 F8:CA:B8:18:67:15 -> 50:3D:E5:31:2B:D2 type:0x800 len:0x36
192.168.0.182:51404 -> 23.49.14.224:80 TCP TTL:128 TOS:0x0 ID:452 IpLen:20 DgmLen:40 DF
***A**** Seq: 0x6ABE562  Ack: 0xC4DB57A6  Win: 0x104  TcpLen: 20

=+=+=+=+=+=+=+=+=+=+=+=+=+=+=+=+=+=+=+=+=+=+=+=+=+=+=+=+=+=+=+=+=+=+=+=+=+=+
```

FIGURE 14.36 Snort in Sniffer Mode

As shown in Figure 14.36, you can see the IP addresses, MAC addresses, packet details, protocols, and more.

9. To stop Snort, press Ctrl+C. At the command prompt, type **exit** and press Enter.
10. Close all remaining open windows. Shut down the machine.

Lab Questions

1. What are the two strategies, or two types of rules, on which an IDS is based?
2. What are the three main modes that can be accomplished in Snort?
3. What is the purpose of adjusting the configuration file?
4. What are the pros and cons of using Snort?

Lab Answers

1. What are the two strategies, or two types of rules, on which an IDS is based?

All IDS devices are based on one of two strategies:

- Signature analysis: Incoming and outgoing traffic is compared with a database of stored, specific code patterns that have been identified as malicious threats.
- Anomaly analysis: Incoming and outgoing traffic is compared to an established baseline of normal traffic for the system. The baseline is "learned" (generated) by applying mathematical algorithms to data the system obtains from the traffic flow.

2. What are the three main modes that can be accomplished in Snort?

   Snort can be configured to run in three main modes, with a variety of complex options. The three main modes include sniffing, packet logging, and network intrusion detection.

3. What is the purpose of adjusting the configuration file?

   The majority of the configurations were performed to enable or disable certain features. Snort offers many functions that Windows doesn't use well. Without going through the configuration file, you would not be able to run Snort.

4. What are the pros and cons of using Snort?

   Although Snort is very effective and widely used, it does not contain a GUI for easy administration. This is both a pro and a con. The benefit is that the administrator has complete control, even being able to create his or her own rules. However, one of the drawbacks of Snort is that it has a steep learning curve and requires strong command-line understanding.

CHAPTER 15

Understanding Network Connectivity Devices

All intelligent devices attached to a network must have a network interface adapter capable of physically connecting the device to the network transmission media. These network connectivity devices provide physical connection schemes (such as plugs and jacks) as well as electrical compatibility between the device and the signals traveling across the transmission media (cables or airwaves). The network typically contains other connectivity devices that connect different portions of the network together and perform different network management functions. These connectivity devices are usually switches or routers. In large or complex networks, you might also find devices, called *bridges,* which are used to interconnect different sections of the network. Although each device provides physical connectivity, each device also features specific methods of operation that make it suitable for use in specific network applications. In some cases, a device with more features might be used to perform the functions of a lower-featured device. In this chapter, you'll learn to:

- **Understand network switches**
- **Understand routers**
- **Understand gateways**
- **Understand network bridges**
- **Understand network connectivity**

Network Switches

Network switches are connectivity devices that function at Layer 2 of the OSI model (see the following note). They are designed to connect network devices together to form a local area network. Enterprise networks (corporate networks designed to support medium and large numbers of users for business activities) typically employ combinations of switches to segment the network and establish efficient data traffic flows. They may be used in combination with other network connectivity devices, or they may be connected directly to the server room through a backbone cabling arrangement.

A Word About Network Switches

Primarily, switches are Layer 2 devices that function at the OSI data link layer. However, there are also Layer 3 switches that act similarly to *brouters* (devices that have the functional capabilities of both routers and bridges, covered in the upcoming sections), Layer 4 switches that include Network Address Translation (NAT) capabilities, and Layer 7 (content) switches that distribute content based on server loading factors.

For example, a company whose organization spans several floors of an office building might employ a separate switch on each floor to provide connectivity for all the devices on that floor. The switches on individual floors would also be connected to each other through a switch or router. Figure 15.1 shows a typical network-switch-connection scheme.

Switches collect MAC address information to keep track of the devices attached to them. As they interact with those devices, they record their MAC information in an onboard memory structure called a *MAC address table.*

When a switch receives a packet of network information at one of its ports, it can direct the information to its intended receiver provided the address of the receiver is known. If the address is not known, the switch will broadcast the information to all of its ports. Because information traveling through the switch is generally only sent to the port where it is intended, the performance of the entire network is improved greatly.

Switches can also be used to create logically secured virtual local area networks (VLANs). A VLAN is a security topology that restricts the visibility of network traffic by limiting the movement of network packets so that they only pass between designated ports.

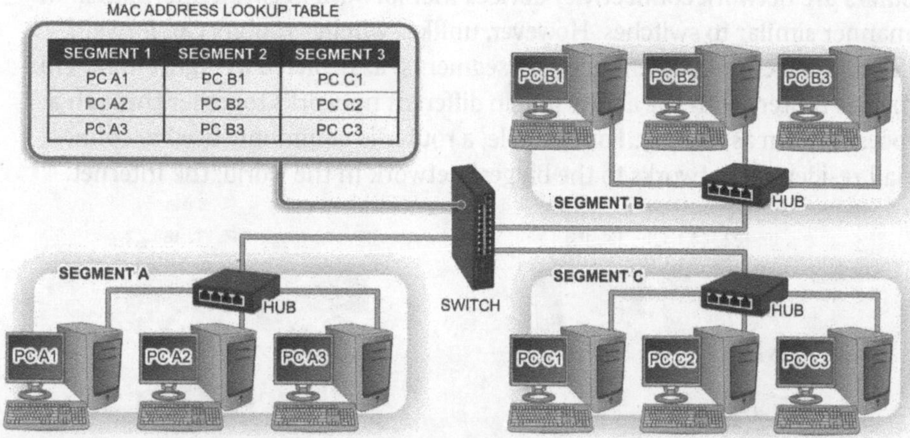

FIGURE 15.1 A Network-Switch Connection

Network switches are typically grouped into one of two categories by their configuration options. Unmanaged switches are Plug and Play (PnP) devices that do not include any options for user configuration. These tend to be low price units intended for use in residential and small office settings, so they are rarely found in business and enterprise networks.

The other category of switches is referred to as *managed switches*. These devices have programmable management functions built into them that enable administrators to configure them for the specific network environment in which they will be used. As such, they provide some type of management console that the administrator can use to set parameters. Common management interfaces include:

Command-Line Programming This format provides a very efficient and direct text-based method of programming the switch's settings. Command-line programming requires the administrator to be aware of the instruction set and parameter variables available for setting the different parameters.

Web-Browser-Based Interfaces These interfaces provide a more graphical, menu-driven tool for setting key switch parameters. A Simple Network Management Protocol (SNMP) tool is used to permit the administrator to access the switch's parameters through a remote client using its web browser.

Routers

Routers are network connectivity devices that forward network information in a manner similar to switches. However, unlike switches routers can forward information across different network segments, as depicted in Figure 15.2. This provides routers with the ability to join different networks together through a process known as *routing*. For example, a router is commonly used to connect small residential networks to the biggest network in the world: the Internet.

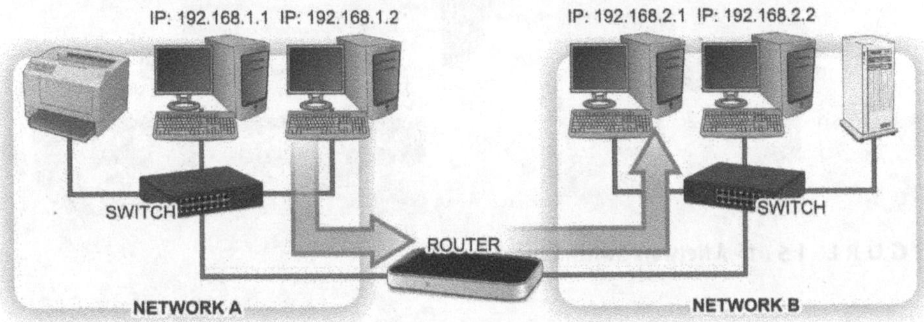

FIGURE 15.2 A Network Router

The internal structure of a typical router is depicted in Figure 15.3. *Routers* are microprocessor-based intelligent devices that control the flow of data between networks. The *microprocessor* is a specialized device optimized to operate as a route processor.

As with other microprocessor-based equipment, routers contain a ROM BIOS for bootup, an NVRAM CMOS configuration area to hold operational configuration parameters, and an onboard operating system stored in a flash memory unit.

A Word About Routers

Routers operate from their own operating systems. The most widely recognized router/switch operating system is Cisco System's Internetwork Operating System (IOS). However, many other Linux/Unix-based router OS distributions are available for use.

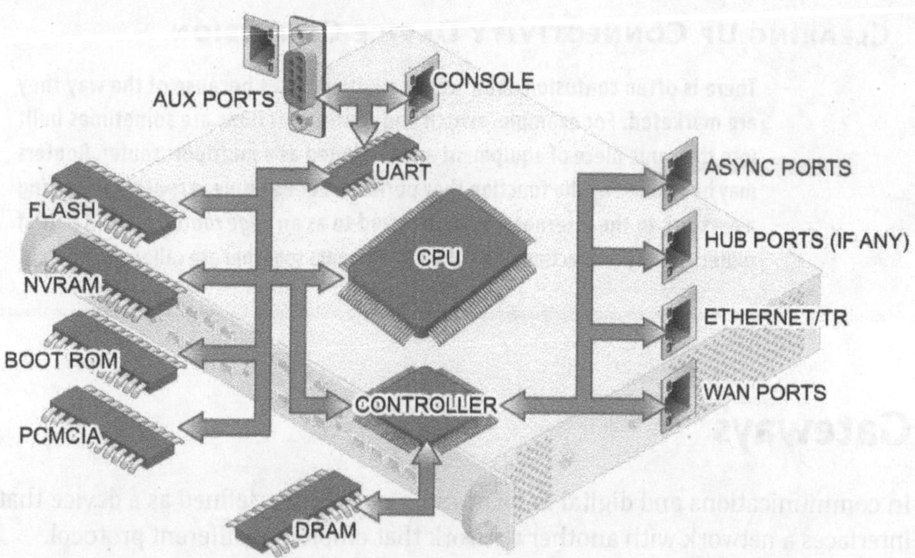

FIGURE 15.3 **Internal Structure of a Network Router**

Routers also contain different sections of DRAM memory to hold message routing information and to buffer data flow between its ports. The routing information is stored and updated in a logical memory table referred to as *routing table*.

Each network segment is connected to the router through one of its physical port interfaces. These interfaces can be implemented as different types of physical/logical interface specifications, such as an 8P8C Ethernet connection port.

In large networks, routers communicate with other routers using a routing protocol to build and maintain their routing tables. These tables are used to record the best route between different network locations. Unlike the MAC tables used in switches, routing tables store address and hop information about the paths between devices.

Almost all routers possess a physical interface that can be used to attach an external console for configuration purposes. They may also contain an asynchronous RS-232 serial hardware port that can be used by administrators to perform remote router-management functions.

Clearing Up Connectivity Device Confusion

There is often confusion about connectivity devices because of the way they are marketed. For example, switch and router functions are sometimes built into the same piece of equipment and marketed as a multiport router. Routers may be labeled by the function they perform. For example, a router connecting a network to the Internet may be referred to as an *edge router,* while a pair of routers simply connecting two network segments together are called *core routers.*

Gateways

In communications and digital networking, a *gateway* is defined as a device that interfaces a network with another network that employs a different protocol. Recall that a *protocol* is a defined set of rules for carrying out communication between different devices or systems.

The protocol may be designed to match differences in physical connections (hardware protocols) or to match different signal logic levels, message formats, or information exchange speeds (software protocols). Some gateway devices are designed to perform both functions, as illustrated in Figure 15.4. The gateway in the figure translates a wired Ethernet/TCP/IP protocol format into a wireless/ZigBee protocol format.

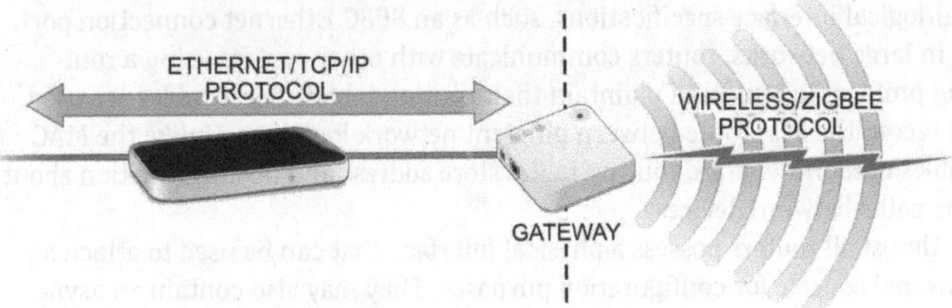

FIGURE 15.4 Gateway Operations

For communications to be successful, both parties must agree to use the same protocol. For example, for two people to communicate verbally, they must both be able to use a common language. If not, you have an example of an old Chinese proverb of the chicken talking to the duck.

When a router is used to connect networks to always-on, broadband Internet connections, it is referred to as an Internet gateway. In addition to performing the routing functions, Internet gateway routers typically supply a number of other Internet-related services, such as automatic address assignments and firewall services. You may also encounter routing switches (called LAN switches) that have built-in routing capabilities.

Network Bridges

A *network bridge* (sometimes referred to as a network switch) bridges network segments together and forwards traffic from one network to another. Like the switch, a bridge uses MAC addresses to guide information to the correct ports. However, it also passes broadcast information to all of its ports. Therefore, the bridge gathers network connections into a single common segment, while a router separates them into different segments. Figure 15.5 illustrates the operation of a network bridge.

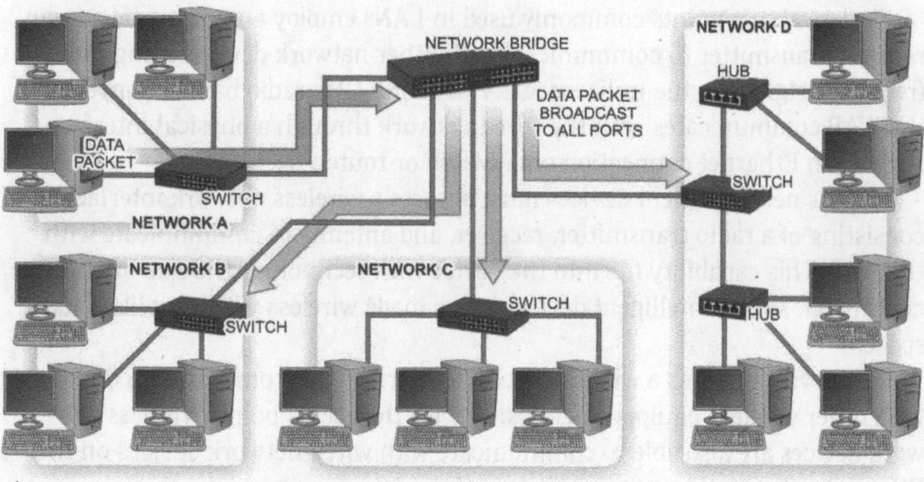

FIGURE 15.5 A Network Bridge Arrangement

Wireless Network Connectivity

In a wireless network, or wireless network segment, the network devices connect to the network through a device known as a wireless access point (WAP). The wireless access point acts as a bridging device that connects the wireless network devices with the wired network, as shown in Figure 15.6.

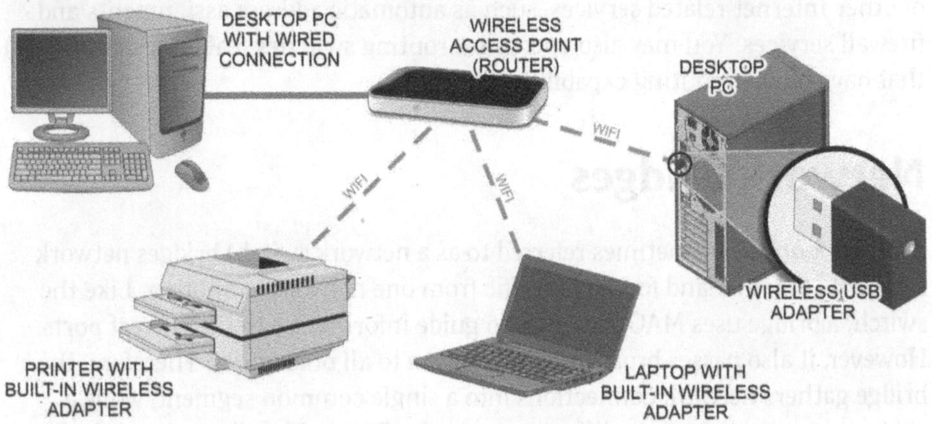

FIGURE 15.6 A Wireless Access Point

Wireless access points commonly used in LANs employ antennas and a radio receiver/transmitter to communicate with other network devices using radio frequency signals in the unlicensed 2.4 GHz or 5 GHz radio bands. Conversely, the WAP communicates with the wired network through a physical interface such as an Ethernet connection on a switch or router.

Wireless network client devices must possess a wireless network interface consisting of a radio transmitter, receiver, and antenna to communicate with the WAP. This capability fits into the device with technology the size of a square centimeter, so any intelligent device can be made wireless with very little added space.

Each device that has a wireless network interface can communicate directly with other wireless-equipped devices, or with the access point. Wireless network devices are also able to communicate with wired network devices on the Ethernet network through the access point.

Network Connectivity Device Vulnerabilities

Because of their positions and functions within the network, connectivity devices are vulnerable to a number of different types of exploitation. If a network connectivity device is successfully attacked, the consequences can include problems ranging from slowed network traffic to a shutdown of the entire network. For this reason, these devices require the same types and levels of security considerations that servers do. General considerations for protecting switches, routers, and other network connectivity devices include:

- Placing connectivity devices in secure wall cabinets or locating them within the security of the server room to provide physical protection.
- Configuring device management settings so that required features are as secure as necessary to provide the performance level needed. Disabling any management features that are not needed.
- Establishing port security through MAC address filtering (manually entering static MAC addresses into the CAM), or by specifying the maximum number of devices allowed on a port. By entering static ARP entries, this removes the possibility of attackers being able to replace them with forged ARP replies.

Network Connectivity Device Attacks

Typical attacks targeting network connectivity devices include:

- Unauthorized accesses
- Packet sniffing attacks

Unauthorized Accesses

Most network connectivity devices possess some level of configuration possibilities. As such, their operation can be manipulated if their configuration parameters can be accessed. As with other types of network and computing devices, passwords should be employed to control access to the connectivity device's configuration data whenever possible.

Because most network administrators configure connectivity devices through Remote Management interfaces, using Telnet or HTTP web services, these communications should be placed behind a firewall for protection. In addition, an encrypting transmission protocol such as Secure Shell (SSH) could be used to secure the configuration data as it moves from the administrator's device to the switch. Or, a directly connected console could be used to configure switch interfaces. Data and configuration information should never be sent across the network in plaintext mode.

Packet Sniffing Attacks

Packet sniffing is the act of listening to packets as they move through a network. This activity is normally conducted using a network analyzer tool referred to as a *packet sniffer*. Attackers use these tools to listen to network traffic looking for items such as passwords and user names sent across the network in a plaintext mode or sensitive information such as credit card or other financial information they can hijack. Typical packet sniffing attacks are detailed in this section.

Address Resolution Protocol (ARP) Spoofing Attacks

In Address Resolution Protocol (ARP) spoofing attacks, the attacker sends fake ARP messages to associate their MAC address with the IP address of another user. Once the association has been established, messages directed to that address will be diverted to the attacker. The attacker can then use information obtained from the intercepted messages to mount other types of attacks, such as DoS or man-in-the-middle attacks (discussed later in this section).

MAC Flooding

A MAC broadcast flood attack can be launched against a Layer 2 device, such as a network switch, from a device connected to one of its ports. The attack software on the controlled device is designed to flood a high volume of different MAC addresses into the switch's CAM table, causing it to fill up. When this state is reached, the switch will run out of room to map the new MAC addresses to its ports. Because all of the MAC addresses in the CAM are now new addresses that have not been mapped, the switch will be forced to broadcast all of the frames it receives to all of its ports.

Router Flood Attacks

As with MAC broadcast flooding attacks associated with switches, routers are vulnerable to flood attacks designed to consume all—or a significant part of—their resources, thereby rendering them nonfunctional. Router resources commonly targeted include onboard memory, processor operation, and internal bus bandwidth.

MAC Duplicating (or Cloning) Attacks

In a MAC duplicating or MAC cloning attack, the attacker updates their own MAC address with the target's MAC address. This will cause the switch to forward traffic to both locations.

Switch Port Stealing

Switch-port-stealing attacks are designed to flood the switch with altered response packets. This will cause the switch to forward all traffic through the switch to the attacker's location.

Denial of Service (DoS) Attacks

DoS attacks (see Figure 15.7) are designed to overuse a host, server, or network resource to the point where it functionally ceases to provide its services. Depending on the exact nature of the attack, the failure may be temporary or indefinite. Distributed Denial of Service (DDoS) attacks involve multiple remote systems being used to simultaneously amass the attack on the targeted resource.

Spoofing Attacks

Spoofing attacks are based on changing a device's MAC or IP address to change its apparent identity. Because a TCP/IP packet contains many different headers, attackers can create a TCP/IP packet and send its contents using a false source IP address. When the addressed recipient receives the message, the response generated is sent to the spoofed address.

This form of spoofing is known as *IP address spoofing,* or simply as IP spoofing, and is often used to create DDoS attacks. These attacks are carried out by sending falsified packets to multiple targets so that their response messages flood the targeted victim and create the designed DoS condition.

Man-in-the-Middle (MITM) Attacks

Man-in-the-middle attacks involve an attacker creating links to two or more victims so they can intercept messages moving between them and insert new information into them before forwarding them, as shown in Figure 15.8. This is accomplished without either victim realizing the attacker is controlling the communications.

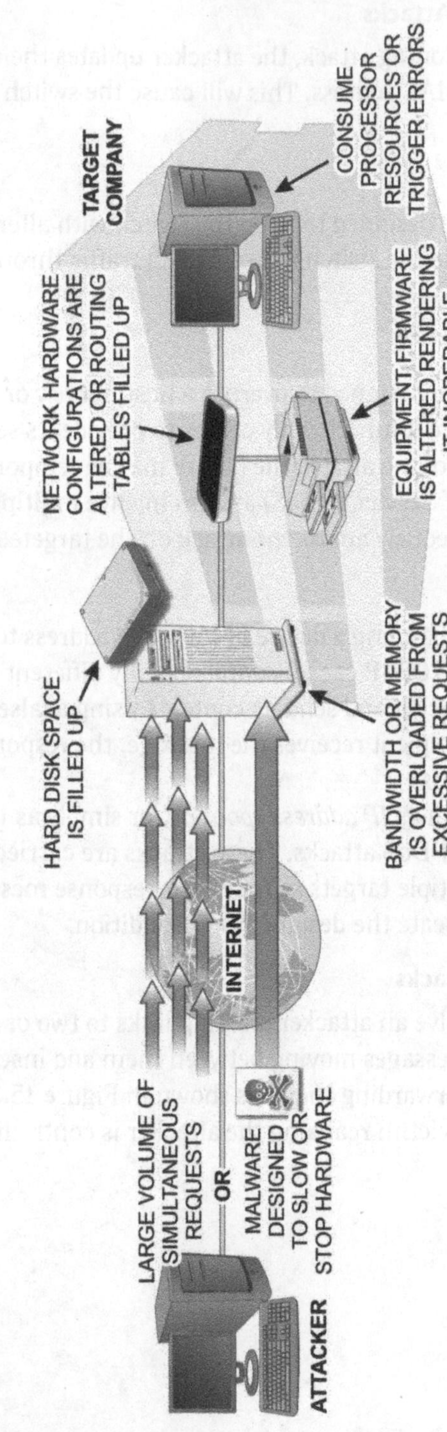

FIGURE 15.7 A Denial of Service Attack

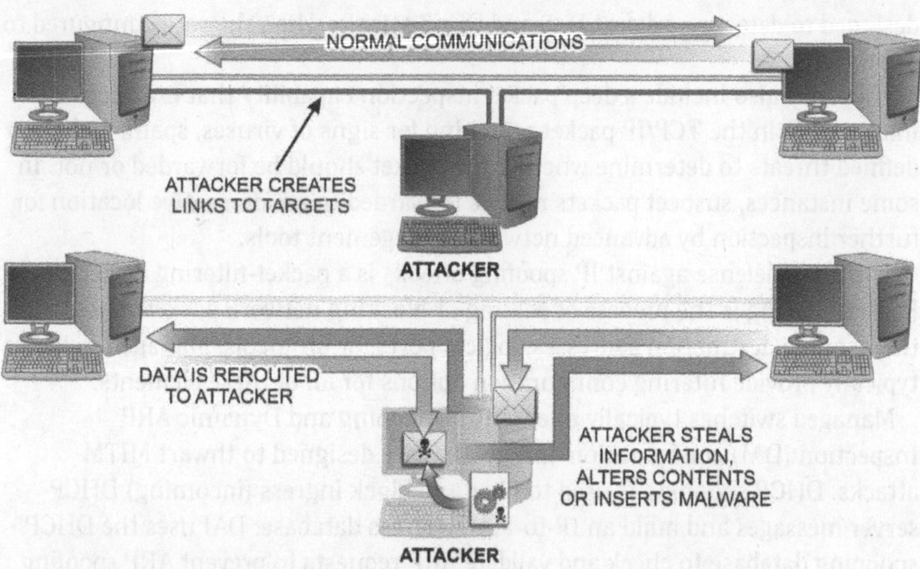

FIGURE 15.8 A Man-in-the-Middle Attack

Session Replay Attacks

In session replay attacks, the attacker records a sequence of IP packets or router commands, manipulates the data in them, and then reintroduces them to the router to gain access or cause undesirable actions to be performed.

Rerouting Attacks

Rerouting attacks are enabled by an attacker gaining access to the routing tables in a network router and reconfiguring it to redirect IP packets to alternative locations. These types of attacks are prevented by using transmission protocols that require route authentication. The can also be thwarted by employing static routers.

Masquerade Attacks

Masquerade attacks involve an attacker manipulating IP packets to create a false IP address so they can gain access to the network or inject false data into it.

Network Connectivity Defense

Network switches and routers typically possess data rate limiting, delayed binding, bogus IP address filtering, and access control list capabilities that are designed to detect and defeat DoS and DDoS attacks when they are configured to do so.

They may also include a deep packet inspection capability that examines the information in the TCP/IP packet searching for signs of viruses, spam, and other defined threats to determine whether the packet should be forwarded or not. In some instances, suspect packets may be forwarded to an alternative location for further inspection by advanced network management tools.

The main defense against IP spoofing attacks is a packet-filtering device. Packet filtering is the process of passing or blocking network packets based on their source/destination addresses, logical ports, or protocols. Managed switches typically provide filtering configuration options for all of these elements.

Managed switches typically offer DHCP snooping and Dynamic ARP Inspection (DAI) configuration options that are designed to thwart MITM attacks. DHCP snooping is used to filter and block ingress (incoming) DHCP server messages and build an IP-to-MAC address database. DAI uses the DHCP snooping database to check and validate ARP requests to prevent ARP spoofing attacks.

Network Hardening

After the operating systems and their file systems have been hardened, administrators must take steps to harden the rest of the network, including network protection and connectivity devices. Typical steps involved in this portion of the system hardening process include:

- Secure the system's servers to the degree called for in the organization's security policies. If possible, place them in a monitored, centralized server room that has a double locking door.
- Check to determine if there are any network devices whose specifications fail to meet current security goals and therefore represent easy access points to the network.
- Verify that the network is configured to perform its communication functions and still provide the security levels called for by the organization's security policies. Make certain that devices such as switches, firewalls, and routers are not still set to their default configuration settings.
- Evaluate the cybersecurity plan to make sure that critical devices such as production servers are installed in the correct network segment, security zone, or subnet.

- Establish and configure ACLs on network connectivity devices to limit or restrict access to assets as required by the organization's security policies.
- Evaluate the roles and responsibilities of personnel against the servers they commonly access.
- Assess residual risks that remain in the network and monitor for changes that may need to be made in the future.

Hands-On Exercises

Objectives

The purpose of this lab is to simulate setting up a small office or home office router. This lab guides you through the process of resetting your router to factory settings. Then you will connect and change the default credentials. After that, you will disable Remote Management and disable the guest network.

You should note that the instructions given here are generalized for any router. Your images, names of settings, places to click, and functionality may be different.

Resources

- Windows 10 PC physically connected to a SOHO router
- SOHO router

Procedures

1. Turn off your router by unplugging the power cable.
2. Leave the router off for approximately 30 seconds.
3. Plug the power back into the router. This should turn on the router. If not, find a power button or switch.
4. Wait until the router indicates power is received.
5. Find a reset button somewhere on your router. This button is usually small and is probably recessed in a small hole in the outer case. A paperclip is typically used to press the button.

6. Push the reset button on the router for 10 seconds and then release it. Be aware that resetting the router's configuration will erase all existing settings, and a completely new configuration will need to be created.
7. Ensure your computer is physically connected to the router.
8. Press and hold the Windows key and press r to open the Run dialog (see Figure 15.9). Then type cmd and press Enter (or click OK).

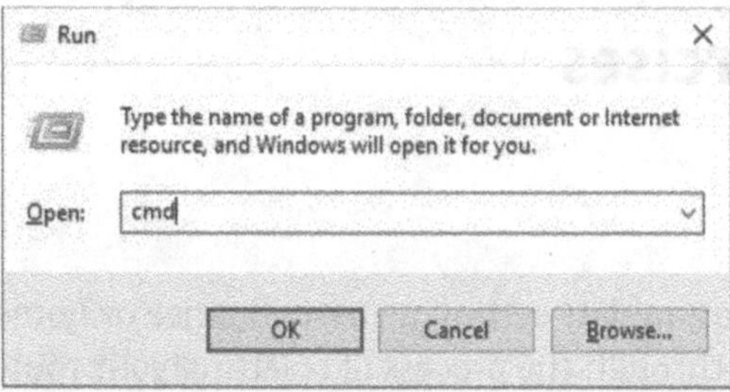

FIGURE 15.9 Run Dialog

9. At the command prompt (see Figure 15.10), type ipconfig. Figure 15.11 shows the output.

FIGURE 15.10 Command Prompt

```
C:\WINDOWS\system32\cmd.exe
Microsoft Windows [Version 10.0.16299.125]
(c) 2017 Microsoft Corporation. All rights reserved.

C:\Users\Marcraft1>ipconfig

Windows IP Configuration


Ethernet adapter Ethernet 2:

   Connection-specific DNS Suffix  . :
   Link-local IPv6 Address . . . . . : fe80::3424:5c5e:17a8:e4%10
   IPv4 Address. . . . . . . . . . . : 192.168.1.3
   Subnet Mask . . . . . . . . . . . : 255.255.255.0
   Default Gateway . . . . . . . . . : 192.168.1.1

Ethernet adapter Npcap Loopback Adapter:

   Connection-specific DNS Suffix  . :
   Link-local IPv6 Address . . . . . : fe80::91d:df5b:1870:b4d3%11
   Autoconfiguration IPv4 Address. . : 169.254.180.211
   Subnet Mask . . . . . . . . . . . : 255.255.0.0
   Default Gateway . . . . . . . . . :

Tunnel adapter Local Area Connection* 3:

   Media State . . . . . . . . . . . : Media disconnected
   Connection-specific DNS Suffix  . :

C:\Users\Marcraft1>
```

FIGURE 15.11 IPCONFIG Output

10. Search for your default gateway entry. The default gateway shown in Figure 15.11 is `192.168.1.1`.

11. Type exit at the command prompt and press Enter to close the Command Prompt window.

12. Open Microsoft Edge and type your default gateway IP address in the address bar.

13. A dialog box should appear, requesting a username and password. The router was reset to factory default settings. However, not all routers have the same default username and password combinations.

14. If you have Internet access, `www.defaultpassword.com` may be able to assist you. Some common username and password combinations are *`admin/admin`* or *`admin/password`*. Sometimes the username is empty and the password is *`admin`*. Sometimes the username is *`admin`* and the password is empty. The username and password may be on a tag on the router. Lastly, you can search for documentation or manuals online for your specific router. When you gain access to your router, proceed to Step 15.

NOTE **Router manufacturers have default usernames and passwords to reduce troubleshooting and manufacturing difficulty.**

15. Your router may offer a "wizard" to help you with the first time set up of your router. Ignore these messages.

NOTE **Remember, you can factory reset your router if something goes awry.**

16. Since routers have default usernames and passwords, they are easy to guess and not secure. Changing the default username and password is the first task.

17. Look for a setting that involves management or administration. The steps used to produce what is shown in Figure 15.12 were Advanced ➢ Administration ➢ Set Password.

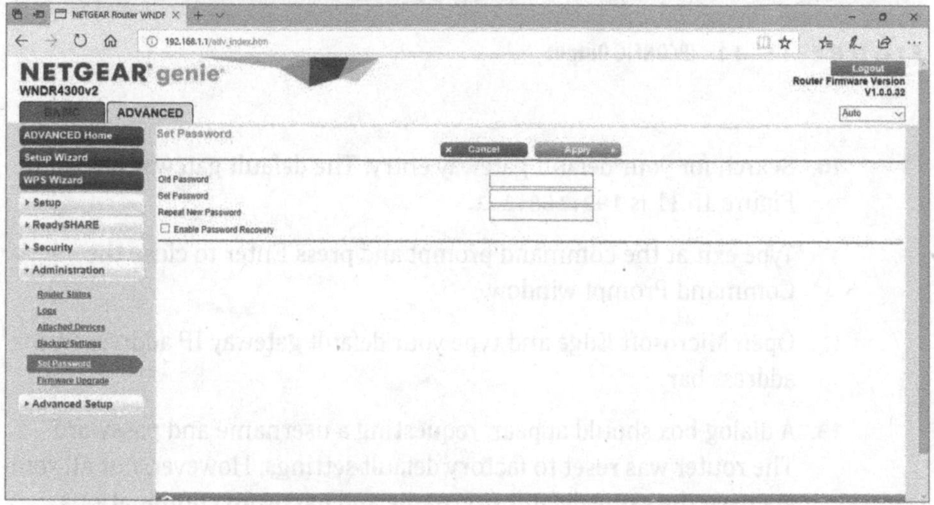

FIGURE 15.12 Setting the Password

18. Change the password. You should choose a password that is reasonably secure and memorable.

19. If possible, click Apply or your equivalent, such as OK.

20. If possible, change the default username. This is a best practice, but the option is not available on all routers.
21. A useful feature to disable is Remote Management.

NOTE **Remote Management is very useful for authorized remote access. However, allowing remote access also allows malicious agents to gain access.**

22. Search for a menu, such as Advanced Setup, Advanced Settings, or More Preferences.
23. Ensure Remote Management is off (see Figure 15.13). This router has Remote Management off by default, but yours may not.

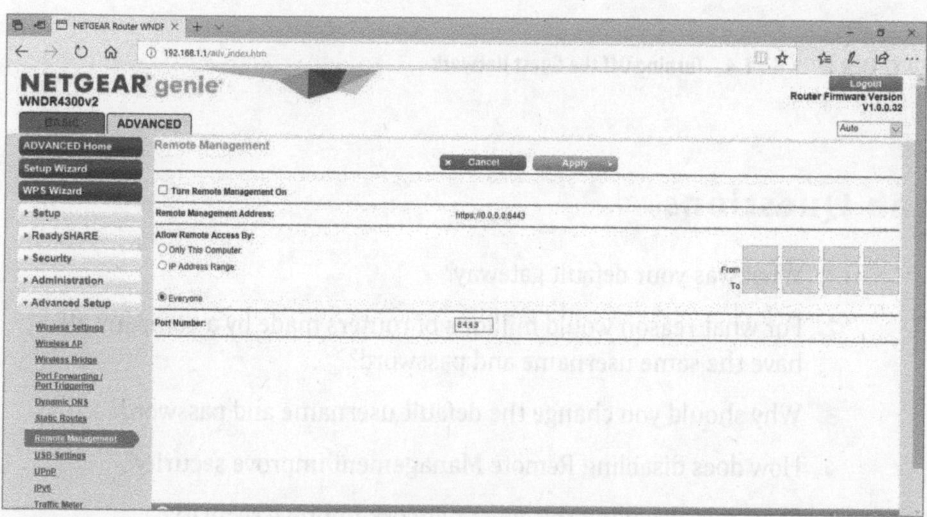

FIGURE 15.13 **Turning Off Remote Management**

24. Many routers have guest networks already enabled. Much like guest accounts on an OS, guest networks hamper Wi-Fi security by allowing anyone access.
25. This router had the Guest Network setting under Advanced ➢ Setup ➢ Guest Network. See Figure 15.14.

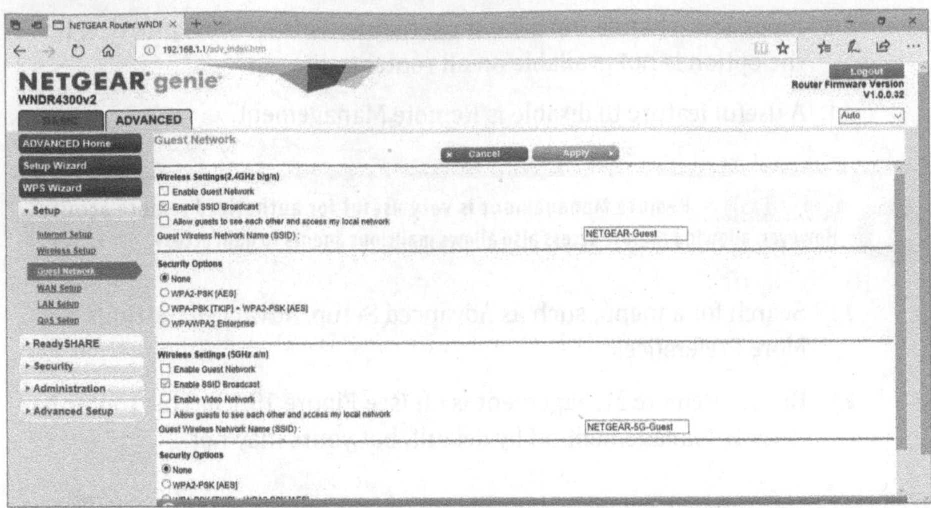

FIGURE 15.14 Turning Off the Guest Network

Lab Questions

1. What was your default gateway?
2. For what reason would millions of routers made by a company all have the same username and password?
3. Why should you change the default username and password?
4. How does disabling Remote Management improve security?
5. How does disabling the guest network improve security?

Lab Answers

1. What was your default gateway?

   The industry standard is `192.168.1.1` by default. If your default gateway is different, insert it here: ____________________.

2. For what reason would millions of routers made by a company all have the same username and password?

   This makes troubleshooting much easier.

3. Why should you change the default username and password?

   Changing the username and password is part of a router initial setup.

4. How does disabling Remote Management improve security?

   It helps prevent malicious agents from gaining access.

5. How does disabling the guest network improve security?

   Guest networks allow anyone access to your network.

CHAPTER 16

Understanding Network Transmission Media Security

Digital data travels from one network device to another across the network communication media. Three general types of transmission media are used to transmit data between networked devices: copper wire, light waves, and wireless radio frequency (RF) signals. In this chapter, you'll learn to:

- **Understand twisted-pair cabling and coaxial cabling**
- **Understand fiber-optic cabling**
- **Understand Bluetooth and WiMAX**
- **Understand transmission media vulnerabilities**
- **Understand wireless network vulnerabilities**

The Basics of Network Transmission Media

Digital data travels using three types of transmission media:

- Copper wire (twisted copper cabling or coaxial cabling)
- Light waves (fiber-optic cabling or infrared light)
- Wireless radio frequency (RF) signals (Wi-Fi, WiMAX, Bluetooth, ZigBee, or Z-Wave)

Each media type offers advantages that make them useful for networking in certain conditions. The main media-related considerations include their cost to implement, maximum data transmission rates, and noise immunity characteristics. Likewise, each media type has some limitations on its ability to transfer information.

This factor is also wrapped up in two considerations: its bandwidth and its attenuation. *Bandwidth* is the media's capacity to carry data. *Attenuation* is a measure of how much signal loss occurs as the information moves across the medium. As you will see in the following sections, some media types can literally carry a signal for miles and still deliver it as recognizable information, while another type loses strength across the house. All individual media types have benefits and disadvantages over others.

The final media-related consideration is its noise immunity capabilities. Stray electrical energy (referred to as *noise*) moves through the atmosphere as a natural course. Electrical machines and devices can also generate electronic noise. These stray signals can interfere with organized data signals and make them unrecognizable. Therefore, cabling used to transmit data is expected to have some resistance to these stray signals.

Copper Wire

Under the heading of copper cabling, there are basically two categories to consider: twisted-pair cabling and coaxial cabling.

Twisted-Pair Cabling

Twisted-pair cabling consists of two or more pairs of wires twisted together to provide noise reduction. The twist in the wires causes induced noise signals to cancel each other out. In this type of cabling, the number of twists in each foot of wire indicates its relative noise immunity level.

When discussing twisted-pair cabling with data networks, there are two basic types to consider: unshielded twisted pair (UTP) and shielded twisted pair (STP). UTP networking cable contains four pairs of individually insulated wires, as illustrated in Figure 16.1.

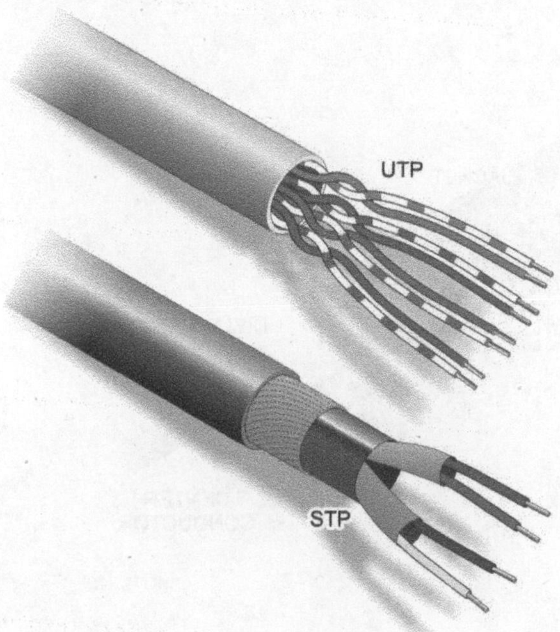

FIGURE 16.1 UTP and STP Cabling

STP cable is similar with the exception that it contains an additional foil shield that surrounds the four-pair wire bundle. The shield provides extended protection from induced electrical noise and cross talk by supplying a grounded path to carry the induced electrical signals away from the conductors in the cable.

Coaxial Cabling

Coaxial cable (often referred to simply as "coax") is familiar to most people as the conductor that carries cable TV into their homes. *Coaxial cable* is constructed with an insulated solid or stranded wire core surrounded by a dielectric insulating layer and a solid or braided metallic shield. Both the wire and shield are wrapped in an outer protective insulating jacket, as illustrated in Figure 16.2.

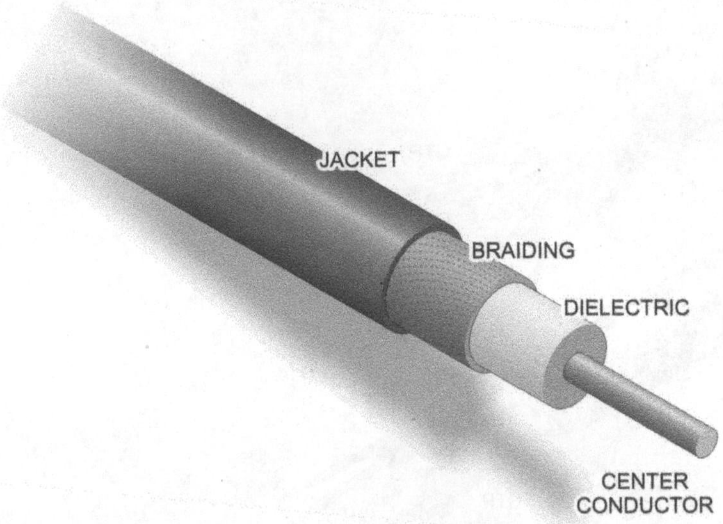

FIGURE 16.2 Coaxial Cable

In the past, coaxial cable was widely used for Ethernet LAN media. However, because the thickness and rigidity of coaxial cable make it difficult and time-consuming to install, the networking industry and network standards development groups have abandoned coaxial cable in favor of unshielded twisted-pair cabling.

Coax cable continues to be used for some applications, such as Internet service delivered to residential settings through the commercial cable television (CATV) system. In addition, several varieties of coaxial cable are available for transporting video and high-data-rate digital information. This comes into play with computers, audio/video equipment, and intelligent home products with residential networks.

Light Waves

Fiber-optic cable is plastic or glass cable designed to carry digital data in the form of light pulses. The signals are introduced into the cable by a laser diode and bounce along its interior until they reach the end of the cable, as illustrated in Figure 16.3. At the end, a light-detecting circuit receives the light signals and converts the information back into an electrical signal. This type of cabling provides tremendous capacity, offering potential signaling rates in excess of 200,000 Mbps. However, current access protocols still limit fiber-optic LAN speeds to 100 Mbps.

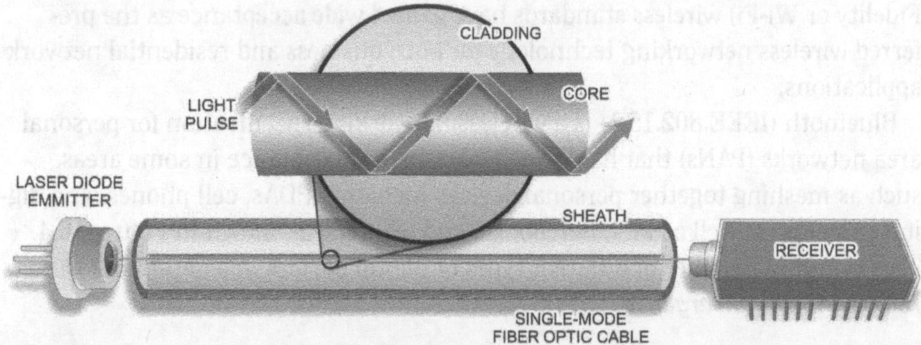

FIGURE 16.3 Transmitting Over Fiber-Optic Cable

Light moving through a fiber-optic cable does not *attenuate* (lose energy) as quickly as electrical signals moving along a copper conductor. Therefore, segment lengths between transmitters and receivers can be much longer when using fiber-optic cabling. In some fiber-optic applications, the maximum cable length can range up to 2 kilometers.

A Fiber-Optic World Speed Record

Researchers from the United States and the Netherlands have broken a world speed record by using a single, multicored piece of glass fiber. They were able to push 255 terabits per second, roughly equivalent to 32 terabytes per second.

Because it cannot be tapped without physically breaking the conductor, fiber-optic cable also provides a much more secure data transmission medium than copper cable. Basically, light introduced into the cable at one end does not leave the cable except through the other end. In addition, fiber-optic cable electrically isolates the transmitter and receiver so that no signal level matching normally needs to be performed between the two ends.

Wireless Signals

Wireless networks connect computer nodes using high-frequency radio waves. The IEEE organization oversees a group of wireless networking specifications under the IEEE-802.xx banner. The IEEE 802.11x (also known as Wireless Fidelity or Wi-Fi) wireless standards have gained wide acceptance as the preferred wireless networking technology for both business and residential network applications.

Bluetooth (IEEE 802.15.1) is a wireless networking specification for personal area networks (PANs) that has gained widespread acceptance in some areas, such as meshing together personal devices including PDAs, cell phones, and digital cameras, as well as PCs, notebooks, and printers, as shown in Figure 16.4. This bringing together of different types of digital devices in a common forum is referred to as *convergence.*

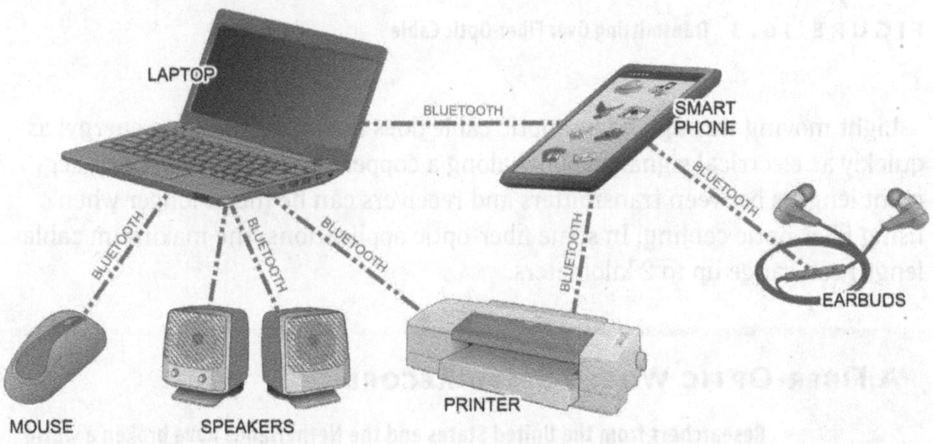

FIGURE 16.4 Bluetooth PAN

Bluetooth devices use low power consumption, short-range radio frequency signals to provide a low cost, secure communication link. The specification provides for three power classes. Thus, Bluetooth devices will be categorized as *Bluetooth class 1, class 2,* or *class 3*. A power class denotes the power level and range of that device. Power classes 1, 2, and 3 can project a power/range of 100 mW/100 meters, 2.5 mW/10 meters, and 1mW/1meter, as shown in Table 16.1.

TABLE 16.1 Bluetooth Parameters

Class	Maximum Power	Operating Range
Class 1	100 mW (20 dBm)	100 meters
Class 2	2.5 mW (4 dBm)	10 meters
Class 3	1 mW (0 dBm)	1 meter

The Bluetooth specification implements Adaptive Frequency Hopping Spread Spectrum (AFHSS) in the license-free 2.4GHz range to provide security and avoid crowded frequency ranges. The Bluetooth protocol divides the 2.4 GHz frequency range into 79 different 1 MHz communication channels. The frequency-hopping mechanism changes channels up to 1,600 times per second. Lastly, the frequency hops channels in one of six predefined patterns. All this frequency hopping is done to lower the effects of other electronic interference.

The data transfer rate for Bluetooth version 1.1 and 1.2 devices is 723.1 Kbps and a big boost of 2.1 Mbps for Bluetooth 2.0 devices.

Bluetooth devices can be connected to only one device at a time; connecting to them will prevent them from connecting to other devices and showing up in inquiries until they disconnect from the other device. However, the standard also provides for constructing multipoint wireless networks using Bluetooth technologies.

Under the Bluetooth specification, up to eight devices can be grouped together to form a piconet. Any device can become the master device and assume control of the network by issuing a request broadcast. The other seven devices become slave devices until the master device releases its position.

The master device uses time division multiplexing to rapidly switch from one slave device to another around the network. In this manner, the Bluetooth network operates like a wireless USB network. Any device in the network can assume the master device role when it is available.

In the computer networking environment, the Bluetooth specification enables several Bluetooth peripheral devices to simultaneously communicate with a host device. In particular, Bluetooth is used with local host computers communicating with wireless input and output devices such as mice, keyboards, and printers.

Like Bluetooth, the ZigBee (IEEE 802.15.4) standard is a wireless, mesh-networked PAN protocol that provides for a 10-meter communication range with data transfer rates at 250 Kbps, as shown in Figure 16.5. The ZigBee standard has been embraced by the smart home automation and industrial controls communities, as well as several areas of the smart grid consortium. It is also being considered for use with personal biomedical sensors to provide secure, remote medical-data acquisition.

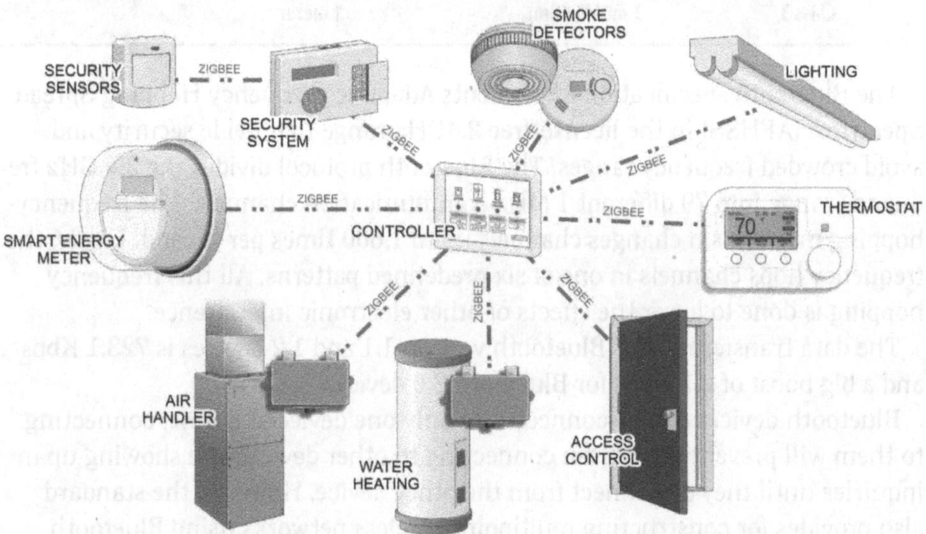

FIGURE 16.5 ZigBee PAN

The IEEE 802.16 – WiMAX specification was established to provide guidelines for wider area wireless networking capabilities. WiMAX is a broadband wireless access standard designed to provide Internet access across large geographic areas such as cities, counties, and in some cases countries, as shown in Figure 16.6. It is also designed to provide interoperability with the 802.11 Wi-Fi standard.

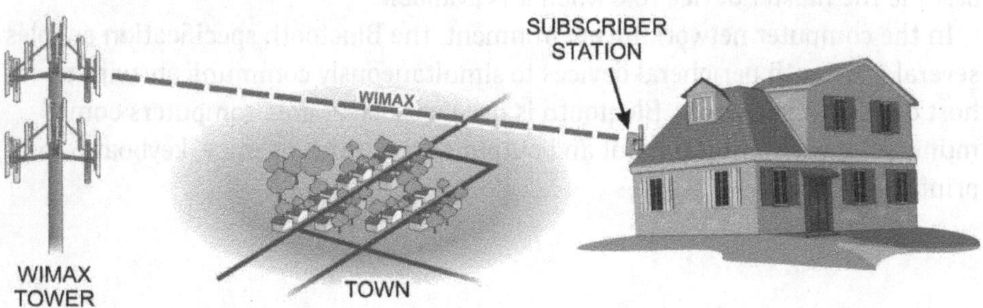

FIGURE 16.6 WiMAX

Transmission Media Vulnerabilities

As with other components of the network, transmission media security must be considered at two levels: physical security and logical security. *Physical security* involves securing the physical medium, along with the communication equipment and physical ports that interconnect the networked equipment. If attackers can gain uninterrupted access to the transmission media, they can find a way to exploit it.

Securing physical media becomes challenging when it leaves the controllable area of a private facility. Within the facility, optical and metal communication media are relatively safe as a physical tapping of the media is required to extract information from it. The same cannot be said for wireless communications because they can be extracted from the air through a simple antenna.

However, when physical media leaves the confines of the private facility, the information they carry becomes vulnerable to interception and capture along their route or at the receiving port of the message.

Securing Wireless Networks

While wireless networks are very popular due to their ease of installation, there are a number of security issues concerning using them to communicate personal or otherwise sensitive information. Transmissions from wireless network devices cannot simply be confined to the local environment of a residence or business.

Although the range of most wireless network devices is typically limited to a few hundred feet, RF signals can easily be intercepted even outside the vicinity of the stated security perimeter. Any unauthorized mobile terminal can accomplish this using an 802.11 receiver. Any intercepted transmissions, being unencrypted, are then easily read.

In order to minimize the risk of security compromise on a wireless LAN, the IEEE-802.11 wireless standard provides for several encryption options. An early security feature called Wired Equivalent Privacy (WEP) provides a 128-bit mathematical key encryption scheme for encrypting data transmissions and authenticating each computer on the network. Enabling the WEP function adds some security for data being transmitted. However, at this time, WEP no longer provides the assurance it had years ago.

You will also need to enter the WEP key value (password), either in the form of hexadecimal number string or as an ASCII character string. Working with the ASCII option is easier for most people. Record this string for use with the network's client computers. Each client computer will need to have the key installed the next time they attempt to connect to the network. When requested by the system, enter and confirm the WEP key.

While WEP was secure enough years ago, a patient or determined attacker today can easily crack it. This vulnerability led the wireless industry to create a stronger WiFi Protected Access (WPA) standard and then create an improved WPA2.

The weakness with WEP is how it encrypts every packet using the same static key. Therefore, a patient hacker only needs to collect enough packets and use brute force to discover the static key. With a reasonable amount of computing power, this is done in minutes or at most a few days. To counter this vulnerability, WPA uses the Temporary Key Integrity Protocol (TKIP) and IEEE 802.1X Extensible Authentication Protocol (EAP) user authentication protocol to provide increased security. This combination requires users to employ usernames and passwords to access the network. After the user logs in, the access point generates a temporary key that is used to encrypt data transfers between the AP and the client computer. WEP, WPA, and WPA2 are included on most APs and are relatively simple to configure.

All of the computers in a network must be configured to use the same key to communicate. Therefore, if you enable encryption on the AP, you will need to input the same key on each computer in the network. For home setups, encryption is enabled and configured by a browser-based configuration wizard. For corporate setups, encryption might be configured by browser or command line. In any case, if the configuration wizard provides for multiple encryption levels, you should select the highest (strongest) level of encryption that doesn't result in a significant drop in throughput.

If possible, you should set up the router to use WPA-PSK along with a strong password. The PSK option enables WPA to use pre-shared keys instead of a separate Certificate Authority (CA) computer to provide user authentication. The PSK permits a password to be set on the router and shared with the rest of the users.

If WPA is simply not an option, you should enable WEP with 128-bit encryption. In addition, after you've installed and authenticated all the wireless clients, you should set the SSID Broadcast option to Disable, so that outsiders do not use SSID to acquire your address and data. Also, change the SSID name from the default value if you have not already done so.

If wireless networking technology is being used within a secure server room, additional physical hardening steps should be taken in securing the room. This may include physically hardening the room's architecture, such as electrically isolating the server room's ceiling and floor, as well as its walls to prevent the wireless signals from escaping.

Hands-On Exercises

Objectives

The purpose of this lab is to examine some of the more advanced security configuration settings of your router. Logs will be examined and turned on. SSID broadcasting will be disabled. Next, antennas will have their power lowered and turned off entirely. Finally, Universal Plug and Play will be disabled.

Resources

- PC with Windows 10 physically connected to your SOHO router
- SOHO router

Procedure

1. Open the Microsoft Edge browser.
2. Type in the IP address of your gateway in the address bar of your browser. Remember, you can find this by going to the command line and issuing IPCONFIG. (See Steps 7 through 12 in Chapter 15's hands-on exercise for additional assistance.)
3. At the login screen (see Figure 16.7), provide your administrator credentials.

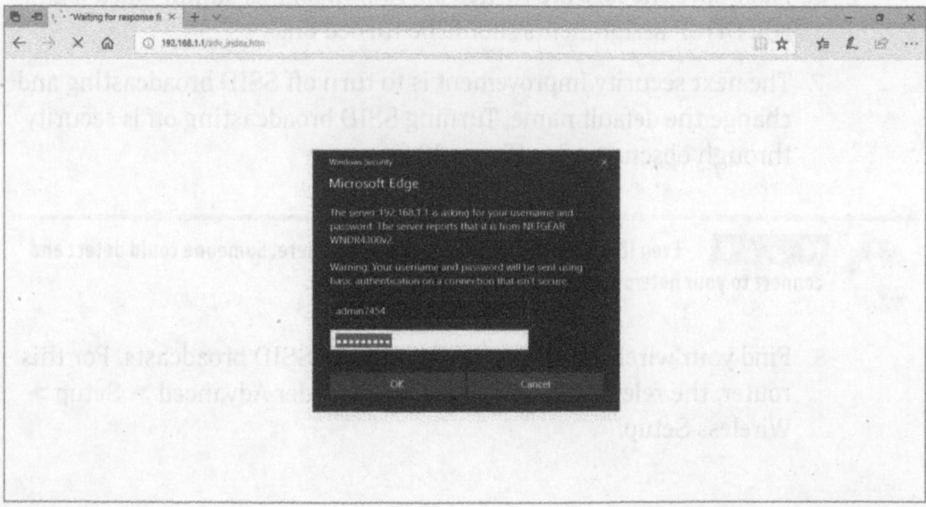

FIGURE 16.7 Enter your credentials.

4. The first advanced setting of interest is to enable logging. Recall that logging is the act of recording events, such as users logging in or recording when software was updated. For a router, who and when someone has connected to the network is of interest.

5. Find the location of the log settings. They may be under some advanced settings. For this example, these logs were found under Advanced ➢ Administration ➢ Logs. See Figure 16.8.

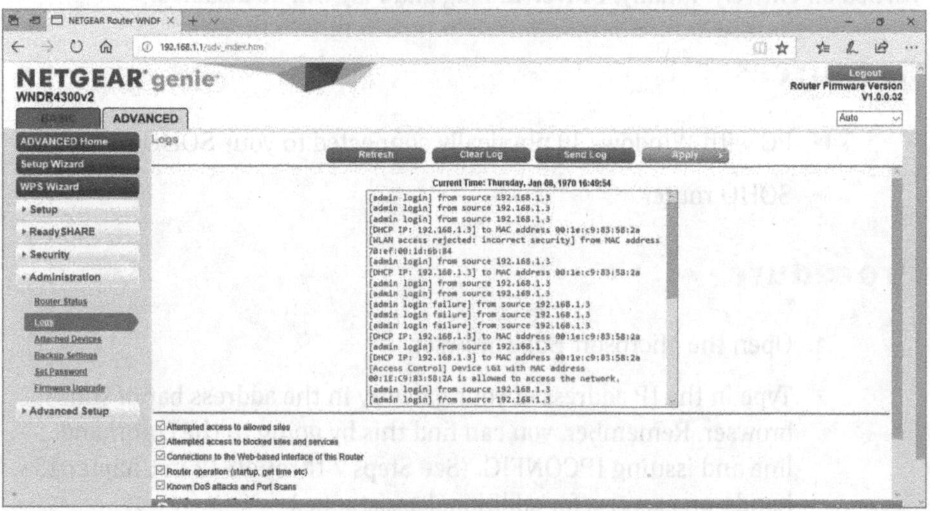

FIGURE 16.8 The Logs

6. Make sure the logs are turned on. Admin logins, admin failed logins, and DHCP assignments should be turned on.

7. The next security improvement is to turn off SSID broadcasting and change the default name. Turning SSID broadcasting off is security through obscurity. See Figure 16.9.

NOTE Even if the SSID isn't broadcast, it's still there. Someone could detect and connect to your network even though the SSID is disabled.

8. Find your wireless settings and disable all SSID broadcasts. For this router, the relevant options were found under Advanced ➢ Setup ➢ Wireless Setup.

9. Change the name to something memorable. Alternatively, write down the SSID somewhere safe.

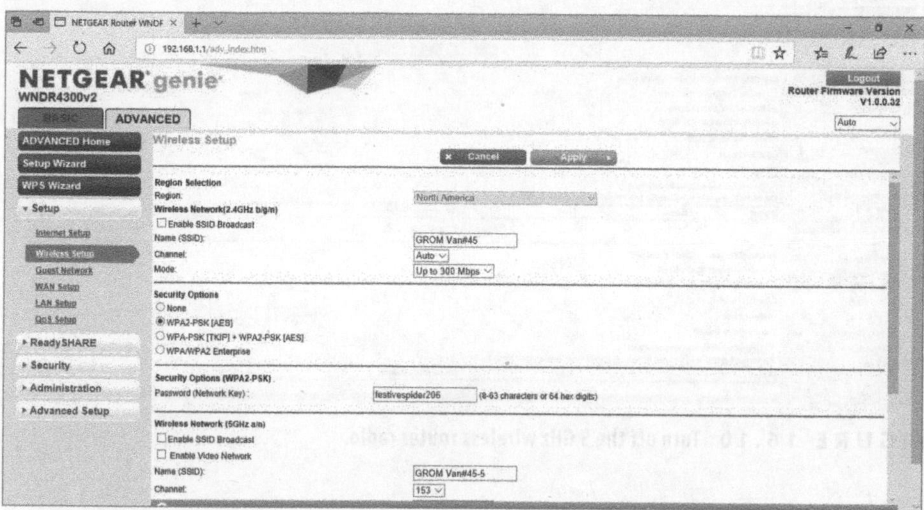

FIGURE 16.9 Turn off all SSID broadcasts and change the default name.

10. Make sure you click Apply or Enable to save your changes.

11. Another, more effective security version of turning off SSID broadcasting is to turn off the antenna entirely. We will turn off only the 5 GHz antenna; the 2.4 GHz antenna will stay on.

NOTE **Some wireless capability is desired; almost all networks these days have at least one wireless device connected to them. Some routers may have only one frequency band antenna; turn it off for demonstration purposes, but remember to turn your antenna back on if you need it.**

12. Find a setting that disables the wireless antenna. It may be called *Disable Wireless Router Radio* or *Disable Wireless Antenna*. For this example, the setting was found under Advanced ➢ Advanced Setup ➢ Wireless Settings. See Figure 16.10.

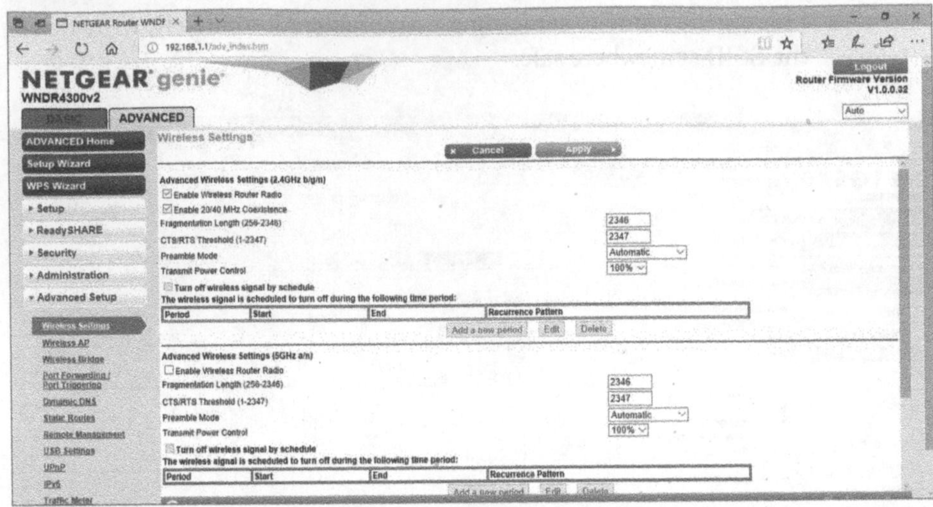

FIGURE 16.10 Turn off the 5 GHz wireless router radio.

13. Yet another antenna-based feature is to lower the transmission power. This improves security by forcing attackers into closer proximity to the router to wirelessly connect. This also retains your ability to connect to your router wirelessly.

14. Find this setting. The name may be different. For this example, the setting is named Transmit Power Control and can be found under Advanced ➢ Advanced Setup ➢ Wireless Settings. In fact, the transmission power setting is in the same area as the settings to turn off the antenna. You can refer to Figure 16.10.

15. The last setting worth turning off is Universal Plug and Play, or UPnP. UPnP is a set of network protocols that allow networked devices to easily discover each other's presence and communicate over a network.

NOTE Because UPnP facilitates communication between devices, it also makes your network easier for the bad guys to move around in.

16. Find and disable the UPnP setting. For this example, the UPnP setting was found under Advanced ➢ Advanced Setup ➢ UPnP. UPnP is standardized; the location of the setting may change, but the name will not. See Figure 16.11.

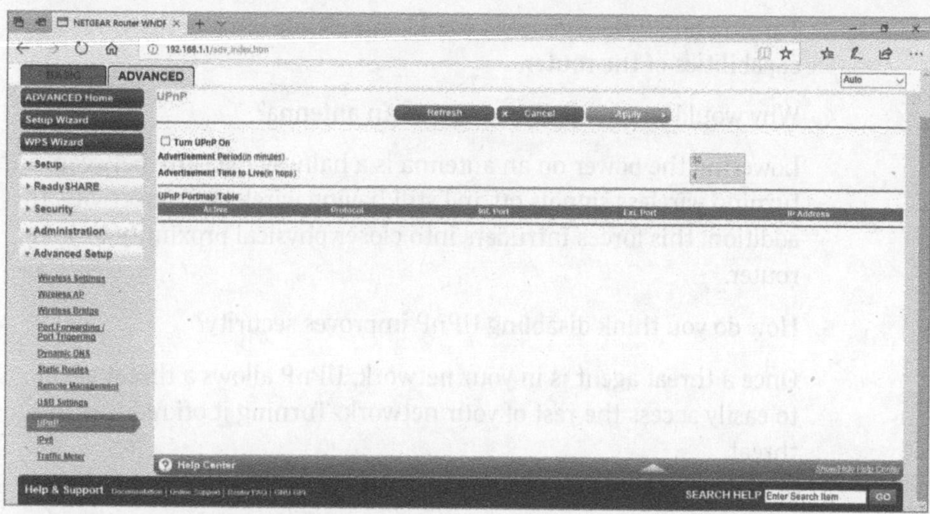

FIGURE 16.11 Disabling UPnP

Lab Questions

1. What are the default log settings for your router?
2. How does turning off SSID broadcasts improve security?
3. Why was only one antenna turned off?
4. Why would you lower the power on an antenna?
5. How do you think disabling UPnP improves security?

Lab Answers

1. What are the default log settings for your router?

   Some of the default settings for the example router are to log router operation and attempted access to blocked sites and services.

2. How does turning off SSID broadcasts improve security?

   It provides security through obscurity.

3. Why was only one antenna turned off?

Turning off all the antennas would completely remove the wireless capabilities of the router.

4. Why would you lower the power on an antenna?

   Lowering the power on an antenna is a halfway measure between turning wireless signals off and still having wireless connectivity. In addition, this forces intruders into closer physical proximity to your router.

5. How do you think disabling UPnP improves security?

   Once a threat agent is in your network, UPnP allows a threat agent to easily access the rest of your network. Turning it off reduces this threat.

CHAPTER 17

Local Network Security: Review Questions

Review the following summary points before proceeding to the "Review Questions" and "Exam Questions" sections at the end of this chapter to make sure you are comfortable with every concept. After completing the review, answer the review questions to verify your knowledge of the material covered in Part III.

Summary Points

- The most widely discussed hierarchical networking initiative is the *open systems interconnection (OSI) model* put forward by the International Standards Organization.
- Every networking course examines the OSI model in terms of what types of devices, protocols, and functions exist at each level. However, different cybersecurity challenges may be present at each level.
- Network topologies are Layer 1—physical or logical—connection strategies that fall into four basic types of configurations: star, bus, ring, and mesh.
- Most networks employ connectivity devices, such as hubs, switches, and routers, which alter the appearance of the actual connection scheme. Therefore, the logical topology will not match the appearance of the physical topology. The particulars of the connection scheme are hidden inside the connecting device.
- A *network protocol* is a set of rules that governs how communications are conducted across a network. In order for devices to

communicate with each other on the network, they must all use the same network protocol.

- The most basic address in networking operations is the Media Access Control address (*MAC address*) that serves as a unique identifier for every device attached to a network. These addresses are typically assigned to the devices by their manufacturers and stored in their firmware.
- Two common types of attacks typically are aimed at the MAC layer of a network: MAC spoofing and MAC broadcast flooding.
- *MAC spoofing* involves changing the device's MAC address to change its identity.
- A *MAC broadcast flood attack* can be launched against a Layer 2 device, such as a network switch, from a device connected to one of its ports. The attack software on the controlled device is designed to flood a high volume of different MAC addresses into the switch's CAM table, causing it to fill up. When this state is reached, the switch will run out of room to map the new MAC addresses to its ports. Because all of the MAC addresses in the CAM are now new addresses that have not been mapped, the switch will be forced to broadcast all of the frames it receives to all of its ports.
- The TCP/IP (Transmission Control Protocol/Internet Protocol) suite of protocols form the most popular network protocol currently in use.
- With the proper tools, it is fairly easy to manipulate the IP headers of TCP/IP packets to falsify addresses to hide an attacker's identity. This manipulation process is known as *IP spoofing* and is the basis for many types of network and internetwork attacks.
- A *SYN flood* that exploits the three-way handshake that TCP/IP employs to initiate connections between network nodes. In this type of attack, the attacker sends the SYN request to the server, but manipulates the handshake to either spoof a different IP address in the SYN packet or simply withhold the ACK packet from the server.
- An IP address is required to make a device a valid member of the Internet. This is how individual users are identified to receive file

transfers, email, and file requests. Two versions of IP addressing are currently in use: IPv4 and IPv6. IPv4 is the internet protocol version typically referenced because it has been around longer and is simpler to understand.

- Sections of the network can be grouped together into subnets that share a range of IP addresses. A protective *gateway* is employed to act as an entry and exit point for the segmented subnet. These groups are referred to as *intranets*. An intranet requires that each segment have a protective gateway to act as an entry and exit point for the segment. In most cases, the gateway is a device called a *router* or a *switch*.
- Alongside TCP/IP being the dominant data packaging and transfer protocol suite, the Ethernet family of standards has become the dominant force in hardware and electrical signaling interfacing as well as for providing media access control.
- Under the Ethernet standard, information is collected into a package called a frame. An Ethernet *frame* brings together many pieces of information required to navigate a network: the source and destination MAC addresses, as well as the IP packet header and data. In addition, the Ethernet frame adds an error-checking and correcting section, which enables the receiver at the destination to check what it receives for correctness.
- The Ethernet protocol is classified as a bus topology that has been implemented across several different network media, including:
    - Coaxial cable (IEEE 802.3 – 10BASE-2 or -5)
    - Twisted-pair copper cable (IEEE 802.3 – 10/100/1000BASE-T)
    - Fiber-optic cable (IEEE 802.3 – 10/100/1000BASE-Fx, Lx or Sx)
    - Wireless RF (IEEE 802.11a-h)
- *Network servers* are specialized computers designed to operate efficiently in a multiuser, multiprocessor, multitasking environment.
- While all servers perform the basic functions described so far, in practice servers may vary significantly in the primary application they are designed to perform for the network's clients.

- Access to a server's shared resources should be limited to users who have both a need and the proper authorization to gain such access. Care should be taken to make sure that unauthorized employees do not gain access to confidential materials.
- Network access to servers should typically be protected by one or more firewalls.
- Subnets or routers may be used to create a network segment for some network servers.
- Because servers are frequently used for user authentication, the server's password should be hashed as a preventative measure. This is typically done by the operating system.
- In network environments, administrators are responsible for implementing the organization's security policies. These policies should be designed to reflect the three objectives associated with the classical model of information security: confidentiality, integrity, and availability (CIA).
- The server admin is responsible for the design, implementation, and maintenance of the server computers, while the network administrator provides the same functions for the network and its media and connectivity devices.
- Division of administrative duties may also involve a special security administrator who is responsible for performing information security tasks for the servers, hosts, and connectivity devices in the network.
- Network administrators must have control over their physical server environment to provide a comprehensive security setting. This is accomplished by strictly limiting physical access to the servers—most commonly by placing them in protected server rooms that have automatic locks on the door and computer chassis.
- After the operating system and the desired applications have been installed, steps need to be taken to harden the security configuration of the entire server software environment. This involves closing as many known vulnerabilities, while still offering acceptable usability to the network's users/customers.
- The *Mandatory Access Control (MAC) system* establishes which users or groups may access files, folders, and other resources.

- With Discretionary Access Control (DAC) strategies and configurations, the user has the discretion to decide who has access to their objects and to what extent.
- *Nondiscretionary, Role-Based Access Control (RBAC)* is based on job roles each user has within the organization.
- The domain's server is responsible for maintaining an *access control list (ACL)* database that tracks each user account, including which group accounts they may be assigned to, as well as what rights and permission they have to different objects.
- In each strategy type, the *principle of least privilege* should be implemented when providing users with access to objects through rights and permissions assignments. Under this rule, each user is granted only the levels of access required to perform their job roles. This principle limits the damage that can be inflicted by a security breach to the initial task, process, or user.
- There are two classes of users in a network: administrators and users. These classes may also exist at two different levels: in local accounts databases located on the individual client devices and in network accounts databases located on network servers.
- Administrators create user and group accounts for network clients that include specific access rights and permissions to the network's resources. Network users are allowed or denied access to read, modify, and examine files and folders based on the access control policy that has been established for them either as individuals or by their position in different network groups.
- An important part of an administrator's tasks and the overall network security plan is auditing. *Auditing* is a preplanned monitoring method to evaluate or determine if problems exist within the area being evaluated or audited.
- Some firewalls, Intrusion Detection Systems, and auditing software can be configured to provide immediate alerts or notifications to administrators when unusual patterns or events are recognized.
- Auditing user privileges is a useful technique for identifying whether a user's computer has picked up a virus that escalates the user's privileges.

- *Privilege escalation* refers to users who are able to execute a program with embedded code that gives them administrative privileges after logging onto the server.
- Local host Intrusion Detection Systems have been the dominant implementation choice. However, similar systems are available for network-wide implementation. Ultimately, the most effective IDS/IDPS defense is a combination of the two types of systems working together in what are referred to as *distributed IDS systems*.
- Several vulnerability scanners are available to test the system and identify vulnerabilities and misconfigurations of computing devices in a network environment.
- When physical media leaves the confines of the private facility, the information they carry becomes vulnerable to interception and capture along their route or at the receiving port of the message.
- Fiber-optic cable provides a much more secure data-transmission medium than copper cable, because it cannot be tapped without physically breaking the conductor.
- The IEEE 802.11x wireless standards (also known as Wireless Fidelity or Wi-Fi) have gained wide acceptance as the preferred wireless networking technology for both business and residential network applications.
- Wired Equivalent Privacy (WEP) provides a basic encryption scheme for encrypting data transmissions and authenticating each computer on the network using a 128-bit mathematical key.
- The Wi-Fi Protected Access (WPA) standard adds improved data encryption, using Temporary Key Integrity Protocol (TKIP) and IEEE 802.1X Extensible Authentication Protocol (EAP) user authentication protocol to provide increased security. This combination requires users to employ usernames and passwords to access the network.
- All the intelligent devices attached to the network must have a network interface adapter capable of physically connecting the device to the network transmission media.
- Switches collect MAC address information to keep track of the devices attached to them. As they interact with those devices, they record their MAC information in an onboard memory structure called a *MAC address table*.

- Switches can also be used to create logically secured Virtual Local Area Networks (VLANs)—a security topology that restricts visibility of network traffic by limiting the movement of network packets so that they only pass between designated ports.
- *Unmanaged switches* are Plug and Play (PnP) devices that do not include any options for user configuration.
- *Managed switches* are connectivity devices that have programmable management functions built into them that enable administrators to configure them for the specific network environment in which they will be used. As such, they provide some type of management console that the administrator can use to set parameters.
- *Routers* are network connectivity devices that forward network information in a manner similar to switches. However, unlike switches, routers can forward information across different network segments. This gives routers the ability to join different networks together through a process known as *routing*.
- Routers contain different sections of DRAM memory to hold message routing information and to buffer data flow between its ports. The routing information is stored and updated in a logical memory table referred to as *routing table*.
- Routers communicate with other routers using a routing protocol to build and maintain their routing tables. These tables are used to record the best route between different network locations.
- A *gateway* is defined as a device that interfaces a network with another network that employs a different protocol. Recall that a *protocol* is a defined set of rules for carrying out communication between different devices or systems.
- A *network bridge* (or a network switch) bridges network segments together and forwards traffic from one network to another. Like the switch, a bridge uses MAC addresses to guide information to the correct ports.
- Most network connectivity devices possess some level of configuration possibilities. As such, their operation can be manipulated if their configuration parameters can be accessed. As with other types of network and computing devices, passwords should be employed to control access to the connectivity device's configuration data whenever possible.

- *Packet sniffing* is the act of listening to packets as they move through a network. This activity is normally conducted using a network analyzer tool referred to as a *packet sniffer*. Attackers use these tools to listen to network traffic looking for items such as passwords and usernames sent across the network in a plaintext mode; they also listen for sensitive information such as credit card or other financial information they can hijack.
- *Address Resolution Protocol (ARP) spoofing* attacks send fake ARP messages to associate their MAC address with the IP address of another user. Once the association has been established, messages directed to that address will be diverted to the attacker. The attacker can then use information obtained from the intercepted messages to mount other types of attacks, such as DoS or man-in-the-middle attacks.
- A *MAC broadcast flood attack* can be launched against a Layer 2 device, such as a network switch, from a device connected to one of its ports. The attack software on the controlled device is designed to flood a high volume of different MAC addresses into the switch's CAM table causing it to fill up. When this state is reached, the switch will run out of room to map the new MAC addresses to its ports. Because all of the MAC addresses in the CAM are now new addresses that have not been mapped, the switch will be forced to broadcast all of the frames it receives to all of its ports.
- Router *flood attacks* are designed to consume all, or a significant part, of the router's resources, thereby rendering them nonfunctional. Router resources commonly targeted include onboard memory, processor operation, and internal bus bandwidth.
- In *MAC duplicating attacks,* also known as MAC cloning attacks, the attacker updates their own MAC address with the target's MAC address. This will cause the switch to forward traffic to both locations.
- *Switch-port-stealing attacks* are designed to flood the switch with altered response packets. This will cause the switch to forward all traffic through the switch to the attacker's location.

- *Denial of Service (DoS) attacks* are designed to overuse a host, server, or network resource to the point where it functionally ceases to provide services. Depending on the exact nature of the attack, the failure may be temporary or indefinite. *Distributed Denial of Service (DDoS)* attacks involve multiple remote systems being used to simultaneously amass the attack on the targeted resource.
- *Spoofing attacks* are based on changing a device's MAC or IP address to change its apparent identity. Because a TCP/IP packet contains many different headers, attackers can create a TCP/IP packet and send its contents using a false source IP address. When the addressed recipient receives the message, the response generated would be sent to the spoofed address.
- *Man-in-the-middle attacks* involve an attacker creating links to two or more victims so they can intercept messages moving between them and insert new information into them before forwarding them. This is accomplished without either victim realizing the attacker is controlling the communications.
- *Session replay attacks* involve the attacker recording a sequence of IP packets or router commands, manipulating the data in them, and then reintroducing them to the router to gain access or cause undesirable actions to be performed.
- *Rerouting attacks* are enabled by an attacker gaining access to the routing tables in a network router and reconfiguring it to redirect IP packets to alternative locations. These types of attacks are prevented by using transmission protocols that require route authentication. They can also be thwarted by employing static routers.
- *Masquerade attacks* involve an attacker manipulating IP packets to create a false IP address so they can gain access to the network or inject false data into it.
- The main defense against IP spoofing attacks is a packet filtering device. *Packet filtering* is the process of passing or blocking network packets based on their source/destination addresses, logical ports, or protocols. Managed switches typically provide filtering configuration options for all of these elements.

Security Challenge Scenarios

Now that you have read Chapters 11 through 16, it's time to revisit the observations you made in Chapter 11. In the following section, complete the information requested and then compare this information to your original Chapter 11 assessments.

Local Network Security Scenario 1

Identify: ______________________________

Protect: ______________________________

Detect: ______________________________

Respond: ______________________________

Recover: ______________________________

Local Network Security Scenario 2

Identify: ______________________________

Protect: ______________________________

Detect: ______________________________

Respond: ______________________________

Recover: ______________________________

Professional Feedback

In this section, you will compare your observations to those of a working security specialist—in this case, Philip Craig, the founder of BlackByte Cyber Security—to improve your understanding of cybersecurity.

About Philip Craig

Philip Craig is the founder of BlackByte Cyber Security, LLC, a consultancy supporting the Pacific Northwest National Laboratory (PNNL) research and national security agendas, as well as the National Rural Electric Cooperative Association and National Rural Telecommunications Cooperative.

For many years, Phil served as a Sr. Cyber Security Research Scientist at PNNL, where he provided engineering and program management support in the fields of cybersecurity, supervisory control, and data acquisition (SCADA) technologies, computing, and communications infrastructure.

This included development of complex system and policy solutions in a variety of critical infrastructures including the nuclear power, electric power, and water sectors. He developed and deployed both strategic and tactical cybersecurity defensive solutions for the electric power and nuclear sectors.

The Insights of a Practicing Professional

Getting the opportunity to design an overall computing environment may be one of the most challenging, frustrating, and rewarding endeavors in your career. It will challenge both your technical and interpersonal skills, keep you bound up in detail after detail, and most importantly force you to learn an immense amount about the whole process from start to end. Whatever the environment, remember some key points:

- Function not feature
- Security over convenience
- Business before desire

Building the Core System

When designing a new environment, always build the core system by defining function, security, and business processes. Don't fall prey to a long list of desired features, the whining about security slowing down progress, or all of the disparate wishes from organizational desires to do things their way. If you do, you might as well get on your horse, throw down the reins, turn around in your saddle, start whacking its backside, and hold on for your life, because you definitely will not be in control of your destiny.

Local Network Security Scenario 1

You have been tasked with making recommendation for equipping a new data network for a small, educational-content development company (fewer than 20 employees). The new company has outgrown its old network and computing equipment and wants to start out in the new facility with a network that meets their current needs.

Because their business is based on the creation of IP (intellectual property) in a market that is highly competitive, they have asked for equipment and configuration recommendations to establish the most secure physical networking environment they can afford.

In particular, the customer has asked that you provide comprehensive recommendations for implementing their server-related security policies and standards. Figure 17.1 provides an overview of the company's electronic workflow structure.

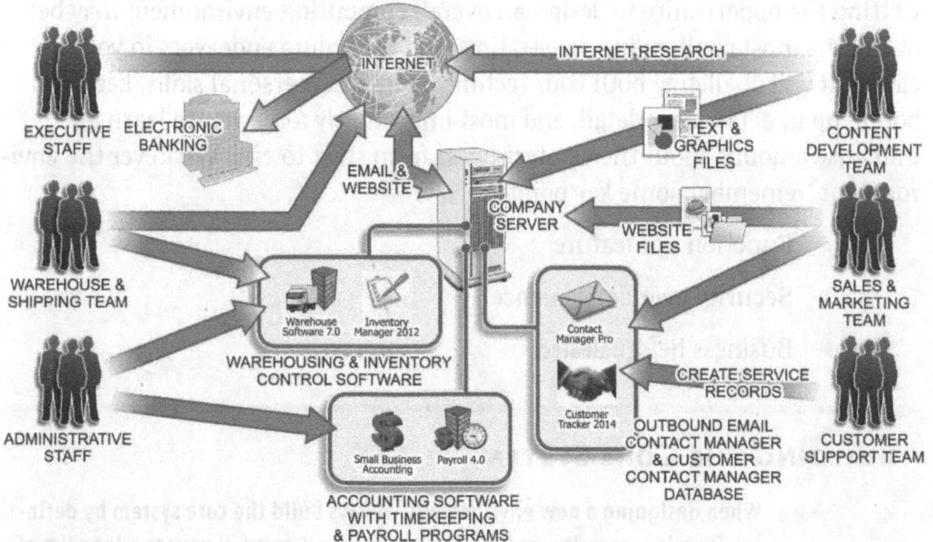

FIGURE 17.1 The Company Layout

The company's major functions can be organized as follows:

- *Executive Staff*: The executive staff conducts the following electronic activities:
  - Conducts electronic banking activities via the Internet
- *Administrative Staff*: The administrative staff is involved in the following electronic functions:
  - Managing a server-based accounting, warehousing, and inventory program
  - Managing electronic employee payroll and timekeeping records

- *Sales and Marketing Team*: The sales and marketing personnel work in house and on the road as required to prospect for customers, interact with outside sales representatives, and make customer visits and presentations. They are involved in the following electronic activities:
    - Handling incoming emails and customer sales calls
    - Operating an outbound email contact manager
    - Tracking customer interactions using a server-based customer management database program
    - Interacting with the home office when traveling to retrieve documents, product updates, emails, and other communications
    - Interacting with their Internet ISP and their internal content-development team to manage and update the company's website.
- *Content Development Team*: This team consists of writers, editors, and artists. Some of these workers are located in the company facility, some live and work remotely and never physically access the facilities, and others combine in-house work with telecommuting so they are in the office one or two days per week. Their electronic activities include the following:
    - Creating text and graphic content on local machines, but they need to share that information among the team members as freely as possible
    - Conducting web-based and hands-on research on technical products within a lab environment
- *Customer Support Team*: These technicians are dedicated to handling customers' technical support calls, testing failure reports, and creating new or updated content for any errors or omissions in the IP. They also arrange and track replacement and update products that must be delivered to the customers. Their electronic activities include the following:
    - Interacting with the customer management program to review past customer interactions and creating service records of problem calls and resolution actions

- Interacting with the content development team to share content problems reported by customers and offering rough revision materials as required

- *Warehouse and Shipping Team*: These workers are involved in the receiving, inventory tracking, storage of, and shipping of products. These employees have the following electronic activities associated with their jobs:
  - Interacting with the warehouse and inventory portion of the company's accounting software to update and track product receiving and shipping, as well as current inventory levels
  - Interacting via Internet with Federal Express, United Parcel Service, and over-the-road trucking companies to schedule and track shipments

With this scenario in mind, provide suggestions as to how you would implement their server functions and what security measures should be set in place to provide security for their corporate resources. Recommendations should include, but are not limited to, physically securing the server and server room, establishing policies to protect the company's intellectual property and personal information, and establishing procedures for maintaining the company's servers.

Functions First

Base your initial network and platform selection on the functionality that everyone may need. Then determine what organizational functionality may be selected by role.

There are six major departments within the organization. Initially mapping them to a basic role profile that can be implemented by a number of domain controllers (Microsoft, Linux, etc.) is important.

- Executive
- Administrative
- Sales/marketing

- Content development
- Customer support
- Warehouse

The existing functions are initially provided by the scenario, so a role-based access program will provide sufficient operational (and security) access controls for them:

- Electronic banking (A)
- Accounting (B)
- Warehouse inventory (C)
- Payroll and timekeeping (D)
- Customer-contact management system (E)
- Company website management (F)
- Content creation/management (G)
- Functional test lab (H)
- Website access (research, email, and so on) (I)

Building role-based access controls is a two-step process. The domain controllers can allow/disallow access to the application, and the application itself can be discriminant of users and privileges. This multi-authentication approach is a good idea. With such a small company, however, there may not be a domain controller, so you'll have to take that into consideration.

With 20 people or so in the company, a central server (and backup preferably off-site) will provide good functionality. Your initial role-based architecture might look like Figure 17.2 (with the capital letters representing the application function).

Usually, almost everyone in the company will need to access the Internet. In reality, giving access to online email, banking, and a few Internet-surfing liberties won't be a burden to your network or your computing platforms. What it can do, however, is challenge productivity! To help prevent employee slacking, disallow excessive content streaming (music services, Amazon Prime video, and so on) that can disrupt your business.

Now that you generally have a role-based, electronically enabled user policy, you can determine how the application itself will provide the separation of roles and duties necessary to maintain the operational integrity of the software systems deployed. As an example, everyone in the timekeeping system would need to input their time but not be able to access or report anyone else's. The "timekeeper," however, would need to have access to those higher-level functions of the payroll software. What you're trying to avoid is the warehouse being able to access the customer contact database.

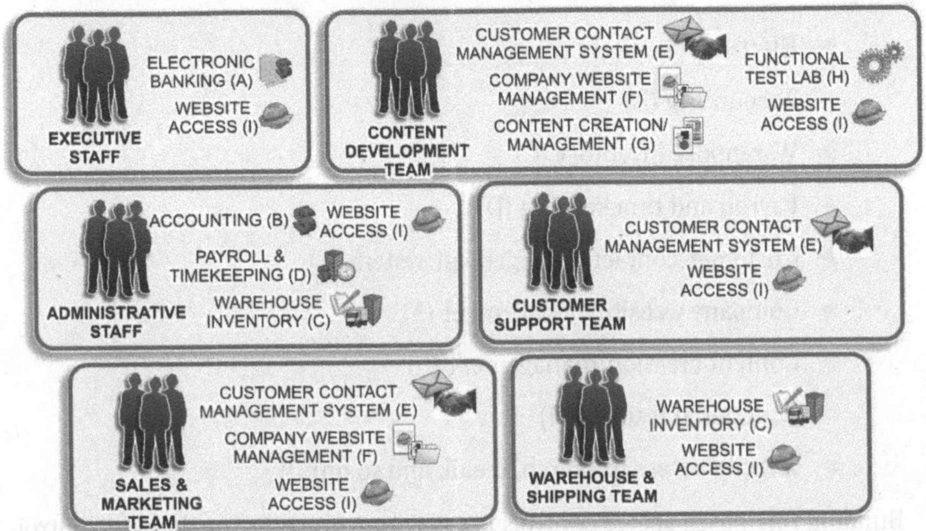

FIGURE 17.2 Role-Based Architecture

Proprietary information and intellectual property are main concerns in this scenario. The role-based access-control methodology will extend into these concerns. The objectives are to limit access to the information, keep it from leaving the company, and ensure that your employees understand that there are serious ramifications if they themselves compromise it. A good document management plan, policy, and procedures will provide a sound basis to protect this information. Some basic principles include keeping the company proprietary and intellectual information inside the system. Don't let employees take it home on a thumb drive, don't email it all over the company, and don't let just anyone access it. Consider the loosely managed environment shown in Figure 17.3.

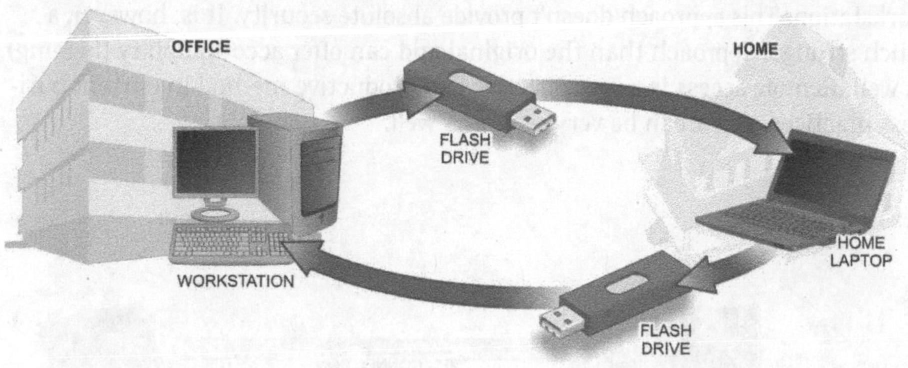

FIGURE 17.3 Loosely Managed Environment

Just a simple "I'll get this done tonight!" scenario will significantly compromise your files or data. In the worst case, data comes off the work computer, onto a removable device, to a laptop, to a home network (or computer if it has the larger screen you want to use), back onto the laptop, and back to the office computer. From a security perspective, this is a nightmare! From a file or data perspective, the sheep have left the pen! Remember, this is a worst case; it can be argued that the employee has malware/antivirus protection, the file is deleted (even wiped) on all devices, and further it is checked before it is put back on the network. Would everyone really take the time to do all of these tasks? Even with these protections, your files have left the premises. This is not what you want to have happen.

The potential solutions are abundantly more secure. As an example, you could implement the simple, cost-effective solution discussed here:

Assume that the employee needs to be off-site for some reason. You want to accomplish the following:

1. Keep the file(s) on the premises.
2. Keep the development/work environment on the premises.
3. Maintain positive control of both while the work is being completed.

This means you need to extend the desktop in a secure fashion. As shown in Figure 17.4, we usually accomplish this with a simple VPN connection back into the office and extend the remote desktop (RDP) session to the employee's workstation. This approach doesn't provide absolute security. It is, however, a much stronger approach than the original and can offer accountability (logging) as well. Remote access is a very effective and productive method in current business practices, and it can be very secure as well.

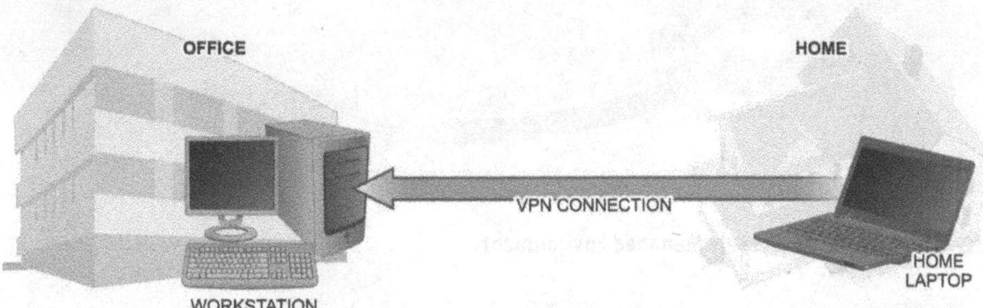

FIGURE 17.4 Maintaining Control

There are other options to remotely operate. From GotoMyPC software to full-blown Citrix desktop virtualization, people are working remotely extensively. For a 20-person company, some simple solutions such as a properly configured VPN and RDP connections can offer ways to be productive remotely.

With the need for remote connectivity—and for that fact, any connectivity—and keeping files and data (especially that which is proprietary) safe comes the need to discuss how to build a safe and secure environment for our electronic files and data. Keeping all of the company business within the physical walls (even virtual walls) of the company goes a long way toward securing that data. To do so, you can implement a simple communications policy that prohibits emailing files and data when unnecessary, especially internally. Email has become the de facto file repository.

Using email as a file cabinet is easy because attachments are surrounded by the context of the message containing the attachment. But now it sits on the email server—forever! Instead of allowing it to sit, you can file share to an individual on the network file server, and then email them the link to the file with instructions to "track changes" or "save a revision with your initials." Now, you have an access record on the file server, and the data will remain on the servers. You can allow a working directory on a locally controlled office computer, but by practice and policy, you should always instruct employees to put the file back on the server and remove any local copies.

Most small networks like the size we're talking about will tolerate simply opening and manipulating the file directly from the file server, so no local copy is necessary. Encryption techniques are extensive! Trying to address them here would consume a lot of space, so we'll keep it simple. Use encryption when it makes sense. If you have highly proprietary documents, then encrypt them and add the public keys only to those documents that absolutely require it. Always use a master public key in addition to individual keys, as shown in Figure 17.5. This will ensure that the company owner always has access to any encrypted information. You can implement simple, electronic-auditing techniques to collect information on what files have whose key associated with them.

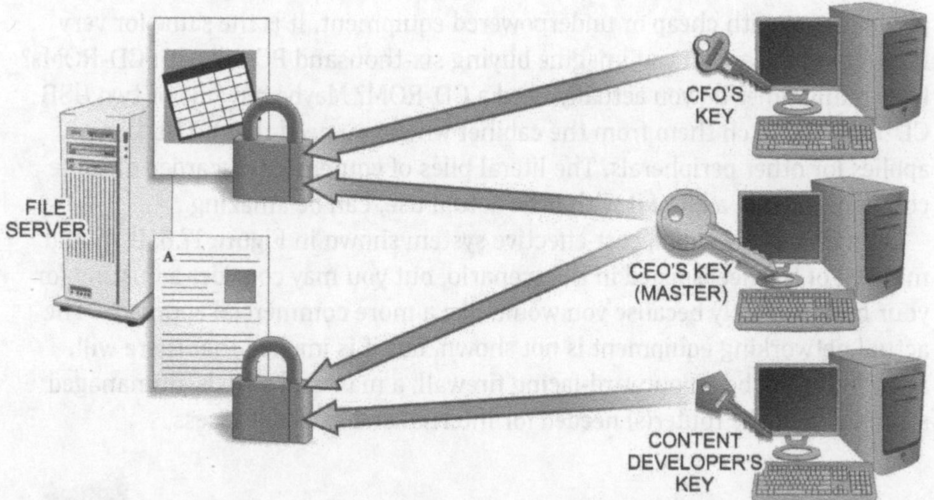

FIGURE 17.5 The Master Key

Now that you understand the basic architecture, you can start to focus on the different requirements for deployment. When you're deploying your resources (that is, hardware, networks, monitors, storage arrays, and so on), there are many novel methods from which to choose nowadays. Let's leverage a scaled approach. This means that the warehouse won't get a 30-inch monitor, and the administrative folks won't get dual screens. As the old saying goes, "the right tool for the right job."

Smaller Hardware Footprints

A system where all of the electronic media is kept within the company means a smaller hardware footprint. That means using file servers to store and distribute everything electronic. No removable drives, thumb drives, CD-ROMs, and so forth. Unless you have the justification for the horsepower, why spend the money on it?

When it comes to personal computers and servers, there are some pretty simple principles to control costs and maintain capability. Only buy what you need for the job. As a small company, you wouldn't want to hinder your employee performance with cheap or underpowered equipment. It is the same for very large companies. Can you imagine buying six-thousand PCs all with CD-ROMs? How many times do you actually need a CD-ROM? Maybe buy one or two USB CD-RWs and fetch them from the cabinet when you need them. The same applies for other peripherals. The literal piles of equipment discarded at some companies, quite a bit of it with little actual use, can be amazing.

Let's look at the small, cost-effective system shown in Figure 17.6. It should meet all of the needs listed in the scenario, but you may consider adjusting for your budget simply because you would like a more commercial approach. The actual networking equipment is not shown, but it is implied that there will, at a minimum, be an outward-facing firewall, a managed switch, unmanaged switches, and the router(s) needed for internal and external access.

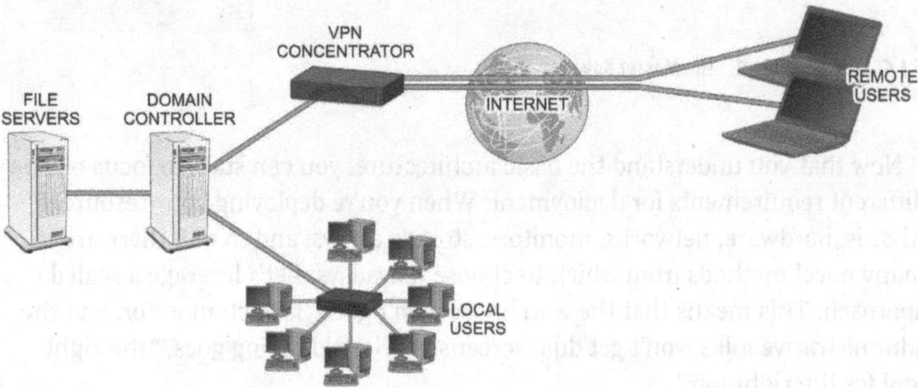

FIGURE 17.6 Suggested Network

It should be no surprise that this looks like almost any other computer network on the planet. After all, there's only so much you can do with what you have. The difference is that you will implement the following:

1. Implement a strict role-based authority and authentication policy and enforcement strategy.
2. Implement a strict keep-it-here policy for company sensitive information. After all, it is the reason you have your job.
3. Design a document management system (including policy) that encourages good utilization of the file server, including file/data access permissions, encryption, auditing, and good work-flow to maintain a tidy source of your company information.
4. Make prudent choices for equipment procurement and use. If you don't need it, don't buy it. If you do need it, can you share a resource?

REMEMBER!

Function not feature. Security over convenience. Business before desire.

Review Questions

The following questions test your knowledge of the material presented in Part III.

1. **_______________ is a set of rules that governs how communications are conducted across a network. In order for devices to communicate with each other on the network, they must all use the same network protocol.**
2. **At what layer of the OSI networking model do MAC addresses work?**
3. **_______________ involves sending so many requests to a server or network connectivity device that its ability to handle these requests is reached, causing it to stop supplying service due to its lack of resources to handle the volume.**
4. **What three steps should be performed after the operating system has been installed, updated, and patched?**

5. **Under what access control strategy does the system establish which users or groups may access files, folders, and other resources?**

6. **Administrators use ______________________ to collectively deal with user accounts that have common needs.**

7. **Describe the two major components of an auditing system.**

8. **______________________ are database-driven tools designed to search computers for known vulnerabilities that have been identified and added to the database.**

9. **What security advantage does fiber-optic cabling have over copper cabling media?**

10. **At what level of the OSI model do network switches primarily operate?**

11. **In what type of attack does the attacker send fake ARP messages to associate their MAC address with the IP address of another user?**

12. **How does a SYN flood attack work?**

13. **Which device typically marks the boundary of an intranet segment?**

14. **______________________ is the process of passing or blocking network packets based on their source/destination addresses, logical ports, or protocols.**

15. **Which type of device is considered the main defense against IP spoofing attacks?**

Exam Questions

1. **Which OSI model layer is responsible for controlling how data is packaged and moved between communication points?**

   A. Data link layer

   B. Network layer

   C. Transport layer

   D. Application layer

   Answer: A

   The data link layer is involved in controlling how the data is packaged and moved between communication points. At this layer, the data is formatted into frames suited for transmission. Components at this level also add error detection and correction functions to the frames, as well as media access protocols and specific information about transmission to specific nodes on the same network segment.

2. **Which of the following is a valid IPv6 address?**

   A. `10000111.10001011.01001001.00110110`

   B. `191.254.0.0`

   C. `2001:0db8:00a7:0051:4dc1:635b:0000.2ffe:`

   D. `13:A2:00:40:6B:8E:66`

   Answer: C

   IPv6 addresses are typically written in the form of hexadecimal digits, separated by colons (`2001: 0db8:00a7:0051:4dc1:635b:0000:2ffe`).

3. **Which type of server acts as an intermediary between network computers and the Internet?**

   A. **Gateway server**

   B. **Router server**

   C. **Web server**

   D. **Proxy server**

   Answer: D

   Proxy servers act as intermediaries between network computers and the Internet.

4. **_______________ servers allow clients to dial in to a computer from a remote site, even if they are not connected to a LAN.**

   A. **SAN**

   B. **NAS**

   C. **RAS**

   D. **FTP**

   Answer: C

   RAS (Remote Access System) *servers* allow clients to dial in to a computer from a remote site, even if they are not connected to a LAN.

5. **In which type of network attack do attackers use network analyzers to listen to network traffic looking for items such as passwords and usernames sent across the**

network in a plaintext mode or seeking sensitive information such as credit card or other financial information they can hijack?

A. Packet sniffing attacks

B. ARP spoofing attacks

C. MAC hijacking attacks

D. DoS attacks

Answer: A

Packet sniffing attacks are normally conducted using a network analyzer tool referred to as a packet sniffer, to listen to network traffic looking for items such as passwords and usernames sent across the network in a plaintext mode, or sensitive information such as credit card or other financial information they can hijack.

6. **In which type of network attack do attackers update their own MAC addresses with the target's MAC address to cause a switch to forward traffic to both locations?**

A. MAC flooding attacks

B. MAC duplicating attacks

C. Rerouting attacks

D. Man-in-the-middle attacks

Answer: B

In a *MAC duplicating* or *MAC cloning* attack, the attacker updates their own MAC address with the target's MAC address. This will cause the switch to forward traffic to both locations.

7. **Which wireless security feature offers the best defense for wireless networking?**

A. Bluetooth

B. WEP

C. WPA

D. WIMax

Answer: C

Although WEP is a strong encryption method, serious attackers can crack it. This has led the wireless industry to create a stronger Wi-Fi Protected Access (WPA) standard. WPA adds improved data encryption, using Temporary Key Integrity Protocol (TKIP) and IEEE 802.1X Extensible Authentication Protocol (EAP) user authentication protocol to provide increased security.

8. **Which Linux group possesses the privilege to execute background processes that run without direction from the user?**

   A. **Users**

   B. **Wheel**

   C. **Root**

   D. **Daemon**

   Answer: D

   Daemon is a standard, default user/group that has privilege to execute daemon programs (background processes) that run without direction from the user.

9. **Which configurable features are offered by managed switches to prevent man-in-the-middle attacks? (Select all that apply.)**

   A. **Packet filtering**

   B. **DHCP snooping**

   C. **Deep packet inspection**

   D. **Dynamic ARP inspection**

   Answer: B, D

   Managed switches typically offer DHCP snooping and Dynamic ARP Inspection (DAI) configuration options that are designed to thwart MITM attacks. DHCP snooping is used to filter and block ingress (incoming) DHCP server messages and builds an IP-to-MAC address database. DAI uses the DHCP snooping database to check and validate ARP requests to prevent ARP spoofing attacks.

10. **Which of the following is the most fundamental step in providing security for network connectivity devices?**

   A. **Placing connectivity devices in secure wall cabinets or locating them within the security of the server room to provide physical protection**

   B. **Configuring device management settings so that required features are as secure as necessary to provide the performance level needed**

   C. **Disabling any management features that are not needed**

   Answer: A

   All security efforts begin at the physical access level. If an unauthorized person can gain physical access to the network servers, media, or connectivity devices, then there is no security.

PART IV

Securing the Perimeter

CHAPTER 18

Perimeter Security in the Real World

The following challenges provide you with contextual reference points for the concepts you will learn in Part IV. Because you have not yet read the chapters in Part IV, the challenges in this chapter are designed to introduce you to the local host scenarios you'll face in the real world. In this chapter, you'll learn to:

- **Understand the relevance of internet perimeter security**
- **Use the NIST Cyber Security Framework to develop specific solutions for the security scenarios presented**

Security Challenges

This chapter will jumpstart your thought processes for what you are about to learn in Part IV. Instead of simply trying to absorb all of the information you're about to learn in these chapters, you'll begin here by gaining a better understanding of the real-world relevance of that information.

In Chapter 25, you will return to these scenarios and apply what you have learned in Chapters 19 through 24. You will also compare your observations to those of the professional security specialists who have provided their observations and solutions for these scenarios.

Internet Security Scenario 1

Because of your company's excellent work in designing the server and local area network systems for the organization in the previous chapter, their contract with the organization has been expanded to also cover their Internet security needs. You have been tasked with the responsibility of researching, designing, and implementing the company's cybersecurity policy.

Figure 18.1 shows the arrangement of the company's current network structure. Use this information to determine how to best protect it from attacks and exploits associated with being connected to the Internet.

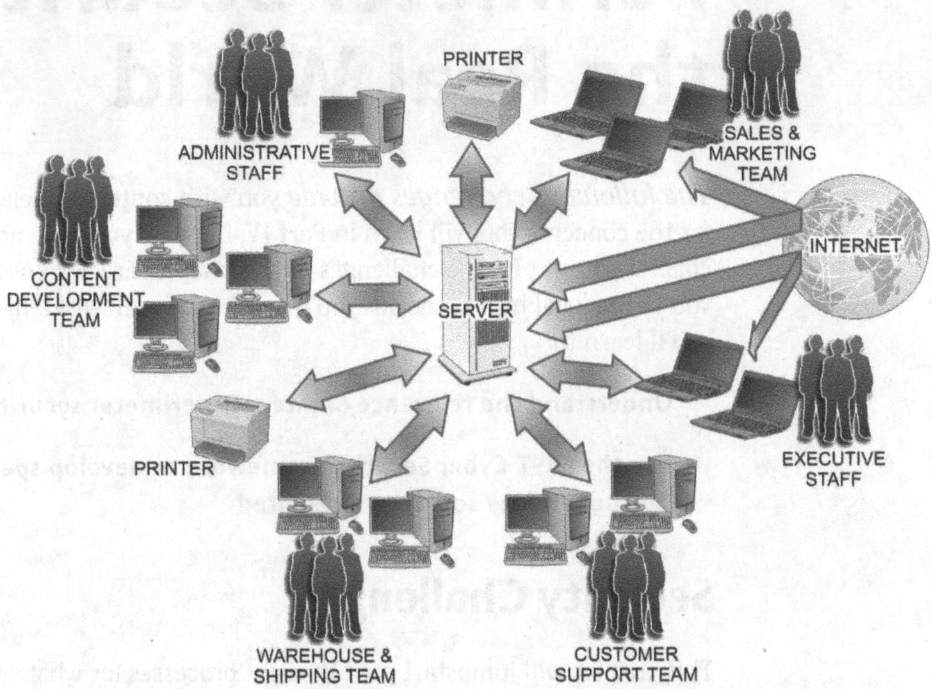

FIGURE 18.1 The Company Network Layout

Risk Assessment 1

From the information provided in this scenario, consider the following National Institute of Standards and Technology (NIST) functions and formulate your thoughts about the selected categories and subcategories listed for each function. You may also want to refer to the copy of the NIST Cyber Security Framework available in Appendix C, as well as the supporting documentation it references for each subcategory, to aid in formulating the responses requested.

With these considerations in place, you will be introduced to specific information about how to implement the functions requested throughout subsequent chapters. Finally, you will also be given a chance to update these original ideas with new options you derive from that material in Chapter 25, as well as compare them to solutions produced by working cybersecurity experts.

Identify

Determine the communications flow between the company's private network and customers who will be accessing the network from the Internet and employees who will be accessing the Internet from the company network. Identify any potential threats and attacks associated with the company network being tied to the Internet along with potential impacts associated with such attacks. (See NIST ID.AM-3, ID.RA-3, 4.)

Protect

Describe potential systems and policies to manage identities and credentials for authorized customers making connections from the Internet as well as employees who need to remotely access the company network. Also suggest ways to protect the network's integrity.

Determine which options are best suited for protecting confidential information as it passes from, to, or through the Internet. Finally, suggest methods, devices, and structures that can be employed to secure the company's network from Internet exploits. (See NIST PR.AC-1, 3, 4, 5, PR.DS -2, PR.PT- 4.)

Detect

Present your suggestions for systems and techniques that can be used to alert network administrators if someone or something attempts to access the network.

How might you detect anomalies and events that might impact the operation of the network without proper authorization? Also, describe what items should be included in the organization's vulnerability assessments related to providing Internet access to customers. (See NIST DE.CM-1, 8.)

Respond

Produce a policy statement suggestion for how detection system notifications should be investigated. Also include suggestions about options for how intrusion incidences can be contained. (See NIST RS.AN-1, RS.MI-1, RS.RP1.)

Recover

Because the company is now handling public information, discuss what actions might be necessary to secure their reputation with the public after a cyber incidence occurs. (See NIST RC.CO-2.)

Use your portfolio to record your observations for this challenge. You will be asked to access this information again at the conclusion of the chapter to assess your original knowledge concerning this scenario and compare it to the information you have acquired through the chapter and its associated lab procedures. You will also be able to compare your observations with those of a working security specialist to improve your understanding of the subject.

Internet Security Scenario 2

From the description of the client organization's operations, it should be apparent that several of their employee groups have legitimate needs to access the company's internal resources from remote locations. As such, you are also expected to generate a policy and architecture for implementing the remote access capabilities they require.

Risk Assessment 2

From the information provided in this challenge, consider the following NIST functions and generate your thoughts about the categories and subcategories listed for each function. With these considerations in place, you will be introduced to specific information about how to implement the functions requested.

Identify

Determine the communications flow between the company's private network and their remote employees. Also, create policy suggestions for employees accessing the company network assets from remote locations. (See NIST ID.AM-3, 4, 6.)

Protect

Describe potential systems and policies to manage identities and credentials for authorized employees who need to remotely access the company network. Also suggest ways to protect the network's integrity after implementing this communications option.

Determine which options are best suited for protecting the company's confidential information as it passes from, to, or through the Internet through these communication channels. Finally, suggest methods, devices and structures that can be employed to secure the company's remote access connections. (See NIST PR.AC-1, 3, 4, PR.DS -2, PR.PT-1, 4, PR.MA-2.)

Detect

Present your suggestions for systems and techniques that can be used to alert network administrators if unauthorized users attempt to access the network through the remote access channels.

How might you detect anomalies and events associated with the remote access system that might impact the operation of the network? Also, describe what items should be included in the organization's vulnerability assessments related to providing remote access capabilities to employees. (See NIST DE.CM-1, 3, 8.)

Respond

Produce a suggested policy statement for how detection system notifications involving remote access incidences should be investigated. Also include suggestions about options for how intrusion incidences can be contained. (See NIST RS.AN-1, RS.AM-MI-2.)

Recover

Because the company is now potentially transmitting proprietary company information outside of its network, create a suggestion for recovering from an exploit related to company data being exploited through the remote access system. (See NIST RC.RP-1.)

Summary

Record your observations for risk assessments presented in this chapter. In Chapter 25, you will compare these original thoughts and observations with those you will generate after reading Chapters 19 through 24. You'll also be able to compare your answers to those of professional security specialists.

## CHAPTER 19

Understanding the Environment

At this point in the book, you have learned about security vulnerabilities and solutions at three general levels: Physical Security, Local Host Security, and Local Network Security. These three levels apply to computing devices, network connectivity devices, network servers, and networking media that is controlled by an owner. This chapter is the last general security chapter in this book, and it deals with Internet security. In this chapter, you'll learn to:

- **Identify the types of players associated with the uncontrolled Internet environment**
- **Identify the components associated with different IP addressing techniques**
- **Relate basic port numbers with regard to network security**
- **Identify key Internet security organizations and standards**

The Basics of Internet Security

In the early days of the Internet, security was mostly about passwords. In many cases, passwords were birthdays or pet names and used a few different technologies. We were impressed with the wonderful interconnected world in which we lived. However, there were those individuals who were intent on causing mischief or hacking networks, but back then this was mostly mischievous rather than malicious.

The Overlap Between Local Network Security and Internet Security

As you move through Part IV, you will notice a great deal of overlap between local network and Internet security because the Internet is merely a collection of interconnected networks. Virtually every security concept appropriate for a network should be applied to these interconnected networks as well. However, we will be less concerned with physical layer or data link layer technologies in this chapter and focus mainly on concepts unique to Internet connectivity.

Hacking was mostly just cracking, which utilized software that looped and guessed at passwords until access was gained. The little real hacking that took place involved direct access or placing malicious code on a floppy disk.

The use of the Internet grew at an amazing rate. In just a few short years, almost every business was using it and even a large percentage of residential users were sending email, shopping, or just probing for knowledge on a daily basis. Access speeds and collaborative software were improving so much that the overall experience became compelling to almost everyone. As networks grew and became the norm, the features used to interact became the norm as well.

Network professionals had to deal with some security issues and some more significant security challenges, giving birth to the cybersecurity industry. Hackers could access lists of email addresses or even guess them and send carefully crafted software that could annoy and inconvenience unsuspecting recipients. We trusted most of our email, blindly clicked on attachments, and essentially were easy prey.

The real shift in security awareness came when the first computer viruses started making the rounds. A single user could run a piece of malicious code and impact an entire company network. A victim could be complicit in furthering that virus's spread by unknowingly sharing that virus with every one of their contacts.

Microsoft wanted to have the most powerful web browser on the market, one that could revolutionize the way we communicated. They built those capabilities into their operating system and amazed us with what we could accomplish using those technologies.

It wasn't long before hackers focused on this new power and created exploit after exploit aimed at those capabilities. Almost immediately, as businesses rushed to adopt newer technology, it was too late to protect against malicious exploits. The world was dependent on interaction and communication. As Microsoft and others rushed to patch new holes that were being discovered almost daily, it became very clear: Internet security is a big deal!

Today, there are so many different software and hardware technologies using the Internet that security needs to be everyone's concern. We can't simply rely on the operating system vendors or the application vendors to keep us safe. We must all be vigilant and make sure security measures are in place. Even the home user who only communicates with their grandchildren via email must have some awareness of security.

After the local hosts and the local area network have been secured, the connection to the Internet must be secured. With this in mind, Internet security involves four primary objectives and three main forms of Internet security to consider:

- Understanding the boundary between the local internal network and the Internet environment. There are many ways to connect to and use the Internet. The goal is to understand how it works so data can be secured against malicious Internet users accessing data on a local computer or accessing it as it moves across the Internet.
- Securing the local hardware. Physical security simply involves securing physical access to the local network hardware.
- Securing the network. Network security includes securing the hardware that controls the transmission of data as well as providing authentication, authorization, and protection.
- Protecting the data. Data security includes protecting the data stored or transmitted over the network.

Cybersecurity is as much a discipline as it is a skill set. A little security paranoia is probably a good thing; but rather than let security concerns influence your health, it is far better to have a strong backup plan so that network resources are preserved and can be redeployed reasonably in even the worst case.

Part IV will cover the basic concepts of Internet security listed here and apply them to several protocols and services to help you understand how to approach Internet security even when relating to a new or tangential technology.

Understanding the Environment

Networks are collections of devices that can exchange information freely, and the Internet is really nothing more than a collection of networks that can exchange information as well. How freely that exchange occurs varies, but the easy exchange of information is what is so compelling about the Internet. It is also what makes the Internet so dangerous.

The Internet has been around in some form for decades, evolving from a government and university concept to the worldwide standard for information exchange as networking has become more mainstream and practical. It wasn't until the creation of the World Wide Web and the web browser that this concept moved into the home and became something both young and old desired and eventually essentially had to have.

To fully understand the Internet environment, you must understand the types of players who reside in the Internet. Individual users typically encounter five types of players involved in Internet activities:

- Service providers
- Businesses that want to advertise and sell
- People and businesses that want to exchange information
- Users who want to access information or use services located on the Internet
- Bad people who want to access computers to steal information, spy on people, or disable their communications

On the other hand, for most businesses, there are typically five types of players on the Internet to consider (as illustrated in Figure 19.1):

- Potential customers who can view their websites and potentially order products over the Internet
- Remote employees who need to access their internal network through the Internet
- Trusted businesses with which they can efficiently exchange information using the Internet
- Internal users who want to access information or use services located in the Internet

- Bad people who want to access their network to steal from them, disrupt their operations, or disable their communications

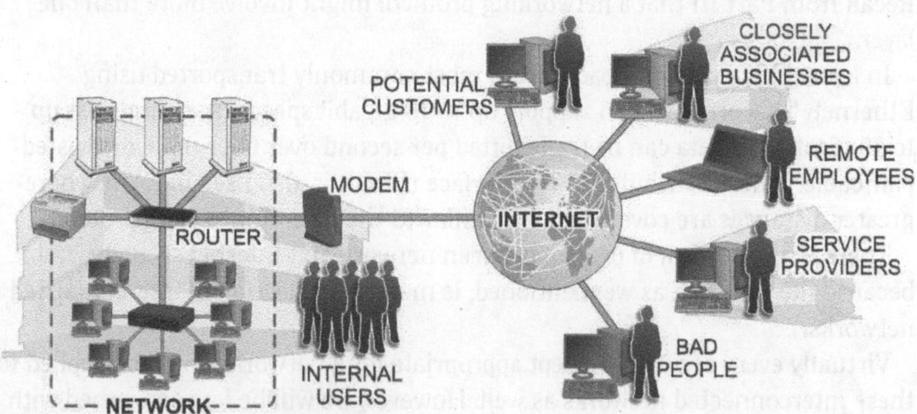

FIGURE 19.1 Internet Players

Basic Internet Concepts

Many people think of the Internet as being nothing more than email and the Web. There have always been many other protocols, and more and more are created every day.

In Part III, you were introduced to the OSI networking model where there are seven *layers* in a system, with each layer interacting only with the layer beneath or above it. We don't really think about these layers that much in network management, but they are the key to understanding that there are different ways to deal with interconnection in a network using different protocols.

Many different protocols are involved in typical Internet activities. But the core protocol suite involved (and the most important one to understand) is the Internet protocol suite commonly referred to as TCP/IP. As the title of the suite indicates, TCP/IP includes the two protocols Transmission Control Protocol (TCP) and the Internet Protocol (IP), which are the most important protocols in the Internet model.

We know that data is transmitted over any network in chunks of data referred to as *datagrams, packets,* or *segments,* depending on what layer the data is moving through. TCP/IP is organized into four layers of its own and specifies how data should be packetized (link layer), addressed (Internet layer), transmitted (transport layer), and received and processed (application layer).

We're not going to spend a lot of time discussing OSI layers in this chapter, but it is common for network technicians to refer to Layer 2 and Layer 3 networking, so we need to make sure you understand what they are referring to. Recall from Part III that a networking protocol might involve more than one layer.

In a local area network, packets are most commonly transported using Ethernet. This protocol can support up to 10 gigabit speeds, meaning that up to 10 gigabits of data can be transmitted per second over fiber-optic or twisted-pair cable. Fiber Distributed Data Interface (FDDI) is also used in LANs where greater distances are covered and is similar to the older Token Ring protocol.

There is a great deal of overlap between network and Internet security because the Internet, as we mentioned, is merely a collection of interconnected networks.

Virtually every security concept appropriate for a network should be applied to these interconnected networks as well. However, we will be less concerned with physical layer or data link layer technologies in this chapter, mainly focusing on concepts unique to Internet connectivity.

IP Traffic

There are two kinds of Internet Protocol traffic: Transmission Control Protocol (TCP) and User Datagram Protocol (UDP). When a TCP connection is established, data can be sent bidirectionally. This connection is highly reliable and features error-checking but adds some bulk to the transmission.

UDP is a much simpler, connectionless protocol where multiple messages are sent as packets in data chunks, without waiting to verify they're received. UDP is great for servers dealing with queries from a large volume of clients or for games where speed is critical. There is no error-checking function with UDP, so there is no real guarantee that transmitted packets will actually arrive at their destinations. Instead, with UDP, data is sent as "best effort."

As we have seen, data can be transmitted in a variety of ways using a variety of technologies. At some level, each technology may include some basic security concepts, but the protocols of the Internet Protocol suite (or TCP/IP) are where most security efforts are focused.

What we are most concerned with is simply host-to-host communication. To facilitate this type of communication, we can use many different protocols depending on what needs to be communicated. For example, which application layer protocol should be used depends on exactly what type of information is being communicated. Email is communicated using the Simple Mail Transfer

Protocol (SMTP), and Hypertext Transfer Protocol (HTTP) is the main web protocol.

As the TCP protocol accepts data, it divides it into chunks and adds a TCP header to each chunk creating a TCP segment, as illustrated in Figure 19.2. That segment is then encapsulated by the Internet Protocol (IP) into a datagram known most commonly as a TCP *packet*. The TCP *header* contains 10 required fields and an optional extension field. Together these fields provide the information needed to ensure proper and reliable delivery of the data that follows the header.

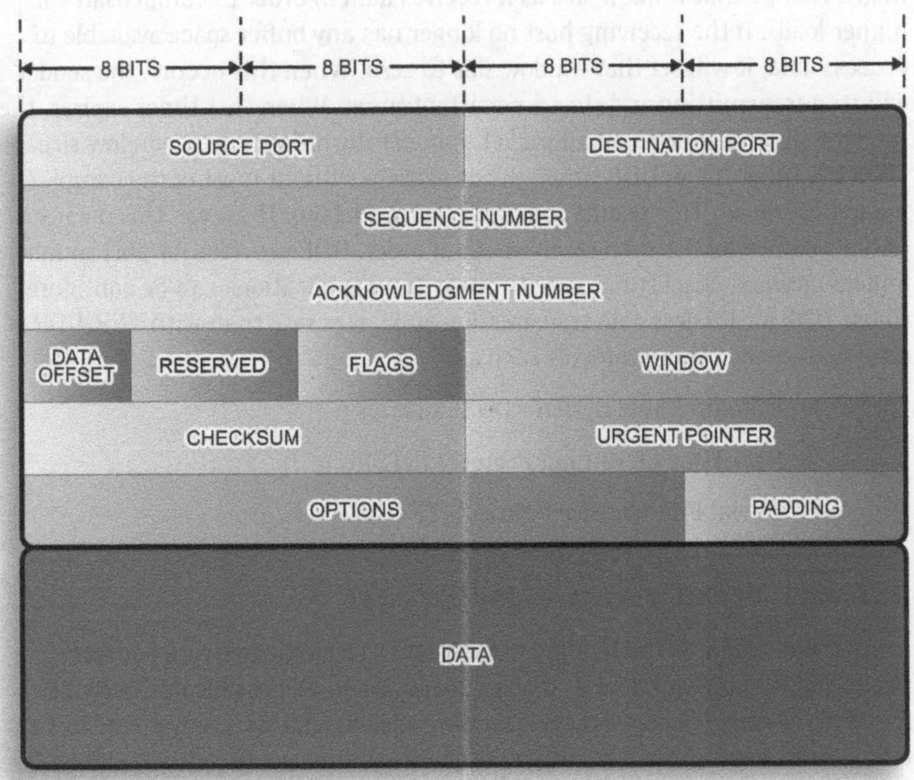

FIGURE 19.2 TCP Segment Structure

The Drawbacks of TCP/IP Packets

The TCP/IP packet provides the backbone of Internet communications (as well as most local area network strategies). Conversely, it also provides the vehicle for most types of cyber attacks. These attacks manipulate the source and destination addresses in different ways to change or hide the origin or destination of messages.

The TCP protocol keeps strict track of all data so that any jumbled or lost packets can be retransmitted or even reordered to maintain reliability. The network device that receives these packets must buffer this data until it can process it. So the protocol must facilitate an agreement between hosts to limit the size of unacknowledged data that can be transmitted at a time. This is known as the TCP *window size* and is found in the TCP header.

To optimize this, TCP uses a flow control protocol where a receiving host might change that window size as it receives data in order to compensate for higher loads. If the receiving host no longer has any buffer space available to process data, it will set that window size to zero. When this occurs, the sender will stop transmitting and start a persistent timer. When that timer expires, the sender will send another small packet to hopefully obtain a new window size.

On the other hand, UDP simply sends packets without most of the complexity and overhead. This results in lower *latency* (delays). However, this means packets can be lost or even received out of order. UDP provides for port numbers and an optional checksum to verify integrity so applications can be configured to use UDP for lossless data transmission at a faster rate than with TCP. UDP is used with many other protocols such as:

- Domain Name System (DNS) lookups
- Real Time Streaming Protocol (RTSP)
- Trivial File Transfer Protocol (TFTP)

Unicasts, Broadcasts, and Multicasts

Unicast messaging is the sending of messages to a single network address. *Broadcast messaging* refers to sending messages to all possible destinations. *Multicast messaging* sends messages using special address assignments to a specific group of addresses. The differences between unicast, broadcast, and multicast are illustrated in Figure 19.3.

FIGURE 19.3 Network Messaging Types

With multicasting, the source only has to send packets once regardless of how many addresses will be receiving it. Network nodes then replicate the packet as needed to reach multiple addresses. Multicast is used for multimedia and content delivery networks. Often UDP is used in multicasts so providers must add error-detection and retransmission schemes to make multicast reliable.

Ports

In addition to the network address, many protocols may also specify a port or a port number. A protocol or application may respond to specific ports in different ways. For example, a web server typically responds to HTTP requests over port 80 but responds to HTTPS requests on port 443.

Ports are seemingly arbitrary conventions, and a large range of port numbers are not generally associated with any particular service so they can be used for a particular application. If a port number is added to a host name or IP address in a web browser, for example, you can create a way to access a particular application or service or even just regular web content.

A port number is a 16-bit number. The first 1,024 port numbers are reserved by convention to identify specific services. Both TCP and UDP protocols use ports. A few common ports and their descriptions are given in Table 19.1.

TABLE 19.1 A Few Common Ports and Their Uses

Port	Protocols	Description
20	TCP/UDP	FTP
22	TCP/UDP	SSH
23	TCP/UDP	Telnet
25	TCP/UDP	SMTP (Simple Mail Transfer Protocol)
80	TCP/UDP	HTTP (Hypertext Transfer Protocol)
88	TCP/UDP	Kerberos authentication system
110	TCP	POP3 (Post Office Protocol v3)
118	TCP/UDP	SQL (Structured Query Language) Services
143	TCP	IMAP (Internet Message Access Protocol)
443	TCP/UDP	HTTPS (Hypertext Transfer Protocol over TLS/SSL)
631	TCP/UDP	Internet Printing Protocol (IPP)

Port numbers from 1024 to 49151 are registered ports assigned by the Internet Assigned Numbers Authority (IANA). For example, Microsoft SQL Server uses ports 1433 and 1434. Microsoft Windows Internet Name Service (WINS) uses port 1512, etc. Private ports are those from 49152 through 65535.

Understanding ports is critical in managing network security. The easiest way to minimize unwanted scans or restrict access is by monitoring specific ports and port blocking. For example, if you are operating a server that is only a web server, you can restrict outside network access so it can only occur through port 80 and maybe port 443. This way, if someone from outside the network tries to access port 22 or 23 attempting to break in, that request will be blocked.

Routing

Routing is simply the process of selecting the best pathway for transmitting data over a network or between networks, as illustrated in Figure 19.4. A router is a complex device that will route data between networks; a router can be hardware, software, or a combination. Routers mostly deal with IP addresses, which can be used as another way of restricting access. Much of the time a human does not know the IP address of the server they want to access, but instead will know the host name and the domain name.

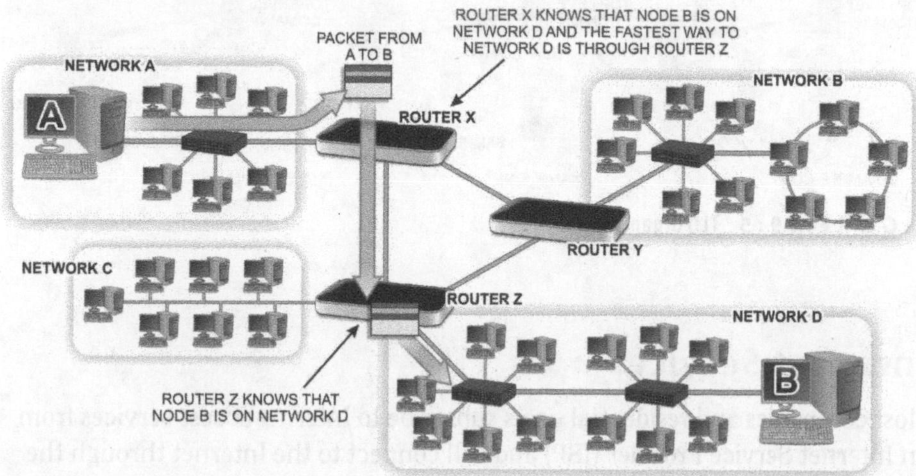

FIGURE 19.4 Routing Operations

Domains

Domains are unique realms assigned by an agent, known as a *registrar*, which has been authorized by the Internet Corporation for Assigned Names and Numbers (ICANN). Some of larger registrars include Network Solutions, GoDaddy, and eNom.

Domains are registered for a renewable period of time, and a root authority can be queried so you can learn the *name servers* in charge of routing that domain. These name servers will respond to queries with the IP associated with various protocols, and you can learn most of the protocols associated with a domain with a specific type of query.

A top-level domain (TLD) is essentially the domain extension, as shown in Figure 19.5. TLDs are established for countries (for example, `US`), descriptive groups (`.people`, `.rocks`, `.attorney`, and so on), and generic TLDs (such as `.com`, `.net`, `.edu`, and `.gov`). Each TLD might have different requirements and could even require that you use a specific registrar to register a domain. The `.edu` domains and some country-code domains often have specific requirements before you can register a domain in that TLD, such as being an actual learning institution or be located in that country. However, most domains are readily available to anyone and can be quickly and inexpensively registered for a period of one or more years through a registrar.

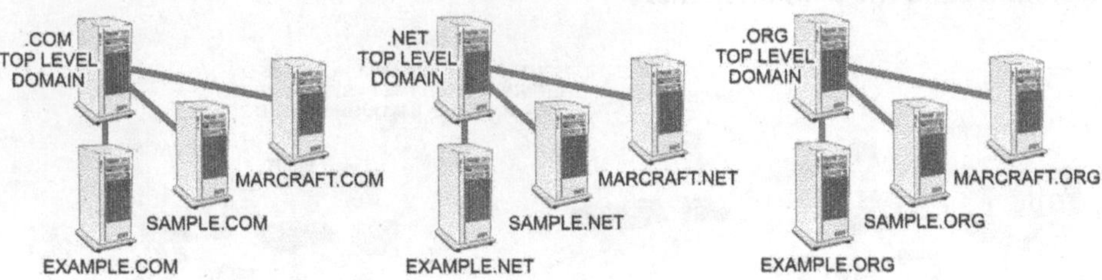

FIGURE 19.5 TLD Organization

Internet Services

Most companies and residential users subscribe to Internet access services from an Internet Service Provider (ISP) and will connect to the Internet through the ISP, as shown in Figure 19.6. This service is typically contracted for a specific service level or potential transfer speed and at least one IP address. However, the service level may also include email, web hosting, some security services, or even a larger block of public IP addresses.

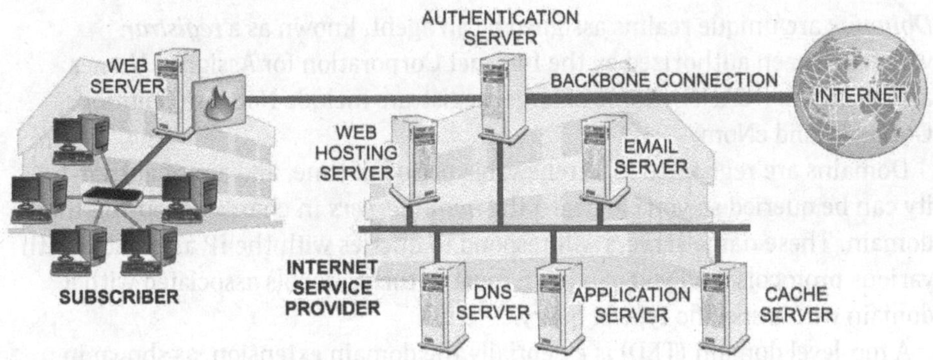

FIGURE 19.6 ISP Position and Services

Many Internet access services are *asymmetrical*, meaning the download potential is different from the upload potential. While most Internet services are *full duplex*, some services may be *half duplex*, meaning that data can only be transmitted in one direction at a time. These service differences are not relevant to security measures, but it is important to be aware of the differences and what type of connection you have when dealing with many security issues.

In addition to controlling the amount of data that may flow through an Internet connection and assigning customers IP addresses, an ISP may provide certain more transparent services about which you should be aware. Many ISPs will proxy your web connections through caching servers or caching devices to minimize bandwidth utilization. Some ISPs will also block certain ports in a misguided attempt to minimize the impact of malware, viruses, and worms.

For example, many cable and DSL providers block port 25 unless the request is directed at their mail servers. If an infected user becomes part of a distributed spam botnet and begins to spew spam, their email will be blocked from using third-party mail servers. This allows the ISP to prevent a major spam outbreak without any sophisticated scanning techniques. It also forces users of that ISP to set their mail software to an alternative port if they want to use a third-party mail provider.

The ISP may also provide customers with certain network hardware. It is important that you understand exactly what this hardware does. Some ISPs provide their customers with a *modem* that also acts as a router, being the border between the Internet and the local network. In some cases, that router may have been preconfigured with certain settings that could conflict with what the local area network administrator is trying to do. This can all be dealt with, but you must understand how your connection is set up so that you can properly configure your network.

The ISP assigns the modem a single public IP address that may be dynamically assigned using Dynamic Host Configuration Protocol (DHCP). Using DHCP does not necessarily mean the network will get a different IP address every time you access the network, or even when the network's gateway device is rebooted. But it also does not guarantee the modem's IP address is fixed, as is the case when assigned a static IP address.

A DHCP server hands out an IP address, one from a pool of available addresses. That IP is associated to a modem's MAC address, for a specified period of time. DHCP can also be used to assign addresses in an internal network as we will discuss later.

Internet services are offered using a variety of technologies, and each technology might impact how you approach security. Dial-up and slower ISDN or cellular connections are not likely ways someone might intrude upon your network simply because of their speeds. The intruder must really want to get into that specific network to have the patience to penetrate it in this way.

Standards and RFCs

The Internet would be like the old Wild West of America if it were not for some rules that dictate how everything should work. As with anything else, there are different standards organizations that oversee some of the protocols. But another, somewhat less formal tool helps guide how these protocols should work.

RFCs, or Request for Comments, are notes submitted to the Internet Engineering Task Force (IETF), the main standards organization for the Internet. An RFC can be submitted by anyone. If the IETF deems the note worthy, the RFC is given a unique number and once published is never revised without a new number given to it. If this RFC attracts enough interest and a consensus emerges, it may evolve into an Internet standard; however, many RFCs are essentially the de facto standards for most Internet protocols. The name might imply that it is a work in progress—and to some extent it is—but these RFCs are often as important as any technical manual when you need to understand a protocol.

Security Organizations and Standards

A number of organizations are involved in maintaining network vulnerability resources not dissimilar from virus and malware resources. A variety of commercial entities have grown to serve this vital need, but there are also many public resources and standards available about which you should be aware:

- Security Content Automation Protocol (SCAP) is a method of using various open standards for evaluating vulnerabilities and measuring the potential impact of these vulnerabilities. You can learn more at `scap.nist.gov`.
- Common Vulnerabilities and Exposures (CVE) is a system for referencing publicly known vulnerabilities. Maintained by MITRE Corporation but backed by the U.S. Department of Homeland Security, CVE is used by SCAP. CVE can be explored in more detail at `cve.mitre.org`.
- Common Vulnerability Scoring System (CVSS) is a system for scoring vulnerabilities from CVE, making it easier to understand your risks. CVSS can be explored in more detail at www.`first.org/cvss`.
- Common Platform Enumeration (CPE) is a standardized method of describing and identifying operating system, hardware devices, and

application classes on the network. CPE can be explored in more detail at `scap.nist.gov/specifications/cpe/`.

- Open Vulnerability and Assessment Language (OVAL) is a security community standard for communicating security information such as configuration, vulnerabilities, patch levels, etc. OVAL is essentially a group of XML schemas that describe a language to provide the details needed to assess a network resource for security vulnerabilities. You can learn more about OVAL at `oval.mitre.org`.

While the Open Checklist Interactive Language (OCIL) has uses beyond security, it provides a conceptual framework for representing nonautomated questions for security checks and is now part of SCAP.

A Word About SCAP

SCAP is overseen by the National Institute of Standards and Technology (NIST)—the organization responsible for the Cyber Security Framework, Medical Device Security and Guide to Industrial Control System (ICS) Security guides on which much of this course is based. NIST offers a SCAP Validation Program for specific versions of vendor products. This is an emerging standard that currently offers validation only for Windows and Red Hat platforms. This type of standardization is designed to help network designers and administrators more clearly understand the vulnerabilities of their networks so they can make them more secure.

Hands-On Exercises

Objectives

- Describe the security options available with Internet Explorer.
- Learn about protecting the system and users from Internet browsing hazards.
- Apply security and privacy options to secure the browser.

Resources

- PC-compatible desktop/tower computer system
- Windows 10 Professional installed
- Internet access through a network connection

Discussion

Because the browser is the portal to the wider outside world, its security settings are a very important part of securing the local host. If the physical device has been secured at the inner and outer perimeters, the browser becomes one of the main points of access for attackers.

In addition, other Internet tools on the machine may rely on browser components to perform their functions. These applications may bring with them enhancements that create additional vulnerabilities. Such features should be evaluated and turned off if they do not contribute to the operation of the system.

Procedures

The Internet Explorer security settings for Windows 10 Pro can be managed in several different ways. In this lab, you will learn where these settings are located and how to adjust them to your specific needs. You will also learn how to control the privacy settings to further control security issues that are often overlooked.

NOTE **In this exercise, you will be working with Internet Explorer (IE). Most browsers have similar security and privacy options or are dependent on the options selected for IE.**

Accessing the Security Settings in Internet Explorer

1. Power on your computer.
2. Log on using your administrative account.
3. In the Search field embedded in your taskbar, type **Internet Explorer**, as shown in Figure 19.7.

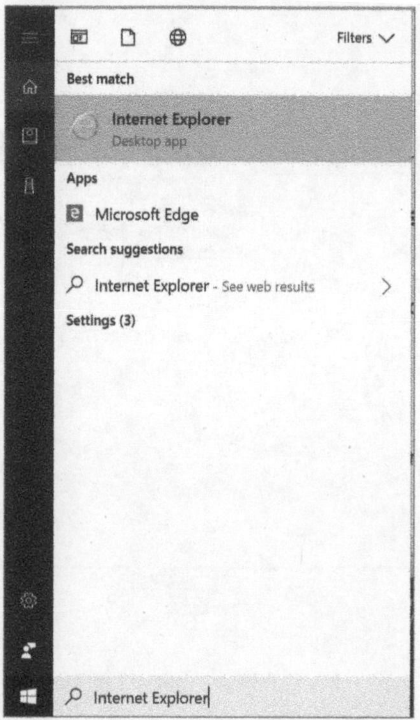

FIGURE 19.7 Locating Internet Explorer

4. Left-click on Internet Explorer to open the browser.
5. In the top-right corner is a small gear icon; click it to open a small options list.
6. Highlight Internet Options, and click to launch the Internet Options window, as shown in Figure 19.8.

The General tab allows you to change the settings affecting items such as the Home page, browsing history, search defaults, tab displays, and the appearance of various displayed web pages. Browsing History includes cookies, cached web pages, and the history of websites you have visited, provided the Delete Browsing History On Exit box is unchecked. Keep in mind that the tabs related to Internet Security options are labeled General, Security, and Privacy.

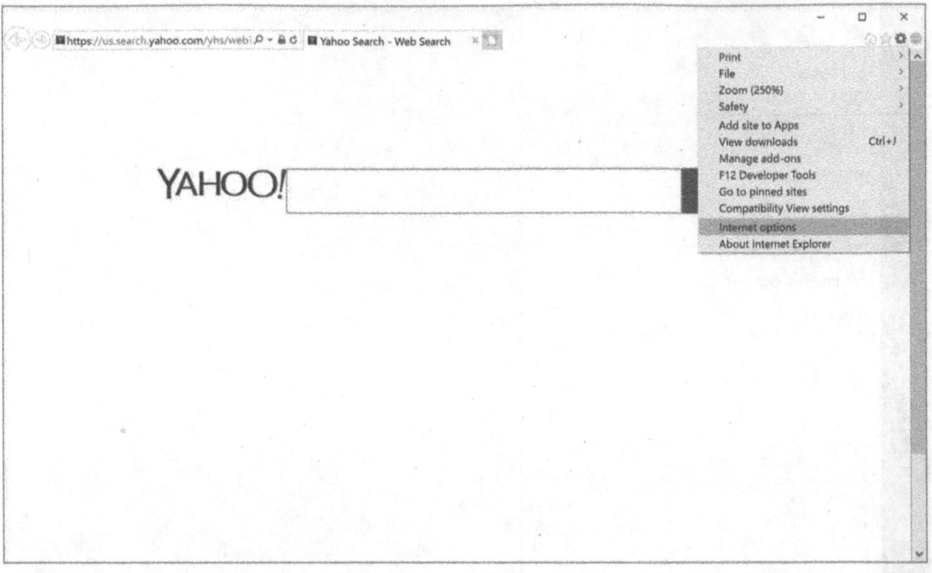

FIGURE 19.8 Accessing Internet Options

Examining Browsing History Options

1. Under the General tab, click on the Settings button located in the Browsing History section to launch the Website Data Settings window.
2. Examine the Temporary Internet Files, History, and Caches And Databases tabs, as shown in Figure 19.9.

This window includes the settings that control how often the system checks for newer versions of visited websites and the location of accumulated web page files. Saving these items helps to load previously visited web pages faster. There is also a setting that controls how much disk space is allocated for saving this information, which can be adjusted for systems where disk space is limited. Notice that you can also change the location of the folder used to store files or to view the files currently contained in it.

3. Click Cancel to close this window. Select Delete, which is also located in the Browsing History section. Figure 19.10 shows the Delete Browsing History window.

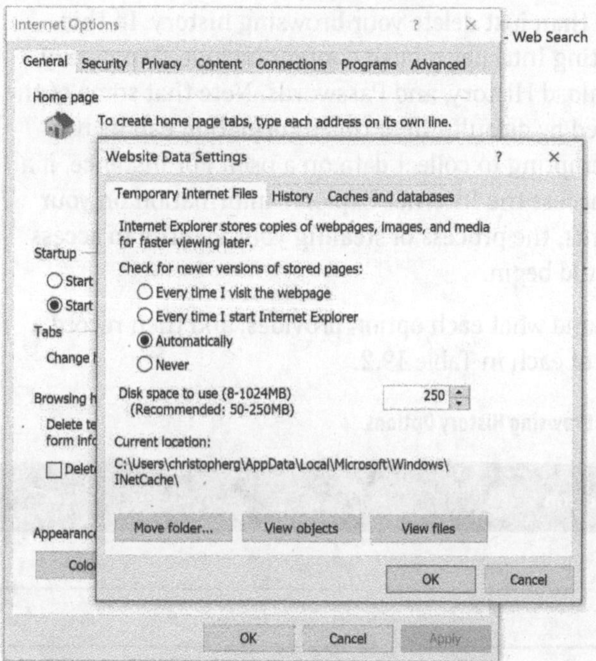

FIGURE 19.9 Website Data Settings

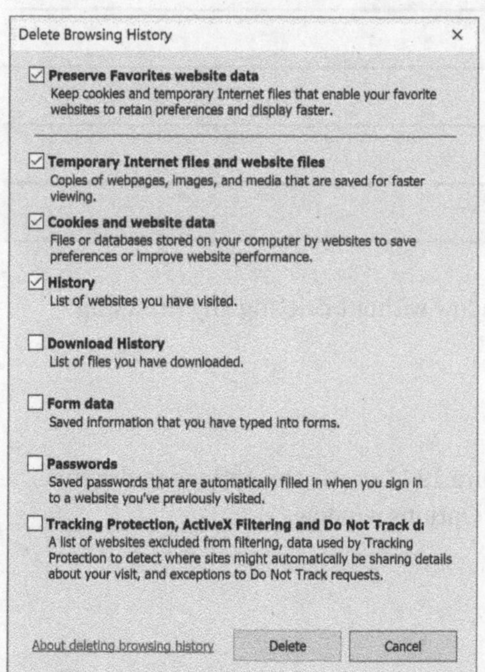

FIGURE 19.10 Delete Browsing History Window

This section does far more than just delete your browsing history. In this window, the options for deleting Internet-related content include: Temporary Internet files, Cookies, Download History, and Passwords. Note that some of the content categories are selected by default. All of this information can be useful to an intruder who is attempting to collect data on a user. For instance, if a malicious user were able to access the Internet Explorer information on your stored Form Data or Passwords, the process of stealing your identity to access resources on the network could begin.

4. Read and understand what each option provides, and then record a short description of each in Table 19.2.

TABLE 19.2 Delete Browsing History Options

Option	Function

5. Click Cancel to exit this window without deleting any Browsing History options.

Comparing Security Zones

1. Select the Security tab. Figure 19.11 shows the options under the Security tab of the Internet Options window.

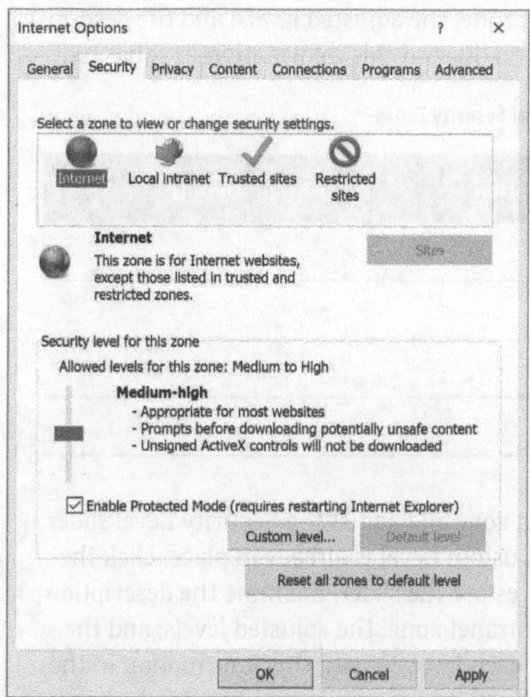

FIGURE 19.11 Security Tab of Internet Options

This window allows you to assign websites to various security zones.

- The Internet zone contains all the websites not assigned to another zone.
- The Local Intranet zone contains all the websites related to a local network (such as internal web pages).
- The Trusted Sites zone will contain all the websites that a user has deemed safe and unlikely to damage the system.
- The Restricted Sites zone will identify websites already known to contain potentially dangerous content.

With the exception of the zone reserved for the Internet, you can include the sites you choose with the Sites button.

2. With the Internet zone selected, under the Security tab, move the Security Level slider to the Medium setting. Examine the description

provided for the Internet zone, the adjusted levels, and the description provided for each level. Record this information in Table 19.3.

TABLE 19.3 Internet Explorer Security Zones

Zone	Description	Level	Details
Internet			
Local Intranet			
Trusted Sites			
Restricted Sites			

3. Select the Local Intranet zone and adjust the Security Level slider to the Low setting. If a Custom Level is already in place, click the Default Level button to restore the slider. Examine the description provided for the Local Intranet zone, the adjusted levels, and the description provided for each level. Record this information in the designated spaces of Table 19.3.
4. Select the Trusted Sites zone and adjust the Security Level slider to the Medium-Low setting. Examine the description provided for the Trusted Sites zone, the adjusted levels, and the descriptions provided for each level. Record this information in the designated spaces of Table 19.3.
5. Finally, select the Restricted Sites zone and try to adjust the slider to a lower setting.

Were you able to adjust it?

6. Examine the description provided for the Restricted Sites zone, the adjusted level, and the description provided for the level. Record this information in the designated spaces of Table 19.3.

Keep in mind that adding sites to the Restricted Sites zone does not block them. However, it prevents them from running programs or any active content. Protected mode can be enabled for both the Internet and Restricted Sites zones, although dong so requires restarting the browser.

If you choose to Enable Protected Mode, it will become more difficult for malicious software to be installed on your computer. Internet Explorer will warn you in the event that a malicious program attempts to install or run itself outside of protected mode.

7. Click the Reset All Zones To Default Level button to restore the security levels to their original settings.
8. Click Cancel to leave the Internet Options window.

Applying Security Zones to Sites

The security zones are a quick and efficient way to broadly define how your browser reacts to various sites, add-ons, programs, and downloads. You have the opportunity, however, to be specific in your choices. You will now test this by adding a website to the Restricted Sites zone, and viewing the results.

1. You should be located at the Home page of your Internet Explorer browser. Navigate to `www.msn.com`.
2. Notice the page, pictures, videos, advertisements, and anything else that catches your eye.
3. Return to the Internet Options page by selecting the gear icon in the upper-right corner, and then select Internet Options.
4. Select the Security tab to return to the Security Zones page. Select Restricted Sites.
5. Beneath the Restricted Sites logo is a button labeled Sites. Click Sites.

You are now located at the Restricted Sites, Add Website window shown in Figure 19.12.

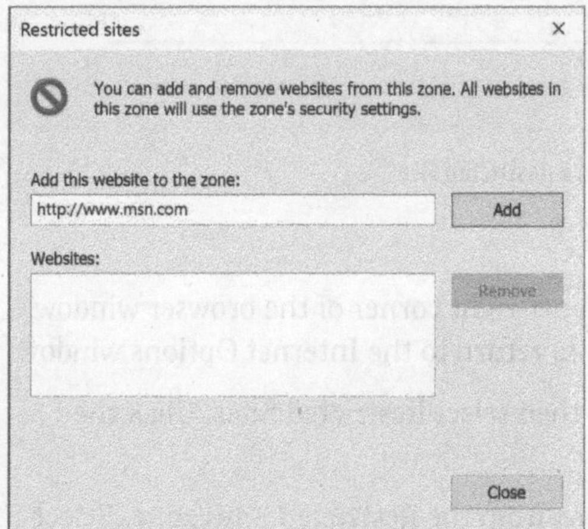

FIGURE 19.12 Restricted Sites Window

6. You can enter any website address you choose, or simply use the Add button to add the current website. Click Add.

7. The website is moved below and is now on the Restricted Sites zone. Click Close, and then click Cancel to exit the Internet Options window.

The same approach can be used to add sites to any of the other types of zones as well.

8. Notice the current website, `msn.com`, has not changed. Click the Refresh button located to the right of the URL or press the F5 button.

Does the site look different?
Figure 19.13 illustrates what `msn.com` looks like as a restricted site.

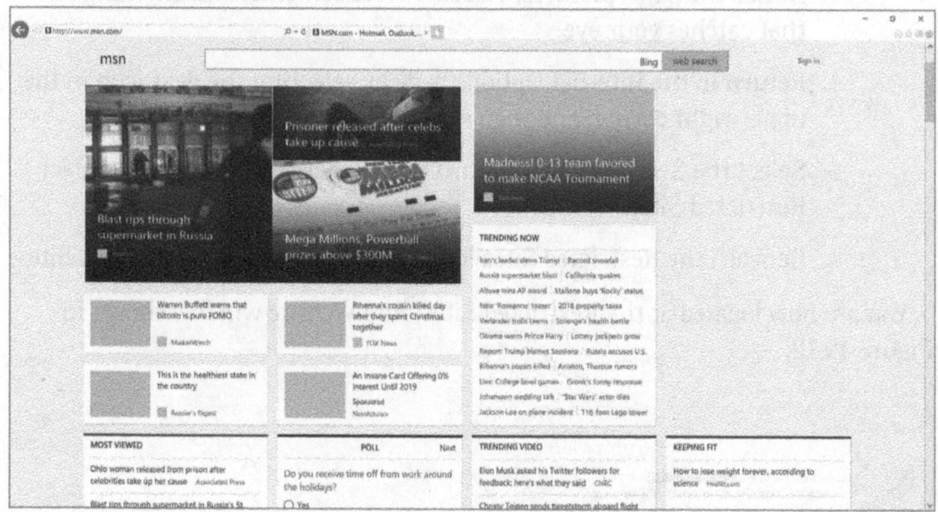

FIGURE 19.13 The msn.com Website as a Restricted Site

9. Click the gear icon in the upper-right corner of the browser window and select Internet Options to return to the Internet Options window.

10. Select the Security tab and then select Restricted Sites. Click the Sites button.

11. Now you can remove `msn.com` from the Restricted Sites zone. Select `msn.com` and then click Remove. Click Close.

12. Back at the Internet Options Security tab, click Custom Level to explore the specific options you can choose from within a security zone.

These settings control how Internet Explorer handles various objects associated with web pages, such as ActiveX controls and Java Scripting. Keep in mind that web pages can contain malicious objects designed to damage your system. Restricting how these objects interact with your system can help prevent viruses, Trojans, or malicious scripts from being downloaded to your system without your knowledge.

13. Explore the options available, but don't change any. Figure 19.14 shows the Security Settings – Restricted Sites Zone window.

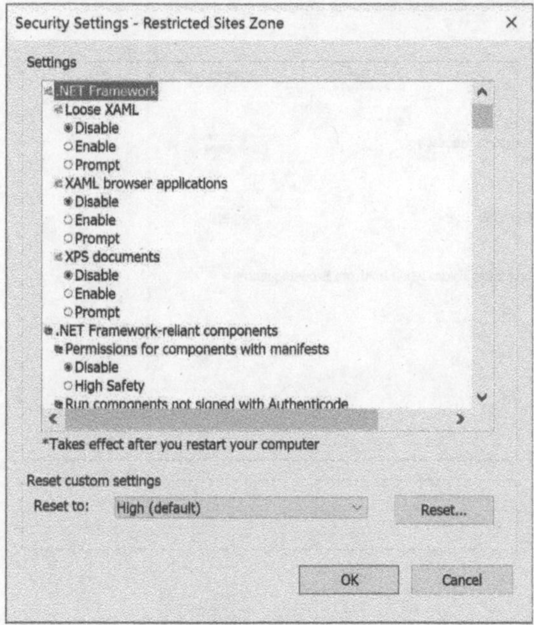

FIGURE 19.14 Security Settings – Restricted Sites Zone Window

14. Click Cancel to exit the Security Settings – Restricted Sites Zone window. Click Cancel again to exit the Internet Options window.
15. Refresh the web page by click the Refresh button to the right of the URL.

Is the `msn.com` website back to normal?

Applying Privacy Controls

Privacy controls for Internet Explorer can help you manage how websites monitor your online activities. You have the opportunity to block all monitoring; however, your online resources will become limited. Beyond malicious software, marketing firms and online shopping outlets use monitoring to make your experience easier and faster.

1. Return to the Internet Options window by clicking the gear icon in the upper-right corner and selecting Internet Options.
2. Select the Privacy tab to reveal the window shown in Figure 19.15.

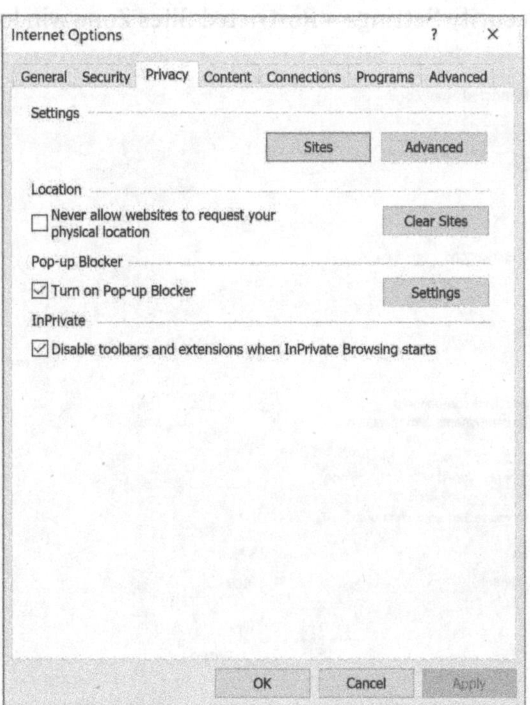

FIGURE 19.15 The Privacy Tab in Internet Options

An attacker only needs to employ a *packet sniffing* utility to monitor the network traffic and capture a cookie in order to gain access to your credentials (username, password, network address, and so on). With this information in hand, the attacker has the ability to imitate you when they access other sites.

The attacker can also use a technique called *cross-site scripting* to cause the returning cookie to be redirected to a third-party server operated by the attacker. The attacker can then use the stolen cookie to spoof the original site posing as the original user. The redirection is typically accomplished by simply hiding the script on the site and using social engineering techniques to trick you into clicking on the code. When you do, your cookie is transmitted to the third-party location specified by the attacker.

3. Click on the Security tab and you will notice a scroll bar on the lower left. The level on this has varying degrees of blocking and denying cookies. Scroll through each, evaluating the information on each. Return it to the Medium setting when you're done.
4. Click on the Privacy tab again and you will see that again you have the ability to select sites to either allow or deny. If you select the Sites button, you will be redirected to another window where you must specify a website. Back on the Privacy Internet Options window, there is an Advanced button. Click on the Advanced button to specify whether you want to allow cookies from them or deny cookies from them.
5. By default, Internet Explorer is set to accept all cookies, in order to permit frequently visited web pages to remember your last visit.
6. For both First-party Cookies and Third-party Cookies, select the Prompt radio button.

Selecting Block will prevent all websites from placing cookies on the machine. However, this may cause problems with websites that require enabled cookies for proper functioning. Selecting Prompt will cause Internet Explorer to ask permission before allowing any cookie to be placed on the system.

Recall that session cookies are cleared when the browser is closed, whereas persistent cookies will remain on the computer until the specified expiration date is reached. You have the option of Always Allow Session Cookies.

7. Click OK to save the changes to cookies. Click OK once more to exit the Internet Options window.
8. Refresh `msn.com` by selecting the Refresh icon to the right of the URL.

Were you prompted to allow or block a cookie?
Were any cookies from a source that was not `msn.com`?
Allow or block the cookies at your discretion.

Recognize that even this one site uses multiple cookies. They can be hard to manage, keep track of, and a nuisance if prompted continuously. For this reason, they are allowed. Attackers know this, and that makes cookies a great target for collecting information.

9. Click the gear icon in the upper-right corner of your web browser. Select Internet Options.
10. Return to the Privacy tab. Click the Default button to reset the cookie settings to their default setting.
11. Under Location, click the check box next to Never Allow Websites To Request Your Physical Location.

Websites will often request this information to keep track of your physical location, in order to provide customized results for local services or searches. Unfortunately, they are provided your IP address or MAC address, along with your signal strength if you are on a mobile device.

12. Select Clear Sites to remove any cookies that already contain this information. The option will now be grayed out.
13. By default, the Turn On Pop-up Blocker option is enabled. Click Settings to view more information about options, as shown in Figure 19.16.

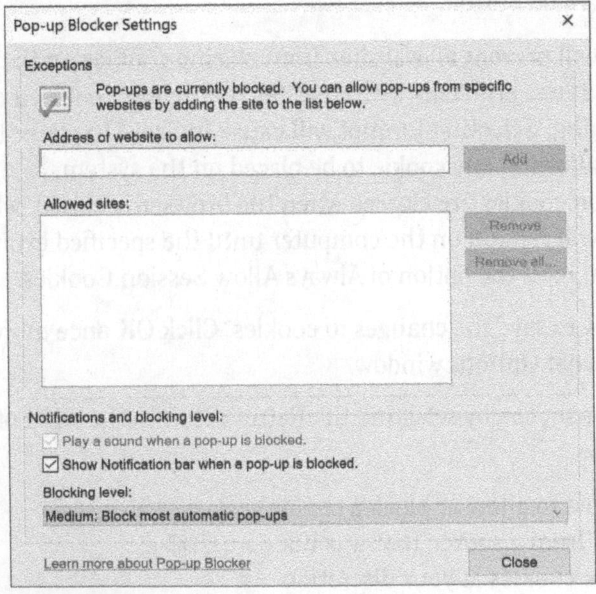

FIGURE 19.16 Pop-Up Blocker Settings

14. Review the settings and then click Close to exit the window.

The last check box is to Disable toolbars and extensions when InPrivate Browsing starts. InPrivate Browsing prevents Internet Explorer from leaving a trail for others to see. This means items such as cookies, temporary Internet files, and history will not be saved. Leaving this check box marked eliminates possible vulnerabilities that toolbars and extensions bring with them.

Exploring Security Settings

1. Select the Advanced tab within the Internet Options window.
2. Scroll down the Settings options until you reach the Security directory. Review the options in this list.

This list requires a more advanced knowledge of how the Internet works as a network. As you work through this book and continue learning about networks, return to these Advanced Security Settings and review the capabilities of each setting.

3. Click OK to save the default cookie settings.
4. Click the gear icon located in the upper-right corner of your browser window and hover the cursor over Safety.

This area of options gives you a common, quick-access list to enable or disable certain features.

5. In Table 19.4, list the available options.

TABLE 19.4 Options

Options

6. Close Internet Explorer.

Lab Questions

1. List the four types of zones into which websites must categorically fall.
2. Which security zone allows for only one level, and what is that level?
3. By default, Internet Explorer is set to accept ________________ cookies.
4. What does InPrivate Browsing accomplish?
5. What is collected when a website requests your physical location?

Lab Answers

1. Internet, local intranet, trusted sites, restricted sites
2. Restricted sites, High
3. All
4. Items such as cookies, temporary Internet files, and history will not be saved.
5. They are provided your IP address or MAC address, along with your signal strength if you are on a mobile device.

CHAPTER 20

Hiding the Private Network

In each of the preceding chapters, security planning was presented as a three-level plan that incorporated different types and levels of security devices, techniques, and policies at each level. Internet security is no different. In this setting, the interior is the local user system or the organization's local area network. Going forward, we will refer to these structures as *private networks*. In this chapter, you'll learn to:

- **Discuss the advantages and disadvantages of implementing Network Address Translation (NAT) and Port Address Translation (PAT) for network security.**
- **Define and describe network segmentation and security zones**
- **Use NAT to create security segments in the network**
- **Use VLANs to implement security zoning**

Understanding Private Networks

After the interior has been secured using the proper devices, techniques, and policies described in the first three chapters, it is necessary to secure the *inner perimeter*, which is the connectivity points between the individual's or organization's private network and the Internet.

The Internet is everything outside your perimeter. The thing is, the Internet is not managed by a single organization, nor is there one organization to secure it for us. Instead, using the Internet means your data is traversing across network devices managed (and maybe secured) by many organizations.

As mentioned earlier, the Internet has customers, employees, and businesses with whom we want to interact more efficiently using the Internet. However, it also has a wide array of different bad people with whom we do not want to interact.

The first security layer to be addressed is the interior. In addition to implementing the devices, techniques, and practices described in the previous chapters, many network security designers also take steps to hide or disguise the private network from the Internet. The following sections will present different techniques and devices that are commonly used for these purposes.

Network Address Translation

Routing is simply the translation of an IP address used in one network to an IP address in another network. Network Address Translation (NAT) is like simple routing, but is when one network is using private addressing, as shown in Figure 20.1. Typically, NAT is used to map a public IP address, such as from the Internet, to an address inside a network.

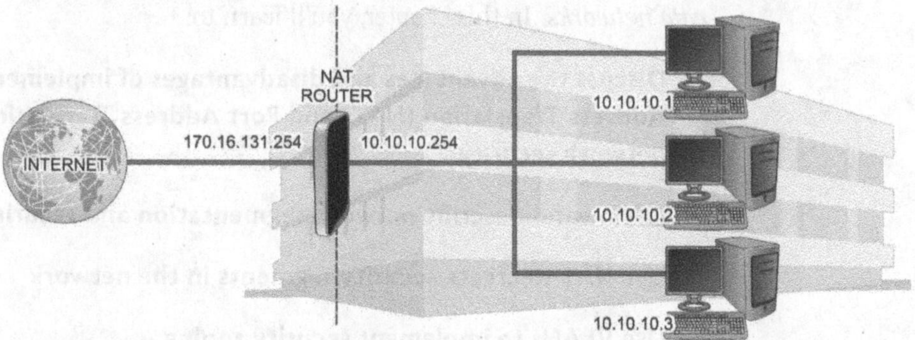

FIGURE 20.1 NAT Configuration

At the time this translation occurs, the network device performing it (generally, a router or firewall) can also authenticate the request or block it. This mapping may be guided by a NAT table that dictates the specific translation or by using a dynamic scheme that assigns translated IP addresses from an available pool of addresses.

NAT can be performed with policy-based routing (PBR) where the mapping decision is determined by any number of rules, which can be based on many different criteria. These rules are critical to security if outside access to a network is desired.

The Dynamic Host Configuration Protocol (DHCP) is commonly used to define a range of IPs that can be dynamically leased to the requesting system for a preconfigured length of time. The device handling this allocation is called the DHCP server, and it will track all address allocations to avoid allocating the same IP twice. The DHCP server can also support static allocation where an IP address may be reserved for a particular MAC address.

Port Address Translation

An extension to NAT known as Port Address Translation (PAT) supports the concept of mapping multiple or private IPs to a single or public IP address, as described in Figure 20.2. The router assigns a port number that is appended to the IP address, effectively making each address a unique address, even though they share an IP address.

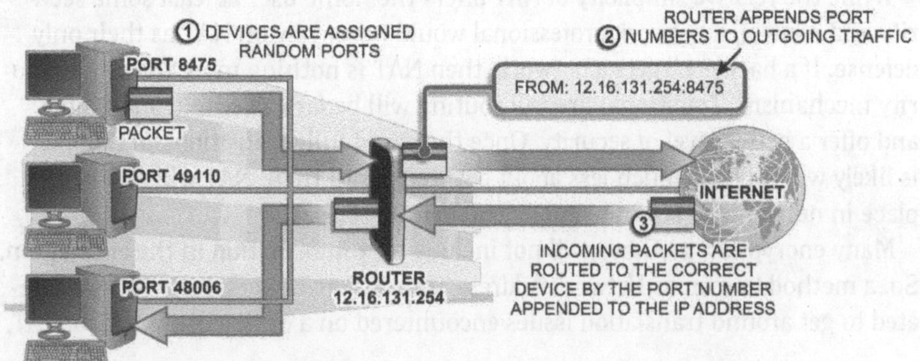

FIGURE 20.2 PAT Configurations

Because IPv4 IP addresses are in such short supply, this concept is currently used almost everywhere. While IP conservation is certainly a main reason for NAT and PAT, these concepts can also help with network security by allowing networks to expose only what is absolutely necessary. Most people think of NAT and PAT as the same thing. Although there is a distinction between these two techniques, the following discussions will treat them this way as well.

Once a connection has been authenticated and all the translation has been done, each packet can be inspected to ensure that the conversation is valid. If an inside client requests something from an outside device, we must know if that packet should be allowed through. Old-school static *packet filtering* looked only at packet headers, but this technique was easily exploited by an attacker that would indicate in the header that the packet was a reply and would be allowed in.

Modern firewall devices use stateful packet inspection or dynamic packet filtering to analyze the packets further—looking at IP addresses, port numbers, and more. They track this information so they can control their ports, only allowing them to be opened when an internal request asks for it. This practice is used to prevent a common hacking technique known as *port scanning*. When a hacker knows which ports are in use, they can focus their exploits on the services commonly associated with those ports.

Most home networks rely on NAT as their only security mechanism. While NAT may not be a true security apparatus, it does essentially shut off access to the internal network, unless the administrator deliberately opens outside access and even then, only to a small number of ports. Some would argue this is really enough for a Small Office/Home Office (SOHO) network—and for some it might be. But as hacker tools become increasingly automated, the risk of a SOHO network being the target of an arbitrary attack becomes more and more likely.

While the relative simplicity of NAT offers the home user at least some security and control, a network professional would never rely on NAT as their only defense. If a hacker targets a network, then NAT is nothing more than an obscurity mechanism. Traditional firewall routing will be far easier to troubleshoot and offer a better level of security. Once the world fully transitions to IPv6, it is likely we will hear much less about NAT; but until then, NAT will still have a place in networks to separate public and private IP space.

Many encryption methods will not include port information in the encryption. So, a method known as Network Address Translation-Traversal (NAT-T) was created to get around translation issues encountered on a device using NAT or PAT.

Port Forwarding or Mapping

The strongest feature of NAT/PAT is that by default nothing is translated or forwarded through the device. To move packets through the device, a rule must be explicitly created on the device to forward (or map) the desired protocol port to a private IP address and port in the local area network, as shown in Figure 20.3. This translation process is transparent in that external clients are unaware of the forwarding.

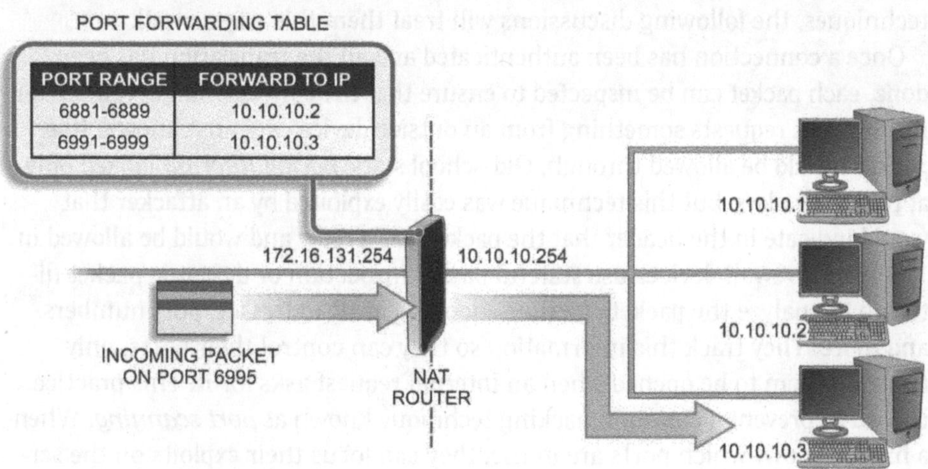

FIGURE 20.3 Port Forwarding

For example, an unusual port mapping could be created that requires web clients to connect using port 4444 instead of the usual port 80. Then, that port could be mapped to port 80 on a private IP in the private network. This might sound like a clever obfuscation, and network administrators do this all the time. However, such a plan really doesn't provide much security. A hacker can easily port scan the network and learn which ports are open.

Many applications can be configured to use arbitrary ports, allowing many different applications to reside behind a single public IP address. Many of these applications may provide a web interface, but others require specific client software for access. Either way, the client or browser software must be configured to access the public IP address and also provide the external port being mapped.

Security Through Obscurity

Most port scans are vanilla and will look at every potential port—all 65,535 of them—but a hacker might be looking for specific open ports in a strobe scan. So, by mapping unusual ports to those services, you could potentially discourage those attackers, but then clients would need to append a nonstandard port to their requests. Security through obscurity will not provide a successful security plan.

The port might be in a separate field or appended to the IP address separated by a colon (:). So, for a web browser, this might be something like:

```
http://203.0.113.86:4444
```

which might map to `192.168.0.4:8888` on the private network, meaning that on the device using `192.168.0.4`, the application being accessed is set up on port 8888.

A Word About Port Forwarding

Previously, some standard port numbers were discussed, and every hacker knows these common ports well. Any time you can easily map nonstandard ports, rather than use common ports, you should. However, serious hackers will still find these open ports, so port forwarding alone can't be thought of as a security technique.

Port forwarding through Secure Shell (SSH) is known as *SSH tunneling*. SSH tunneling creates a connection between a remote host and a local device or computer through which services can be relayed. This can be a great way of encrypting protocols that are normally not encrypted. SSH tunneling can be quite complex and can be a way to bypass normal filtering or blocks.

Network Segmentation

Network segmentation, also known as *zoning*, can be a useful concept for multiple reasons. It is essentially the separation of the network into subnetworks, each of which becomes a segment, as illustrated in Figure 20.4.

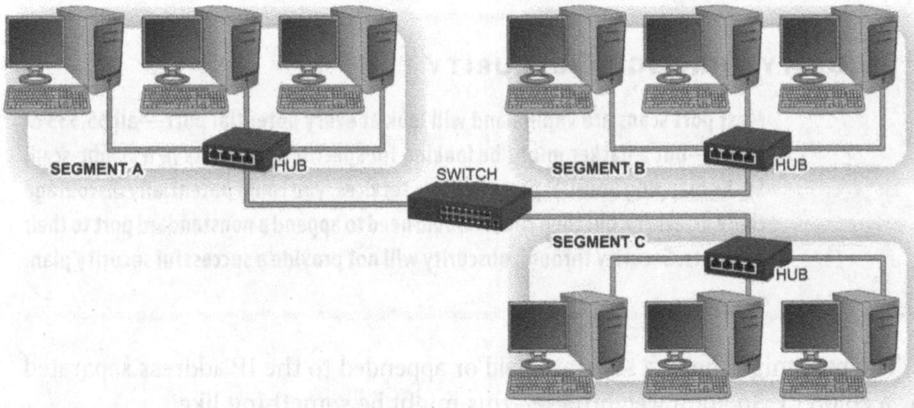

FIGURE 20.4 **A Segmented Network**

Segmenting networks is typically considered when connecting them across different geographical areas, interconnecting different network topologies (such as Ethernet and FDDI), or extending a network that has reached limitations in numbers of nodes or cable length.

While convenience and organizational simplicity can make segmentation a sensible solution, security considerations should drive decisions about network segmentation. From a security perspective, the main reason to deploy network segmentation is to limit the access capabilities of intruders. Each segment will also benefit from reduced congestion and broadcast traffic in addition to containing network problems to a single segment.

These security considerations may also be driven by requirements from outside entities. For example, credit card vendors require that any business that accepts credit cards adhere to the Payment Card Industry Data Security

Standard (PCI-DSS). This standard requires the use of firewalls and other security concepts, such as network segmentation, to ensure that all stored credit card information is securely stored both physically and electronically. This requirement even impacts businesses that don't store credit card data but accept credit cards using a point-of-sale device.

To achieve PCI-DSS compliance, all Point of Sale (POS) terminals and all stored cardholder data must be on a network completely separated from any network area where third parties might have access. Some users may need access to some of the network but certainly not every segment.

Segmentation is critical in the medical field where network administrators must deal with Health Insurance Portability Accountability Act (HIPAA) compliance to ensure the confidentiality of patient medical information.

Access to a network segment is often provided through an access control list, where only users matching some criteria or authentication are allowed access. This is known as a *whitelisting*. Alternatively, when access is denied only to users matching given criteria this is known as *blacklisting*. The latter scheme is far less secure, and you should always try to whitelist an ACL rather than blacklist it.

Segmentation can also be used to restrict access between zones by internal users. Sales people may not need to be given access to a server used by the accounting department. However, the accounting staff may need to access sales data on the sales server. These zones need to be connected with each other, but access between zones can be controlled by implementing segmentation.

When allowing outside users into a network, always use the principles of "least privilege" and "need to know" to establish access levels. Give each user the least amount of access possible and only to the areas of the network they must have.

Network segmentation might look to be one of those "set it and forget it" initiatives, but it actually requires continuous management and enforcement. In a large enterprise, segmentation can be a major challenge due to the many different policies and rules involved in such network environments.

We won't get into the nuances of managing segments and dealing with internal application requirements in this chapter.

As you will see going forward, segmentation is a key component of overall Internet security schemes in many different network environments. If for no other reason, segmentation is so widely employed because of its abilities to minimize the depth of penetration that an intruder might obtain, should they gain entry to the network through the Internet.

Software-Defined Networking

Network virtualization changes the way we must look at network segmentation. A relatively new concept of software-defined networking (SDN) is emerging that essentially analyzes the connection between any two nodes and can filter that connection based on a defined policy. This micro-segmentation will make security more powerful when it is widespread but will certainly make certain management aspects more complex.

Network Virtualization

Computer platforms have evolved enough that we can simulate hardware platforms such as servers, routers, and most any other network resource using software. Through software, a single piece of hardware can support multiple virtual instances, as shown in Figure 20.5. Each instance has the ability to function like the original host hardware. Virtual instances can be enabled as needed to handle demand and scalability, or to provide tremendous amounts of portability.

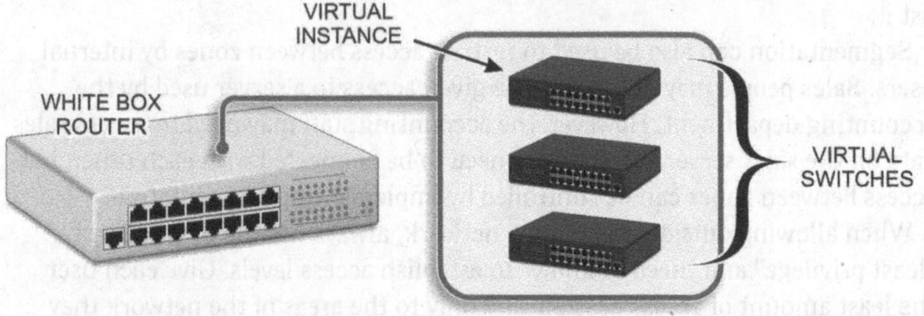

FIGURE 20.5 Virtual Instances

Network *virtualization* is also a way to segment your network by creating overlay networks, (essentially a network built on top of another, physical or underlay, network). It is possible to use white box switches (generic routing and switching hardware) in these overlay networks.

Network virtualization can provide a virtual network completely separate from other network resources, creating a zone just as you would with traditional network hardware. Network virtualization can also be used to implement software-driven virtual network storage units. This is seen in storage area network (SAN) deployments.

VLANs

A VLAN, or virtual LAN, is simply a software-configured network where hosts will behave as if they are all connected to the same physical network even when they are not. This allows several networks or broadcast domains to work, virtually, as a single LAN and broadcast domain, as shown in Figure 20.6. This reduces latency and can often make network segmentation much simpler to understand and maintain. However, you now have to deal with additional security issues such as the spread of viruses and malware across your new logical network rather than within a single physical network.

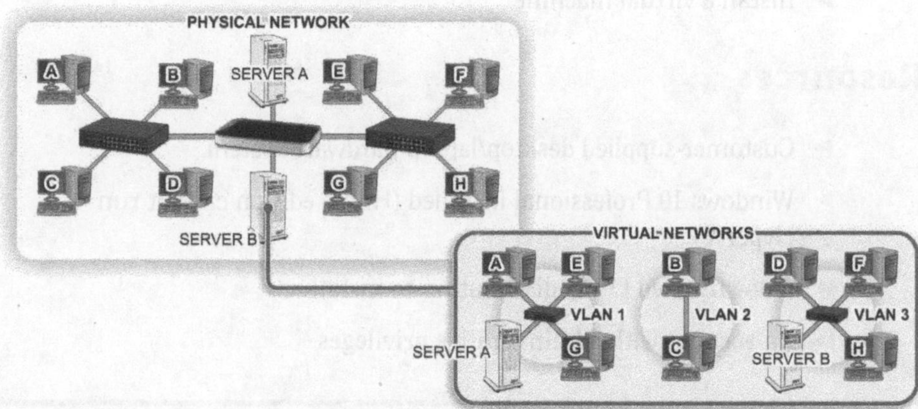

FIGURE 20.6 A VLAN

VLANs are typically set up on a router or a switch; but to pass traffic from one VLAN to another, you must have hardware that will support VLANs or VLAN tagging. VLANs can be port-based or tagged/untagged. The Ethernet frame header contains a VLAN ID and part of this is the Tag Protocol Identifier (TPID).

If a packet contains VLAN information, then it is considered a tagged packet or an untagged packet if it does not. A port-based VLAN could simply be a group of ports on an Ethernet switch that form a segment, or it could span multiple switches.

A managed Layer 2 switch may be configured to forward or block traffic to or from specific VLANs and can add the VLAN tag to the header or encapsulate the frame within another type of transmission frame if you are exchanging data with different network technology. The switch might even support trunk lines between switches, and a trunk port will carry all of the traffic accessible by that switch. A Layer 3 switch (or a router) supporting VLAN tagging can support all of the routing and blocking of data between VLANs as well.

Hands-On Exercises

Objectives

- Check system for compatibility with Hyper V.
- Enable Hyper V on a Windows 10 Professional computer.
- Install and explore a virtual switch Hyper-V Manager.
- Install a virtual machine.

Resources

- Customer-supplied desktop/laptop hardware system
- Windows 10 Professional installed (Home edition cannot run Hyper-V)
- A downloaded Linux distribution to install
- An account with administrative privileges

NOTE For this lab, we recommend downloading an Ubuntu distribution at `https://www.ubuntu.com/download`.

Discussion

Computer platforms have evolved enough that we can simulate hardware platforms such as servers, routers, and most any other network resource using software. Through software, a single piece of hardware can support multiple virtual instances. Each instance has the ability to function like the original host hardware. Virtual instances can be enabled as needed to handle demand and scalability, or to provide tremendous amounts of portability.

Network virtualization is also a way to segment your network by creating overlay networks (essentially a network built on top of another, physical or underlay, network). It is possible to use white box switches (generic routing and switching hardware) in these overlay networks.

Procedure

In this procedure, you will learn how to enable virtualization technology, configure a virtual switch, and install a virtual machine (VM) on your Windows 10 Professional computer.

Checking Hyper-V Compatibility

Check your Windows 10 Professional computer for compatibility with Hyper-V.

1. Turn on your computer.
2. Log on using your account with administrative privileges.
3. On your desktop in the embedded search bar on your taskbar, type cmd and press Enter to open the Command Prompt window.
4. In the Command Prompt window, type systeminfo.exe and press Enter.
5. After a few moments, your system information should be listed in the Command Prompt window, as shown in Figure 20.7.

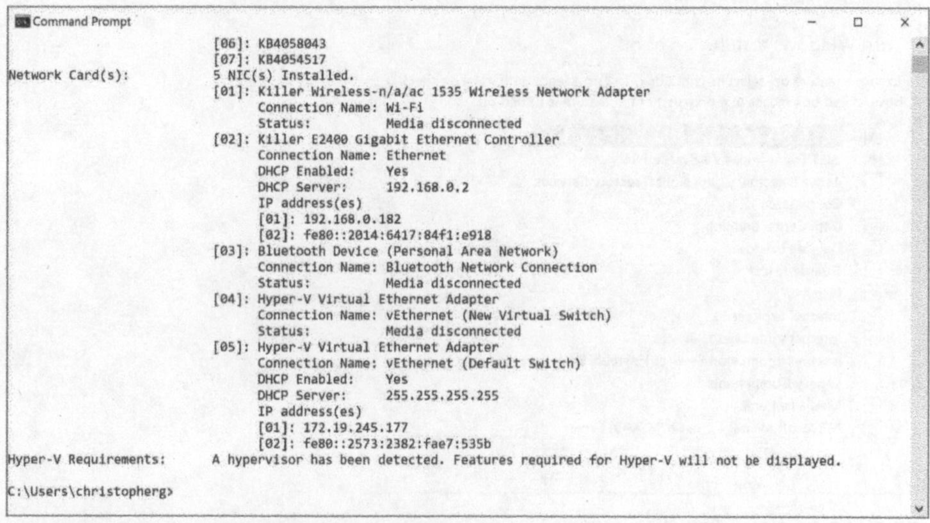

FIGURE 20.7 Systeminfo Command Output

NOTE This system already has Hyper-V installed, so no information is provided in the output field.

6. Under Hyper-V Requirements, if the results indicate Yes, you may enable Hyper-V without any further steps. If the results read No, you may need to go into your BIOS to enable hardware features or your hardware may be incompatible with Hyper-V.

Enabling Hyper-V in Windows 10 Professional

Once the compatibility verification has been completed and any required adjustments have been made in the BIOS, proceed with the following steps to enable Hyper-V on your Windows 10 Professional computer.

1. If you have not done so already, boot your computer and log on using an account with administrative privileges.
2. On your desktop in the search bar embedded in your taskbar type **turn windows features on or off** and press Enter.
3. The Windows Features window should appear, and it should look similar to the one displayed in Figure 20.8.

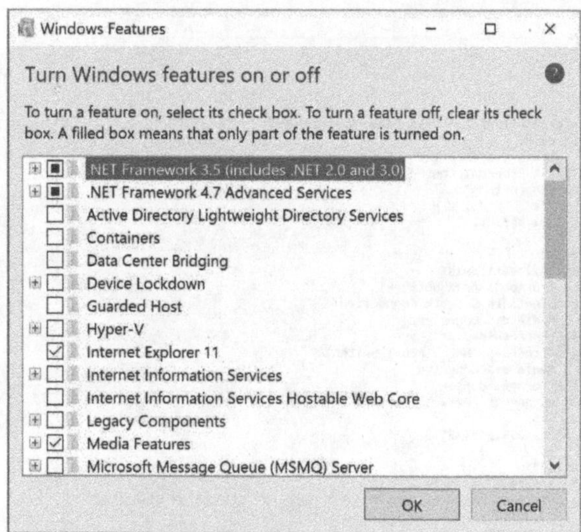

FIGURE 20.8 Windows Features

4. Locate and click the box next to Hyper-V to tell Windows to turn on this feature, as shown in Figure 20.9.
5. Click OK.

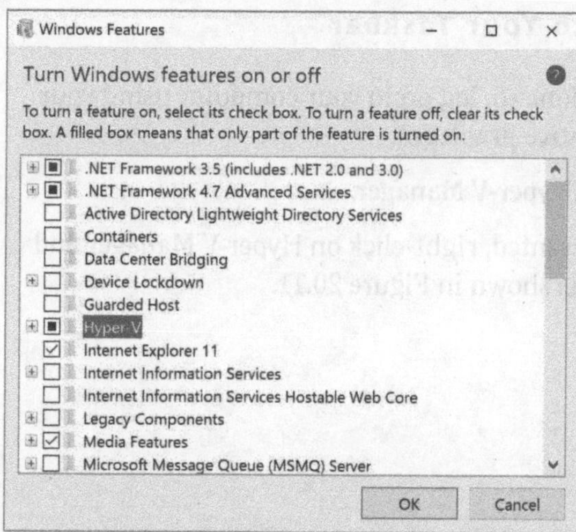

FIGURE 20.9 Enabling Hyper-V

6. Windows will process the change and provide a prompt indicating that you need to reboot to finish installing the requested feature, as shown in Figure 20.10. Click the Restart Now button.

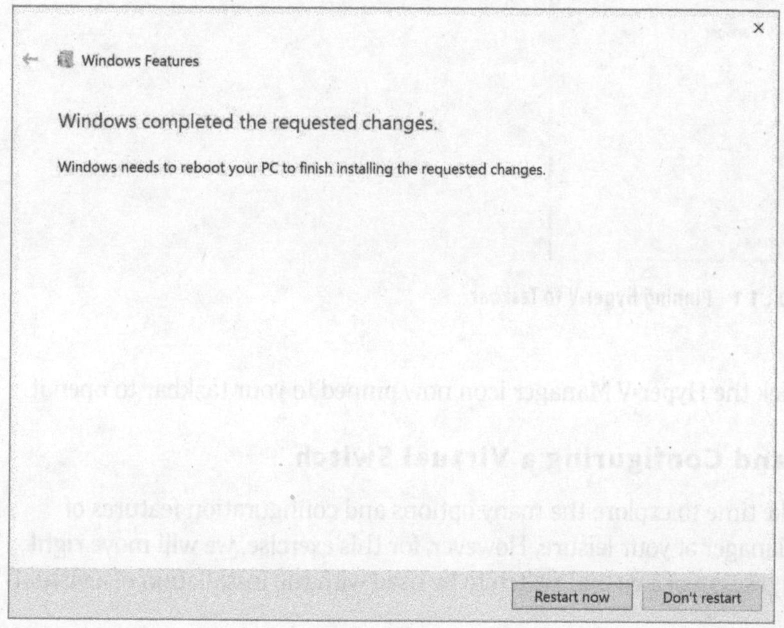

FIGURE 20.10 Ready for the Reboot

Congratulations on enabling virtualization technology on your computer.

Pinning Hyper-V Manager to Your Taskbar

1. If you have not already done so, log on to your computer using your account with administrative privileges.
2. In your search bar, type Hyper-V Manager.
3. In the menu options presented, right-click on Hyper-V Manager and choose Pin To Taskbar, as shown in Figure 20.11.

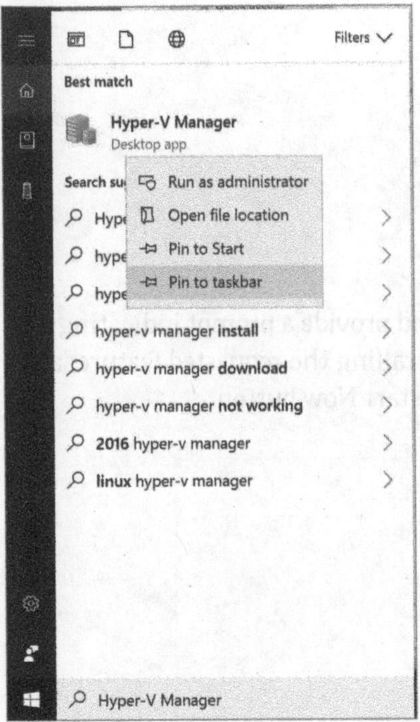

FIGURE 20.11 Pinning Hyper-V to Taskbar

4. Click the Hyper-V Manager icon now pinned to your taskbar to open it.

Installing and Configuring a Virtual Switch

You should take time to explore the many options and configuration features of the Hyper-V Manager at your leisure, However, for this exercise, we will move right into the configuration of a virtual switch to be used with the installation of a virtual machine.

1. In the right Actions pane of the Hyper-V Manager window, click Virtual Switch Manager.

A new window titled "Virtual Switch Manager for 'Your Computer's Name'" should appear, as shown in Figure 20.12.

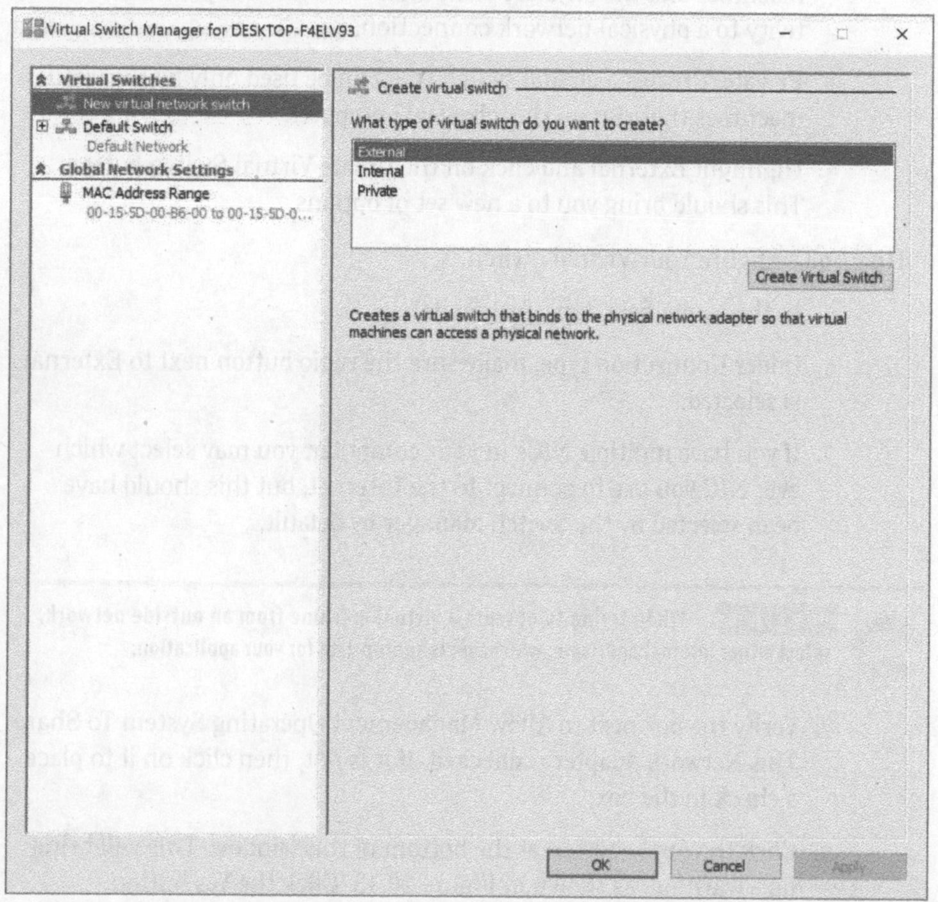

FIGURE 20.12 Virtual Switch Manager

2. A virtual switch is installed by default and is associated with your active NIC. But let's examine the options provided when setting up a switch for use with your VMs.
3. If it is not already selected, click New Virtual Network Switch, under Switches in the left pane of the window.

When creating a virtual switch, you should be presented with three options:

- **External:** Creates a virtual switch that binds to the physical network adapter so that virtual machines can access a physical network.

- **Internal:** Creates a virtual switch that can be used only by the virtual machines that run on this physical computer, and between virtual machines and the physical computer. This does not provide connectivity to a physical network connection.
- **Private:** Creates a virtual switch that can be used only by the virtual machines that run on this physical computer.

4. Highlight External and click on the Create Virtual Switch button. This should bring you to a new set of options

How To Configure Your Virtual Switch.

5. In the Name field, type **Test Switch.**
6. Under Connection type, make sure the radio button next to External is selected.
7. If you have multiple NICs in your computer, you may select whichever NIC you use to connect to the Internet, but this should have been selected by the Switch Manager by default.

NOTE **When trying to obscure a virtual machine from an outside network, select either Internal or Private, whichever is appropriate for your application.**

8. Verify the box next to Allow Management Operating System To Share This Network Adapter is checked. If it is not, then click on it to place a check in the box.
9. Click the Apply button at the bottom of this window. This will bring up a warning, as shown in Figure 20.13. Click the Yes button.

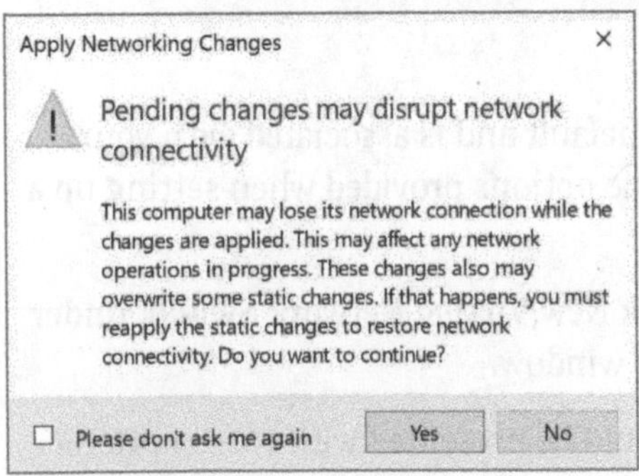

FIGURE 20.13 **Apply Network Changes Warning**

10. At the bottom of the Virtual Switch Manager window, click the OK button. This should take you back to the Hyper-V Manager window.

Installing a Linux Distribution in Hyper-V

1. Download an Ubuntu distribution and save it to a location where you can find it. For this example, we are using Ubuntu 16.04.3.
2. If Hyper-V is not open, click on the Hyper-V Manager icon on the taskbar to open it.
3. In the right-hand pane under Actions, locate and click New. This should present a side menu to create a new virtual machine, hard disk, or floppy disk.
4. Click on Virtual Machine to bring up the New Virtual Machine Wizard, as shown in Figure 20.14.

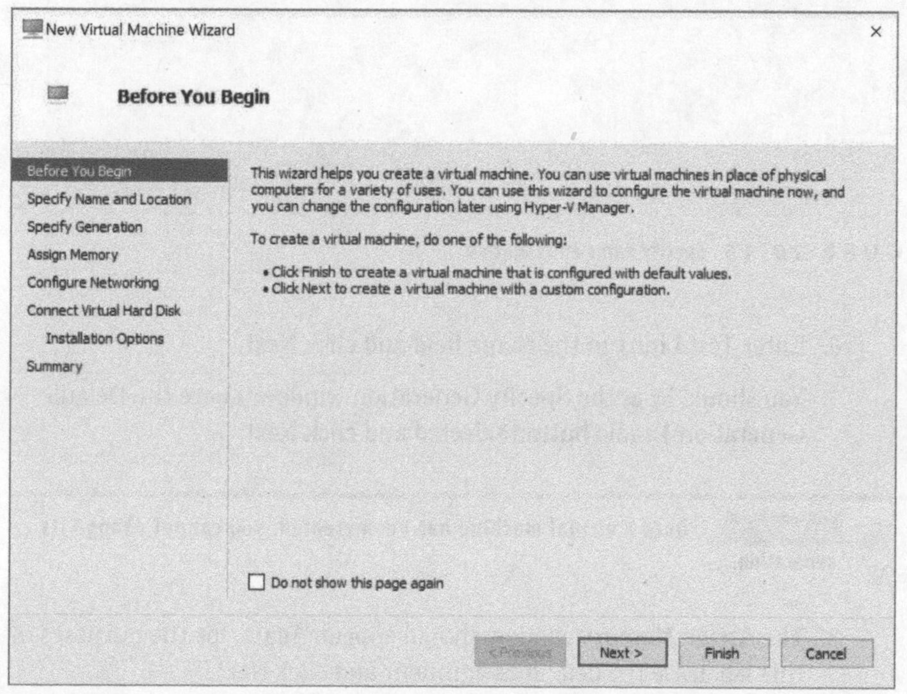

FIGURE 20.14 New Virtual Machine Wizard – Before You Begin Window

5. Click Next. This should take you to the Specify Name And Location window, as shown in Figure 20.15.

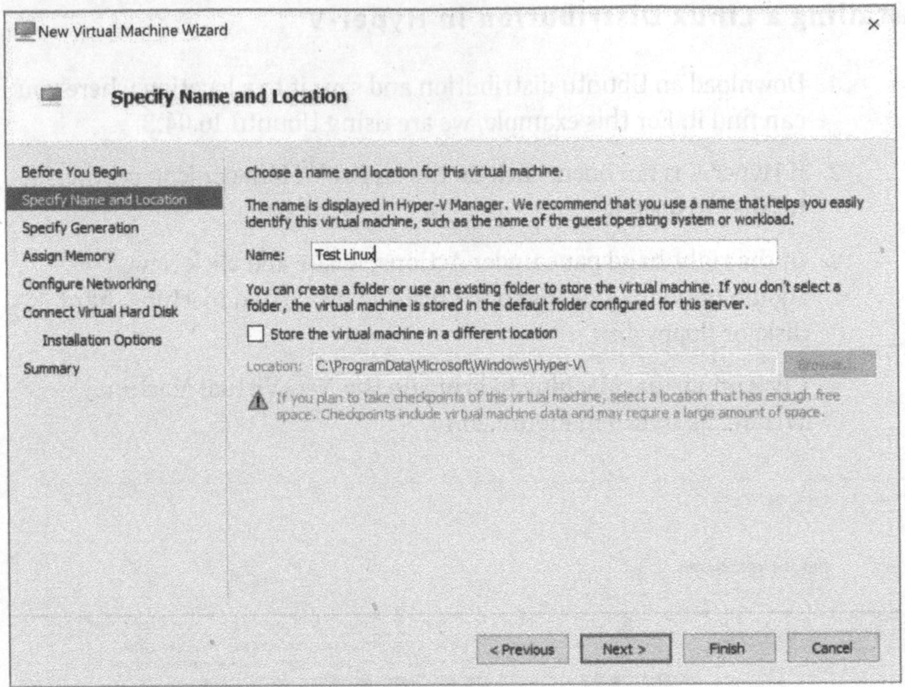

FIGURE 20.15 Specify Name and Location

6. Enter Test Linux in the Name field and click Next.
7. You should be at the Specify Generation window. Leave the Default Generation 1 radio button selected and click Next.

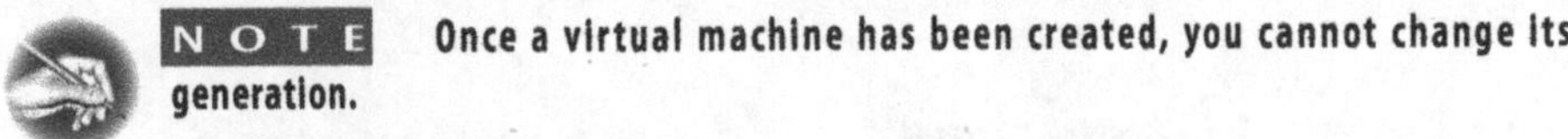

NOTE Once a virtual machine has been created, you cannot change its generation.

8. The Assign Memory window should appear. Again, for the purposes of this lab, leave the default assignment and click Next.

9. The Configure Networking window should appear. In this window, the default setting is Not Connected. Click on the drop-down menu and select the Test Switch we previously created, as shown in Figure 20.16.

10. The Connect Virtual Hard Disk window should appear. In this window, you will select whether to create a virtual HD, use an existing Virtual HD, or attach a virtual HD later. For this exercise, leave the default values and click Next.

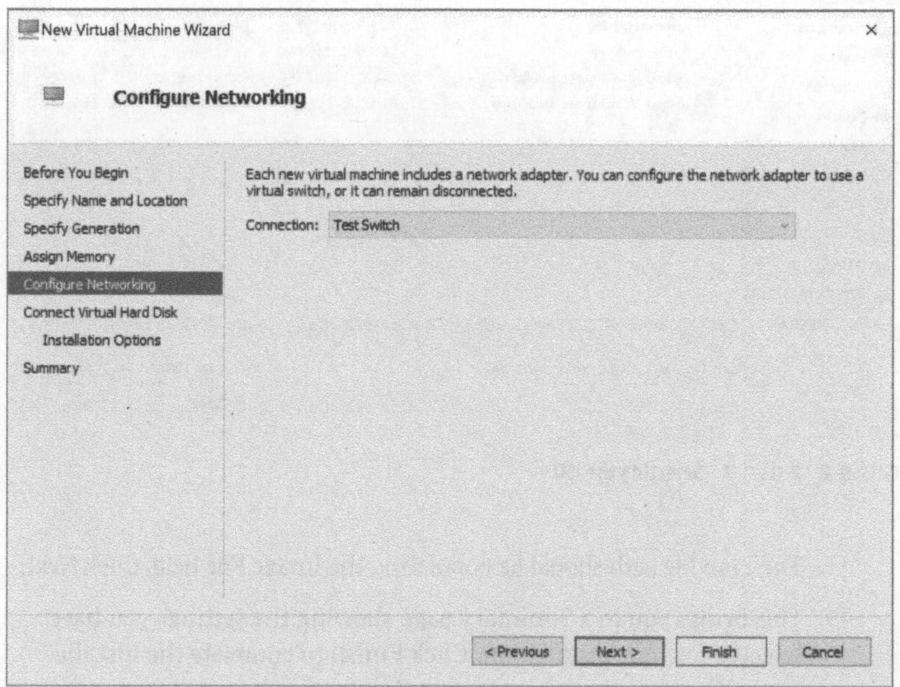

FIGURE 20.16 Selecting the Network Connection

11. At the installation option, click the radio button next to Install An Operating system From A Bootable CD/DVD-ROM.

12. Click the radio button next to Image File (`.iso`) and click the Browse button next to the File Location field.

13. Browse to the location of your downloaded Linux ISO, click on the file to select it, and then click the Open button, as shown in Figure 20.17.

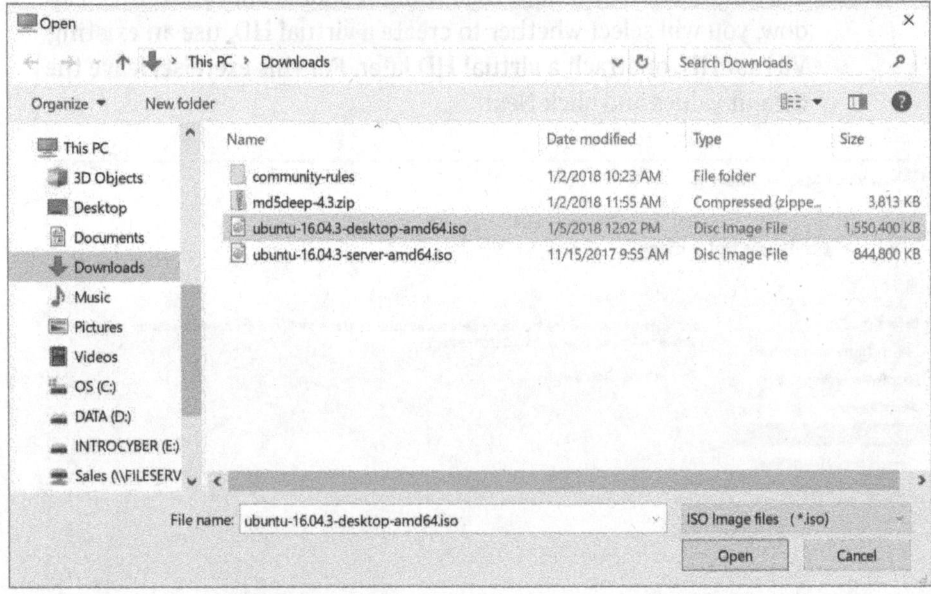

FIGURE 20.17 Selecting the ISO

14. The .iso file path should be populating the Image File field. Click Next.

15. This brings you to a Summary page showing the settings you have selected for your installation. Click Finish to complete the installation of the virtual machine.

16. Your new Linux virtual machine should now appear in your Hyper-V Manager, as shown in Figure 20.18.

17. You will still need to install the OS from your image file onto this virtual machine to make it usable, but you have now enabled and applied a virtual machine to your Windows 10 computer.

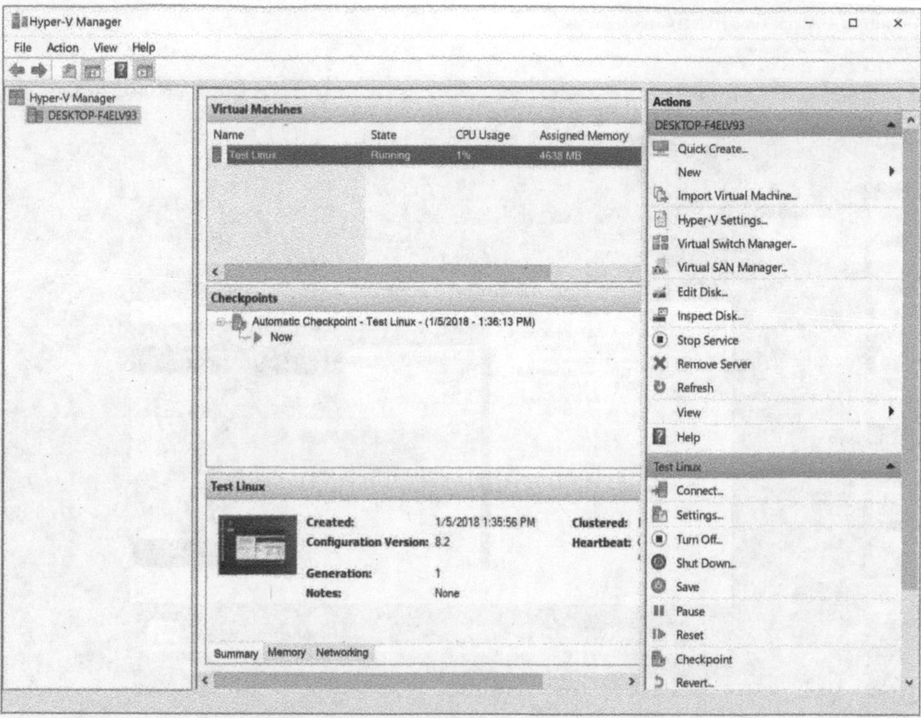

FIGURE 20.18 Virtual Machine Installed in Hyper-V

If you power on your virtual machine, you will be prompted to install your Linux distribution on the virtual machine. Upon completion, it should look like Figure 20.19.

You may also use Hyper-V Manager to import and export existing virtual machines. This is useful in terms of saving an uncorrupted backup of your existing virtual machine installations, as well as troubleshooting issues on existing VMs within your enterprise structure.

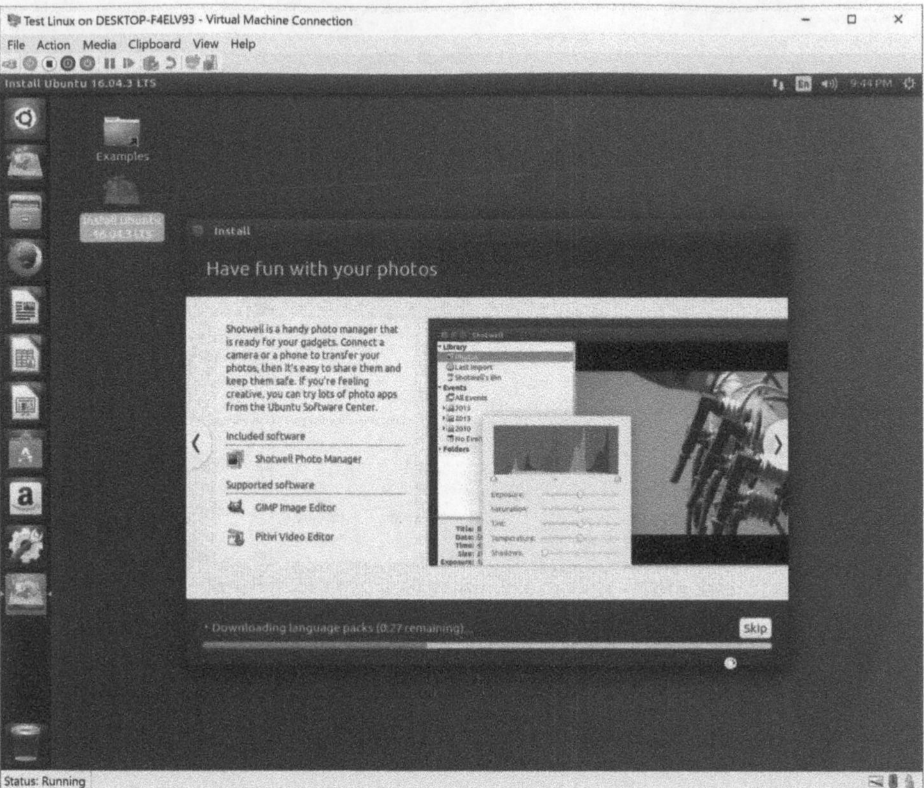

FIGURE 20.19 Ubuntu Linux 16.04.3 LTS Running as a VM

Lab Questions

1. What command prompt utility program is used to verify a Windows computer's compatibility with Hyper Visor?
2. As there is no installation file for Hyper Visor on Windows 10 Professional, where do you go to enable Hyper-V in this operating system?
3. What three configuration options are available when you're creating a virtual switch in Hyper-V?
4. Once a virtual machine has been created, can you change its generation?

Lab Answers

1. What command prompt utility program is used to verify a Windows computer's compatibility with Hyper Visor?

   `systeminfo.exe`

2. As there is no installation file for Hyper Visor on Windows 10 Professional, where do you go to enable Hyper-V in this operating system?

   Turn Windows features on or off.

3. What three configuration options are available when you're creating a virtual switch in Hyper-V?

   External, Internal, and Private.

4. Once a virtual machine has been created, can you change its generation?

   No.

CHAPTER 21

Protecting the Perimeter

The second level you need to secure is the inner perimeter, where the private network meets the Internet. What defines a perimeter is the boundary where you have control, versus where you don't have control. The perimeter is where your private network touches those individuals and companies with which you want to interact. In this chapter, you'll learn to:

- **Implement firewalls and other intrusion-prevention devices and structures**
- **Describe common enterprise-network structures, including intranets, extranets, DMZs, and honeypots**
- **Describe the purpose and limitations of firewalls**
- **Describe the use of honeypots as an intrusion-prevention technique**
- **Understand the role of DMZs (demilitarized zones) in cybersecurity topologies**
- **Explain the configuration and operation of a demilitarized zone (DMZ) host, including the key services contained within the zone**

Understanding the Perimeter

The inner perimeter is the point where we want to stop the bad people on the Internet from accessing the private network, as depicted in Figure 21.1.

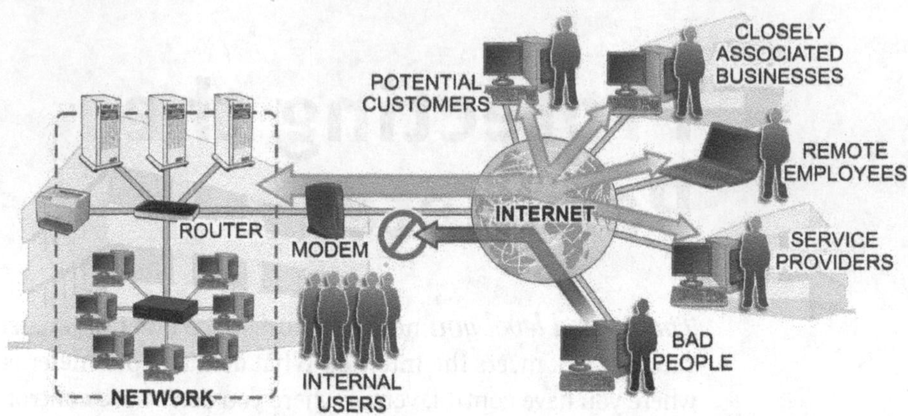

FIGURE 21.1 The Perimeter

Network hardware is the integral component in Internet access and can usually serve a dual purpose in providing a certain amount of network security. Whether access is controlled via something as simple as a modem or as complex as a router or firewall, there is always at least one and generally two or more critical pieces of hardware between the user's computer or device and their ISP, as shown in Figure 21.2.

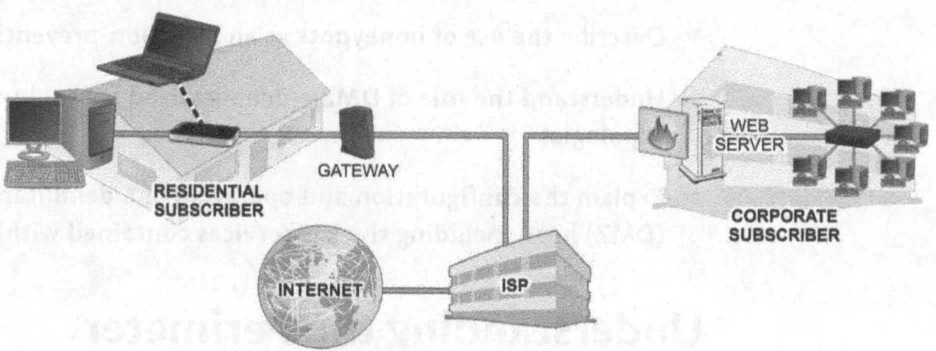

FIGURE 21.2 Internet Connectivity

It is critical to understand that these devices can be the *single point of failure* or the portal to network tragedy when it comes to design, troubleshooting, and maintenance. These are the devices that technical support personnel will typically target initially while troubleshooting because they really are the most common trouble spots. They are also important in any security initiative.

Gateway devices often provide good security capabilities and even out-of-the-box and unconfigured, they will usually provide "good enough" security for the average residential or small office user. These days, the typical ISP-provided modem also functions as a router and packet-level firewall. However, if your modem does not function as a router, you will need to run security software to create a software firewall on your computer. Both Mac and Windows systems include basic firewall capabilities built-in and many dedicated software firewall products or firewall features bundled with antivirus software exist to help these users.

Every standalone computer or local area network that connects to the Internet will connect through some type of gateway device, as shown in Figure 21.3. This gateway device is often a router but may also be a switch that features some protocol conversion or translator to allow your Ethernet or wireless clients access to the technology your ISP provides at your location. This gateway device could also be a modem, an access point, or even a Voice over Internet Protocol (VoIP) adapter.

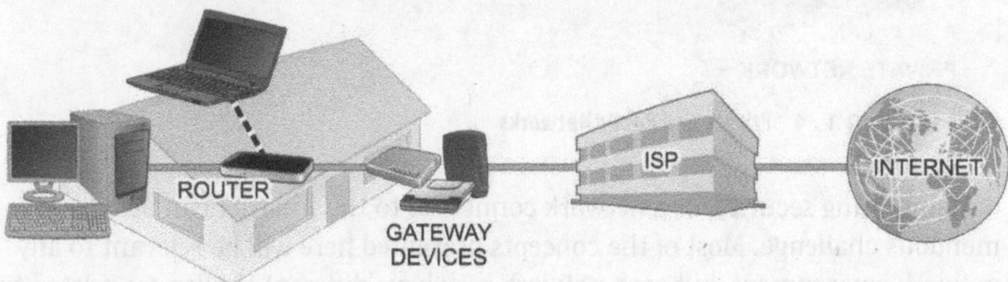

FIGURE 21.3 **Gateway Connection Options**

If the gateway is not also a router (or at least a switch), generally, you will need a router operating behind that gateway. If the gateway does not feature a router, it likely connects to a network that provides routing services, so going forward we will assume that all networks connect to the Internet through a router or routing device.

It is important that you understand exactly what features any network hardware between your router and your ISP performs. Security is not just about a single device; you might have to deal with many devices to further secure the environment. For example, many networks have key network components connected to their routers. These devices might act as a firewall or be a network appliance that provides some specific features for users.

In many networking environments, it is common to create some outwardly facing network services that provide available access to external users. These services might include web servers or mail servers that users can access easily while the organization maintains control of the content. Such networks that are insulated from the private network but that can be seen from the Internet, as illustrated in Figure 21.4, are referred to as *public networks*. Most organizations do this by creating a managed, externally accessible network called a *demilitarized zone* (DMZ) between their private network and the Internet. DMZs are discussed in greater detail later in this chapter.

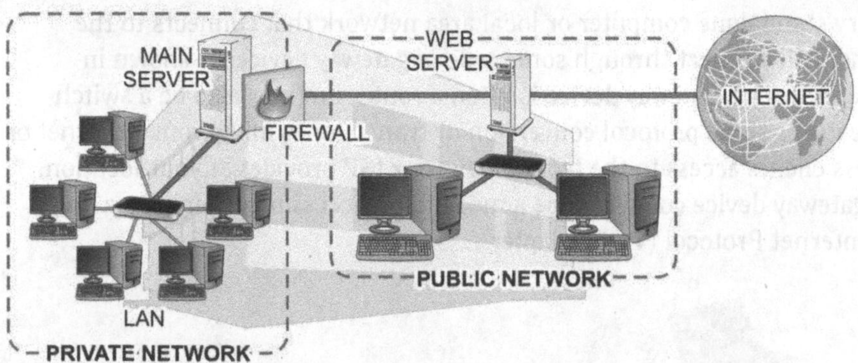

FIGURE 21.4 Private and Public Networks

Maintaining security for a network connected to the Internet can be a tremendous challenge. Most of the concepts presented here will be relevant to any network environment, but each network may have different challenges related to the services and applications featured on that network.

Going forward, we will focus on security for devices that must live on a public network and not so much about protecting the private network from threats originating from the Internet, even though many of those concepts are the same. Much like any other kind of security, the amount of emphasis placed on Internet security should be related to what stands to be lost. Important questions that must be answered to arrive at a satisfactory solution include:

- How important is what you are protecting?
- What is the worst-case scenario?
- How much will it hurt you or your company if the network is compromised?
- Do you have private data that must be protected or are there any liability concerns if data is obtained by outside users?
- Are there regulations or laws requiring you to protect your data?

Everyone should participate in a certain level of Internet security, but after you answer these questions you should realize how much additional security is needed.

Firewalls

The most common first line of defense in a network connected to the Internet is a *firewall*. These devices usually consist of some combination of hardware and software used to protect a private network from unauthorized access by way of the Internet. This is accomplished by limiting security exposures, enforcing the organization's security policy, and sometimes logging or monitoring Internet activity.

Firewalls can be implemented in various ways in different network arrangements. A firewall might be a mission-specific hardware device, or it may be a function that is built into a router or switch, or it may be implemented in a computer that has multiple Ethernet interfaces. It can even be a pure software firewall installed on a host computer like any other application. Many network appliances are available that offer firewall and security capabilities along with other network features.

In a corporate or industrial network environment, the administrator controls firewall installations and configurations. The advantage of the network firewall is that it enables the administrator to control the flow of information to all the devices attached to their network, as illustrated in Figure 21.5.

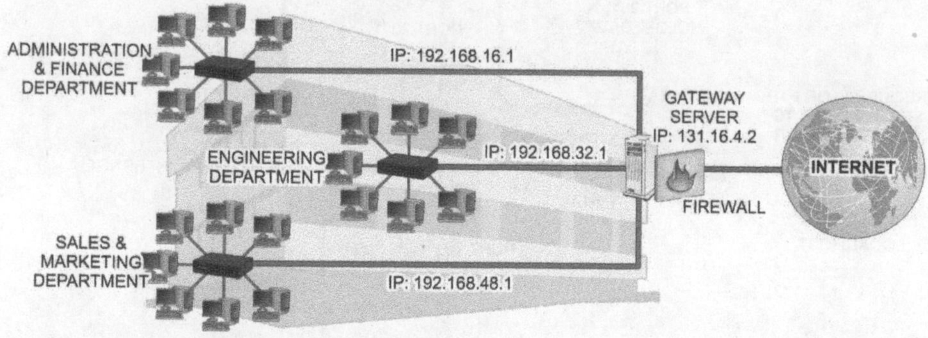

FIGURE 21.5 Network Firewall

Firewalls must act as gateway devices, authorizing and granting access to both network applications and protocols. They might also act as proxy servers, provide Network Address Translation, and act as DHCP servers. Firewalls typically also filter both incoming and outgoing traffic.

A good firewall will provide packet filtering using defined rules to reject or accept both incoming and outgoing packets. This can be more challenging to configure, but effective firewall rules are really critical to security.

A packet-filtering firewall can be established through routers by configuring them with packet-filtering rules to allow or deny client access based on factors such as their source address, destination address, or port number. There are generally two types of packet-filtering firewalls to consider: static packet filtering and stateful packet filtering.

Static (or *stateless*) packet-filtering firewalls do not keep track of the state of a connection between two computers. They actually operate in much the same manner as any ACL does. This makes this variety of firewalls relatively faster than other firewall options. They also tend to be relatively inexpensive and easy to maintain. Conversely, static packet-filtering firewalls offer fewer security features than other firewall options.

Stateful packet-filtering firewalls do keep track of the connection state between entities. These firewalls collect network connection information and maintain dynamic state tables that are used for subsequent connections. As illustrated in Figure 21.6, this enables ports to be opened and closed as needed. Once a client has completed a communication session, the stateful packet-filtering firewall closes the specific port used until it is requested again.

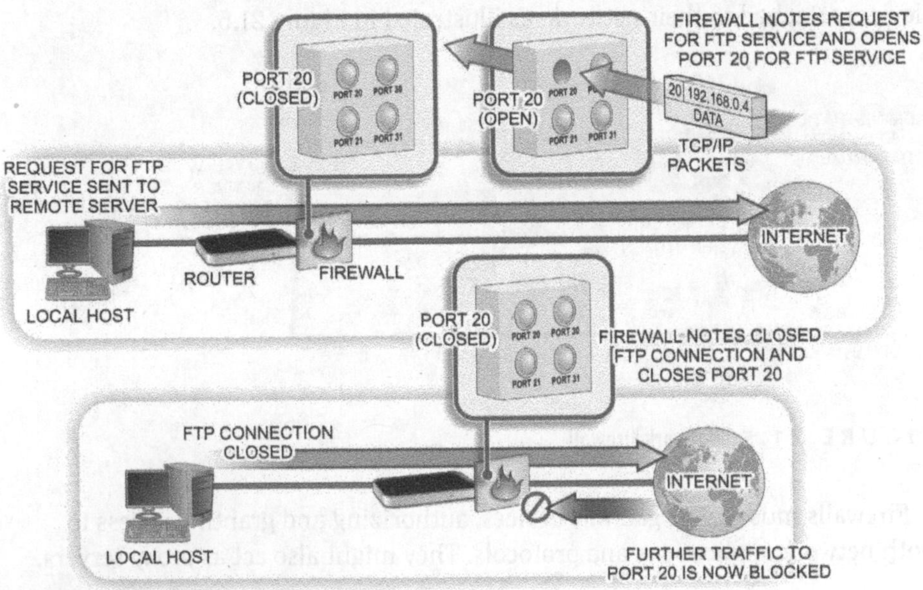

FIGURE 21.6 Stateful Firewall Operations

As described earlier, *proxy servers,* or proxy-filtering firewalls, are servers configured to filter out unwanted packets. Proxy filtering is a much more complex process than packet filtering. During this filtering process, each packet is disassembled, evaluated, and reassembled, making this type of connection significantly slower than other firewall types.

Proxy-filtering firewalls or application-level firewalls are configured to view entire packets for consistency, type of application, and appropriate ports. The data that is attempting to travel through these ports to a client must match what the proxy-filtering firewall expects, or the unknown packet will be dropped and the connection will be lost.

Newer firewalls will also provide *Quality of Service (QoS)* functionality, which allows for the prioritization and differential treatment of network traffic based on special rules or policies. A common use for QoS is to ensure that a Voice over IP (VoIP) phone system will always have enough bandwidth for phone service, regardless of how busy the network is.

Some applications are more sensitive to latency, and using Quality of Service (QoS) can make sure those applications always have enough priority to keep packets flowing to them, so that connections do not drop. QoS can also be a way to share or allocate bandwidth effectively on a busy network. Some firewalls will separate this sort of traffic management from QoS, but they are similar concepts.

Firewall Considerations

The firewall is generally the place to start when implementing or evaluating Internet security. Most administrators configure the firewall features they need and then try to make them secure. However, security really needs to be the first consideration. For instance, before configuring the firewall features, you should consider:

- What applications do outside users need to access?
- Will outside users be using a VPN or not?

You are almost always going to enable NAT and proxy server functionality on a firewall. But the design of the network and configuration of the firewall should be based on the applications to which outside users will need to connect.

If no one needs to access the network from the Internet, then the firewall configuration can be tightened up to disallow any packet that originates from the outside world. For example, if you disallow Internet Control Message Protocol (ICMP) and don't respond on any port, then the firewall is better secured.

However, at the tightest security levels, that firewall configuration might enrage network users as they typical want zero-configuration protocols, such as Universal Plug and Play (UPnP) enabled. As with other aspects of business, use of security controls is governed by the needs of the users and the business.

Before you can configure a network or a network appliance, you have to evaluate your needs as well as consider acceptable use policies and balance all of this against the available network resources. The network administrator who fails to consider all of these things will become unpopular with both management and staff quickly. A sound and organized approach to network design and security is imperative for efficient and effective management of the network. Many questions must be answered before you can create and organize a network properly:

- Resources:
  - What are the available network resources?
  - How many users will be sharing those resources?
  - If you are working with limited bandwidth, you will need to consider traffic management and QoS features.
- What are the most critical network services?
  - Configure QoS to prioritize those services.
- What is considered acceptable use to management?

It can be difficult to filter all the kinds of content that users can access. Sure, you can block access to Facebook, but what about streaming video? Netflix? Sporting events? You can spend time determining where your bandwidth was used and adding new blocking rules to keep users from accessing bandwidth intensive applications. On the other hand, you could simply set up QoS policies that fairly share bandwidth so that in periods of high demand, everyone gets their fair share of the resources. If that fair share will still support streaming, then maybe that's OK.

Often management wants to make sure users can't do anything but their work. So, the acceptable use policy is simple: only work-related activities are to be tolerated on the network. The degree to which you can block all nonwork-related access will largely be determined by the network hardware available. Hardware procurement is done according to business needs (per policy).

- Which remote access needs to be supported?
  - VPN support will depend on the network hardware.

- ▶ Do you need to run an email server behind the firewall that can also be accessed by Internet users who aren't connecting through a VPN?
- ▶ How will you segment the network to minimize risks?

Network Appliances

Increasingly, routers and switches are being integrated into smart switches, or even coupled with a traditional operating system to create smart network appliances. The degree to which each of these devices functions as a router varies, but often they offer a great deal of router functionality coupled with software that can ease the management of the network.

Generally, network appliances offer significant firewall capability, but many are specialized and focus on a single task, such as email, spam, or antivirus and malware detection. These devices can offer a strong arsenal of tools against attacks and ease the chore of managing access and network security.

Security appliances are also known as unified threat management (UTM) devices featuring gateway, antivirus, firewall, intrusion prevention and detection, and possibly more in a single product, as shown in Figure 21.7. Not only are many security features presented in a unified platform, but the solutions are streamlined and simplified to minimize the need for extensive training or security knowledge. Enterprises are increasingly relying on these appliances and expect their IT staff to manage them effectively.

FIGURE 21.7 A UTM Device

Probably one of the more complex aspects of a network appliance is choosing one. There are a number of big names in the industry—names such as Cisco, Barracuda, and Juniper—that are popular with midsize companies. However, many other companies—such as WatchGuard, Cyberroam, and Check Point—offer solutions for smaller organizations.

Beyond purchase price, it is important to evaluate a prospective device by carefully looking at the amount of training required, support for all of the features required by the network, as well as remote access and ongoing support and subscription costs.

Although UTM devices may seem like the best solution to Internet security issues, they also represent a single point of failure on the network and can potentially have vulnerabilities themselves. The device must also be able to handle all the network traffic or it will become a network bottleneck.

Selecting an appliance that is appropriate for your network needs is crucial, and you must consider many factors to ensure the product will be able to handle the demands of your networks rather than just focusing on security features.

Proxy Servers

A *proxy server* is a barrier that prevents outsiders from entering a local area network and prevents insiders from directly connecting to outside resources, as illustrated in Figure 21.8. Instead, it allows clients to make indirect network connections that are routed through it. The client connects to the proxy server, with or without any conscious authentication, and makes a request for a resource from a different server. The proxy server will handle the request by either returning the requested resource from its own cached copy or by forwarding the request to the other server (after potentially modifying the request).

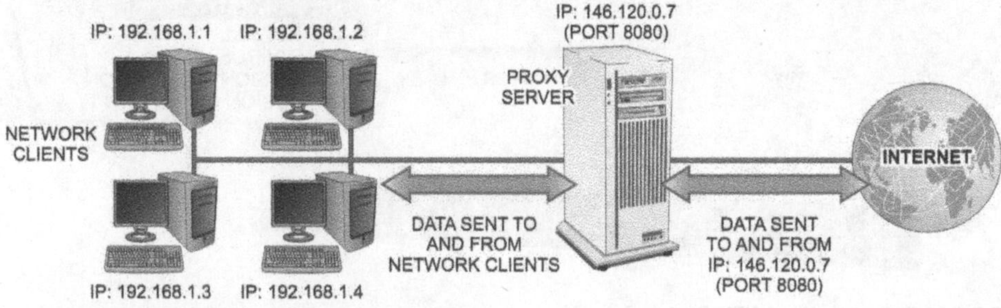

FIGURE 21.8 Operation of a Proxy Server

All addressing information sent to the Internet will use the IP address of the proxy server. Because the IP address of the client that's requesting the resource isn't used, an outside intruder has no way of accessing the local host.

When fully configured, the proxy server will supply the client with the addresses and port numbers for Internet services (HTTP, FTP, and so on) that are available to it. Client access is configured from the local web browser. Most operating systems and web browsers provide for proxy configuration.

Probably the most common use of this concept is with caching web proxies where a local server will cache web resources and then expire them intelligently. Web proxies help conserve Internet bandwidth and speed up connections, but they can also be used to filter content or even reformat that content.

A proxy server might be an anonymous proxy that provides client anonymity by concealing their original IP address.

A *transparent proxy* makes the original IP address available but only in the HTTP headers. Typically, the user is not even aware they are using a transparent proxy. Many ISPs will transparently proxy connections so they can provide a customized "404 page" or search result filter.

A *distorting proxy* acts in a manner very similar to a transparent proxy, but it includes incorrect IP information in the HTTP headers.

Data communication through proxies is typically unencrypted and can be hacked. So, you need to be careful using nonlocal proxy services.

Malicious proxy servers have been used for various purposes including malware delivery, ad injection, and for simple information gathering. While these proxy servers may not pass on your IP address, they will know your IP address and could use this information for other purposes.

There are a great many open proxies on the Internet offering to conceal your IP address while you browse the Web in the name of privacy, etc. Before considering such a service, research them well and only use proxy servers that are known and trusted.

It is common to put a cluster of web servers behind a *reverse proxy server* that handles public requests for web resources and then forwards them to one or more of the servers, as illustrated in Figure 21.9. To the requestor, this process appears as if those web servers are being accessed directly. This arrangement can be beneficial for load balancing, effectively distributing requests for a single site among a number of servers.

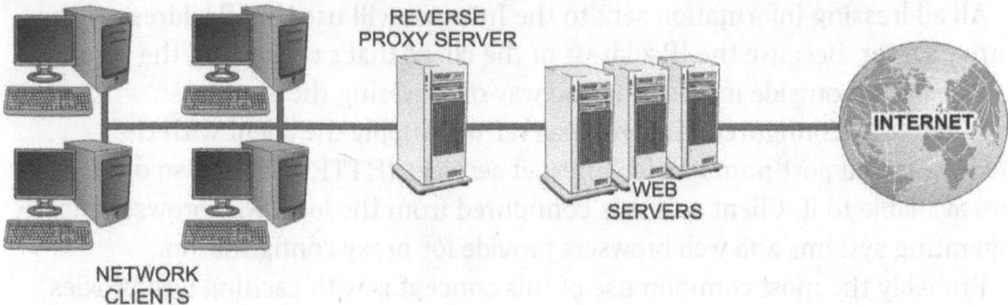

FIGURE 21.9 Reverse Proxy Operations

A reverse proxy can also be used to provide an SSL connection to allow the web server cluster to share a single secure certificate. They can also be used to cache static content, for data compression, filtering, and more. They also offer some additional security for the servers and can help with some types of attacks.

Demilitarized Zones (DMZs)

In addition to creating secure links to other trusted businesses, other organizations want to extend their business directly to their customers for Business-to-Customer (B2C) operations. This normally involves hosting web pages that advertise products and services to the general public over the Internet. While the organization wants these customers to access their site, they do not want them to be able to access their secured intranet zones. Therefore, the outward-facing web servers or computers that host the service cannot be linked directly with those zones.

Some organizations dedicate a portion of their network to a security structure called a demilitarized zone (DMZ). The DMZ is a separate perimeter network that isolates the secure intranet from the outside world, yet enables public access to outward-facing dedicated resources. Figure 21.10 shows a typical DMZ implementation.

As the figure illustrates, select servers and other resources dedicated to customer traffic are located in the DMZ. These resources are referred to as *bastion hosts*. A bastion host may be a firewall, a router, a server or a group of computers that are not protected behind another firewall, but that have direct access to the Internet.

The most common bastion hosts found in a DMZ are servers that provide public access services, such as:

- Web servers
- Mail servers

- FTP servers
- VoIP servers

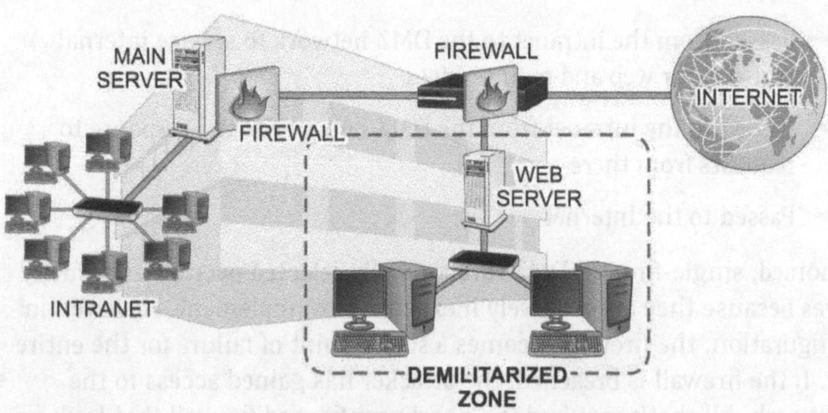

FIGURE 21.10 A DMZ

Single-Firewall DMZs

Access to the DMZ is controlled by one or more firewalls. In a single-firewall DMZ, like the one depicted in Figure 21.11, the firewall must be a multihomed device that can provide three separate network interfaces:

- One interface for the Internet (external, uncontrolled network)
- One interface for the intranet (internal, controlled network)
- One interface for the DMZ network (external, controlled network)

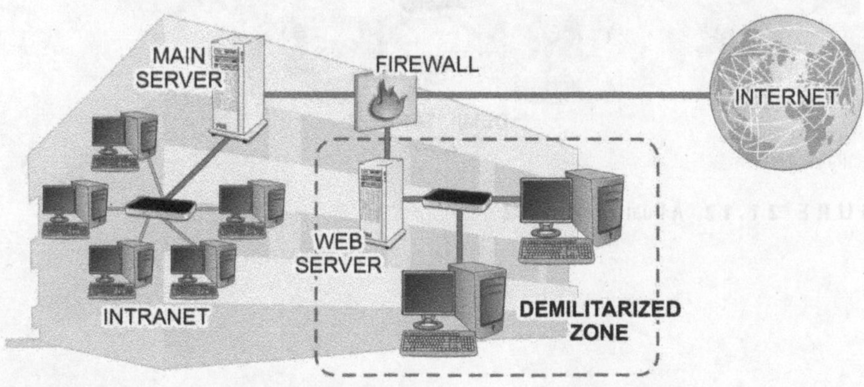

FIGURE 21.11 A Single-Firewall DMZ

In this configuration, the firewall examines all incoming traffic to determine whether it should be routed over to the DMZ or passed to the intranet. Likewise, the DMZ examines all outgoing traffic from the intranet to determine whether it should be:

- Passed from the intranet to the DMZ network to service internal requests for web and mail services
- Passed to the intranet from the DMZ network as the response to requests from there
- Passed to the Internet

Multihomed, single-firewall DMZs are typically selected over other security structures because they are relatively inexpensive to implement. However, in this configuration, the firewall becomes a single point of failure for the entire network. If the firewall is breached, the attacker has gained access to the entire network. All that's required is a poorly configured firewall that leaves a port open to attack.

Dual-Firewall DMZs

In a dual-firewall DMZ, such as the one shown in Figure 21.12, firewalls are positioned on each side of the DMZ to filter traffic moving between the intranet and the DMZ, as well as between the DMZ and the Internet. These firewalls are used to route public traffic to the DMZ and internal network traffic to the intranet.

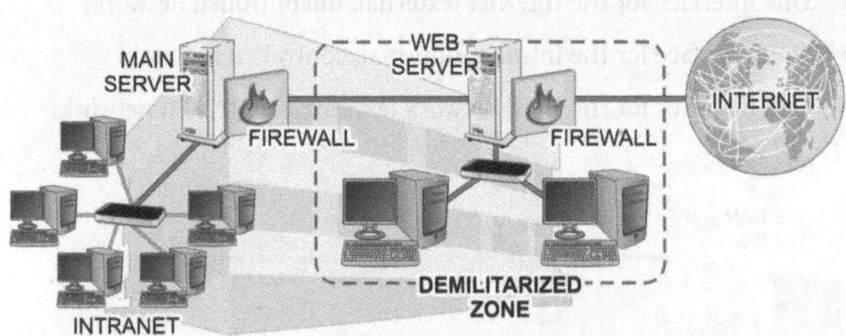

FIGURE 21.12 A Dual-Firewall DMZ

Dual-firewalled DMZ configurations offer a much higher level of security in that an attacker would have to hack multiple devices to compromise the intranet. If they are successful at compromising the first firewall, they only gain access to the public-facing resources in the DMZ.

Honeypots

Honeypots are another perimeter network-security structure used to lure attackers away from gaining access to legitimate intranet resources. A honeypot is a decoy server, network device, or network segment designed to attract attackers away from the real network. This is accomplished by providing attackers with relatively easy access to decoy systems on the network and hiding truly critical systems.

Typically, honeypot servers are designed as poorly configured production servers, making them appear to be easy high-value targets. These servers are normally placed in a DMZ to separate them from other sections of the intranet. Figure 21.13 depicts a generic honeypot implementation.

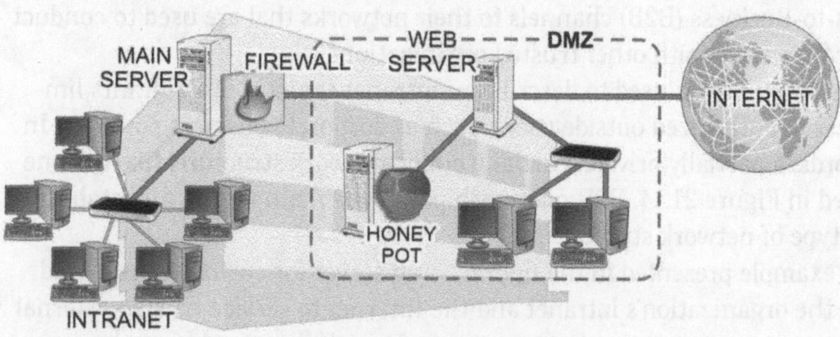

FIGURE 21.13 Honeypot Implementation

The honeypot typically includes monitoring software that is configured to initiate alerts to the network administrator when an attack occurs. They also include some type of passive IDS (intrusion-detection system) to collect forensic information. This information normally includes attacker signature data, attack methods, and legal support information that can be used to pursue legal prosecution for attempted cracking activities.

Honeypots can be valuable as training or research tools. However, given their vulnerable nature, it is critical to stay vigilant in monitoring a honeypot. Otherwise, a compromised honeypot can be turned into a hacking platform from which more attacks are made, perhaps even internally. The risk of a honeypot being used against yours and others' networks demands constant monitoring.

A security structure referred to as a *honeynet* extends the concept of the honeypot to establish a small decoy, production network to attract would-be attackers. This structure is used in some larger networks that have extremely critical resources. However, the cost of implementing and managing such a security system becomes prohibitive in medium and smaller networks.

Extranets

While an intranet is designed to provide a secure network structure for authorized members within the organization, many businesses add one or more Business-to-Business (B2B) channels to their networks that are used to conduct secure transactions with other trusted organizations.

The term *extranet* is used to describe an intranet structure that grants limited access to authorized outside users, such as corporate business partners. In other words, a partially private, partially public network structure, like the one illustrated in Figure 21.14. B2B relationships are the main reason for establishing this type of network structure.

In the example presented in the figure, a web server for customers is placed between the organization's intranet and the Internet to service trusted external users. The server must authenticate requests from these users before they can access the server's contents. A firewall is typically positioned between the web server and the intranet to block outside users from accessing the organization's internal network structures.

The extranet creates a special security zone that extends the network to the other trusted organization. This zone can also employ secure communication techniques such as VPNs or tunnels between the two organizations.

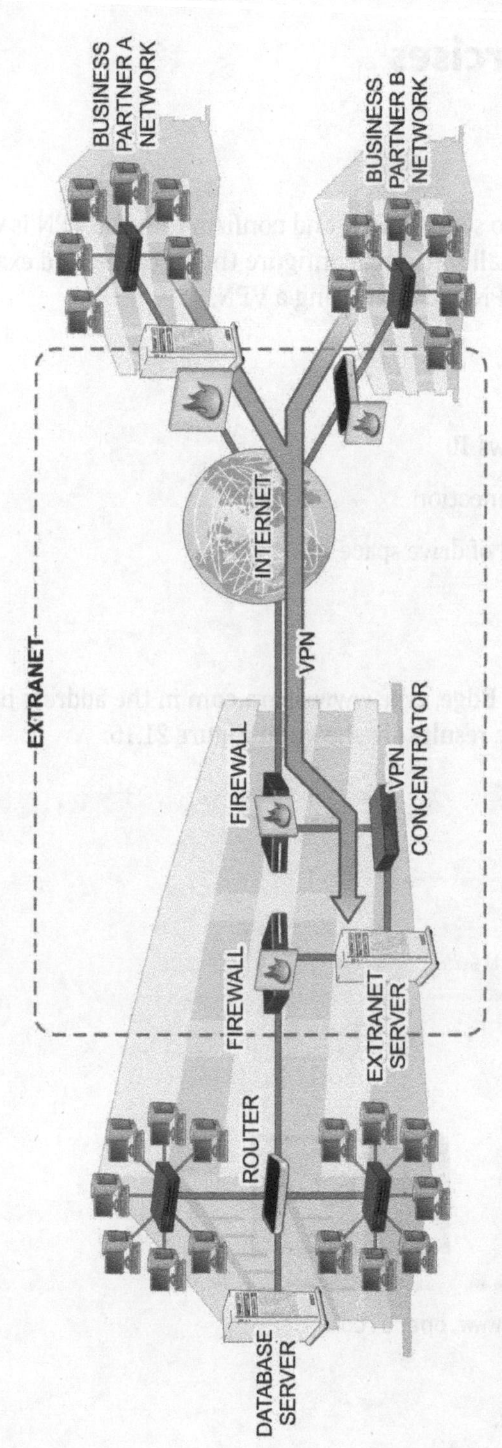

FIGURE 21.14 An Extranet

Hands-On Exercises

Objectives

The purpose of this lab is to set up a VPN and confirm that the VPN is working. You will download and install software, configure the software, and examine the difference before using a VPN and after using a VPN.

Resources

- PC with Windows 10
- An Internet connection
- At least 200 MB of drive space

Procedures

1. Open Microsoft Edge, type **www.opera.com** in the address bar, and press Enter. The results are shown in Figure 21.15.

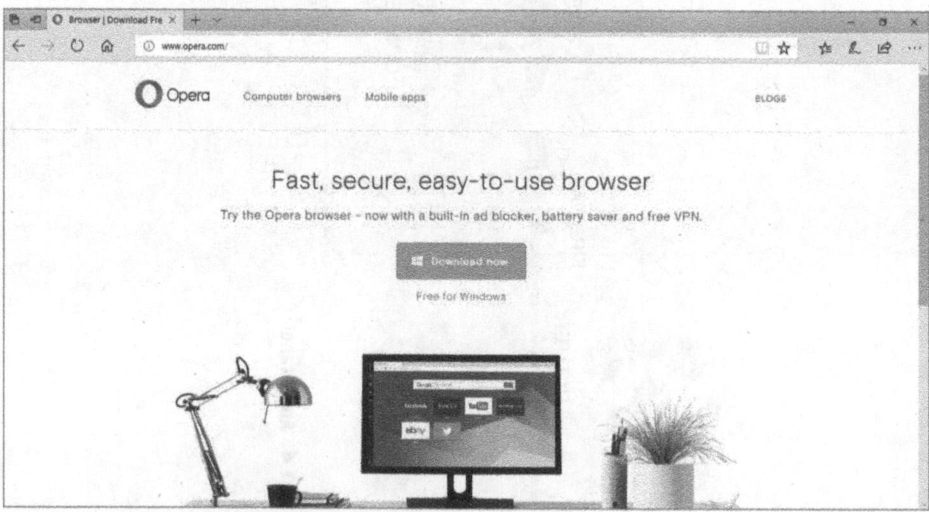

FIGURE 21.15 Viewing `www.opera.com`

2. Click Download.

3. Click Run in the dialog box.

4. Click Accept And Install when the installer appears, as shown in Figure 21.16. Allow the software to make changes if necessary.

FIGURE 21.16 Using the Installer

5. If there is a message to close Edge, as shown in Figure 21.17, click Skip Import.

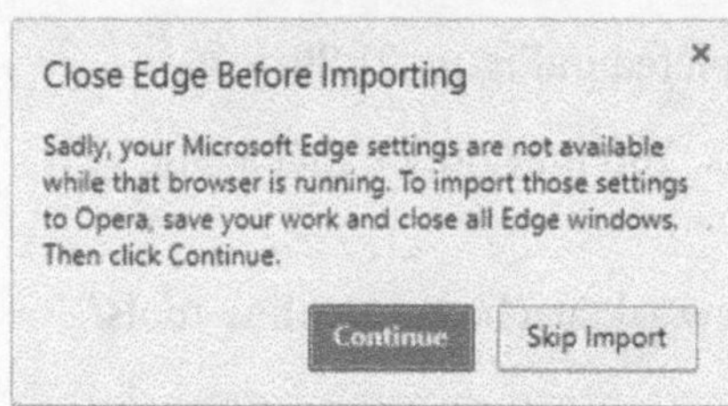

FIGURE 21.17 Skipping the Import

6. Open a new tab by pressing Ctrl+T.

7. Close the other two tabs by clicking on the X on the tabs you want to close.
8. Your Opera browser should look similar to Figure 21.18.

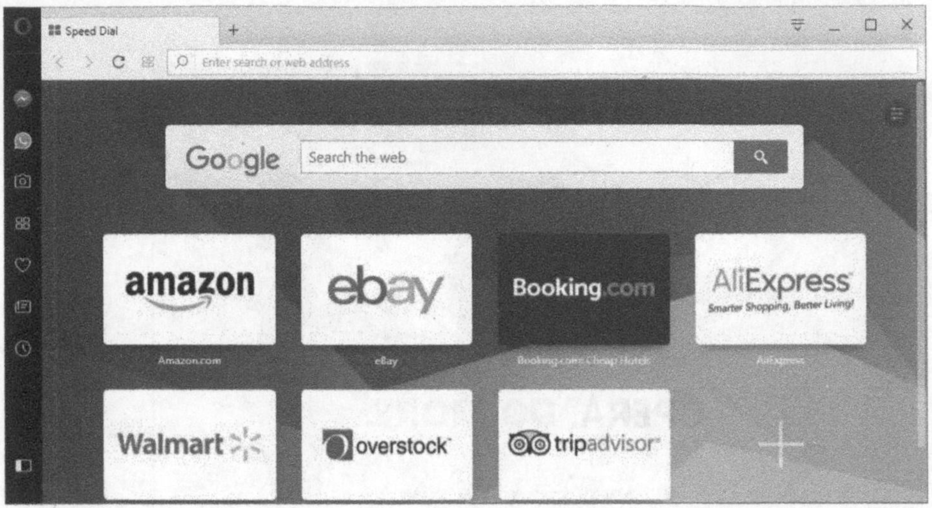

FIGURE 21.18 Opera Browser

9. Click on the Settings icon in the top-right corner. This icon looks like a set of three sliders.
10. Scroll to the bottom and select Go To Browser Settings. This should bring up a window similar to that shown in Figure 21.19.
11. Click Privacy & Security in the Settings window.
12. Scroll down to VPN section, as depicted in Figure 21.20.
13. Click on the Enable VPN check box. You may notice that a blue VPN icon has appeared in the address bar.
14. In the address bar, type **https://www.askapache.com/online-tools/whoami**.

Your Internet connection may seem slower. This is normal when using a VPN. The VPN creates more routing and encapsulation requiring more time and bandwidth to facilitate communications. If this website doesn't work, you can try using the keyword "whoami" in an Internet search engine.

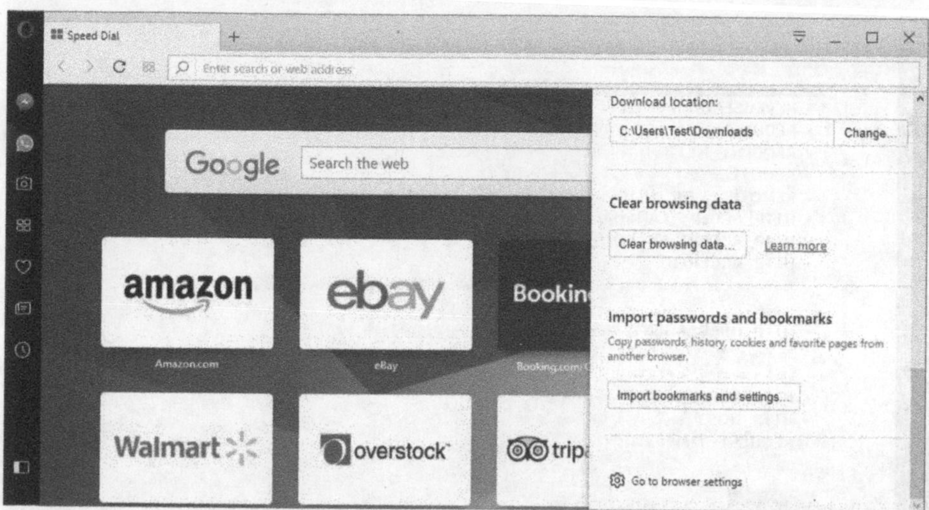

FIGURE 21.19 The Browser Settings Gear

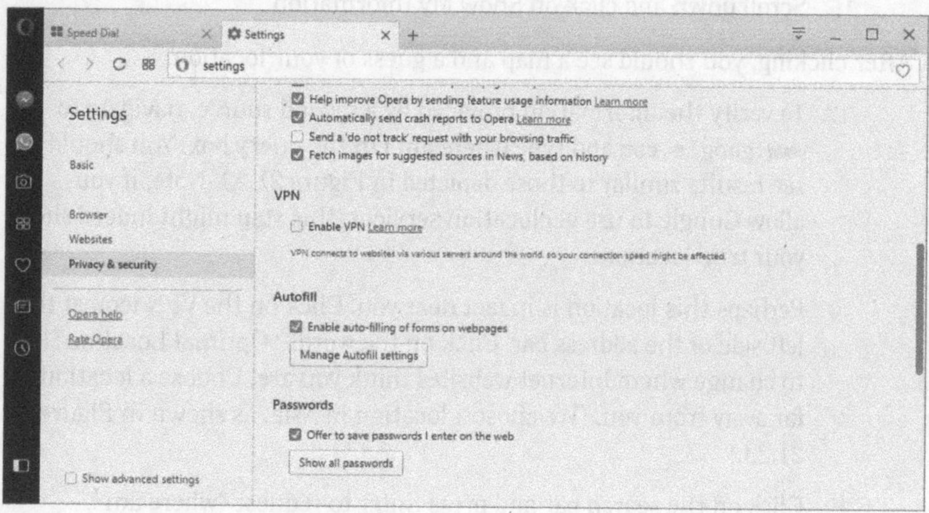

FIGURE 21.20 The VPN Settings

15. Examine the information displayed; see Figure 21.21 for an example. The REVERSE_DNS listing is the most important information.

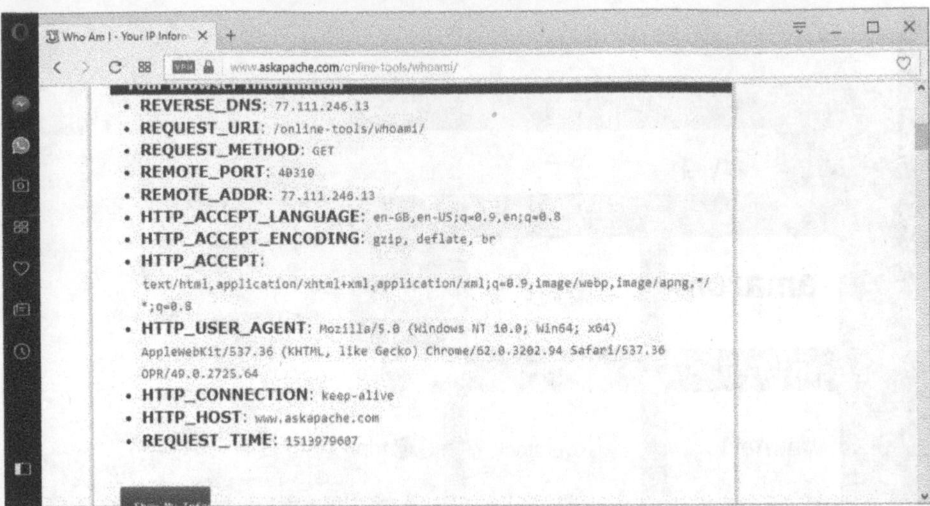

FIGURE 21.21 The Results of Apache "Whoami"

16. Scroll down and click on Show My Information.

After clicking, you should see a map and a guess of your location.

17. To verify the information provided by a second source, navigate to `www.google.com` and type where am i in the query box. You should see results similar to those depicted in Figure 21.22. Note, if you allow Google to use geolocation services, this step might indeed show your true location.
18. Perhaps this location is in fact near you. Click on the VPN icon at the left side of the address bar. Click on the words "Optimal Location" to change where Internet websites think you are. Choose a location far away from you. (We chose a location in Asia, as shown in Figure 21.23.)
19. Click on the search bar and press Enter to request "where am i."

Where are you now? Your reported location should be different, although it could be nearby.

20. Close your browser.

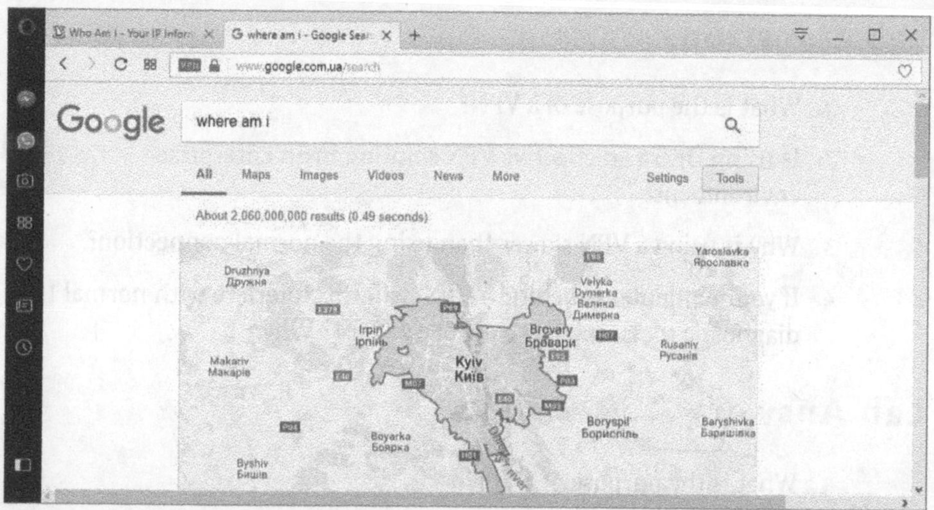

FIGURE 21.22 The Results of "Where Am I"

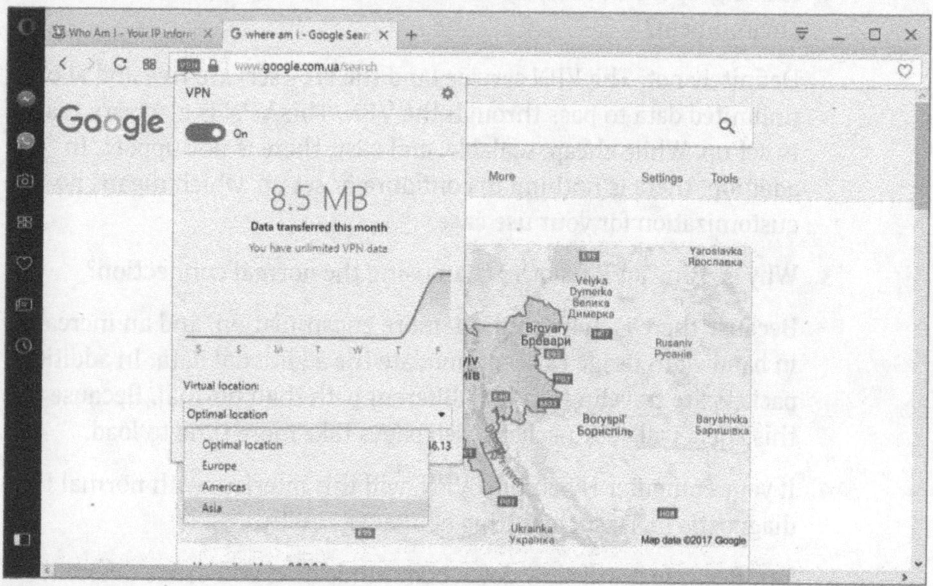

FIGURE 21.23 Choosing Location in Asia

Lab Questions

1. What is the purpose of a VPN?
2. Is using Opera an effective VPN solution in an enterprise environment?
3. Why is using a VPN slower than using the normal connection?
4. If your computer is behind a VPN, will this interfere with normal IP diagnostic tools, such as `ping` or `TRACERT`? Why?

Lab Answers

1. What is the purpose of a VPN?

   The purpose of a VPN is to provide secure communication with another server over a nonsecured network.

2. Is using Opera an effective VPN solution in an enterprise environment?

   Definitely not. The VPN service (and the browser) are free and allow unlimited data to pass through the VPN. This VPN is also very easy to set up. While cheap, scalable, and easy, there is no support. In addition, there is nothing to configure or set up, which means no customization for your use case.

3. Why is using a VPN slower than using the normal connection?

   Because there is more routing, more encapsulation, and an increase in bandwidth usage to accommodate the additional data. In addition, packets are traveling a much different path than normal. Because this affects all your packets, web pages take more time to load.

4. If your computer is behind a VPN, will this interfere with normal IP diagnostic tools, such as `ping` or `TRACERT`? Why?

   Yes. Because it will slow down communication and cause different routing than normal based on the identified different connectivity node location.

CHAPTER 22

Protecting Data Moving Through the Internet

As previously discussed, most users and organizations want to use the Internet to interact with different types of people. These interactions can involve activities such as exchanging information through email, social media, FTP transmissions, and other transport mechanisms. They can also involve activities that include sending sensitive personal information, conducting financial activities, or transferring medical information that typically calls for heightened security measures. In this chapter, you will learn to:

- **Describe typical Internet access control strategies, including authentication methods and protocols**
- **Define basic cryptography implementations used to secure data in motion, including encryption, digital signatures, certificate management, PKI, public versus private keys, hashing, and key management**
- **Describe the two major components involved in creating a virtual private network (VPN)**

Securing Data in Motion

Because the Internet is public and based on TCP/IP, strangers and bad people can potentially examine these interactions. So, transmission-specific security features must be added to these messages to protect the data while it is in motion between the secure environment of the sender and the secure environment of the intended receiver.

The NIST Cybersecurity Framework standards specifically call for establishing security for data in motion (as opposed to data at rest, which is stored in some device that may be more protected). The following sections of this chapter deal with devices, tools, protocols, and policies involved in securing data as it moves across the Internet.

Often, security is implemented as we initially configure services. Sometimes we really don't even think of it as security per se but rather simple configuration. It is important to be thinking about security throughout the configuration process because this is typically where many security features are enabled. To properly implement security concepts, it is important that you have a basic understanding of authentication and encryption.

Authentication

As illustrated in all of the previous chapters, security at all levels always involves some type of authentication process. Recall that authentication is simply a way to know the identity of a user through some means. You will certainly want to authenticate outside users who want to access your network, and you will generally also want to authenticate internal users as they venture out to locations unknown on the Internet.

Users can be authenticated by asking them to provide a username and password, examining their MAC address, or by their network address if they are assigned a static IP address. A combination of factors may be used, and it is becoming more common to involve other factors unrelated to the network in the authentication scheme. If unauthenticated users are allowed on the network, you will have no way of tracking their activities.

After a user is authenticated, you will generally want to determine their authorization, which essentially involves the resources that the authenticated user has permission to access, and what actions they can perform. Often, these credentials and permissions are stored in some sort of database, but sometimes authentications are stored in simple text files. The security of these files and databases are critical aspects of network security.

After a user has been authenticated and authorized, their activities need to be accounted for by means of some type of logging process. This is an often-overlooked concept related to authentication. However, logging is a key component of the security process, as security is never a purely preventative activity. Administrators must wade through logs from time to time to evaluate what events have happened, might have happened, or may yet happen in their networks, as well as to whom it happened.

Single-Factor Authentication

From the previous three chapters, you should be aware that the most well-known authentication method is certainly password authentication. It can be as simple as prompting the user for a password and nothing else. This is commonly seen when wireless users connect to an access point. The user is able to browse available access points around them and then only needs to provide a password or authentication key to connect. This is single-factor authentication and represents the lowest level of security available.

Single-factor authentication may be fine for restricting access to resources but can make it more challenging to verify the identity of the actual user. It may also be sufficient for guest access in a residential network, but this conveys a certain amount of trust in those users because they can now access the network and its Internet connection with much the same access as the owner.

You can configure restrictions, but at some point users will have access capabilities that increase your liability. When that liability is too great, you must find another way to authenticate. If passwords are a part of your security plan, you also must consider policies related to those passwords. A poor password may be enough for home networks, but every business should have strict policies relating to password quality and perhaps even password history.

Multifactor Authentication

Two-factor authentication involves asking for authentication using a second, different method. For example, one factor is something physical or in the user's possession such as:

- An RFID key
- A USB key dongle
- A card swiped

Another factor is some physical characteristic, such as:

- A fingerprint or iris scanned
- A spoken phrase, analyzing the user's voice

The different factors used can be set apart as one of the following:

- Something you know (a password or PIN)
- Something you have (a physical token or card)
- Something you are (physical characteristic like fingerprint)

Having a bank card and knowing your PIN code is an example of two-factor authentication. If authentication using some physical attribute cannot be implemented, an identifier that is not easily guessable could be used as a second factor. If both components are difficult to guess, the likelihood of a brute-force attack being successful is dramatically less than with single-factor authentication or with an email-password pair.

Additional authentication factors can be added to the login sequence to increase security by making it less and less likely that an attack will be successful. However, with more challenging login sequences, users will become dissatisfied and resort to scribbling credentials on sticky notes and desktop calendars, or just simply not using the service. This is a huge challenge for any website designer or security engineer where user satisfaction is an issue. When users are inconvenienced enough, they will find a way to bypass security.

A Word About Public Access to Credential Systems

If a credential system is easily accessed by the public, it is also a good idea to provide some sort of test to determine that the user is, in fact, human. The often seen but despised CAPTCHA prompt is one such test.

Password Management

Passwords are a huge nuisance to users. The majority of users can remember only one or two passwords, and if each login requires a unique scheme or authentication factor, they might just give up and not participate.

Administrators must balance their need for security against the user's willingness to comply with strong password requirements. There will almost always be grumbling, but this balance must be established and enforced—there will be much more grumbling if the user's account is compromised.

Password manager applications can be employed to ease user's password woes. These applications run on computers and mobile devices and will remember user authentication parameters so users don't have to remember them. While using such applications places all of the user's passwords behind one authentication scheme, that scheme is stored on a more personal device to which the user can control access.

This single-credential system can be made more secure by using a challenging password; fortunately, most users can learn a single secure password. Password managers generally suggest long and secure passwords that you can use that you couldn't possibly remember. This can be a great solution so long as the password manager always works, although not every application or gateway will work with these systems conveniently.

IP and MAC Authentication

Access control lists are commonly used by servers and routers to grant a certain amount of access. When all that's required is to ensure that access to a system is granted only to users from a particular network (or through a particular piece of hardware), IP address authentication or MAC address authentication can be effective.

However, be aware of IP *address spoofing,* where IP packets are created with a header containing a forged source IP address. Generally, this is done to conceal the source of a denial-of-service or other attack, but this can also be a way of defeating IP address authentication.

IP spoofing won't work in all authentication schemes, as often something must be sent back to the user and that information is sent to the spoofed IP and not the actual source of the connection. Only in the case where the "spoofer" is on the same broadcast network can the spoofer eavesdrop for the reply.

IP authentication should be used only in combination with other authentication methods or to allow a connection to merely have the opportunity to communicate with a protocol or device and not for any specific access privileges whenever possible. This is generally best used in a LAN environment where spoofing should be less of a concern.

As you learned in Part I, a MAC address can also be spoofed. While this address is embedded in the hardware device network controller, a computer can mask this address to impersonate a different device. This can be far more effective than IP spoofing because it happens before the IP connection is established. MAC address authentication may be used in combination with other authentication schemes but should not be used for any serious authentication alone.

Authentication Protocols

A number of protocols are used on the Internet for validating access and facilitating secure communications between clients and a server-based system. These schemes are based on the use of authentication protocols. The following section discusses a few of the more common authentication protocols in use.

Password Authentication Protocol (PAP) is a standard username and password combination scheme that operates with or without an encrypted password. With both parameters set and rarely, if ever, changed, this leaves the system subject to simple guessing, especially if the username is easily obtainable as is the case with email addresses and sequential ID usernames.

Challenge-Handshake Authentication Protocol (CHAP) creates a random string, a challenge phrase, or a secret. It then combines that with something else, such as the username or host name, and sends the combined information to the requesting system. The requestor, in turn, hashes the string and returns the result. The server then checks to see that the hashed result is correct and authenticates or denies the requestor.

With CHAP, the server might make this request periodically and use different challenge phrases to revalidate the connection. Because the secret must be known to both sides and is never sent over the connection, this method is much more secure. Every possible secret must be maintained in plaintext at each end, so this protocol does have its limitations.

Kerberos authentication gets its name from a mythological three-headed dog. Kerberos involves relying on a trusted third-party Ticket Granting Server (TGS) to authenticate client/server interaction. The exact process varies with implementation, but essentially the client exchanges cleartext information with the Authentication Server (AS), which then uses keys shared with the client to encrypt messages that include keys shared between the AS and the TGS, as illustrated in Figure 22.1.

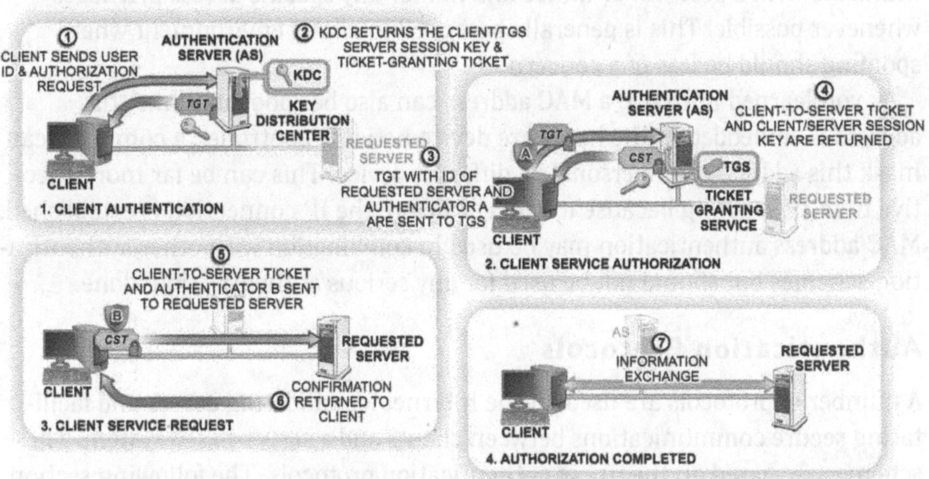

FIGURE 22.1 Kerberos Authentication

The client then validates these messages and decrypts them using the shared key and encrypts messages that include the TGS keys with keys shared between the client and the TGS. The TGS then decrypts the messages with those shared keys, which then allow the TGS access to the message from the AS, which it can decrypt using the keys shared between the TGS and the AS.

Then a similar process happens in reverse where encrypted authentication information is sent back to the client where it is partially decrypted and sent back to the AS for final authentication.

This has been oversimplified, but you can see the role the TGS or Kerberos server has in the process. Since this Kerberos server would represent a single point of failure, it is also possible to have multiple Kerberos servers. Each of these messages is time-stamped and given a strict expiration time and can be problematic on congested networks. This type of authentication also requires a lot of key management and can be a nightmare for administrators.

Remote Authentication Dial-In User Service (RADIUS) was a common protocol used in the dial-up modem days of the Internet, but it is also used as a simple method of user authentication and accounting on Wi-Fi and other modern networks. RADIUS uses the AAA protocol (Authentication, Authorization, and Accounting), which can use different link layer protocols but usually uses PPP and authenticates using PAP or CHAP, but the RADIUS server can use Kerberos or other protocols.

A Word About RADIUS

RADIUS is mentioned here for completeness. From a security perspective, the issues with RADIUS are related to the authentication schemes used.

Password-Authenticated Key Agreement (PAKE) is essentially encrypted authentication using *shared keys*. Keys can be shared by multiple servers to allow a user to visit other servers using the same authentication.

Secure Remote Password (SRP) protocol is an augmented form of PAKE that uses a large, private shared key derived from a random number. The random number is partially generated by the client and partially generated by the server, which makes the number unique to each login attempt. This prevents attackers from simply brute-force-guessing passwords, even if the server is hacked.

Some email authentication schemes use a Challenge Response Authentication Mechanism (CRAM) based upon the MD5 message-digest algorithm. MD5 uses a 128-bit hash value expressed as a 32-digit hexadecimal number. CRAM-MD5 has largely fallen into disfavor because the passwords are stored on the server in plaintext, making them vulnerable to dictionary and birthday attacks.

The Lightweight Directory Access Protocol (LDAP) is a popular protocol often used for authentication in enterprise networks. LDAP offers a single login system that can lead to access to many services. A nonstandard Secure LDAP version is available that offers LDAP over SSL.

Encryption

Encryption is nothing more than the conversion of electronic data into a form called *ciphertext*. This involves applying a secret code, called a cipher, to the data to produce a scrambled message that cannot be understood without the knowledge of the cipher that was used to create it. It won't matter how secure the password is if a third party can easily capture it electronically.

On the Internet, data passes across many systems and lines that you do not control. As such, any credentials passing through external networks in the form of cleartext may end up in the wrong hands if the bad guys are examining the data packets as they pass through specific nodes. This practice is known as *packet sniffing*, as shown in Figure 22.2. Adding encryption to the credential system is critical in any network security scheme.

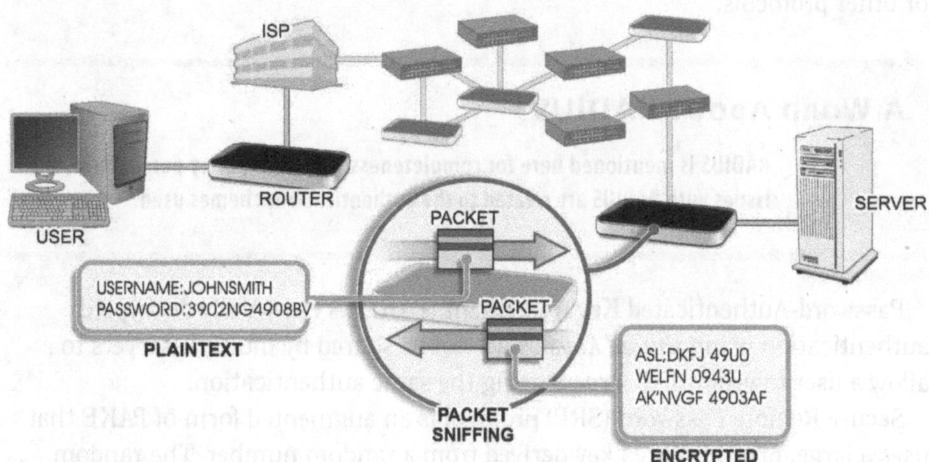

FIGURE 22.2 Viewing Credentials

Any password mechanism can employ good security techniques. If the following three conditions exist, then that system can be considered somewhat secure:

- At least some of the credentials are never stored anywhere without encryption,

- The encryption keys or secrets are not stored anywhere.
- The connection between the client and server is secure and encrypted.

That same system can be made more secure by including more factors and by adding physical factors, such as fingerprint scanning or another biometric authentication system, as described in Chapters 1 and 2. However, while the industry has been producing device solutions for years, mainstream acceptance by users takes a much longer time.

If you use a credential-based access system that does not use good security techniques, then you must understand the risk associated with that activity. If very little is at risk, then just using good password policy might provide enough security.

Cryptography

Cryptography is the term used to describe the concepts and methods for securing information. Many researchers have built their careers on a single cryptographic algorithm. Some of these methods are interesting historically and can be fascinating to read about, but we will deal with only a few of the modern areas of cryptography.

Many cryptographic techniques involved the use of keys. A *key* is merely a data string used to encrypt or decrypt information. How the key is used in this way and how large the string is does impact the strength of the encryption. Encryption keys can be based on a "secret" string that is known only to the software that encrypts and decrypts the data, or it may be randomly generated. It could also be a combination of known and random factors.

The algorithm that performs this encryption or decryption is known as a *cipher.* A cipher might be a stream cipher dealing with one character at a time or a block cipher that deals with multiple blocks of an input string at one time.

If the same key is used for both encryption and decryption, then it is a *symmetric* key. If a different key is used for encryption than decryption, then these are known as *asymmetric* keys even if the keys are based on one another. The difference is shown in Figure 22.3.

Public-key cryptography uses asymmetric keys incorporating a public key and a private key (or secret key). Public and private keys are different. A person's public key is widely shared, while their private key must be kept secret to them only. Asymmetric key cryptography when used correctly offers two services: encryption and *authentication* (proving someone is who they say they are).

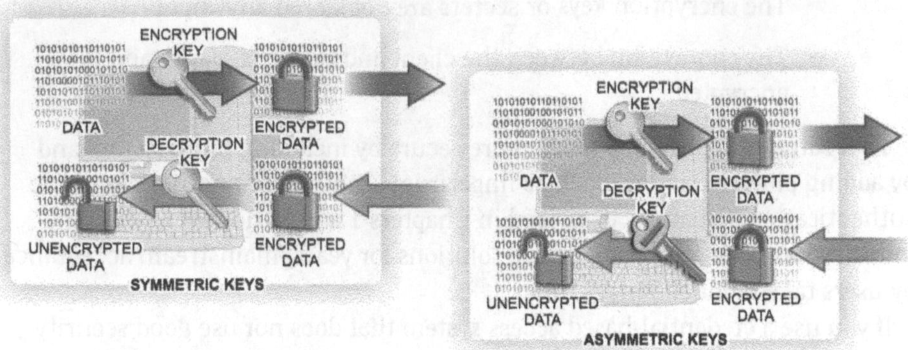

FIGURE 22.3 Symmetric vs. Asymmetric Keys

The strength of this type of cryptography obviously is related to how impossible this calculation is to *reverse engineer*. The initial authentication process typically involves processing some credential with the private key to produce a digital signature. Subsequent verification is then done by processing the public key against this signature to validate the original credential or message.

Public-key cryptography is used in a number of different encryption protocols and systems including:

- Transport Layer Security and Secure Sockets Layer (TLS and SSL)
- Secure Shell (SSH)
- PGP (Pretty Good Privacy)
- GNU Privacy Guard (GPG)
- Secure/Multipurpose Internet Mail Extensions (S/MIME)
- Digital Signature Standard (DSS)
- RSA encryption algorithm

Symmetric-key cryptography uses the same or easily transformed key for both encryption and decryption. These keys are known as a *shared secret* between the two sides of the transaction. Symmetric-key encryption is used in Advanced Encryption Standard (AES) encryption, Blowfish, RC4, 3DES, and many other schemes.

Simple stream ciphers are less secure, so most use 64-bit or better block ciphers. Some schemes will tout their strength by mentioning the block size of their encryption (such as 256-bit encryption). The original plaintext input must be padded so that it is an even multiple of the block size.

Symmetric-key ciphers are mostly vulnerable to brute-force attacks where the attacker systematically guesses the key based on a known list or a predictive mathematical scheme, so the authentication scheme should try to identify these activities and automatically employ appropriate measures to thwart them. This typically means limiting the number of authentication attempts in a period of time, which can be an inconvenience to users but a necessary feature nonetheless.

Another component of the strength of a key-based security scheme is the degree of randomness used in key generation. Randomized keys may be generated algorithmically using applications called *pseudorandom key generators*. Randomizers employ some source of entropy (or a degree of uncertainty) as a seed for randomization. The degree of entropy can be measured, generally in bits, and is sometimes mentioned in the strength analysis of an encryption scheme.

Ideally, the entropy is the same size as the key. The source of this entropy is typically a combination of data readily available to the system, possibly transformed by some multiplier or algebraic equation. For example, a randomizer might combine the milliseconds of time since some time in the past divided by the process ID padded to length.

If the time is somewhat randomly calculated (say, randomly chosen between 1,001 and 4,017 seconds ago) and the process ID would be difficult for anyone to predict, you would have an easily generated random key. Some key generation algorithms use wild math to transform keys, but at the heart of entropy is some source of pseudorandom data.

Ultimately, it is desirable to work with asymmetric keys using 256-bit block ciphers where the keys are generated by high entropy randomizers. Today you are unlikely to see this frequently. For large scale systems, processing such calculations can be processor intensive and the management of such schemes can be arduous.

Digital Certificates

Digital certificates, also known as public key certificates, are digital verifications that the sender of an encrypted message is who they claim to be. To obtain a digital certificate, you must apply to a trusted Certificate Authority (CA). The applicant must create a private key and provide a Certificate Signing Request (CSR) to the CA.

Depending on the type of certificate involved, the CA will verify your identity in some manner, which might be as simple as verifying an email account on that domain but could involve the verification of public company documents or even a personal interview.

The CA then issues an encrypted digital certificate containing a public key for the applicant, along with their digital signature and an expiration date. When the applicant receives the encrypted message, they must use the CA's public key to decrypt the digital certificate attached to the message and verify that it was issued by the CA.

Next, the applicant uses the CA's public key and identification to encrypt a reply indicating their trust of this encryption. Finally, the server uses its private key to decrypt the response in order to obtain the symmetric public key that will be used for the data exchange. This process is illustrated in Figure 22.4.

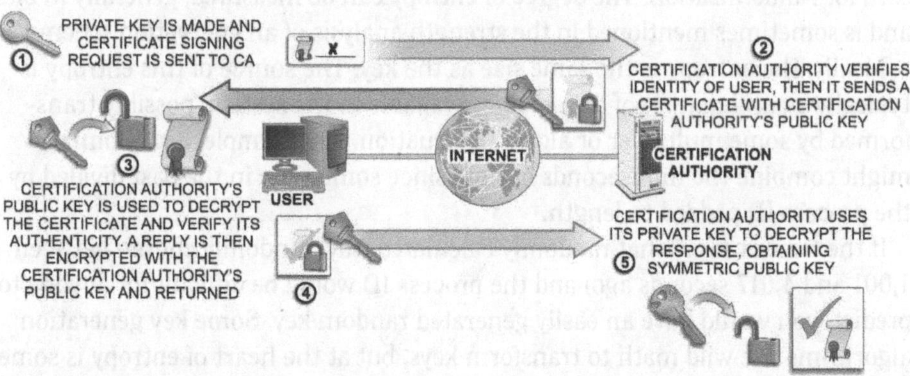

FIGURE 22.4 Digital Certificates

Public Key Infrastructure (PKI) supports the distribution of these public keys and certificates to enable trusted connections and secure data exchange based on the information from the CA signer. CAs must obtain their own certificates from a higher ranking CA. At the top of this hierarchy there must be a root certificate or self-signed certificate identifying the Root Certificate Authority.

A Word About Revoking Certificates

Security issues such as the Heartbleed OpenSSL bug have made it necessary to revoke certificates because the private keys have been compromised on affected servers.

Software such as web browsers may contain CA keys to facilitate the handling of certificates. However, they should also reference a Certificate Revocation List (CRL) or use the Online Certificate Status Protocol (OCSP) to query for revoked certificates. Increasingly, browsers are employing OCSP, but there are still those providers that simply include a CRL with each update of their browser software.

A certificate chain is the list of certificates starting with the root certificate followed by every other certificate where the issuer or signer of one certificate is the subject of the next. While a certificate can have only one issuing CA signature, different certificate chains may exist for some certificates because more than one certificate can be created using the same public key.

Secure certificates should be obtained only from known and respected CAs, or you risk having the certificates revoked. CAs are increasingly pushing Extended Validation (EV) certificates where the identity of the entity is verified much more extensively. EV certificates are no stronger or structurally different than other certificate types, but they imply a greater trust because the site being visited is owned by the certificate holder.

Web browsers typically have some visual indication that the SSL/TLS connection is using an EV certificate. This usually involves displaying information using a green color. EV certificates are typically used only on sites that accept credit cards or other private data (rather than those that handle email or other services).

It is possible to generate and use a self-signed certificate for encryption. This can be useful for testing. However, client software will inform the user that this certificate is not trusted.

Secure Sockets Layer (SSL)

Secure Sockets Layer (SSL) is a protocol for managing both authentication and communication between clients and servers using both a public key and a private key. SSL uses the sockets method to exchange data between client and server program. A socket is bound to a specific port number and once created will listen for a connection request. Web requests using SSL use the HTTPS protocol designation rather than HTTP.

In 2014, SSL version 3.0 was considered vulnerable due to a repeatable, man-in-the-middle attack method called Padding Oracle on Downgraded Legacy Encryption (POODLE). Therefore, SSL v3.0 is now considered obsolete.

Transport Layer Security (TLS)

Transport Layer Security (TLS) is the successor to SSL even though the two are often referred to interchangeably or even together as SSL/TLS. They are not, however, interoperable. The TLS Handshake Protocol allows the client and server to exchange keys and handle an encryption algorithm prior to any exchange of data.

Hash Tables

A *hash table* is simply a lookup table that maps keys to values using a hash function that converts the keys into hash values. Rather than sequentially searching a table of data looking for a particular value, a hash function can be performed on the lookup key, which will return the index to the hash value being searched for. This can save a tremendous amount of time searching for data.

A distributed hash table (DHT) is a similar type of function, but the mapping from keys to values is distributed among the different nodes across the network. The node that stores this map can be found by hashing that key.

Cookies

Cookies are a bit of text stored on a system after visiting a particular website. Because web protocol is largely "stateless," the saved cookie text allows some information to remain, such as a password or preference, about the website for future visit.

In many cases, users hear about privacy concerns and decide that cookies are a bad thing and simply block them in their browser. This will likely cause a number of issues with some sites, including the inability to log in to private areas or even the creation of a requirement to constantly reenter simple identity data. Most cookies aren't malicious and should be accepted.

Browsers offer the ability to block cookies from sites that the user isn't visiting. While this partially solves the tracking cookie issue, older browsers may still allow some scripting that can circumvent this privacy feature.

Often, some compelling offer on a particular site will bring up a pop-up window from a different domain (which you are now visiting) and load the cookie in that way. While blocking popups can help, educating users about the pitfalls of aggressive clicking before thinking is a more effective way to prevent these issues.

More recently, *super cookies* have emerged as another privacy nuisance. Super cookies are simply third-party cookies that are harder to remove than other types of cookies. Many of them do not use the traditional cookie storage methodology, but rather use local browser HTML5 database storage or even Adobe Flash data storage.

These Flash cookies and super cookies heighten the already bad reputation of cookies, but browser vendors have responded well and modern browsers now control these storage options. Conceptually, this is done in the same manner as traditional cookies offering a way to block cookies from third party sites.

CAPTCHAs

Everyone should be aware of the reality that almost anything available publicly can be exploited in some manner. While this exploration might come from actual humans, a larger threat comes from automated tools that can be used to carry out the exploitation. Often, the purpose of the exploitation is simply to inject unsolicited commercial advertisements into a message through a form.

However, this can also be a way to carry out brute-force password attacks where an automated device might repeatedly try different credentials to obtain access. This is frequently seen on many web forms where the site owner is merely trying to minimize spam. However, a similar concept can be used on authentication forms to thwart automated attacks.

CAPTCHA is an acronym for Completely Automated Public Turing test to tell Computers and Humans Apart. These are generally a form input request for a word or phrase or maybe even random characters and numbers but can also be a simple request to perform a simple test that cannot easily be automated, such as identifying colors by name. Often, these CAPTCHAs feature obscured text, making it hard for automated tools to interpret them, as illustrated in Figure 22.5.

FIGURE 22.5 CAPTCHA Examples

Adding a CAPTCHA to a traditional authentication scheme can potentially eliminate any kind of automated password attack. While these tests tend to annoy users, they are generally very effective. However, they are also a barrier to some users with certain disabilities, unless alternative mechanisms are included that target those users.

Authentication is a key part of any security conversation and can be done in many different ways. Network administrators must find the proper balance of security for access for their particular network or application, and the ease of use for users. The more at risk, the more security that should be deployed. At a minimum, it is best to find multiple ways to authenticate users.

Virtual Private Networks

An important networking concept is that of the Virtual Private Network (VPN). A remote user can connect to a private network over a public network, such as the Internet, and then authenticate and perform tasks on the private network as if they were connected directly, as illustrated in Figure 22.6.

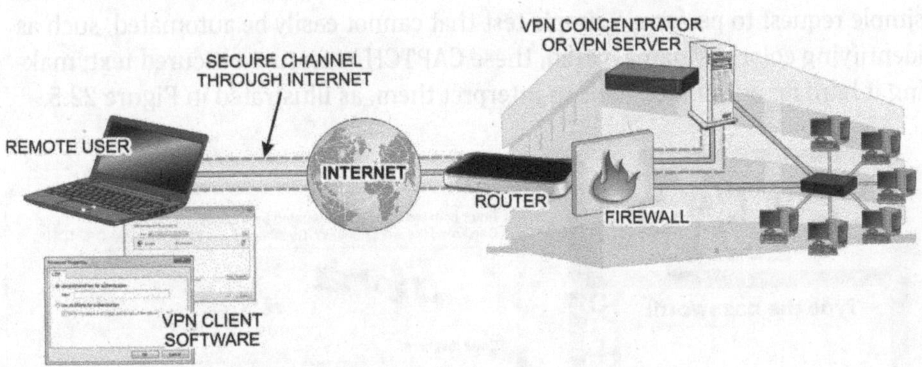

FIGURE 22.6 VPN Connections

Basically, a virtual private network consists of two components: a communication point-to-point tunnel established between the sender and the recipient and an encryption scheme for encoding the data so that it cannot be understood even if it is intercepted. For this reason, VPNs often involve the use of two different protocols: a tunneling protocol and an encryption protocol.

VPNs may be established using a variety of protocols and encryption, and can be one of the more complex things with which a network administrator has to deal. Many VPNs are simply point-to-point connections over IP or MPLS and do not support Layer 2 protocols such as Ethernet. Therefore, most networking is limited to TCP/IP, but newer VPN variants like Virtual Private LAN Service (VPLS) or Layer 2 Tunneling Protocol (L2TP) can provide Ethernet-based communication.

VPNs may be either trusted VPNs or secure VPNs. Trusted VPNs do not use cryptographic tunneling but rather trust the underlying network to handle security beyond authentication. Secure VPNs handle the encryption of the connection.

Many different types of VPNs are available, but the most widely used protocol is the Point-to-Point Tunneling Protocol (PPTP). PPTP does not provide any encryption and uses the simple password authentication taken from the Point-to-Point Protocol (PPP).

Layer 2 Tunneling Protocol (L2TP) also uses PPP and is unencrypted but can pass another encryption protocol in the tunnel. Often, the underlying protocol will be combined with L2TP as with L2TP/IPsec.

Internet Protocol Security (IPsec) is an open standard commonly used in VPNs that actually employs a suite of protocols for encrypting and authenticating IP communications. Protocols in this suite include:

- Authentication Headers (AH) provides data integrity and origin authentication to protect against *replay attacks* (attacks where a recorded transmission is replayed by an attacker to gain access).
- Encapsulating Security Payloads (ESP) offers origin authentication as well as encryption. ESP encrypts and encapsulates the entire TCP/UDP datagram within an ESP header that does not include any port information. This means that ESP won't pass through any device using port address translation.
- Security Associations (SAs) offer a number of algorithms and frameworks for authentication and key exchange.
- Internet Key Exchange (IKE) is the protocol used to set up a security association in IPsec.

Hands-On Exercises

Objectives

The purpose of this lab is to implement file hashes, compare file hashes, describe the usage and importance of file hashing, and define file integrity.

Resources

1. Customer-supplied desktop/laptop hardware system
2. Windows 10 Professional installed
3. MD5deep installed

MD5deep may be obtained from `https://sourceforge.net/projects/md5deep/files/md5deep/md5deep-4.3/md5deep-4.3.zip/download`. Download, extract, and move the MD5deep folder to your desktop.

Discussion

Hashing is a basic type of cryptography. It employs a one-way algorithm that creates a unique hash (also known as a *message digest*). The purpose of a hash is not to create a cryptographic message to be decrypted later; instead, it is used to compare a file before and after a certain set of circumstances has arisen.

Hashing does not ensure confidentiality, rather it confirms file integrity. File integrity proves the file has not been altered in any way while the file or message was in transit.

A common use of file hashing is used with downloads from the Internet. Perhaps a freeware item is available, but you are worried that a malicious user has tampered with the file on the site. The owner of the site, however, has provided a hash of the original file in case you want to compare it once downloaded. Examining the string of characters on the site, you create a hash of the downloaded file and compare. If they are exactly the same, you have confirmed file integrity.

Procedures

In this procedure, you will create and compare hashes. You will also tamper with the file to witness the differences in hashing so you'll better understand what ensuring file integrity really means.

Locating MD5deep

MD5deep is a command-line tool that supplies hashing algorithms that include MD5, Whirlpool, and Sha-1. The noticeable differences in the hashing algorithms occur in the padding and length (in bits) of the digest.

1. Power on your machine.
2. Log on to your computer using your administrative account.
3. Double-click the `md5deep-4.3` folder, located on the desktop.

To help navigate which files are which, you will change the view option to show the file extensions of each file.

4. Click the View tab near the top left of the window and place a check in the box next to File Name Extensions; this will add the extensions to each file to help you navigate which files are which, as shown in Figure 22.7.

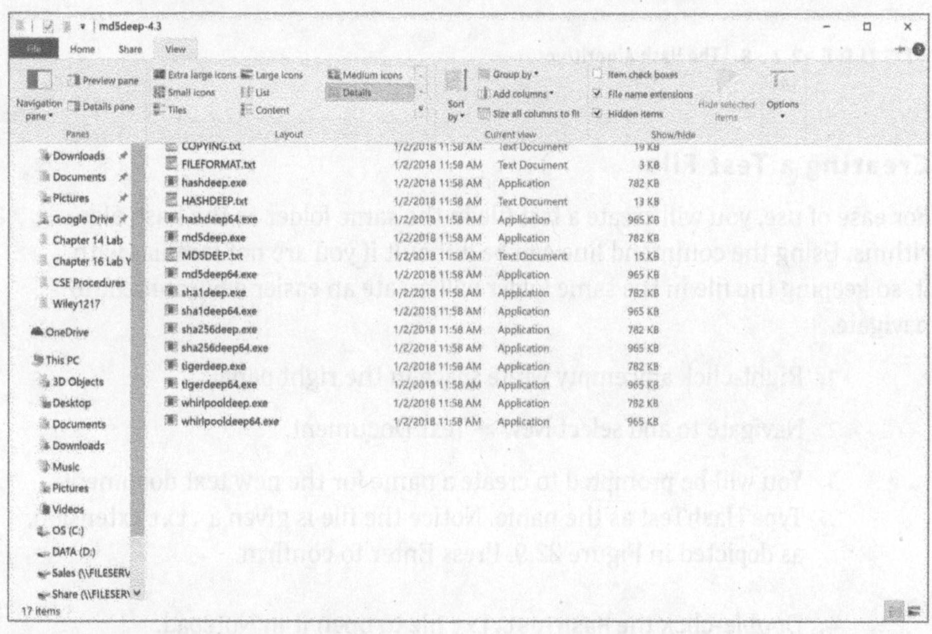

FIGURE 22.7 Show File Extensions

5. Locate `md5deep.exe`, `sha1deep.exe`, and `whirlpooldeep.exe`, as depicted in Figure 22.8. These will be the hash algorithms you will test.

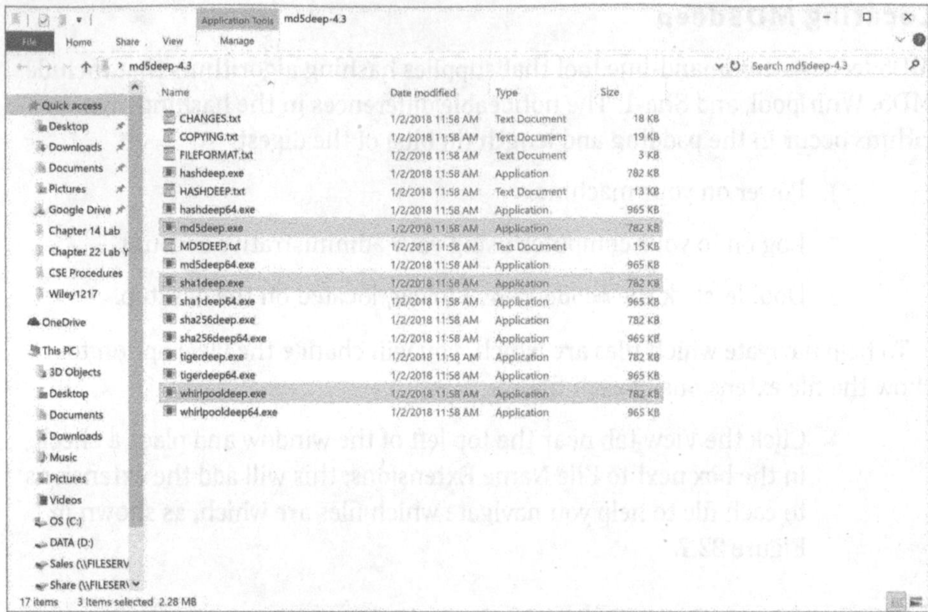

FIGURE 22.8 The Hash Algorithms

Creating a Test File

For ease of use, you will create a test file in the same folder as the hash algorithms. Using the command line can be difficult if you are not familiar with it, so keeping the file in the same folder will create an easier environment to navigate.

1. Right-click any empty white space in the right pane.
2. Navigate to and select New ➢ Text Document.
3. You will be prompted to create a name for the new text document. Type HashTest as the name. Notice the file is given a `.txt` extension, as depicted in Figure 22.9. Press Enter to confirm.
4. Double-click the `HashTest.txt` file to open it in Notepad.
5. Type This is my Hash Test!, as shown in Figure 22.10.

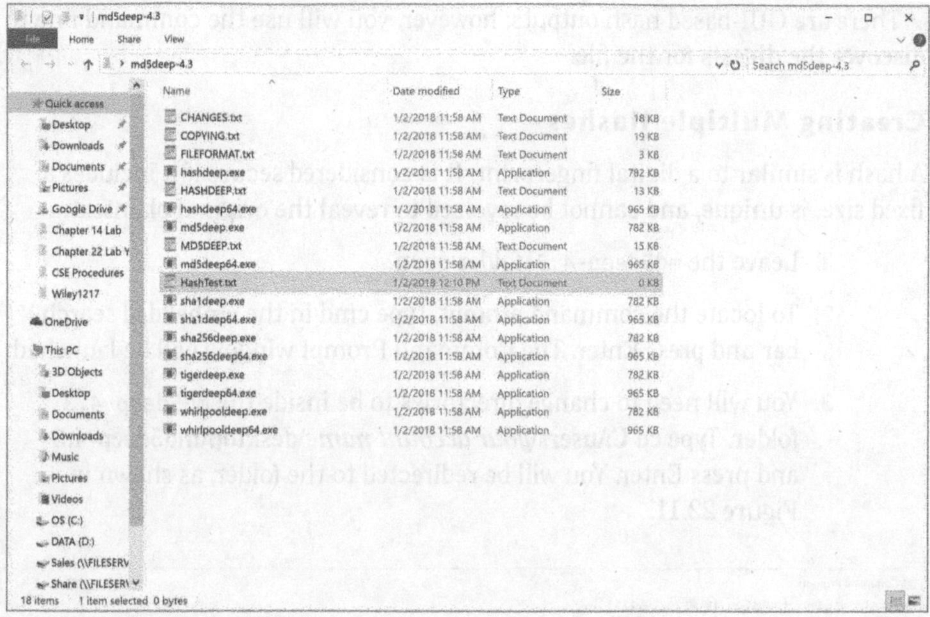

FIGURE 22.9 Creating the `HashTest.txt` File

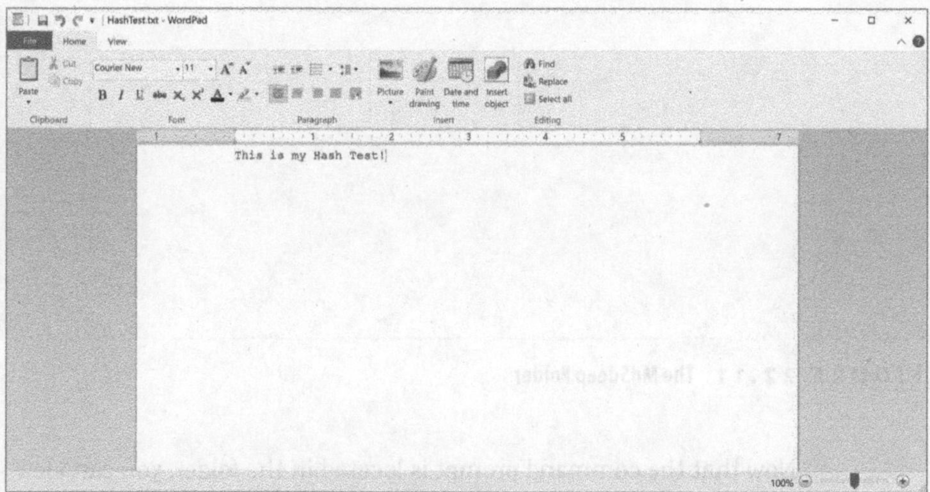

FIGURE 22.10 Contents of HashTest File

6. Click File, and then select Save to save the contents. Exit Notepad by clicking on the red X in the top-right corner of the window.

There are GUI-based hash outputs; however, you will use the command line to discover the digests for the file.

Creating Multiple Hashes

A hash is similar to a digital fingerprint. It is considered secure if it includes a fixed size, is unique, and cannot be reversed to reveal the original plaintext.

1. Leave the `md5deep-4.3` folder open.
2. To locate the command prompt, type **cmd** in the embedded search bar and press Enter. The Command Prompt window will be launched.
3. You will need to change directories to be inside the `md5deep-4.3` folder. Type **cd C:\users*your account name*\desktop\md5deep-4.3** and press Enter. You will be redirected to the folder, as shown in Figure 22.11.

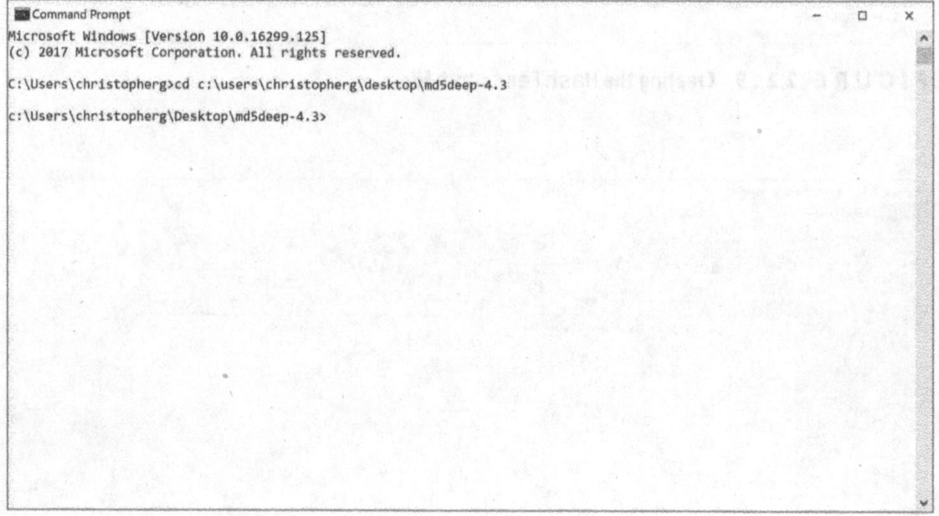

FIGURE 22.11 The Md5deep Folder

4. Now that the command prompt is located in the folder, you can view the contents by typing dir and pressing Enter. The contents of the folder will be displayed, as shown in Figure 22.12.

Here you can see the same contents as within the Windows Explorer. Locate the hash algorithms you will be using, along with the `HashTest.txt` file. Understand that to use these command-line tools you will need to type the entire filename with its associated extension.

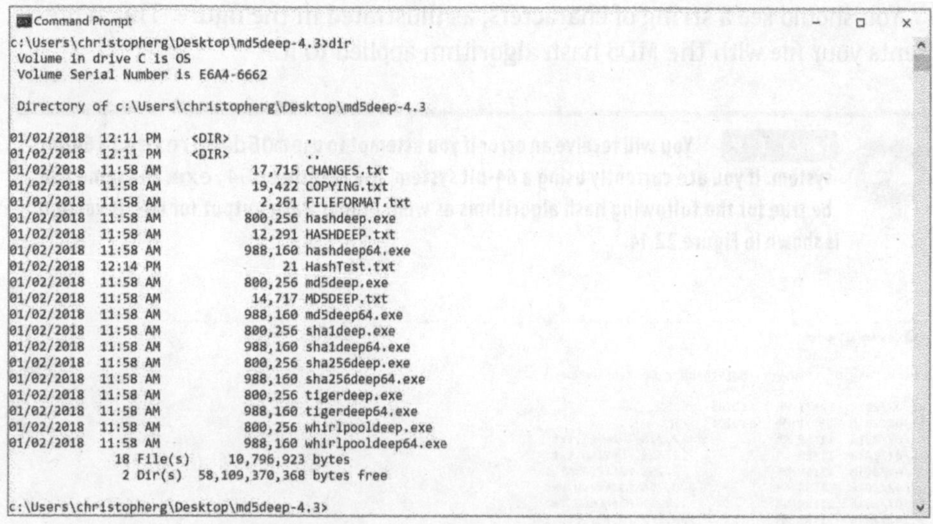

FIGURE 22.12 Md5deep Contents in the Command Prompt

5. To create your first hash, type **md5deep.exe HashTest.txt**. This tells the computer to use MD5 to create a hash of `HashTest.txt`. Press Enter to create the hash, as shown in Figure 22.13.

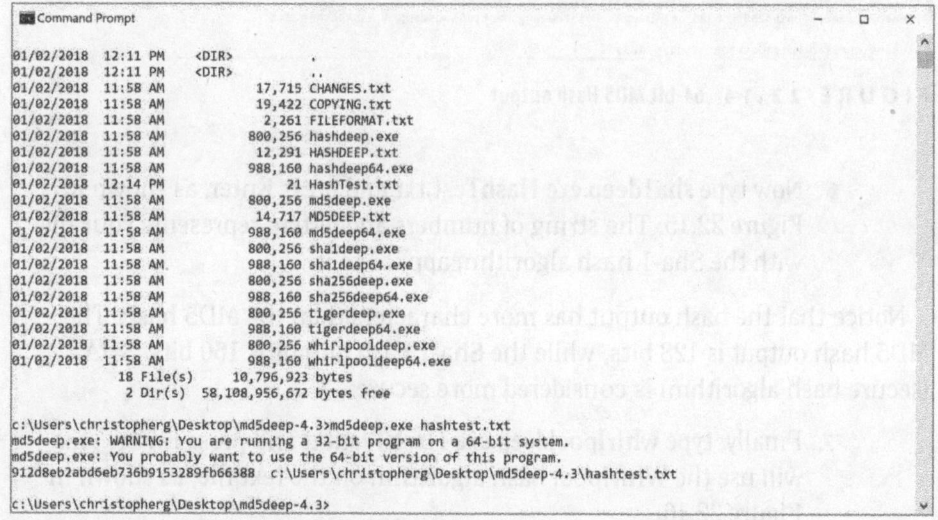

FIGURE 22.13 MD5 Hash Output

You should see a string of characters, as illustrated in the figure. This represents your file with the MD5 hash algorithm applied to it.

NOTE **You will receive an error if you attempt to use `md5deep.exe` on a 64-bit system. If you are currently using a 64-bit system, use `md5deep64.exe`. The same will be true for the following hash algorithms as well. Proper Hash output for 64-bit version is shown in Figure 22.14.**

```
Command Prompt

 Directory of c:\Users\christopherg\Desktop\md5deep-4.3

01/02/2018  12:11 PM    <DIR>          .
01/02/2018  12:11 PM    <DIR>          ..
01/02/2018  11:58 AM            17,715 CHANGES.txt
01/02/2018  11:58 AM            19,422 COPYING.txt
01/02/2018  11:58 AM             2,261 FILEFORMAT.txt
01/02/2018  11:58 AM           800,256 hashdeep.exe
01/02/2018  11:58 AM            12,291 HASHDEEP.txt
01/02/2018  11:58 AM           988,160 hashdeep64.exe
01/02/2018  12:14 PM                21 HashTest.txt
01/02/2018  11:58 AM           800,256 md5deep.exe
01/02/2018  11:58 AM            14,717 MD5DEEP.txt
01/02/2018  11:58 AM           988,160 md5deep64.exe
01/02/2018  11:58 AM           800,256 sha1deep.exe
01/02/2018  11:58 AM           988,160 sha1deep64.exe
01/02/2018  11:58 AM           800,256 sha256deep.exe
01/02/2018  11:58 AM           988,160 sha256deep64.exe
01/02/2018  11:58 AM           800,256 tigerdeep.exe
01/02/2018  11:58 AM           988,160 tigerdeep64.exe
01/02/2018  11:58 AM           800,256 whirlpooldeep.exe
01/02/2018  11:58 AM           988,160 whirlpooldeep64.exe
              18 File(s)     10,796,923 bytes
               2 Dir(s)  58,108,608,512 bytes free

c:\Users\christopherg\Desktop\md5deep-4.3>md5deep64.exe hashtest.txt
912d8eb2abd6eb736b9153289fb66388  c:\Users\christopherg\Desktop\md5deep-4.3\hashtest.txt

c:\Users\christopherg\Desktop\md5deep-4.3>
```

FIGURE 22.14 64-bit MD5 Hash output

6. Now type **sha1deep.exe HashTest.txt** and press Enter, as shown in Figure 22.15. The string of numbers and letters represents your file with the Sha-1 hash algorithm applied to it.

Notice that the hash output has more characters than the MD5 hash. The MD5 hash output is 128 bits, while the Sha-1 hash output is 160 bits. SHA (secure hash algorithm) is considered more secure.

7. Finally, type **whirlpooldeep.exe HashTest.txt** and press Enter. This will use the Whirlpool hash algorithm on the text file, as shown in Figure 22.16.

```
Command Prompt
01/02/2018  12:11 PM    <DIR>          .
01/02/2018  12:11 PM    <DIR>          ..
01/02/2018  11:58 AM            17,715 CHANGES.txt
01/02/2018  11:58 AM            19,422 COPYING.txt
01/02/2018  11:58 AM             2,261 FILEFORMAT.txt
01/02/2018  11:58 AM           800,256 hashdeep.exe
01/02/2018  11:58 AM            12,291 HASHDEEP.txt
01/02/2018  11:58 AM           988,160 hashdeep64.exe
01/02/2018  12:14 PM                21 HashTest.txt
01/02/2018  11:58 AM           800,256 md5deep.exe
01/02/2018  11:58 AM            14,717 MD5DEEP.txt
01/02/2018  11:58 AM           988,160 md5deep64.exe
01/02/2018  11:58 AM           800,256 sha1deep.exe
01/02/2018  11:58 AM           988,160 sha1deep64.exe
01/02/2018  11:58 AM           800,256 sha256deep.exe
01/02/2018  11:58 AM           988,160 sha256deep64.exe
01/02/2018  11:58 AM           800,256 tigerdeep.exe
01/02/2018  11:58 AM           988,160 tigerdeep64.exe
01/02/2018  11:58 AM           800,256 whirlpooldeep.exe
01/02/2018  11:58 AM           988,160 whirlpooldeep64.exe
              18 File(s)     10,796,923 bytes
               2 Dir(s)  58,108,608,512 bytes free

c:\Users\christopherg\Desktop\md5deep-4.3>md5deep64.exe hashtest.txt
912d8eb2abd6eb736b9153289fb66388  c:\Users\christopherg\Desktop\md5deep-4.3\hashtest.txt

c:\Users\christopherg\Desktop\md5deep-4.3>sha1deep64.exe hashtest.txt
673e9b61a16c0f0fae52b857ddf2590a73218145  c:\Users\christopherg\Desktop\md5deep-4.3\hashtest.txt

c:\Users\christopherg\Desktop\md5deep-4.3>
```

FIGURE 22.15 Sha-1 Hash Output

```
Command Prompt
01/02/2018  11:58 AM             2,261 FILEFORMAT.txt
01/02/2018  11:58 AM           800,256 hashdeep.exe
01/02/2018  11:58 AM            12,291 HASHDEEP.txt
01/02/2018  11:58 AM           988,160 hashdeep64.exe
01/02/2018  12:14 PM                21 HashTest.txt
01/02/2018  11:58 AM           800,256 md5deep.exe
01/02/2018  11:58 AM            14,717 MD5DEEP.txt
01/02/2018  11:58 AM           988,160 md5deep64.exe
01/02/2018  11:58 AM           800,256 sha1deep.exe
01/02/2018  11:58 AM           988,160 sha1deep64.exe
01/02/2018  11:58 AM           800,256 sha256deep.exe
01/02/2018  11:58 AM           988,160 sha256deep64.exe
01/02/2018  11:58 AM           800,256 tigerdeep.exe
01/02/2018  11:58 AM           988,160 tigerdeep64.exe
01/02/2018  11:58 AM           800,256 whirlpooldeep.exe
01/02/2018  11:58 AM           988,160 whirlpooldeep64.exe
              18 File(s)     10,796,923 bytes
               2 Dir(s)  58,108,608,512 bytes free

c:\Users\christopherg\Desktop\md5deep-4.3>md5deep64.exe hashtest.txt
912d8eb2abd6eb736b9153289fb66388  c:\Users\christopherg\Desktop\md5deep-4.3\hashtest.txt

c:\Users\christopherg\Desktop\md5deep-4.3>sha1deep64.exe hashtest.txt
673e9b61a16c0f0fae52b857ddf2590a73218145  c:\Users\christopherg\Desktop\md5deep-4.3\hashtest.txt

c:\Users\christopherg\Desktop\md5deep-4.3>whirlpooldeep64.exe hashtest.txt
68b5d714f3a445e3d966e84c40c1bd486743a129a4ca7edd91526ed84b4277a0d57924c6970fb05a36526693bcb2232959d8679e76b1d7926a9cf0e9
3668922a  c:\Users\christopherg\Desktop\md5deep-4.3\hashtest.txt

c:\Users\christopherg\Desktop\md5deep-4.3>
```

FIGURE 22.16 Whirlpool Hash Output

The Whirlpool hash algorithm employs an astounding 512-bit digest to the file, much larger than the previous two hashing algorithms.

Tampering with a File

The purpose of the hash is verify file integrity. Now let's tamper with the file in a minimal way so you can later attempt to discern the subtle difference.

1. Leave the Command Prompt window open and return to the Windows Explorer window with the `md5deep-4.3` folder open.
2. Double-click the `HashTest.txt` file to open it. Notepad will launch.
3. Delete the exclamation point and insert a period. The contents should now read, *This is my Hash Test.*, as shown in Figure 22.17.

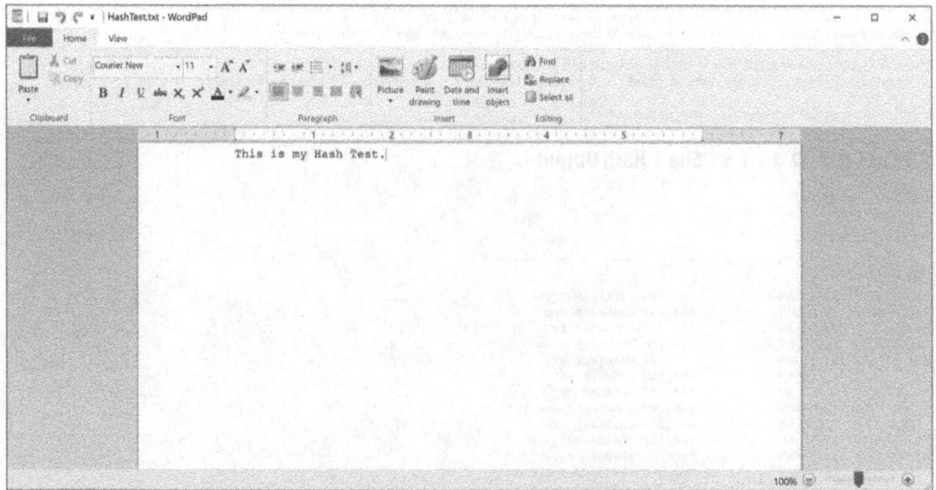

FIGURE 22.17 New Contents of HashTest File

4. Click File and select Save to save the file. Exit Notepad by clicking on the red X in the top-right corner of the window.
5. Exit the Windows Explorer window by clicking on the red X in the top-right corner of the window.

Comparing Hash Values

You might think with such a subtle change to the contents of the file that a hash output might be similar. You will now discover the importance of hash output by comparing the before and after of the file hashes.

1. Return to the command prompt. You should be able to view the three previous hashes.

2. At the prompt, type **md5deep.exe HashTest.txt**. This will create a hash of the newly tampered with HashTest file. Press Enter.

Is there a difference between your new hash and your previous hash?

____

As illustrated in Figure 22.18, comparing this hash to the first hash reveals a completely different set of characters. This verifies the file's integrity.

```
Select Command Prompt
01/02/2018  11:58 AM           988,160 hashdeep64.exe
01/02/2018  12:14 PM                21 HashTest.txt
01/02/2018  11:58 AM           800,256 md5deep.exe
01/02/2018  11:58 AM            14,717 MD5DEEP.txt
01/02/2018  11:58 AM           988,160 md5deep64.exe
01/02/2018  11:58 AM           800,256 sha1deep.exe
01/02/2018  11:58 AM           988,160 sha1deep64.exe
01/02/2018  11:58 AM           800,256 sha256deep.exe
01/02/2018  11:58 AM           988,160 sha256deep64.exe
01/02/2018  11:58 AM           800,256 tigerdeep.exe
01/02/2018  11:58 AM           988,160 tigerdeep64.exe
01/02/2018  11:58 AM           800,256 whirlpooldeep.exe
01/02/2018  11:58 AM           988,160 whirlpooldeep64.exe
              18 File(s)     10,796,923 bytes
               2 Dir(s)  58,108,608,512 bytes free

c:\Users\christopherg\Desktop\md5deep-4.3>md5deep64.exe hashtest.txt
912d8eb2abd6eb736b9153289fb66388  c:\Users\christopherg\Desktop\md5deep-4.3\hashtest.txt

c:\Users\christopherg\Desktop\md5deep-4.3>sha1deep64.exe hashtest.txt
673e9b61a16c0f0fae52b857ddf2590a73218145  c:\Users\christopherg\Desktop\md5deep-4.3\hashtest.txt

c:\Users\christopherg\Desktop\md5deep-4.3>whirlpooldeep64.exe hashtest.txt
68b5d714f3a445e3d966e84c40c1bd486743a129a4ca7edd91526ed84b4277a0d57924c6970fb05a36526693bcb2232959d8679e76b1d7926a9cf0e9
3668922a  c:\Users\christopherg\Desktop\md5deep-4.3\hashtest.txt

c:\Users\christopherg\Desktop\md5deep-4.3>md5deep64.exe hashtest.txt
6d69a8765af50f2c99c3984d4bce1e6f  c:\Users\christopherg\Desktop\md5deep-4.3\hashtest.txt

c:\Users\christopherg\Desktop\md5deep-4.3>
```

FIGURE 22.18 Comparing the MD5 Hash Outputs

3. Type **sha1deep.exe HashTest.txt** and press Enter. The resulting hash will be displayed and should be different from the earlier hash, as illustrated in Figure 22.19.

When you compare your Sha-1 outputs, is there a difference?

____

4. Finally, type **whirlpooldeep.exe HashTest.txt** and press Enter. As shown in Figure 22.20, there should be a difference between the previous hash and the new hash.

Is there a difference between your hashes?

____

```
Command Prompt
01/02/2018  11:58 AM            14,717 MD5DEEP.txt
01/02/2018  11:58 AM           988,160 md5deep64.exe
01/02/2018  11:58 AM           800,256 sha1deep.exe
01/02/2018  11:58 AM           988,160 sha1deep64.exe
01/02/2018  11:58 AM           800,256 sha256deep.exe
01/02/2018  11:58 AM           988,160 sha256deep64.exe
01/02/2018  11:58 AM           800,256 tigerdeep.exe
01/02/2018  11:58 AM           988,160 tigerdeep64.exe
01/02/2018  11:58 AM           800,256 whirlpooldeep.exe
01/02/2018  11:58 AM           988,160 whirlpooldeep64.exe
              18 File(s)     10,796,923 bytes
               2 Dir(s)  58,108,608,512 bytes free

c:\Users\christopherg\Desktop\md5deep-4.3>md5deep64.exe hashtest.txt
912d8eb2abd6eb736b9153289fb66388  c:\Users\christopherg\Desktop\md5deep-4.3\hashtest.txt

c:\Users\christopherg\Desktop\md5deep-4.3>sha1deep64.exe hashtest.txt
673e9b61a16c0f0fae52b857ddf2590a73218145  c:\Users\christopherg\Desktop\md5deep-4.3\hashtest.txt

c:\Users\christopherg\Desktop\md5deep-4.3>whirlpooldeep64.exe hashtest.txt
68b5d714f3a445e3d966e84c40c1bd486743a129a4ca7edd91526ed84b4277a0d57924c6970fb05a36526693bcb2232959d8679e76b1d7926a9cf0e9
3668922a  c:\Users\christopherg\Desktop\md5deep-4.3\hashtest.txt

c:\Users\christopherg\Desktop\md5deep-4.3>md5deep64.exe hashtest.txt
6d69a8765af50f2c99c3984d4bce1e6f  c:\Users\christopherg\Desktop\md5deep-4.3\hashtest.txt

c:\Users\christopherg\Desktop\md5deep-4.3>sha1deep64.exe hashtest.txt
dd4df487960579e50ea0136913336a628c08e95d  c:\Users\christopherg\Desktop\md5deep-4.3\hashtest.txt

c:\Users\christopherg\Desktop\md5deep-4.3>
```

FIGURE 22.19 Comparing the Sha-1 Hash Outputs

```
Command Prompt
01/02/2018  11:58 AM           800,256 sha256deep.exe
01/02/2018  11:58 AM           988,160 sha256deep64.exe
01/02/2018  11:58 AM           800,256 tigerdeep.exe
01/02/2018  11:58 AM           988,160 tigerdeep64.exe
01/02/2018  11:58 AM           800,256 whirlpooldeep.exe
01/02/2018  11:58 AM           988,160 whirlpooldeep64.exe
              18 File(s)     10,796,923 bytes
               2 Dir(s)  58,108,608,512 bytes free

c:\Users\christopherg\Desktop\md5deep-4.3>md5deep64.exe hashtest.txt
912d8eb2abd6eb736b9153289fb66388  c:\Users\christopherg\Desktop\md5deep-4.3\hashtest.txt

c:\Users\christopherg\Desktop\md5deep-4.3>sha1deep64.exe hashtest.txt
673e9b61a16c0f0fae52b857ddf2590a73218145  c:\Users\christopherg\Desktop\md5deep-4.3\hashtest.txt

c:\Users\christopherg\Desktop\md5deep-4.3>whirlpooldeep64.exe hashtest.txt
68b5d714f3a445e3d966e84c40c1bd486743a129a4ca7edd91526ed84b4277a0d57924c6970fb05a36526693bcb2232959d8679e76b1d7926a9cf0e9
3668922a  c:\Users\christopherg\Desktop\md5deep-4.3\hashtest.txt

c:\Users\christopherg\Desktop\md5deep-4.3>md5deep64.exe hashtest.txt
6d69a8765af50f2c99c3984d4bce1e6f  c:\Users\christopherg\Desktop\md5deep-4.3\hashtest.txt

c:\Users\christopherg\Desktop\md5deep-4.3>sha1deep64.exe hashtest.txt
dd4df487960579e50ea0136913336a628c08e95d  c:\Users\christopherg\Desktop\md5deep-4.3\hashtest.txt

c:\Users\christopherg\Desktop\md5deep-4.3>whirlpooldeep64.exe hashtest.txt
a931b1bc89f4ca97987c7d6e9b3b2faf0706bc383ed1f54452c7a36894da357053dc3e278e40f4fb0d4821814f24834e144881f3b0bd5d44128a2ae8
e2a2df86  c:\Users\christopherg\Desktop\md5deep-4.3\hashtest.txt

c:\Users\christopherg\Desktop\md5deep-4.3>
```

FIGURE 22.20 Comparing the Whirlpool Hash Outputs

5. Exit the command prompt by typing exit and pressing Enter.
6. Shut down the computer.

It is important to remember that file hashing only verifies integrity. It does not provide confidentiality, availability, authenticity, or nonrepudiation. Therefore, it is only one part in the security scheme.

Lab Questions

1. What is the purpose of a file hashing?
2. Hashing provides confidentiality. True or False?
3. Does a hash change only a little if the file is changed only a little?
4. Of the three hash algorithms used, which has the longest digest?

Lab Answers

1. The purpose of a hash is to be able to verify file integrity.
2. False.
3. No, it is completely changed even with a small change to the data in the file.
4. The Whirlpool hash.

## CHAPTER 23

Tools and Utilities

Network administrators must be armed with a wide variety of software tools to monitor, diagnose, and control the network around them. In this chapter, you will learn the basic tools of this arsenal. Certain tools are known by slightly different names in different operating systems but essentially accomplish the same tasks. In this chapter, you will learn to:

- **Apply different tools and utilities to various cybersecurity situations**
- **Identify commonly used network monitoring tools**
- **Use a software packet sniffer to examine different types of network traffic**

Using Basic Tools

There are certain basic administrative, troubleshooting-and-monitoring tools and utilities that every cybersecurity specialist should have in their toolbox. The following sections describe some prominent versions of the basic tools required. Some are tools already available through the installed operating system, while others are third-party tools for download or purchase.

IFconfig/IPconfig

The first tool you need to be familiar with is either `ifconfig` or `ipconfig`, depending on your operating system. The former is used on Unix/Linux systems, while `ipconfig` accomplishes the same function on Windows systems.

This tool is used at the command line and presents you with the local system's IP address and other basic network-configuration information. This tool is your first stop when you want to know the gateway's IP address, where the system sends DNS queries, whether the system was served its IP address by DHCP or it was assigned statically, along with other useful information.

Whois

Frequently, you will need to know some information about a domain. As shown in Figure 23.1, you can go to the website of virtually any domain registrar and use their Whois search tool to find information concerning ownership, administrative and technical responsibility, and the name of the server responsible for providing host information. `Whois` is also a command-line utility in some operating systems.

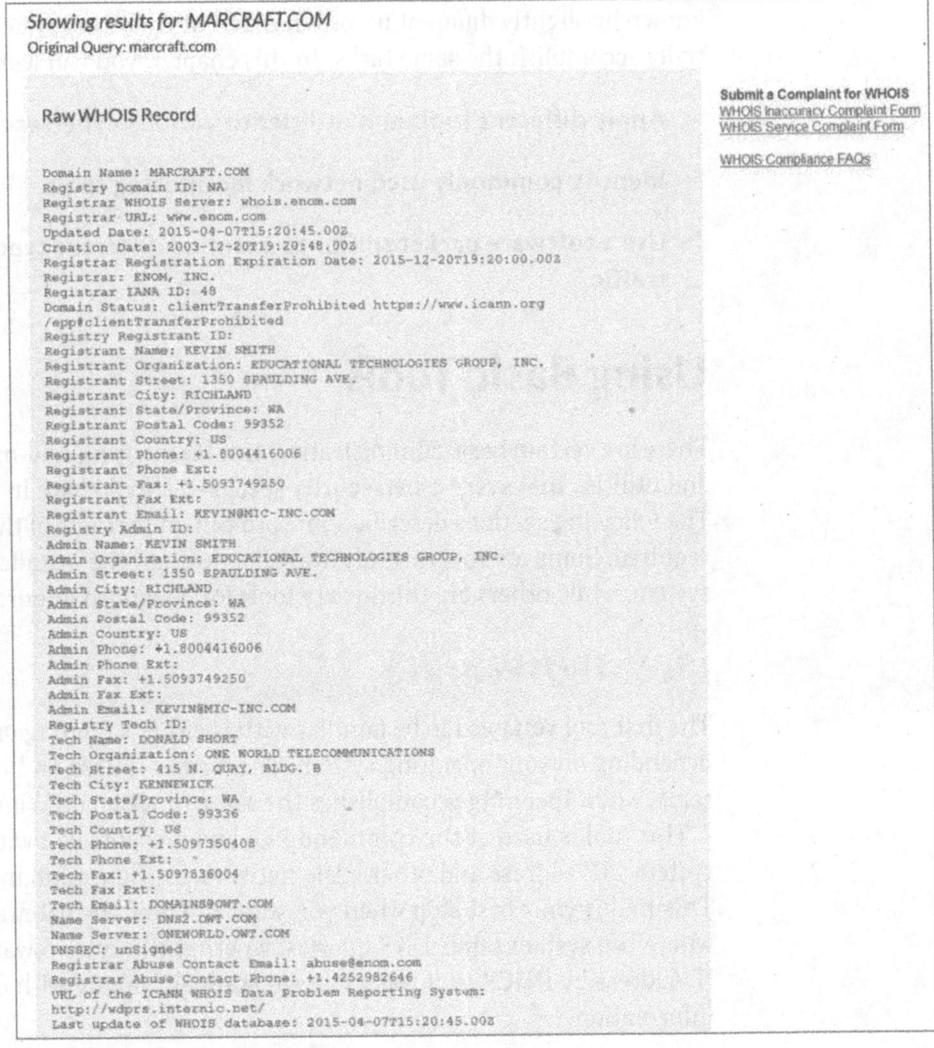

Showing results for: MARCRAFT.COM

Original Query: marcraft.com

Raw WHOIS Record

```
Domain Name: MARCRAFT.COM
Registry Domain ID: NA
Registrar WHOIS Server: whois.enom.com
Registrar URL: www.enom.com
Updated Date: 2015-04-07T15:20:45.00Z
Creation Date: 2003-12-20T19:20:48.00Z
Registrar Registration Expiration Date: 2015-12-20T19:20:00.00Z
Registrar: ENOM, INC.
Registrar IANA ID: 48
Domain Status: clientTransferProhibited https://www.icann.org
/epp#clientTransferProhibited
Registry Registrant ID:
Registrant Name: KEVIN SMITH
Registrant Organization: EDUCATIONAL TECHNOLOGIES GROUP, INC.
Registrant Street: 1350 SPAULDING AVE.
Registrant City: RICHLAND
Registrant State/Province: WA
Registrant Postal Code: 99352
Registrant Country: US
Registrant Phone: +1.8004416006
Registrant Phone Ext:
Registrant Fax: +1.5093749250
Registrant Fax Ext:
Registrant Email: KEVIN@MIC-INC.COM
Registry Admin ID:
Admin Name: KEVIN SMITH
Admin Organization: EDUCATIONAL TECHNOLOGIES GROUP, INC.
Admin Street: 1350 SPAULDING AVE.
Admin City: RICHLAND
Admin State/Province: WA
Admin Postal Code: 99352
Admin Country: US
Admin Phone: +1.8004416006
Admin Phone Ext:
Admin Fax: +1.5093749250
Admin Fax Ext:
Admin Email: KEVIN@MIC-INC.COM
Registry Tech ID:
Tech Name: DONALD SHORT
Tech Organization: ONE WORLD TELECOMMUNICATIONS
Tech Street: 415 N. QUAY, BLDG. B
Tech City: KENNEWICK
Tech State/Province: WA
Tech Postal Code: 99336
Tech Country: US
Tech Phone: +1.5097350408
Tech Phone Ext:
Tech Fax: +1.5097836004
Tech Fax Ext:
Tech Email: DOMAINS@OWT.COM
Name Server: DNS2.OWT.COM
Name Server: ONEWORLD.OWT.COM
DNSSEC: unSigned
Registrar Abuse Contact Email: abuse@enom.com
Registrar Abuse Contact Phone: +1.4252982646
URL of the ICANN WHOIS Data Problem Reporting System:
http://wdprs.internic.net/
Last update of WHOIS database: 2015-04-07T15:20:45.00Z
```

Submit a Complaint for WHOIS

WHOIS Inaccuracy Complaint Form

WHOIS Service Complaint Form

WHOIS Compliance FAQs

FIGURE 23.1 Whois Tool

These days many registrations are private, which means you can't learn anything about ownership, administrative, or technical contacts; you can only obtain information about the name server. This information is subject to ICANN rules but may not always be accurate. Still, this can be a great place to learn something about a domain.

Many websites offer this service and all Unix-like operating systems offer this command-line tool. Not all Whois tools will access information for every top-level domain, however. In some instances, you may have to go to a specific registrar to fully query a particular top-level domain.

Nslookup

The `nslookup` command is a command-line DNS query tool that is typically the first tool used to gain DNS information about a website. The basic `nslookup` command returns the IP address information associated with a specified domain name.

The basic command can be modified by adding specific parameters to obtain other types of information, such as Name servers or Mail exchanges.

Although `nslookup` is a great tool for troubleshooting DNS hostname resolution problems, it is also one of the most commonly used tools in the information-gathering process of the enumeration phase of a cyber attack.

PING

PING is software utility used to evaluate the ability to reach any other IP host. The `PING` command will measure the round-trip time for packets sent from the originating host to the target host. The PING utility will send Internet Control Message Protocol (ICMP) request packets to the target host and wait for a response measuring the trip time and any packet loss.

`PING` and `ping6` for IPv6 hosts are available as command-line tools in many operating systems, and a variety of software products will also offer this capability often packaged with `traceroute` features.

The `PING` command can be a great way to determine if a host is alive, as well as the quality of the connection between your network and a host. However, ICMP traffic is generally considered low-priority traffic; therefore, busy networks may ignore it. In addition, because it is possible to flood a network with `PING` requests (referred to as a *ping flood*), ICMP traffic is often blocked. Most firewall devices can be used to block ICMP traffic completely.

Some options available with the PING utility, such as adjusting the packet size or sending without waiting for a reply, which can be used to create a ping flood that results in a denial-of-service (DoS) attack. Such a ping flood would certainly consume incoming bandwidth. However, if the network replies to the ICMP requests, then outgoing bandwidth will be consumed as well.

Sadly, it is also possible to send malformed `PING` packets maliciously. Older systems, for example, could not handle a packet larger than 65,535 bytes, and any packet larger than that would crash the computer. Modern routers should examine these packets for size and fragmentation and enforce rules that prevent any problems from a "ping of death."

While it is typically good practice to allow ICMP traffic on public networks for a variety of reasons, it is critical that your firewall block ICMP traffic, and for most networks, you may even want to set the firewall to not even reply to these requests itself. A `PING` request should look something like the one depicted in Figure 23.2:

```
ping www.google.com
```

```
PING www.google.com (173.194.33.115): 56 data bytes

64 bytes from 173.194.33.115: icmp_seq=0 ttl=54 time=15.323 ms
64 bytes from 173.194.33.115: icmp_seq=1 ttl=54 time=13.566 ms
64 bytes from 173.194.33.115: icmp_seq=2 ttl=54 time=15.056 ms
64 bytes from 173.194.33.115: icmp_seq=3 ttl=54 time=13.076 ms
^C

--- www.google.com ping statistics ---
4 packets transmitted, 4 packets received, 0.0% packet loss
round-trip min/avg/max/stddev = 13.076/14.255/15.323/0.955 ms
```

FIGURE 23.2 PING

Traceroute

A TRACEROUTE utility will display the *route* (path) that packets will travel from one IP to another. As with `PING`, the round-trip time of the ICMP packets (also known as *latency*) is measured; however, with `traceroute` this time is measured between each successive host in the route.

Each segment of the route is known as a *hop*. `Traceroute` will send three packets and measure the time required to complete each hop. The cumulative latency at each hop is recorded, usually in milliseconds, along with the IP and host name (acquired through a reverse lookup) of each node.

This can be a great way to look at latency issues between hosts and evaluate the connection to determine where excessive latency exists or a route fails.

`Traceroute` is available in most operating system command-line interfaces. Windows uses the TRACERT utility. Some utilities, such as `tcptraceroute`, may use TCP packets.

A Word About TCP Packets

The PathPing utility is found on many Windows systems that combines `ping` and `traceroute`. Using TCP packets may be useful when a router along the route is blocking ICMP traffic.

A typical `traceroute` operation should look something like the one shown in Figure 23.3.

```
traceroute www.google.com
traceroute to www.google.com (216.58.216.132), 30 hops max, 40 byte packet

1    out-66-119-213-1.out.com (66.119.213.1) 0.232 ms 0.216 ms 0.234 ms
2    64.146.233.193 (64.146.233.193) 0.757 ms 0.746 ms 0.735 ms
3    core00.noa-ben.kenn.bentonbb.org (64.146.233.213) 0.724 ms 0.763 ms 0.746 ms
4    64.146.233.105 (64.146.233.105) 1.330 ms 1.323 ms 1.306 ms
5    bentonpud-gw.ge-1-2-0.89.col-cor1.noanet.net (66.119.207.241) 5.300 ms 5.296 ms 5.269 ms
6    xe-0-1-0.3002.sea-bdr0.noanet.net (64.184.178.101) 10.040 ms 9.959 ms 9.054 ms
7    google.xe-0-0-1.sea-bdr0.noanet.net (64.184.133.70) 8.631 ms 8.619 ms 8.607 ms
8    66.249.94.212 (66.249.94.212) 8.585 ms 8.560 ms 8.555 ms
9    216.239.51.159 (216.239.51.159) 8.546 ms 8.571 ms 8.560 ms
10   sea15s01-in-f4.1e100.net (216.58.216.132) 9.623 ms 8.997 ms 10.634 ms
```

FIGURE 23.3 Traceroute Operation

Telnet

Telnet is an application client-server protocol that can use Telnet client software to establish a connection between a computer (or device) and any remote Telnet server listening on port 23, typically. This is very much a text-based command-line interface that allows the remote user to perform operations as if they had logged into the server locally, as shown in Figure 23.4.

```
Please Enter IP/Domain..........:www.tiptop.com

Please Enter Port..........23 :23

Red Hat Linux release 7.1
Kernal 2.2.16-22enterprise on i686
login: abhorr
Password:
Last login: Sat Jan 25 08:19:42 from 210.56.9.252
You have mail.
[abhorr@shotelx abhorr1$ ls
1.zip
report.txt
[abhorr@shotelx abhorr1$ _
```

FIGURE 23.4 Telnet Operation

Many types of Telnet emulations are available via custom client software, but most have no encryption available; therefore, there is no guarantee that your communication will not be intercepted while in transit. Some older network devices may only support Telnet, but whenever possible you should use SSH instead.

Secure Shell

Secure Shell (SSH) is an encrypted network protocol for secure client-server connections. Designed to replace nonsecure shell protocols—such as Telnet—SSH employs public-key cryptographic authentication. Users can authenticate with a password as with Telnet, or they can use key pairs—or both. Administrators responsible for SSH connections should be well versed in SSH key management.

File transfer is also possible using the associated SSH File Transfer Protocol (SFTP) or Secure Copy Protocol (SCP). SSH supports tunneling and port forwarding, so it can be an important tool in some network security schemes. SSH is included in all Unix-like distributions but not with Windows, although you can obtain versions for most versions of Windows.

Even if you aren't administering an SSH server, you will most likely use an SSH client at some point. Despite rumors of NSA decrypting SSH connections and some past vulnerabilities, SSH is considered to be a secure and reliable protocol that all but eliminates potential eavesdropping of your network traffic.

Monitoring Tools and Software

To truly secure a network, you must have some way of monitoring and testing it. Over time, increasingly powerful network monitoring tools and services have become available. These tools can be used to ensure that servers (or even specific services on those servers) are up and running, or they can be used to simply monitor data flow.

Typically, server- or service-monitoring products will send requests to that service (such as an HTTP request to a web server) and measure the response. If the request yields no reply or the reply is too slow, then a message may be sent to a network administrator via email, SMS, or some other alert methodology. It is important to have at least one monitor that is independent of the network being monitored to ensure that an alert will be generated when the network is down.

Much of this monitoring requires nothing more than sifting through logs to find errors or other issues, which can be a more-than-daunting task for network administrators. Software tools that summarize or even graph this log data can be tremendous productivity aids.

Network monitoring tools can be divided into two main types:

- Uptime and performance monitoring utilities
- Packet analyzers

Just about any protocol can be monitored for uptime and performance, and the period that it is tested can be adjusted to match the importance of that service. From a single network location, you can monitor all local services and even remote services such as a distant web server or mail server.

A *packet analyzer* is typically inserted into the network so that network traffic flows through it allowing packets to be captured in real time, as shown in Figure 23.5. As the network traffic passes through the analyzer, it "sniffs" the packets looking for malicious activity or it just logs what's going on.

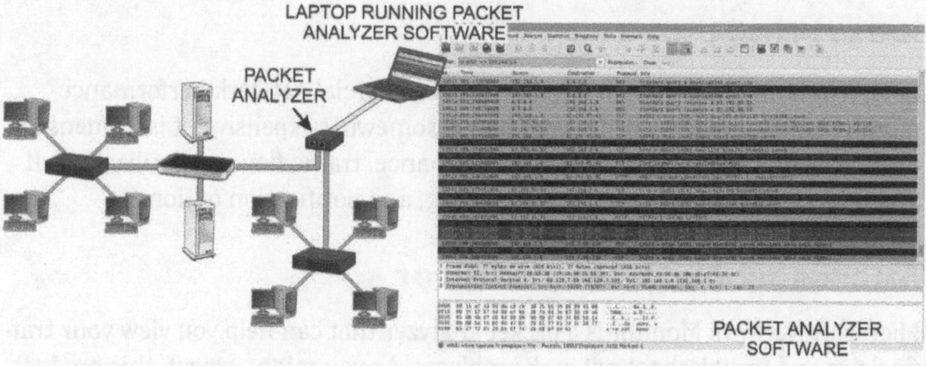

FIGURE 23.5 A Packet Analyzer Tool

Normally, only network traffic intended for a specific system is viewable on that system; therefore, to be able to view all traffic, the analyzing system is set to "promiscuous" mode in order to view traffic flowing on the attached network.

Packet and protocol analyzers require two network interfaces so they can examine the network activity as it flows through them.

Because they do not require tremendous CPU resources, an older laptop that can support two Ethernet interfaces can be ideal. Performance monitoring products can run on older hardware as well, and they can be a great way to use unwanted, aging computer hardware.

There are a number of free and commercial products, as well as a growing service industry, ready to provide these monitoring services. Free products are a great place to start because they are fairly easy to set up and don't require a lot of resources.

The following sections discuss just a few of these products for you to consider. Using these and other network testing tools will enable you to more easily audit a network in order to understand its resources, evaluate its risks, assess its vulnerabilities, and create a plan for mitigating these risks and vulnerabilities.

Nagios

Nagios is probably the most well-known network monitoring tool that still has a free version; however, it has grown and offers a full-featured commercial enterprise version as well. A fork of this project, Icinga, is an interesting open-source alternative that is more full-featured than the free version of Nagios. Both products have plenty of monitoring, reporting, and notification options that are best suited to uptime monitoring but can monitor performance as well.

SolarWinds

SolarWinds offers an incredibly powerful commercial network-performance-monitoring product. While this product is somewhat expensive, it is immensely powerful and can monitor uptime, performance, traffic flow, and utilization. It also offers a plethora of reporting, graphing, and notification options.

Microsoft Network Monitor

Microsoft Network Monitor is a packet analyzer that can help you view your traffic flows and troubleshoot network problems. As you might expect, this product does a wonderful job interacting with proprietary Microsoft protocols, but most common public protocols are supported as well.

Wireshark

Wireshark is a mature, open-source, and cross-platform network protocol analyzer. It is probably the most well-known protocol analyzer, and it supports just about every protocol and runs on nearly any platform. For more information about Wireshark, visit `www.wireshark.org`.

Wireshark, shown in Figure 23.6, is a valuable tool for capturing and subsequently analyzing traffic to discover, as well as for troubleshooting network issues. It can be used to learn more about the protocols used on a given network. This tool is easy to employ, but it requires experience and practice to accurately analyze the results it produces. However, every network admin should have this product in their arsenal.

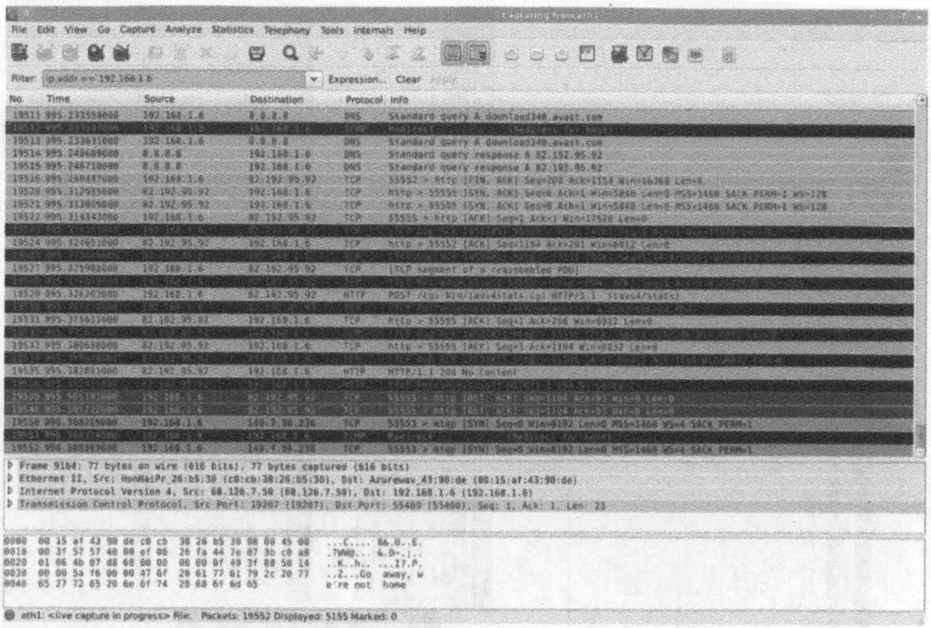

FIGURE 23.6 Wireshark

Snort

Snort is an open-source, cross-platform intrusion-detection system that provides real-time traffic analysis, packet logging, and protocol analysis as well as active detection for worms, port scans, and vulnerability exploit attempts. This, of course, is useful in monitoring the network in real time. It is well suited to identifying probes and attacks, but it can act as a network sniffer as well. Snort, shown in Figure 23.7, is an excellent product for networks that feature public services. For more information about Snort, visit `www.snort.org`.

Perhaps more than any other tool listed here, Snort has many complementary products with which it can be used to extend its detecting and reporting capabilities.

As with any intrusion-detection/prevention system, Snort is effective only if properly "tuned" to the network on which it is being used. Without due diligence in tuning an IDS/IPS, administrators will battle both too many *false negatives* (wrongly accused alerts) and too many *false positives* (missed real concerns).

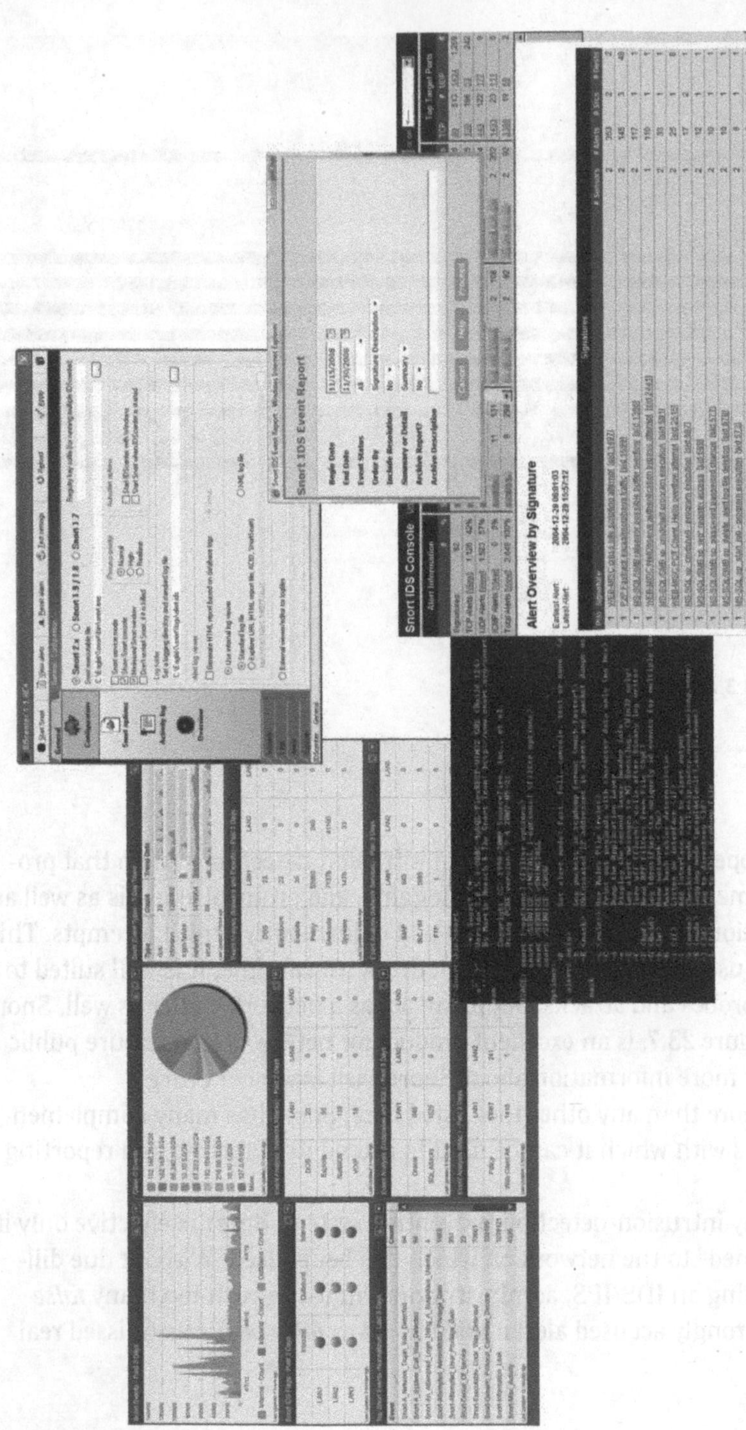

FIGURE 23.7 Snort

Nmap

Nmap, shown in Figure 23.8, is an open-source and cross-platform network-mapper utility for discovery and security-auditing performing network inventory, as well as monitoring and upgrade scheduling. This is a highly flexible tool used to examine, profile, and assess the systems in any network. It is particularly useful for discovering ports and service versions. For more information about Nmap, visit `www.nmap.org`.

As shown in Figure 23.8, Nmap can be used with both a command-line and a GUI interface.

Nikto

Nikto is an open-source web server scanner that can identify issues on a web server. For more information about Nikto, visit `cirt.net/nikto2`.

OpenVAS

OpenVAS is an open-source vulnerability scanner for Linux and Windows that is a fork of the last free version of the now-commercial Nessus. Built as a full vulnerability-management solution, this tool uses SCAP and can perform a number of network vulnerability tests (NVT); it can look for common vulnerabilities and exposures (CVE). This product has a bit of a learning curve, but it is a well-respected and powerful tool worth considering. For more information about OpenVAS, visit `openvas.org`.

Metasploit

Metasploit is one of the most popular open-source penetration-testing frameworks available. It is available for both Windows and Linux environments. It is commonly used to identify and validate network vulnerabilities, including simulating attacks that prey on human vulnerabilities, as shown in Figure 23.9. Metasploit can also be used to prioritize responses to any network vulnerabilities that are discovered. For more information about Metasploit, visit `www.metasploit.com`.

FIGURE 23.8 Nmap Utility

Metasploit is normally a command-line-based tool. However, as portrayed in Figure 23.9, there are also commercial tools that provide a GUI front end.

The Browser Exploitation Framework (BeEF)

The Browser Exploitation Framework (BeEF) is another notable open-source penetration-testing tool, but it focuses on web-borne attacks through a web browser. BeEF is available for MacOS, Windows, and Linux. For more information about BeEF, visit `www.beefproject.com`.

Other Products

Some other security products that are worth evaluating include Nessus, Core Impact, and Nexpose. There are also dedicated hardware solutions, such as Netscout from nGenius, that offer serious solutions for monitoring network services and performance. Every network should have some sort of monitoring enabled at all times, and every network administrator should have access to a dependable packet-sniffing tool as well.

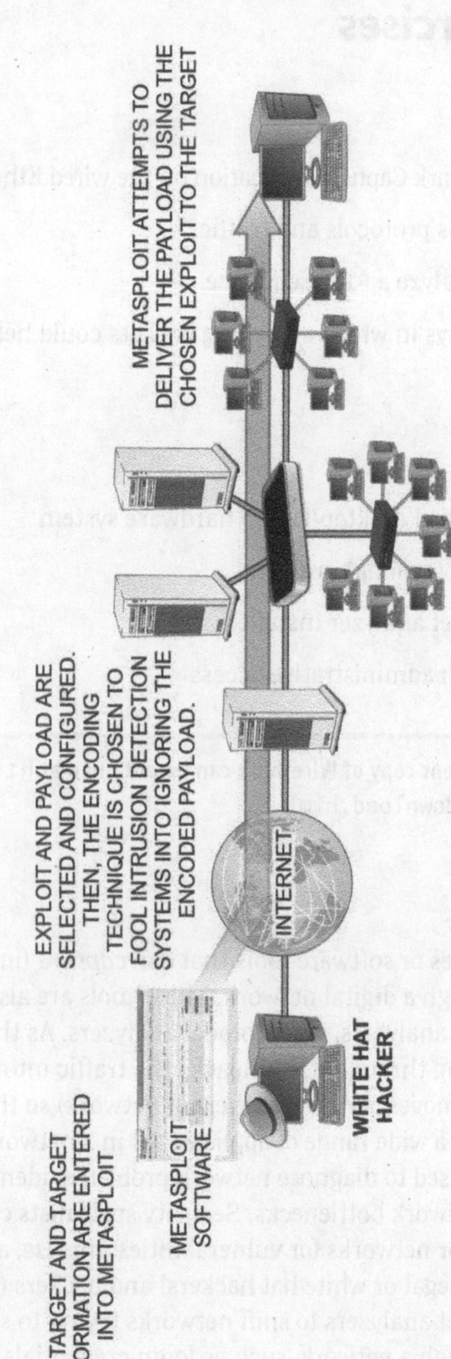

FIGURE 23.9 Metasploit Operation

Hands-On Exercises

Objectives

- Initiate a Wireshark Capture application on the wired Ethernet interface.
- Examine various protocols and traffic.
- Capture and analyze a `PING` sequence.
- Describe the ways in which analyzing packets could help detect malicious activity.

Resources

- Customer-supplied desktop/laptop hardware system
- Windows 10 Professional installed
- Wireshark packet analyzer installed
- An account with administrative access

NOTE **A current copy of Wireshark can be obtained at** `https://www.wireshark.org/download.html`.

Discussion

Packet analyzers are devices or software tools that can *capture* (intercept and log) data as it moves through a digital network. These tools are also known as packet sniffers, network analyzers, and protocol analyzers. As the analyzer examines the traffic moving through it, it unpacks the traffic into packets (such as the TCP/IP packet that moves across an Ethernet network) so that it can be analyzed. These tools have a wide range of applications in a networked environment. They are routinely used to diagnose network problems, identify configuration issues, and resolve network bottlenecks. Security specialists can also use packet analyzers to monitor networks for vulnerabilities, misuse, and attempted cyber attacks. Pentesters (legal or white hat hackers) and hackers (illegal or black hat hackers) also use packet analyzers to sniff networks trying to steal unencrypted data moving through a network, such as login credentials, financial information, or email messages. They may also use these tools to perform reconnaissance for setting up future attacks. Wireshark is a network-packet analysis tool that is commonly used to capture packets as they move across a network and display them in as great of detail as possible. Wireshark is a free and open-source program that is used for troubleshooting, analysis, debugging protocol implementations, and examining security concerns.

Procedures

In this procedure, you will explore the uses of Wireshark as it applies to cybersecurity. Analyzing traffic can give you great insight into the activity on your network. Wireshark is one of many tools you should employ to secure your network.

Launching Wireshark

You will begin by launching Wireshark and becoming familiar with the interface.

1. Power on your machine.
2. Log on using an account with administrative privileges.
3. Locate the Wireshark shortcut icon on your desktop. Right-click the icon and select Run As Administrator. Wireshark will launch, as shown in Figure 23.10.

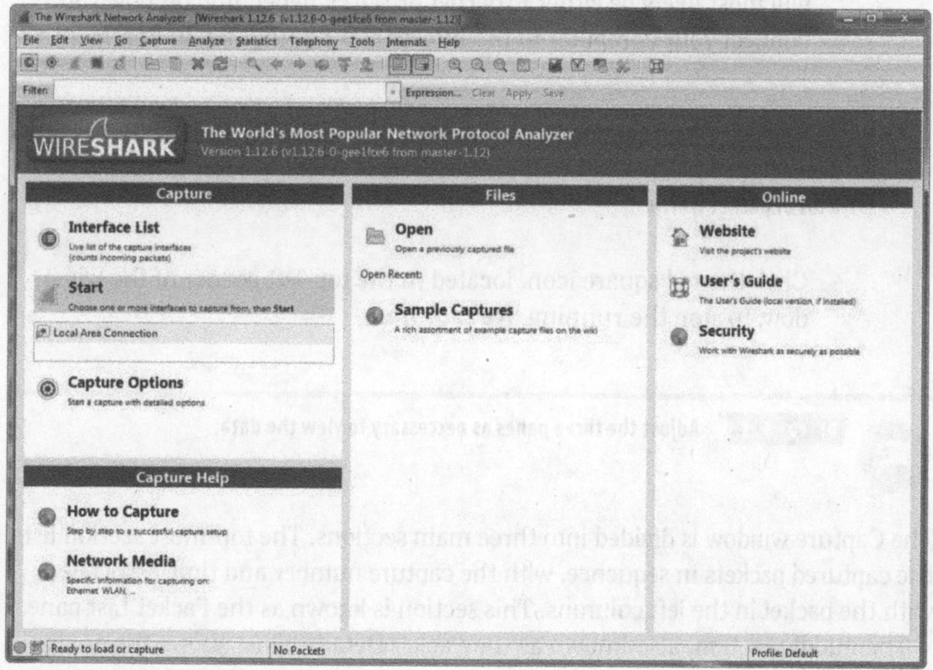

FIGURE 23.10 Wireshark Interface

NOTE **If you receive the error "The NPF driver isn't running," follow these instructions:**

1. **Click on the Start icon and select the search bar.**
2. **Type cmd and *do not* press Enter.**
3. **Right-click `cmd.exe` under Programs and select Run As Administrator.**
4. **Select Yes when prompted to elevate privilege.**
5. **At the command prompt, type net start npf and press Enter.**

You should see that The NetGroup Packet Filter Driver service started successfully. You will need to restart Wireshark.

Generally, you should not run Wireshark with an administrative account. For this scenario, however, it will be fine; but in normal environments, you should run it with a lower privileged account and escalate when prompted.

4. Explore your options by reading each heading and subheading. Many configuration options are available.
5. To begin capturing live packets, click on the network device appropriate for your particular network configuration. The device you choose will most likely be either Ethernet or Wi-Fi, depending on how you connect your computer to the Internet, as highlighted in Figure 23.11.

NOTE **Your captured data should look similar to Figure 23.12. However, depending on your network traffic and network structure, you may or may not see a lot of packet traffic.**

6. Click the red square icon, located in the top-left corner of the window, to stop the running live capture.

NOTE **Adjust the three panes as neccessary to view the data.**

The Capture window is divided into three main sections. The top-most section lists the captured packets in sequence, with the capture number and time associated with the packet in the left columns. This section is known as the Packet List pane.

The middle section, also known as the Packet Details pane, shows the analysis of the highlighted packet.

The bottom section, known as the Packet Bytes pane, provides the packet in its transmitted hexadecimal form.

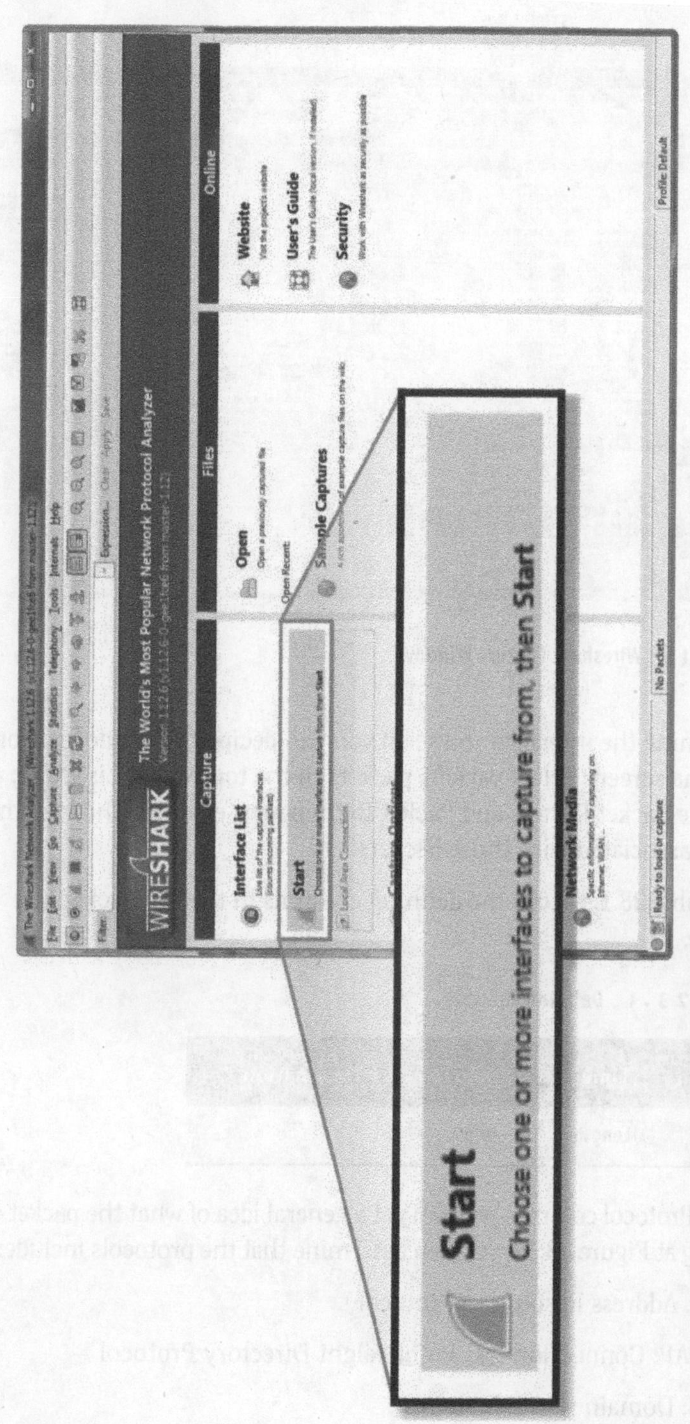

FIGURE 23.11 Starting to Capture Packet Traffic

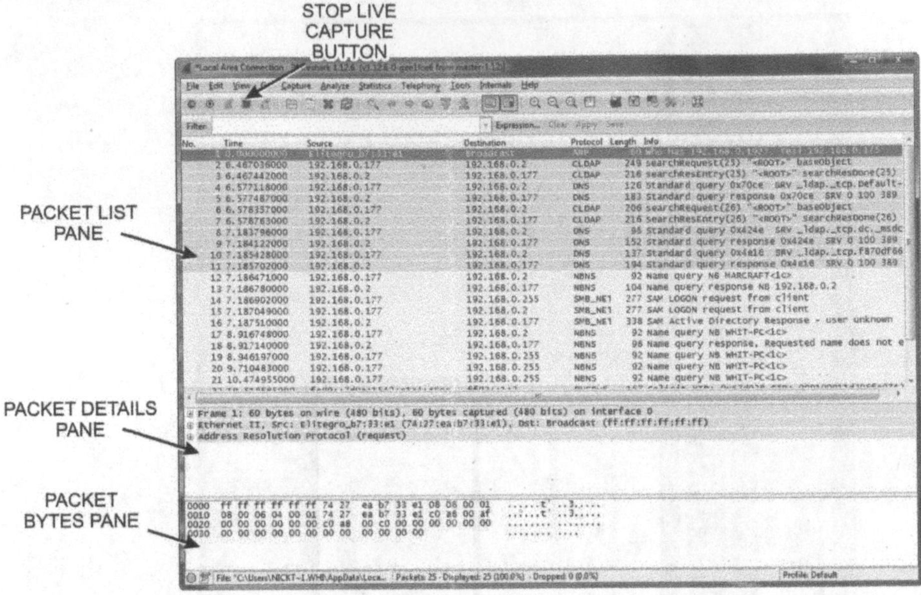

FIGURE 23.12 Wireshark Capture Window

7. Examine the interface and see if you can decipher the information on the screen. Select various packets in the top Packet List pane; and in the Packet Details and Packet Bytes panes, examine the information associated with those packets.

8. In Table 23.1, record the defining columns in the top Packet List pane.

TABLE 23.1 Defining Columns

No.	Time	Source	Destination
Protocol	**Length**	**Info**	

By locating the Protocol column, you can get a general idea of what the packet contains. By looking at Figure 23.12, you can determine that the protocols include:

- ARP: Address Resolution Protocol
- CLDAP: Connection less Lightweight Directory Protocol
- DNS: Domain Name System
- NBNS: NetBIOS Name Service

- SMB: Server Message Block9

9. In the Packet List pane, locate one IP address that is not your own and record it on the following line:

NOTE **You can locate your own IP Address by entering ipconfig into the command prompt.**

Capturing a PING

For this exercise, you will `ping` another IP address and attempt to locate its packet while running Wireshark.

1. Click on the search bar on your desktop taskbar.
2. Type **cmd** and press Enter. The command prompt will launch.
3. Using the IP address recorded earlier, type **`ping`** ***`[IP address]`***, but do not press Enter. This will produce a screen like the one shown in Figure 23.13.

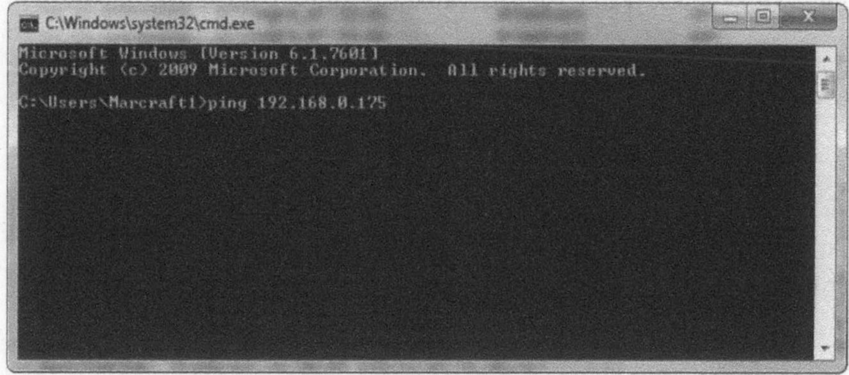

FIGURE 23.13 Sending a `PING` Request

4. Return to the Wireshark window. In the top-left corner of the window, you will notice a bright-green shark fin (Start icon). Click on it to Start a new live capture.
5. You will be prompted to save your captured packets. Select Continue Without Saving.
6. After the capture has begun, return to the command prompt and press Enter to initiate the `PING` process depicted in Figure 23.14.

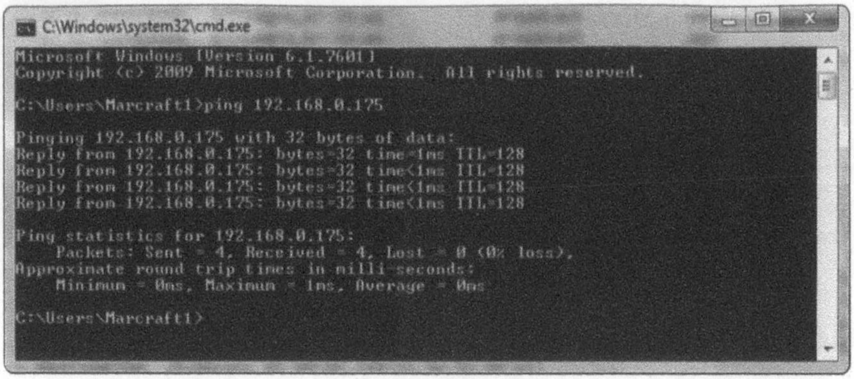
C:\Windows\system32\cmd.exe
Microsoft Windows [Version 6.1.7601]
Copyright (c) 2009 Microsoft Corporation. All rights reserved.
C:\Users\Marcraft1>ping 192.168.0.175
Pinging 192.168.0.175 with 32 bytes of data:
Reply from 192.168.0.175: bytes=32 time=1ms TTL=128
Reply from 192.168.0.175: bytes=32 time<1ms TTL=128
Reply from 192.168.0.175: bytes=32 time<1ms TTL=128
Reply from 192.168.0.175: bytes=32 time<1ms TTL=128
Ping statistics for 192.168.0.175:
Packets: Sent = 4, Received = 4, Lost = 0 (0% loss),
Approximate round trip times in milli-seconds:
Minimum = 0ms, Maximum = 1ms, Average = 0ms
C:\Users\Marcraft1>

FIGURE 23.14 Ping

7. When the PING process has completed, return to Wireshark and stop the live capture by selecting the red square located near the top-left corner of the window.

You will notice at least one new protocol present on the list. The ICMP protocol should be listed, as depicted in Figure 23.15. (You may have to scroll up depending on how much traffic your network is pushing.)

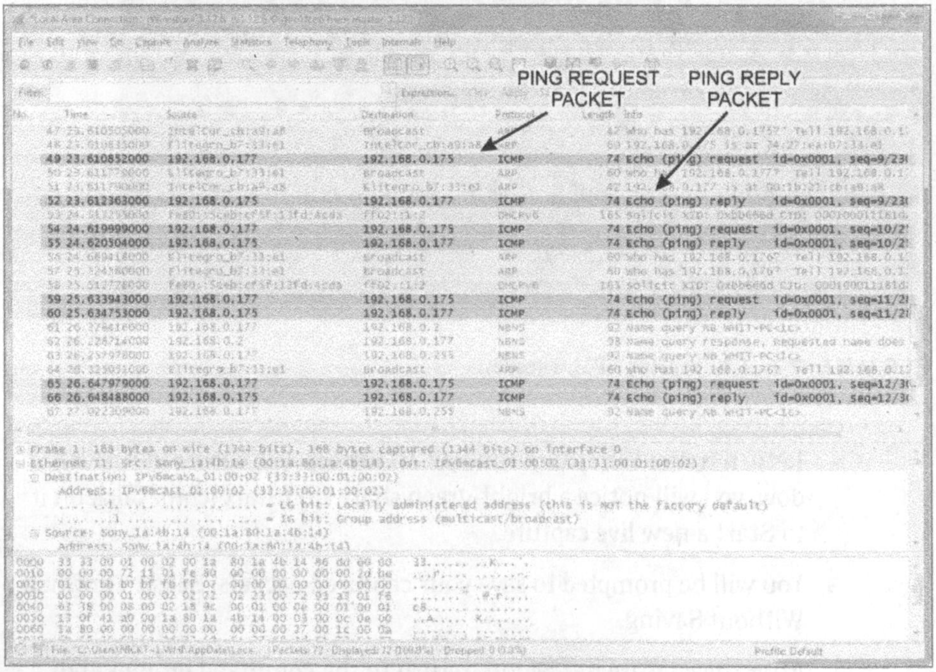
PING REQUEST PACKET
PING REPLY PACKET

FIGURE 23.15 Wireshark Capture Window with ICMP Packets

NOTE **For every one `PING`, you will see two ICMP-related packets. Echo (`PING`) requests and Echo (`PING`) reply.**

8. Select the Filter: field box. Type **icmp** and press Enter.

This filters all the traffic to that of only the ICMP protocol. Here you can view the `PING` much more easily, as illustrated in Figure 23.16.

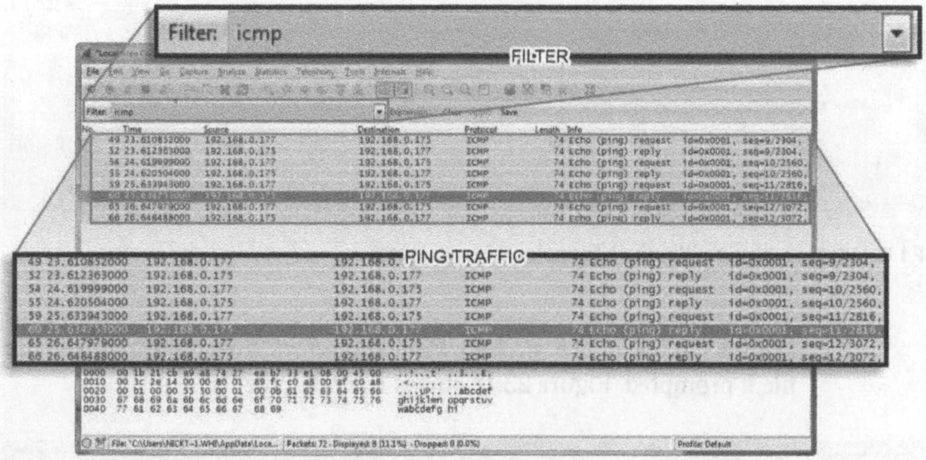

FIGURE 23.16 Viewing the `PING`

Exploring Attacks in Wireshark

Starting an attack just so that you can view the traffic in Wireshark would be unwise. Performing an attack at this stage could render your local machine unusable. Therefore, you will have to examine previously captured traffic that represents different attacks.

You can download some example attacks at: `https://wiki.wireshark.org/SampleCaptures`. Store them in a Wireshark Examples folder on your desktop.

For the purposes of this lab, locate and download the following:

- `arp-storm.pcap` (`https://wiki.wireshark.org/SampleCaptures#ARP.2FRARP`)
- `teardrop.cap` (`https://wiki.wireshark.org/SampleCaptures#Crack_Traces`)

1. Locate the folder labeled Wireshark Examples on your desktop. Double-click to open the folder and view its contents, as shown in Figure 23.17.

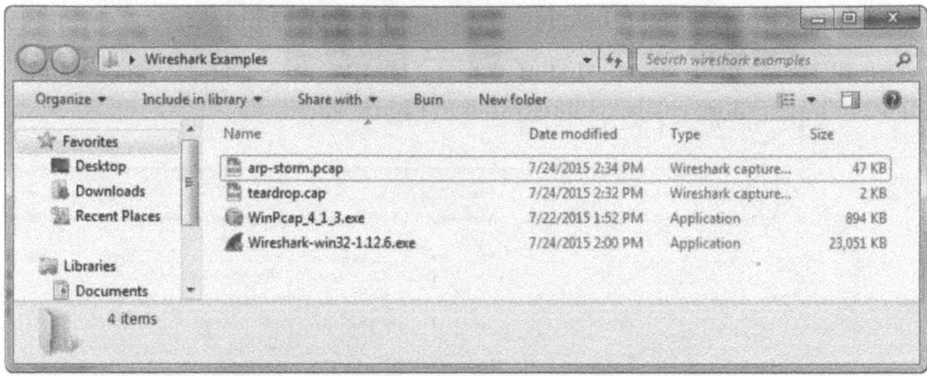

FIGURE 23.17 Wireshark Examples Folder Contents

2. Double-click `arp-storm.pcap`. Find and select Wireshark to open this file if prompted. Figure 23.18 shows the open file.

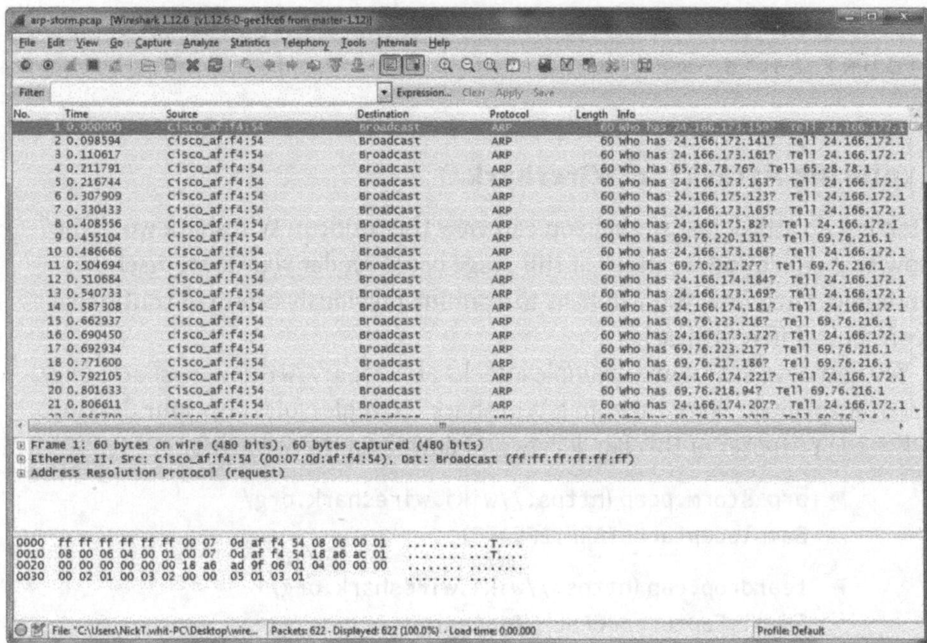

FIGURE 23.18 Arp-Storm Example

When broadcast or multicast traffic overwhelms a network, it is known as a *broadcast storm* or a *network storm*. Because broadcast traffic is rebroadcasted by every network device, continuous traffic can quickly overload switches and routers if they are not up to the task.

As with DoS attacks, it is important to monitor networks for broadcast storms. However, it is also important to make sure the network is properly configured and that it has hardware robust enough to move data quickly and learn routes fast enough to meet organizational needs.

3. Examine the traffic by scrolling through the Packets List pane. See if you can discover any important information.
4. After you are finished examining the arp-storm example, close the Wireshark window by clicking the X in the top-right corner of the window.
5. Return to the Wireshark Examples folder and double-click `teardrop.cap`.

A *teardrop attack* is another type of DoS attack that involves sending fragmented packets to a targeted machine. The targeted machine will not be able to reassemble packets of this nature. This will cause packets to overlap one another and eventually crash the targeted network device.

6. Examine the traffic, specifically Packets 8 and 9, as illustrated in Figure 23.19, by using the middle pane (Packet Details). Packet 8 is considered to be the setup, while Packet 9 is the overlapping hit. In this example, the difference is subtle; however, Packet 8 is 36 bytes and Packet 9 starts at offset 24, thereby causing the attack.
7. Close out any remaining Wireshark windows. If prompted to save before quitting, select Quit Without Saving.
8. Close the Command Prompt window, along with the Wireshark Examples folder.
9. Shut down the computer.

Wireshark is a powerful and popular tool for analyzing traffic. This exercise was only an introduction to its basics; it has many more options, including I/O graphs, advanced filtering, and the ability to analyze traffic captured elsewhere. For more information, visit `wireshark.org`.

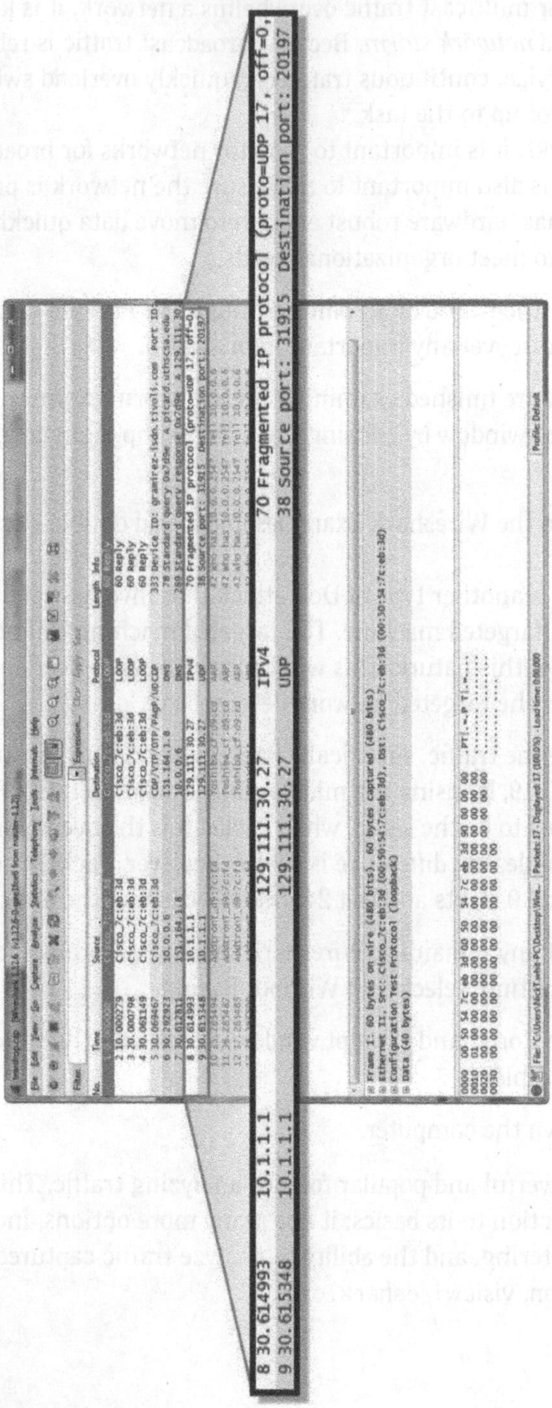

8 30.614993 10.1.1.1 129.111.30.27 IPv4 70 Fragmented IP protocol (proto=UDP 17, off=0,
9 30.615348 10.1.1.1 129.111.30.27 UDP 38 Source port: 31915 Destination port: 20197

FIGURE 23.19 Teardrop Attack Example

Lab Questions

1. What three panes are in the Wireshark Capture window?
2. How many packets are involved with a PING?
3. Should you run Wireshark with an administrative account?

Lab Answers

1. What three panes are in the Wireshark Capture window?

   The Packet List pane, the Packet Details pane, and the Packet Bytes pane.

2. How many packets are involved with a PING?

   For every one PING, you will see two ICMP-related packets: Echo (PING) requests and Echo (PING) reply.

3. Should you run Wireshark with an administrative account?

   It is not generally recommended. Instead, run Wireshark with a lower privileged account and escalate when prompted.

CHAPTER 24

Identifying and Defending Against Vulnerabilities

One of the realities of the modern Internet is that new network vulnerabilities will be discovered almost daily. You can also count on those vulnerabilities being exploited soon after they are discovered. An entire industry is growing and profiting from these discoveries, whether they are used maliciously or used to lead to the prevention of future exploitation. In this chapter, you will learn to:

- **Identify common computer and network vulnerabilities associated with being connected to the Internet**
- **Discuss common cybersecurity exploits and defenses**

Zero Day Vulnerabilities

When discussing vulnerabilities, you will often hear the term *zero day vulnerability* or *zero day attack*. These terms refer to a vulnerability unknown to the product vendor and, therefore, no patch is available to fix it yet. Once the vulnerability is made public, the vendor must scramble to release a patch.

Vulnerabilities can be discovered a number of ways. They might be found by accident, perhaps when someone used the application in some way the app's developers didn't anticipate. But the way we're most concerned with are the vulnerabilities researched and targeted for exploitation. Those can be found either by "fuzzing" or interacting with the application in an unexpected way, hoping to escape the application's control. Another way to find a vulnerability is to *reverse-engineer* the application, working backward from the finished product's files to hopefully find a weakness.

Many of us are familiar with the second Tuesday of the month as being "Patch Tuesday" when Microsoft typically releases their security patches.

When you are dealing with many vulnerabilities, this schedule might be adequate. However, some vulnerabilities are severe enough to warrant an unscheduled patch.

Web browsers typically offer easy or automatic upgrade methods. While this might be annoying to users, these updates should always be applied as soon as possible just the same as you would keep your antivirus software up-to-date.

A Word About Hackers

You might wonder who finds these zero day vulnerabilities. This is typically done by individuals referred to as hackers. The term *hacker* has come to represent computer programmers who operate with malicious intent. However, the original term referred to people tasked with finding problems in software programs. Today, hackers actually come in different "shades" as not all hackers are motivated to cause harm.

Software Exploits

Hardly a day goes by that you don't see a notice about some popular software package having an update available. Of course, the accepted method for obtaining these updates is by downloading them through a web browser. This makes them an issue on desktop as well as on application servers.

PHP-based software such as WordPress, WordPress plugins, or PHPMyAdmin have frequent updates as new exploits are discovered frequently. There have been single months where three or more critical WordPress security updates were released to deal with security-issue discoveries. To their credit, WordPress has dealt with this by making auto-updates a reality. But administrators must remain ever vigilant if they hope to have any of these packages and keep their software up-to-date.

Plugins may also be affected by different exploits, and their updates are not yet automatic. Therefore, it is important to manually check for updates on all server software packages frequently. If server security is absolutely critical, it might also be prudent to reconsider the use of these packages as they are so commonly exploited.

Most computer users are at least somewhat aware of the many exploits to Adobe's Flash Player over the years. Most will attest that this is the single piece of software they have updated the most over the years. Adobe has done an admirable job trying to keep up with new zero day vulnerabilities, but they have not been winning this war by any means.

Are You Hosting a PHP Product?

If you are hosting a PHP product, consider using suPHP (`suphp.org`), which can limit PHP execution.

While some exploits may do nothing more than inject advertising into the browser, others install ransomware on vulnerable computers, as discussed in Part II. Once installed, the ransomware will encrypt all or part of the user's data and demand large sums of money to decrypt the files.

While statistically more of a threat on Windows systems, Mac and Linux users are vulnerable to Flash exploits as well. The Flash software will check for updates frequently, but many users forgo these updates or at least delay them because they do take some time to complete. Sometimes several updates in rapid succession will cause some update-weary users to disable auto-updates or simply cancel and ignore the update warnings.

Because Flash runs within the browser, users may not realize they are even viewing some Flash content. They may think that, because they aren't watching a movie or presentation, it isn't being used. Educate users about the importance of updating this software in a timely manner and not disabling auto-updates.

Adobe has more to worry about than just Flash exploits, as Adobe Reader (formerly Acrobat Reader) exploits are becoming increasingly common. These exploits may lead to arbitrary code execution, sandbox bypassing, or simple denial-of-service usually through memory corruption.

Using what they learned from Flash, Adobe has developed a good update mechanism; but, as with Flash Player, this update may require user intervention and, therefore, may be ignored. This product should be included in your user-education presentations.

Microsoft updates their software frequently as well, and not just on "Patch Tuesdays" as described earlier. Windows is not the only product at risk here either, as application software can also be exploited. Therefore, it is critical to encourage users to allow their Microsoft updates to run and be completed. Each new version of Windows tries to make this less obtrusive and transparent, but users who continue to circumvent this process will become aware at some point why these updates are critical.

An issue that some administrators overlook is the user who has a portable PC that they use only when they travel. This machine may go weeks or months without updates and then, when the user is finally prompted for updates, they cancel them as they are in a hotel or on an airplane. Portable PC users should always be encouraged to prepare for travel in advance by connecting their laptops to the network at least a day before they travel and allow all updates to proceed.

SQL Injection

Perhaps the most common (and also most preventable) software exploit is known as *SQL injection*. As shown in Figure 24.1, hackers may attempt to inject SQL commands into a public-facing form, such as a login form, in hopes that they will lead to their being granted access to the data stored in an underlying database.

Much of the power of the modern web is related to the use of online databases, and many web designers use SQL (or SQL-like) database engines to power them. Websites are often powerful web applications that may store enormous amounts of information. With SQL, you can often chain queries and commands as easily as just adding a semicolon (;) and then an SQL command. The semicolon acts to "escape" from the need to enter data, to an opportunity to instruct the application to execute what you add next. You don't need to understand SQL programming fully to see the problem SQL injection presents.

Imagine a web form that might look up resources based on a zip code. It would use a single query such as:

```
SELECT * FROM Locations WHERE Zip='$zipcode';
```

Where `$zipcode` actually comes from an input field supplied by the user. If the hacker were to enter: **`99336; DROP TABLE Locations`** instead of just `99336`, then the database might chain those commands and delete (drop) the Locations table entirely.

A common way that hackers determine whether the application is subject to SQL injection is to look for a single quote exploit on login forms. An authentication query might be something like this:

```
SELECT ID FROM Users WHERE Username = '$username'
AND Password = '$password';
```

If a hacker knows or can guess that you have a user named Steve, he can try the simple trick of entering a password of:

```
something' OR 'a'='a
```

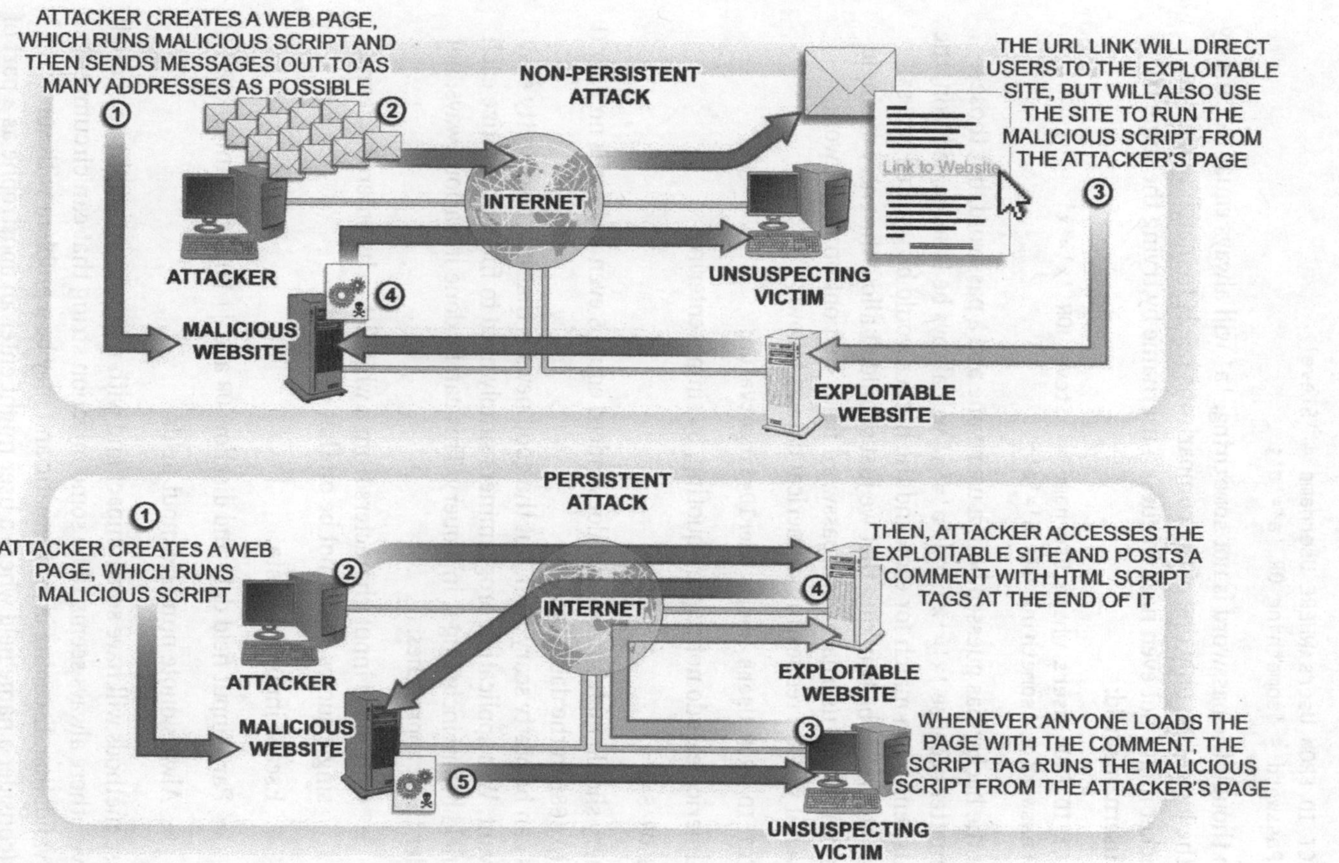

FIGURE 24.1 SQL Injection

Note that there is no beginning or ending single quote as the application query will provide that. Now the query that might be executed looks like this:

```
SELECT ID FROM Users WHERE Username = 'Steve'
AND Password = 'something OR 'a'='a';
```

Even though the password is not `something`, `'a'` will always equal `'a'` and by using the logical `OR`, only one of the comparisons needs to match to be true. The hacker might not even need to guess a username by trying the same trick in the username field:

```
SELECT ID FROM Users where Username = 'Steve' OR 'x'='x'
AND Password = 'something OR 'a'='a';
```

Here the hacker has guessed both a username and a password, but those won't matter because `'x'='x'` and `'a'='a'` will always be true. In addition, the `OR` clause ensures a match for each and the hacker would be granted access. You might already be thinking that we just shouldn't allow the entry of single quotes. With both username and password fields that option might work. However, if you are requesting numerical data as follows:

```
SELECT ID FROM Users where UserID=$inputValue;
```

and numeric fields do not require quoting, by simply entering:

```
8686 OR 5=5
```

the query should match because `5` does indeed equal `5` even if there is no `UserID` equal to `8686` in the database.

This can be pretty scary stuff, but the good news is that it is also pretty easy to prevent. Web application programmers simply need to filter or sanitize each input field before including it in a query. This can be done in various ways, but consider these approaches:

- Only allow input characters from a whitelist to be entered. Clearly, single quotes would not be on that whitelist.
- Escape input field data.
- Parse input field data and disallow `OR` and `||` (and certainly `DROP`).
- Always quote numeric input fields.

These methods will have some impact and with many forms might be enough. However, there always seems to be some injection string that can circumvent input validation. Escaping is problematic and may be a problem with some fields (consider a name field where a user might enter an apostrophe as a part of their name). If a hacker enters a backslash (\) character to escape their input or uses, Unicode, or other encodings, they may end up defeating your sanitization routines.

The best way to prevent SQL injection is to employ SQL parameters. Modern SQL systems support parameterized queries where the parameters are evaluated strictly as data and will not allow any command execution. For example:

```
SELECT ID From Users where Username='@user' AND
Password='@pass';
```

Somewhere in the code, the server will have stored procedures that handle these parameters and enforce strict data typing and validation to ensure that no code but your own is executed. You still need to be careful when crafting queries and also understand that tables and columns can't be parameters. However, this is considered the best practice when using SQL systems.

There are two other vulnerabilities that are similar to SQL injection: Cross-Site Scripting (XSS) and LDAP injection attacks. In a *cross-site scripting attack*, the attacker installs JavaScript in input fields. If that input is echoed, then the user's browser might execute that code. This type of thing can easily be avoided by simply not echoing that input or by converting all HTML entities in your input sanitization, which will convert <script> to <script> and render it harmless. To prevent LDAP injection attacks, it is important that public-facing forms that perform LDAP queries use some type of input validation.

While modern browsers protect against cross-site scripting, they cannot completely defend against it. This attack, like many others, requires a hacked or otherwise maliciously crafted webpage, as shown in Figure 24.2. Educating users about this risk and logging into social media manually rather than from web links can help. Hosted web pages should be periodically scanned for this type of exploit using a utility such as BeEF or Metasploit described earlier.

Java

Statistically, Java may be targeted with exploits more than any other software package. Many feel Oracle has not reinforced Java enough and have taken the stance that Java should be avoided. Java runs in its own virtual environment and standard operating-system protection schemes offer no protection against Java exploits.

Most modern operating systems offer Data Execution Prevention (DEP) and Address Space Layout Randomization (ASLR), as well as other application sandboxing schemes, which make exploits considerably more difficult. These schemes can't protect the user from Java exploits. Combined with the ubiquity of Java, this makes it a great target for hackers.

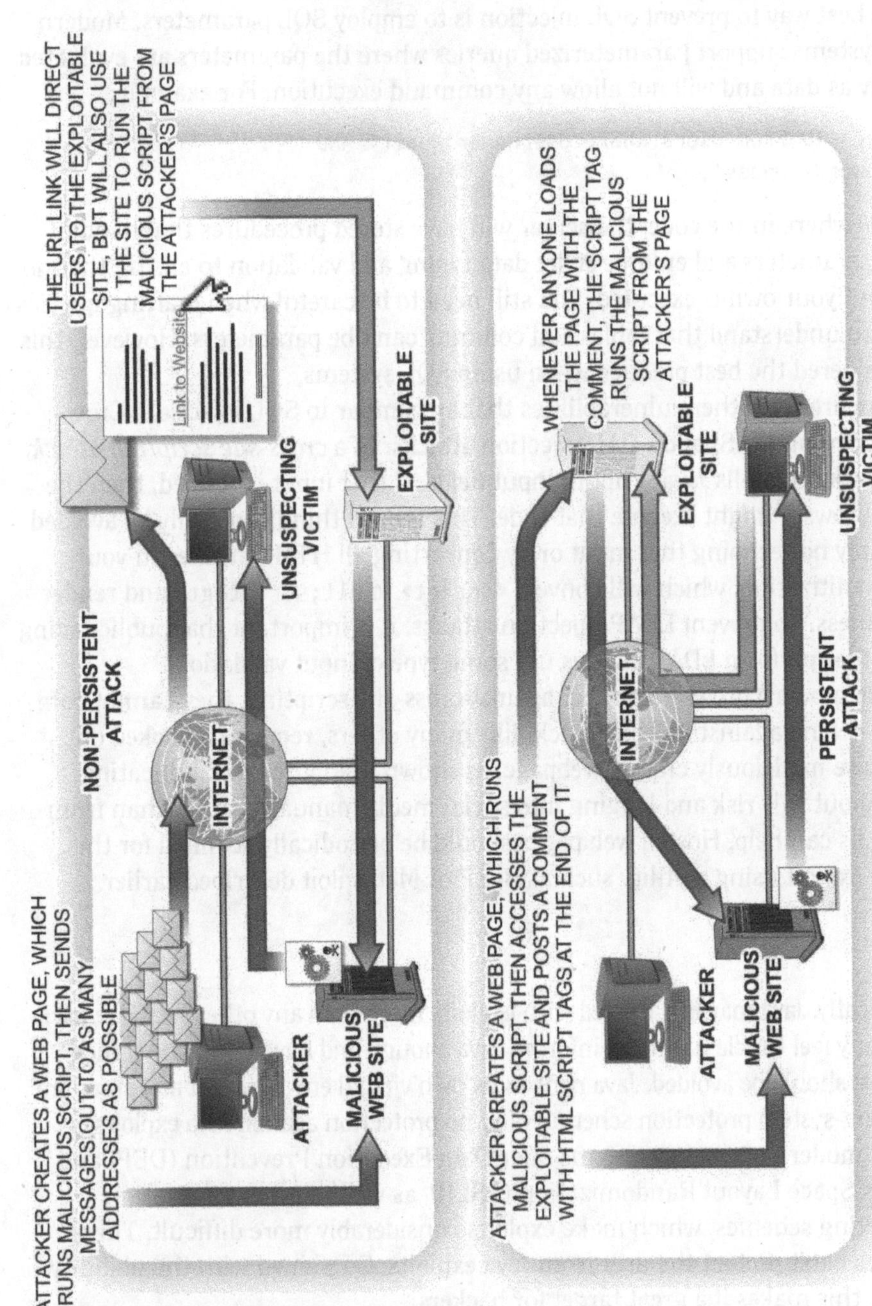

FIGURE 24.2 Cross-Site Scripting

For those users who don't really need Java, simply disabling Java is a great solution. For those who must run Java, it is possible to restrict the files that can be used somewhat. This makes it even more important that users must keep Java patched. Oracle updates tend to lag behind the published exploits a bit more than the cybersecurity industry would like, but promptly updating when these patches are made available is crucial.

Other Software Exploits

Despite the efforts of everyone involved, it seems almost any software can be exploited if given enough attention by the right hackers. The same concepts apply to all software in that users must be vigilant about where they obtain their software and data files and they must perform all software updates in a timely manner.

Microsoft Office applications support macros that have many possible exploits. Because most users don't use these macros, turning off macro support is a good solution in these cases.

Web browsers seem to excel at updating themselves, and more and more software packages are moving toward auto-updating mechanisms, so collectively good progress is being made. Browser extensions are a growing concern as they are becoming more popular and must be taken as seriously as other types of software.

Users must be well informed about software threats and be responsive to update requests.

Simple antivirus and anti-malware software cannot fully protect users or servers from software exploits. Some exploits may come through higher risk web adventures or through social engineering (or user gullibility); but at the end of the day, it is important to realize there is only so much anyone can do to prevent every exploit.

When you combine that reality with the nastiness of some exploits like CryptoLocker and other ransomware, the best defense might be a strong backup solution. Frequent and incremental backups are the best way to minimize the impact of these exploits. Simple backups are not a perfect solution because you might not be aware of an exploit and could back up the exploited software or data over top of the good copy.

Using incremental backup solutions that offer time-based data retrieval are the best solution. Apple's Time Machine and Microsoft's File History are excellent backup solutions that allow retrieval back to a point in time before the exploit occurred.

Social Engineering Exploits

When we think of network vulnerabilities, we don't initially think of human vulnerabilities, but they are the targets of many cybersecurity attacks. *Social engineering* essentially exploits human interactions to circumvent normal security. As traditional security improves and network exploits are increasingly difficult to implement, hackers are turning to psychological manipulation to achieve their goals.

We tend to laugh off this concept, and often it may seem amazing that users can be deceived in this way, but social engineering works surprisingly well without needing to be overly detailed or sophisticated. The crux of the problem is that people err on the side of being overly helpful and trusting. When someone encounters a well-crafted attack, without proper awareness training, people can be gullible.

Some social engineering deceptions are so realistic it is only with extreme scrutiny that they can be recognized. Users will not be able to provide this level of review or specific understanding, so educating them regarding the general concepts is the best way to combat these activities.

Phishing Attacks

Phishing is a social engineering technique that attempts to acquire sensitive information, usually login credentials or credit card data, by masquerading as a trustworthy organization. These attacks generally involve emails that direct the user to a bogus website that looks like the real thing, as shown in Figure 24.3.

Such sites prompt the user to enter their credentials or other sensitive information so that the information can be harvested and used for identity theft. Often, we think these things are so obviously ridiculous that no one would ever fall for the deception. However, someone always falls for these deceptions, which is why they are so popular.

The first and best way to combat phishing is to educate your users. Rather than shame them for being gullible noobs, it is far better to offer simple ways to recognize the difference between a real and a bogus email or website including:

- The look of an email or website can be deceptive. Logos and official disclaimers and legalese do not provide any legitimacy because they can be faked or copied easily.

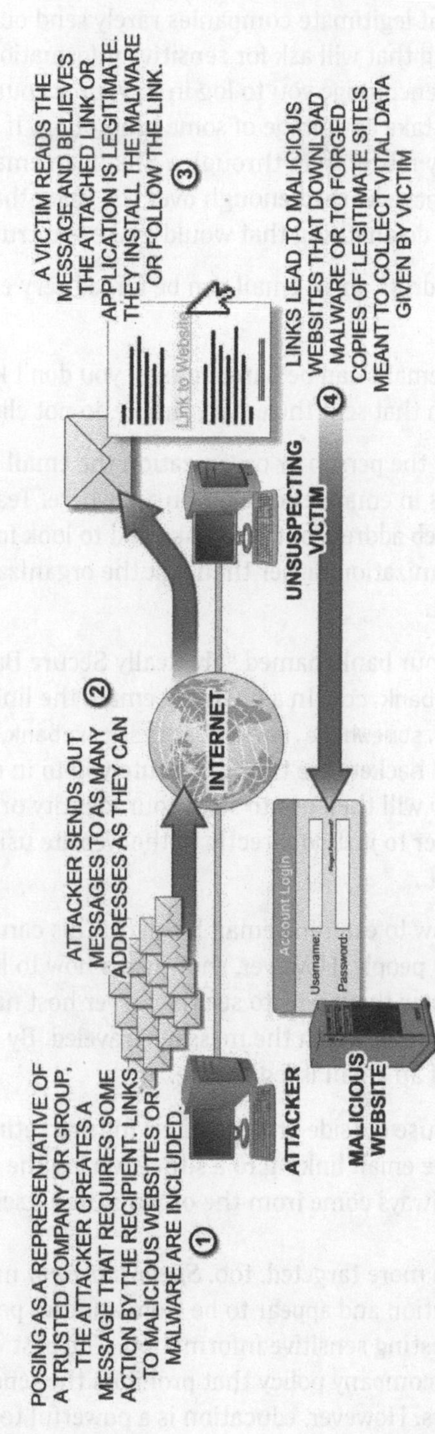

FIGURE 24.3 An Example Phishing Attack

- Understand that legitimate companies rarely send out email that will link to anything that will ask for sensitive information. These organizations may encourage you to log in to your account to enjoy some new feature or take advantage of some promotion. If so, do that in the normal way rather than through a link in an email. Legitimate organizations have learned enough over the years that they just aren't going to do anything that would make you trust them less.
- The "From" address on an email can be forged very easily and anyone can do that.
- Hyperlinks in emails can be dangerous. If you don't know the person or organization that sent the email, simply do not click on the link.
- If you do know the person or organization the email is from, realize that hyperlinks in emails can take you anywhere. Teach users how to examine the web address of these links and to look for the URL of the legitimate organization rather than just the organization name as part of the URL.

For example, a link to your bank, named "My Really Secure Bank," is `https://myreallysecurebank.com`. In a phishing email, the link might be presented as: `https://bogus.somewhere.ru/myreallysecurebank`, where *bogus* and *somewhere* are places hackers are trying to route you to in order to get you to reveal information they will then use to steal your identity or access your accounts. It is always better to just go directly to the website using your bookmark or by typing the URL.

- Teach users how to examine email headers. This can be a little difficult for many people. However, show users how to look at the email headers and show them how to see the server host names for each mail server through which the message traveled. By doing so, you can often see if an email is legitimate.

While some companies use outside organizations for marketing or even support emails, any legitimate email linking to a site requiring the entry of sensitive information should always come from the organization itself. If it doesn't, don't trust it.

Phishing attacks can be more targeted, too. *Spear phishing* may target a single user in an organization and appear to be from another person in that organization who is requesting sensitive information. The best way to solve this type of attack is to create company policy that prohibits the sending of sensitive information between users. However, education is a powerful tool here as well.

Replying to an email such as the one described here would be more problematic than sending that information to an address in their address book. If users not only understand the risks, but also know a few simple ways to avoid deception, the network will be more secure.

There are a number of different variations of the phishing exploit, including pharming, spear-phishing, whaling, and a number of others. You can learn more about these variations by searching for these terms online.

Network Threats and Attacks

Part III introduced you to several different types of network vulnerabilities and associated attack types as they apply to local area network connectivity devices. In this chapter, these vulnerabilities and attack types are being revisited as they apply to Internet-related activities.

Broadcast Storms

In Part III, you learned that when broadcast traffic is rebroadcast by every network device, the continuous broadcast or multicast traffic can quickly overload switches and routers and overwhelm the network. This type of activity is referred to as a *broadcast storm* or a network storm, which is depicted in Figure 24.4.

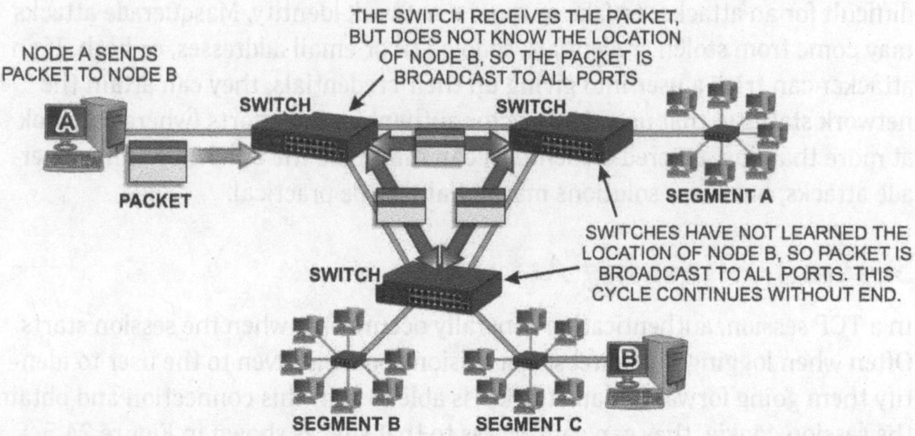

FIGURE 24.4 Broadcast Storm

It is important to monitor networks for broadcast storms. However, it is also important to make sure the network is properly configured. If a network node communicates directly with more than one switch, lookup tables may get confused, causing packets to be flooded between segments. This can represent a major weakness in network implementation.

It also important to have hardware that is robust enough to move data quickly and learn routes fast enough to meet the organization's needs. As networks increase to gigabit and faster speeds, it is increasingly important that all network hardware is appropriate for that data rate.

While it may be possible to segment a network in such a way as to minimize the risks of a broadcast storm, the spanning-tree protocol (STP) was created to deal with this issue. STP employs the spanning-tree algorithm (STA) to understand that a switch may have more than one way to communicate with a network node and manage the optimal pathway while still being able to fall back to a secondary path. Mission-critical networks must utilize STP to minimize broadcast storms.

STP will act to establish one of the switches in the multipath network as its *root bridge,* by manipulating its priority level. It does this by exchanging Layer 2 *Bridge Protocol Data Units* (BPDUs) between all of the network's switches until a winner is selected. Once established, all other switches in the network are then subject to the root bridge switch and all the network traffic will pass through it. Each nonroot bridge switch is connected to its own root port on the root bridge switch.

Many network vulnerabilities focus on obtaining valid credentials in some way. Spoofing was discussed earlier, so it should be apparent that it isn't terribly difficult for an attacker to fake or spoof a network identity. Masquerade attacks may come from stolen credentials, spoofed IP or email addresses, or both. If an attacker can trick a user into giving up their credentials, they can attain the network status of that user. Multifactor authenticating efforts (where you look at more than just entered credentials) can minimize the efficiency of masquerade attacks, but these solutions may not always be practical.

Session-Hijacking Attacks

In a TCP session, authentication generally occurs only when the session starts. Often when logging into a website, a session cookie is given to the user to identify them going forward. If an attacker is able to sniff this connection and obtain the session cookie, they can gain access to that site, as shown in Figure 24.5. This sort of attack is known as *session hijacking.*

Man-in-the-Middle (MITM) Attacks

In Part III, you were also introduced to man-in-the-middle (MITM) attacks or fire brigade attacks. These attacks are a type of session hijacking that involves intercepting or sniffing and modifying communication between users, as shown in

Figure 24.6. You can think of them as a form of network eavesdropping. As such, the attacker is usually on the same network or broadcast domain as the other two parties and will proxy communications between the parties, inserting or altering data in the process. In an SSL connection, the attacker might use ARP spoofing to divert traffic though the attacker rather than the normal network router.

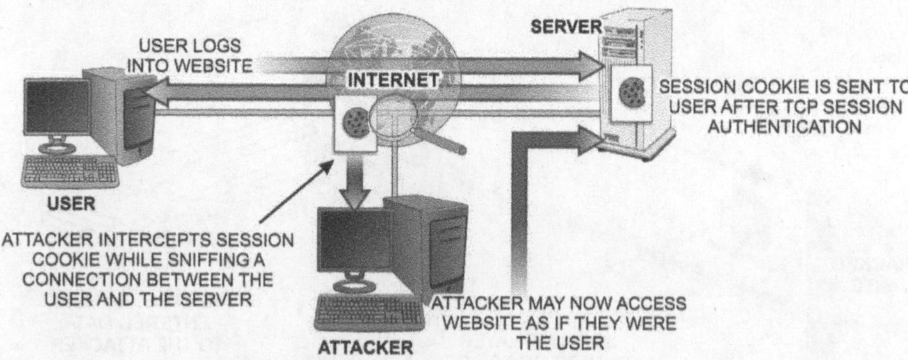

FIGURE 24.5 Session Hijacking

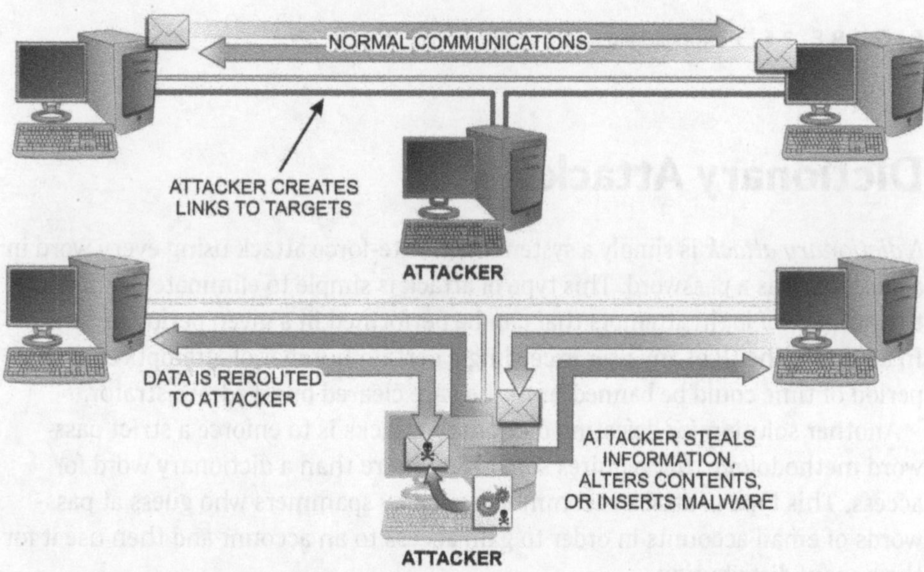

FIGURE 24.6 MITM Attack

Clickjacking Attacks

A *clickjacking attack* employs deceptive frame techniques to trick the user into clicking on their content rather than the intended content. This is a popular trick deployed on hacked websites because it is easy to do and can yield high rewards, as shown in Figure 24.7. The attacker mostly conceals the legitimate frame so the user clicks on the attacker's frame. This is often done to social media frames. It is possible for the web page developer to add a little frame-busting code to their web documents, but that can be defeated as well.

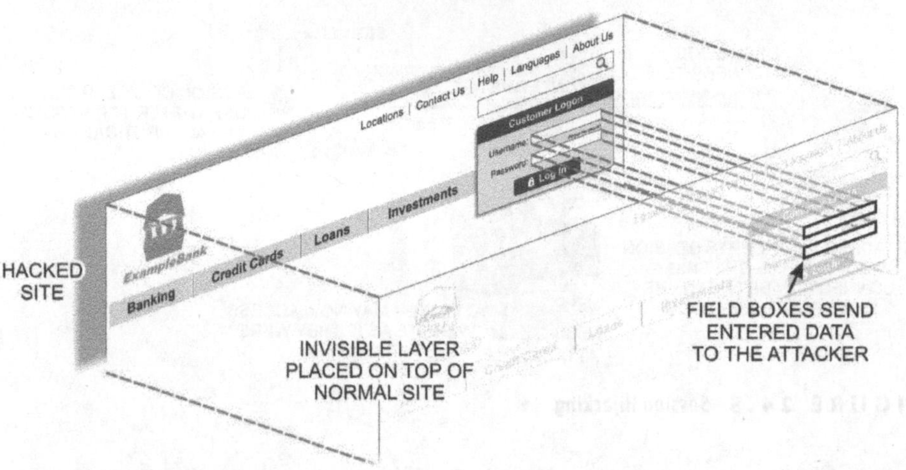

FIGURE 24.7 Clickjacking

Dictionary Attacks

A *dictionary attack* is simply a systematic, brute-force attack using every word in a dictionary as a password. This type of attack is simple to eliminate by limiting the number of login attempts that can be performed in a given period of time. In addition, the IP of any user exceeding a certain number of attempts over that period of time could be banned until they are cleared by an administrator.

Another solution for defeating dictionary attacks is to enforce a strict password methodology that requires something more than a dictionary word for access. This type of attack is commonly used by spammers who guess at passwords of email accounts in order to gain access to an account and then use it for their spam distribution.

Denial of Service (DoS) Attacks

Probably nothing disrupts a network administrator's dreams more than the DoS attacks (see Figure 24.8) you were introduced to in Part III. They are disruptive not simply because these attacks often occur in the middle of the night, but because there is really no way to be completely immune to them. As you are aware from those previous DoS discussions, there are many ways to flood a network or a service with requests that can ultimately bring down even the most robust network hardware. The best that can be hoped for is to minimize their impact and have a plan to deal with them.

Would You Like Fries with That DoS Attack?

DoS attacks are now available as services known as *booter* services, which charge customers for providing a distributed Denial of Service attack on demand.

A distributed DoS (DDoS) attack uses multiple compromised systems on many different networks (referred to as *botnets*) to provide the attack. The botnet systems are typically infected with a Trojan, but there are many ways to get malware into a computer these days.

Because the attack could come from hundreds or even thousands of computers, a distributed attack is much more difficult to stop, as it's not as simple as just blocking a single IP. In addition, DDoS attacks are so easy to perform that even an unsophisticated attacker, commonly called a *script kiddie,* can launch an attack that will wreak havoc on a network. The botnet-for-rent service is a real concern for network administrators as well.

Many incorrectly think they are unlikely targets for a DoS attack of any kind. Security through obscurity is no longer a rational approach to network protection. There is some degree of randomness to DoS attacks these days, so every network will be affected eventually.

Networks normally rely on firewalls to defend their resources. Some firewalls offer protection against DoS attacks, but a better approach is to employ a specialized device that examines all incoming traffic before it gets to the firewall. These specialized network appliances offer better DDoS mitigation and monitoring and perform much better than normal firewalls because of their singular focus. These products are very expensive and probably not practical for smaller organizations.

Monitoring for any kind of DoS attack is critical, and having a plan to deal with this sort of thing is important because the network will be down before administrators can even start to deal with it. Because a DoS can be initiated in so many different ways, simply monitoring for slow network performance is the first place to start. Usage spikes or even a large jump in email volume should get an administrator's attention.

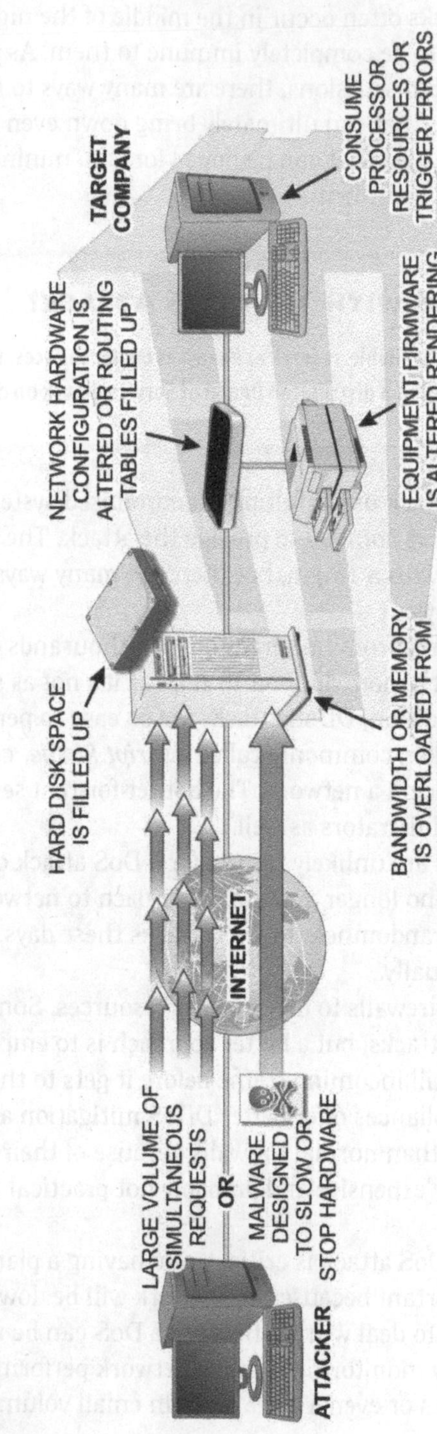

FIGURE 24.8 A Typical DoS Attack

If the network has a public web server, ensure that it is patched with the latest security and software updates. Also consider implementing transaction limits and monitoring so that any surges in activity can be reacted to in a rapid manner as well. Ensure the network's authentication schemes are strong and web servers ideally should be protected with firewall software that incorporates some level of IP filtering and automatically block excessive activity.

For Linux/Apache systems, a product such as Fail2ban can be used to reject IP addresses and services for a specified time to help thwart basic attacks. Nondistributed attacks are easier and, therefore, more common, making this type of protection from brute-force attacks very helpful.

A new DDoS protection and mitigation service industry is on the rise, offering more affordable solutions for organizations. These are not on-premise solutions and they are not for everyone. However, this type of solution is certainly something to consider when running mission-critical Internet applications. While CloudFlare (`cloudflare.com`) offers a free plan that may help many organizations, the monthly costs associated with most plans make them very attractive as well.

Often a DoS attack may be a diversion for some other criminal activity and should always be considered as a possibility when investigating an attack. If no sort of DDoS mitigation process is in place, you may simply have to endure the attack. When these attacks occur, some administrators pointlessly attempt to block IP after IP.

Once such an attack has been initiated, the remaining option is to simply shut down the network. The attacker might proclaim victory and move on if you are very lucky. Also consider blocking every incoming port that you possibly can. If the attack targets a particular port, it may be possible to move this service to a different port.

A newer DoS attack scheme, known as a *Distributed Reflection and Amplification Denial of Service (DRDoS) attack,* is becoming more common. Attackers are able to use a relatively small botnet in a distributed attack on reflection servers that redirect the queries they receive, making it appear as though the reflection server is the actual source. This type of attack is illustrated in Figure 24.9.

The reflection server is then overwhelmed by the combination of incoming queries and resulting responses. Often this sort of attack targets DNS services as the attacker forges a DNS request and the server responds to the spoofed IP that is the actual target of the attack. This means that the reflection servers may not even be part of a botnet or be compromised at all.

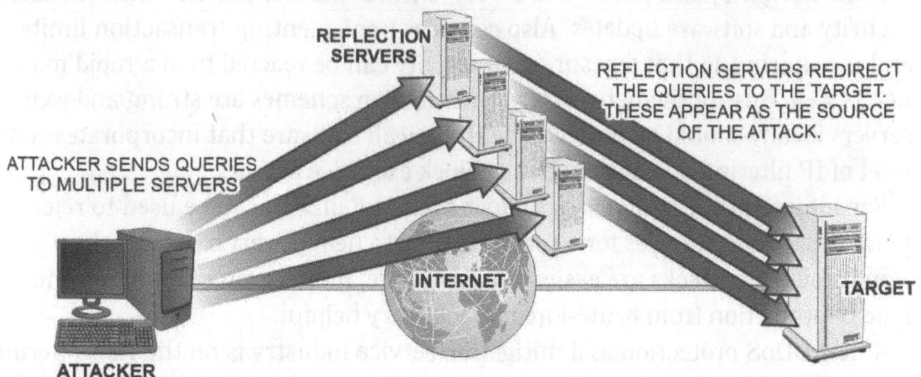

FIGURE 24.9 A DRDoS Attack

The impact of this DNS amplification attack is much stronger when the DNS server is authoritative for the domain being queried where the attacker will make a `DNS ANY` request, which will return all known information about that DNS zone. A name server is authoritative if it provides definitive answers to DNS queries rather than from a cache or by requesting that information from another name server. By leveraging a botnet of DNS servers configured to allow unrestricted recursive resolution for any client, known as open DNS resolvers, a small number of servers can amplify the DDoS attack.

The Open DNS Resolver Project (`openresolverproject.org`) has a compilation of DNS servers that are known to serve as globally accessible resolvers so you can block them. However, you should also make sure that the network's DNS servers are not open recursive resolvers. Some free tools are available to test DNS servers (`dns.measurement-factory.com`, `dnsinspect.com` and others).

Make sure that all caching name servers respond only to local queries and any authoritative DNS servers do not offer recursion and instead use DNS RRL (DNS Response Rate Limiting), which limits the rate at which authoritative servers respond to queries.

Most DDoS attacks target the transport and network layers. Layer 7 attacks focus on the application layer and generally target specific areas of a website in hopes of exhausting resources. This type of attack can be difficult to recognize because it appears as normal network traffic up to a point. The attacker will find a form or a feature of the website that might employ more resources and target that feature from a botnet.

Popular content management systems such as WordPress are targeted with this sort of application layer attack, often exploiting the search function of the site that appears to be normal requests. The sheer volume of these requests will bring the site down. DDoS mitigation services will help with this, and you could also consider using proxy servers that can provide some sort of rate limiting.

Ultimately, the battle to block IP addresses is rarely won, as these attacks typically come from thousands of IP addresses, depending on the size of the botnet. If a dynamic IP blocking system, such as Fail2ban, is in place some progress might be made. However, a large botnet will probably prevail. IP blocking is a fundamental mitigation concept, but the more distributed the attack the less likely this single tactic will help.

Tarpitting

Another possible solution to this sort of attack is known as *tarpitting,* sometimes known as a *sticky honeypot*. To mitigate an HTTP attack, the concept here is to initially respond to a connection as normal but with a very small TCP window size. The host replies to a SYN packet with a SYN/ACK, but ignores the sender's ACK, as shown in Figure 24.10. The sender starts to send data, but the host will never receive it, or the host might just set their TCP window size to zero, effectively stopping incoming traffic.

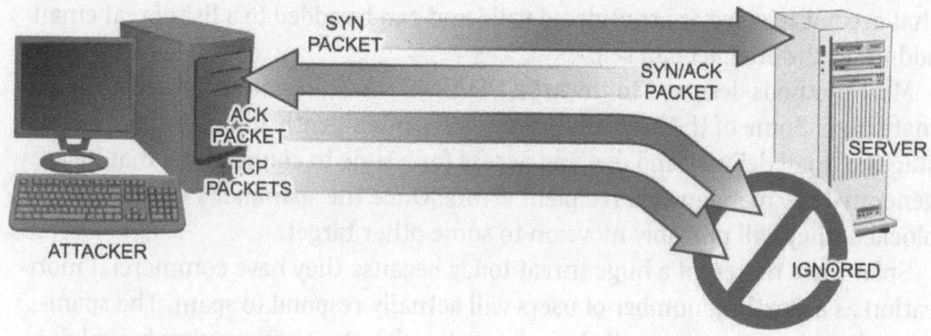

FIGURE 24.10 Tarpitting

Clearly, you can't do this for all connections, so the challenge is to identify the attackers and only tarpit those connections. This is far better than simply dropping packets because the sender will just send again rather than wait.

To thwart bulk email attacks, the concept is to deliberately slow down bulk-delivered emails compared to normal traffic. This may have some impact but typically will just force the spammer to send smaller batches with a longer delay between batches.

More sophisticated tarpitting software is used to monitor ARP requests looking for consecutive requests spaced several seconds apart without any ARP replies. When such requests are discovered, the software creates an ARP reply, using a bogus MAC address, on an unused IP address on the network.

The software then creates a virtual machine that watches for SYN packets for that bogus MAC address and replies with a SNY/ACK that tarpits the connection. This virtual machine might even respond to pings to further the charade.

Sophisticated tarpitting software packages are created to thwart specific worm attacks, but it is an ongoing battle. Sadly, you can't just enable tarpitting and be fully protected—but this type of software is a great addition to the arsenal.

Spam

Spammers are generally considered the lowest form of hacker and often perform directory harvest attacks (DHAs), where they simply guess email addresses at a domain and then connect to the email server of that domain. Any addresses that are not rejected are considered valid and can be added to a list of real email addresses the attacker can sell.

Most methods designed to thwart a DHA will result in slower service for legitimate mail. Some of the best solutions involve intelligently monitoring the early stages of mail delivery and denying access for a time to connections that have generated too many invalid recipient errors. Once the spammer's efforts are blocked, they will probably move on to some other target.

Spammers represent a huge threat today because they have commercial motivation as a startling number of users will actually respond to spam. The spammers don't have to necessarily breach a network but rather can simply exploit a single user to serve their purposes.

Using social engineering, deceptive emails, clickjacking, or whatever means they can, spammers gather credentials for one of the network user's email accounts. Even if there is no public webmail server on the network, it isn't difficult for spammers to figure out server settings for most networks and send email through the mail server as if they were the compromised user.

Protecting Against Spam Exploits

Strong passwords and education can provide only so much protection. Once exploited, the spammer can send spam freely through the network and worse yet could even send out false or misleading information that could create liability (or at least embarrassment) for an organization. This type of *repudiation attack* is becoming more and more common. It is far from trivial to limit this sort of attack, but there are some things you can do.

Require Authentication for the Outgoing Mail Server

Make sure the outgoing mail server requires some sort of authentication. If you don't allow users to send from outside your network, this is simple. You can constrain sending to a subnet, but most organizations don't do this. If the outgoing password is different than the incoming mail password, the user base will scream—but it will make it less likely for spammers to achieve this goal. If you require outside users to log in through a VPN to be able to send email, that can help as well provided the VPN is secure.

Limit Outgoing Email Recipients

You should limit the number of recipients for any outgoing email to a reasonable number. Spammers will want to send large batches of emails as quickly as they can before spam-detection blocks your mail server. If a single email can be sent to only 20 users at a time, this will slow down their progress. If possible, do this per user and accomplish even more while still allowing internal mailing lists and services to function normally.

Configure Notifications for Email Volumes

You should trigger notification of an administrator when an unusual volume of email is sent by a single user or overall. Generally, when administrators review the logs, they can tell by the email subjects that the message is spam. If you can quarantine bulk email until it can be reviewed, you are in the best position to stop this sort of thing.

Restrict Webmail Servers

When a public-facing webmail system is used, you should restrict that server more than a normal outgoing mail server because these servers are the favorite targets of spammers. By restricting bulk email sending to traditional email client software rather than webmail systems, you can remove one variable from the equation.

Pay Close Attention to Email Blacklists

You should monitor email blacklists carefully and respond to complaints immediately. The sooner a rogue account is discovered and disabled, the better. Blacklist-monitoring services that can really help are available. Even though it is too late to prevent a release of spam and subsequent blacklisting by the time the alerts come in, you will at least be in a better position to deal with the issue.

Many email providers and administrators fail to check these lists, assuming they should be above reproach. Blacklisting is a mostly automated activity and what isn't automated is not governed particularly well.

Spam-weary users may report the mail server and some systems can trigger a blacklisting with very few complaints. Utilize services such as `mxtoolbox.com`, `blacklistmonitoring.com`, `debouncer.com`, and others to assist with blacklisting.

Other Exploits

There are many other types of attacks and hackers are busy dreaming up new ones every day. Some attacks are just malicious to be malicious, and there is no real commercial gain for the attacker, but others may have commercial motives. With any attack you should look for what possible commercial gain could be available as it may not be immediately obvious.

Transport Layer Security (TLS) Exploits

As encrypted communication using Transport Layer Security (TLS) is becoming more the rule rather than the exception, it should come as no surprise that more security attacks are focusing on it.

After a secure connection has been negotiated and keys exchanged, there isn't much that can be exploited, so these attacks focus on this key exchange.

Often, these vulnerabilities exploit weaknesses in both the browser and server that can lead to a connection with weakened encryption. Patching both the client browser and the server SSL/TLS libraries was necessary after an OpenSSL bug was discovered in early 2015 that would allow a man-in-the-middle attack to downgrade connections from strong RSA encryption to an "export-grade" 512-bit RSA encryption.

Export-grade encryption was created to be good enough but still allow the National Security Agency to decrypt communication outside the United States. The NSA lifted this export requirement in the late 1990s, but those cipher suites have remained in both client and server libraries.

FREAK Exploits

More than 15 years later, when a vulnerability known as *FREAK* (Factoring attack on RSA-EXPORT Keys) was discovered, it became clear that this export-grade feature was still available in many web clients, as well as in OpenSSL. This led to a scramble to patch the product.

While this still means an attacker would have to crack a 512-bit encryption, it is well known that this can be done in a matter of hours. However, 1024-bit encryption would take an impractically long time, and today encrypted services are often using 2048-bit encryption, which, for now anyway, seems uncrackable using contemporary technologies.

Because the FREAK flaw required a susceptible browser and server, its discovery also exposed another area of concern when it was learned just how many mobile browsers were susceptible. Many mobile platforms are simply and frequently updated, leading Microsoft, Apple, and Google to scramble and make software solutions available soon after the issue was discovered.

However, not all devices have upgrades available. Many older devices never had or no longer have software upgrade paths, so those browsers remain susceptible. The same can be said for the many painfully old desktop computers that are running obsolete operating systems, which will not support modern browsers. It is not that uncommon for employees to use personal mobile devices or laptops on their work networks, and these devices could create some risk for their organization.

Logjam Exploits

Another popular cryptographic algorithm used in many Internet protocols rather than an RSA key exchange is the Diffie-Hellman key exchange (DHE). A *logjam attack* is similar to the FREAK attack but instead targets this Diffie-Hellman key exchange, convincing the connection to use DHE Export ciphers.

This attack exploits the *prime number sieve* (algorithm for determining all prime numbers up to a specified limit) used in the key-generation process, forcing it to use a 512-bit prime. Similar to FREAK, upgrade patches have been made available for modern browsers and software suites leaving obsolete systems vulnerable.

Hands-On Exercises

Objectives

- Create a new software restriction policy.
- Describe the difference between whitelisting and blacklisting.
- Create a new hash rule.

Resources

- Customer-supplied desktop/laptop hardware system
- Windows 10 Professional installed (not the Home edition)
- An account with administrative access

Discussion

Software-restriction policies provide another layer of defense by limiting the use of specified applications. Using the methods of whitelisting or blacklisting, you can successfully block attempts made by viruses, Trojans, and other malicious software from running a program without your knowledge.

Whitelisting is the practice of assigning access to the known good and denying all others, while blacklisting involves allowing everyone except those on the known bad list. In reference to applications, as with most listing options, whitelisting is the preferred and recommended method.

Procedures

In this procedure, you will investigate the types of rules you can create to enforce software-restriction policies. You will test the new policy and new rule locally but understand that the same method can be used within a domain environment.

Locating Software-Restriction Policies

1. Power on your machine.
2. Log on using an account that has administrative access.

3. At the desktop, select the search bar. Type **secpol.msc** and then press Enter. The Local Security Policy MMC will launched, as shown in Figure 24.11.

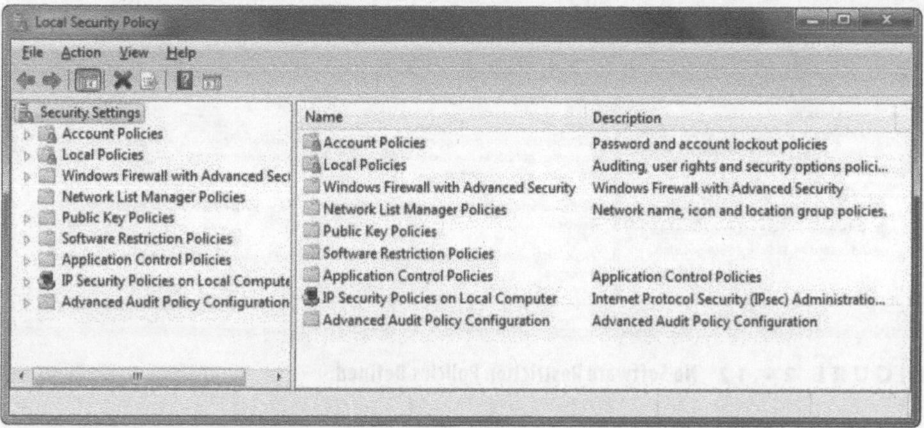

FIGURE 24.11 Local Security Policy

NOTE These settings can also be accessed under the Local Group Policy Editor. Type **gpedit.msc** into the search bar and press Enter to launch.

NOTE The MMC, or the Microsoft Management Console, provides an interface for users to configure the system. The MMC hosts tools and displays these tools in a console as a snap-in.

4. Click Software Restriction Policies to view the contents. The right pane should show No Software Restriction Policies Defined, as illustrated in Figure 24.12.

5. In the left pane, right-click Software Restriction Policies and select New Software Restriction Policies. The contents of the folder will be displayed in the right pane, as shown in Figure 24.13.

6. In the right pane, the bottom three object types can be adjusted by double-clicking each. Without adjusting any settings, explore Enforcement, as shown in Figure 24.14. When finished, click Cancel

and then explore the Trusted Publishers and Designated File Types options.

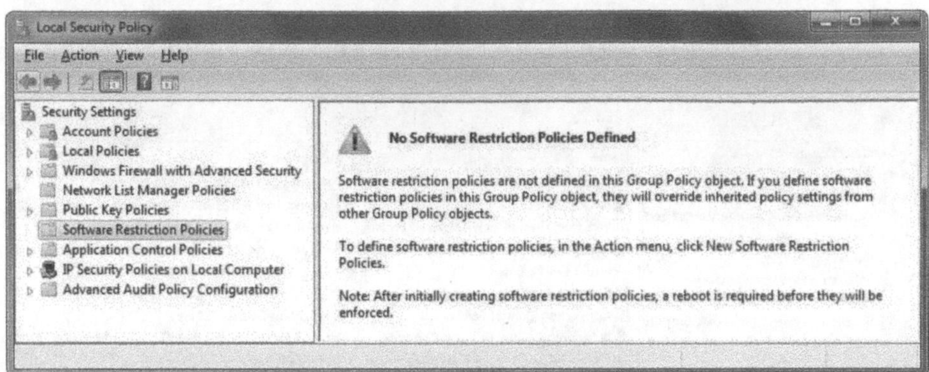

FIGURE 24.12 No Software Restriction Policies Defined

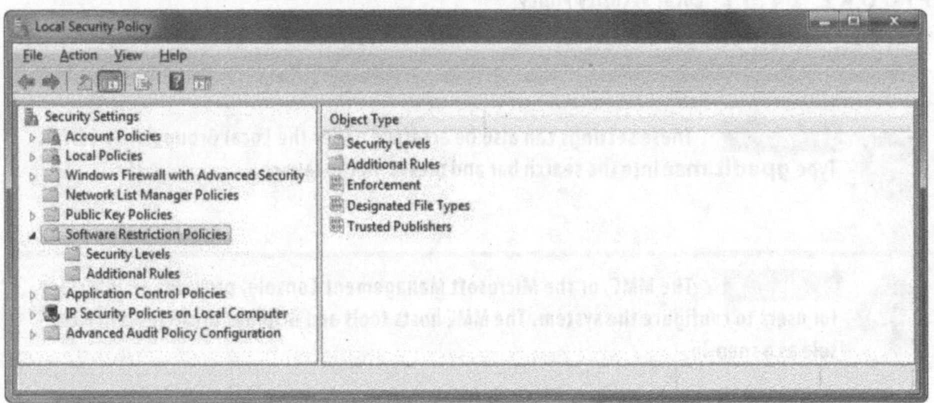

FIGURE 24.13 Software Restriction Policies with Contents

7. In the left pane, select Security Levels under Software Restriction policies. There are three security levels, as illustrated in Figure 24.15.

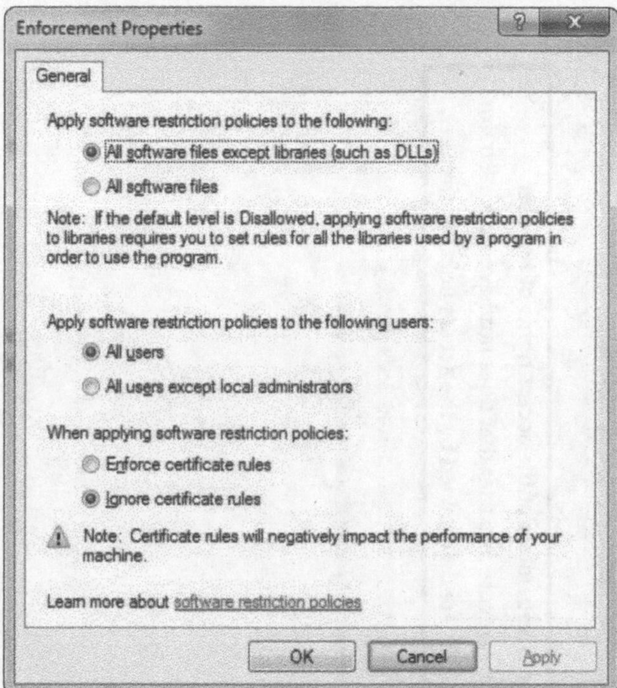

FIGURE 24.14 Enforcement Properties

NOTE The default security level is Unrestricted.

8. In the left pane, select Additional Rules under Software Restriction Policies to view the contents, as illustrated in Figure 24.16.

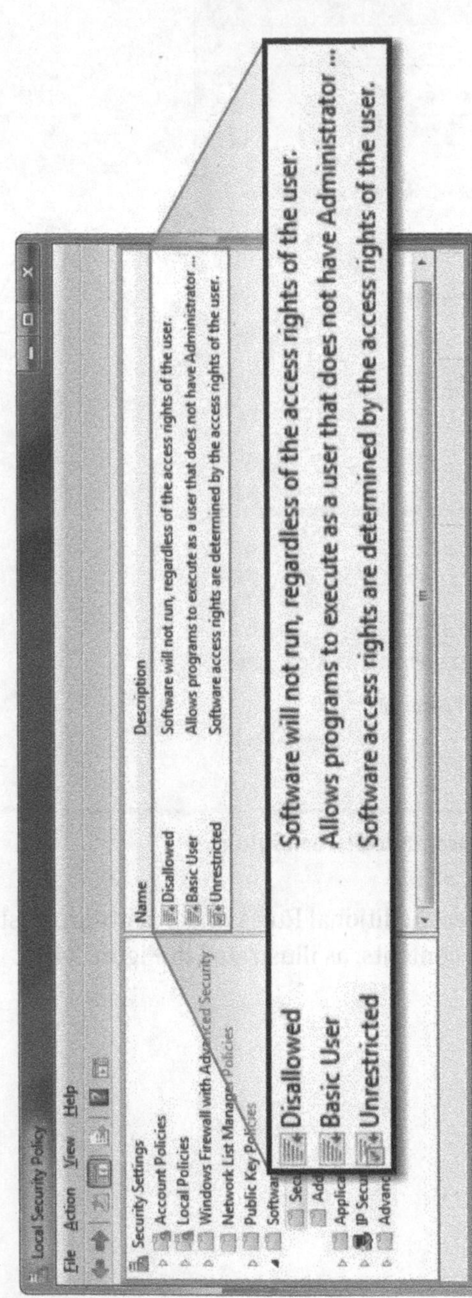

FIGURE 24.15 Security Levels

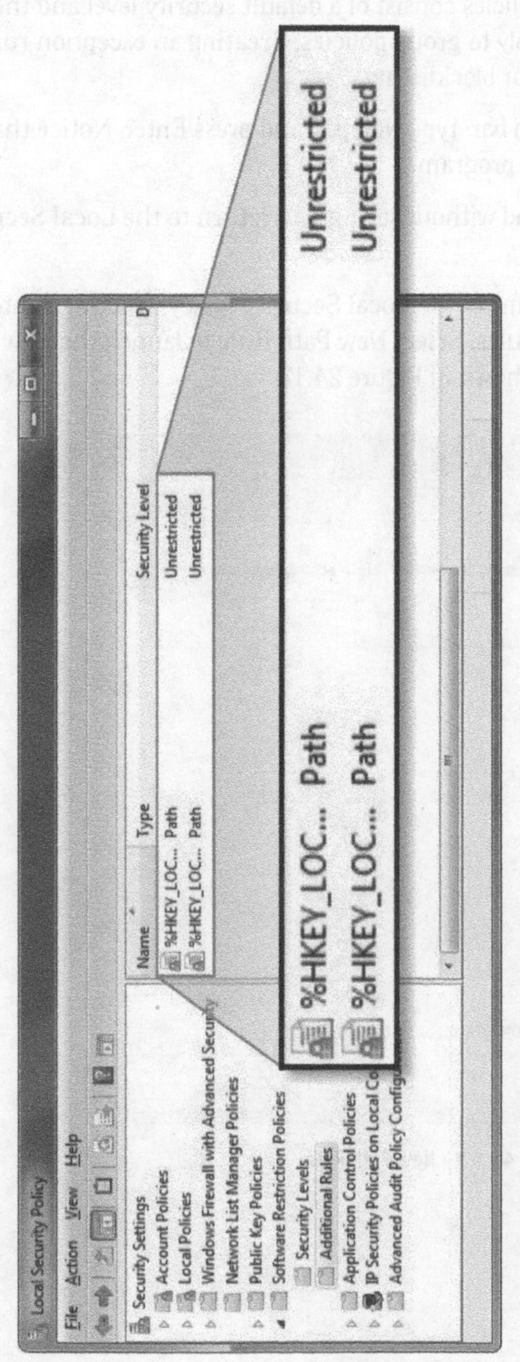

FIGURE 24.16 Additional Rules

Creating and Testing a New Path Rule

Software Restriction Policies consist of a default security level and the associated exception rules that apply to group policies. Creating an exception rule is necessary when whitelisting or blacklisting.

1. In the search bar, type **Notepad** and press Enter. Notice that this executes the program.
2. Close Notepad without saving and return to the Local Security Policy MMC.
3. In the left pane of the Local Security Policy window, right-click Additional Rules. Select New Path Rule to launch the New Path Rule window, as shown in Figure 24.17.

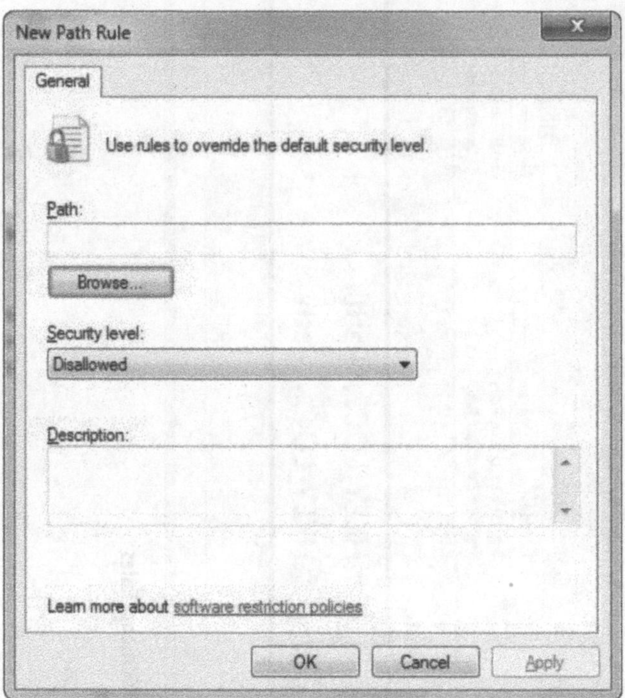

FIGURE 24.17 New Path Rule

A path rule will identify a program by its file path. For example, you can use this type of rule to prevent users from running email attachments, by specifying the mail program's attachment folder.

4. Click Browse to launch the Browse For File Or Folder window. Locate Notepad by navigating to This PC ➢ Local Disk (C:) ➢ Windows ➢ System32. Select Notepad, as depicted in Figure 24.18. (This will take a bit of scrolling down.)

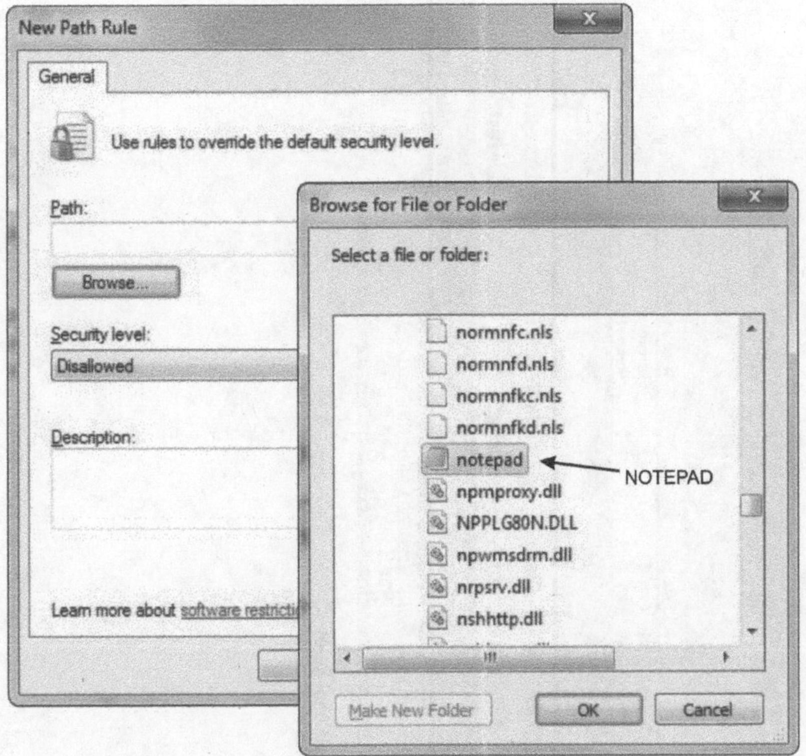

FIGURE 24.18 Notepad Selected in Browse for File or Folder

5. Click OK to select Notepad and return to the New Path Rule window. The path to Notepad is located under Path.
6. Select the Security Level drop-down menu to view its choices. Leave it at Disallowed and click OK. The new rule should be located in the right pane of Additional Rules with a Security Level of Disallowed, as illustrated in Figure 24.19.

FIGURE 24.19 New Rule in Additional Rules

NOTE The user must log off and log back on for the rules to apply.

7. Close the Local Security Policy MMC by clicking File and then selecting Exit.
8. Right-click the Windows/Start icon on the taskbar. On the menu, locate and hover your mouse over the Shut Down Or Sign Out option, and then on the options that are presented, select Sign Out.
9. Log back on with the same credentials you used at the beginning of this procedure.
10. Type Notepad into the search bar and press Enter.

Were you able to execute Notepad? ___________

As shown in Figure 24.20, you should see the software restriction rule prompting a blocked message. This is considered blacklisting, as you blacklisted the program you didn't want others to access.

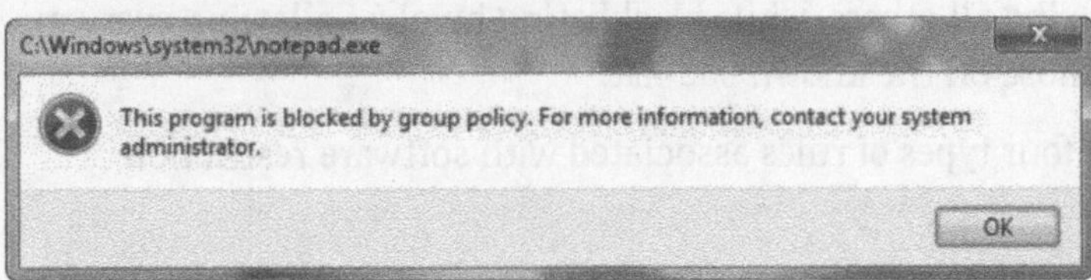

FIGURE 24.20 Notepad Blocked

11. Click Close to continue.
12. Return to the Local Security Policy MMC by typing **secpol.msc** in the search bar on your taskbar and pressing Enter.
13. Navigate to Software Restriction Policies ➢ Additional Rules.
14. Locate the path rule you created and right-click it. Select Delete. When prompted, select Yes to permanently delete the selected rule.

Exploring the Rule Types

The remaining rule types accomplish the same output, in different ways. The four rules types include:

- Path Rule: Identifies software by its file path.

- Network Zone Rule: Identifies software through a specified zone in Internet Explorer.
- Hash Rule: Identifies programs based on their initial hash output.
- Certificate Rule: Identifies software based on its certificate signing.

Lab Questions

1. What is the difference between whitelisting and blacklisting?
2. List the four types of rules associated with software restriction policies.
3. What are the three security levels and what is the default?

Lab Question Answers

1. What is the difference between whitelisting and blacklisting?

   Whitelisting is the practice of assigning access to the known good and denying all others, while blacklisting involves allowing everyone except those on the known bad list.

2. List the four types of rules associated with software restriction policies.

   Path Rule, Network Zone Rule, Hash Rule, and Certificate Rule

3. What are the three security levels and what is the default?

   The three security levels are Disallowed, Basic User, and Unrestricted. The default security level is Unrestricted.

## CHAPTER 25

Perimeter Security: Review Questions and Hands-On Exercises

Review the summary points before proceeding to the "Review Questions" and "Exam Questions" sections to make sure you are comfortable with each point. After completing the review, answer the review questions that follow to verify your knowledge of the material covered in this chapter.

Summary Points

- There are two kinds of Internet Protocol traffic: Transmission Control Protocol (TCP) and User Datagram Protocol (UDP). When a TCP connection is established, data can be sent bidirectionally. This connection is highly reliable and features error checking but adds some bulk to the transmission. UDP is a much simpler, connectionless protocol where multiple messages are sent as packets in data chunks.
- *Unicast messaging* is the sending of messages to a single network address. *Broadcast messaging* refers to sending messages to all possible destinations. *Multicast messaging* sends messages using special address assignments to a specific group of addresses.
- In addition to the network address, many protocols may also specify a *port* or a port number. A protocol or application may respond to specific ports in different ways.
- Understanding ports is critical in managing network security. The easiest way to minimize unwanted scans or restrict access is by using specific ports and *port blocking*.

- *Routing* is simply the process of selecting the best pathway for transmitting data over a network or between networks.
- *Routers* deal with IP addresses mostly, but they can also deal with MAC addresses, which can be another way of restricting access.
- *A domain* is a unique realm assigned by an agent known as a *registrar* authorized by the Internet Corporation for Assigned Names and Numbers (ICANN).
- Most companies and residential users subscribe to Internet access services from an Internet Service Provider (ISP). This service is typically contracted for a specific service level or potential transfer speed and at least one IP address. However, the service may also include email, web hosting, some security services, or even a larger block of IP addresses.
- Many ISPs will *proxy* your web connections through caching servers or caching devices to minimize bandwidth utilization.
- Some ISPs will also block certain ports in a misguided attempt to minimize the impact of malware, viruses, and worms.
- The Internet Engineering Task Force (IETF) is the main standards organization for the Internet.
- A number of organizations are involved in maintaining network vulnerability resources not dissimilar from virus and malware resources. A variety of commercial entities have grown to serve this vital need, but many publicly available resources and standards are available.
- The real shift in security awareness came when the first computer viruses started making the rounds. With this shift, a single user could run a piece of malicious code and impact an entire company network and even be complicit in the furthering of that virus's spread by unknowingly sharing that virus with every one of their contacts.
- Network hardware is the integral component in Internet access and can usually serve a dual purpose in providing a certain amount of network security.
- *Gateway* devices often provide good security capabilities and even out-of-the-box, unconfigured, they will usually provide "good enough" security for the average residential or small office user.

- Every standalone computer or local area network that connects to the Internet will connect through some type of gateway device. This gateway device is often a router but may also be a switch that features some protocol conversion (or translator) to provide Ethernet or wireless clients access to the technology the ISP provides.
- The router may also support a DMZ that provides relatively free access from external networks. Often, this is where web servers or mail servers are located so that offsite users can have easy access, while you can still control the content and hardware.
- A *proxy server* allows a client to make an indirect network connection. The client connects to the proxy server, with or without any conscious authentication, and makes a request for a resource from a different server. Then, the proxy server will handle the request by either returning the requested resource from a cache or by forwarding the request to the other server.
- Probably the most common use of this concept is with caching *web proxies* where a local server will cache web resources and then expire them intelligently.
- Web proxies help conserve Internet bandwidth and speed up connections, but they can also be used to filter content or even reformat that content.
- A *transparent proxy* makes the original IP address available but only in the HTTP headers. A transparent proxy is typically not something the user is even aware they are using.
- Malicious proxy servers have been used for various purposes including malware delivery, ad injection, and for just simple information gathering. Although the proxy server may not pass on your IP address, it will still know your IP address and could use this information somehow as well.
- It is common to put a cluster of web servers behind a *reverse proxy server* that will handle public requests for web resources and then forward them to one or more servers. To the requestor, this process appears as if those web servers are being accessed directly.
- The most common first line of defense in a network connected to the Internet is a *firewall*.

- A good firewall will provide *packet filtering* using defined rules to reject or accept both incoming and outgoing packets. Firewall rules are critical to security on most networks.
- The firewall is generally the place to start when implementing or evaluating Internet security. Most administrators configure the firewall features they need and then try to make them secure. However, security really needs to be the first consideration.
- Increasingly, routers and switches are being integrated into *smart switches* or even coupled with a traditional operating system to create devices referred to as *smart network appliances.*
- Security appliances are also known as *Unified Threat Management (UTM) devices* featuring gateway, antivirus, firewall, intrusion prevention and detection, and possibly more in a single product.
- *Data security* is deployed to prevent data misdirection through encryption or live capture. It is also implemented to prevent scanning of incoming packets or files, as well as monitoring and scanning data on a computer after it has been accepted.
- *Encryption* is a simple way to make sure data isn't intercepted by a third party and used inappropriately. It is rapidly becoming an almost required step in securing any network.
- Security at all levels always involves some type of authentication process.
- Users can be authenticated by asking them to provide a username and password, by examining their MAC address, or by their network address if they are assigned a static IP address.
- After a user is authenticated, we generally want to determine their authorization, which essentially involves the resources that the authenticated user has permission to access and what actions they can perform.
- The most well-known authentication method is certainly password authentication, which is a *single-factor authentication* and represents the lowest level of security available.
- *Two-factor authentication* involves asking for another authentication component—ideally one that is something physical or in the user's possession.

- Additional authentication factors can be added to the login sequence to increase security by making it less and less likely that an attack will be successful. However, with more challenging login sequences, users will become dissatisfied and resort to scribbling credentials on sticky notes and desktop calendars or just simply not using the service.
- *Password Authentication Protocol (PAP)* is a standard username and password combination scheme with or without an encrypted password.
- *Challenge-Handshake Authentication Protocol (CHAP)* creates a random string, a challenge phrase, or a "secret." It then combines this with something else—such as the username or host name—and sends this information to the requesting system, which in turn hashes the string and returns the result.
- *Kerberos* authentication is based on a trusted third-party Ticket Granting Server (TGS) to authenticate client/server interaction.
- *Password-Authenticated Key Agreement (PAKE)* is essentially encrypted authentication using shared keys. Keys can be shared by multiple servers to allow a user to visit other servers using the same authentication.
- The *Lightweight Directory Access Protocol (LDAP)* is a popular enterprise protocol often used for authentication. LDAP offers a single login system that can lead to access to many services, and a nonstandard Secure LDAP is available offering LDAP over SSL.
- Encryption is nothing more than the conversion of electronic data into a form called *ciphertext* that is created by applying a cipher or secret code to the data to produce a scrambled message that cannot be understood without the knowledge of the cipher used to create it.
- *Cryptography* is simply the concepts and methods for securing information. Many cryptographic techniques involved the use of keys. A *key* is merely a data string used to encrypt or decrypt information. How the key is used in this way and how large the string is will impact the strength of the encryption.
- *Public-key* cryptography uses asymmetric keys incorporating a public key and a private key (or secret key). The strength of this type of cryptography obviously is related to how impossible this calculation is to reverse engineer.

- *Digital certificates,* also known as public key certificates, are simply a digital verification that the sender of an encrypted message is who they claim to be. To obtain a digital certificate, you must apply with a trusted Certificate Authority (CA).
- *Secure Sockets Layer (SSL)* is a protocol for managing both authentication and communication between clients and servers using a both public key and a private key.
- *Transport Layer Security (TLS)* is the successor to SSL even though the two are often referred to interchangeably or even together as SSL/TLS. They are not, however, interoperable. The TLS Handshake Protocol allows the client and server to exchange keys and handle an encryption algorithm prior to any exchange of data.
- A *hash table* is simply a lookup table that maps keys to values using a hash function that converts the keys into hash values. Rather than sequentially searching a table of data looking for a particular value, a *hash function* can be performed on the lookup key, which will return the index to the hash value being sought. This can save a tremendous amount of time searching for data.
- *Super cookies* have emerged as another privacy nuisance. Super cookies are simply third-party cookies that are harder to remove than other types of cookies. Many of them do not use the traditional cookie storage methodology, but rather use local browser HTML5 database storage or even Adobe Flash data storage.
- Adding a *CAPTCHA* to a traditional authentication scheme can potentially eliminate any kind of automated password attack.
- *Network segmentation,* also known as zoning, can be a useful concept for multiple reasons. Network segmentation is essentially the separation of the network into subnetworks, each of which becomes a segment.
- Access to a network segment is often provided through an access control list, where only users matching some criteria or authentication are allowed access. This is known as a *whitelisting.*

- Access to a network segment where only users matching some criteria or authentication are denied access is known as *blacklisting.*
- When allowing outside users into a network, always use the principles of "least privilege" and "need-to-know." Give each user the least amount of access possible and only to the areas of the network they must have.
- Network *virtualization* changes the way we must look at network segmentation. A relatively new concept of software-defined networking (SDN) is emerging that essentially analyzes the connection between any two nodes and can filter that connection based on a defined policy.
- Through software, a single piece of hardware can support multiple *virtual instances,* each of which has the ability to function like the original host hardware. Virtual instances can be enabled as needed to handle demand and scalability, or to provide for a tremendous amount of portability.
- A *VLAN,* or virtual LAN, is simply a software-configured network where hosts will behave as if they are all connected to the same physical network even when they are not. This allows several networks or broadcast domains to work, virtually, as a single LAN and broadcast domain.
- *Network Address Translation (NAT)* is simply the translation of an IP address used in one network to an IP address known within another network. Typically, this is used to map an IP address from outside a network to an address inside a network.
- NAT can be performed with policy-based routing (PBR) where mapping decisions are determined by any number of rules, which could be based on many different criteria. These rules are critical to security if outside access to a network is desired.
- *Port Address Translation (PAT)* supports the concept of mapping multiple inside (or private) devices or IPs to a single outside (or public) IP address. The router assigns a port number that is appended to the IP address, effectively making each address a unique address, even though they share an IP address.

- Firewall devices use *stateful packet inspection* or dynamic packet filtering to analyze the packets further—looking at IP addresses, port numbers, and more. They track this information so that they can control the ports, only allowing them to be opened when an internal request asks for it.
- *Virtual Private Networks (VPNs)* enable a remote user to connect to a private network over a public network, such as the Internet, and then authenticate and perform tasks on the private network as if they were connected directly.
- The most widely used protocol with VPNs is the *Point-to-Point Tunneling Protocol (PPTP)*. PPTP does not provide any encryption and uses the simple password authentication taken from the *Point-to-Point Protocol (PPP)*.
- *Layer 2 Tunneling Protocol (L2TP)* also uses PPP and is unencrypted but can pass another encryption protocol in the tunnel. Often, an underlying protocol will be combined with L2TP, such as in an L2TP/IPsec arrangement.
- *Internet Protocol Security (IPsec)* is an open standard commonly used in VPNs that actually employs a suite of protocols for encrypting and authenticating IP communications.
- The strongest feature of NAT/PAT is that by default nothing is translated or "forwarded" through the device. To move packets through the device, a rule must be explicitly created on the device to forward (or map) the desired protocol port to a private IP address and port in the local area network.
- Network monitoring tools can be used to ensure that servers (or even specific services on those servers) are up and running or they can be used to simply monitor data flow.
- Network monitoring tools can be divided into two main types: uptime and performance monitoring utilities and packet analyzers.
- The terms *zero day vulnerability* and *zero day attack* refer to a vulnerability unknown to the product vendor and, therefore, no patch is available to fix it yet. Once the vulnerability is made public, the vendor must scramble to release a patch.

- Perhaps the most common (and also most preventable) software exploit is known as *SQL injection*. Hackers may attempt to inject SQL commands into a public-facing form, such as a login form, in hopes that they will lead to their being granted access to the data stored in an underlying database.
- While some exploits do nothing more than inject advertising into the browser, others install ransomware on vulnerable computers. Once installed, the *ransomware* will encrypt all or part of the user's data and the attacker will demand large sums of money to decrypt the files.
- *Social engineers* exploit people's human nature to fool them into providing information about themselves, their business, or their computer/network. They accomplish this by using trickery, deceit, lies, gifts, or acts of kindness to first establish a level of trust. They then use this trust relationship to gain information.
- *Phishing* is the attempt to acquire sensitive information, usually login credentials or credit card data, by masquerading as a trustworthy organization.
- *Spear phishing* may target a single user in an organization and appear to be from another person in that organization who is requesting sensitive information. The best way to solve this type of attack is to create company policy that prohibits the sending of sensitive information between users.
- When broadcast or multicast traffic overwhelms a network, it is known as a *broadcast storm* (or sometimes as a network storm). Because broadcast traffic is rebroadcast by every network device, the continuous traffic can quickly overload switches and routers.
- In a TCP session, authentication generally occurs only when the session starts. Often when logging into a website, a session *cookie* is given to the user to identify them going forward. If an attacker is able to sniff this connection and obtain the session cookie, they can gain access to that site. This sort of attack is known as *session hijacking*.
- A *man-in-the-middle (MITM) attack* is a type of session hijacking that involves intercepting or sniffing and modifying communication between users.

- A *clickjacking attack* employs deceptive frame techniques to trick the user into clicking on their content rather than the intended content.
- A *dictionary attack* is simply a systematic, brute-force attack using every word in a dictionary as a password. This type of attack is simple to eliminate by limiting the number of login attempts that can be performed in a given period of time.
- A *teardrop attack* is a DoS attack where fragmented packets are sent to a target system. Older operating systems had bugs in their TCP/IP reassembly mechanisms that caused the fragmented packets to overlap and crash the device.
- A *distributed DoS (DDoS) attack* uses multiple compromised systems on many different networks (referred to as botnets) to provide the attack.
- In a *Distributed Reflection and Amplification Denial of Service (DRDoS) attack,* the attackers are able to use a relatively small botnet in a distributed attack on reflection servers that redirect the queries they receive, making it appear as though the reflection server is the actual source. The reflection server is then overwhelmed by the combination of incoming queries and resulting responses.
- *Smurf attacks* are similar to DoS attacks in that they employ an intermediary amplifier. The attacker will send a large amount of ICMP traffic to the broadcast address of the intermediary system using a target's spoofed source IPs.
- *ICMP tunneling* can also be used to deliver malicious packets. The best defense here is to configure network devices not to respond to ICMP echo requests. Another option is to simply block all ICMP traffic as well as inbound broadcast traffic.
- A *Fraggle attack* uses UDP packets instead of ICMP but is otherwise similar in concept and mitigation to a Smurf attack.
- *Layer 7 attacks* focus on the application layer and generally target specific areas of a website in hopes of exhausting resources. This type of attack can be difficult to recognize as it appears as normal

network traffic up to a point. The attacker will find a form or a feature of the website that might employ more resources and target that feature from a botnet.

- Another possible solution to DoS attacks is through a technique known as *tarpitting,* also referred to as a sticky *honeypot.* To mitigate an HTTP attack, the concept here is to initially respond to a connection as normal but with a very small TCP window size.
- *Spammers* are generally considered the lowest form of hacker and often perform Directory Harvest Attacks (DHAs), where they simply guess email addresses at a domain and then connect to the email server of that domain.

Security Scenario Review

Network Security Scenario 1

Identify: ____________________

Protect: ____________________

Detect: ____________________

Respond: ____________________

Recover: ____________________

Network Security Scenario 2

Identify: ____________________

Protect: ____________________

Detect: ____________________

Respond: ____________________

Recover: ____________________

Professional Feedback

At this point, compare your observations with those of a working security specialist to improve your understanding of the subject.

About Donald Short

Donald Short is the President of One World Telecommunications, Inc., an Internet Service Provider in Kennewick, Washington, where he both manages the business and programs web and database applications.

Don has been has been both a pharmacist and computer scientist for over 35 years working in many programming languages on a variety of network architectures and has developed large and complex online content and learning management systems.

Risk Assessment 1

Identify

With plenty of assets to protect, the network will need a good firewall, and users will only be allowed to access the Company Network using an encrypted VPN.

Before we go any further let's not forget the biggest internal threat on any network—the users themselves. Review all related company policies to determine how we should proceed and to what extent new policies and procedures must be created. Study the physical layout and access to each network asset.

The main internal threats we are worried about are data harvesting from unauthorized visitors or the ability for unauthorized users (whether visitors or even certain company employees) to intentionally or inadvertently infect a workstation, server, or the entire network by accessing these assets.

From the Internet we are worried about unauthorized access obviously but also the potential for Denial of Service (DoS) attacks on the network. If the main server must be made available to the public and not just employees, we have a huge risk to mitigate. Even if mail or other services must be available, we have significant risks to deal with.

Protect

From within the Company Network physical security must be provided so that visitors do not have easy access to servers or workstations and certainly are not able to plug into any USB ports. While we can update security policies and procedures, we will probably need to make some changes so that certain workstations cannot be easily compromised or accessed by visitors.

At some point we may need to consider security checkpoints and keypads, etc.

With a large number of internal users in different departments accessing the network, we need to make sure the network is segmented using switches to facilitate the creation of access control procedures throughout the entire network.

Clearly a substantial firewall router will be needed. Here we will disallow all IP traffic from the WAN (Internet) side of things and then only allow specific services and ports that we may need.

If public access is needed to a server, then we need to create a perimeter network or DMZ and move those functions to a server located within that network. If they main firewall cannot handle an additional interface, then a simpler firewall is a good idea for the perimeter network as well, so that we can both provide VPN access to the public server(s) but also restrict the services that can enter the DMZ.

All authorized users must use an encrypted VPN to access DMZ or internal network assets. Once a user has VPN access, then other assets must be protected with access control using credentials or IP-based controls. Ideally your VPN can assign users to a unique IP address, so that you can protect and monitor the network on a per-user basis by IP and therefore only rarely have to resort to credentials.

For the DMZ firewall or interface we will only enable the ports needed, such as 80 and 443 for a web-based system and the minimum mail services ports we need to make available. Ideally mail is only made available via VPN, but if a webmail service is made available on the DMZ server and that server is responsible for accepting mail, then the appropriate ports must be opened.

All sensitive information stored on the DMZ server must be stored encrypted. If any breach does occur you want to ensure the data is protected by some good encryption.

For the network firewall or interface we hopefully can disallow every service and only allow VPN access. We then create firewall rules that restrict access to the various network segments by the users' VPN IP address. Turn off ICMP and other unnecessary services on the firewall as well. Even though we have restricted access to the network, it is still a good idea to lock down every service on the server as well.

Detect

Our firewall router or appliance is going to play an important role in protection but not so much with detection. DMZ assets should be locked down as tight as possible, but generally if some intrusion does happen the intruder will be looking for certain PHP exploits and trying repeatedly to log in with simple credentials. Security software can be configured to look for such things and block the access and notify an administrator.

Simple down detection is a great idea for both the internal and DMZ servers with a protected asset polling critical servers and notifying an administrator when they become unavailable or even overloaded.

I suggest using an open-source intrusion detection system (IDS) or maybe even more than one to assist in this process. Products such as Snort and Tripwire can help detect intrusion early on so that it can be dealt with in a timely manner. Linux packages such as Security Onion can provide an arsenal of tools that can supplement the capabilities that you may have with your security appliance or firewall.

Respond

When creating policies and policy statements, assume your audience is nontechnical and keep the jargon to a minimum. They will need to understand certain concepts such as VPNs, but they may need to be educated along the way about why some issues are important. Your network is more secure when your users understand security better.

IT staff will need to be educated about intrusion notifications and given strict policies on how to proceed when a notification is received. If you are using a mitigation service for DDoS attacks, then policies related to how to proceed during an attack are important as well. These same IT staff must also be educated to provide user-friendly advice to the network users, so they understand how to handle certain more subtle attacks such as phishing requests.

Education is so very important and so you should create educational materials to supplement the network policies and procedures. Your users need to understand why good passwords are important and why they should be suspicious of anything that could be a phishing attack and why they should not share credentials with anyone, etc.

Make sure you have robust backup procedures in place, ideally backup to servers not available to the network per se. The backup servers may access the servers but not the other way around, so minimize the impact of any intrusion. Cloud based and offsite backup mechanism should ideally supplement onsite backups.

Recover

If you are experiencing a denial of service type of attack and do not use a mitigation service, then you should disconnect the network from the Internet while you work to identify the attack. If the attack is well distributed there may not be anything you can do but to wait it out. A smaller attack may respond to blocking a few IPs if you are very lucky.

If you have a more powerful router you may be able to do a certain amount of filtering, and you can always move network access to different IPs, etc., but this can often be impractical depending upon the nature of your business.

The more critical your publicly available services are, the more you should consider a DDoS mitigation service. If you are adept at DNS settings you can make zone changes to dance around attacks, but this will still result in some network availability issues. A mitigation service can help minimize this.

Recovery from many attacks or intrusions is simply restoring from backup. This is where you don't want to have to rely on a cloud-based backup ideally, as it usually takes a long time to restore. Ideally you have a drive you can access locally that you can use to restore your data while the services are offline.

If you have been breached and data has been compromised, you must assess the damage quickly. Review your logs and determine what data may have been accessed and generally assume the worst. While of course you will probably need to change credentials on your network, you may also need to notify your customers. If all customer data was encrypted you should be OK though, since you would never have stored the key on anything that could be breached.

Risk Assessment 2

Identify

These days remote access is much simpler as you just have to select a VPN scheme and use it. This really depends upon the firewall or appliance you are using on your network. Regardless of VPN scheme, try to assign the credential management chore to the IT staff so that you never have to worry about a user using a weak password.

You will need to create policies that your organization can tolerate, so work with management to create policies that are as strict as is practical for your network.

Some policies cannot really be enforced, but that doesn't mean you should create them. Strongly urge your employees to follow these policies, and try to educate them about the reasons for and the importance of these policies. Requiring that your employees not access your network from public Wi-Fi, for example, can eliminate many security risks, but it is nearly impossible to enforce.

Stressing good credentials, being alert for phishing attacks, and always being aware of security in general to your users will pay off.

Protect

Use a good encrypted protocol suite such as IPSec, and create the credentials for each user adhering to strict good password concepts. Your options may be dictated by your firewall or appliance, but you should be able to find a scheme that all of your users and their devices can support.

Your policies should include some expiration of credentials generally in months not years. Ideally you assign cryptic passwords to each user, but many organizations fight this because users cannot remember cryptic passwords and many don't use password management software. If you must use less cryptic passwords, use a mixture of common words plus a short number that the employee can remember, such as Jumpbranch92 or better yet Jump$Branch92. I tend to put the capital letters at the beginning or end for ease of typing.

If a user has access to many assets and therefore presents a higher security risk, then those policies should be tighter, with cryptic passwords more frequently changed. If a remote user will always come from a fixed IP, include that in their access profile to add another layer of protection.

Be sure to enable as much logging as you can so that you have access to robust reports of user activity.

If users will access shared files remotely, try to find a way to limit or eliminate the remote user's ability to delete files or even write files if that is possible. Read only access is ideal. If the remote user must access confidential information stored in internal databases, make sure the database content is encrypted. Much of this depends upon the operating system of the server and the database technology, but look for these solutions as they will minimize your risk.

While security through obscurity is a weak concept in general, be smart when you create hostnames for remote employee access. `vpn.yourcompany.com` is terribly obvious. It could also be worth registering a separate domain for this kind of thing that doesn't give away the company name.

Simply creating access schemes where the user only has access to the resources they need and not the entire network is always wise. The best way to reduce your risk is to manage the worst-case scenarios and minimize what can possibly be accessed remotely. If sensitive information must be accessed remotely, then you must inconvenience those users a bit more with extra password challenges or force them to access from a fixed IP address.

Detect

With good credentials and everything locked as tightly as you can on a fully hardened network, your main risk is mostly limited to an unauthorized user obtaining legitimate credentials through phishing or just poor user security. Even though you have done what you could, this can still happen. This is why you want to minimize what any user can do after login.

On many systems you can force the user to upgrade to some temporary superuser status with yet another password to do many functions (e.g., sudo on Unix systems). Some systems include security features that allow administrators to be notified of any and all remote access, but this isn't often practical. Some systems also email the user after login or logout reporting the access. This doesn't offer any protection of course, but if the user becomes aware that their account was used by someone else, they can at least contact the network administrator and minimize the damage. On networks that need extra security, reports from the logs can be generated and made available internally as well.

You can use intrusion detection software (IDS), but this is better suited to alerting administrators to hacking attempts rather than account misappropriation, as it is just so hard to manage a large volume of alerts to every access granted. This type of monitoring may only be required for a small group of users to be practical, however. Ideally you can configure the system to only alert for anomalies rather than simple access.

If you are using an IDS, then your vendor can help with simplifying the configuration, as IDS sensors have swamped many IT staffs and much has been learned over the years. The goal is to only alert IT staff to the highest risk events.

If you are running a detection system that merely scans logs, this will need to be done frequently. Ultimately this will only show you what has happened and is too late to be mitigated, but it can still be useful for uncovering network weaknesses and users who have been compromised.

Respond

No matter how much you have done to protect your network, there will always be some sort of security event. If any suspicion of a user account being compromised is seen, then those credentials should immediately be changed or at least locked. Contact the user and find out if they accessed the network or not.

If you are unable to determine the extent of any breach or fully comprehend how significant any unauthorized access was, you should disable remote access completely until this can be determined.

If your network has not only been breached but confidential data has been accessed, you must determine which data was involved. The server logs should show exactly what was accessed. If confidential information for you or your customers was accessed, you will most likely need to contact your legal department after you have made sure remote access has been stopped.

Recover

Recovery of damaged or deleted data is a technical function you can handle fairly easily with good backups. Changing credentials and access rules can be easily handled as well.

If confidential information has been accessed, however, nothing will be easy. Coordinate with legal counsel always, but generally it is better to be open about the breach and the potential that confidential information was viewed by unauthorized personnel.

Sadly, it is often only after a breach that management will be open to stricter network policies. Now is the time to address policies and procedures and do everything possible to prevent or at least minimize the damage from future security events.

Review Questions

The following questions test your knowledge of the material presented in this chapter.

1. **Name the two types of Internet Protocol traffic and describe the benefits and deficiencies of each.**

   Answer: There are two kinds of Internet Protocol traffic: Transmission Control Protocol or TCP and User Datagram Protocol or UDP. When a TCP connection is established, data can be sent bi-directionally. This connection is highly reliable and features error-checking but adds some bulk to the transmission. UDP is a much simpler, connectionless protocol where multiple messages are sent as packets in data chunks. UDP is great for servers dealing with queries from a huge volume of clients or games where speed is critical. There is no error-checking function with UDP, so there is no real guarantee that transmitted packets will actually arrive at their destinations.

2. **What is the main standards organization for the Internet and how does it go about establishing the standards that are used on the Internet?**

   Answer: The Internet Engineering Task Force (IETF), the main standards organization for the Internet. RFCs, or Request for Comments, are submitted by anyone to the Internet IETF, and if the IETF deems the note worthy the RFC is given a unique number. If this RFC attracts enough interest and a consensus emerges, it may evolve into an

Internet standard, but many RFCs are essentially the de facto standards for most Internet protocols.

3. **What category of connectivity devices is involved in every type of connection to the Internet and what types of physical devices can assume this role?**

   Answer: Every stand-alone computer or local area network that connects to the Internet will connect through some type of gateway device. This gateway device is often a router but may also be a switch that features some protocol conversion or translator. The gateway device could also be a modem, an access point, or even a Voice over Internet Protocol (VoIP) adapter.

4. **Describe the security function provided by a proxy server.**

   Answer: A proxy server allows a client to make an indirect network connection. The client connects to the proxy server, with or without any conscious authentication, and makes a request for a resource from a different server. Then, the proxy server will handle the request by either returning the requested resource from a cache, or by forwarding the request to the other server (after potentially modifying the request).

5. **How do firewalls determine which packets to allow to go through and which ones to deny?**

   Answer: A good firewall will provide packet filtering using defined rules to reject or accept both incoming and outgoing packets. This can be more challenging to configure, but firewall rules are really critical to security on most networks.

6. **What is the purpose of encrypting data that must be transmitted through or from the Internet?**

   Answer: Encryption is a simple way to make sure that if data is intercepted by a third party it will be very challenging to decipher. It is rapidly becoming an almost required step in securing any network.

7. **After a user has been authenticated, what activity is performed to determine what resources they have permission to access and what actions they can perform on those resources after accessing them?**

   Answer: Authorization. After a user is authenticated we will generally want to determine their authorization, which essentially involves the resources that the authenticated user has permission to access, and what actions they can perform.

8. **What is the eventual drawback of using overly complex multifactor authentication schemes?**

   Answer: Additional authentication factors can be added to the login sequence to increase security by making it less and less likely that an attack will be successful. However, with more challenging login sequences, users will become dissatisfied and resort to scribbling credentials on sticky notes and desktop calendars, or just simply not using the service. This is a huge challenge for any website engineer where user satisfaction is an issue.

9. **Which two administrative principles should be practiced any time outside users are allowed to access a network?**

   Answer: When allowing outside users into a network, always use the principles of "least-privilege" and "need-to-know." Give each user the least amount of access possible and only to the areas of the network they must have

10. **How does adding a CAPTCHA to a login scheme increase security?**

    Answer: Adding a CAPTCHA to a traditional authentication scheme can potentially eliminate any kind of automated password attack. While these tests tend to annoy users, they are generally very effective. However, they are also a barrier to some users with certain disabilities, unless alternative mechanisms are included that target those users.

11. **What is the advantage of choosing a static packet filtering firewall device for a given position in a network?**

    Answer: Static packet filtering firewalls do not keep track of the state of a connection between two computers. This makes this variety of firewalls relatively faster than other firewall options. They also offer fewer security features than other firewall options. On the other hand, a static packet filtering firewall is relatively inexpensive and easy to maintain.

12. **Describe the process involved in a dictionary attack, as well as actions that can be taken to defeat such an attack.**

    Answer: A dictionary attack is simply a systematic, brute-force attack using every word in a dictionary as a password. This type of attack is simple to eliminate by limiting the number of login attempts that can be performed in a given period of time. In addition, the IP of any user exceeding a certain number of attempts over that period of time could be banned until they are cleared by an administrator.

13. **Why is it so difficult to stop DDoS attacks by blocking the attacking IP addresses?**

    Answer: Ultimately, the battle to block IP addresses is rarely won, as these attacks typically come from thousands of IP addresses depending on the size of the botnet. If a dynamic IP blocking system, such as *fail2ban*, is in place some progress might be made. However, if a large botnet is used, it will probably prevail. IP blocking is a fundamental mitigation concept, but the more distributed the attack the less likely this process will help.

14. **If no one in a given organization needs to access the network from the Internet, what firewall configuration can be established to make the network more secure?**

    Answer: If no one needs to access the network from the Internet, then the firewall configuration can be tightened up to disallow any packet that originates from the outside world. If you disallow ICMP and don't respond on any port, then the firewall is better secured.

15. **What networking technique is typically used to separate networks into smaller segments for security and performance reasons?**

    Answer: Network segmentation, or zoning, is essentially the separation of the network into sub-networks, each of which becomes a segment. From a security perspective the main reason to deploy network segmentation is to limit the access capabilities of intruders. Each segment will also benefit from reduced congestion and broadcast traffic in addition to containing network problems to a single segment.

Exam Questions

1. **You have been tasked with presenting a defense strategy to protect the organization's network from Internet-based threats. What type of device is at the top of your list as the first line of defense for the network?**

    A. **Proxy servers**

    B. **Firewalls**

    C. **L2 Switches**

    D. **Routers**

Answer: B. The most common first line of defense in a network connected to the Internet is a firewall. These devices usually consist of some combination of hardware and software used to protect a private network from unauthorized access by way of the Internet. This is accomplished by limiting security exposures, enforcing the organization's security policy, and sometimes logging or monitoring Internet activity.

2. **The organization wants to establish a secure connection with a trusted supplier. You have recommended establishing a Virtual Private Network (VPN) between the two company networks. Which of the following protocols are typically combined to accomplish this goal? (Select two.)**

   A. S/MIME

   B. TACACS+

   C. IPSec

   D. L2TP

   Answer: C, D. The Layer 2 Tunneling Protocol (L2TP) uses PPP and is unencrypted but can pass another encryption protocol in the tunnel. Often the underlying protocol will be combined with L2TP as with an L2TP/IPsec combination.

3. **Telnet is used for remote login purposes, but it offers little security. Which of the following encrypted network protocols should be used instead?**

   A. SSH

   B. Secure Telnet

   C. SSL

   D. Secure login

   Answer: A. There are many types of Telnet emulations available via custom client software, but most have no encryption available and so there is no guarantee that your communication will not be intercepted while in transit. Some older network devices may only support Telnet, but whenever possible you should use SSH instead.

4. **Which of the following are the main elements of the Kerberos authentication protocol?**

   A. Ticket, authentication, and encryption

   B. Key, ticket, and authentication

   C. Key, ticket, and encryption

   D. Key, authentication, and encryption

Answer: C. Kerberos involves a trusted third party Ticket Granting Server (TGS) to authenticate client/server interaction. The exact process varies with implementation, but essentially the client exchanges clear text information with the Authentication Server (AS), which then uses keys shared with the client to encrypt messages that include keys shared between the AS and the TGS.

5. **Which of the following attack types employs deceptive frame techniques to trick the user into clicking on their content rather than the intended content?**

   A. **MITM**

   B. **DDoS**

   C. **Clickjacking**

   D. **Fraggle attack**

   Answer: C. A clickjacking attack employs deceptive frame techniques to trick the user into clicking on their content rather than the intended content.

6. **The Challenge-Handshake Authentication Protocol (CHAP) is used primarily for what?**

   A. **Network layer encryption**

   B. **Remote access**

   C. **LAN server configuration**

   D. **WAN ISDN connection**

   Answer: B. creates a random string, a challenge phrase, or a *secret*. It then combines that with something else, such as the username or host name, and sends the combined information to the requesting system. The requestor, in turn, hashes the string and returns the result. The server then checks to see that the hashed result is correct and authenticates or denies the requestor

7. **Of the various firewall types available for use in a business network, which type disassembles each packet, evaluates it, and then reassembles it, making this type of connection significantly slower than other firewall types?**

   A. **Stateful packet-filtering firewalls**

   B. **Static packet-filtering firewalls**

   C. **Proxy filtering firewalls**

   D. **MAC filtering firewalls**

   Answer: C. Proxy servers, or proxy filtering firewalls, are servers configured to filter out unwanted packets. Proxy filtering is a much more complex process than packet filtering. During the filtering process, each packet is disassembled, evaluated, and reassembled, making this type of connection significantly slower than other firewall types.

8. **Which protocol in the IPSec protocol suite is valuable for preventing replay attacks?**

   A. AH

   B. ESP

   C. SA

   D. IKE

   Answer: A. Authentication Headers (AH) provides data integrity and origin authentication to protect against replay attacks (attacks where a recorded transmission is replayed by an attacker to gain access).

9. **Of the various firewall types available for use in a business network, which type collects network connection information and maintains dynamic state tables used for subsequent connections, which enables ports to be opened and closed as needed?**

   A. Stateful packet-filtering firewalls

   B. Static packet-filtering firewalls

   C. Proxy filtering firewalls

   D. MAC filtering firewalls

   Answer: A. Stateful packet-filtering firewalls do keep track of the connection state between entities. These firewalls collect network connection information and maintain dynamic state tables that are used for subsequent connections. This enables ports to be opened and closed as needed. Once a client has completed a communication session, the stateful packet-filtering firewall closes the specific port used until it is requested again.

10. **Even though passwords can be sent as hashed values rather than as cleartext, several hacking tools are available that can be used to obtain user passwords. Which types of attacks would these tools be used to perform? (Select two.)**

   A. Logic bomb

   B. Dictionary

   C. Buffer overflow

   D. Brute force

   Answer: B, D. Dictionary and brute force attacks use tools to guess user passwords.

Glossary

3DES

Also known as Triple DES, 3DES is a block cipher encryption algorithm that employs symmetric keys. It applies the DES algorithm three times to each block.

A

AAA protocol

Authentication, Authorization, and Accounting that uses different link layer protocols such as PPP and authenticates using PAP or CHAP.

access codes

Numerical sequence, typically four numbers long that identifies the authorized client(s) or user(s). Once properly authenticated, access codes may arm, disarm, or access the security system for other features.

access control

Security precautions that ensure resources are granted only to those users who are entitled to them.

access control gate

An opening in a wall or fence that functions as a passageway between two open spaces (as opposed to a door, which provides access into or between enclosed spaces).

access control list

A list that controls access to a network segment via whitelisting or blacklisting.

access control policy

The method by which an access control list is generated.

Acknowledge (ACK)

Part of the second and third (final) step of the Three-Way Handshake of the TCP/IP protocol. This part of the segment acknowledges the request for synchronization.

Active Directory

A directory service provided by Microsoft that handles domain management, which includes authentication, authorization, certificate management, and more.

Active RFID tags

These self-powered tags provide a longer range but are much more expensive. Active Radio Frequency Identifier tags transfer identifying information by way of electromagnetic fields.

ActiveX

A Microsoft utility that enables web applications to build extended, interactive features and functionality in the browser. ActiveX automatically downloads without involving the user, which creates a potential security vulnerability that can be used by crackers to embed malicious code in hacked websites.

Adaptive Frequency Hopping Spread Spectrum (AFHSS)

The Bluetooth specification implements this in the license-free 2.4GHz range to provide security and avoid crowded frequency ranges, by hopping between previously divided subfrequencies.

Address Resolution Protocol (ARP) spoofing attacks

An attack where the attacker sends fake ARP messages to associate their MAC address with the IP address of another user. Once the association has been established, messages directed to that address will be diverted to the attacker. The attacker can then use information obtained from the intercepted messages to mount other types of attacks, such as DoS or man-in-the-middle attacks.

Address Space Layout Randomization (ASLR)

This is a technique used to prevent or lessen the impacts of buffer overflow attacks.

administrative tools

These tools include programs designed to control the usage of the computer's memory, administer and optimize hard-disk-drive usage, configure OS services running on the computer, control the hardware/OS handoff during startup, and troubleshoot operating system problems.

Adobe Reader

Adobe's PDF software. Exploits may lead to arbitrary code execution, sandbox bypassing, or simple denial-of-service usually through memory corruption.

Advanced Encryption Standard (AES)

A block-level encryption algorithm that uses symmetric keys. Announced by NIST in 2001, it has been adopted by the United States government and supersedes DES.

Advanced Persistent Threats

These threats target very specific and very secure systems over a continuous period of time.

adware

Unwanted, unsolicited advertising usually displayed in web browsers.

algorithm

As related to computer security, an algorithm is code used to alter a message so that unauthorized people cannot read it.

analog camera

A camera that requires a separate coaxial cable to connect to a monitor or to the recording device. Analog cameras are susceptible to quality degradation of the information being transmitted.

Android

An operating system that was developed for use with tablet and smart phone devices. It primarily uses touchscreen gestures for operation and control. It is currently the most popular mobile operating system in use.

annunciators

An alarm system device that signals the operating condition of the system by sound, light, or other indication.

anomaly analysis

This analysis system applies statistical analysis techniques to the data stream in order to determine whether it is "normal" or "anomalous" at any given time.

anomaly-based IDS/IDPS

Intrusion-detection systems that use anomaly analysis to detect and prevent unauthorized access to a network.

anonymous proxy

A proxy server that provides client anonymity by concealing the original IP address.

antispyware

Programs that defend against spyware by either detecting and then removing the spyware and/or blocking it in the first place.

antivirus

Programs that defend against computer viruses by either detecting and then removing them and/or blocking them in the first place.

Apple OS X

The Apple operating system, which is Unix-based.

Apple's Time Machine

Apple's backup software application.

appliance-based virtualization

These are closed storage management systems that are placed between the user network and the storage network.

application-level encryption

One method of applying encryption at the application level, providing a broader security standard.

application packages

These operate as extensions of the operating system. Depending on the type of operating system being used, an application program may directly control some system resources, such as printers and network interfaces, while the operating system lends fundamental support in the background. In more advanced systems, the operating system supplies common input, output, and disk management functions for all applications in the system.

application servers

Servers configured to provide a specific role in the organization's business activities provided for the organization's internal users.

Application Service Provider (ASP)

The ancestor of modern cloud computing. An enterprise that provides application-based services to paying customers across a network.

Application zone

A delegated zone defined by the usage of applications within an Intranet environment. The zone is created by use of firewalls, routers, and switches.

asset

Something of value can be tangible—e.g., a flash drive or intangible such as the data on said flash drive.

asymmetric keys

Used in encryption algorithms, defined by two keys; one key is used for encryption and another key is used for decryption.

asymmetrical (out-of-band) virtualization

The virtualization device is installed outside the actual data path between the network and the storage system.

attack surface

The sum of the different opportunities for being attacked.

attenuation

A measure of how much signal loss occurs as the information moves across a transport medium such as a fiber optic cable.

audit entries

Items added to the security log when an audited event occurs.

audit event log files

These are where the audit entries are stored.

audit policy

This defines the types of events that will be monitored and added to the system's security logs.

audit trail

A record of a user's computer usage.

auditing

A form of accounting that is a preplanned monitoring method to evaluate or determine if problems exist within a specific area.

authentication

The process of determining that someone is who they say they are.

Authentication, Authorization, and Accounting (AAA)

A framework that network administrators can use to control access, enforce security policies, and track usage.

Authentication Header (AH)

A protocol used by IPsec to prevent packet changes in transport. This provides integrity and authentication.

Authentication Server (AS)

A server whose function is to provide network users with authentication.

authentication system

A network system used to provide authentication.

authoritative

A server that provides definitive answers to DNS queries rather than from a cache or by requesting that information from another name server.

authorization

The resources that a user has permission to access, and what actions they can perform.

authorized

Being recognized as a person who has the right to access an asset.

automated access control

A design feature that requires authentication of the identity of a user attempting to access a security zone or computer system from a distant location.

automated provisioning

Similar to Rule-Based Access Control, this is a method where a rule is the basic element. The rule defines what operations can perform be performed.

Autorun

A featured that automatically runs executable programs found on removable media devices as soon as it detects the presence of the media in the drive or reader. This feature provides a very serious security threat because malware programs located on the media will run automatically and infect the host device.

B

backup media

This is what the data backups are stored on—e.g., DVD-Rs.

backup policy

A policy that defines what to back up, when to back up, and where to store the backups. Also includes who has authorization over the backups and how they are made.

bandwidth

This is the media's total ability to carry data at a given instance.

barriers

These impede the ability of an intruder to advance from the outer perimeter to the interior region.

Basic Input/Output System (BIOS)

The program that boots up the computer and controls input and output operations.

bastion host

A bastion host is located in the DMZ and may be a firewall, a router, a server, or a group of computers that are not protected behind another firewall, but that have direct access to the Internet.

beacon frames

These let nearby clients know what networks they are broadcasting.

beacon interval

This determines the amount of time between beacon frames.

biometric solutions

Using the unique physical features of a person, fingerprints, voiceprints, and/or retinal scans to provide identification and authentication.

biometrics

These are access control mechanisms that use human physical characteristics to verify individual identities.

BitLocker

A native utility on some newer, high-end Windows OS versions that provides full disk-level encryption.

black hat hacker

An individual who possesses extensive programming skills and uses them for the purpose of breeching or bypassing network security structures for malicious or criminal purposes.

blacklisting

When access is denied only to users matching given criteria.

blacklists

Lists of users who are untrusted.

block cipher

A cipher that applies an algorithm to a block of data, rather than a single bit at a time.

Blowfish

A block-level encryption algorithm that uses symmetric-key encryption.

Bluebugging

A type of Bluetooth attack where a hacker can gain total control over the device if it is left discoverable.

Bluejacking

This is the act of sending unsolicited messages to Bluetooth devices that are set to be automatically discoverable.

Bluesnarfing

This is running special software on a nearby Bluetooth device that requests information from the mobile device.

Bluetooth

A wireless networking specification for personal area networks (PANs) that meshes together personal devices including PDAs, cell phones, digital cameras, PCs, notebooks, and printers.

boot files

These take over control of the system hardware from the ROM BIOS during start-up. They bring the OS kernel files into RAM memory so they can be used to control the operation of the system.

booter services

Services that perform DOS attacks for a price.

bot herder

The unauthorized person in control of a botnet.

botnet

A large collection of zombies, or bots, controlled by a bot herder.

bots (zombie computers)

PCs controlled by an unauthorized person.

bring-your-own-device (BYOD)

Authorizing the use of an employee's own device instead of providing one, for business-related activities.

broadcast storm

This is when broadcast traffic is rebroadcast by every network device, eventually causing traffic delivery failure. This can quickly overload switches and routers and overwhelm a network.

broadcast traffic

This is sending messages to all possible destinations on a network.

Browser Exploitation Framework (BeEF)

A notable open-source penetration testing tool that focuses on web-borne attacks through a web browser.

brute-force attack

This is where the attacker systematically guesses the key based on a known list or a predictive mathematical scheme. This can involve hundreds and thousands of attempts.

buffer overflow

An anomaly where a program overruns the buffer boundary, thereby resulting in erratic behavior, memory access errors, and/or system crashes. The system is effectively disabled to the point where the user cannot use it.

buffer overflow attack

Causing a system to have a buffer overflow.

bus topology

The nodes, or stations, of the network connect to a central communication link.

Business-to-Business (B2B)

Network channels that organizations use to conduct secure transactions with other trusted organizations.

Business-to-Customer (B2C)

This is a specialized DMZ that's used by an organization to communicate with their customers.

bypass mode

A mode available for many alarm systems designed to let someone through the alarm area without triggering the alarm.

bypassing

Turning off or disabling a sensor, device, or an entire zone without affecting the rest of the system.

C

cabinetry

Specialized furniture used to secure physical computing assets.

cache poisoning

When an attacker establishes a rogue DNS server and then uses that server to feed false information back to the primary DNS server, thereby poisoning the primary DNS server's cached resources.

caching device

A device that stores certain data for quicker responses to future requests.

caching servers

Using cached web pages, a proxy server will serve already-accessed web pages placed in its cache to requesting clients without requiring outside access to the Internet.

caching web proxies

Local servers that cache (store) web resources for quicker access.

camera deployment strategy

Determining where security cameras will be placed.

candela

A measure of foot-candles.

cantenna

A home-built tin-can waveguide antenna that can amplify Wi-Fi signals.

certificate chain

This is the list of certificates starting with the root certificate, followed by each subsequent certificate, where the issuer or signer of one certificate is the subject of the next.

Challenge-Handshake Authentication Protocol (CHAP)

An authentication method using a three-way handshake (syn, syn-ack, ack) to identify remote clients.

Charged Coupled Device (CCD)

A surveillance camera technology featuring high-resolution, low-operating light requirements, less temperature dependence, and high reliability.

chokepoint

A place where people or other traffic must pass through a portal—such as a gate, doorway, hallway, or access street/road—that may lead to a single point of failure.

chroot

A Linux-based command that adjusts the root directory location of a currently running process. May also be used for creating and managing multiple virtualized copies of an operating system.

cipher

In cryptography, a cipher is the algorithm used to encrypt data.

cipher locks

Locks that operate by unlocking magnetic door locks when the correct programmed code is entered by the user on the cipher lock keypad.

ciphertext

The text of any data after it has been encoded by a cryptographic key.

Cisco Discovery Protocol (CDP) attacks

The CDP protocol enables Cisco devices to communicate with other Cisco devices to exchange information. Attackers can use this protocol to gather information about the switches and other network devices running CDP on the network.

cleartext

Stored or transmitted data that has not been encrypted.

clickjacking attack

This attack employs deceptive frame techniques to trick the user into clicking on their content rather than the intended content.

client-server

This is a number of users using multiple workstations that has the data stored on a server.

client/server network

Where dependent workstations, referred to as clients, operate in conjunction with a dedicated master computer called a server.

closed-circuit television (CCTV)

Electronic security and surveillance technology that often provides real-time monitoring of exterior and interior residential areas. The signals produced from a CCTV system are not publicly distributed.

cloud-based services

Clouds are hosted services with special client application software that extends the users' desktops or mobile files and data storage to an Internet service.

cloud computing

Utilizing remote, networked, servers for resources. These resources may include data storage, data processing, and others, thereby reducing the hardware needs of a local machine.

coaxial cable

A transmission cable consisting of two conductors insulated from one another and enclosed in a polyethylene jacket.

Common Criteria for Informational Security Evaluation (Common Criteria or CC)

This establishes Evaluation Assurance Levels that can be used to certify equipment reliability or assure levels of security. The greater the organizational security need, the higher the specific EAL value should be for any given network hardware or software asset.

Common Internet File System (CIFS)

A network protocol developed to provide shared access to files and devices, along with network communications.

Common Platform Enumeration (CPE)

This is a standardized method of describing and identifying operating systems, hardware devices, and application classes on a network.

Common Vulnerabilities and Exposures (CVE)

This is a system for referencing publicly known vulnerabilities. Maintained by MITRE Corporation and backed by the US Department of Homeland Security.

Common Vulnerability Scoring System (CVSS)

This is a system for scoring vulnerabilities from CVE, making it easier to understand the associated risks.

communication media

The hardware, firmware, and software used to physically store and/or transport the data information that exits and enters computers. This media includes magnetic, optical, or floptical disks, tapes, and drives, either internal or removable.

Completely Automated Public Turing test to tell Computers and Humans Apart (CAPTCHA)

These are generally a form input request for a word, phrase, random characters and numbers, or a simple request to perform a simple test that cannot easily be automated.

complexity

As it relates to passwords, it is the combination of the length, width, and depth of an input.

Conficker

This worm targeted thumb drives and would automatically execute as soon as it was connected to a live USB port.

Confidentiality, Integrity, and Availability (CIA)

This is the classic model of information security.

connectivity devices

Devices used to create network connections, including hubs, switches, and routers.

contingency planning

Planning for disasters/emergencies before they happen.

controller

The controller is responsible for taking the input information, comparing that information to a predetermined condition or a reference, making decisions about what action should be taken, and finally sending corrective error signals to the final element, which adjusts the manipulated variable.

cookie poisoning

An attacker steeling a cookie, altering it, and then sending the altered cookie back as an attack vector.

cookie theft

An attacker acquiring unauthorized access to a site by obtaining a cookie.

cookies

These are small files that web servers send to web browsers when their pages are accessed.

copper cabling

One of the primary physical transport mediums for network data transfer.

crackers

These individuals break computer security in order to gain access to software without purchasing.

cracking

Utilizing software that would guess at passwords in loops until access is granted.

CRAM-MD5

Email authentication system that transfers passwords in a hashed form.

credential harvesting

Any method used to collect another user's authentication information.

cross-site scripting (XSS)

An attack method that allows the injection of client-side script into a web page that may be used by other, unsuspecting, users.

crypt

The original encryption utility included with older versions of Unix.

cryptography

The procedures, processes, and techniques used to convert data into secret code.

CryptoLocker

This is a ransomware Trojan.

cryptology

The study of cryptography.

current loop

The amount of electrical current flowing between a zone's two connection points.

Cyber Kill Chain®

This is a process that was developed by Lockheed Martin to address attacks from threats considered Advanced Persistent Threats (APT).

cyber security policy

The company's security policy explains the overall requirements needed to protect an organization's network data and computer systems.

cyber warfare

A virtual conflict that involves politically motivated attacks on an adversary's IT or ICS networks.

cybercriminals

These individuals are typically motivated by greed and seek financial gain. This group of hackers is probably the most notable hacker type, as they tend to generate the most notice.

cybersecurity

This is securing physical access to property, systems, and equipment ports while securing intangible assets including electronic, optical, and informational access to the system's data and controls.

cyberterrorists

These individuals are typically not motivated by money, but rather by furtherance of a political agenda or ideology. The goal is to cause harm and chaos to the general public.

D

daemon

This is a standard, default user/group that has privilege to execute programs (background processes) that run without direction from the user.

data concentrators

These are used to group multiple smart meters together and aggregate their data transmissions for delivery to the utility servers in the central office.

data diode

A device that creates a one-way connection between networks or network segments that possess different security classifications.

data encoding

The process of converting data into a format used for transmission and storage.

Data Encryption Standard (DES)

A symmetric-key algorithm used for the encryption of data.

Data Execution Prevention (DEP)

A sandboxing scheme that isolates a given program to a specific memory region to protect the rest of the system from potential attack.

data in motion

The process of data that is being transmitted through a wired or wireless network.

data in use

Data that is in the process of being created, updated, retrieved, or deleted.

Data Segmentation for Privacy (DS4P)

Creates constraints to standards for meaningful use, consistent with federal and state privacy policies and regulations. In other words, it tries to clarify how to apply the standards in a way that is consistent with the intent of the regulation. DS4P supports a secret exchange of EHRs and privacy annotations applied to documents, messages, atomic data, and metadata.

deadband

Also known as a neutral zone or dead zone, a deadband is a band of inactivity above and below the set point of IPC.

deauthentication flood attack

This involves an attacker sending a deauthentication packet to an access point, which in turn removes any previously authenticated devices connected to it.

decrypt

Using the relevant key to unlock the scrambled ciphertext into plaintext so that it might be understood.

decryption

The process of converting previously encrypted data back to its original form.

decryption key

The key used to decrypt a secret code.

deep packet inspection (DPI)

Examining the actual data in a TCP/IP packet searching for signs of viruses, spam, and other defined threats to determine whether or not the packet should be forwarded.

default user accounts

As it applies to Microsoft, the accounts provided on every new installation of the Windows OS.

defense-in-depth

A defense strategy that includes a number of different overlapping security mechanisms, which potentially minimizes the effects of a single mechanism being overcome by an attacker.

demilitarized zone (DMZ)

The DMZ is a separate perimeter network that isolates the secure intranet from the outside world, yet enables public access to outward facing dedicated resources.

Denial of Service (DoS)

Attacks designed to overuse a host, server, or network resource to the point where it functionally ceases to provide its services.

desktop/single user

This is a single computer, possibly shared by a small group of users.

detection-specific audit records

Records generated to provide specific information about desired actions or events. These actions or events can be based on operating system activities, application events, or security events.

Dynamic Host Configuration Protocol (DHCP) server

A server that uses the network protocol to distribute network parameters such as IP addresses.

Dynamic Host Configuration Protocol (DHCP) snooping

A security technology built into an operating system to filter and block ingress (incoming) DHCP server messages that are deemed unacceptable.

dictionary attack

A systematic, brute-force attack using every word in a dictionary as a password for a given username.

digital cameras

These convert the images they detect directly into digital signals that can easily be transmitted to and manipulated by digital computing devices.

digital certificates

These are digital verifications that the sender of an encrypted message is who they claim to be.

digital IP device

Any digital device that can be identified by an IP address and, therefore, can be accessed by a network.

Digital Video Recorder (DVR)

The preferred type of recording system (rather than VCRs) for surveillance cameras. DVR technology for CCTV permits images to be transferred to disk, lessening the negative impact of poor quality video storage media.

direct-attached storage

This technique employs additional disk drive storage devices that are attached directly to the DVR via USB or eSATA connections.

directory harvest attacks (DHAs)

A spammer simply guesses email addresses at a domain and then connects to the email server of that domain. Any addresses that are not rejected are considered valid.

directory traversal

As it relates to an attack, directory traversal exploits poorly secured software applications to access files that should not be accessible. This is done by traversing to a higher level folder or directory.

Discretionary Access Control (DAC)

Configurations where the user has the discretion to decide who has access to their objects and to what extent.

discretionary access control list (DACL)

A list of rights that an object or user has to a specific resource within a network.

disk-level encryption

Involves using technology to encrypt an entire disk structure. This technique offers value in that it protects everything on the disk from unauthorized access, including the operating system files and structure.

disk operating system (DOS)

A collection of programs that run in the background and control overall computer operation.

distorting proxy

A proxy server that hides or modifies your IP address and related information.

Distributed Denial of Service (DDoS) attacks

Involve multiple remote systems being used to simultaneously perform a mass DoS attack on the targeted resource.

distributed IDS systems

Local hosts attached to a network have their own IDS modules installed. Additionally, there is an IDS management module installed on a network server that coordinates the flow of information to and from the individual local IDS modules.

Distributed Reflection and Amplification Denial of Service (DRDoS)

The attacker uses a relatively small botnet in a distributed attack on reflection servers that redirect the queries they receive, making it appear as though the reflection server is the actual source.

distributions

Linux-speak for versions.

diversion

This is a tactic intended to distract an individual from monitoring something. Typically, diversions are created so that an attacker can either view sensitive information without being seen or gain entry into a secure area without being questioned.

DNS RRL (DNS Response Rate Limiting)

A mitigation attempt that limits the rate at which authoritative servers respond to large volumes of queries.

docking stations

Accessories designed for use with portable computing devices. The primary function of the docking station is to enable portable users to travel with their portable devices, yet still employ full-size peripheral and connectivity devices when they are in the office environment.

documentation

Official material that provides a record or evidence.

domain

A computer environment where all of the members of the network share a common directory database and are organized into various levels. The domain is identified by a unique name and is administered as a single unit having common rules and procedures.

domain controller

A centralized server that controls the objects, rules, and procedures of a domain.

Domain Name System (DNS) servers

These contain DNS databases (*.dns files) that are used to resolve computer names to IP addresses. These servers also contain mappings between Fully Qualified Domain Names and the IP addresses they represent.

Domain User and Group accounts

User and Group accounts that are defined with a domain environment.

Double Encapsulation VLAN Hopping attack

This attack results in two headers being added (double tagged) to the original frame. One of the tags represents the target's VLAN ID, while the other is the VLAN ID of the attacker's switch. When the packet hits the attacker's switch, the first tag is stripped out but the second tag remains with the packet. The packet is then forwarded to the target's switch, which reads the tag and forwards the packet to the target host.

downstream interface

The interface that allows traffic to enter a network from the Internet.

dual-firewall DMZ

Firewalls are positioned on each side of the DMZ to filter traffic moving between the intranet and the DMZ as well as between the DMZ and the Internet. These firewalls are used to route public traffic to the DMZ and internal network traffic to the intranet.

Dynamic ARP Inspection (DAI)

A configuration feature that is designed to thwart MITM attacks. DAI uses the DHCP snooping database to check and validate ARP requests to prevent ARP spoofing attacks.

Dynamic Host Configuration Protocol (DHCP)

This is commonly used to define a range of IPs that can be dynamically leased to the requesting external IP address for a preconfigured length of time.

dynamic trunking protocol (DTP) request

An attacker sends a request to a network switch that would configure the attacker's port as a trunk connection.

dynamic variable

This physical parameter can change spontaneously from external influences or internal influences.

E

eCryptfs

A built-in package that the major Linux operating systems possess, which provides file system–level encryption services. This level of encryption enables the encryption service to be applied at the individual file or directory without significant disk management overhead.

egress

The action of leaving a place, whether physically or logically.

electric deadbolts

Electronically operated locks used in securing a closed door.

electronic signatures

A technique used to validate the authenticity of an individual, usually attached to an electronic document, indicating the sender's intent or agreement.

email servers

Email servers are client/server application servers used to receive and store electronic mail messages in individual mailboxes, even when users are not actually logged directly onto the network.

EMV chip-and-PIN technology

This technology adds extra layers of payment card protection for customers.

Encapsulating Security Payloads (ESP)

This offers origin authentication as well as encryption. ESP encrypts and encapsulates the entire TCP/UDP datagram within an ESP header that does not include any port information.

Encrypting File System (EFS)

The Window's file- and folder-level encryption service.

encryption

Encrypting data involves taking the data (plaintext) and processing it with a key code (cipher) that defines how the original version of the data has been manipulated (ciphertext).

encryption key

The key or algorithm used to convert plaintext to ciphertext, and vice versa.

enterprise networks

A computer network designed to support medium and large numbers of users for business to interconnect its activities and share resources.

entropy

Any lack of predictability and order, leaving to a degree of uncertainty.

entry delay

A delay that a security zone can be configured with that gives those entering the premises time to access an internal security panel to deactivate an alarm before it activates.

enumerate

Establishing a map of any network or determining what devices and hosts can be found.

eSATA

External SATA (Serial AT Attachment), or eSATA, ports are physical interfaces that link eSATA-compatible devices with the system's internal SATA bus.

escort

Someone charged with controlling the movement of one or more visitors.

Ethernet

This is the dominant transmission media force in hardware and electrical signaling interfacing as well as for providing media access control.

Ettercap

A free and open source software tool used to perform a number of network and security analyses.

EV certificates

Extended Validation (EV) certificates require verification of an individual by a Certificate Authority. These are typically used on sites that are using SLL/TLS.

exclusion

This is a method, device, or system security professionals use to forbid, prohibit, or remove access to excluded assets.

eXecute Disable (XD) bit

A feature built into microprocessor hardware to protect certain areas of memory that contain specific blocks of instruction code, such as the kernel.

exFAT

Microsoft's extended File Allocation Table file system for flash memory devices.

exit delay

A time delay on the activation of a security system to give an individual time to leave the premises without triggering the alarm.

exploits

Software programs or tools designed to take advantage of particular vulnerabilities or flaws in a computer system.

export-grade encryption

This was created to be good enough, yet still allow the NSA to decrypt communication outside the United States. The NSA lifted this export requirement in the late 1990s, but those cipher suites have remained in both client and server libraries.

Ext#

The ext# series of Extended File Systems are the primary file management systems designed for the Linux kernel. Ext2 is also widely used in SD cards and other flash-based storage devices.

extensible

Signifies when something can be expanded without bounds. As it applies to software, future growth is taken into consideration, allowing the system to function normally.

extranet

An intranet structure that grants limited access to authorized outside users, such as corporate business partners. In other words, a partially private, partially public network structure.

F

F2FS

Samsung's Flash-Friendly File System (version 2) is an open-source Linux file system for flash storage devices.

fail-safe

Also known as fail-secure, it is a method that responds to certain types of failures in a way that will cause minimum harm to personnel or devices.

fail-secure

Also known as fail-safe, it is a method that responds to certain types of failures in a way that will cause minimum harm to personnel or devices.

fail-soft

This mode will terminate any nonessential processing when a hardware or software failure occurs.

false negative

This is a report that produces an incorrect rejection of the individual, thereby locking them out of a facility or security area to which they should have access.

false positive

This is a report that incorrectly authenticates the individual, which could lead to providing access to equipment or data to which this person should not have access. Of the two types of authentication failure, this is the most significant in that it could grant access to malicious people.

Fiber Optic cabling

Plastic or glass cable designed to carry digital data in the form of light pulses.

field of view

Also known as field of vision, field of view is the extent a given surveillance camera can see.

file- and folder-level encryption

Encryption applied to individual files and folders. File- and folder-level encryption tools enable users to encrypt files stored on their drives using keys only the designated user (or an authorized recovery agent) can decode. This prevents theft of data by those who do not have the password or a decoding tool.

file and print servers

These provide employees with quick access to shared applications, folders, specific files, and networked printers.

FileVault

This is the disk-level-based data encryption service included with the Apple OS X operating systems.

fire brigade

These cyber attacks are a type of session hijacking that involves intercepting or sniffing and modifying communication between users.

fire detection and reporting system

A standalone fire alarm system used by larger organizations.

fire detection sensors

Sensors that detect the presence of fire by using heat and/or smoke sensors.

firewall rules

The rules by which a firewall determines what communication will be filtered.

firewalls

These devices usually consist of some combination of hardware and software used to protect a private network from unauthorized access by way of the Internet. This is accomplished by limiting security exposures, enforcing the organization's security policy, defining rules for filtering, and sometimes logging or monitoring activity.

FireWire

Similar to a USB cable, FireWire provides a connection on which up to 63 devices can be daisy-chained. This interface standard was first deployed with Apple products.

firmware

As opposed to software and hardware, firmware is permanent software that has been programmed into read-only memory.

fisheye lens

An ultra wide-angle lens that forgoes straight-line perspective for the purpose of viewing a larger area. Images from a fisheye lens are often distorted near the edges.

fixed focal length lens

Lenses whose focal length is fixed and cannot be adjusted like common zoom lenses.

foot-candle

A measure of luminance (or light intensity) used by the lighting industry.

Fraggle attack

A Denial of Service attack, much like a Smurf attack, where the attacker sends spoofed UDP packets to a broadcast address in a network.

frame

A digital data transmission unit that contains indicators informing of the beginning and ends of blocks of data.

FTP server

A centralized server, with specialized software, that manages file sharing and storing. Requires the use of the File Transfer Protocol.

G

gate

An opening in a wall or fence. Typically refers to a passageway between two open spaces (as opposed to a door, which provides access into or between enclosed spaces). Like doors, gates can be used to control access by presenting a barrier across the perimeter's passageway.

gateway

A device that interfaces a network with another network.

gateway device

A gateway device is often a router, but could also be a switch, a modem, an access point, or even a Voice over Internet Protocol (VoIP) adapter.

GEOM-Based Disk Encryption (GBDE)

A block device-layer disk-level encryption system.

glass breakage detection

A sensor that detects breaking glass. They come in two types. The vibration type is mounted on the glass or on a nearby wall. Acoustical or sound discriminators sense the sound of breaking glass.

graphical user interface (GUI)

A type of interface that allows the user to interact with graphical icons and visual interpretations, as opposed to text-based interfaces.

grayware

Software applications that may not have malware assigned to them, yet still contain undesirable functions.

group accounts

A collective set of users who use the same criteria for permissions. Used for ease of management.

guests

This default group typically has minimized access to the system, and all of its members share the same user profile. The Guest user account is automatically a member of this group.

H

hacker

An individual who uses their skills in computers to gain unauthorized access to data and resources.

hardening

The process of making any device (hardware and software) more secure. Often involves many steps and procedures, while taking into account acceptable usability.

hardware firewall device

A device specifically and solely designed to operate as a firewall.

hardware ports

An interface between various computer and networking devices.

hardware token

Also known as a security token, a hardware token is a physical device that can provide authentication.

hash table

Also known as a hash map, a hash table is a lookup table that maps keys to values using a hash function that converts the keys into hash values.

Hierarchical File Systems

These are proprietary Apple file systems developed as the primary file system for their Macintosh line of computers using MAC OS. It is also used in Apple's line of iPod music devices.

Home Area Network (HAN)

A specialized LAN made up of automated electrical device controllers, usually within or in close proximity of a home.

honey pots

A honey pot is a decoy server, network device, or network segment designed to attract attackers away from the real network. This is accomplished by providing attackers with relatively easy access to decoy systems on the network and hiding truly critical systems.

host address

The portion of the IP address that defines the identity of a device.

host-based authentication

This form of authentication relies on information (such as MAC addresses and hostnames) to authenticate to a network, as opposed the user's credentials.

host-based IDS (HBIDS)

An intrusion-detection system that is installed on and protects a single system.

Hypertext Transfer Protocol (HTTP)

This is the main web application protocol.

hypervisor

The hypervisor is a virtual operating platform (similar to a virtual operating system) that hosts other guest operating systems.

I

Icinga

An open source network-monitoring application.

ICMP

The Internet Control Message Protocol is commonly used to test connectivity to a network from a device.

identity proofing

The process in which a particular individual is associated and verified with an existing identity.

identity theft

Obtaining, by subterfuge, a person's various pieces of identification, usually for financial gain.

IEEE-1394

The FireWire bus specification.

illegal

Contrary to the law.

in-band

This virtualization scheme has the appliance located in a direct path between the storage servers and the disk farm. This configuration eliminates the need to install appliance-related software on each server, as required by an out-of-band configuration.

Information and Communications Technology (ICT)

A blanket term that encompasses any communication device or application.

informative references

Documents that contain specific standards, guidelines, and practices from various organizational security stake holders to accomplish the goals of the functions, categories, and subcategories listed.

infrastructure security

The physical security initiatives applied to providing security for the basic physical and organizational structures needed for the operation of an enterprise, an organization, or society.

ingress

The right of an individual to enter a property.

inherited access

Nonexplicit access, usually granted due to being part of a group.

inner perimeter

This perimeter typically involves physical barriers such as walls, doors, and windows—either exterior or interior, depending on the context of the outer perimeter.

input devices

A device that is used to introduce information into electronic devices.

Input/Output (I/O) controller

The part of a smart meter responsible for providing physical connectivity compatibility between the other system components and the outside world.

insider threat

This type of threat exists inside the network, usually as an employee.

intangible asset

Any nonphysical asset, defined as having a use greater than one year.

intangible property security

This involves securing property that is not physical in nature, such as patents and trademarks.

interior security

This is the innermost level of infrastructure security and involves monitoring the area inside the inner perimeter.

interior sounders

These are designed to operate at maximum sound levels to frighten an intruder into making a fast exit.

Internet Assigned Numbers Authority (IANA)

The organization that oversees the allocation of IP addresses to ISPs.

Internet Engineering Task Force (IETF)

The main standards body of Internet protocols, such as TCP/IP.

Internet gateways

Routers that are used to connect a network to always-on, broadband Internet connections.

Internet Key Exchange (IKE)

The protocol used to set up a security association in IPsec.

Internet of Things (IoT)

The network composed of any physical object that has network connectivity and can communicate with other objects to collect and exchange data.

Internet Protocol Security (IPsec)

An open standard commonly used in VPNs that actually employs a suite of protocols for encrypting and authenticating IP communications.

Internet zone

This zone includes all networks (including the Internet) that are not controlled by an individual or organization. As such, the content can be public, or it can be confidential data that belongs to trusted partners or customers.

interoperability

The ability for devices made by one company to interface with the related devices of another company.

intranet

A local or restricted network within the realm of a single organization.

intruders

Unauthorized people who gain access to an asset to which they do not have access rights.

intrusion detection and reporting system

The collective components of a basic, commercial security system.

Intrusion Detection and Prevention System (IDPS)

Designed to monitor the system (local computer or network environment), log key events, policy violations, report them, and prevent them as directed.

Intrusion Detection System (IDS)

These systems are designed primarily to monitor the system (local computer or network environment), log key events and policy violations, and report them as directed.

iOS

This is Apple's mobile operating system designed to support Apple's line of iPhones and iPads. While iOS shares many structures with OS X, it is not compatible with OS X applications.

IP address

A unique string of numbers that identifies each device that communicates using the Internet Protocol, over a network.

IP address spoofing

The process of using a forged source IP address to create IP packets for the purpose of concealing an identity.

IP-based

Any device that has an IP address and relies on wireless communications or traditional network cabling for communication.

IP-based notification

Notifying a monitoring station via an IP network, such as the Internet, concerning an alarm condition.

IP blocking

A form of security that blocks a specific IP, or range of IPs, from establishing a connection.

IP cameras

Digital IP (Internet Protocol) devices that have IP addresses that can be connected directly to a network, or to the Internet, rather than directly to a host controller or computer.

IP header manipulation

A technique used to change the information contained in the header portion of an IP or TCP network packet in order to conceal one's identity over a network.

IPsec

A protocol suite to establish secure communications. IPsec employs AH and ESP to authenticate and encrypt each IP packet.

IPv4

IPv4 addresses exist in the numeric format of `XXX.YYY.ZZZ.AAA`. Each address consists of four 8-bit fields separated by dots (.).

IPv6

IPv6 is a newer IP addressing protocol developed to cope with the anticipated shortage of available IPv4 addresses in the future. Under IPv6, the IP address has been extended to 128 bits and has a hexadecimal format, separated by colons (:).

ISO 15408

The Common Criteria for Information Technology Security Evaluation international standard.

ISO 2700xx

A group of ISO information security management systems standards designed to provide management with explicit information security control.

isolation

Physical or logical segmentation used to isolate or separate parts of a network.

J

jamming

An intentionally transmitted stream of arbitrary noise on the same frequency that a device or network operates on.

JavaScript

An object-oriented programming language, often used in web browsers to create interactive websites.

JFFS2

The Android default Journal Flash File System (version 2). This FS version replaced the YAFFS2 (Yet Another Flash File System) as the default Android flash file system used in earlier kernel versions.

journaling file system

A file system that keeps track of changes in a circular log file, referred to as a journal, before committing them to the file system.

K

Kerberos

A network authentication protocol that involves a trusted third-party Ticket Granting Server (TGS) to authenticate client/server interaction.

kernel files

The fundamental logic files of the operating system responsible for interpreting commands obtained from software programs for the central processing unit.

key

Having ownership of a key signifies that the entity either possesses or knows the information required to gain access to a given asset.

keyfob

A wireless keychain device that can be used to lock, unlock, and alarm a device.

keypad

Input devices that are typically equipped with a set of numerical push buttons. Keypads are used to program, control, and operate various access controls and management devices.

keys

As it relates to cryptography, cryptographic keys are data strings used to encrypt or decrypt information. Encryption keys can be based on a secret string that is known only to the software that encrypts and decrypts the data, or may be randomly generated. It could also be a combination of known and random factors.

KillerBee

Framework for exploiting ZigBee and other 802.15.4 networks. KillerBee offers sniffing, packet decoding, and manipulation, as well as injection techniques.

L

latency

The delay of an input system to the desired output.

laws

The system of rules that a country or community recognizes to regulate the associated members.

Layer 7 attacks

A type of DDoS attack that focuses on the application layer and generally targets specific areas of a website in hopes of exhausting resources.

least privilege

Under the principle of least privilege, users are granted only the levels of access required to perform their specific job roles.

legal

Actions permitted by the law.

Lightweight Directory Access Protocol (LDAP)

An application protocol used for queries and modifying items in directory service providers. LDAP offers a single login system that can lead to access to many services.

Linux

This is a freely distributed, open-source operating system based on Unix.

Local Area Networks (LANs)

Networks that exist in a relatively confined geographical area (e.g., a room or building).

local firewall

A firewall that is designed and implemented only on the host.

lock

Any device or technique used to restrict access to an asset.

locked condition monitoring

Locked monitoring is a feature that allows the security supervisor to confirm that a door is locked. In addition to monitoring the locked status of a door or gate, the condition monitoring system can also provide details as to how long and during what time periods the door or gate has remained locked.

lockout policy settings

These enable administrators to enact password policies that prevent attackers from repeatedly trying to access the system via brute-force attacks.

logic bomb

A logic bomb is computer code that, much like other malware, is attached to a legitimate program. The code sits idle until a specific logical event is concluded, after which a harmful effect may occur.

logical perimeter

An established virtual boundary that involves computing and control systems, networks, and the Internet.

logjam attack

A security vulnerability that targets the Diffie-Hellman key exchange, convincing the connection to use DHE Export ciphers.

lux rating

Lux is a measure of the amount of light that falls on an object. One lux is approximately the amount of light falling on one square meter from one candle measured from one meter away.

M

MAC address

Media Access Control (MAC) addresses are unique identifiers for every device attached to a network. These addresses are typically assigned to the devices by their manufacturers and stored in their firmware.

MAC address filtering

A filtering technique that requires the manual entering of static MAC addresses into the CAM or specifying the maximum number of devices allowed on a port.

MAC address table

Switches collect MAC address information to keep track of the devices attached to them. As they interact with those devices, they record their MAC information in an onboard memory structure called a MAC address table.

MAC duplicating attacks

In a MAC duplicating or MAC cloning attack, the attacker updates their own MAC address with the target's MAC address. This causes the switch to forward traffic to both locations.

MAC flooding

A technique used to compromise the security of network switches. An attacker connected to a switch port floods the switch interface with a large number of fake MAC addresses, causing the switch to broadcast the frames.

MAC learning and discovery

As connectivity devices interact with other devices connected to their physical ports, they read message headers to acquire the sending and receiving device MAC addresses and record them in the CAM along with their port information.

MAC spoofing

A technique used to change a factory-assigned MAC address of a device on a network.

magnetic contact switches

Consisting of a two-part magnetic switch, one piece of the sensor is a magnet while the other side is a switching mechanism that is sensitive to a magnetic field. The switch portion is mounted on the fixed structure (frame) of the barrier. Wires from the switch are routed to the security system's control panel.

magnetic stripe card

This is a physical credit-card-like device that contains authentication information in the form of magnetically coded spots on a magnetic stripe. The cardholder uses the information on the card to access physical spaces or assets by passing the stripe on the card through a magnetic card reader.

malicious proxy servers

These are proxy servers that are used for various purposes including malware delivery, ad injection, and simple information gathering. While these proxy servers may not pass on your IP address, they will know your IP address and could use this information for other purposes.

malware

A term used to describe any number of intrusive software programs, designed to be malicious in nature.

man-in-the-middle (MITM) attacks

Man-in-the-middle attacks involve an attacker creating links to two or more victims so they can intercept messages moving between them.

managed switches

Devices have programmable management functions built into them that enable administrators to configure them for a specific network environment.

Mandatory Access Control (MAC)

A type of access control that utilizes the operating system to establish which users or groups may access files, folders, and other resources.

masquerade attack

An attack that involves an attacker assuming the identity of another system.

MDK3

A penetration testing tool used to exploit common 802.11 protocol weaknesses.

mesh network

In this decentralized topology, each node relays data for the network.

metadata

This defines information about data. The term is used to describe all data that might be considered secondary to the purpose of the record. Typically, metadata is thought of as automatically generated, often embedded, data that is created by the information system to supplement or even validate the record.

Metasploit

One of the most popular open-source penetration testing frameworks available. It is commonly used to identify and validate network vulnerabilities, including simulating attacks that prey on human vulnerabilities.

microcontroller

A small computer located on a single integrated circuit.

Microsoft Network Monitor

A network packet analyzer that can help view traffic flows and troubleshoot network problems.

mid-tier servers

Servers that act between the highly secure database layer and the less secure presentation layer. Servers in this tier are responsible for controlling application functionality and moving data between the other two layers.

monitors

Video display systems similar to computer displays or televisions, used to observe or record a process.

motion detector

A device that detects moving objects, often integrated in a infrastructure security system.

multifactor authentication (MFA)

A method of access control that requires at least two of the following: knowledge, possession, inherence.

N

Nagios

One of the most well-known network monitoring tools that helps to ensure systems, applications, and processes.

National Institute of Standards and Technology (NIST)

The federal technology agency responsible for development of the Cyber Security Frameworks, Medical Device Security, and Guide to Industrial Control System (ICS) Security guides.

native audit records

Event records generated by a host machine in most modern multiuser operating systems.

natural access control

Using natural design elements, such as structures and landscaping, to guide people as they enter and exit spaces.

Need-to-Know policy

Similar to a Separation of Duties policy, it limits the employee's knowledge of the entire network system.

network

A group of system, people, and devices that can connect and operate with each other.

network address

An identifier that defines the network in any given system.

Network Address Translation (NAT)

The translation of an IP address used in one network to an IP address known within another network.

network administrator

In network environments, administrators are responsible for implementing the organization's security policies. These policies should be designed to reflect the three objectives associated with the classic model of information: confidentiality, integrity, and availability (CIA).

network analyzer

Also referred to as a packet sniffer. Penetration testers use these tools to listen to network traffic, looking for items such as passwords and usernames sent across the network in a plaintext mode, or sensitive information such as credit card or other financial information.

Network-Attached Storage (NAS)

A virtualized storage system that provides both storage and a file system structure within a network.

network bridge

A piece of hardware that connects multiple network segments.

network connectivity devices

Any device that has connectivity purposes, such as routers, hubs, switches, and bridges.

Network File System

Enables client computers to access files across a network. It is used primarily in Unix OS versions, but is also supported in Microsoft Windows and Apple's MAC OSs.

network firewall

A firewall that performs security on an entire network by granting or rejecting access to specific traffic flows between trusted and untrusted networks.

network hardening

All processes and techniques involved in securing a network.

network interface adapter

Also known as a network interface controller (NIC), it is hardware that allows a device to connect to a network.

network monitoring tools

Any tool that can be used to ensure that servers or other devices are up and running appropriately.

Network Operating Systems (NOS)

Operating systems designed to run on specialized server computers that function as the center of a client/server network environment.

network packet

A unit of data that is routed on a network.

network segmentation

The process of separating or splitting a network into one or more subnetworks, resulting in each being its own network segment.

network servers

Specialized computers designed to operate efficiently in a multiuser, multiprocessor, multitasking environment. Typically, they employ multiple processors and large disk drive arrays; they support the network in its operations, authentication, and processes.

network topologies

Layer 1: Physical (or logical) connection strategies that fall into four basic configurations: Star, Bus, Ring, and Mesh.

network virtualization

The process of creating a software-based administrative entity, utilizing hardware and software network resources, along with network functionality.

network vulnerability scanner

Used to scan a network for different types of common vulnerabilities, such as system misconfigurations and default password usage.

Nikto

An open-source web server scanner that can identify issues on a web server.

nmap

A popular security scanner tool that enumerates networks.

No eXecution (NX) bit

NX-bit technology is used to separate areas of memory into regions for distinct uses. For example, a section of memory can be set aside exclusively for storing processor instruction code, while another section can be marked only for storage of data.

NTFS permissions

New Technology File System permissions are those that can set parameters for operations, which users can perform on a designated file or folder.

O

OAuth

An authentication protocol that allows applications to act on the behalf of a user without sharing passwords.

octet

A grouping of eight, typically referring to eight bits of data.

Open Checklist Interactive Language (OCIL)

A defined framework for expressing a set of nonautomatable security checks.

open/close conditions

The state, or condition, of an alarm sensor indicated as open being off and closed being tripped.

open systems interconnection (OSI) model

The primary networking model that defines and characterizes the communication functions in a network environment.

Open Vulnerability and Assessment Language (OVAL)

This is a security community standard for communicating security information such as configuration, vulnerabilities, patch levels, and more. OVAL is essentially a group of XML schemas that describe a language to provide the details needed to assess a network resource for security vulnerabilities.

OpenVAS

The Open Vulnerability Assessment System is an open-source framework of several services and tools that provide vulnerability scanning and management.

operating system (OS)

The software programs designed to control and coordinate the operation of the computer system, including scheduling tasks, executing applications, and controlling peripherals.

operators

Humans who operate or supervise a process.

out-of-band

The virtualization device is installed outside the actual data path between the network and the storage system.

outer perimeter

The first line of defense in a given area or boundary, which can be physical or logical in nature.

overlay networks

This is when a network is built on top of another, physical or underlay, network.

overview

This camera viewpoint generally covers a wide field of view, such as over a parking lot or warehouse floor.

owner

The rightful possessor of an asset.

owning group

Linux permission term that refers to a group of users who collectively have access to data.

owning user

Linux permission term that refers to an individual who has control and access over data.

P

packet

A unit of data that can be carried and transferred by a packet-switched network.

packet analyzer

Also known as a packet sniffer, it is a computer program used to analyze network traffic.

packet filtering

The process of passing or blocking network packets based on their source/destination addresses, logical ports, or protocols.

packet-filtering firewall

Firewalls configured with packet-filtering rules to allow or deny client access based on factors such as their source address, destination address, or port number.

packet-sniffing attacks

Attackers use packet sniffers to listen to network traffic looking for items, such as passwords and usernames, sent across the network in a plaintext mode, or sensitive information such as credit card or other financial information.

pagers

Mobile RF devices that receive messages and signal their user.

pairing process

The process of connecting two Bluetooth devices together.

panning

Traversing a camera left and right; tilting, inclining, or declining a camera up and down.

passageway

An enclosed path from one room/area to another; it is often a chokepoint.

passive controls

Controls that are in place, but are not adjusted based on any action.

passive infrared (PIR) detectors

PIR detectors use a lens mechanism in the sensor housing to detect any change in infrared energy across the horizontal sectors covered by the sensor. This type of detector is insensitive to stationary objects but reacts to rapid changes that occur laterally across the field of view.

Passive RFID tags

Tags that are powered by the electromagnetic energy transmitted from the RFID reader and allow for authentication.

passphrase

A sequence of words or text used to control access, much like a password; however, generally longer in the number of characters.

password

A secret word or random string used as an authentication tool.

password attack

Any password attempt that successfully authenticates through a password prompt without originally knowing the correct password.

Password-Authenticated Key Agreement (PAKE)

An interactive method for two or more entities to establish cryptographic keys based on one entity's knowledge of a password.

Password Authentication Protocol (PAP)

Used with PPP, it is an authentication protocol that utilizes passwords.

password capturing

A technique used to view and save (capture) a password as it is transferred for authentication.

password cracking

The process of attempting to recover passwords from stored data or data in transit, for the purpose of later use.

password encryption

The process of taking a standard password and applying an algorithm to it in such a way as to make it meaningless to sniffers, crackers, or other eavesdroppers.

password management policy

A policy put into place to manage the passwords of users in a networked environment.

password managers

Software applications that store and organize a user's passwords.

Patch Tuesdays

Microsoft's primary patch release day.

patches

General improvements to a given operating system or application that has been released for distribution. Many patches and updates are purely cosmetic and convenient add-on features, while others are critical security upgrades designed in response to a particular virus, discovered threat, or weakness.

PathPing

A utility, found on many Windows systems, that combines the `ping` and `traceroute` command-line tools.

Payment Card Industry Data Security Standard (PCI-DSS)

This standard requires the use of firewalls and other security concepts, such as network segmentation, to ensure that all stored credit card information is securely stored both physically and electronically.

peer-to-peer network

This is where each computer is attached to the network in a ring or bus fashion and is equal to the other units on the network.

perimeter area inputs

These include sensors at every perimeter opening including doors, windows, garage doors and windows, and doors to crawl spaces.

permissions

Defined privileges and authorization on specific data and assets.

persistent cookie

Also known as a permanent cookie, a cookie that will remain on the computer hard drive until the specified expiration date is reached.

personal area networks (PANs)

A type of network that combines personal devices such as PDAs, cell phones, digital cameras, PCs, notebooks, and printers.

pharming

A type of malicious activity that redirects an unsuspecting user to a forged website, in hopes obtaining personal information.

phishing

A social engineering technique that attempts to acquire sensitive information, usually login credentials or credit card data, by masquerading as a trustworthy organization. These attacks generally involve emails that direct the user to a bogus website that looks legitimate.

physical-intrusion-detection system

Any device whose purpose is to detect and signal intrusions, including motion sensors, card readers, cameras, and alarms.

physical security

Any process or device that is concerned with protecting physical boundaries and property.

physical topology

The placement of the various components of a network, including network cables and devices.

piconet

Up to eight devices can be grouped together to form a piconet, a small Bluetooth network.

PING

A network utility used to evaluate the ability to reach another IP host. The PING utility will send Internet Control Message Protocol (ICMP) request packets to the target host and wait for a response measuring the trip time and any packet loss.

ping flood attack

A simple DoS attack where an attacker overwhelms a victim with ICMP Echo Request (ping) packets.

pinhole lens

A lens that's a very small hole, possibly made by a pin, that forces the light into parallel lines to create a clear image.

plugins

Adding new features to existing software applications, such as search engines and antivirus functions, these script controls are similar to ActiveX controls but cannot be executed outside of a web browser.

Point-of-Sale (POS)

The hardware and software used in a retail transaction.

Point of Sales (POS) terminals

Intelligent and networked terminals used for the time and place where a retail transaction takes place.

policies

The rules and procedures adopted by an individual or business.

polyinstantiation

In this database management solution, an additional server is configured to act as a third party between users and the database server. The mid-level server acts as an interpreter and guardian that limits database access to only authorized users and only to requested database files.

port-based VLAN

A range of ports on an Ethernet switch that are defined as a network segment.

port scan

The process of probing or scanning a server, client, or host for open ports.

port scanner

A software application that performs the probing of a network device, for open ports.

portal system

A web-based interface to a portion of the HCP communication system.

Poseidon POSIX (Portable Operating System Interface)

This is a set of interoperability standards developed to standardize variations of Unix and Unix-like operating systems. POSIX-compliant systems (Unix, Linux, and Apple OS X systems) support some type of ACL for managing traditional Unix file access permissions.

Power over Ethernet (PoE)

Power is provided through the UTP network cable, rather than from a dedicated power supply, for each intelligent device.

pressure mats

A type of sensor that can be placed under rugs, in hallways, or on stair treads. They react and alarm due to pressure from footsteps activating the alarm.

Pretty Good Privacy (PGP)

A widely used Unix encryption tool. This tool does both private and public key encryption/decryption and offers a very strong method to secure data.

Privacy Rule

The Privacy Rule is intended to limit the circumstances in which an individual's protected health information may be used or disclosed.

private key

In cryptography, it is an encryption/decryption key known only to the specified recipient.

Private VLAN (PVLAN) attacks

PVLAN attacks involve an attacker sending packets into a PVLAN that contain a destination IP address of a targeted computer and a MAC address of the PVLAN router. The switch sees the destination MAC address and forwards the packet to the router's switch port (a promiscuous port type that can communicate with any port). The router in turn directs the packet to the targeted host.

privilege escalation

The act of exploiting a vulnerability that enables an unauthenticated user to gain elevated administrative access.

privilege management

Through the privilege management policy, an administrator is provided with guidelines as to how the organization's privileges should be implemented. As discussed in previous chapters, access control privileges can be role-based (RBAC), discretionary (DAC), or mandatory (MAC).

procedures

Often used to enforce policies, procedures are an established way of performing an action.

profile-based anomaly-detection systems

Systems that use mathematical algorithms to monitor normal data traffic and develop a profile of rules that describe what normal traffic for that system looks like. The profile developed reflects evaluations of users' past behaviors and is configured to signal when deviations from these behaviors reach a certain level (or threshold).

programmable zone

A zone can be programmed to encompass a single point of protection, such as a motion detector, or multiple points can be combined into a single zone.

promiscuous mode

The operation of a network device able to listen or capture traffic moving through a medium, but not sourced from or targeted to that device.

protocols

A set of rules that governs how communications are conducted across a network. In order for devices to communicate with each other on the network, they must all use the same network protocols.

promiscuous port

A port configured to be able to communicate with any other port, usually in a VLAN instance.

proxy-filtering firewalls

Servers configured to filter out unwanted packets. During this filtering process, each packet is disassembled, evaluated, and reassembled, making this type of connection significantly slower than other firewall types.

proxy server

A server that acts as a barrier, as it allows clients to make indirect network connections that are routed through a proxy.

psychological engineering

Using psychology and human weaknesses, hackers can craft many different attacks that trick people into believing what they want them to believe and giving up important information that they would not normally give out.

public key

A cryptographic key that can be obtained and used by anyone to encrypt messages intended for a particular user.

public key certificates

Digital verifications that the sender of an encrypted message is who they claim to be.

public-key cryptography

Also known as asymmetric cryptography, it incorporates a public key and a private key (or secret key) for encryption and decryption purposes.

Public Key Encryption (PKE)

This encryption technique employs two keys to ensure the security of the encrypted data: a public key and a private key. The public key (known to everyone) is used to encrypt the data, and the private or secret key (known only to the specified recipient) is used to decrypt it.

Public Key Infrastructure (PKI)

This infrastructure supports the distribution of public keys and certificates to enable trusted connections and secure data exchange based on the information from the CA.

public switched telephone network (PSTN)

Also referred to as the Plain Old Telephone Service (POTS), these systems use physical cabling to interconnect and transmit voice grade signals between a sender and a receiver.

purging

The process of separating and deleting inactive records within a database.

Q

Quality of Service (QoS)

Allows for the prioritization and differential treatment of network traffic based on special rules or policies. A common use for QoS is to ensure that a VoIP phone system will always have enough bandwidth for phone service, regardless of how busy the network is.

R

race condition attack

A race condition exists when an attacker exploits the timing of consecutive events in a multiuser/multitasking environment to insert malicious code into the system between the events.

radio frequency identification (RFID)

RFID systems utilize self-powered RFID tags that can be used as beacons to track location or authenticate proximity.

rainbow tables

Pregenerated tables that contain millions of passwords that have already been hashed, used to compare for the purpose of cracking passwords.

ResearchKit

An open-source software framework made by Apple, intended specifically for medical research. Ease of application creation and use provides researchers and developers alike the opportunity to revolutionize medical studies.

reflection servers

Used in DDoS attacks, forged echo requests are sent out and the echo replies are aimed toward the victim.

regress

As it relates to security, the term is used to describe the legal right to reenter a property.

remote access control

A design feature that requires authentication of the identity of a user attempting to access a security zone or computer system from a distant location.

remote access monitoring

Systems that are used to notify supervisory security personnel when an event or incident has occurred.

Remote Authentication Dial-In User Service (RADIUS)

A network protocol that provides centralized AAA protocol (Authentication, Authorization, and Accounting).

remote control access

A design feature that works with remote monitoring systems to monitor, control, and supervise doors, gates, and conveyances from a distance.

Remote Desktop Connection (RDC)

Uses the Remote Desktop Protocol (RDP) to provide a user with a GUI-based interface to connect to another computer over a network.

Remote Desktop Services (RDS)

Formally known as Terminal Services, RDS is a component that allows a user the ability to take control of a remote computer over a network.

remote monitoring

Monitoring or the measurement of devices from a remote location or control room.

remote notification systems

When an alarm condition exists, this set of systems will coordinate and inform the appropriate parties.

Remote Telemetry Unit (RTU)

Small intelligent control units deployed at selective locations within a process, or set of processes, to gather data from different sensors and deliver commands to control relay outputs.

repeater

A network hardware device that extends the range and reach of a network.

replay attack

A network attack where a recorded transmission is replayed or delayed by an attacker to gain access.

Request for Comments (RFC)

These are notes submitted by anyone to the Internet Engineering Task Force (IETF), the main standards organization for the Internet.

rerouting attack

A network attack that attempts to redirect (reroute) traffic from a valid destination to a false one.

resolution

The number of pixels displayed or within a camera sensor.

reverse proxy server

A server that handles public requests for web resources and then forwards them to one or more of the servers.

right

A legal privilege or permission granted to someone, or some group, by some recognized source of authority.

ring topology

A network topology that connects devices in a circular fashion, in which each node is connected to exactly two other nodes.

risk

Defined as the potential loss of an object of value. It can also be expressed as an intentional interaction with uncertainty. Risk can also be calculated as a quantity that can be communicated to the organization's internal and external stake holders.

Role-Based Access Control (RBAC)

An access control method that uses job roles to differentiate permissions and privileges.

rootkit

A type of software designed to gain administrative control of a computer system while remaining undetected. Normally, the purpose is to enable malicious operations to occur on a target computer without the knowledge of its users or system administrators. Rootkits can occur in hardware or software by going after the

BIOS, boot loader, OS kernel, and sometimes applications or libraries.

router flood attacks

Routers are vulnerable to flood attacks designed to consume all or a significant part of their resources, thereby rendering them nonfunctional. Router resources commonly targeted include onboard memory, processor operation, and internal bus bandwidth.

routers

Network connectivity devices that, unlike switches, can forward information across different network segments. This gives routers the ability to join different networks together through a process known as routing.

routing

The process of selecting the best path for transmitting data over a network or between networks.

routing protocol

A set of rules used by routers to determine appropriate paths in which data should be transmitted.

routing table

A database where routers store and update routing information.

rule

To move packets through the device, a rule must be explicitly created on the device to forward (or map) the desired protocol port to a private IP address and port in the local area network.

Rule-Based Access Control (RBAC)

Also known as automated provisioning, a rule is the basic element of a role. The rule defines what operations the role can perform.

rule-based anomaly detection

This detection method analyzes audit records to generate rules based on past usage patterns to generate a rules set. The system then monitors the traffic looking for patterns that do not match the rules created.

rule sets

Used to control what types of information can move between security zones. These rules are normally based on data source and destination information, data type, or data content.

S

sanitize

Making data on an HDD unrecoverable, either by overwriting the data multiple times and/or physically destroying the drive so that it cannot be reassembled.

script

A list of commands able to be executed without user interaction.

Secure Remote Password (SRP)

A protocol that is an augmented form of PAKE, designed to work around existing patents.

Secure Shell (SSH)

An encrypted network protocol for secure client-server connections. Designed to replace insecure shell protocols such as Telnet, SSH employs public-key cryptographic authentication.

Secure Sockets Layer (SSL)

A protocol for managing both authentication and communication between clients and servers, using both a public key and a private key. SSL uses the sockets method to exchange data between client and server program, usually as a website and a browser.

security

The science, technique, and art of establishing a system of exclusion and inclusion of individuals, systems, media, content, and objects.

security administrator

In networked environments, administrators are responsible for implementing the organization's security policies. These policies should be designed to reflect the three objectives associated with the classic model of information security: confidentiality, integrity, and availability (CIA).

Security Associations (SAs)

The establishment of shared attributes between two network devices in order to support a secure connection.

security baseline

This baseline defines the minimum security requirements necessary to protect the confidentiality, integrity, and availability (CIA) of the organization's information systems, along with the data processed, stored, and transmitted by those systems.

Security Content Automation Protocol (SCAP)

A method of using various open standards for evaluating vulnerabilities and measuring the potential impact of those vulnerabilities.

security patches

Updates issued for the specific purpose of correcting an observed weakness to prevent exploitation of a vulnerability.

security policy

Documentation stating how security should be implemented at each level. Businesses and organizations develop comprehensive security policies that define who is authorized to access different assets and what they are allowed to do with those assets when they do access them.

segregated

In a network, a physical or logical separation. Often used to separate individuals, data, and other assets.

server

A centralized computer or computer program that manages resources on a network.

server administrator

An individual who is responsible for the design, implementation, and maintenance of the server.

Server Message Block (SMB)

Also known as Common Internet File System, this network protocol was developed to provide shared access to files and devices, along with network communications.

server rooms

Secured rooms where servers are protected.

service pack

Major Windows updates and/or collections of many individual Windows updates.

session cookie

Stored in temporary memory, this cookie is erased when the web browser is closed.

Session Replay attack

This attack involves the attacker stealing a user's session ID, then gaining access to do anything an authorized user would be able to do on a given website.

side channel attack

An attacker on one virtual machine obtains private key information from another virtual machine running on that same physical server.

signature analysis

Incoming and outgoing traffic are compared to a database of stored specific code patterns (signatures), which have been identified as malicious threats.

signature-based IDS/IDPS

These systems work by looking for specific patterns in content, known as signatures. If a known bad pattern is detected, then the appropriate actions can be taken to protect the host.

single authentication

Authentication that requires the possession of only one form of verification. This represents the lowest level of security available.

single firewall DMZ

A network DMZ that has a lone firewall associated with it.

siren

An audible enunciator, made to be very loud.

smart card

Card device that often resembles magnetic stripe cards. They typically contain information about their owners, such as their passwords, personal identification numbers (PINs), network keys, digital certificates, and other PII that can be used in the authentication process.

smart phone applications

Applications that run specifically on mobile devices, such as tablets and phones.

Smurf amplifiers

A computer network that lends its usefulness to amplify the effects of a Smurf attack.

Smurf attack

A DDoS attack that floods a victim with ICMP reply packets. This attack builds on the ping flood attack by adding a reflective property. This reflective property is created by using more participants, known as Smurf amplifiers, in the attack.

Snort

An open source, cross-platform intrusion-detection system that provides real-time traffic analysis, packet logging, and protocol analysis, as well as active detection for worms, port scans, and vulnerability exploit attempts.

social engineering

Using psychological manipulation is a non-technical method to exploit human interactions in hopes of circumventing normal security.

Social Engineering Toolkit (SET)

Used in penetration testing, this Linux software package can be used to perform advanced attacks against a target.

socket

One endpoint of a two-way communication. A socket is bound to a port number.

soft targets

Devices that are vulnerable to disruption because they have little or no built-in security features and few options for adding security features. If they can be accessed directly or virtually, they can easily be manipulated.

softphone

A software program that enables a user to make telephone calls over the Internet.

software exploitation

Cyber attacks designed to take advantage of vulnerabilities or weaknesses in software products, operating systems, and applications.

software-defined networking (SDN)

An approach to computer networking that analyzes the connection between any two nodes and can filter that connection based on a defined policy.

software firewall

Firewalls that are installed on a host computer, much like any other application.

SolarWinds

This software is a commercial network performance-monitoring product. It can be used to monitor uptime, performance, traffic flow, and utilization; it offers a plethora of reporting, graphing, and notification options.

spanning-tree attack

If packets are circulated just between the Layer 2 switches in this type of topology, their Time-To-Live (TTL) field never gets decremented—instead, continuing to loop through the redundant links. This creates a broadcast storm that floods the network with traffic.

spanning-tree Protocol (STP)

This protocol provides loop-free, redundant links for switches in multiple path networks. It accomplishes this by configuring switch ports so they forward or block traffic depending on the type of segment to which they are connected.

spear phishing

Whereas phishing attacks are sent to a broad range of targets seemingly at random, spear-phishing attacks target a specific organization or individual within that organization to attempt to gain unauthorized access to confidential data. Spear-phishing attacks are more likely to be conducted by attackers who are seeking large financial gain, industry secrets, or military information.

spoof

Any form of forging a false identity, thereby gaining access to assets.

spoofing attacks

These attacks are based on changing a device's MAC or IP address to change its apparent identity.

spyware

A software program that monitors the system's operation and collects information such as usernames, passwords, credit card numbers, and other PII.

SQL injection

A technique malicious users employ to manipulate SQL input fill boxes on web pages. In particular, the SQL literate hacker will input valid SQL commands through the field boxes that cause the SQL database to reveal information other than what the input was created to do.

SSH tunneling

Creates a secure connection between a remote host and a local device or computer, through which unencrypted traffic can be transferred through an encrypted channel.

star topology

This logical layout where all the nodes are connected in branches that eventually lead back to a central unit. Nodes communicate with each other through the central unit.

stateful packet-filtering firewalls

These firewalls collect network connection information and maintain dynamic state tables that are used for subsequent connections, enabling ports to be opened and closed when defined against packet filtering rules.

stateless packet-filtering firewalls

Acting more as an ACL, they do not keep track of the state of a connection between two computers; however, they compare packets against filtering rules.

Storage Area Networks (SANs)

A network-based storage system that appears to the host machine as a locally attached.

stream cipher

A symmetric-key cipher that converts each plaintext character one at a time.

subnet

A segregated network that is ultimately part of a larger network.

super cookies

Third-party cookies that are harder to remove than other types of cookies. Many of them do not use the traditional cookie storage methodology, but rather use local browser HTML5 database storage or even Adobe Flash data storage.

supervisory password

Used to establish a password that can be employed to access the CMOS setup utility.

suPHP

A tool for executing PHP scripts with the permission of the owner.

switch-based virtualization

This is implemented through the managed switches used to connect the SAN devices together. These devices also sit between the user and storage networks but may employ different techniques to provide storage management functions.

switch port stealing

A technique used to alter the direction of switch traffic, causing a switch to send traffic intended for another recipient to an attacker.

switches

Network connectivity devices that function at Layer 2 of the OSI model. They are designed to connect network devices together to form a local area network, forwarding packets based on destination addresses.

symmetric key

A cryptographic algorithm will use the same key to perform both encryption and decryption.

SYN flood

A form of Denial of Service attack, where an attacker takes advantage of the TCP handshake that uses SYN and ACK messages to establish a reliable connection between two hosts.

T

tagged packet

A packet that has a VLAN ID inserted into the packet header, in order to identify the VLAN to which the packet belongs.

tangible assets

Any physical assets.

tangible property security

Classically known as physical security, which consists of protecting physical boundaries and property.

TCP segment

The Transmission Control Protocol accepts data, divides it into sections, and then adds a TCP header to the data, creating a TCP segment.

TCP/IP

A suite of protocols, primarily the Transmission Control Protocol (TCP) and the Internet Protocol (IP), which form the basic and most important protocols of the Internet model.

TCP window size

The maximum size of received data that can be buffered at a time, on the receiving side of a TCP connection.

teardrop attack

A type of DoS attack where fragmented packets are sent to a target system. Older operating systems had bugs in their TCP/IP reassembly mechanisms that caused the fragmented packets to overlap and crash the host.

telephoto lens

A lens with a longer focal length, providing a magnified view.

Telnet

An application client-server protocol that can establish a connection between a computer (or device) to any remote Telnet server.

territorial reinforcement

This employs structures, systems, and devices to prevent unauthorized entry and creates a clear difference between what is public and private.

threat

The potential to perform actions, with the intent to inflict pain, injury, damage, or other hostile action.

threat agent

Indicates an individual, group, or device that has the knowledge and intent to establish an attack.

threat vector

A common security term that refers to a method an attacker may employ to get to a desired target.

threshold-based anomaly-detection systems

These IDS systems are designed to track the number of occurrences of specific events over time, and then generate an intrusion warning if the number of events exceeds a predetermined number.

time of check to time of use (TOCTOU)

This condition exists when an operating system creates a temporary file. During the time between which the OS checks to see if a file exists and when it actually writes the file, the attacker executes a program to save a malicious code package using the file name of the temp file.

time-of-day settings

Most automated access control systems base decisions about valid or invalid entry requests, also called transactions, on preconfigured time of day settings.

time of use (TOU)

A type of electrical billing schedule that assigns higher costs to energy consumed during certain times of the day and seasons of the year.

top-level domain (TLD)

The highest level domain preceding the rightmost dot (.), as defined in the Domain Name System of the Internet. TLDs are generally divided between commercial and country-specific.

Top Secret

Usually the highest level of a three-tiered security clearance.

topology

A physical and/or logical definition of a network connection structure.

TRACEROUTE

This networking utility will display the route (path) packets travel from one IP to another.

tracking cookies

Nonmalicious text files placed on a host computer, designed to track a user's web browsing habits.

transparent proxy

This proxy server communicates on the behalf of a host machine, without modifying requests, as opposed to most proxy services. A transparent proxy is typically not something the user is even aware they are using.

Transport Layer Security (TLS)

A successor to the SSL protocol, TLS is a protocol used to ensure privacy between communicating applications.

Trojans

Malware that appears to be a legitimate application so that users will be tricked into using them. Although they function and work properly, they have malicious code that initiates when the application is launched.

TrouSerS

An open-source daemon that controls all of the communications with the TPM through a single module.

trunk

A communication link designated to handle and combine multiple traffic signals, often to other network devices, for the purpose of consolidating physical port usage.

Trusted Platform Module (TPM): Many computer motherboard designs include a built-in microchip called a Trusted Platform Module (TPM) that is used to store cryptographic information, such as the encryption key (also known as start-up key).

Trusted VPNs

These VPN's do not use cryptographic tunneling but rather trust the underlying network to handle security beyond authentication.

TrustedGrub

This Linux module is capable of detecting and supporting TPM functionality in Linux systems. It is a downloadable extension of the Grub bootloader that has been modified for this purpose.

tunneling

Allows remote users to securely connect to internal resources after establishing an Internet connection. This is accomplished by securing the data in motion using data transfer encryption.

two-factor authentication

A process that requires two differing factors to grant authorization, based on what you know, what you have, and what you know.

two-man control

Requires that two users must review and approve each other's work in order to complete a project. Although this may not be practical for many tasks, it offers a high level of security for those tasks where it is implemented.

U

UDP flood attack

A DoS attack, similar to a ping flood attack, that uses User Datagram Protocol packets.

unauthorized

Any user or device that does not have permission to access a network or asset.

unauthorized access

An individual gains access to a service, application, network, or device without owning proper credentials.

unicast

Communication between a single sender and a single receiver or a network.

unidirectional security gateways

Used to create a one-way connection between networks, or network segments, that possess differing security classifications.

unified threat management (UTM) devices

Security appliances that feature gateway, antivirus, firewall, and intrusion prevention and detection services within a single product.

Universal Disk Format (UDF)

An open, vendor-neutral file system for data storage in a wide range of media.

Universal Plug and Play (UPnP)

A zero-configuration network architecture that brings a certain amount of compatibility between different brands and types of network hardware. While primarily intended to help the unskilled home networker, UPnP is supported by some nonconsumer hardware manufacturers as well.

Universal Serial Bus (USB)

The most popular hardware port found in modern personal computers is the Universal Serial Bus (USB) port. This high-speed serial interface has been developed to provide a fast, flexible method of attaching up to 127 peripheral devices to the computer.

Unix

The Unix line of operating systems provide a modular, multitasking, multiuser OS environment originally developed to run on main frame and mini-computers. Proprietary versions of the Unix OS include several BSD (Berkley Software Distribution) variations, along with Apple's OSX and iOS operating systems and Google's Android OS.

Unix File System

The first file structure designed for the original Unix operating system, and it is still in use with Unix and its derivatives. The structure of this file system standard presents a unified tree structure beginning at a main director known as the root (/).

unlocked condition monitoring

The condition monitoring system can record and signal each time a specific gate or door is unlocked (granting access), indicating and recording which type of access was granted.

unmanaged switches

Plug and Play (PnP) devices that do not include any options for user configuration. These tend to be low price units, intended for use in residential and small office settings.

untagged packet

A packet that does not have a VLAN ID inserted into the packet header.

update

A service pack, or patch, that improves the reliability, security, or attractiveness of an operating system. The most reliable source of operating system updates is the OS manufacturer. Some updates may make the OS more convenient, but it may not necessarily be more secure.

UPnP AV

Universal Plug and Play – Audio Visual. This was released to support consumer media devices such as TVs, home audio systems, cameras, and other digital media devices.

upstream interface

The interface allowing traffic to transfer in the direction from client to server, or client to Internet.

user password

This BIOS option enables administrators to establish passwords that users must enter during the startup process to complete the boot process and gain access to the operating system.

utility files

Programs that permit the user to manage system resources, troubleshoot the system, and configure the system.

V

varifocal lens

Optical assemblies containing several movable elements, to permit changing of the effective focal length (EFL) of a surveillance camera. Unlike a zoom lens, a variable focal lens requires refocusing with each change. If it has a varifocal lens, and it can focus at multiple millimeter settings based on the user's preference.

VBScript

Another scripting language that is unique to Microsoft Windows Internet Explorer. VBScript is similar to JavaScript, but it is not as widely used in websites because of limited compatibility with other browsers.

video surveillance system

An important element of most commercial security systems. The system employs cameras for prevention and recovery.

videocassette recorders (VCRs)

CCTV has traditionally been recorded using videocassette recorders (VCRs); such systems tend to be highly labor intensive.

virtual access control lists (VACLs)

Access lists that filter traffic entering the VLANs, as well as filter traffic moving between members of the VLANs.

virtual LAN (VLAN)

Software configured network that is segregated at the data link layer.

Virtual Private Network (VPN)

Remote users can connect to a private network over a public network, such as the Internet, and then authenticate and perform tasks on the private network as if they were connected directly. It enables users to communicate between another device across a public network, as if it were a private network, ensuring security.

viruses

Malware programs designed to replicate and spread within a local computer environment. This most often happens when users download programs from the Internet or open email attachments.

VLAN hopping attacks

These attacks, also known as Switch Spoofing Attacks, involve an attacker sending a dynamic trunking protocol (DTP) request to a switch to configure the attacker's port as a trunk connection. Once configured, this connection routes all traffic in the VLANS to the attacker.

VLAN Management Policy Server (VMPS)

VMPS is used to dynamically assign VLANs based on MAC addresses. It is based on the Cisco VQP protocol for client/server exchanges and is vulnerable to attack because it is an unauthenticated protocol that runs under UDP.

VLAN Trunking Protocol attacks

These attacks target Cisco's layer-2 VLAN Trunking Protocol (VTP). This protocol provides automated ISL/802.1Q trunk configuration between switches across an entire network so they can share packets. The automated nature of VTP provides access to all of the network's VLAN by default. It can be used to add or remove a VLAN from the network. This makes switches with the trunk ports vulnerable to attack.

voice recognition

Applications that utilize the voice and speech patterns of a user to perform a variety of actions.

vulnerability

Any weakness that may allow an attacker access to network assets.

vulnerability emulators

Training simulators for penetration testing.

vulnerability scanners

Database-driven tools designed to search computers for known vulnerabilities that have been identified and added to the database. They are designed to assess computer, systems, networks, and applications.

W

web browser

A software application that provides the retrieval, presentation, and traversing of resources on the Internet.

web proxy

A computer or server that functions on behalf of a host, or network of hosts, that are accessing the web.

web server

Enterprises employ web servers to host web pages that advertise their organization on the Internet. These are frontend servers that deal directly with the Internet.
engineering tactics.

whitelisting

The process of permitting only the users who match some criteria or authentication.

whitelists

Registries of users who are trusted to have specific privileges, services, or access to an asset.

wide angle lens

A lens that provides the ability to see a wider image in confined areas, as opposed to other standard lens types.

Wide Area Networks (WANs)

Networks distributed over a wide geographical area.

Wi-Fi

Wireless Fidelity (Wi-Fi) is a wireless network technology that provides electronic devices the access to connect to a LAN.

WiGLE

An online database that users use and contribute to, to track and log wireless network information.

WiMAX

Worldwide Interoperability for Microwave Access (WiMAX) is a broadband wireless access standard designed to provide Internet access across large geographic areas, such as cities, counties, and in some cases countries.

Wired Equivalent Privacy (WEP)

A security protocol designed to provide security to a wireless LAN.

Wireless Access Point (WAP)

A network connectivity device that allows wireless clients to connect to a wired network.

wireless networks

Any network that is connected, not using a traditional cabling scheme. It connects computer nodes together using high-frequency radio waves. The IEEE organization oversees a group of wireless networking specifications under the IEEE-802.xx banner.

Wireshark

A mature, open-source, and cross-platform network protocol analyzer. One of the most well-known protocol analyzers, and it supports nearly every protocol.

worms

Sometimes referred to as network viruses, these malware programs are circulated through a network connection. Worms search for vulnerabilities to exploit in an application, and once the worm has taken advantage of the vulnerability, it seeks to replicate to another computer on the network.

Z

zero day attack

An attack that exploits a zero day vulnerability.

zero day vulnerability

A vulnerability unknown to the product vendor and, therefore, no patch is available to mitigate the effects.

Z-Force

A packet interception and injection tool, used to compromise and exploit Z-Wave AES encryption.

ZigBee

This standard is a wireless, mesh-networked PAN protocol that provides for a 10-meter communication range with data transfer rates at 250 Kbps. The ZigBee standard has been embraced by the smart home automation and industrial controls communities, as well as several areas of the smart grid consortium.

ZigBee Alliance

An open, nonprofit association working to develop new ZigBee standards.

zombies

Infected computers that can be placed under the remote control of a malicious user. Zombies can be used to create Denial of Service attacks that flood targeted networks. Computers are often infected and become a zombie by way of viruses, worms, and Trojans.

zooming

A function of a telescopic lens to get a closer view.

Z-Wave

A wireless communication standard created to support communication between devices in the home automation market. It was designed for simple monitoring and control as well as interdevice wireless communication.

APPENDIX B

Acronyms

μC
Microcontroller

AAA
Authentication, Authorization, and Accounting

ACK
Acknowledge

ACL
Access Control List

AES
Advanced Encryption Standard

AFHSS
Adaptive Frequency Hopping Spread Spectrum

AH
Authentication Header

AIM
Apple/IBM/Motorola

ASLR
Address Space Layout Randomization

ASP
Application Service Provider

ARM
Acorn RISC Machine/Advanced RISC Machine

ARP
Address Resolution Protocol

B2B
Business-to-Business

B2C
Business-to-Customer

BAA
Business Associate Agreement

BeEF
Browser Exploitation Framework

BES
Bulk Electric System

BIOS
Basic Input/Output System

BPDU
Bridge Protocol Data Units

BSD
Berkley Software Distribution

BYOD

Bring-Your-Own-Device

CA

Certificate Authority

CAM

Content Addressable Memory

CANs

Campus Area Networks or Corporate Area Networks

CAPTCHA

Completely Automated Public Turing test to tell Computers and Humans Apart

CATV

Commercial Cable Television

CCD

Charged Coupled Device

CCTV

Closed-Circuit Television

CDFS

Compact Disc File System

CDP

Cisco Discovery Protocol

CHAP

Challenge-Handshake Authentication Protocol

CIA

Confidentiality, Integrity, and Availability

CIFS

Common Internet File System

CIP

Critical Infrastructure Protection

CISC

Complex Instruction Set Computing

CMS

Centers for Medicare and Medicaid Services

CPE

Common Platform Enumeration

CPTED

Crime Prevention Through Environmental Design

CRAM

Challenge Response Authentication Mechanism

CRL

Certificate Revocation List

CSMA/CD

Carrier Sense Multiple-Access with Collision Detection

CSP

Cloud Storage Provider

CSR

Certificate Signing Request

CVE

Common Vulnerabilities and Exposures

CVSS

Common Vulnerability Scoring System

DAC

Discretionary Access Control

DACL

Discretionary Access Control List

DAI

Dynamic ARP Inspection

DAS

Direct-Attached Storage

DCS

Distributed Control System

DDoS

Distributed Denial of Service

DEA

Drug Enforcement Administration

DEP

Data Execution Prevention

DES

Data Encryption Standard

DHA

Directory Harvest Attack

DHCP

Dynamic Host Configuration Protocol

DHE

Diffie-Hellman Key Exchange

DHT

Distributed Hash Table

DMZ

Demilitarized Zone

DNP3

Distributed Network Protocol

DNS

Domain Name Service

DOS

Denial of Service

DOS

Disk Operating System

DRDoS

Distributed Reflection and Amplification Denial of Service

DRP

Disaster Recovery Plan

DS4P

Data Segmentation for Privacy

DTP

Dynamic Trunking Protocol

DVR

Digital Video Recorder

EAP

Extensible Authentication Protocol

EAL

Evaluation Assurance Levels

EFL

Effective Focal Length

EFS

Encrypting File System

eSATA

External Serial AT Attachment

ESIGN

Electronic Signatures in Global and National Commerce Act

ESP

Encapsulating Security Payload

EV

Extended Validation

FAT

File Allocation Table

FIPS

Federal Information Processing Standard

FMS

File Management System

FREAK

Factoring attack on RSA-EXPORT Keys

FTA

Fault Tree Analysis

FTP

File Transfer Protocol

GBDE

GEOM-Based Disk Encryption

GPRS

General Packet Radio System

GUI

Graphical User Interface

HAN

Home Area Network

HBIDS

Host-Based IDS

HFS

Hierarchical File Systems

HTTP

Hypertext Transfer Protocol

IANA

Internet Assigned Numbers Authority

IC

Integrated Circuit

ICANN

Internet Corporation for Assigned Names and Numbers

ICCP

Inter-Control Center Communications Protocol

ICMP

Internet Control Message Protocol

ICT

Information Communication and Technology

ID

Identify

IDF

Intermediate Distribution Frame

IDPS

Intrusion Detection and Prevention System

IDS

Intrusion-Detection Systems

IED

Intelligent Electronic Device

IEEE

International Electrical and Electronic Association

IETF

Internet Engineering Task Force

IGD

Internet Gateway Device

IKE

Internet Key Exchange

IoT

Internet of Things

IP

Internet Protocol

IPsec

Internet Protocol Security

IRP

Incident Response Policy

ISP

Internet Service Provider

IT

Information Technology

IV

Initialization Vector

L2TP

Layer 2 Tunneling Protocol

LAN

Local Area Network

LDAP
Lightweight Directory Access Protocol

LOIC
Low Orbit Ion Cannon

LOPA
Layer of Protection Analysis

MAC
Mandatory Access Control

MAC
Media Access Control

MAN
Metropolitan Area Network

MDF
Main Distribution Frame

MIT
Massachusetts Institute of Technology

MITM
Man-in-the-Middle

NAN
Neighborhood Area Network

NAS
Network Attached Storage

NAT
Network Address Translation

NAT-T
Network Address Translation-Traversal

NBIDS
Network-Based IDS

NFC
Near Field Communication

NIST
National Institute of Standards and Technology

NOS
Network Operating System

NS
Name Servers

NVT
Network Vulnerability Tests

NX
No Execution

OCIL
Open Checklist Interactive Language

OCSP
Online Certificate Status Protocol

OPC
Open Platform Connectivity

OSI
Open Systems Interconnection

OS

Operating System

OTP

One-Time Passwords

OVAL

Open Vulnerability and Assessment Language

PAKE

Password-Authenticated Key Agreement

PAN

Personal Area Network

PAP

Password Authentication Protocol

PC

Personal Computer

PEFS

Private Encrypted File System

PF

Packet Filter

PGP

Pretty Good Privacy

PIN

Password or Personal Identification Number

PIR

Passive Infrared

PKE

Public Key Encryption

PKI

Public Key Infrastructure

PnP

Plug and Play

PoE

Power over Ethernet

POODLE

Padding Oracle on Downgraded Legacy Encryption

POS

Point-of-Sale

POSIX

Portable Operating System Interface

PR

Protect

PSTN

Public Switched Telephone Network

PTZ

Pan/Tilt/Zoom

PVLAN

Private VLAN

QoS

Quality of Service

RADIUS

Remote Authentication Dial-In User Service

RARP

Reverse ARP

RAT

Remote Access Trojan

RBAC

Role-Based Access Control

RC

Recover

RDC

Remote Desktop Connection

RF

Radio Frequency

RFC

Request for Comments

RFID

Radio Frequency Identification

RISC

Reduced Instruction Set Computing

RS

Respond

SA

Security Association

SAAS

Software as a Service

SAN

Storage Area Network

SATA

Serial AT Attachment

SBS

Small Business Server

SCP

Secure Copy Protocol

SDN

Software-Defined Networking

SDO

Standards Development Organization

SET

Social Engineering Toolkit

SFTP

SSH File Transfer Protocol

SiIQ

Silicon Intelligence

SLE

Single Loss Expectancy

SMBFS

Server Message Block File System

SMTP

Simple Mail Transfer Protocol

SNMP

Simple Network Management Protocol

SQLi

SQL injection

SRK

Storage Root Key

SRP

Secure Remote Password

SSH

Secure Shell

SSL

Secure Socket Layer

SSO

Single Sign-on

STA

Spanning-Tree Algorithm

STP

Shielded Twisted Pair

STP

Spanning-Tree Protocol

SYN

Synchronize

SYN/ACK

Synchronize/Acknowledge

TCP

Transmission Control Protocol

TCP/IP

Transmission Control Protocol/Internet Protocol

TGS

Ticket Granting Server

TKIP

Temporary Key Integrity Protocol

TLD

Top-Level Domain

TLS

Transport Layer Security

TO

Transmission Owner

TOCTOU

Time Of Check-Time Of Use

TOP

Transmission Operator

TOU

Time of Use

TPID

Tag Protocol Identifier

TPM

Trusted Platform Module

TTL

Time-To-Live

UDP

User Datagram Protocol

UETA

Uniform Electronic Transactions Act

UL

Underwriters Laboratories

UPnP

Universal Plug and Play

USB

Universal Serial Bus

UTM

Unified Threat Management

UTP

Unshielded Twisted Pair

VACL

Virtual Access Control List

VCR

Videocassette Recorder

VLAN

Virtual Local Area Network

VMD

Video Motion Detection

VMPS

VLAN Management Policy Server

VNA

Vendor Neutral Archive

VoIP

Voice over IP

VPLS

Virtual Private LAN Service

VQP

VLAN Query Protocol

VTP

VLAN Trunking Protocol

WAN

Wide Area Network

WAP

Wireless Access Point

WBAN

Wireless Body-Area Network

WEP

Wired Equivalent Privacy

Wi-Fi

Wireless Fidelity

WLAN

Wireless Local Area Network

WPA

Wi-Fi Protected Access

WSDL

Web Services Description Language

XD

eXecute Disable

XN

Execute Never

XSS

Cross-Site Scripting

APPENDIX C

NIST Preliminary Cybersecurity Framework

The national and economic security of the United States depends on the reliable functioning of critical infrastructure. To strengthen the resilience of this infrastructure, President Obama issued Executive Order 13636 (EO), "Improving Critical Infrastructure Cybersecurity," on February 12, 2013. This Executive Order calls for the development of a voluntary Cybersecurity Framework that provides a "prioritized, flexible, repeatable, performance-based, and cost-effective approach" for assisting organizations responsible for critical infrastructure services to manage cybersecurity risk.

Critical infrastructure is defined in the EO as "systems and assets, whether physical or virtual, so vital to the United States that the incapacity or destruction of such systems and assets would have a debilitating impact on security, national economic security, national public health or safety, or any combination of those matters." Due to the increasing pressures from external threats, organizations responsible for critical infrastructure need to have a consistent and iterative approach to identifying, assessing, and managing cybersecurity risk.

The critical infrastructure community includes public and private owners and operators, and other supporting entities that play a role in securing the nation's infrastructure. Each sector performs critical functions that are supported by information technology (IT), industrial control systems (ICS), and, in many cases, both IT and ICS. To manage cybersecurity risks, a clear understanding of the security challenges and considerations specific to IT and ICS is required. Because each organization's risk is unique, along with its use of IT and ICS, the implementation of the Framework will vary.

The Framework, developed in collaboration with industry, provides guidance to an organization on managing cybersecurity risk. A key objective of the Framework is to encourage organizations to consider cybersecurity risk as a priority similar to financial, safety, and operational risk while factoring in larger systemic risks inherent to critical infrastructure.

The Framework relies on existing standards, guidance, and best practices to achieve outcomes that can assist organizations in managing their cybersecurity risk. By relying on those practices developed, managed, and updated by industry, the Framework will evolve with technological advances and business requirements. The use of standards will enable economies of scale to drive innovation and development of effective products and services that meet identified market needs. Market competition also promotes faster diffusion of these technologies and realization of many benefits by the stakeholders in these sectors. See Figure C.1.

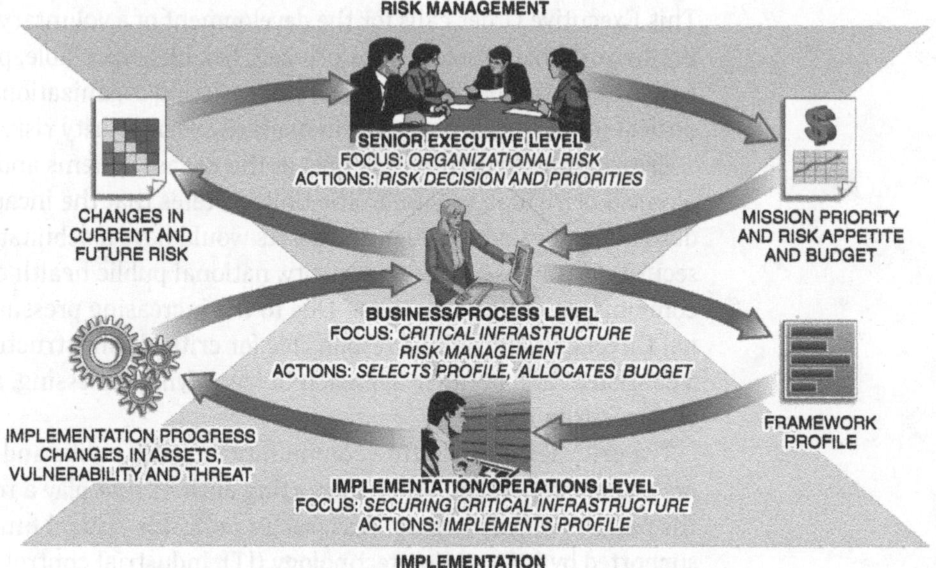

FIGURE C.1: The NIST Framework Stakeholders

IDENTIFY

Category	Methodology	Subcategory
Asset Management (ID.AM)	The data, personnel, devices, systems, and facilities that enable the organization to achieve business purposes are identified and managed consistent with their relative importance to business objectives and the organization's risk strategy.	ID.AM-1: Physical devices and systems within the organization are inventoried. ID.AM-2: Software platforms and applications within the organization are inventoried. ID.AM-3: The organizational communication and data flow are mapped. ID.AM-4: External information systems are catalogued, ID.AM-5: Resources (e.g., hardware devices, data, and software) are prioritized based on the classification, criticality, and business value. ID.AM-6: Cybersecurity roles and responsibilities for the entire workforce and third-party stakeholders (e.g., suppliers, customers, partners) are established.
Business Environment (ID.BE)	The organization's mission, objectives, stakeholders, and activities are understood and prioritized; this information is used to inform cybersecurity roles, responsibilities, and risk management functions.	ID.BE-1: The organization's role in the supply chain is identified and communicated. ID.BE-2: The organization's place in critical infrastructure and its industry sector are identified and communicated. ID.BE-3: The organizational mission, objectives, and activities are established and communicated. ID.BE-4: Dependencies and critical functions for delivery of critical services are established. ID.BE-5: Resilience requirements to support delivery of critical services are established.

(Continues)

IDENTIFY *(Continued)*

Category	Methodology	Subcategory
Governance (ID.GV)	The policies, procedures, and processes to manage and monitor the organization's regulatory legal, risk, environmental, and operational requirements are understood and inform the management of cybersecurity risk.	ID.GV-1: Organizational information security policy is established, ID.GV-2: Information security roles and responsibilities are coordinated and aligned with internal roles and external partners. ID.GV-3: Legal and regulatory requirements regarding cybersecurity, including privacy and civil liberties obligations, are understood and managed. ID.GV-4: Government and risk management processes address cybersecurity risks.
Risk Assessment (ID.RA)	The organization understands the cybersecurity risk to organizational operations (including mission, functions, image, or reputation), organizational assets, and individuals.	ID.RA-1: Asset vulnerabilities are identified and documented. ID.RA-2: Threat and vulnerability information is received from information sharing forums and sources. ID.RA-3: Threats, both internal and external, are identified and documented. ID.RA-4: Potential business impacts and likelihoods are identified. ID.RA-5: Threats, vulnerabilities, likelihoods, and impacts are used to determine risk. ID.RA-6: Risk responses are identified and prioritized.
Risk Management Strategy (ID.RM)	The organization's priorities, constraints, risk tolerances, and assumptions are established and used to support operational risk decisions.	ID.RM-1: Risk management processes are established, managed, and agreed to by organizational stakeholders. ID.RM-2: Organizational risk tolerance is determined and clearly expressed. ID.RM-3: The organization's determination of risk tolerance is informed by its role in critical infrastructure and sector-specific risk analysis.

PROTECT

Category	Methodology	Sub-Category
Access Control (PR.AC)	Access to assets and associated facilities is limited to authorized users, processes, or devices, and to authorized activities and transactions.	PR.AC.1: Identities and credentials are managed for authorized devices and users. PR.AC.2: Physical access to assets is managed and protected. PR.AC.3: Remote access is managed. PR.AC.4: Access permissions are managed, incorporating the principles of least privilege and separation of duties. PR.AC.5: Network integrity is protected, incorporating network segregation where appropriate.
Awareness and Training (PR.AT)	The organization's personnel and partners are provided cybersecurity awareness education and are adequately trained to perform their information security–related duties and responsibilities consistent with related policies, procedures, and agreements.	PR.AT-1: All users are informed and trained. PR.AT-2: Privileged users understand roles and responsibilities. PR.AT-3: Third-party stakeholders (e.g., suppliers, customers, partners) understand roles and responsibilities. PR.AT-4: Senior executives understand roles and responsibilities. PR.AT-5: Physical and information security personnel understand roles and responsibilities.

(Continues)

PROTECT *(Continued)*

Category	Methodology	Sub-Category
Data Security (PR.DS)	**Information and records (data) are managed consistent with the organization's risk strategy to protect the confidentiality, integrity, and availability of information.**	**PR.DS-1: Data-at-rest is protected.** **PR.AT-2: Data-in-transit is protected.** **PR.AT-3: Assets are formally managed throughout removal, transfers, and disposition.** **PR.AT-4: Adequate capacity to ensure availability is maintained.** **PR.AT-5: Protections against data leaks are implemented.** **PR.AT-6: Integrity-checking mechanisms are used to verify software, firmware, and information integrity.** **PR.AT-7: The development and testing environment(s) are separate from the production environment.**

Category	Methodology	Sub-Category
Information Protection Processes and Procedures (PR.IP)	Security policies (that address purpose, scope, roles, responsibilities, management commitment, and coordination among organizational entities), processes, and procedures are maintained and used to manage protection of information systems and assets.	PR-IP-1: A baseline configuration of information technology/industrial control systems is created and maintained. PR-IP-2: A System Development Life Cycle to manage systems is implemented. PR-IP-3: Configuration change control processes are in place. PR-IP-4: Backups of information are conducted, maintained, and tested periodically. PR-IP-5: Policy and regulations regarding the physical operating environment for organizational assets are met. PR-IP-6: Data is destroyed according to policy. PR-IP-7: Protection processes are continuously improved. PR-IP-8: Effectiveness of protection technologies is shared with appropriate parties. PR-IP-9: Response plans (Incident Response and Business Continuity) and recovery plans (Incident and Disaster Recovery) are in place and managed. PR-IP-10: Response and recovery plans are tested. PR-IP-11: Cybersecurity is included in human resources practices (e.g., deprovisioning, personnel screening). PR-IP-12: A vulnerability management plan is developed and implemented.

(Continues)

PROJECT *(Continued)*

Category	Methodology	Sub-Category
Maintenance (PR.MA)	Maintenance and repairs of industrial control and information system components are performed consistent with policies and procedures.	PR-MA-1: Maintenance and repair of organizational assets are performed and logged in a timely manner, with approved and controlled tools. PR-MA-2: Remote maintenance of organizational assets is approved, logged, and performed in a manner that prevents unauthorized access.
Protective Technology (PR.PT)	Technical security solutions are managed to ensure the security and resilience of systems and assets, consistent with related policies, procedures, and agreements.	PR-PT-1: Audit/log records are determined, documented, implemented, and reviewed in accordance with policy. PR-PT-2: Removable media is protected and its use restricted according to policy. PR-PT-3: Access to systems and assets is controlled, incorporating the principle of least functionality. PR-PT-4: Communications and control networks are protected.

DETECT

Category	Methodology	Sub-Category
Anomalies and Events (DE.AE)	Anomalous activity is detected in a timely manner and the potential impact of events is understood.	DE-AE-1: A business of network operations and expected data flows for users and systems is established and managed. DE-AE-2: Detected events are analyzed to understand attack targets and methods. DE-AE-3: Event data are aggregated and correlated from multiple sources and sensors. DE-AE-4: Impact of events is determined. DE-AE-5: Incident alert thresholds are established.

Category	Methodology	Sub-Category
Security Continuous Monitoring (DE.CM)	The information system and assets are monitored at discrete intervals to identify cybersecurity events and verify the effectiveness of protective measures.	DE-CM-1: The network is monitored to detect potential cybersecurity events. DE-CM-2: The physical environment is monitored to detect potential cybersecurity events. DE-CM-3: Personnel activity is monitored to detect potential cybersecurity events. DE-CM-4: Malicious code is detected. DE-CM-5: Unauthorized mobile code is detected. DE-CM-6: External service provider activity is monitored to detect potential cybersecurity events. DE-CM-7: Monitoring for unauthorized personnel, connections, devices, and software is performed. DE-CM-8: Vulnerability scans are performed.
Detection Processes (DE.DP)	Detection processes and procedures are maintained and tested to ensure timely and adequate awareness of anomalous events.	DE-DP-1: Roles and responsibilities for detection are well defined to ensure accountability. DE-DP-2: Detection activities comply with all applicable requirements. DE-DP-3: Detection processes are tested. DE-DP-4: Event-detection information is communicated to appropriate parties. DE-DP-5: Detection processes are continuously improved.

(Continues)

RESPOND

Category	Methodology	Sub-Category
Response Planning (RS.RP)	Response processes and procedures are executed and maintained, to ensure timely response to detected cybersecurity events.	RS-RP-1: Response plan is executed during or after an event.
Communications (RS.CO)	Response activities are coordinated with internal and external stakeholders, as appropriate, to include external support from law enforcement agencies.	RS-CO-1: Personnel know their roles and order of operations when a response is needed. RS-CO-2: Events are reported consistent with established criteria. RS-CO-3: Information is shared consistent with response plans. RS-CO-4: Coordination with stakeholders occurs consistent with response plans. RS-CO-5: Voluntary information sharing occurs with external stakeholders to achieve broader cybersecurity situational awareness.
Analysis (RS.AN)	Analysis is conducted to ensure adequate response and support recovery activities.	RS-AN-1: Notifications from detection systems are investigated. RS-AN-2: The impact of the incident is understood. RS-AN-3: Forensics are performed. RS-AN-4: Incidents are categorized consistent with response plans.
Mitigation (RS.MI)	Activities are performed to prevent expansion of an event, mitigate its effects, and eradicate the incident.	RS-MI-1: Incidents are contained. RS-MI-2: Incidents are mitigated. RS-MI-3: Newly identified vulnerabilities are mitigated or documented as accepted risks.

Category	Methodology	Sub-Category
Improvements (RS.IM)	Organizational response activities are improved by incorporating lessons learned from current and previous detection/response activities.	RS-IM-1: Response plans incorporate lessons learned. RS-IM-2: Response strategies are updated.

RECOVER

Category	Methodology	Sub-Category
Recovery Planning (RC.RP)	Recovery processes and procedures are executed and maintained to ensure timely restoration of systems or assets affected by cybersecurity events.	RC.RP-1: Recovery plan is executed during or after an event.
Improvements (RC.IM)	Recovery planning and processes are improved by incorporating lessons learned into future activities.	RC.IM-1: Recovery plans incorporate lessons learned. RC.IM-2: Recovery strategies are updated.
Communications (RC.CO)	Restoration activities are coordinated with internal and external parties, such as coordinating centers, Internet Service Providers, owners of attacking systems, victims, other CSIRTs, and vendors.	RC.CO-1: Public relations are managed. RC.CO-2: Reputation after an event is repaired. RC.CO-3: Recovery activities are communicated to internal stakeholders and executive and management teams.

INDEX

B

C

D

E

G

H

I

O

P

Q

R

T

U

K

Z